JESUS AND THE LAST DAYS

JESUS
AND THE
LAST DAYS

*The Interpretation of the
Olivet Discourse*

GEORGE R. BEASLEY-MURRAY

REGENT COLLEGE PUBLISHING
Vancouver, British Columbia

To Ruth
To mark fifty years
of life together

Jesus and the Last Days
Copyright © 1993 The Estate of George R. Beasley-Murray

This edition published 2005 by
REGENT COLLEGE PUBLISHING
5800 University Boulevard
Vancouver, BC V6T 2E4 Canada
Email: info@regentpublishing.com
Website: wwww.regentpublishing.com

Library and Archives Canada Cataloguing in Publication Data

Beasley-Murray, G. R. (George Raymond), 1916–2000
Jesus and the last days : the interpretation of the Olivet
discourse / George R. Beasley-Murray.

Reprint of the ed. published: Peabody, Mass. : Hendrickson Publishers,
c1993, which was a revision of the author's
Jesus and the future, published 1954.
Includes bibliographical references and indexes.

ISBN 1-57383-351-7

1. Bible. N.T. Mark XIII—Criticism, interpretation, etc.—History.
2. Eschatology—Biblical teaching. I. Beasley-Murray, G. R. (George
Raymond), 1916-2000. Jesus and the future. II. Title.

BS2585.2.B42 2005   226.3'06   C2005-902387-2

TABLE OF CONTENTS

Preface   vii

Abbreviations   ix

1.   The Presuppositions and the Formulation of the Little Apocalypse Theory   1

2.   The Development of the Little Apocalypse Theory   32

3.   Other Theories Concerning the Origin of Mark 13   80

4.   Attempts to Vindicate the Eschatological Discourse   110

5.   Contributions Since the Rise of Redaction Criticism   162

6.   A Fresh Approach to the Discourse of Mark 13   350

7.   A Commentary on Mark 13   377

Select Bibliography   477

Index of Modern Authors   492

Scripture Index   499

PREFACE

IN THE SUMMER OF 1952 I COMPLETED the writing of a dissertation entitled "The Eschatological Discourse of Mark 13, with particular reference to the rise and development of the Little Apocalypse Theory." The theme had been selected in view of the notorious difficulty and complexity of the task of interpreting the chapter. In my innocence I set out to read all the literature on Mark 13 that had been produced since the rise of modern criticism of the New Testament. I speedily discovered that I had embarked on an all but impossible task. The literature on the subject was enormous. That was due in part to the immense interest in the eschatological discourse in the mid-nineteenth century and the years that followed. In view of the nature of the discussions that had appeared, the discourse was not merely notoriously difficult; it had become just simply notorious, and a stumbling block to faith. On the other hand the appearance of Albert Schweitzer's *Quest of the Historical Jesus* early in the present century demonstrated the importance of eschatology in the proclamation of Jesus; inevitably that led many to examine afresh the teaching of Mark 13, and the solutions of its problems became increasingly diversified.

My investigation was divided, like Gaul and all good sermons, into three parts: a historical review of the criticism and interpretation of Mark 13 from the rise of modern criticism to the time of writing; the theology of Mark 13 and its relation to other eschatological passages in the New Testament; and finally a commentary on the chapter. The British publisher Macmillan agreed to issue the work in an abbreviated form and without the commentary. It appeared under the title *Jesus and the Future* and went into two editions. At the urging of several scholars, notably W. G. Kümmel and G. D. Kilpatrick, I revised and expanded the original commentary, and it was published by Macmillan with the simple title *A Commentary on Mark Thirteen.*

Various colleagues in later years have suggested that *Jesus and the Future* should be reissued. That, I knew, was impossible without serious revision, which I was unable to give. Curiously, in spite of all the discussions on Mark 13 that continued for over a century, only one book had been written on the discourse prior to my own work—a slender but splendid little volume by F. Busch entitled *Zum Verständnis der synoptischen Eschatologie: Markus 13 neu untersucht.* Perhaps due to its appearance shortly before World War II, the book was little known in the English-speaking world, but it was widely discussed in Germany. A few years after the publication of *Jesus and the Future,* books on the eschatological discourse began to flow in an unprecedented manner. Since the mid-1950s no less than twenty works on the discourse, some very lengthy, have appeared, most of them on Mark 13, but some on the versions in Matthew 24 and Luke 21. But a further factor emerged: while I was writing my dissertation, Bornkamm, Marxsen, and Conzelmann were busily engaged in formulating redaction criticism of the Gospels. Significantly, a considerable portion of Marxsen's book *Mark the Evangelist: Studies on the Redaction History of the Gospel* was devoted to a study of Mark 13 to demonstrate how redaction criticism worked in practice. Since then the method has informed and stimulated a large number of studies on the eschatological discourse.

In revising and updating the original work it was necessary to modify its structure. The first four chapters, surveying the investigation of Mark 13 up to 1950, have been allowed to remain. They reflect a certain liveliness of style, not to say impudence, characteristic of the young. A historical review of studies that appeared between 1950 and 1991 is contained in chapter 5. In view of the extraordinary diversity of views on the origin and interpretation of Mark 13 that has continued to manifest itself, it has seemed right to present the contributions of scholars separately, and not summarily to categorize their views. This is particularly important with regard to the monographs on the discourse, some of which have made unique contributions to our understanding of the discourse. In place of a section on the relations of Mark 13 to the rest of the New Testament I have given an account of my own thoughts on the origin and development of the discourse, and of some theological issues discernible within it. Above all, the book concludes with a fresh commentary on the discourse. It has been written in the light of the labors of many scholars during the past forty years. It is intended as a monument to their toil, and I hope not an unworthy one.

ABBREVIATIONS

AB	Anchor Bible
AnBib	Analecta biblica
BAGD	Bauer, W., W. F. Arndt, F. W. Gingrich, and F. W. Danker, *Greek-English Lexicon of the New Testament and Other Early Christian Literature*
BBB	Bonner biblische Beiträge
BDB	Brown, F., S. R. Driver, and C. A. Briggs, *Hebrew and English Lexicon of the Old Testament*
BETL	Bibliotheca ephemeridum theologicarum lovaniensium
BHK	*Biblia hebraica*, ed. R. Kittel
Bib	*Biblica*
BJRL	*Bulletin of the John Rylands Library*
BZ	*Biblische Zeitschrift*
BZNW	Beihefte zur *ZNW*
CBQMS	Catholic Biblical Quarterly Monograph Series
CGTC	Cambridge Greek Testament Commentary
CJT	*Canadian Journal of Theology*
ConBNT	Coniectanea biblica, New Testament
EKKNT	Evangelisch-katholischer Kommentar zum Neuen Testament
ETL	*Ephemerides theologicae lovanienses*
EvQ	*Evangelical Quarterly*
ExpT	*Expository Times*
FB	Forschung zur Bibel
FRLANT	Forschungen zur Religion und Literatur des Alten und Neuen Testaments
HKNT	Handkommentar zum Neuen Testament
HNT	Handbuch zum Neuen Testament
HTKNT	Herders theologischer Kommentar zum Neuen Testament
IB	*Interpreter's Bible*

ICC	International Critical Commentary
IDB(Sup)	Interpreter's Dictionary of the Bible, 4 vols., ed. G. A. Buttrick (1962); Supplementary volume, ed. K. Crim (1976)
Int	*Interpretation*
JBL	*Journal of Biblical Literature*
JRS	*Journal of Roman Studies*
JSNT	*Journal for the Study of the New Testament*
JSNTSup	Journal for the Study of the New Testament, Supplement Series
JSS	*Journal of Semitic Studies*
JTS	*Journal of Theological Studies*
LD	Lectio divina
LTK	*Lexikon für Theologie und Kirche*
MeyerK	H. A. W. Meyer, Kritisch-exegetischer Kommentar
MNTC	Moffatt New Testament Commentary
MT	Masoretic Text
NCBC	New Century Bible Commentary
NICNT	New International Commentary on the New Testament
NIGTC	New International Greek Testament Commentary
NIV	New International Version
NovTSup	Novum Testamentum, Supplements
NRSV	New Revised Standard Version
NTD	Das Neue Testament Deutsch
NTS	*New Testament Studies*
OTP	*Old Testament Pseudepigrapha*, 2 vols., ed. J. H. Charlesworth
RB	*Revue Biblique*
RE	*Realencyklopädie für protestantische Theologie und Kirche*
REB	Revised English Bible
RechBib	Recherches bibliques
RHPR	*Revue d'histoire et de philosophie religieuses*
RNT	Regensburger Neues Testament
SBT	Studies iη Biblical Theology
SE	*Studia evangelica*
SJT	*Scottish Journal of Theology*
SNTSMS	Society for New Testament Studies Monograph Series
ST	*Studia Theologica*
Str-B	Strack, H. L. and P. Billerbeck, *Kommentar zum Neuen Testament aus Talmud und Midrasch*, 6 vols.
TBl	*Theologische Blätter*
TDNT	*Theological Dictionary of the New Testament*, ed. G. Kittel and G. Friedrich, 10 vols.
THKNT	Theologischer Handkommentar zum Neuen Testament
TLZ	*Theologische Literaturzeitung*
TZ	*Theologische Zeitschrift*
WBC	Word Biblical Commentary
ZNW	*Zeitschrift für die neutestamentliche Wissenschaft*
ZWT	*Zeitschrift für wissenschaftliche Theologie*

1

THE PRESUPPOSITIONS AND THE FORMULATION OF THE LITTLE APOCALYPSE THEORY

"NO MATTER HOW ORIGINAL A SCHOLAR'S IMAGINATION, no matter how penetrating and critical his judgment, society does far more of the writing of any book that lives than the author himself."[1] However humiliating it may be to formulate such a principle, its justification scarcely requires demonstration. We can no more escape the influence of our cultural climate than people at the equator or in the Arctic regions can remain unaffected by their physical conditions. This seems plain enough when pointed out, yet in theological discussion it is rarely thought necessary to take account of the environment in which ideas are formulated and of the motives of their sponsors. A book is cited and a name mentioned in connection with an attractive theory; let it be endorsed by a few impressive authorities and it rapidly spreads; in due time it may be regarded as critically orthodox. But how did that theory come to be formulated? What precedents did it have in its own field, and what prompted the author to put it forward? Most significant advances in thought are the product of long processes, brought to an issue by a gifted person. Such is the case with Timothy Colani's theory that the eschatological discourse of the Gospels is built around the nucleus of an apocalypse of independent origin. It has been assumed that this hypothesis came out of the blue, like the image of Diana that fell from heaven to Ephesus; we have not paused to ask whether it may first have been thrown into the air and why, if that did happen, Colani was ready to receive it. This question we desire to examine.

---

[1] C. C. McCown, *The Search for the Real Jesus* (New York, 1940), 18.

1. Criticism from D. F. Strauss to F. C. Baur

D. F. Strauss

We must go back at least as far as David Strauss. The extent to which NT studies have been affected by this writer, both for good and for ill, has been strangely overlooked in English-speaking countries, though his ghost still haunts the theological literature of Germany. No book concerning Christian origins had such an explosive effect upon the world as his *Life of Jesus,* published in 1835–1836; the scars inflicted on the edifice of the church remain to this day, though their origin has been forgotten. The book created an immediate sensation and sustained for years its position as a focal point of controversy. "During the year 1836 the *Tübingen Review* contained some four hundred pages of attack upon Strauss," wrote McCown. "Other theological and religious periodicals paid the book an equal amount of attention. . . . Nearly thirty years later a writer in the *Westminster Review* could say, 'The name of Strauss has long been a bugbear in the English religious world. High Churchmen and Low Churchmen hush naughty children with the name of Strauss.' "[2] Naughty children were not alone in their uneasiness at that name. For large numbers of scholars NT studies had been thrown into confusion; old positions were felt to be impossible, and a question mark had been set alongside everything formerly taken for granted. In the year that followed Strauss's *Life,* a German scholar declared that the result of this work was "to turn into a problem the great gospel history to an extent and with a completeness such as no earlier investigation had done."[3] It is not without significance that the same abiding result was felt in Germany three generations later. In 1911 Wellhausen wrote, "*The Life of Jesus,* which formerly stood on the programme of theological literature and of theological lecture courses, has dwindled lately, under the silent influence of Strauss, to *Problems from the Life of Jesus.*"[4] We shall find reason to believe that Wellhausen himself came under that "silent influence," in directions little suspected by him.

The issues Strauss raised were fundamental to all aspects of Gospel criticism, and we are here concerned with one only, namely with his views on eschatology. For most scholars of the day the eschatology of Jesus meant the consideration of the discourses of Matthew 24–25; indeed, for a large part of the nineteenth century the eschatological question centered upon the problem of what to do with these

---

[2] Ibid., 7–9.
[3] Cited by C. H. Weisse, "Die Evangelienfrage," *Blätter für literarische Unterhaltung* (March 1836): 1.
[4] Wellhausen, *Einleitung in die drei ersten Evangelien,* 2d ed. Berlin, 79.

chapters, notably with ch. 24 (= Mark 13). Here Strauss found a peculiarly vulnerable point in the armor of the orthodox, for the second coming of Christ seemed to be set in the context of his own time. "It is impossible," Strauss wrote, "to evade the acknowledgment that in this discourse, if we do not mutilate it to suit our own views, Jesus at first speaks of the destruction of Jerusalem and farther on, and until the close, of his return at the end of all things, and that He places the two events in an immediate connexion."[5] Such an admission naturally calls into question the reliability of the teaching of Jesus. "As it will soon be eighteen centuries since the destruction of Jerusalem, and an equally long period since the generation contemporary with Jesus disappeared from the earth, while his visible return and the end of the world which he associated with it, have not taken place, the announcement of Jesus appears so far to have been erroneous."[6]

Strauss reviewed the attempts to meet this difficulty. The "mountain-peak" theory compared the crises of history with the summits of distant mountains that hide from view intervening distances; but if one is anxious to preserve the authority of Jesus, it will not do. "We may here cite the appropriate remark of Paulus, that as one, who in a perspective externally presented, does not know how to distinguish distances, labours under an optical illusion, i.e. errs; so likewise in an internal perspective of ideas, if such there be, the disregard of distances must be pronounced an error; consequently this theory does not show that the above men did not err, but rather explains how they easily might err."[7] The theory thus illustrates the nature of the error of Jesus, but it in no way absolves him from it. What, then, of the view that it is necessary to make people think that the end is ever at hand, in order to allow the belief to exercise its full moral influence upon them? Was it not necessary for Jesus to impress on people at least the probability of the nearness of the second coming, lest it find them unprepared? No, for that also incurs difficulties. "One whose mind is in a healthy state conceives the possible to be possible, the probable as probable; and if he wishes to abide by the truth, he so exhibits them to others; the man, on the contrary, by whom the merely possible or probable is conceived as the real, is mistaken; and he who, without so regarding it himself, yet for a moral or religious reason so represents it to others, permits himself to use a pious fraud."[8] On such a view, therefore, Jesus was either mistaken or a deceiver. Strauss does not mind which alternative is chosen; it satisfies him to be able to present the dilemma.

---

[5] Strauss, *Life of Jesus* (ET London, 1846) 3:95.
[6] Ibid., 85.
[7] Ibid., 98.
[8] Ibid., 98–99.

One last resort remains: is it not possible that the prophecy is unauthentic, composed by disciples to show the ability of the Master to predict coming events? Here Strauss speaks with two voices. It suits him to maintain the authenticity of the discourse, for he is anxious to prove the fallibility of Jesus. He accordingly agrees with those theologians who seek the origin of the prophecies, not in the events leading up to the fall of Jerusalem, which would make the whole prophecy a *vaticinium ex eventu,* but in the well-known predictions of OT prophecy. Strauss is prepared to apply this even to the Lukan version of the discourse, though not without a sting in the tail: "Even those particulars in which Luke surpasses his fellow narrators in definiteness are not of a kind to oblige us to suppose either a supernatural knowledge, or a *vaticinium post eventum.*" The result is plain: that which Jesus predicted concerning Jerusalem and which came true is due to no superior insight, it is merely a collocation of OT ideas; that which he predicted, but which did not happen, is due to a similar, but indiscriminate, use of the OT. Alike in his true predictions and false ones, Jesus possesses no originality!

Strauss hints at a different possibility, however, the mention of which is fortunate since it reveals the source of his ideas. He cites the *Wolfenbüttel Fragmentist,* i.e., Reimarus, for the view that the idea of the second coming was due not to Jesus, but to his disciples:

> No promise, throughout the whole Scriptures . . . , he thinks, is on the one hand more definitely expressed, and on the other has turned out more flagrantly false, than this, which yet forms one of the main pillars of Christianity. And he [Reimarus] does not see in this a mere error, but a premeditated deception on the part of the apostles (to whom, and not to Jesus Himself, he attributes that promise, and the discourses in which it is contained). . . . Such inferences from the discourse before us would inflict a fatal wound on Christianity.[9]

Strauss makes no comment on this suggestion; it is enough to have provided another reason for shaking the confidence of the orthodox. It did not occur to him that if the suggestion were true, it would have the effect of absolving Jesus from the great "error," but neither did it occur to anyone else. His allegation stood forth with a pitiless clarity. It cut to the quick the theologians of his day. Jesus had been charged with a blunder of the greatest magnitude. Somehow the situation had to be retrieved. But what could be done? The suggested employment of the critical knife, inadvertently put forward by Strauss, was too violent for the mood of that day. The idea of a "kenosis" of the Christ, by which it might be possible to admit the presence of an intellectual error in the Incarnate Lord, was not yet abroad. There seemed but one path left free:

---

[9] Ibid., 86.

Jesus was accurately reported, in the main, but his conceptions were loftier than those of his contemporaries; his disciples had confused distinctions drawn by him and in their reports mingled the various elements of his teaching.

C. A. Hase

The first critical writer in whom this interpretation becomes plain is the noted Professor at Jena, C. A. Hase. His *Life of Jesus* was published in 1829; the second edition was issued in 1835, the year that saw the publication of the first part of Strauss's *Life*; a third edition appeared in 1840, and the English translation was made from this, corrected from the fourth edition. It will be instructive to compare what Hase wrote about the eschatology of Jesus (i.e., the great discourse) before Strauss's book came on the scene and what he wrote after its appearance.

Hase's earlier exposition is typical of that of many who did not appreciate eschatology in the raw and endeavored to refine it for "modern" taste. His summary of Matthew 24–25 commences thus:

> As He now sat on the Mount of Olives and looked down on the Holy City, his view of the future, proceeding from a very clear comprehension of the history of the world and from the deepest understanding of the kingdom of God, disclosed itself to the apostles in prophetic pictures . . . (viz. concerning) the destruction of Jerusalem, the ruin of the Roman Empire through the migration of the nations and the victory of Christianity. . . . He spoke as prophet in the highest sense of the term, i.e., as one who, in faith in the victory of the kingdom of God and in full consciousness of the present, hurrying on with a glance at his contemporaries, possessed of a presentiment as to the course of Providence, takes in at a glance the coming centuries according to his spirit and comprehends them with his plan.[10]

It is admitted that if Mark 13:32 (= Matt 24:36) were taken strictly it could be regarded as a revocation of previous definitions as to the time of the end (as, e.g., Matt 16:28), but on the whole he thought that, "in view of the generally attested prudence of Jesus, who . . . consistently respected the tranquil passage of history and of providence, the symbolic understanding of his prophecy is the most probable."[11] The second coming is accordingly a symbolic representation of the triumph of the messianic kingdom; the prophets had similarly portrayed the glory of the theocracy as a coming of Yahweh among his people.

In the third and fourth editions of his work, Hase considerably modified his views. In the preface he stated that the alterations had been mostly occasioned by Strauss's *Life* and the literature occasioned

---

[10] Hase, *Leben Jesu* (Leipzig, 1835), 224.
[11] Ibid., 225–26.

by it. The greatest benefit he had evidently received from his skeptical contemporary was a measure of realism in interpreting eschatological language. All that had appeared in the earlier editions about Jesus' disclosure of the course of world history was excised. Still more significantly, his former interpretation of Mark 13:32 was withdrawn and the presence of a time limit was frankly affirmed in the sayings of our Lord: "Ascribing to God the sole knowledge of the day and hour, he nevertheless fixed his return during that generation."[12] But that Jesus could have held the hope of his coming in any literal sense is strenuously denied: "Since Jesus from the first had elevated the national notion of a Messiah to a religious idea which could not be injured by his death, he did not need to frame out of visions of a pretended prophet[13] the fantastic hope of such a pretended return." The view is reiterated more strongly that the second coming is simply the victory of Christ's kingdom.[14]

Three notable features are involved in these modifications of Hase: (1) the "tranquil passage of history and of providence" disappears, to be replaced by an acknowledgment of an eschatological view of history; (2) the limitation of the time interval constituted by "that generation" is admitted; (3) the notion of a second coming is rejected as "fantastic." The battle over the "enthusiasm" of Jesus has begun.

C. H. Weisse

The tendencies apparent in the discreet Hase came to full expression in the writings of C. H. Weisse, who first plainly demonstrated the priority of Mark. He wrote two books, both of which, though separated by a distance of eighteen years, were prompted by the Strauss controversy. With regard to Mark 13, the fundamental principle of interpretation enunciated by Weisse was that in this discourse we have material, authentic in itself, but uttered on various occasions and with varied needs in mind; the duty of criticism is to consider each segment of tradition by itself. In advancing this contention, in which he anticipated Lohmeyer by a full century, he found few followers, due to his unwise use of it. He divided Mark 13 into vv. 1–20, 21–23, 24–27, 28–30, 31, 32–37. Each section was presumed to be originally independent, and to each he endeavored to give "a meaning worthy of the divine Speaker." With regard to the first section, he denied that it related to the fall of Jerusalem (Luke has interpreted wrongly here); its real concern was the struggles and trials that the movement initiated by Jesus was to encounter generally. The counsel to flight in Mark 13:14–

---

[12] Hase, *Life of Jesus*, 201.

[13] Dan 7:13. This characterization of Daniel is taken from C. H. Weisse, "Evangelienfrage," 594–95; see p. 7 below.

[14] Hase, *Life of Jesus*, 201–2.

16 is accordingly interpreted as "decisively to turn one's back on the old order, that has irremediably perished, and to seek salvation only in a completely new order of things." The lament over mothers with children in 13:17 refers to "those who insist on being occupied with or still producing within *(erzeugen)* the old order." The "winter" of 13:18 signifies "a raw, barren time that yields no fruit for the spirit."[15]

It is the parousia passage, however, that evokes the eloquence of Weisse. He insists that 13:24–27 should never have been connected with the foregoing; the words are genuine, but the context is unauthentic. To retain it here is to destroy the meaning of the earlier passage. Weisse remarks:

> "That which makes it difficult to attribute so quixotic an aberration [i.e., the second coming conception] to the exalted Master is not merely a so-called 'Christian feeling' or 'Christian consciousness' which, without clear insight into its reason and its justification, wishes to put forward a *mulier taceat in ecclesia* (the citations and the Latin tag are both from Strauss). It is the plain recognition that, as surely as a vine does not bear thorns or a fig tree thistles, even so certainly a spirit of such greatness as Jesus had preserved, even in the foregoing discourse, cannot have degenerated to imagining such a fancy as only originates in a sick brain. Out of the same mouth that announced the preaching of the gospel in conditions of affliction and distress of every kind . . . it was impossible that in the next moment there could proceed an utterance constructed out of the most narrow and superstitious belief in the symbolic saying of a fantastic book, which ignorance or deceit had attributed to a renowned old prophet, and out of the most extravagant, half-insane imagination!"[16]

It is difficult to understand how a Christian scholar could bring himself to employ such unrestrained language regarding Gospel sayings, but it reveals how deeply he had been affected by the contentions of his opponent. What, then, is the meaning of Mark 13:24–27? "He himself incontestably meant," wrote Weisse, "on the one hand the judgment that world history carries out every day and at every hour, in which he as head and center of history could name himself with perfect right as Judge, and on the other hand the judgment at the end of time, in regard to which, however, we dare not presume that he represented himself in so external and sensual a form as subsequent church doctrine has represented it."[17] Most interpreters of the Gospels will admit that apocalyptic language should be accorded some latitude in interpretation, but Weisse has gone beyond what is reasonable. In his later book, the position is a little more soberly put, but there is no essential

---

[15] Weisse, *Die evangelische Geschichte, kritisch und philosophisch bearbeitet* (Leipzig, 1838), 590–92.

[16] Weisse, *Evangelische Geschichte*, 594–95.

[17] Ibid., 596.

modification, save for the significant suggestion that Mark 13:1–20 is not a unit, but is composed of originally disparate fragments uttered on different occasions; the entire discourse, 13:1–37, thus comes to be of that order. As an example of the later treatment of these isolated segments, we may cite Weisse's view of the "abomination of desolation," 13:14; removed from this context it is susceptible of a sense, "more worthy of its exalted Speaker"; it represents the corrupt Jewish religion, and so corresponds to the condemnatory sayings of which Mark has preserved but few (Mark 12:38–39).[18]

That Weisse revealed marks of genius is not to be denied, but they are disfigured here. It is the motive of his interpretation that is significant. He was impelled by the explicit desire to counter the teaching of Strauss, in particular to evade the mocking appeal to a speedy coming of Christ in glory. The very extravagance of his protestations must have afforded no little satisfaction to his opponent.

F. C. Baur

Between the publication of Weisse's two books appeared the celebrated work of F. C. Baur on the Gospels. The critical spirit that Strauss had applied to Gospel dogma he applied to Gospel documents. He had no hesitation in pronouncing the discourse of Matthew 24 as spurious. "It is impossible that Jesus can have spoken as the evangelist makes him speak."[19] This is proved by the book of Revelation, in which the fall of Jerusalem plays no part at all. "Of a destruction of Jerusalem the apocalyptist knows nothing."[20] The prediction of the fall of Jerusalem in Matthew 24 is accordingly regarded as a *post eventum* prophecy and due to the evangelist. Baur is unique in dating the prophecy in the time of the Bar Cochba rebellion, on the ground that no messianic pretender after the death of Jesus is known before this man, and that the "abomination of desolation" suits best the erection of the statue of the Capitoline Jupiter by Hadrian on the site of the ruined temple. This becomes for Baur the one fixed point for the dating of the Gospels; he assigns Matthew to the period AD 130–134, and the other Gospels according to their supposed deviations from the first one.[21]

The argument, both in its comparison with the book of Revelation and the exploits of Bar Cochba, is most dubious. The reference to the second-century Jewish revolt is needless. Nor is there any necessity to

---

[18] Weisse, *Die Evangelienfrage in ihrem gegenwärtigen Studium* (Leipzig, 1856), 171–72.

[19] F. C. Baur, *Kritische Untersuchungen über die kanonischen Evangelien* (Tübingen, 1847), 604.

[20] Ibid., 604–5.

[21] Ibid., 608–9.

relate the predictions of Mark 13 to the events of the latter part of the first century; if any should insist on so doing, it is still necessary to explain how the late "compiler" could have omitted the events of AD 70 from his prophetic review. Further, since the temple had been destroyed sixty years before Hadrian's attack, Baur is forced to place Matt 24:1–3 earlier and to presuppose a gap thereafter, of which there is no hint in the text. It is not surprising that contemporary opinion did not take kindly to Baur's views, but their ventilation contributed to the atmosphere that made the later hypotheses possible.

2. Criticism from H. A. W. Meyer to T. Colani

H. A. W. Meyer

From the time of Baur and Weisse to Colani the strictly critical treatment of the eschatological discourse remained in abeyance. It was a period in which a settled interpretation of the eschatology of Jesus gained currency. We see it clearly defined in the commentaries of H. A. W. Meyer, which exercised a widespread influence. In his commentary on Matthew, Meyer provides a summary of his views on this subject.[22] Jesus spoke of his parousia in the threefold sense. By it he meant: (1) the impartation of the Holy Spirit, which should happen shortly (John 16:16, etc.), and did happen; (2) the historical revelation of his sovereignty and might in the victory of his work on earth, experienced immediately after his exaltation to the Father (cf. Matt 26:64); (3) his parousia in a literal sense for the resurrection, judgment, and the setting up of the kingdom. Confusion arose because Jesus used prophetic language in describing the first two senses, so that what he taught as to the impending entry of the ideal kingdom was mistakenly applied by his disciples to the appearance of the final kingdom; admittedly they were not to be blamed, in that Jesus used the latter as a foil to set off the former. In particular, "Jesus had most definitely set the destruction of Jerusalem in the lifetime of that generation; and at the same time he had seen and proclaimed in prophetic symbol what could not be hidden from him, the connection in which the victory of his ideal kingdom would stand to this catastrophe; nothing was more natural therefore than that the further the time of the generation declined to its expiration, the more surely was the parousia awaited as occurring immediately after the destruction of Jerusalem. . . . Inevitably the form of the expectation reflected on the form of the promise; the ideal parousia and founding of the kingdom were identified with the real, so that the former was obliter-

---

[22] Meyer, *Kritisch exegetisches Handbuch über das Evangelium des Matthäus,* 3d ed. (Göttingen, 1855), 409ff.

ated in the tradition and only the latter remained the object of expectation."[23] By relating Matt 24:1–28 to the fall of Jerusalem and vv. 29ff. to
the various forms of the parousia, Meyer was able to explain satisfactorily the exegetical puzzle that had so distressed his contemporaries.

H. J. Holtzmann

The interpretation was heartily adopted by H. J. Holtzmann and
by his master F. Bleek, whose exposition of the Gospels Holtzmann
edited.[24] Bleek added to the threefold view of the parousia a strong
emphasis on the misinterpretation of their Teacher by the disciples. He
appears to be the first to call attention to the difficulty of reconciling
teaching on the suddenness of the coming of Christ, as given in Luke
17:22ff., with the view of the eschatological discourse, wherein the
coming is preceded by signs. Variety of materials and varieties of
comings smooth out for him the difficulty.[25]

Holtzmann worked on the assumption that the eschatological
discourse was derived from Ur-Markus (i.e., a primitive version of
Mark), and that therefore it is preserved best in Mark. His division of
Mark 13 was adopted by almost all subsequent exegetes: it narrates (1)
archai ōdinōn, the beginnings of the woes, represented first according
to their "world-historical" character, 13:5–8, and next according to
their significance for the development of the kingdom of God (the time
of the mission), vv. 9–13; (2) *hē thlipsis*, the tribulation, including the
destruction of Jerusalem, vv. 14–23; (3) *hē parousia*, the coming of
Christ, vv. 24–27. Divergencies in Matthew and Luke are due to editorial modification, a process particularly noticeable in Luke, who writes
with the history of the church, notably that of Paul, in view, and after
the fall of Jerusalem (hence Luke 21:20–24 is wholly *ex eventu*). Holtzmann emphasizes, nevertheless, that the original version contained in
Ur-Markus gave "genuine prophecies of Jesus, which were written
down before the fulfillment had happened."[26] The threefold view of the
parousia is enunciated more simply than by Meyer; it is said to consist
of: (1) the literal parousia at the end of the age; (2) the historical
parousia, "a series of evident historical acts of power"; (3) a spiritual
coming, shortly to happen after the death of Jesus, "a provable,
energetic beginning of the realization of God's kingdom." Mark 13:30
is now in a misleading context and really relates to the second

---

[23] Ibid., 411–12.

[24] Holtzmann, *Die synoptischen Evangelien, ihr Ursprung und geschichtlicher Charakter* (Leipzig, 1863); Bleek, *Synoptische Erklärung der drei ersten
Evangelien*, ed. H. Holtzmann (Leipzig, 1862).

[25] Bleek, *Synoptische Erklärung*, 357–69.

[26] Holtzmann, *Synoptischen Evangelien*, 235ff., 405ff.

view.[27] We shall see later that Holtzmann in his maturer years renounced this idea of the historical parousia; it requires mention here
since it affected in no small measure the views of his generation.

The year in which Holtzmann's work on the Synoptic Gospels was
issued witnessed an event which was to prove as decisive in this
controversy as the appearance of Strauss's *Leben Jesu.* C. H. Weisse in
his later volume had lamented that the promise of a new day in NT
critical studies, apparently dawning with the publication of Strauss's
book, did not come to fulfillment; the situation had remained disap-
pointingly the same. The cause of this stagnation seemed to him to be
that of fear; the old dogmatic system had been threatened, and it had
evidently been felt safer to ignore the issues raised by the heretic. A
"conspiracy of silence" had been promoted within the theological
world.[28] Weisse himself had attempted to break the silence by a positive
contribution. He was aided in a startling fashion by the forcing of battle
on the unwilling theologians by a romantic agnostic, whose charm
captured the public imagination: Ernest Renan.

E. Renan

Renan issued his *Vie de Jésus* in 1863 and scored an immediate
success. Of the influence of Strauss on Renan there can be no question;
the former thinker was much the more original of the two. Renan said
little that his predecessor had not provided for, but his style was far
more appealing. His treatment of the eschatology of Jesus fundamentally agreed with that of his master, except that he recognized a development in Jesus' thought. The prime idea of the Lord throughout his
ministry was felt to be the establishment of the kingdom of God. But
sometimes in his preaching Jesus appeared to be simply a democratic
leader, toiling for the emancipation of the poor and outcast; at other
times he was the herald of the apocalyptic kingdom of Daniel and
Enoch, while on occasions the approaching deliverance was conceived
in purely spiritual terms. The three views in reality were but two, the
temporal-eschatological and the spiritual; their coherence simulta-
neously in the mind of Jesus was the reason for his greatness. If he had
been merely an apocalyptist he would have been forgotten, if only a
puritan he would have failed.[29] Jesus gave no detailed prediction such
as the book of Revelation contains, yet Mark 13:30 shows that "his
declarations on the nearness of the catastrophe leave no room for any
equivocation."[30] This fundamental error shows that his system is dis-

---

[27] Ibid., 409–10.
[28] Weisse, *Evangelienfrage*, 1–7.
[29] Renan, *Life of Jesus* (ET London, 1935), 145–46.
[30] Ibid., 147.

credited. "The world, in continuing to exist, caused it to crumble. One generation of man at the most was the limit of its endurance. The faith of the first Christian generation is intelligible, but the faith of the second generation is no longer so. After the death of John, or of the last survivor, whoever he might be, of the group which had seen the Master, the word of Jesus was convicted of falsehood."[31]

Renan was generous enough to feel that Jesus should be pardoned for this unfortunate error. Perhaps the mistake was not his, but that of his disciples. If he did share the "general illusion," at least it nerved him to a struggle which might otherwise have been too strong for him.[32] The same may be said of its value in inspiring his followers through the centuries. "Let us not despise this chimera which has been the thick rind of the sacred fruit on which we live. This fantastic kingdom of heaven, this endless pursuit after a city of God, which has constantly preoccupied Christianity during its long career, has been the principle of that great instinct of futurity which has animated all reformers. . . . The idea of the kingdom of God, and the Apocalypse, which is the complete image of it, are thus in a sense the highest and the most poetic expression of human progress."[33] These are kindly words, no doubt, and are meant to soothe ruffled feelings, but they must have seemed to the orthodox like serpent's venom flavored with vanilla. They stung contemporary theologians to indignant response, as the attacks of Strauss had done a generation before.[34]

D. Schenkel

The first of the Christian protagonists to arise was the gentle Daniel Schenkel. He himself had undergone a considerable change of views over the years, not without much heart searching, and up to this point he had preserved a discreet silence. The sensation over Renan's *Life* compelled him to an answer, and in 1864 he issued his "character study" of Jesus.[35] His views on the eschatology of our Lord were almost a return to those of Hase, a noteworthy coincidence in view of the relation of Hase to Strauss. Mark 13 was to him "the most impressive

---

[31] Ibid., 149.

[32] Ibid., 149–50.

[33] Ibid., 151.

[34] Goguel tells us that Renan's *Vie de Jésus* created a greater sensation than that of Strauss and elicited a host of replies. Renan's book was as easy to read as that of Strauss was difficult; consequently it was read by multitudes who were neither initiated into nor prepared for exegetical research. According to Girard and Monckel, up to the year 1923 the *Vie de Jésus* went through 205 editions in French and 216 in other languages. See Goguel, *Life of Jesus* (London, 1933), 50.

[35] Schenkel, *Das Charakterbild Jesu. Ein biblischer Versuch* (Wiesbaden, 1864), iv.

and powerful utterance that Jesus made."[36] The prediction of the over-throw of the temple (Mark 13:2) is an expression of "prophetic grief," although he knew that his own triumph was therein involved. That he announced it at all is proof that his messianic vocation had nothing in common with Jewish hopes. Judaism was crippling the Jewish national life. The religions and cultures of other nations were similarly enslaving their members. The new order therefore had to come about in a catastrophic manner. Jesus foresaw the course of history and warned his disciples to be faithful to the end. This "end," however, was not the "end of the world," of which he never spoke at all. "He simply used that expression to indicate the conclusion of the earlier Jewish and heathen era, the final point of the so-called old world, after which the period of the kingdom of God, or as we express it, the Christian era, the new world, should follow."[37] For this reason the preaching of the gospel is regarded as an eschatological event; by means of it Jesus achieved his "second coming" on earth. Naturally the disciples misunderstood his language. . . .

The one point of interest in Schenkel is his recognition that Jesus linked his own return with the fall of Jerusalem. "All attempts to deny such a connection in apologetic interests are mere sophistry and merit no refutation."[38] If the Synoptists have rightly reported Jesus, then he has erred in this respect. If other evidence compelled us to accept their accounts, we would have to bow before it, but surely it is obvious that the notion of a glorious parousia is Jewish, not at all in the spirit of Jesus. "If he had taught that, several years after his departure to the heavenly Father, he would come down from heaven to set up an external kingdom, he would then have acknowledged that theocratic misconception which he had fought throughout his entire life, i.e. he would have opposed his own life's work and the goal of his vocation with an indissoluble contradiction."[39] Once again the hope of a speedy coming has proved a stone of stumbling and rock of offense to the theologian. That Renan should have been the man to set the stone in the path of the church seemed to provide the greater reason for casting it away.

T. Colani

A champion now arises who is not content to remove this rock only; he orders the entire mountain to depart into the depths of the sea. Timothy Colani will have no half-measures. If timid predecessors are

---

[36] Ibid., 183.

[37] Ibid., 183–85.

[38] It is worthwhile observing the strong language that theologians employ when they are sure they have an explanation of this datum!

[39] Ibid., 280.

content to postpone or spiritualize the second advent of Christ, he will eradicate eschatology root and branch from the teaching of Jesus. Only so can the offensiveness of this doctrine be removed.

In dealing with the views of Colani and his book, we beg a little patience on the part of the reader. Colani's name is indelibly associated with the "little apocalypse" theory, but it is not sufficient to narrate his views on this matter alone. His treatment of the discourse of Mark 13, unlike that of his predecessors, was not the starting point of his study of the eschatology of the Gospels but its conclusion; it forms the climax of his exposition of the teaching of Jesus and cannot be understood apart from this wider context. This we must examine.

The first major point which Colani sought to establish is that there is no connection between Jewish messianism and the gospel. The Jewish messiah before the time of the Christian church was always merely human, and the Jewish hope was always bound up with temporal and political aims. If one should cite the Son of man against this contention, it is answered that he was a symbolic figure for the Israelite nation; and in any case the Son of man ascends to heaven, according to Daniel 7, not descends.[40] The Similitudes of Enoch were composed by a Christian (perhaps a Gnostic); the Son of man in that book is none other than Jesus, the Christian Messiah. So also the Messiah of 4 Ezra has borrowed features from the Christians' Christ. The revolts of AD 70 and 132, particularly the acceptance of Bar Cochba's claims by Rabbi Akiba, show plainly that the Jewish messiah was simply "a hero of a political revolution."[41]

For this reason Jesus avoided the application to himself of the term "Messiah." The episode of Peter's confession at Caesarea Philippi shows that Jesus could never have made a claim to be Messiah before that occasion. Nor did he think in such terms of himself. The preaching in the synagogue at Nazareth reveals it as the time when he felt himself called to be a prophet.[42] The defiant words "I say to you," repeated five times in the Sermon on the Mount, are no more messianic than many an utterance of Luther.[43] The call for sacrifice recorded in such passages as Matt 10:37ff. is such as any champion of a noble cause would send forth.[44] "Jesus could utter all these sayings without believing that he was the Messiah, purely in considering himself as a great prophet charged with initiating people into the kingdom of God."[45]

---

[40] Colani, *Jésus Christ et les croyances messianiques de son Temps*, 2d ed. (Strasbourg, 1864), 20.

[41] Ibid., 45.

[42] Ibid., 125.

[43] Ibid., 85–86.

[44] Ibid., 86.

[45] Ibid., 87.

The kingdom was first preached by Jesus as yet to come (Mark 1:14–15), but he soon taught that it had arrived, the watershed of the two periods being the conclusion of the ministry of John (Matt 11:11). It is no kingdom such as the Jews had anticipated; it is synonymous with his doctrine and way of life. "The gospel, working invisibly but all powerfully, is the real kingdom of God which gradually extends itself over humanity."[46] Note the term "gradually." There is no thought of a denouement in this teaching; on the contrary, Jesus "substituted in his views of the future an organic development for the catastrophes of the apocalypses."[47] It is impossible therefore that Jesus could have conceived of a time when he himself would bring his kingdom to a victory and exercise universal sway. The whole life of Jesus is a contradiction of the second coming idea. "Why should he return to earth? To triumph, when he hates success? To conquer by force, when he wishes to conquer by weakness and resignation? What? Would he be considered as his own precursor? A humble and sweet precursor of a violent and terrible Messiah? Can one find in the religious teaching of Jesus a single line that does not contradict explicitly or implicitly such a point of view? It would be really absurd to attribute it to him."[48] The blame for this attribution in the Gospels is to be laid at the door of the disciples, who applied to Jesus the traditional features of the Jewish messiah.[49] It was Paul's contribution to the common stock of mounting errors to imagine Jesus as the Judge at the last day.

Statements in the Gospels purporting to teach an advent of Christ in glory must therefore be eliminated. Either they are to be understood in a figurative sense or they are to be viewed as unauthentic, on the ground of their unworthiness of Jesus. For example, Mark 14:25 is a "saying impregnated with a materialism worthy of Papias." To take Mark 14:62 literally would be to impute to Jesus an unsupported illusion.[50] The apocalypse of Luke 17:22ff. deals solely with the ruin of Jerusalem and the Jewish nation: "All the sayings to the contrary which try to relate this discourse to the coming of the Son of man are necessarily glosses of the evangelist, glosses which have passed into the text and which miss the sense."[51]

So we arrive at Mark 13. In view of the foregoing discussion, no doubt need be entertained as to the treatment it must receive at Colani's hands. Every eschatological saying in the Gospels thus far has been eliminated by the twin methods of reinterpretation and the pronounce-

---

[46] Ibid., 125.
[47] Ibid., 103.
[48] Ibid., 146–48.
[49] Ibid., 144.
[50] Ibid., 195.
[51] Ibid., 204.

ment "unauthentic." In the discourse of Luke 17 both expedients were employed, with emphasis on reiteration. Here that method is sparsely used; resort is had in the main to the other method. As the references in Luke 17 to the parousia were said to be "glosses," so the eschatological passage in Mark 13 is regarded as an "interpolation." It is a rigid application of an undeviating principle, that of "thoroughgoing noneschatology."

Colani notes that the limits of parallelism in the three Synoptic Gospels extend to Mark 13:32 (Matt 24:36; Luke 21:33). These thirty verses "constitute the entire discourse, to which each evangelist, but especially Matthew, adds other sayings which relate, in appearance at least, to the coming of Christ."[52]

The disciples, on being informed of the coming destruction of the temple, ask when it will occur. "We expect a precise reply. But no; beginning with a long discourse, he starts off with words which suit well enough Matthew's authentic question, but not at all Mark's." The section ends at v. 31, after which we read, "As to that day and that hour, nobody knows anything of it, neither the angels, nor the Son, but the Father." "Is not that the direct reply to what has been asked, viz. 'When will it be?' In other words we have here a great interpolation which extends from v. 5 to v. 31. The primitive text is composed of the question of the disciples, 'When will it be?' and the simple reply of Jesus, 'I do not know,' a reply followed by counsels of vigilance. . . . Nothing could be more simple, more natural, more evangelical than this original text."[53]

As to the discourse proper, Colani adopts Holtzmann's division of the end time into three periods, "the sorrows of childbirth" (*hai ōdines*), "the affliction" (*hē thlipsis*), and "the end" (*to telos*). "Our discourse presents not only this division, but it uses precisely these three technical words. . . . We have here a very complete summary of the apocalyptic views spread among the Jewish Christians of the first century, such as we know them by John's book. They are not the views of the Jews contemporary with Jesus, for the Messiah here descends from the heavens, as he will do much later in the book of Esdras. They are not the views of Paul and of the Catholic Church, for the Christ does not come to judge the living and the dead; he comes 'to gather the elect,' evidently with the intention of founding with them his kingdom. To demonstrate the unauthenticity of this fragment, it could suffice to establish that it contains the eschatology of the Jewish Christians, since in any case (as we have seen) Jesus could not have shared their opinions."[54]

---

[52] Ibid., 201.
[53] Ibid., 202–3.
[54] Ibid., 204–5.

In one respect at least the compiler of the discourse has given himself away—"Let the reader reflect." The reader of what? Not of Daniel, for Mark does not mention him; it must refer to the discourse itself. Then it originally had not been spoken but written. "We have under our eyes a short apocalypse by an unknown author, which the Synoptics have taken for a discourse of Jesus and inserted into their compilations."[55] As to its date, its origin among Jewish Christians, in a time of severe persecution which forces them to leave Judea, fixes the period clearly enough. It is the time immediately preceding the retreat of the church of Jerusalem to Pella. Probably the "oracle" which, according to Eusebius, commanded the Jerusalem Christians to flee, was precisely this discourse. We can see that it was written before the siege of the city, for that which is predicted from the "abomination of desolation" passage onwards never took place, while what precedes is an accurate narration of events: up to v. 14 therefore history is related, from v. 14 on a prediction is given. It was composed probably a little before the Apocalypse of John (written in AD 68 according to Colani). Luke's version is a redaction of the discourse after the fall of Jerusalem and reflects its events.

It has seemed necessary to reproduce Colani's views at length, both on account of their intrinsic worth (it is notable how many ideas regarded as original to later writers were anticipated by him), and still more to show how completely his whole outlook influenced his interpretation of the eschatological discourse. Admittedly he adduced some plausible reasons to support his view, which will occupy our attention later, but most of them had been accounted for by earlier scholars. It is ironical, however, that this king of glosses and interpolations should have stressed the clause "Let him that reads understand" (Mark 13:14); for here the hypothesis of gloss is very plausible.[56] His real objection to the discourse has already been cited: "It contains the eschatology of the Jewish Christians. . . . Jesus could not have shared their opinions." Colani had in fact so mutilated the Gospels that his Jesus could not have shared these views. But this is a Jesus of his own imagining, constructed on the basis of a horror of eschatology. For this reason above all Mark 13 could have no place in Colani's expurgated Gospels; all lesser reasons are auxiliary, adduced to add plausibility to the main contention.

What was the cause of this aversion of Colani to eschatology? C. C. McCown suggested that it was due to a reaction from the traditionalism of his day. "If for no other reason, reaction against the excesses of pietistic Chiliasm, such as the great theologian Bengel had fostered in Wurtemburg and the uneducated farmer William Miller had excited in

---

[55] Ibid., 207.
[56] But see below pp. 224–26 for R. A. Clements' interpretation.

America, drove the 'modern' exegete to seek for some way out which would rescue Jesus from such unworthy associates."[57] Doubtless "pietistic excesses" would have been a contributory factor in forming the attitude of Colani and his like-minded contemporaries, though to bracket the sober Bengel with the unbalanced sectarian Miller is scarcely just to the former. Nevertheless, it was not the chiliasts who were engaging the attention of theologians in the mid-nineteenth century in Europe; it was the agnostics, and if any name is to be singled out at this juncture it will not be Bengel but Renan.

It will have been noted how almost every writer considered by us has had some relation to Strauss or Renan. The scholars concerned explicitly mention one or the other of these two men, frequently in their prefaces when explaining why their books were written, and in the course of their expositions. We have seen how Strauss caused a change in Hase's views, how violently C. H. Weisse reacted to him, how Schenkel was moved to oppose Renan, etc. Is there any ground for thinking that Colani reacted to the latter in this way? Assuredly there is. If he does not polemicize against Renan in the development of his argument, he does better by devoting the final chapter of his book to refuting the agnostic's views, particularly his eschatology. Demanding how it is that Renan has been able to secure so large a following, he concludes that it is because the humanity of Jesus, which the church had forgotten, had been laid bare once more by him. The church should learn this lesson and "cut out from the figure of the Christ the traits which are incompatible with this humanity taken seriously."[58] In particular, the question of the second coming of Christ must be faced anew. "Let someone tell me, without using flowery language, if he believes—seriously and in a literal sense—in a return of Jesus on the clouds to judge the living and the dead. . . . A man (and Jesus was a man) who legitimately attributes to himself this role, is he still our brother, subject to the same temptations as we, our pattern in the fight? Take care! If you succeed in carrying conviction that he really was our brother, the legitimacy of such pretensions would be neither desirable nor believable, and they would be viewed as M. Renan has viewed them, which is one stage worse."[59] The mere mention of Renan's name here proves nothing, but the words immediately following on that passage should be particularly noted:

> Is it not time to impose silence on the sophistries of exegesis and to acknowledge that which leaps to the eye? Jesus, in the discourses which are attributed to him, does not announce in general that he will come again

---

[57] McCown, *Search for the Real Jesus*, 243.
[58] Ibid., 250.
[59] Ibid., 251.

on the clouds of heaven—one day, in 2,000 years perhaps or in 100,000; he announces that he will return before the death of the persons present, that he will come again immediately after that Jerusalem will have been defiled. If the words which are placed in his mouth have any sense, they have this sense; and if they do not have it, it is because for theologians white means black and black means white. But for everyone who is not a sophist this dilemma poses itself categorically: either Jesus is mistaken or these discourses are not from him. The Christian Church cannot without disloyalty escape this dilemma.[60]

This language is familiar to us by now. It is the language of Reimarus. It is the language of Strauss. It is the language of Renan. Two points are made: (1) the idea of an appearance of Jesus in glory is impossible, for it involves the thought of a man discharging divine functions; (2) he promised he would come soon, according to the documents, and he has not done so. It is the latter consideration here stressed, as it was that of Renan, following upon his predecessors. Surely it is no coincidence that immediately after the mention of Renan's attitude comes that extravagant dilemma, based upon the very point that Renan had striven to make. This dilemma has been provoked by the agnostics. They elected to regard Jesus as discredited. Colani could never do that. If it is a choice of Jesus or eschatology, what Christian could pause for one moment? He will choose Jesus and reject the discourses. And so Colani did.

It seems, therefore, that Gospel critics must face the following proposition: the theory of a "little apocalypse" in Mark 13 was not the product of a dispassionate analysis of the text; it was the last stage of a developing emotional reaction to a theological problem propounded by agnostics.[61]

Lest it be thought that we do injustice to Colani, we would urge that this is no isolated phenomenon, but is observable both before and after him. What else can account for C. H. Weisse's passionate denials

---

[60] Ibid., 251–52.

[61] It is, naturally, not claimed that Colani suddenly developed his views on eschatology when Renan's *Life* appeared, but undoubtedly it provided a spur to him and conditioned his treatment of the theme, in so far as he stressed those elements that seemed to rebut Renan's views. Colani was forty years old when he wrote the book we have reviewed. His interest in the controversy roused by the agnostics dated from the commencement of his literary work. When he was but twenty-three he wrote a prize essay on the principles and results of the apologetic developed against Strauss's criticism. Three years later he founded, and continued to edit, a journal for the "new theology" of his day, in which his interest in Christology found frequent expression. It is significant that for the two years 1863–1864 he wrote a lengthy criticism of Renan's work. His own book would have appeared immediately on finishing those articles. See the article by Th. Gerold on Colani in *RE* (1898), 3:210–15.

of eschatology but an intense opposition to the views of Strauss? As he felt, so did a multitude of others. We will now go on to demonstrate a further proposition, in the light of which the above statement ought to be judged, viz. that this chain of emotional reaction to these problems has worked continuously in the history of exegesis and abides in measure to this day. In order to present our evidence concisely and to avoid scattered references to it in our subsequent discussion, we will anticipate the course of our review and assemble the evidence at once.

3. The Fanaticism of Jesus

D. Strauss

The "villain of the piece" is Strauss again. The year of Colani's book saw the publication of his work, *Das Leben Jesu für das deutsche Volk bearbeitet.* His former *Life* had been written for scholars, and was a full generation old. He now set down his views in more popular style, but how different was the mood! Years of strife had embittered his soul, and the tone of the book showed it. With regard to eschatology, what he had hinted at earlier he now emphasized with utmost violence: the expectation of a second advent of Christ is sheer folly and the final proof of the falsity of Christianity. Writing of our Lord's teaching on his parousia he states: "Such a thing as he has here prophesied of himself cannot happen to a man. If he prophesied the like of himself and expected it, then to us he is a fanatic [*(Schwärmer)*]; if he uttered it of himself without any real conviction, then he was a braggart and a deceiver."[62] Strauss anticipates the indignation of his readers: they may reply that the language of Jesus is purely symbolic, or even that he never spoke such things. Nevertheless, he insists, it must be recognized that Jesus may have said them and that he may have meant them seriously; in which case, "However sourly it may be received by our Christian ways of thinking, if it becomes established as historic fact, then our Christian ways of thinking must be given up."[63]

What makes Strauss feel so strongly that the Christian faith cannot legitimately exist with its parousia teaching? He himself supplies an answer, and in more reasonable language. Apparently it is not the mistaken view of time which Jesus is regarded as maintaining. Strauss frankly admits that if Jesus truly distinguished between this present earthly existence and one to be lived in a future kingdom of God, then "it is irrelevant at which nearer or remoter point of time he removed

---

[62] Strauss, *Das Leben Jesu für das deutsche Volk bearbeitet* (Leipzig, 1864), 236.

[63] Ibid., 237.

this act"; it would be but a human mistake for Jesus to have put the end nearer instead of further than he should.[64] One can hardly overestimate the importance of this admission. For the first time, at least in the modern debate, it has been recognized that this embarrassing matter of the time of the second coming is of no consequence; and it was put forward not by a theologian in defense of the faith, but by its most relentless opponent. It is extraordinary that the theologians did not seize on this clue. Failure to recognize it had been responsible for most of the unrealistic interpretations of biblical eschatology.

On the other hand the same failure had been equally responsible for the attacks of Reimarus, Strauss in his earlier work, and Renan, to say nothing of the misunderstanding of Colani. The theologians had been given a rod with which to measure their own deficiencies, and then to beat the backs of their opponents; to their irreparable loss they declined it. They continued to be obsessed with an irrelevancy, wandering in every conceivable bypath meadow to avoid it, and to this very day the process continues. Naturally Strauss maintained a discreet silence as to the effects of this admission on his earlier writings, and in fact he conveniently forgot the admission when he wrote *Der alte und der neue Glaube* in 1872 (see below on Weiffenbach). The point he now stresses is the monstrosity of a man claiming the power to judge his fellows and introduce a new creation:

> What gives us offense in all these sayings is simply the one factor that Jesus joined that wonderful transformation, and the introduction of the ideal state of reward, on to his own person; that he should have claimed that he himself was that one who is to come with the clouds of heaven, accompanied by angels, in order to awaken the dead and to hold the judgment. To expect that for himself is something quite different from expecting it in a general sense. Whoever expects it of himself and for himself not only appears to us as a fanatic; we see therein an unallowable self-exaltation that a man (and only of such do we speak here) should let it get into his head to divide himself off from all others and set himself over against them as the future judge; in this respect Jesus must especially have forgotten that he once refused the predicate "good" as one allowable only to God.[65]

The position is now clear; the real offense in the doctrine of the parousia is that it unveils the glory of the divine Son. In this Strauss has but clarified the position of Colani as expressed above. It is a remarkable confirmation of the contention of William Sanday, made fifty years later: "The great point about apocalyptic, and the great value of its recognition to us at the present day, is that it postulates through-

---

[64] Ibid., 242.
[65] Ibid.

out a real manifestation of God upon earth, and not merely a teacher more eminent than the rest."[66]

In comparison with the issue raised by Strauss over the "fanaticism" of Jesus, the withdrawal of his former view that Mark 13 was authentic is of small moment; to him in his present mood the whole discourse is contrived by Jewish Christians after AD 70, to put their Jesus on a par with the OT prophets, especially with Daniel.[67] That allegation was speedily forgotten, but not so the charge of fanaticism. It shook his generation, and the next, and the one after that. Subsequent discussion of the eschatology of Jesus was affected by the accusation of Strauss to an extent that has never been recognized; never, that is, with the exception of one man, H. J. Holtzmann. Here I may be permitted to state that as this phenomenon dawned on me when reading the literature of this period, its total lack of recognition on the part of previous writers perplexed me. The question suggested itself whether I was misconstruing the facts, although they seemed unambiguous. Holtzmann's *Lehrbuch der neutestamentlichen Theologie* (1897) set my mind at rest, for the great exegete had seen it. Holtzmann has a footnote, commencing on p. 326 of that book and extending over two more pages, in which he cites writer after writer to prove that the question of the *Schwärmerei*[68] of Jesus has been the determining factor between the two parties in the eschatological debate. Those who wish to see how Holtzmann illustrates the point are referred to his book; I will use his own store and continue beyond Holtzmann.

W. Weiffenbach

Next to Timothy Colani, the man who most popularized the "little apocalypse" theory is Wilhelm Weiffenbach, to whom the theory is sometimes mistakenly attributed. The first half of his work on the eschatology of Jesus is concerned with the history of the critical interpretation of Mark 13. He was an enthusiastic follower of Colani, and after portraying the developments of his theory in subsequent writers he suggested his own modifications. Weiffenbach makes it plain that his work has been called forth by Strauss's charge as to the *Schwärmerei* of Jesus. In the introduction to the book he gives a lengthy extract from Strauss's *Der alte und der neue Glaube,* expressing the sentiment ob-

---

[66] Sanday, "The Apocalyptic Element in the Gospels," *Hibbert Journal* 10 (1, 1914): 84.

[67] Strauss, *Leben Jesu . . . bearbeitet,* 240.

[68] The German term is ambiguous. Luther pronounced rival teachers in his Reformation as "Schwarmer." The translator of Frantz Funck-Brentano's biography of Luther defines it as "a word meaning *enthusiast, visionary and mountebank,* for which there is no precise English equivalent" (*Luther* [London, 1936], ch. 19, "The Heavenly Visionaries").

served in the above quotation from the popular *Life*.[69] To Weiffenbach the reputation of Jesus is at stake.

> Should all attempts prove idle to protect Jesus from the objection of a perpetually unfulfilled promise to come again, then in our opinion there remains for any honest Bible-student only this one unambiguous confession—Jesus has made a mistake in regard to his coming again, he is found in a state of self-delusion in respect to the consummation of the kingdom of God! It is also evident, as already Keim, Weizsäcker, etc., as well as Strauss in his way, have made clear, that the consequences of this thesis must be drawn absolutely and on all sides; before all else the question must be faced whether, along with that "necessary" confession, the religious-moral greatness of Jesus remains unimpaired, and his position as Lord and Leader remains the same for our religious thought, faith, and life.[70]

Weiffenbach writes to propound a solution, whereby Jesus can be relieved of the promise: Jesus spoke of his coming again, but by it he meant his resurrection; the disciples misunderstood his language. That is the burden of his book. To identify the parousia with the resurrection, however, raises a difficulty: the parousia is said in the eschatological discourse to be preceded by events following the resurrection, affecting both the church and the world; how are they to be accounted for on this view? One answer alone is possible: the eschatological discourse is spurious and misrepresents the teaching of Jesus. Hence a major portion of Weiffenbach's book has to be devoted to a detailed proof that Mark 13 is composite. Once again, despite a long and tedious discussion of critical opinions, we are presented with an interpretation fundamentally based on an a priori argument, designed to meet the objections of the scoffers.

G. Volkmar

The sentiments of Strauss are expressed by Gustav Volkmar in almost identical language, although the unbelief of the former was by no means shared by the latter. To him, as to Strauss, the concept of the parousia is bound up with that of a deified Christ and therefore unacceptable. Speaking of the presentation of Jesus in Matthew, he comments:

> So long as he was regarded as in this book, as one who was born Son of God, or a demi–god, such an announcement of the hope can be sustained; a divine being can ascend to heaven or descend. But when the "divine Son" has become the Son of man, born an Israelite, who became the Son

---

[69] That Holtzmann reproduces precisely this section of Strauss's book is presumably due to his dependence on Weiffenbach here.

[70] Weiffenbach, *Die Wiederkunftsgedanke Jesu* (Leipzig, 1873), iii–iv.

of God in spirit after his baptism, this hope of the clouds of heaven can be explained as nothing else than a piece of fanaticism. Admittedly a certain amount of fanaticism can be taken for granted in any great man, and it is equally to be excused in Jesus in view of his sublimity in other respects. But this view savours more of an uncontrolled enthusiasm wafted in the air of fantasy than of a life on solid earth such as our documents reveal.[71]

Not surprisingly, in Volkmar's estimate the kingdom of God is the community of those who respond to the preaching of Jesus and become God's children like him; by their consecration of the marriage relationship and unwearied toil they create a holy people, able by God's grace to bring in "the victory of the true worship of God over all forms of idolatry and to unite the world in one divine kingdom of peace."[72] In such a system there is as much room for eschatology as there is for an Incarnate Redeemer—none at all.

H. J. Holtzmann

H. J. Holtzmann has already been cited as one who perceived the nature of the eschatological controversy revolving about the person of Christ. With clear insight he saw that Jesus attributed to himself a central place in the eschatological future, but he believed that this was offset by Jesus' preaching of a present kingdom, wherein alone his original and abiding message is to be sought. If anyone will look "beyond the prospect of those earth colors" (i.e., of the eschatological kingdom) to the advancement of humanity wrought in history through the preaching of the present kingdom, one will easily distinguish the permanent element in our Lord's "prophetic fantasy" from "the dissolving views of a purely idle fanaticism."[73] Holtzmann, then, recognized an element of *Schwärmerei* in Jesus, but refused all that was bound up with it. Beyschlag, on the other hand, equally recognizing the issue at stake, rejected this interpretation. The idea of Jesus coming to judgment is essential: "It seals Christianity as the absolute religion." If Jesus was simply a guide among other guides, or if he could merely initiate, but not finish, redemption, "then certainly the very idea of his office as Judge of the world would be a fanatical presumption." But if the Son is the true revelation of the Father, "then is Christ also born judge of the world."[74] Here we see contemporaries taking opposite sides on this

---

[71] Volkmar, *Jesus Nazarenus und die erste christliche Zeit* (Zürich, 1882), 154–55.

[72] Ibid., 74–75.

[73] Holtzmann, *Lehrbuch der neutestamentlichen Theologie* (Leipzig, 1897), 337.

[74] Beyschlag, *New Testament Theology* (ET 1895, from the German of 1891, Edinburgh), 191.

issue, in full consciousness of what was involved. Beyschlag was not alone in the position he adopted.

P. Schwartzkopff

Paul Schwartzkopff similarly defended Jesus against *Schwärmerei* in his anticipation of a second coming. Whether Jesus was wrong or right in that expectation, it involves him in neither fanaticism nor self-exaltation. "He recognized in himself the absolute Mediator of salvation, hence the perfected salvation must be mediated through his Person." That Jesus described the advent as taking place in divine glory is not surprising; it corresponds with the majesty of God revealed in the consummated kingdom. "Self-exaltation would have been involved if he had ascribed that majesty to his own human ability. But as everywhere, he knew himself in this respect not as originator, but only as mediator and instrument of the execution of the divine plan of salvation."[75] Fanaticism is therefore ruled out. The humility of Jesus and his spirit of self-sacrifice are plainly seen in the way he gave himself for the setting up of the kingdom: "He whose cleanness of heart had ever preserved the purest sobriety of feeling, untouched by fantasy, found in the conception of his coming again in divine glory the manner worthy of God in which God himself should lead mankind to its highest goal through him." If there is nothing fanatical in the conception of a new creation for the eternal state, neither is there anything fanatical in the thought of Jesus coming in a glorified spiritual body to the renewed earth.[76]

A. Réville

A return to Colani's views is observable in the French writer Albert Réville. He stressed two points: the speedy advent and the fantasy of the whole conception.

> The ancient exegetes never wished to recognize that if Jesus held the language which the evangelists attribute to him, he was gravely deceived in his outlook. . . . They had recourse to mystical applications, saying that this return is permanent in the heart of his believers, as if this idea had anything in common with the unique return, visible, at a fixed day, which is propounded to us. They have tried to represent this sudden coming of the Son of man as simply the death which comes to greet us so often unexpectedly; as if there was any question of death in this description of the reappearance of the Christ, of which the living will be the witnesses. We admit that preachers can give this edifying turn to the synoptic

---

[75] Schwartzkopff, *Die Weissagungen Jesu Christi von seinem Tode, seiner Auferstehung und Wiederkunft und ihre Erfüllung* (Göttingen, 1895), 192–93.
[76] Ibid., 193.

apocalypse in their exhortations, but do not let us pretend that they are thus reproducing the real sense.[77]

The acuteness of this criticism can hardly be denied, but Réville will not stop here. If Jesus spoke as he is represented in the eschatological discourse, then judgment must be passed on him.

Jesus would then have taken back in an imaginary future this theatrical and violent messianism which he had so flatly repudiated during his earthly life. He would only have adjourned the date, and in an intoxicating dream of grandeur, he would have contemplated the prospect of coming to inaugurate his dominion over the kingdoms of the earth and all their glory, with the traits of the heavenly emperor. After beginning by announcing essential religion, drawn from the conscience of religious humanity . . . he would have finished by giving it over to a mere chimera. If this is not impossible, we must assert that it is very strange.[78]

Réville naturally does not wish to pass such a judgment on Jesus; accordingly he pronounces the eschatological discourse, and all in the Gospels that accords with it, as unauthentic.

A. Merx

The Syriac scholar A. Merx, whose commentaries we shall have occasion to notice later, by no means shared the presuppositions of Réville, but his attitude to *Schwärmerei* led him to similar conclusions respecting the eschatological discourse.

I do not understand what false interest for the written word, which molds together the most common stock ideas of Jewish apocalyptic, makes theologians want violently to fix on Jesus a total mistake, where a little textual criticism and a little higher criticism are sufficient to enable us to see in Jesus no self-deceiving *Schwärmer* but a Seer who knows the true forces of history clearly and makes them known. And yet many theologians are pursued by the painful feeling that this pseudo-eschatology inserts into the wholesome picture of Jesus such unwholesome fantastic elements![79]

His own view of the discourse leads him to accept that section in which Jesus warns his disciples against "false messianic *Schwärmerei*" (Matt 24:4–6). The "fantastic idea" that Jesus is the Son of man who is to come on the clouds at the end is not to be put to his account; it is mere Jewish apocalypticism.[80] Here is involved a kind of modification of the "little

---

[77] Réville, *Jésus de Nazareth*, 2 vols. (Paris, 1897), 2:314–16.

[78] Ibid., 316–17.

[79] Merx, *Das Evangelium Matthäus nach der syrischen im Sinaikloster gefundenen Palimpsesthandschrift* (Berlin, 1902), 354–55.

[80] Ibid., 355.

apocalypse" theory which will occupy us later; the earlier sections of that so-called apocalypse are accepted as authentic; the section dealing with the coming of the Son of man is refused (i.e., Matt 24:29–31/Mark 13:24–27). But on what grounds is the major part accepted and the latter rejected? Fundamentally both decisions proceed from one and the same consideration, viz. the wish to save Jesus from fanaticism! In so deciding Merx will satisfy nobody.

A. Jülicher

Jülicher felt obliged to assign no small part of his contribution to the compendious volume *Die christliche Religion* to the aspect of fanaticism in the eschatology of Jesus. He affirmed that the "inconcinnity" of our Lord's views on the kingdom as present and future is reconciled in his Person, which belongs to both present and future; but he insists that Jesus "cannot be made out, on this ground, to have been an apocalyptic *Schwärmer,* consuming himself in ardent longing."[81] In his creative hands the old views are filled with a new content, but it is through the new spirit alone that the old have survived; consequently it is the new element that is of real worth. "In the case of Jesus the serious man must choose between the admission of a new spirit full of new power, naturally claiming for itself the future, or a crazy self-exaltation that no eschatological enthusiasm excuses, a blinded understanding of his time that forbids any confidence in the judgment of so disappointing a man."[82] Presumably the "new spirit" primarily refers to the moral teaching of Jesus, by which his kingdom will claim the world, and that futurist eschatology as such is mere *Schwärmerei.* Inasmuch as no one wishes to claim that Jesus' eschatology is separable from the rest of his teaching, the observation is not very helpful. If it is a negation of eschatology completely, then Jülicher must have his view and we have ours. Jülicher has occasion later to mention how deeply impressed he is with the wisdom of our Lord's counsel for his church; it could not have been improved, even had he anticipated centuries of development, and it has stood the test of time. "Therein lies the best proof how little his thinking was ruled by eschatological *Schwärmerei.*"[83] Most would agree, but we suspect that what Jülicher meant by "eschatological fanaticism" is not what the church as a whole would view as such.

The story is continued in the expositions of Julius Wellhausen, regarded by Creed as containing the germinal ideas of all subsequent

---

[81] Jülicher, *Die christliche Religion,* part 1, "Die Religion Jesu und die Anfänge des Christentums bis zum Nicaenum" (Berlin and Leipzig, 1906), 58.
[82] Ibid., 59.
[83] Ibid., 61.

exegesis of the Synoptic Gospels. Wellhausen, it will be recalled, paid tribute to the "silent influence" of Strauss on the theologians of his time. He appears to have felt that the only way to rebut Strauss's charges was to tread in the path marked out by Colani: as far as the east is from the west, so far hath Jesus removed Jewish messianism from him. Jesus neither regarded himself as Messiah, nor predicted an atoning death and resurrection. Accordingly, "it can safely be asserted that if Jesus did not once speak beforehand to his disciples of his sufferings and resurrection, he certainly did not of his parousia. . . . He ought therefore to be relieved of the charge of fanaticism and false prophecy. In fact, he had nothing of an ecstatic *Schwärmerei* in himself, not even of a prophet."[84] The presence of *Schwärmerei* in primitive Christianity cannot be denied; indeed, "Enthusiasm begat Christianity, but it was the enthusiasm of the disciples, not the enthusiasm of Jesus."[85] Wellhausen's argument is plausible only if its fundamental presupposition be accepted, that Jesus had no thought of a messianic mission. For most of us the evidence of the life and teaching of Jesus is too serious to warrant such drastic treatment of the sources as this demands.[86]

British Writers

So far no mention has been made of British writers. Prior to the opening of this century there is nothing to say about them in this matter, for the eschatological controversy had no counterpart in this country until the work of Schweitzer revealed what had been transpiring in Germany. There is an interesting contact with this movement in the writings of L. A. Muirhead, the Presbyterian theologian. In articles and

---

[84] Wellhausen, *Einleitung in die drei ersten Evangelien*, 96.

[85] Ibid., 150.

[86] Wellhausen appends a curious footnote on p. 150 of his *Einleitung,* probably to counterbalance his citations of Strauss's earlier works, in which the latter had voiced his confidence that the teaching as to the second coming was the surest thing we know about Jesus. He quotes a letter of Strauss, written in 1862, and another in 1864, in which Strauss expresses hesitation to ascribe this view to Jesus, for "It is difficult to imagine so much fanaticism alongside so much reasonableness." In the second letter Strauss wrote that the "crumb of the second coming" is too bulky for him to swallow—that is, he cannot accept the authenticity of this teaching attributed to Jesus—since "that idea in my view stands quite near to madness." As Wellhausen read these letters in Ziegel's biography of Strauss, he might have been candid enough to add what Ziegel himself said about this matter. The letters are given on p. 609 of the biography; on p. 684 Ziegel summarizes Strauss's teaching in *Der alte und der neue Glaube,* in which the old assertions about the *Schwärmerei* are vehemently renewed. Ziegel then comments: "Thus the eschatological crumb that eight years earlier he could not get down him, Strauss has now swallowed." The hesitation as to the *Schwärmerei* of Jesus was a merely temporary aberration on Strauss's part.

in his book *The Eschatology of Jesus* (1904), he had defended the discourse of Mark 13 against the supporters of the "little apocalypse" theory. But he capitulated in his work *The Terms Life and Death in the Old and New Testaments and Other Papers* (1908). As Moffatt draws attention to this convert to the critical theory, we should note the reason for the change: "We are now disposed to accept the theory," wrote Muirhead, "on the ground that it offers an escape from the views in which our Lord appears to be entangled in the meshes, if not the trivialities, of Jewish apocalyptism."[87] Doubtless that is a common enough motive, but whether it is legitimate documentary criticism is another matter. The position is more closely stated by Muirhead in his summary of the main types of eschatological exegesis; he describes them as the pictorial view, represented by Haupt; the pronounced view, seen in Johannes Weiss; and the protective view. Of the last-named he writes: "It is meant to cover views of the eschatological phenomena of the Gospels that may be mutually so diverse as to have hardly anything in common but a repudiation of the exaggerations of the pronounced view. These views we may call protective in that they guard a right and reverent sense of our Lord's sanity of mind, and equip us against the 'neurotism' which mistakes the reflection of itself for the historic Jesus, and sees in his messianic consciousness what Strauss called a dosis of *Schwärmerei*."[88] From this point Muirhead proceeds to expound his fresh view of the eschatological discourse. It is surely not without significance that one of the first British scholars to expound the "little apocalypse" theory with conviction should do it in that context. The "silent influence of Strauss" has entered fresh waters.

Latimer Jackson gave passing mention to this aspect of our subject when he defended the Jewish apocalyptists against the charge of *Schwärmerei*.[89] He similarly refused to regard Jesus as a "dreamer, the enthusiast of his day."[90] This feature of eschatological controversy was not typical of British discussion, however; yet it found a strange echo in the 1940s. T. F. Glasson in his work *The Second Advent* (London, 1945) returned to the views of Colani, in a similar fashion as Martin Werner has followed in the paths laid out by Schweitzer, though naturally he has developed those views in the light of recent trends. The burden of the book is an attempt to prove that Jesus rejected in toto Jewish messianism, which was solely of a this-worldly order, and that

---

[87] Cited by Moffatt, *An Introduction to the Literature of the New Testament*, 3d ed. (Edinburgh, 1918), 208 n. 3; Muirhead, *The Terms Life and Death in the Old and New Testaments, and Other Papers* (London, 1908), 125.

[88] Ibid., 120.

[89] Jackson, *The Eschatology of Jesus* (London, 1913), 244. Jackson actually uses this word without translating it.

[90] Ibid., 320.

consequently Jesus had no thought of a parousia; that belief arose in the primitive church through the application to Jesus of OT texts relating to the theophanies of God. By an extraordinary coincidence Glasson commences his introduction with a quotation from T. H. Huxley: "In his *Collected Essays*, T. H. Huxley refers to the view that Jesus foretold his speedy return to the earth in glory, and makes comment: 'If he believed and taught that, then assuredly he was under an illusion, and he is responsible for that which the mere effluxion of time has demonstrated to be a prodigious error.' " Glasson returns to this citation later,[91] and proceeds to demonstrate its error by showing that Jesus never taught this doctrine. The parallel with Colani is striking. Like his predecessor, Glasson cites the atheist who must be rebutted; like him he adopts the method of denying entirely the authenticity of Jesus' teaching on the future kingdom and parousia, and pays careful attention to Mark 13; like him he caricatures the orthodox belief in the second advent, as when he denies that Jesus was "a distraught, wild-eyed apocalyptist shrieking out the vain message that millions now living will never die," as though the creeds of the church set forth that view of Jesus! Like Colani, too, Glasson maintains that Jesus replaced Jewish apocalyptic by belief in the slow development of God's kingdom. In a scheme of this sort, there is no need to discuss whether Mark 13 is authentic; indeed, it cannot be allowed to remain, for if Mark 13 is authentic, this view cannot stand. In this case, as in all we have been reviewing, Mark 13 is the victim, and the cherished hypothesis stands.

American Writers

In American literature the attitude we have traced in earlier theologians makes an appearance in F. C. Grant's work, *The Gospel of the Kingdom* (1940). This writer combats the notion that Jesus believed himself to be the Messiah. In particular, the title Son of man could not have been adopted by him. "For any human being to identify himself with the Son of Man of the visions of Enoch, taken literally, and without reinterpretation, could suggest little else than an *unsound mind*—certainly not the supreme and unquestioned sanity of the Man of Galilee; yet of any 'reinterpretation' or 'spiritualisation' of the concept there is not one hint in the Gospels."[92] The term "Son of man," and the identification of Jesus with the Messiah, are said to have arisen after his death. "Only on some such hypothesis as this can we relieve the historical Jesus of intolerable contradictions and an unsupportable burden of unreality. He was certainly no mad fanatic, no deluded pretender to a celestial and really mythical title, no claimant to a throne

[91] Glasson, *The Second Advent* (London, 1945), 10.
[92] Grant, *The Gospel of the Kingdom* (New York, 1940), 63.

which did not exist, no prophet of a coming Judgment, to be carried out by a heavenly figure seated on the clouds with whom he identified himself—which judgment never took place, never could take place."[93] Grant concludes by suggesting (as N. Schmidt had done more than a generation earlier) that the term "Son of man" entered Christian theology through Mark 13, which once circulated without the reference to the parousia in v. 26, but which was sufficient to influence the rest of the Gospel tradition in this respect.

It is extraordinary how this motif of *Schwärmerei*, with its accompanying extravagance of language, has persisted so long. The influence it has had on eschatological studies is incalculable, for the interpretation to which it gave birth became accepted in circles in which its presence was overlooked. This particularly applies to the "little apocalypse" theory, which was born of this horror of *Schwärmerei*, but which speedily forsook its parent. We recognize that to uncover the origin of this theory is no proof of its mistakenness. Colani may have stumbled on a true discovery, even though his approach was deeply prejudiced. Not all his successors were animated by the same spirit. Yet the fact remains that whatever may have been the subsequent history of this hypothesis, the claim that it was the impartial conclusion of scientific criticism, in search of truth at all costs, can no longer be sustained. The majority of present-day NT scholars repudiate the assumptions on which this theory was erected. Perhaps it is time they scrutinized more carefully the structure itself. We propose, accordingly, to examine the subsequent developments of this hypothesis in detail, not in the lurid glare of controversies with agnostics, but with all the aids that criticism can give to us.

---

[93] Ibid., 67–68.

2

THE DEVELOPMENT OF THE LITTLE APOCALYPSE THEORY

1. From C. Weizsäcker to W. Weiffenbach

C. Weizsäcker

The importance of Colani's criticism of the eschatological discourse was immediately recognized. From this time on, no major work on the theology of the Gospels, the criticism of the documents, or the life of Jesus could afford to neglect it. It was paid the compliment of instant attention by the Tübingen scholar Carl Weizsäcker in his extensive work on the Gospel history.[1] Colani had treated Mark 13:5–31 as a

---

[1] Weizsäcker, *Untersuchungen über die evangelische Geschichte* (Tübingen, 1864). I do not know on what authority von Dobschütz, writing in 1910, could state: "It was in the year 1864 that Colani and Wiezsäcker, one independent of the other, came to the conclusion that this is not the report of an original sermon of Jesus, but a composite work" (*Eschatology of the Gospels* [London, 1910] 85–86). Both Weiffenbach, who wrote his detailed survey of the criticism of Mark 13 as early as 1873, and Busch in the only book devoted to the consideration of Mark 13 since that date (*Zum Verständnis der synoptischen Eschatologie* [Gütersloh, 1938]), make it plain that Weizsäcker depended on the impetus provided by Colani and attempted to define the original source more closely. The above citation from von Dobschutz hints that he inferred the independence of Weizsäcker on Colani because both writers issued their books in 1864. I have not been able to trace the precise dates of the appearance of these two works, but since Colani's book went through a second edition in the same year, it is plain that the first edition must have appeared early in 1864. For a similar example of the ability of a book to rouse immediate response from writers already engaged on their research we may cite Haupt's *Die eschatologischen Aussagen Jesu in den synoptischen Evangelien* (Berlin, 1895). Both Paul Schwartzkopff (*Die Weissagungen Jesu Christi*) and Arthur Titius (*Jesu Lehre vom Reiche Gottes*

single document, forming in three scenes a self-contained Jewish-Christian apocalypse (vv. 5–8, the "sorrows of childbirth"; vv. 9–13, the "affliction"; vv. 14–31 the "end"). He attempted no further analysis. The problem of accounting for the presence of authentic sayings of Jesus within that document was neglected. The history of the criticism of Mark 13 now becomes the record of the endeavors of Gospel critics to solve this problem as precisely as possible.

Weizsäcker recognized at least some of the sayings in Mark 13:5–31 as genuine; he particularly cites the parable of the Fig Tree, vv. 28–29. The problem of authenticity was solved by stressing the three-fold division of the chapter, mentioned above; the passages which plainly set forth this division, vv. 7–8, 14–20, 24–27, presumably make up the actual apocalypse. To this group has been attached an introduction concerning false prophets (v. 6), repeated between the second and third groups (vv. 21–23), a parabolic epilogue (vv. 33–37), and warnings concerning persecution which must last till the gospel is preached to the heathen (vv. 9–13). It is a neat analysis, and to it a significant number of commentators have returned, after half a century or more of variations.[2] Weizsäcker differed from Colani in thinking that the discourse emanated from Jewish, rather than Jewish-Christian, sources. The objective description of the "Son of man" prophecy of vv. 24–27 seemed to demand a Jewish origin. So also did the Jewish standpoint apparently observable in vv. 14–20, with its scruples concerning the Sabbath; and most important of all, the mention of the "abomination of desolation" presupposes the continuance of the temple, not its destruction. With that in mind Weizsäcker was greatly interested in a "citation" of Enoch in the Epistle of Barnabas, which he read as follows: "The last offense is at hand, concerning which the Scripture speaketh, as Enoch saith, 'For to this end the Master hath cut the seasons and the days short, that his beloved might hasten and come to his inheritance' " (Barn 4:3). The likeness of this to Mark 13:20 is striking. Weizsäcker concluded that the little apocalypse, which he had distinguished within Mark 13, had come from the source quoted by Barnabas, viz. the apocalypse ascribed to Enoch.[3] The date of the synoptic apocalypse must be prior to AD 70, as there is no hint of the fall of Jerusalem in Mark 13. Weizsäcker sought to mitigate the offense of his view by suggesting that there is no reason why Jesus should not have made use of such writings, as may be seen in the citation from Enoch concerning the fruitfulness of the vine and wheat in the kingdom, attributed by Papias and Irenaeus to Jesus. The circulation of this logion explains

---

[Freiburg and Leipzig, 1895]) devoted considerable attention to Haupt's views in their books, both of which appeared in 1895.

[2] Weizsäcker, *Untersuchungen*, 121–22.

[3] Ibid., 135–36.

how easily this apocalypse was ascribed to the Lord.[4] Nevertheless, the teaching of Jesus as to his ignorance of the time and the suddenness of his coming shows that "Jesus himself gave no apocalypse of the history of the future."[5]

Weizsäcker applied himself again to this matter in his later work, *The Apostolic Age of the Christian Church*. In this he withdrew his former contention that the little apocalypse was of Jewish origin, for it would seem that it was addressed expressly to disciples, to whom the scruples for the Sabbath would apply equally as to Jews. The exodus of the Christians had not yet taken place; "they still lived as Jews in Jerusalem."[6] The triple division of the apocalypse is a common feature of Jewish-Christian eschatology, as may be seen in the three woes of the book of Revelation (9:12; 11:14). The first subject there is also war, the second the distress of Jerusalem; under the third the end can alone be understood. The consequence of this change of opinion should be noted, for it is often overlooked, since Weizsäcker's earlier work was republished in the present century and he is still known by the opinions expressed therein. The change of view automatically removes several objections earlier expressed, particularly the supposed reference to Enoch. Indeed, Weizsäcker had wrongly construed the quotation from Barnabas, as the editors of that epistle unanimously recognize. The punctuation usually adopted makes Enoch concur with the Scripture: "The last offense is at hand, concerning which the Scripture speaketh, as Enoch saith. For to this end the Master hath cut the seasons and the days short, that his Beloved might hasten and come to his inheritance" (so J. B. Lightfoot, *The Apostolic Fathers*, revised texts ed. J. R. Harmer [London, 1926]). Whether this is a free rendering of Mark 13:20, as Weiffenbach later believed, is not easily determined, for the motives in the two statements are quite different. In any case there is no ground for imagining the dependence of Mark 13 on 1 (Ethiopic) Enoch; no such statement can be found in the book that has survived under that name. It is a fair instance of the kind of suggestion adduced for proving the "Jewish" origin of Mark 13, which, however, is not easily demonstrated if by that designation we mean "Jewish," in distinction from "Jewish-Christian."

We cannot forbear noting that Weizsäcker's later comparison of the triple division of Mark 13 with Revelation 9–11 is as unfortunate as the comparison with Barnabas. The threefold woes of Revelation 9–11 are quite different from the descriptions of Mark 13. The first woe affects the abyss; the second the loosing of the 200,000,000 horsemen, not

---

[4] Ibid., 128, 551.

[5] Ibid., 552.

[6] Weizsäcker, *The Apostolic Age of the Christian Church* (ET London, 1895, from the German of 1886), 23.

Jerusalem; 10:1–11 is an interlude, having no direct connection with the three woes; the third woe is left for description until 16:17–21, with the further unveiling in chs. 17–19, and denotes the destruction of anti–Christian civilization. Such a scheme has no contact with Mark 13; like many other comparisons, its impressiveness disappears upon investigation. When Weizsäcker's contentions are weighed carefully, the one plausible feature in them is the "contradiction" between Mark 13:32 and the chapter in which it is set. That we may leave for later consideration.

O. Pfleiderer

A more brilliant investigation of Mark 13, which nevertheless would hardly have been possible without Weizsäcker's work, was that of Otto Pfleiderer.[7] To him the eschatological discourse is the key to the eschatology of Jesus. Assuming the threefold division of Mark 13 announced by his predecessors (vv. 5–13, 14–23, 24–27), he adjudges each section to contain two subdivisions: vv. 7–8, 14–20, 24–27 describe world events that affect the nations and natural life and constitute an apocalypse; vv. 9–13, 21–23, 28–32 warn Christian believers of threatening dangers and exhort them to faithfulness. In the apocalypse, vv. 14–20 form the central act, a Jewish catastrophe; the cosmic scenes of vv. 7–8, 24–27 form the introductory foreground and concluding background respectively. Against Weizsäcker, Pfleiderer argues that this apocalypse is Christian, for Jewish Christianity also observed the Sabbath, and, still more decisively, Jewish apocalyptic does not know of a messiah coming from heaven, nor of the messianic use of the term "Son of man" (here Pfleiderer clearly depends on Colani). It is altogether likely that the little apocalypse was composed in the troubles of the seventh decade, prior to the fall of Jerusalem, and that the abomination of desolation relates to the murderous acts of the Zealots. In support of this Pfleiderer cites Josephus, who said of the Zealots, "Their blood alone was a defiling of the sanctuary," and in his appeal to them urged, "Is not the city and the whole temple full of the corpses of those you have murdered? God thus, God himself it is who brings on this fire to purge the city and temple through the Romans."[8] This apocalypse is identical with that "oracle" mentioned by Eusebius as commanding the flight of the Christians from Jerusalem, for Eusebius referred to it as a command *di' apokalypseōs dothenta pro tou polemou*.[9] The portents of the closing section of the apocalypse are to be explained as those in the

---

[7] Pfleiderer, "Über die Composition der eschatologischen Rede, Mt. 24.4ff.," *Jahrbücher für Deutsche Theologie* (vol. 13, 1868), pp. 134–49.

[8] Josephus, *Wars* 4.3.12; 6.2.1.

[9] Eusebius, *Eccl Hist* 3.5.

book of Revelation; they supply a cosmic background for the initiation
of the sovereignty of Christ with his elect, rather than the end of the
universe.

Having thus dealt with the sayings that constitute the little apocalypse, Pfleiderer seeks an explanation of the other series, Mark 13:9–
13, 21–23, 28–32. Whereas an observable sequence of thought enables
us to divide the apocalypse into beginning of sorrows, tribulation, and
climax, no such progression is discernible in the other series. Not only
are they a heterogeneous group, but by their insertion into the other
series the original progression is obscured and confusion is produced.
For example, after the characterization of vv. 7–8 as the beginning of
sorrows, the "then" of v. 9 should introduce the real distress and v. 14
the end, but it is not so;[10] similarly 14–20 narrate a quite short time of
tribulation (v. 20), yet v. 10 speaks of an indefinitely long period in
which the heathen are evangelized; the same feature is seen in a
comparison of 24ff. with 21ff., for v. 24 speaks of something that
happens 'immediately' (so Matthew) after the distress of 14–20, yet
21ff. obtrude another indefinite period of delay; finally we note that
whereas 24–27 describe the end, we are taken back into the period of
signs once more by 28ff.

The conclusion from this is "irresistible"; not only are the two
series of sayings distinct, not only is the second series unrelated, it has
been interpolated into the first series to check the immediate temporal
succession of its members, i.e., to retard the swift course of the apocalyptic process described therein. There is the key to the understanding
of the entire composition.[11] The eschatological discourse has been
drawn up by Mark, as the Pauline addition of 13:10 shows, with a view
to tempering the impatient expectation of an immediately impending
parousia. Jesus did not contemplate a worldwide preaching of the
gospel, as Matt 10:23 proves. "The 'immediately' of the apocalypse
(Matt 24:29) was tempered first by the addition of genuine eschatological sayings of Jesus, and then by the introduction of the universalism
taught by Paul, the realization of which postulated a longer time for the
development of Christianity than had been anticipated in the eschatological reckoning of primitive Christianity."[12]

---

[10] Pfleiderer worked on the basis of Matthew's version of the discourse and
Matt 24:9 begins with *Tote*. The genuine text of Mark 13:9 does not do so,
although in some Western authorities, including D, it is assimilated to the
Matthean text. We have let Pfleiderer's reference stand, so as not to prejudice the
issue as to which version is original. We shall, however, later show reason to
question that the description of the distress of Jerusalem was bound up with that
of the parousia in the earliest tradition.

[11] Pfleiderer, "Composition," 144–46.

[12] Ibid., 148–49.

It is curious that while Weizsäcker in later years modified his original view that the little apocalypse was Jewish and came to regard it as Jewish-Christian, Pfleiderer performed the opposite volte-face and subsequently considered the presumed Jewish-Christian document to be Jewish. The chief reason prompting this change was a fresh consideration of the abomination of desolation, Mark 13:14. The most natural interpretation of that enigmatic phrase is now considered to be one akin to its original use in Dan 9:27; 12:11, where it refers to the setting up of an idol in the temple. Nothing of the kind took place during the war under Titus, yet the event nearly happened in AD 40, when Caligula commanded that his own statue be erected in the temple. The order was not carried out, but Mommsen is cited as saying, "Since that fateful decree (of Caligula), the anxiety never ceased that another Caesar would command the same thing." The whole situation is now plain to Pfleiderer: the abomination has not been set up, according to 13:14, but it nearly was erected, and 13:14ff. reflect the fears of the country populace of Judea, who were ready to fly to the mountains when the next, and successful, attempt was made. "In the circles of the country populace, for whom this saying was given, the introduction of the same was vividly feared, and precisely this fear was maintained in those years of growing Jewish fanaticism before the destruction of Jerusalem."[13]

Pfleiderer suggests that Mark 13:24–27, the coming of the Son of man, could have been derived directly from Dan 7:13; the fact that it is not a Christian description is seen in the lack of suggestion that the Son of man is the crucified Jesus (cf. Rev 1:7). This Jewish apocalypse was probably written in the seventh decade. How, then, did it come to be adopted by the Christians? The answer lies in its approximation to Christian eschatology; it came so near their own hopes, they could not ignore it. "The simplest thing was to change the Jewish apocalypse into a Christian one through the addition of such exhortations as seemed fitting for the Christians of that time." The chief requirements were to warn the Christians against popular leaders who sought to win them to the Jewish national movement (vv. 5f., 21ff.), and to prepare them for persecutions, which in reality contributed to the spread of the gospel and the coming of the end (vv. 9–13, 28ff.). "So the Christian editor sets over against the fanatical Jewish messianic hope the exhortation to patient waiting, courageous testimony, and faithful suffering in the service of the Lord Jesus, whose coming in any case was to be hoped for shortly, within the lifetime of the present generation."[14]

---

[13] Pfleiderer, *Das Urchristentum* (Berlin, 1887), 403–5.
[14] Ibid., 405–6.

This is all very interesting, and it contains some plausible features now widely accepted; but what becomes, on this scheme, of the brilliant explanation of the Christian interpolations, set in the apocalypse to retard the apocalyptic process? There is no place for it, for now Christian and Jew alike expect the end soon, only for different reasons. Pfleiderer thus has silently abandoned the view which was the main inspiration of his earlier contribution to the subject. Yet as in the case of Weizsäcker, fate has decreed that the retraction in *Das Urchristentum* should be forgotten by posterity, and that the view Pfleiderer abandoned should become, in a modified form, generally adopted. The specific notion of the "Christian interpolations" as a brake on the apocalyptic wheel was forgotten, but the intention of the evangelist as allaying the impatience of ardent believers was destined to become the normal view, through the advocacy of Johannes Weiss.

W. Weiffenbach

The most detailed examination that our chapter was to receive for fully sixty-five years was that of Wilhelm Weiffenbach, whose work began with a review of the criticism of Mark 13 to his time. He, too, accepted Pfleiderer's analysis of the little apocalypse, together with the reason adduced by him for the evangelist's insertions between its members, viz. the retarding of the apocalyptic process. He admitted, however, that this latter consideration does not suffice to account for all the facts.[15] To the sections Mark 13:7–8, 14–20, 24–27, Weiffenbach added vv. 30–31, which join on to vv. 24–27 very well. Mark 13:30 declares that "everything," i.e., in the apocalypse thus defined, will happen in the contemporary generation, especially the final denouement at the parousia. To give assurance on this point the apocalyptist added v. 31 as a "ceremonious concluding formula, confirming the truth of the prophecies."[16] This means, of course, that the apocalypse is not anonymous, as had hitherto been supposed, but deliberately pseudonymous; that need occasion no surprise, for apocalyptists "love to conclude their prophecies with solemn formulas of the conclusion and confirmatory endings that impart assurance."[17] That the apocalypse cannot have proceeded from Jesus is obvious, for (1) it is a characteristic representative of that "restless calculating of the future on the part of the later Jews and Jewish-Christians," such as we see in Daniel, Enoch, Ezra, the Sibyls, the Ascension of Moses, the Revelation of John; (2) the first two sections of the little apocalypse, vv. 7–9a, 14–20, are merely historical facts in an apocalyptic disguise, i.e., they

---

[15] Weiffenbach, *Der Wiederkunftsgedanke Jesu*, 133–34.

[16] Ibid., 152–53.

[17] Ibid.

are history written as prophecy; (3) all the features of this apocalypse can be paralleled in Jewish eschatology and are demonstrably derived from it. The one exception to this judgment allowed by Weiffenbach is the expectation of a near return of Jesus as Son of man (v. 26), which can be abundantly paralleled in the authentic teaching of Jesus and which does not fit in with the fundamental scheme of the apocalypse.

As to the insertions between the members of this document, Weiffenbach regards vv. 9b–13 as authentic and given on one occasion, apart from v. 10, which intrudes into the flow of thought but which is, nevertheless, a genuine saying; he rightly observes that Pfleiderer's objection that a worldwide evangelism does not fit an early expectation of the parousia is nullified by Paul, who held to the latter and is credited by Pfleiderer with originating the former idea. If Paul could do that, why not Jesus?[18] Verses 21–23 cannot be genuine in their present form, for Jesus had no special knowledge of future events; Weiffenbach will accept v. 22 if we amend it (cf. v. 6) to *polloi pseudoprophētai eleusontai epi tō onomati mou, kai pollous planēsousin*, which is comprehensible on the lips of Jesus and which the evangelist will have filled out in the light of events.[19] The parable of the Fig Tree (vv. 28–29) is "a characteristic and significant expression of the well-attested, spontaneous, and thoughtful view of nature that Jesus held; because of this and because of its simplicity and clarity, it carries the stamp of genuineness and originality in itself."[20] Mark 13:32 clearly refers to the parousia, the terms "day" and "hour" being synonymous, in accordance with their normal use to denote the time of the end. The exhortations in vv. 33–37 well fit on to this confession of the ignorance of Jesus as to the date of the parousia; their relation to this coming is so plain, "only pure arbitrariness can overlook it."[21]

Weiffenbach follows Keim in regarding the prophecy of the temple's destruction, 13:2, as authentic, because in fact the temple buildings were not demolished but burned, so that "everything combustible went to ashes, but the stones remain standing; actually only the walls and the gates of the city were 'thrown down' after Jerusalem's capture."[22] This assertion has been frequently repeated by expositors, but in reality the temple was both burned and demolished. It is fortunate, however, that exegetes thought that Jesus predicted this wrongly, for at least the point of departure of the discourse (i.e., v. 2) could then be allowed to him!

---

[18] Ibid., 137–38.
[19] Ibid., 142–44.
[20] Ibid., 149.
[21] Ibid., 157–62.
[22] Ibid., 166.

Mark 13:5–6 are regarded as the same as v. 22 and are interpreted accordingly. Since they have nothing to do with 13:2ff., their function is to provide "an improvised temporary bridge which binds two sharply separated river banks, the one side being vv. 2–4 (destruction of the temple and the question about the *pote* and *sēmeion* of the same), the other side vv. 7–8 (apocalyptic description of international wars and natural calamities)."[23]

Pfleiderer had maintained that the "insertions" vv. 5–6, 9–13, 21–23 were wholly disconnected. Weiffenbach, however, relates them to the introduction, vv. 1–4, and the conclusion, vv. 28–29, 32, 33–37. Is it right to regard all these as fragments haphazardly thrown together? No, he replies. While the synoptists diverge widely in their disposition of the gospel material generally, "in the eschatological discourse they agree in a most decided manner, in the sequence and on the basis of a very definite and tenaciously strong oral and written tradition, which energetically forbad any violent departure." This agreement extends to locality, sequence, and content of the discourse. Without laying it down dogmatically, therefore, Weiffenbach thinks it likely that the "unapocalyptic" sections of Mark 13 form a discourse originally given by Jesus on the Mount of Olives, as related by the evangelists.[24] This position of Weiffenbach became the basis of Wendt's investigation and through him it became widely adopted.

It remains to note Weiffenbach's conclusions as to the value of this interpretation of Mark 13. He cites with approval Pfleiderer's estimate of the discourse as the "key" to most of the other eschatological sayings of Jesus and states how he proposes to use it. "Our guiding point of view in the employment of that key is that everywhere we meet with similar apocalyptic ideas and formulas as those in our 'little apocalypse' we shall account them as unauthentic and without hesitation deny them to Jesus; we except the one idea, discovered by us to be decisively genuine, that of the near and personal second coming."[25] From that viewpoint Weiffenbach considers the other eschatological sayings of Jesus, in order finally to show that what Jesus meant by the parousia was his resurrection. Of this procedure Schweitzer characteristically wrote: "In the end Weiffenbach's critical principle proves to be merely a bludgeon with which he goes seal-hunting and clubs the defenceless Synoptic sayings right and left. When his work is done you see before you a desert island strewn with quivering corpses!"[26] If this does not settle the question whether these sayings deserved to be other than

---

[23] Ibid., 167–68.

[24] Ibid., 180–82.

[25] Ibid., 190–91.

[26] Schweizter, *Quest of the Historical Jesus* (ET London, 1910; the original was titled *Von Reimarus zu Wrede* [1906]), 231.

"corpses," at least it does not give confidence in the method by which their execution was determined.

2. From G. C. B. Pünjer to H. H. Wendt

G. C. B. Pünjer, G. Volkmar, and H. J. Holtzmann

The next few years are barren as to productive ideas on the discourse. G. C. B. Pünjer wrote a good review of the problems entailed, without shedding much more light on them.[27] Renan in his work on the antichrist gave an account of the origin of Mark 13 more "bizarre" than the apocalypse he saw behind it.[28] Adopting the "little apocalypse" hypothesis he seems to have set the rest of the chapter to the credit of the "presidents" of the infant church, the whole account reflecting contemporary incidents.

Gustav Volkmar's view of Mark 13 is conditioned by his reading of the story of primitive Christianity as a struggle between the Peter and Paul parties; the Revelation of John was written on behalf of the former party in AD 68, the Gospel of Mark came to the defense of Paul shortly after.

Volkmar reads the eschatological discourse as sustained polemic against the author of Revelation, and analyzes it accordingly:

> The whole discourse cries out, Have care! (1) Verses 5–9, Have care above all for bold and ensnaring proclamations of the future by alleged emissaries of Jesus Messiah like the author of the book of Revelation! Cf. Rev 1:1–3, 9–19. (2) Have a care for yourselves in respect of your commission to preach the gospel to all, though you suffer for it! (3) Verses 14–23, 24–27, Have especial care, you Christians of Judea, lest in the last distress anyone makes you trust in Jerusalem, as Rev 14:1ff. suggests, and thereby leads you to expect a parousia on earth. (4) Verses 28–32, Learn finally to judge the time of the end rather from what God tells you in creation (vv. 28–29), than from apocalypses that give boasting calculations in the name of Jesus Christ and his angel![29]

Constructions of this kind are ingenious and intriguing, but we can scarcely be asked to take them seriously.

Despite the immensity of his learning, H. J. Holtzmann added little to the discussion on the eschatological discourse. He was unwise enough in his introduction to commit himself to the view that the words "Let the reader understand" (Mark 13:14) suffice to identify the entire discourse with the "flyleaf" of the Jewish War, referred to by Eusebius.[30]

---

[27] Pünjer, "Die Wiederkunftsreden Jesu," *ZWT* 2 (1878): 153ff.

[28] Renan, *L'Antéchrist* (Paris, 1873); ET *The Antichrist* (London, 1890).

[29] Volkmar, *Jesus Nazarenus*, 280; cf. 281–88.

[30] Holtzmann, *Lehrbuch der historisch-kritischen Einleitung in das Neue Testament* (Freiburg, 1885), 362.

He agrees with Volkmar that the terminus a quo for the composition of Mark, on the basis of that of ch. 13, is AD 73.[31] With Weiffenbach he inclines to regard Mark 13:30–31 as the conclusion of the little apocalypse, and the latter as characteristic of "the restless reckoning of the future seen in contemporary Judaism."[32] He subscribes to Pfleiderer's idea that Mark 13:10 serves to put back the over-rapid world clock of the apocalyptist.[33] In his textbook on theology he concludes his discussion on the little apocalypse by affirming, "There are few hypotheses which, in their fundamental features, have proved to be so unavoidable and have experienced such illuminating confirmation."[34] The real value of his work is the supreme honesty with which he approaches the whole question of the eschatology of Jesus. He castigates exegetes, traditionalist and liberal, who handle this matter "as if they were dealing with a professional solution of a prize question set on the quickest and most elegantly executed elimination of all eschatological motives."[35] The chief concern appears to be "to preserve the Hero of the gospel history from the Jewish worldview, with its materialistic hopes for the future, and to deprive him of the most obvious point of departure in this respect." From this viewpoint he severely criticizes the effort to interpret the parousia as a "world-historical" process, although he himself had expounded it as a younger man; not only is it "as far removed as possible from the whole construction of biblical pictures of the end," it cannot stand alongside well-attested parousia sayings like Luke 17:23–25, parousia parables like Luke 17:26–35, and especially the classic saying as to the thief in the night, Luke 12:39.[36] It is strange that Holtzmann, with his candid perception of the anti–eschatological motives of his contemporaries, did not perceive that this "unavoidable" hypothesis of a little apocalypse is the most notable instance of this same tendency.

H. H. Wendt

With H. H. Wendt we return to the main line of development of the little apocalypse theory.[37] He builds directly on Weiffenbach's distinction of two discourses in Mark 13, defining the little apocalypse

---

[31] Ibid., 363.

[32] Idem, *Die Synoptiker*, HKNT (Freiburg, 1889), at Mark 13:31.

[33] Ibid.

[34] Idem, *Lehrbuch der neutestamentlichen Theologie*, 327n.

[35] Ibid., 325. Holtzmann has in mind the German practice of setting essays on specified subjects by way of contest, the winner gaining prize money.

[36] Ibid., 315.

[37] Wendt, *Die Lehre Jesu* (Göttingen, 1886). In the ET of this work, *The Teaching of Jesus* (New York, 1892), Wendt entirely recast his material and omitted what he had written on the eschatological discourse.

as vv. 7–9a, 14–20, 24–27, 30–31, and the authentic discourse of Jesus as vv. 1–6, 9b–13, 21–23, 28–29, 32–37. He proposes to transfer vv. 21–23 before vv. 9b–13, as the connection is thereby improved. Three reasons are adduced for separating the two discourses and assigning them to different sources: (1) the nature of the views expressed therein and (2) their worth differ widely; (3) the coherence of each group is destroyed through their combination. These points are elaborated by Wendt with persuasive power. Under the first point he contrasts the nature of the impending evils described in each discourse. One tells of temptations which Christians alone will experience, and that because of their faith in Jesus; their persecutors appear to be Jews, who try to make them apostatize; warnings are given to enable the disciples to overcome their temptations; their consolation is no promise of escape from trial but of divine aid for their proclamation and assurance of final salvation after endurance of the worst (v. 13b). The other discourse, on the contrary, is concerned with distant wars and natural calamities; they affect Christians only in so far as all human beings are involved in them; the watchword is not endurance but flight, so that counsel is given to the Christians to enable them to escape the affliction; their consolation is an assurance given of divine preservation from the worst affliction, since God for their sakes will shorten the period of trial. The second point has in mind the practical application of the discourses to the church generally. The first group of sayings is thoroughly religious and therefore has an enduring value. The second group lacks any Christian orientation; its provisions and demands are so bound up with specific outward conditions that nothing permanent can be extracted from them. The third point is confined to the different reference of *tauta*, "these things," in vv. 29 and 30: in v. 29 it cannot refer to the parousia of vv. 24–27, nor to vv. 21–23 which are *ex hypothesi* displaced, but to the temptations narrated in vv. 5–6, 21–23, 9b–13; in v. 30 it presumably refers in the first place to the parousia of vv. 24–27 or to the whole description of vv. 7–9a, 14–20, 24–27. Wendt places much weight on this distinction; it appears to be sufficient proof that the authentic sayings formed a discourse ready to Mark's hand and that he merely combined it with the little apocalypse; how otherwise would he have used in v. 29 the term *tauta*, which manifestly cannot relate to the immediately preceding context in which it is set? If it originally referred to the temptations of the genuine discourse all is explained; the faulty reference is due to Mark's separating the two discourses and combining them into one.[38]

Probably the "little apocalypse" theory has never been more attractively stated than by Wendt. The force of his contentions depends

---

[38] *Die Lehre Jesu*, 15–21.

on the assumption that the two series of sayings thus distinguished were at one time connected wholes, an assumption we have yet to examine. While deferring the matter for a time, we would point out that Wendt did not help his case by laying so much stress on the use of *tauta* in v. 29; while it is true that it is unnatural to relate "these things" in this verse to the climax of vv. 24–27, who is to deny that it can refer to all that precedes that paragraph? On what grounds can one insist that it must refer to vv. 9b–13 but not vv. 14–20? The distinction is possible only because the little apocalypse has already been delimited on the basis of what Jesus could not have said; but this is a circuitous argument.

On one aspect of the discourse Wendt made a significant contribution which had wider repercussions than he realized. His belief that one of the two discourses of Mark 13 was authentic caused him to face the question, How does the genuine group of sayings relate to the question asked by the disciples in 13:4? He gave two answers: (1) The disciples were assured that precisely the experience of these trials will be the sign of the nearness of the coming of Christ. In the nature of the case, these supply only a relative, not a precise definition of the time of the end, and on this uncertainty the renewed exhortation to remain in a state of preparedness is based (vv. 32–37). (2) The question had been framed in this way because Jesus had earlier made statements which appeared to show a connection between the destruction of the temple and the judgment which would accompany the glorious appearing of the Messiah; the fresh establishment of this connection was part of the new revelation which Jesus imparted in this answer; so that vv. 5–6, 21–23, 9b–13 give a real answer to the question as to the signs of the catastrophe, vv. 28–29 underline the fact, while vv. 32–37 answer the question as to the time of the same.[39] On the basis of Wendt's presuppositions (overlooking the fragmentary nature of the original tradition) these two answers given by Wendt are admirable, but how did he fail to notice that they answered the two major objections voiced against the authenticity of Mark 13? The two most frequently posed questions, in our day as in Wendt's, are: (1) How can a sudden coming be reconciled with one announced by signs? (2) How can the discourse be related to 13:1–4, seeing that it deals with a different subject? Wendt supplied a reasonable answer to both questions. It is ironical in the highest degree, and thoroughly in keeping with the strange course of this controversy, that the writer who supplied the most convincing exposition of the "little apocalypse" theory at the same time destroyed the foundations on which it was built.

---

[39] Ibid., 13.

3. From W. Baldensperger to E. Wendling

W. Baldensperger and W. Bousset

The blow struck by Wendt at the foundations of the critical theory of Mark 13 was unperceived by his contemporaries, and the "little apocalypse" theory was now entrenched. W. Baldensperger did not feel it necessary to discuss the matter in his treatment of the eschatology of Jesus. For him, the fact that Mark 13 is a free composition is not to be contested; it consists of two sayings groups, one of which is similar to the rabbinical expositions of the signs of the end and so is unauthentic.[40] W. Bousset in all his writings accepts the theory, though not always ostensibly for the same reasons. In his book on the antichrist he insists that to interpret Mark 13 aright, "the first thing to be done is to get rid of all interpretations based on current events." That is to say, we are not to presume that the excitement raised by the Caligula episode could create the idea that the antichrist would sit in the temple of God; this figure is simply the old Dragon-foe of God, who storms the abode of God in heaven and ejects God from his sanctuary, as Rev 13:6 shows.[41] Mark 13:14ff. is therefore "a fragment of some apocalypse of the Antichrist."[42] The utmost that Bousset would allow to the influence of the scare due to Caligula is that it revived the memory of the old tradition. This estimate was reversed in a later writing, in that Bousset came to think that the idea of antichrist enthroned in the temple of God was due to the precedent of Caligula's command to erect his own statue in the temple.[43] On such a reading, it is no longer likely that Mark 13:14ff. represents an old "antichrist document," resurrected for the occasion, since the very core of it has been created by the occasion. If Bousset still thought that this passage described the "rule and reign of Antichrist,"[44] his only evidence is later Christian writings, which ought not to be adduced to prove an earlier and foreign origin for Mark 13.[45] Bousset evidently regarded the rest of the chapter as the product of Jesus.[46]

---

[40] Baldensperger, *Das Selbstbewusstein Jesu im Lichte der messianischen Hoffnungen seiner Zeit* (Strassburg, 1888), 146 n. 1.

[41] Bousset, *The Antichrist Legend* (ET London, 1896), 163–66.

[42] Ibid., 214.

[43] Idem, *Die Religion des Judentums im späthellenistischen Zeitalter*, 3d ed. (Tübingen, 1926), 256.

[44] Ibid., 255.

[45] For the evidence adduced by Bousset, see *Antichrist Legend*, 143ff., 163ff., 213ff.

[46] Idem, *Jesus* (ET London and New York, 1906), 121–22.

A. Schweitzer

The chief features in Albert Schweitzer's construction require but brief mention. In his view the sending out of the Twelve as narrated in Mark 10, was "to set in motion the eschatological development of history, to let loose the final woes, the confusion and strife, from which shall issue the parousia, and so to introduce the supra-mundane phase of the eschatological drama."[47] Matthew 10:23 shows that Jesus did not expect the mission of the disciples to be completed before his own translation and parousia took place. The failure of this expectation caused a change in his views; he became convinced that his vocation was to bear the messianic woes in his own person that the kingdom might come in power. "He had thought to let loose the final tribulation and so compel the coming of the kingdom. And the cataclysm had not occurred. . . . That meant not that the kingdom was not near at hand but that God had appointed otherwise in regard to the time of trial. . . . God in his mercy and omnipotence had eliminated it from the series of eschatological events, and appointed to him, whose commission had been to bring it about, instead to accomplish it in his own person."[48] This was the secret that Jesus revealed to the disciples of Caesarea Philippi. A difficulty arises for this interpretation, in that after that revelation, Jesus spoke of the necessity of his disciples to bear their cross and take their share of suffering. Schweitzer, however, is unabashed: Mark has wrongly placed that paragraph, with the ensuing narrative of the transfiguration; they together belong to the era before his decision to die, and so should have preceded the confession. This cool piece of modifying the data to fit the conclusion is given by Schweitzer in a footnote, and he proceeds to the following observation: "For the same reason the predictions of suffering and tribulation in the Synoptic Apocalypse in Mark 13 cannot be derived from Jesus."[49] Apart from a passing notice of Colani's theory on p. 225, this is the sole reference Schweitzer gives to the contents of Mark 13 in his entire work. Obviously none of the reasons adduced by Colani against the authenticity of the eschatological discourse would have been acceptable to Schweitzer, but he could no more receive it than Colani could; it would have ruined his scheme if it had been allowed to remain.[50]

---

[47] Schweitzer, *Quest of the Historical Jesus,* 369.

[48] Ibid., 387.

[49] Ibid., n. 1.

[50] A major weakness in Schweitzer's interpretation is his deliberate ignoring of the generally acknowledged conviction that Matthew used sources for the construction of his discourses. This is as manifestly true of the sermon on mission in ch. 10 as it is of the Sermon on the Mount in chs. 5–7, as also of the parables discourse of ch. 13 and the eschatological discourse of chs. 24–25. Most

M. Werner

The same basic attitude to the chapter is adopted by Martin Werner, Schweitzer's exponent and disciple. His book on the origin of Christian doctrine commences with a lengthy vindication of "thorough-going eschatology," as providing an adequate basis for a history of doctrine, but it contains no discussion of Mark 13.[51] Whereas Werner is at pains to demonstrate that Matthew 10 is a historically situated unity, the significance of the sayings in Mark 13 is not considered. The detailed treatment of the one source and the ignoring of the other would be puzzling and irritating, were it not for the plain fact that on Werner's scheme, Mark 13 must not even be considered, for the two views cannot subsist together. Where one's own belief and Mark 13 clash, so much the worse, evidently, for Mark 13.

E. Wendling

Very different is the treatment accorded to this chapter by E. Wendling in his discussion as to the origin of Mark.[52] Admittedly he provides no fresh ideas about the apocalyptic document; its existence is taken for granted, and it is defined as vv. 7–8, 9a, 12, 13b–20a, 24–27, 30. Wendling's interest lies in the other sayings in the discourse, and he painstakingly discusses each one. The change of scene between vv. 1–2 and 3–4 is "naturally not original"; the second situation is conditioned by the necessity of giving privacy to the eschatological discourse; it must be due to the evangelist. The questions raised in v. 4 ask (1) the point of time, (2) the sign, when the great event will take place. The discourse proper does not answer them, but they find an answer in the

---

critics, accepting the priority of Mark, hold that the mission charge in Mark 6:7–13 and the Q charge in Luke 10:3–12 have been conflated in Matt 10:5–16; they further note that Matt 10:17–22 is paralleled in Mark 13:9–13, and see v. 23 as an isolated saying. These latter sayings reflect a relentless opposition to Jesus and his followers uncharacteristic of Jesus' early ministry. Schweitzer's rejection of critical principles in Gospel study went back to the period prior to his theological studies. During his military service Schweitzer read Holtzmann's work on the Gospels; the suggestion that Matthew brought together sayings of Jesus to form the discourse of ch. 10 appeared to Schweitzer an all too easy device for explaining away an embarrassing text, so he rejected the source-critical approach to the Gospels. That would have been no sin had he provided a plausible alternative explanation for the relationship of the Gospels; in the event he substituted a thoroughly implausible exposition of Matthew 10 for one in accord with Matthew's mode of composing his Gospel, and thereby provided a warning for all subsequent generations of theological students.

[51] Werner, *Die Entstehung der christlichen Dogmas* (Bern-Leipzig, 1941).

[52] Wendling, *Die Entstehung des Marcus-Evangeliums* (Tübingen, 1908), 155ff.

two parables of vv. 28–29 (= the sign), 33ff. (= the time). Wendling therefore suggests that the original source of Mark (Ur-Markus) contained the sayings group vv. 1–2, 33, 28–29, 34–36, a little "discourse." The rest of the sayings are added by the evangelist and mainly come from the "logia." The treatment accorded them by Wendling is not always illuminating; vv. 5b–6, for example, are repeated in 21–22; both passages are said to have a common pattern which the evangelist has already used in 9:38–39 (!). Verses 21–23 are freely composed by the aid of 7–8, as a comparison is thought to show:

7. *hotan de akousēte . . . mē throeisthe*	21. *ean tis hymin eipē . . . mē pisteuete*
8. *egerthēsetai . . .*	22. *egerthēsontai . . .* [53]

As the two uses of *egeiromai* in these passages are quite distinct the parallelism is not very impressive, and we were probably never intended to see any. Of the group, vv. 9–13, 9a, 12, 13b have already been assigned to the "little apocalypse," leaving vv. 9b–11, 13a. These find a close parallel in Matt 10:17–20, except that Mark 13:10 is only represented in Matthew by the phrase *eis martyrion autois*; "clearly" the Markan saying is an expansion of this and must therefore be eliminated as an addition of the evangelist's own composition. Verses 9b and 11 will then come from Q.[54] As to Mark 13:31, 32, Wendling points out that *hoi logoi* as a designation of sayings of Jesus occurs only in two previous places, both being additions of the evangelist (8:38; 10:24). Verse 32 is an appendix; the *oudeis oiden* anticipates *ouk oidate* of vv. 33, 35; it is based on Matt 11:27 and 1 Thess 5:1–2. The final analysis of the chapter thus appears to be:

Ur-Markus: 1–2, 33, 28–29, 34–36.

Little Apocalypse: 7–8, 9a, 12, 13b–20a, 24–27, 30.

Additions of Evangelist: 3–4, 5–6, 21–23, 9b, 11, 10, 13a, (19?), 20b, 31, 32, 37.

We are not sure whom to admire most: Mark for putting together his discourse out of such materials, or Wendling for discovering how he did it. We suspect that Mark would have handed the bouquet to Wendling.

4. From A. Loisy to J. Moffatt

A. Loisy

With Loisy we enter upon a period of more skeptical criticism, an attitude toward the text of the Gospels by no means confined to Mark

---

[53] Ibid., 157–58.
[54] Ibid., 155–57.

13. Loisy perceives that the eschatological discourse has a function of its own in its setting in the Gospel; it serves "to show the significance and essential importance of the life of Jesus, to correct by anticipation the horror of his death, as the resurrection mitigates it afterwards. . . . In this sense it could be said that a Synoptic Gospel could no more be conceived without the discourse on the parousia than the Johannine Gospel without the discourse after the supper."[55] But the discourses in both cases are the result of wishful thinking, not of historical reminiscence. Loisy implies that no discourse of any kind was given by Jesus on this occasion; from this time on we scarcely hear of Wendt's authentic "discourse" combined with the little apocalypse.

Loisy himself strikes deep in his demonstration of the unauthenticity of the discourse as it stands. (1) The setting is suspect: if the evangelist represents it as delivered to four disciples only, it is because he knows it had no place in the primitive tradition; he is conscious of attributing something to Christ unknown in earlier years; consequently he "has not dared directly to present it as the teaching of Christ."[56] (2) Fundamentally the discourse is neither a conversation, nor a short address to the disciples, nor a public utterance, but a written document, as v. 14 shows. To regard the clause "Let the reader understand" as an insertion of the evangelist, calling attention to what is written so as to be prepared for the occasion, is "an artificial and mechanical conjecture." "As we have other reasons to admit that this apocalyptic description is not originally a discourse of Jesus, it is more natural to attribute it to the first redaction."[57] (3) The request of the disciples is not *en rapport* with their situation shortly before the crucifixion, but rather with the preoccupations of believers who, fifty years later, were forced to reconcile the delay of the parousia with what Jesus had said of its imminence. (4) The belief of Jesus in the imminence of the end is irreconcilable with the view that it will be preceded by signs: "Instead of the flash of light which spreads in an instant through all the earth, instead of the Judge who in an instant ravishes to himself the righteous and abandons the wicked to their destiny, it is the divine King who, after a long series of preliminary signs, comes to look on the earth in its ruins, using the celestial spirits to search for the elect."[58] This habit of exegetes, to exaggerate the meaning of a passage they do not like, has been observable from Weisse onwards in our studies; if Loisy really thought that a fair representation of Mark 13:24–27, then we understand Loisy better than we do Mark.

---

[55] Loisy, *Les Evangiles Synoptiques*, 2 vols. (Ceffonds, 1908), 2:393.

[56] Ibid., 398; idem, *Evangile selon Marc* (Paris, 1912), 366–67.

[57] Idem, *Evangiles Synoptiques*, 421.

[58] Idem, *Marc*, 380–81.

The little apocalypse is defined as vv. 6–8, 12, 13b–14, 17–19, 22–23, 24b–27, 30–31. It will be observed that it has now become more fragmentary. Like Holtzmann before him, Loisy has recognized that vv. 15–16 cannot be attributed to a Jewish apocalypse, for they occur in Luke 17:31, so that no longer can Mark 13:14–20 be regarded as a connected whole. But v. 20 itself is viewed as a Pauline idea; consequently that verse must be omitted from the "apocalypse." What remains is not a very satisfactory document, as Loisy seems to realize. How can an independent writing commence with v. 6? It is an impossible beginning. Loisy therefore suggests "Since the description commences a little brusquely by the announcement of false messiahs, that which prepared for this announcement in the source was probably not a suitable item to reproduce in the Gospel."[59] The flight to the mountains in v. 14 is also very briefly narrated, vv. 15–16 being unrelated to it, so we must presume that the evangelist has here shortened his source again. Indeed, the flight to the mountains is quite unmotivated; if the whole world is engulfed in the final catastrophe, what is the use of running off to mountains? Apart from the soundness or otherwise of Loisy's interpretation, we should note that we have been here moved to a different level of discussion as regards the little apocalypse. The long chain of argument initiated by Weizsäcker and continued by his followers had the purpose of demonstrating that the apocalypse embedded in Mark 13 was self-contained, revealing itself to be a complete description of the end, based on the usual division of Jewish apocalypses. Loisy now recognizes that the element of "completeness" cannot be sustained, and he must call on further hypothetical clauses to explain the incomplete extracts given in Mark 13.

The view, represented by Wendt, that the destruction of the city and temple will occur at the end of the age is reproduced by Loisy, with even plainer contradiction than with the former writer. Of the disciples' question, 13:4, he states: "The question has a double object; he is asked when the end will come and by what sign its imminence would be recognized. As the ruin of Jerusalem, the end of the world, the glorious manifestation of the Messiah, and the great judgment are bound up in the apocalyptic belief of the earliest time, no special indication is asked for each one of these eschatological items."[60] How can Loisy, in the light of that, proceed to comment on 13:5ff.: "In view of the character of the introduction (i.e., the privacy of the discourse), there is no need to be surprised that the discourse of Jesus is not in direct and natural relation with the question posed by the disciples"?[61] If the end of Jerusalem is

---

[59] Ibid., 369.
[60] Idem, *Evangiles Synoptiques*, 399.
[61] Ibid., 407.

bound up with the end of the age, and all that ushers it in, then the discourse is certainly related to the disciples' question. Loisy must have forgotten what he had already written. To complete this summary we should notice that Loisy classed vv. 28–29 as belonging to earlier gospel redaction; v. 32 is an apologetic statement, justifying Jesus for having announced as imminent a coming which had not taken place at the time when the Gospel was composed; vv. 33–37 are a mixture of elements from various sources, not blended together. The only sections of the chapter certainly to be ascribed to Jesus are vv. 9bc, 11, 15–16, 21, a meager harvest for such toil.

From the latest of Loisy's published works, we infer that even this harvest must not be gathered. To explain his latest ideas on Mark 13 it will be necessary to digress. Loisy lays it down, "with the minimum risk of error," that Jesus was "the prophet of a single oracle," like John the Baptist, and that oracle was "Repent, for the kingdom of God is at hand."[62] After the death of Jesus the belief arose among his followers that he was the Messiah about to return; their ideas turned wholly on eschatological anticipations of his coming; they were not interested in his earthly life. Thus the parousia was "the essential object, if not the unique object, of faith."[63] Not unnaturally, all the instruction concerning this event, the "eschatological catechesis" as Loisy calls it, was represented as given by the immortal Christ in heaven. "It was only at a later period that this teaching was antedated and thrown back into the life of the Christ on earth, and . . . his exaltation as Messiah was treated in the same manner."[64]

A clear instance of this transfer of events is seen in the account of the transfiguration, which was originally regarded as a communication of the Risen Christ.[65] The manner of its transfer to the earthly ministry, however, was complicated. The eschatological catechesis threw up, toward the end of the first century, the parable of the Wicked Husbandmen as a piece of anti–Jewish polemic; it was eventually pushed back into the earthly life of Jesus to serve as the last discourse of Jesus in Jerusalem. From this position it was ousted by the eschatological discourse, evidently regarded as a more suitable conclusion to the ministry of Jesus. That the first draft of Mark's Gospel did not know this discourse is plain: for one thing, its existence conflicts with the original use postulated for the parable of the Wicked Husbandmen as a piece of anti–Jewish polemic; for another, Mark represents it as given in secret and on the Mount of Olives, just as the Apocalypse of Peter places it in this setting after the resurrection. "We have equal ground for believing

---

[62] Idem, *The Origins of the New Testament* (ET London, 1950), 289.
[63] Ibid., 313.
[64] Ibid., 313–14.
[65] Ibid., 53.

that the artificial introduction to the Book of Acts contains the rudiments of a similar discourse with the scene set exactly as in the Apocalypse of Peter. Thus our hypotheses are not groundless imaginations; they are inductions as solid as the matter permits of."[66] Did this last assertion proceed from an uneasy conscience? Be that as it may, we must add one observation: despite the late date assigned to ch. 13, Loisy is still convinced that it contains a Jewish apocalypse, dating probably from the time of Caligula.[67] Evidently it is believed that the "abomination" prophecy demands a historical event for its occasion; if, on such a view, we can point to an event in the lifetime of Jesus that will account for the "abomination" prophecy, the nucleus of these sayings must logically be put back still further. This possibility will later be explored.

J. Wellhausen

In J. Wellhausen, Loisy found a helpmate for him. Wellhausen's fundamental view of Jesus, that he was a teacher, claiming to be neither Messiah nor Son of man, who gave no instructions as to his coming death, nor dreams of his resurrection and second coming, naturally affected his view of Mark 13. He could no more assent to the authenticity of this chapter than Schweitzer, although their views had no other point of contact. At least Wellhausen was willing to provide two reasons for his views, and his manner of stating them is worth noting. First, if vv. 1–2 are authentic, as they are in essence, then vv. 3–37 are not, for in the former the temple is destroyed, but in the latter it is merely desecrated.[68] This desecration, however, is only temporary and partial. "In the Jewish prophecy taken over, Jerusalem is oppressed most severely, but is rescued finally 'out of this tribulation' at the appearance of the Son of man; there is no mention of the destruction of the temple, and the meaning will be as in a remarkable fragment of the Apocalypse of John (11:1–2) that the temple, perhaps with the exception of the outer forecourt, will not fall into the power of the heathen."[69] As in the case of some of the exegesis we have earlier encountered, we grudge no admiration at such ingenuity, but it remains difficult to understand why it was thought relevant. The interpreting of Mark 13:14 by means of Rev 11:1–2 would not have been dreamed of were it not that the former is regarded as belonging to a Jewish apocalypse; their presuppositions are totally different.

---

[66] Ibid., 298–99.
[67] Ibid., 97.
[68] Wellhausen, *Das Evangelium Marci*, 2d ed. (Berlin, 1909), 100.
[69] Idem, *Einleitung in die drei ersten Evangelien*, 2d ed. (Berlin, 1911), 97.

The second count against Mark 13 from Wellhausen is that "it sets forth the scheme of Jewish eschatology built on Daniel."[70] But a significant limitation is set to this likeness to Jewish apocalypses: "The form of address with 'You' is not Jewish; by this the 'beholding' is changed into teaching and stripped of all apocalyptic frippery. For it belongs to the form of real Jewish apocalypses that the seer himself, who receives the revelation, is addressed, whether by God or an angel of God, or that he recounts with an 'I' what he has been permitted to see and hear."[71] If this be so, why must one assert with Wellhausen that the greatest part of 13:3–27 is "purely Jewish"? Does it not leave open the possibility that the echoes of Daniel, and of the OT generally, in ch. 13 may have been derived directly and not mediated through Jewish apocalyptic sources? Those who believe that Jesus used the title Son of man, and that it is not wholly unrelated to Dan 7:13, will not be so inclined to dismiss that possibility as Wellhausen did.

The little apocalypse receives an extension from Wellhausen to include vv. 7–8, 12, 14–22, 24–27. The intermediate verses, 5–6, 13, 23, are "Christian," but naturally not from Jesus, for they all presume the messianic status of Jesus; though vv. 9–11 are not closely defined, the same presumably applies to them; certainly it will to v. 10. What of the prologue and epilogue of the discourse? Verses 1–2 contain at least authentic ingredients; the prophecy was not spoken to disciples alone, "that appears to me to be a toning down of the saying"; the real occasion and prophecy is given in Mark 14:58, which brought the condemnation of Jesus by the Sanhedrin: "With the prophecy of the destruction of the temple, he placed the knife in the hands of his enemies."[72] Accordingly the entire setting of 13:1–4 is a fiction of the evangelist. Verses 28–29 are due to a misunderstanding; the tree of v. 28 is that of 11:11–14 (the cursed fig tree), of which Jesus simply said that that withered tree will not, as the Jews think, revive again, but will always remain dry, i.e., the hope of a reconstituted Zion in its old splendor will never be fulfilled. In 11:18 Jesus thus rejects the Jewish hope, in 13:28 he is made to take it over, while v. 29 has changed the meaning entirely.[73] Verse 30 attaches to v. 28, being spoken before AD 70 with the Jewish hope in mind. Verse 31 refers to the consolation of having Jesus' words, even though he has departed. Verse 32 is suspicious in view of its antithetic "the Father and the Son." The whole section, vv. 32–37, presupposes the destruction of Jerusalem, for the disciples no longer wait for Christ to come there.[74] Thus all that remain to us from ch. 13 are two sayings

---

[70] Idem, *Marci,* 100.
[71] Ibid.
[72] Ibid., 99.
[73] Ibid., 106–7.
[74] Ibid.

poorly handed down (vv. 2, 28), one scarcely recognizable (v. 28), both in their wrong context. As to the soundness of the method by which that result was obtained we pass no further comment.

C. G. Montefiore

The Jewish scholar C. G. Montefiore follows closely in the steps of Loisy and Wellhausen. He does not give his own views at length; he is frankly not interested in the chapter, for like many liberal Jews he has an aversion to apocalyptic writings; in the main he reproduces Loisy's arguments from *Les Evangiles Synoptiques,* interspersed with some from Johannes Weiss that by no means give an accurate reflection of Weiss's position. His mood will be gathered by the following statement:

> This apocalyptic oration is, as a whole, certainly unauthentic. Much of it is built upon the familiar lines of Jewish apocalypses from Daniel onwards. It has very slight interest for us today, and little or no religious value. . . . How much of the oration from 5 to 37 goes back to Jesus is very doubtful. Verse 32 seems most likely to be authentic. As regards the rest, the portions which are of Jewish origin, or of Christian origin, or lastly, which proceeded from the mouth of Jesus, can never be distinguished with certainty. The oldest parts, representing the original Jewish apocalypse, may be 7–8, 14–20 and 24–31. Christian editors, including the evangelist, will account for what remains. It is even questionable whether any part was said by Jesus of what we now possess.[75]

With reference to the last sentence, it should be noted that in the second edition of the commentary the earlier estimate of v. 32 is modified and doubts are expressed as to its authenticity. Montefiore affirms that as the chapter is of little or no religious value, it is not worth discussing the question of its origin. Nevertheless, he offers one reason for rejecting its genuineness: Loisy is cited with approval that the viewpoint of the discourse is inconsistent with Jesus' teaching on the suddenness of the coming of the kingdom,[76] and he agrees that it is the strongest argument against its authenticity. Curiously enough, when commenting on vv. 28–29 he opposes Weiss's (earlier) view that a contradiction exists between v. 29 and Luke 17:20, as also between vv. 30 and 32: "Both points of view were current in the oldest Church, and perhaps even both were combined side by side in the mind of Jesus. Signs were important, and yet not too important. Too much stress must not be laid on them. In the last resort the precise hour was unknown and unknowable."[77] How did Montefiore reconcile that statement with

---

[75] Montefiore, *The Synoptic Gospels,* 1st ed. (London, 1909), 299.
[76] Ibid., 301.
[77] Ibid., 306.

his citation of and agreement with Loisy, as mentioned above? Presumably he did not perceive the necessity to do so. Once more we see the spectacle of a scholar demolishing his own case for the little apocalypse hypothesis.

J. Moffatt

James Moffatt gave a very well-documented account of the discussion concerning Mark 13, at least on the critical side, but he added little on his own account.[78] He declared: "The details of the reconstructed apocalypse are not quite certain, but its general contour is unmistakable; it parts, as a whole, readily from the context and forms an intelligible unity, whatever were its original size and aim."[79] As to the limits of the document, "If the introductory passage Mark 13:5–6 is added, probably Mark 13:21–23 should also be incorporated"; that would make the apocalypse to consist of vv. 5–8, 14–27, a very considerable section of the chapter. On that score, we are not surprised that Moffatt feels that the little apocalypse forms "an intelligible unity"; he has omitted only vv. 9–13 from the body of the chapter! On the other hand, if one keeps to the more orthodox critical view and defines the apocalypse as vv. 7–8, 14–20, 24–27, how can one be so sure that "it parts readily from its context," when one is not certain of the context of vv. 7–8, nor where vv. 14–20 end or vv. 24–27 begin? And what if, as is very probable, vv. 14–20 be not an original unity? It is one thing to assert that certain portions part readily from their context; it is another thing to claim that together they form an original whole. Moffatt may have felt himself justified in making his celebrated statement, "This hypothesis of the small apocalypse . . . is now a sententia recepta of synoptic criticism,"[80] but whether he should have made it so confidently is questionable.

5. From B. H. Streeter to R. H. Charles

B. H. Streeter

B. H. Streeter's exposition of the eschatology of the Gospels seems to have oscillated between hostility and sympathy. His two contributions to the Oxford *Studies in the Synoptic Problem* (Oxford, 1911) advocate debatable positions, mainly directed against a serious view of the evangelical material on eschatology. He was responsible for a

---

[78] Moffatt, *An Introduction to the Literature of the New Testament,* 3d ed. (Edinburgh, 1918; 1st ed. 1911), 207ff.

[79] Ibid., 207.

[80] Ibid., 209.

curious error in respect of Mark 13; he wrote, "Mark 13 dominates the eschatology of the Second Gospel, and through him that of the two later Gospels, which so largely depend on Mark, especially that of Matthew. It is the citadel of the extreme eschatological school of interpretation."[81] This presumably refers to Schweitzer and his sympathizers, but we have noted that such exegetes could not accept Mark 13 and retain their own views. C. H. Turner perpetuated this mistake in his commentary on Mark.[82]

Streeter repeated the older view that the little apocalypse is "a complete and carefully articulated apocalypse of the conventional type," a view which we have seen reason to question. On this basis, however, he feels that this apocalypse can be interpreted on exactly the same lines as ordinary Jewish apocalypses: it is pseudonymous, like the rest of such writings; it embodies older materials; it reflects a series of recent events, viz. famines, earthquakes, wars, Paul's sufferings and testimony before rulers, the activity of the delators in Rome who betrayed Christians, and above all the fall of Jerusalem, which had recently taken place.[83] The conviction that the end of the world was about to occur is said to be the motive for the writing of this apocalypse, to encourage the faithful who have endured such fearful sufferings, lest they be led astray by false christs at the eleventh hour. "The lengthy and elaborate character of the apocalypse of ch. 13 shows the importance assigned to it by the author—naturally, if the end of the world is coming in a few months, details on that subject are of surpassing interest."[84]

While Streeter adduces the usual objections to Mark 13, in an appendix on this matter he makes plain the real basis of his views: he is convinced that there may be discerned within the NT a twofold evolution of eschatological thought, proceeding *pari passu*; the line from Paul to John starts from crude eschatology to its virtual elimination, the line from Q to Matthew travels from vague eschatological conceptions to sheer apocalypticism, and in this process Mark stands halfway. Since "vagueness and reserve are the characteristic notes of the apocalyptic sayings of Q," Mark 13 is condemned, with its concrete view of the end of the world coming in a few months.[85] The same thing, however, applies to Mark 8:38; 9:1; 14:62, "the last being particularly

---

[81] Streeter, *Studies in the Synoptic Problem* (Oxford, 1911), 425.

[82] Turner, "The Gospel according to St. Mark," *A New Commentary on Holy Scripture*, ed. C. Gore et al. (London, 1928), part 3, 102.

[83] Streeter, *Studies in the Synoptic Problem*, 179–81. Streeter follows the example of many earlier exegetes and explains the wars, famines, etc., from contemporary experiences as narrated by the historians of the day.

[84] Ibid., 428.

[85] Ibid., 425–26.

unreliable since it comes from a version of the trial circulated by the enemies of Jesus."[86]

This view was modified in Streeter's essay in *Foundations* (1912). While still adhering to his belief in the development of eschatology in Q, Mark, and Matthew, he admitted, "The conclusions I was then inclined to draw from it were, I now think, somewhat too sweeping."[87] He felt that the authenticity of sayings like Mark 13:30; Matt 10:23; 24:34 cannot be denied without grave risk of losing the historical character of the Gospels altogether.[88] Nevertheless, Mark 13 is still unauthentic. From this position Streeter did not move, and in his work on the Four Gospels the sympathy with eschatology which showed itself temporarily in *Foundations* disappears.

He seems to have been peculiarly susceptible to the views of other writers; we note, for example, the ready way he took up Charles's idea that the book of Revelation was written in the belief of an impending invasion of the Roman Empire by the Parthians led by Nero redivivus; Streeter thought that the Gospel of Matthew was written with the same fear in mind,[89] a most improbable suggestion. In the case of Mark 13 he seems to have become aware, since writing his earlier essays, that Bousset had written a book on the antichrist, and again he takes up that writer's ideas with enthusiasm. He admitted he had been mistaken in thinking that Mark 13 was written after the fall of Jerusalem, and that the author had written with that event in mind; he now recognizes that the abomination of desolation is a personal antichrist who will sit supreme in the temple of Jerusalem till he is destroyed by the Christ at the parousia.[90] There is no need to date the little apocalypse about AD 70, for the same doctrine appears in 2 Thessalonians 2. "I would venture the suggestion that it, or something very like it, was known to Paul, and was accepted by him, too, as an authentic utterance of Jesus. That at any rate would explain the teaching about the Man of Sin in II Thess."[91] The admission is noteworthy. If Paul in the earlier days of his ministry knew the contents of the little apocalypse, we are taken back to the primitive period of Christian history; how is it that a pseudonymous writing, attributed to Jesus as to some worthy of the distant past, has been able to arise so soon and gain so widespread a circulation? And what of the multitude of "contemporary events," such as wars, famines, earthquakes, etc., of which the apocalypse is supposed to be the reflection? Streeter seems to have forgotten about them. Yet he still

---

[86] Ibid., 429–30.
[87] Idem, *The Historic Christ. Essay in Foundations* (London, 1912), 112 n. 2.
[88] Ibid., 113.
[89] Idem, *The Four Gospels* (London, 1924), 523.
[90] Ibid., 462.
[91] Ibid., 493.

maintains that Mark 13:9–13 reflect Paul's persecutions, delators in Rome, etc.[92]

If we are to put these ideas together we reach the remarkable conclusion that the pseudonymous author of the little apocalypse was a better prophet than Jesus. For his prognostications, according to Streeter's earlier writings, were so impossibly accurate, they must be *vaticinia ex eventu.* On this changed view they were written before the events took place, so they must be regarded as real predictions, although they came true. But the predictions of vv. 9–13, generally ascribed to Jesus, must not be allowed to him because they came true! Naturally Streeter did not intend to imply such an absurdity. Nevertheless, this phenomenon is continually met with in our investigation: a writer lays down uncautious views and realizes later that some modification is necessary; the change is made, in oblivion that thereby his earlier positions are rendered intolerable. We suspect, however, that when the implications of the reflection of Mark 13 in 2 Thessalonians 2 are realized, the little apocalypse theory will encounter heavy seas.

R. H. Charles

R. H. Charles revised his Jowett lectures on eschatology in 1913, and left all students on the subject in his debt for the resultant work. That the first edition of the book had appeared prior to 1900 probably accounts for his continued adherence to Wendt's view that Mark 13 contains two separate discourses, the one directed to persecuted disciples, the other to Jews facing the tribulation of Judea. As always, Charles is very emphatic; the representation of the advent as a sudden, surprising event and that which views it as preceded by admonitory signs are declared to be "mutually exclusive." The two discourses of Mark 13 badly contrast with each other: "Whereas faithfulness unto the death of the body is required from the disciples in one source, in the other they are exhorted to pray that the attack on Jerusalem, which is the beginning of the end, may not be in the winter, lest they should suffer bodily discomfort!"[93] A lengthy list of parallels between the little apocalypse and the Jewish apocalypses is provided, together with a few OT passages charitably thrown in, to demonstrate the derivation of the former from the latter. The identification of the fall of Jerusalem with the parousia in Mark 13 is final proof that the discourse is unauthentic, for "Christ often prophesies his parousia in connection with his death and resurrection, but the destruction of Jerusalem invariably by itself."[94]

---

[92] Ibid., 493–94.

[93] Charles, *A Critical History of the Doctrine of a Future Life,* 2d ed. (London, 1913; 1st ed. 1899), 381.

[94] Ibid., 384.

Unfortunately, none of these considerations may be left as they are. We are not quite sure what Charles means by the first point, for later on he states with reference to the parousia: "Certain signs were to precede it, such as persecution of the disciples and their condemnation before Jewish and heathen tribunals, 13:9–13. This persecution, moreover, was conceived as lasting continuously from the founding of the Church to the parousia. The experience of Christ was to be likewise that of his disciples, Mt. 10:24–25, Jn. 15, 20."[95] Then how can a "sudden" coming and one preceded by signs be "mutually exclusive"? Is it that the signs of persecution extend throughout the Christian dispensation? But the wars, earthquakes, etc., similarly extend through the Christian era. Or does Charles take exception to the specific prediction about the "abomination" and the flight which follows? That, too, is a groundless objection if the prophecy relates to the fall of Jerusalem, for Charles accepts 13:1–2 as authentic. It would seem that the real offense is contained in v. 18, where Jesus descends to the apparently trivial concern that the apocalyptic event should not happen in cold weather. Doubtless Jesus would not descend to this level, but no careful reader of Mark 13:14–20 imagines he did. "Pray that it may not happen in the winter": even Bengel realized that something more than temperature was involved here when he defined *cheimōn* as "winter, or cold and tempestuous weather." It is the heavy rains in view here, rains that turn the wadis into impassable torrents and make flight from danger difficult, if not impossible.[96] If an exhortation to flight in face of impending slaughter be granted as reasonable, 13:17ff. is hardly pandering to comfort.

The relation of Mark 13 to Jewish writings, whether canonical or noncanonical, must be left for the present, as also the relation between the fall of Jerusalem and the parousia, but Charles's statement of the latter cannot go unchallenged. How did this most deeply versed scholar in eschatological thought come to say that Jesus often predicted his parousia in connection with his death and resurrection?[97] A real difficulty in interpreting our Lord's eschatology devolves upon the fact that, in the Synoptic reports at least, he never once plainly did this. Luke 17:25 comes near to it, but the resurrection is not there mentioned; the saying in Mark 14:62 is better, but unfortunately it is not unambiguous.

---

[95] Ibid., 385.

[96] Schlatter translates *cheimōn* as "the rainy season" (*Das Evangelium nach Matthäus* [Stuttgart, 1947] 356).

[97] Charles, of course, was writing on the eschatology of the Synoptic Gospels and was not considering the Fourth Gospel. But since writing the above we can answer our own question. It is plain that he is citing Schwartzkopff, *Die Weissagungen Jesu Christi* (Göttingen, 1895), 160–61, where the same assertion is made in similar language and the same countersuggestion is given.

By contrast, if Matt 23:38–39 be preserved in true sequence, we have the desolation of the temple linked with the parousia! Finally, if we add that Charles in one place defines the little apocalypse as vv. 7–8, 14, 17–20, 24–27, 30–31, but when reproducing it for the reader includes vv. 14–20 as a whole,[98] we shall find it difficult to avoid the conclusion that his exposition of Mark 13 is not the most careful piece of writing he produced in his long years of labor.

In view of the importance attached to Charles's writings, we must not overlook his references to our subject in his commentary on Revelation. Like other commentators on the book of Revelation, Charles does not fail to be impressed with the parallels to be observed between Mark 13 and Revelation 6. He sets them out in columns, to show the likenesses more plainly.[99] Two points emerge: on the one hand, as Rev 6:7–8 makes "pestilence" to be one of the plagues, and only Luke's version of the discourse contains that item, we see contact with Luke rather than Mark and Matthew; on the other hand, the denouement apparently combines Mark's and Luke's versions. To Charles this indicates that John knew the original little apocalypse and used it, rather than the Gospels. But a difficulty is raised by the fifth "plague" of Revelation 6, for it presumes that persecutions of the saints were mentioned in the little apocalypse, and in that document there are none! Charles solves the problem thus: "In this Little Jewish Apocalypse, so far as it is preserved in the Gospels, there is no reference to the persecution of the faithful. But since in the Psalms, Daniel and late apocalyptic literature this is a constant subject of complaint to God, it cannot have been wanting in the original form of the Little Apocalypse."[100] Can one find a better example of *petitio principii?* Observe the presuppositions of this argument: (1) Charles sees close parallels between portions of Mark 13, Luke 21, and Revelation; he assumes on the basis of the little apocalypse theory that John would know them as the little apocalypse, for if such an apocalypse existed John would be sure to know it.[101] (2) Revelation 6 makes persecutions of the faithful an integral part of the last distress; as the other "plagues" are taken from the little apocalypse, presumably this one will be no exception; then the original little apocalypse contained a section on the persecution of the faithful. Such a view implies both that John knew a longer version of the little apocalypse than the evangelists knew, and that the evangelists or their source cut out the original references to persecution in order to replace them by other references to persecution. A very curious

---

[98] Charles, *Future Life*, 381, 382–83.

[99] Idem, *A Critical and Exegetical Commentary on the Revelation of St. John*, 2 vols., ICC (Edinburgh, 1920), 1:158.

[100] Ibid., 159.

[101] Ibid.

procedure if the little apocalypse was taken to be an authentic utterance of Jesus! Why make such a conjecture, when the desired element is already contained in the discourse? And what becomes of the original view of Charles, that the little apocalypse was concerned only with political events, and the Christian discourse with suffering disciples? We see here with transparent clarity the implausibility of the belief that Mark 13 is composed of two independent sources that have been combined; if it is affirmed that their substance must have overlapped in this manner, it surely suggests that neither postulated discourse existed.

6. From E. Meyer to F. Hauck

E. Meyer

The work of a historian on Christian origins is always viewed with interest and respect; that of Edward Meyer has been accorded more than ordinary attention. His specialized training, however, does not find much scope in Mark 13. It is significant to note, after what we find in Charles, that Meyer should affirm, "The preliminary signs and the catastrophe are described entirely with the familiar features of Judaism, drawn from Ezekiel and Daniel as well as the eschatological sections in Isaiah."[102] Where Charles, understandably enough, is anxious to bring in his beloved apocalypses, Meyer is content to see the influence of the OT. Nevertheless, this was hardly said to inspire confidence in the little apocalypse, for Meyer thinks that Jesus did not use the OT in this manner. The only other instances of Jesus directly citing the OT, apart from occasions of exposition, are said to be Mark 4:12 (= 8:18); 7:6; 9:48; 12:10; 14:27. The discourse, accordingly, is "an eschatological tract about the coming world-judgment and the question as to the point of time of the parousia," and since this question of the time of the advent, particularly its delay, was characteristic of the interests of the early community, "it is quite clear that this whole proclamation has nothing to do with the historical Jesus, but is a product of the first generation of the Christian community, whose fortunes are prophesied."[103] That means, of course, that not only the little apocalypse is of alien origin, but the section concerning the disciples in the rest of the chapter is unauthentic. To Meyer that position is inevitable, since we have insufficient data on which to base the true teaching of Jesus. "That Jesus, like all OT prophets, also spoke of the future, of impending overthrow of

---

[102]Meyer, *Ursprung und Anfänge des Christentums* (Stuttgart and Berlin, 1921), 1:127.
[103]Ibid., 126, 129.

earthly things, and of the setting up of the kingdom of God, no one will
doubt; but how he thought of that can no longer be known; it is
completely overgrown by the development of Christian views.... What
Mark offers us in ch. 13 is the tradition which formed itself in the
narrow circle of the leaders of the primitive community, and is laid in
the mouth of their Messiah on the ground of the expectations which
they had fastened on him."[104] The date is determined by such considerations as absence of mention of the conflict with Rome in the sixties,
and of the struggle with the empire as reflected in the book of Revelation; while the Gentile mission is quite unimportant in this group.
"This circle is still ruled wholly by Jewish ideas; Judaism and Jerusalem with its Christian community stand in the middle point dominating
all. Here the composition must have arisen, probably in the fifties, or
at the latest about the time of the persecution in which James the Lord's
brother fell as an offering."[105]

It is of interest that this eminent historian, unlike many theologians, cannot trace the situation of the Roman Christians in Mark 13,
and that in his view the situation presupposed is that of the Palestinian
church. But what of this denial of the authenticity of the chapter in
toto? It raises the question whether Jesus anticipated an interval between his death and second coming; if he did, the denial that he could
have made provision for his disciples in that period is unreasonable,
and unlike what we would have expected of him who spent so much
time in training the apostles for their ministry. We are not convinced
that there are no means for discovering what our Lord really taught
about his advent; the sources for the teaching of Jesus are not wholly
unreliable, and in the end it may be found that we are more at fault than
the documents that instruct us.

A. Piganiol

Following on E. Meyer, and basing himself on his conclusions,
A. Piganiol gave careful consideration to the date of the little apocalypse. Meyer's date, in the fifties or at the time of the death of James in
62, is taken to be the terminus ad quem. "The *terminus a quo* is
furnished by the beginning of the persecution of the Jews against the
Christians," i.e., the end of Tiberius's reign, the persecution reaching
its climax in the death of Stephen. The real clue to the point of time at
which the apocalyptist stood is the past tense used in Mark 13:19–20:
"If the Lord had not shortened the days no flesh would have been saved,
but for the sake of the elect whom he chose he did shorten them."
Clearly, then, at the moment of writing, this event had already hap-

---

[104]Ibid., 129.
[105]Ibid., 130.

pened. The time can only be that of Caligula's threat to erect his statue in the temple. It will be recalled that when the order was first made known, the Roman commander Petronius was persuaded by the Jews to write to Caligula in an attempt to dissuade him from his purpose. "It is precisely during this crisis that the redactor of the Synoptic apocalypse held his pen. The Jews did not remember having traversed days of such mortal anguish. It seemed the winter would not pass before the temple had been profaned ('Pray that these things may not happen in the winter,' 13:18). . . . When the anguish was at its height, the magnanimous decision of Petronius 'shortened the days.' " According to Schürer, this took place in November AD 40.[106] Nevertheless, the jubilation of the Jews was short-lived; Caligula repented of his decision and two months later announced his intention of making a voyage to Syria. The Jews were in dread. Caligula sent an order to Petronius to kill himself. Fortunately for Petronius, Caligula was murdered, and the news of the emperor's murder reached him before the fateful message. Piganiol agrees with Spitta that 2 Thessalonians may well have been composed in this period of anxiety; "We believe that the apocalyptic passage [in 2 Thessalonians] is contemporaneous with the discourse of the parousia (Mark 13), and that it was written in the midst of Jewish Christians among whom Paul then found himself." The apocalypse of Mark 13 was written (*ho anaginōskōn noeitō*) by a Jewish Christian and presented as a prophecy of Christ, in the conviction that the first act of the drama was finished and the rest was speedily to come. "It should be considered as the most ancient document of Christianity; it shows us the spirit of the Jewish Christians less than ten years after the death of Christ."[107]

   This interpretation of Piganiol, attractive though it be, has certain serious defects. (1) It assumes that to issue a document in the light of events for which it is relevant means that it must be composed by the aid of those events; this is unnecessary. If it was known that Jesus had related his prophecy of the ruin of the temple with the Danielic prophecy of the abomination that desolates, there would have been an intense desire in the time of the Caligula crisis to know what he had said about the doom of Jerusalem and his parousia, since in Jewish minds the two events would have inevitably been closely related. (2) It assumes that it was natural for a Christian in Palestine in the year AD 40–41 to compose a writing in the name of the historical Jesus, in distinction from a revelation of the Risen Lord, and equally natural that such a

---

[106]Piganiol, "Observations sur la date de l'apocalypse synoptique," *RHPR* 4 (1924): 247–48. The description of the crisis may be found in the new English translation of Schürer's *History of the Jewish People in the Age of Jesus Christ* (Edinburgh, 1973), vol. 1, 394–97.
   [107]Ibid.

document would gain widespread currency in the presence of the apostles. The former supposition is highly questionable, and the latter, since the document claims to be addressed to the four leading apostles, asks too much at so early a date. (3) It assumes that every element in this prediction reflects events that have happened, for the phenomenon of prediction is inadmissible. This all too commonly accepted canon of criticism is rigorously applied by Piganiol: vv. 7–8 are said to relate to the war between the Arabian Aretas and Herod Antipas, the strained relations between Parthia and Rome, Caligula's expedition to Germany in AD 40 and his intended visit to Syria in 41; Luke's replacement of *akoas polemōn*, "rumors of wars," by *akatastasias*, "disorders," reflects the troubles following Nero's death. As an example of the false prophets, mentioned in 13:22, Bar-Jesus is cited, who withstood Paul (Acts 13:6). And so the process continues. This method surely is erroneous; it overlooks the precedents of OT prophecy, the influence of which was never stronger than in the first century of our era; and it forgets the existence of "prophets" in the NT community (Eph 4:11), the greatest example of whom was our Lord himself. If these three assumptions of Piganiol are called in question, the force of his conclusions is dissipated, insofar as they are intended to prove that the apocalypse of Mark 13 was created by the circumstances of AD 40–41.

A. E. J. Rawlinson

The question of the relation of the gospel traditions to the circumstances of the primitive community was given special attention by A. E. J. Rawlinson, both throughout his commentary on Mark, and specifically as it applied to the problems of our chapter. To him the entire Gospel is both "a record of the story of Jesus . . . and a message addressed to the contemporary Church." His aim as an expositor was therefore twofold: (1) to show the significance of a saying or event in the setting of our Lord's life; (2) to show the significance of this material to the Christians of Rome for whom the Gospel was written.[108] As to Mark 13, Rawlinson cites Luke's words, "Men's hearts failing them for fear, and for looking after those things which were coming on the earth" (22:26), as a description of the period in which Mark wrote. "It is intelligible that in such terrible circumstances the Church clung to and cherished the tradition of the Saviour's apocalyptic words."[109] The substance of Mark 13 is a message for the contemporary church, introduced in the form of instruction given privately to a group of disciples, so conforming to the common pattern of apocalypses as well as to the other "esoteric" passages in Mark 4:10–12; 8:27–33 "Though this may

---

[108]Rawlinson, *St. Mark,* Westminster Commentaries (London, 1925), xviii.
[109]Ibid., 178.

hold good as regards the arrangement, setting and adaptation of the discourse in its present form, it does not follow that its contents may not represent substantially our Lord's own general outlook upon the future, or that it does not contain a good number of sayings which are authentically his."[110]

Apart from these "authentic" sayings (e.g., on persecution, 13:9–13), Rawlinson is generous in his estimate of the extent to which the discourse represents "substantially our Lord's general outlook upon the future," for the general drift of the discourse is evidently regarded as correct: "It is probable that, looking upon future in terms of prophetic symbolism, his mind passed beyond the immediate to the ultimate future, in such a fashion that the coming doom of Jerusalem was thrown (as Bishop Gore expresses it) 'upon the background of the final and universal judgment.' "[111] The representation of the parousia in v. 26 is also believed to be authentic. Rawlinson's objection to the discourse appears to be that instead of indicating generally the nature of this age and the climax to which it is heading, it purports to provide a map of the future; that cannot be reconciled with the professed ignorance of Jesus in 13:32, the unexpectedness of the end assumed in 13:35–37, and our Lord's refusal to provide signs when demanded, 8:11–12:

> It is not surprising that the hypothesis first suggested by Colani in 1864, viz. that a sort of independent apocalypse of Jewish or Jewish-Christian origin has been combined in this chapter with genuine sayings of our Lord, has found wide acceptance among critics even of a generally conservative type. The passages which it is reasonable to assign to such a document are three, viz. vv. 7–8, 14–20, 24–27. . . . Assuming that these three passages really did at one time form parts of a separate document, which has come to be wholly or partly incorporated in the Gospels, it is more probable that the document in question was of Jewish-Christian than of purely Jewish origin (as Colani supposed).[112]

Rawlinson thinks that the advice in 13:14, "Let the reader understand," cannot be taken as evidence of a written apocalypse, but is a remark added by either Mark or the original apocalyptist.[113] Verses 30–32 may be authentic, but if so they were probably spoken on more than one occasion.

We have reproduced Rawlinson's views because they are typical of most English commentators. Probably he numbers himself among the "critics of a generally conservative type," as compared with scholars like Wellhausen, Loisy, and Bultmann. He believes that the drift of

---

[110]Ibid., 179.
[111]Ibid., 180.
[112]Ibid., 181.
[113]Ibid., 188.

Mark 13 is correct, that Jesus prophesied the fall of Jerusalem, the persecution of his disciples, the denouement at the advent, on the background of which the disaster of Jerusalem is set. What, then, has he to do with Colani? It would seem that to the Bishop, as to most, Colani is but a name attached to a theory but his works he has not read. Colani did not believe in the little apocalypse theory in the form apparently imputed to him by Rawlinson, and he certainly did not regard 13:3–31 as composed by a Jew; that section was rejected fundamentally on the ground that it represents Jewish-Christian eschatology, which differs from the beliefs both of Jesus and of the Jews. Most of the grounds on which Colani based his theory were explicitly repudiated by Rawlinson; the chief exception is the feeling that Mark 13 presents us with a map of the future, and that we believe to be a misconception. One element of the discourse on which Colani did not dwell is rejected by Rawlinson—the view of antichrist in 13:14ff. Jewish apocalyptic tradition is said to have viewed antichrist either as a God-opposing tyrant (as in Revelation) or as a seductive agency, the incarnation of Beliar (as in 2 Thessalonians). "It is probable that the roots of the conception are to be found ultimately in the legend of the battle of God with a dragon-like monster, of which traces are to be found in various parts of the Old Testament."[114]

We have yet to discuss the significance of the "abomination of desolation" in 13:14, but we must not be misled by premature reflections on the origins of eschatological conceptions. If it be true that the antichrist of Jewish apocalyptic is adumbrated in the Babylonian goddess, Tiamat, it is equally true that the messiah who overcomes the anti–god power is adumbrated in the god Marduk. On what basis do we preserve the concept of the Christ and reject that of the antichrist, if it be merely a question of origins? Zimmern paralleled every element of Christology in Babylonian mythology, from the Virgin Birth to redemption by death and resurrection and the final victory at the parousia. On the basis of the attitude adopted by Rawlinson in this one matter only, he rejected the whole christological scheme as mythological.[115] In reality the parallels between the Christology, soteriology, and eschatology of the Bible and the mythologies of the religions of the Near East are far more complex than the relations of Judeo-Christian and Babylonian religions, and it simply will not do to take one isolated element and deal with it in this fashion. It goes to the roots of our faith, and demands a treatment commensurate with the problems involved. When it is dealt with on that scale, it may be that Oesterley's contention will be justi-

---

[114]Ibid., 187.

[115]See Schräder, *Die Keilinschriften und das Alte Testament,* rev. H. Zimmern (Berlin, 1903), 370–96.

fied, that the myths of Oriental religions are part and parcel of yearnings native to the human heart and as such integral elements of "natural" religion, or general revelation.[116] Meanwhile, we note that Rawlinson's belief in the irreconcilability of an advent preceded by signs with one that is sudden is an insufficient basis on which to construct a Jewish-Christian apocalypse in Mark 13.

B. S. Easton

The interest of B. S. Easton's exposition of the eschatological discourse centers on his conviction that Luke's version of the discourse is independent in the main of Mark's. He regards Luke 21:5–9 as coming from Luke's special source (L) with some Markan insertions.[117] Luke 21:10–36 is also mainly independent: "Verse 11 differs so much from Mark that 'contacts' and 'common omissions' are illegitimate terms; in fact, from this point down to v. 29, Luke agrees with Mark only in occasional sentences."[118] Easton describes Luke 21:20–24 as "the form Mark's 'Little Apocalypse' took in southern Palestine."[119] The date of Luke's version is determined by the consideration that the Gospel as a whole was written ca. AD 55–65, "when the 'rich' were enjoying undisturbed power, rather than a time when the visitation of the Roman conquest had fallen on them";[120] Luke 21:12–19 is placed earlier, however, since it is "a prediction of persecution in the Palestinian community, with a promise of preservation from the death sentence; through the aid of the Son of Man the disciples would always emerge victorious in their struggles with the Jewish courts. This is an accurate reflection of conditions in Palestine ca. AD 50; there were many persecutions (1 Thess. 2:24f.), but practically no martyrdoms."[121] On this basis Luke's version is earlier than Mark's, for Easton thought that Mark 13 was bound up with the fall of Jerusalem.[122] Our views on the validity of this method of treating a Gospel document purporting to give predictions have already been expressed in our discussion of Piganiol's work. But Easton's view of the independence of Luke 21 is of first importance.

---

[116]Oesterley, *The Doctrine of the Last Things* (London, 1909), 216–19.
[117]Easton, *The Gospel according to St. Luke* (Edinburgh, 1926), xxiv.
[118]Ibid., 310.
[119]Ibid., 311.
[120]Ibid., xxviii.
[121]Ibid., 311.
[122]Idem, *Christ in the Gospels* (New York and London, 1930), 4: "The phenomena of Chapter 13 tie us up to a time close to the Fall of Jerusalem; this is almost universally acknowledged."

V. Taylor

Vincent Taylor's study of Luke appeared in the same year as Easton's commentary. His position was remarkably similar to that of Easton. He differed from the latter in regarding Luke 21:5–11 as derived from Mark's discourse, but 21:12–19, 20–36 are believed to be non-Markan passages containing Markan "insertions" in vv. 16–17, 21a, 23a, 26b–27, 29–33. It is unnecessary to summarize the discussion by which this result is reached, but Taylor's comments on these "Markan insertions" into Luke 21:20–36 are noteworthy. They are said to be "no patchwork or mosaic, but a well-articulated whole."[123] The passages in Mark from which they are taken, 13:19–20, 22–23, 27, 32–33 "constitute a compact body of thought which gives definite tone and meaning to the Markan discourse. Unlike the four passages which St. Luke has undoubtedly taken over, these passages are not fringes and cuttings; they are of the very pattern of the Markan fabric; they make it what it is."[124] This is interesting, for Taylor presumably accepted at this time the usual analysis of the little apocalypse, vv. 7–8, 14–20, 24–27.[125] If vv. 19–20, 22–23, 27, 32–33 constitute "a compact body of thought," what are the grounds for omitting vv. 22–23, 32–33 from the little apocalypse when vv. 19–20, 27 are included? Alternatively, what are the grounds for assigning vv. 19–20, 27 to that source, when they are of a piece with vv. 32–33, which hardly any writer has assigned to the little apocalypse? We leave for the present the contention of Taylor that Luke's version is independent of Mark and that the omissions by Luke are of the same stamp, but we fail to see how one can maintain this hypothesis and that of the little apocalypse at the same time. Later we shall see that this distinguished scholar has since repented of both views, in that he rejects the little apocalypse theory and assigns the one "compact group" of sayings to three different groups.

F. Hauck

The sole reason adduced by F. Hauck for his adherence to the little apocalypse theory is that the discourse gives partly objective prophecy (in the third person, hence the *eklektoi* of vv. 20, 22, 27) and partly exhortation to disciples (in the second person).[126] He believes the "apocalyptic groundwork" to be vv. 7–8, 12, (13b?), 14–22, 24–27. In

---

[123]Taylor, *Behind the Third Gospel: A Study of the Proto-Luke Hypothesis* (Oxford, 1926), 113.

[124]Ibid., 116.

[125]So in his book *The Gospels: A Short Introduction* (London, 1930); in the 4th ed. (1938) this is stated on p. 57.

[126]Hauck, *Das Evangelium des Markus*, THKNT (Leipzig, 1931), 153.

contrast to Rawlinson's view he writes: "It is to be admitted that the apocalyptic basis, despite its strongly Jewish coloring, maintains the spirit of Jesus in its reserve in depicting the future, its lack of Jewish world-sovereignty ideas and all feeling of hatred and revenge. The tendency of ch. 13, despite all tension of thought as to the great hope of the end, is directed more to holding back extravagant views as to the near expectation of the end."[127]

7. From R. Bultmann to R. Heard

R. Bultmann

In considering the views of Rudolf Bultmann, readers will no doubt be more interested to learn what he accepts rather than what he rejects; for Bultmann to receive a Synoptic saying as authentic is something of an event. Alas, the event does not occur in this chapter. Without offering any reason, Bultmann states that Mark 13:7–8, 12, 14–22, 24–27 are "apocalyptic words which formed a connection even before they were worked up by Mark, who preserved them essentially intact."[128] Verses 5–6, 9–11, 13a, 23 are Christian additions, connecting the little apocalypse with the person of Jesus and introducing "predictions" concerning historic events and the mission and persecution of the church. This satisfactorily deals with vv. 5–27. As to the parable of the Fig Tree, Bultmann is not sure; at one point he seems to think v. 28 is authentic, and v. 29 a mistaken application; at another he expresses doubt concerning both verses—28–29 could very well derive from Jewish tradition.[129] Verse 30 may be a variant of 9:1, but it is also possible that it originally formed the conclusion of the Jewish apocalypse (with v. 32?). Verse 31 is a Christian formation. Verse 32 is perhaps a Jewish saying, apart from the Christian conclusion; with v. 30 it could have formed the end of the Jewish apocalypse.[130] Verses 33–37 are to be compared with Matt 15:1–13; Mark 9:1, etc., as Christian compositions that express the Christian view of the person of Jesus.[131] Returning to the beginning of the discourse, Bultmann thinks that vv. 1–2a are a scene composed for the prophecy in v. 2b; its form therefore is determined by the wording of v. 2b.[132] As to v. 2b, Bultmann cannot

---

[127]Ibid., 154.

[128]Bultmann, *Die Geschichte der synoptischen Tradition*, 2d ed. (Göttingen, 1931), 129. ET *History of the Synoptic Tradition*, Oxford 2d ed. 1968, 122. Remaining citations of the work are from this edition.

[129]On the former see ibid., 123; on the latter see 125.

[130]Ibid., 123.

[131]Ibid., 127.

[132]Ibid., 36.

make up his mind whether to accept it. At one time he writes: "With regard to the prophecy of the destruction of the temple, 13:2, there exists at least the possibility that it was first put in the mouth of Jesus by the community."[133] Later, in kinder mood, he states: "The temple saying [in the wording of Mark 13:2?] may perhaps be considered as a word of Jesus, even if with reserve."[134] Verse 3 is placed alongside 4:11, etc., as a secondary question of disciples, composed to give life and interest to apophthegmata.[135] Thus every verse of Mark 13, with the possible exception of v. 2b, is judged to be unauthentic. The same treatment is accorded to the great majority of the other "prophetic and apocalyptic words."

What is the ground for this attitude? Partly it is due to Bultmann's skeptical attitude toward the gospel traditions generally. Nevertheless, a motive is supplied in his book *Jesus and the Word*, where he affirms that Jesus repudiated all apocalypticism.

> It should be noted that he neither depicts the punishments of hell nor paints elaborate pictures of the heavenly glory. The oracular and esoteric note is completely lacking in the few prophecies of the future which can be ascribed to him with any probability. In fact, he absolutely repudiates all representations of the kingdom which human imagination can create when he says, "When they rise from the dead, they neither marry nor are given in marriage, but are as the angels in heaven" (Mark 12:25). In other words, men are forbidden to make any picture of the future life. Jesus thus rejects the whole content of apocalyptic speculation, as he rejects also the calculation of the time and the watching for signs.[136]

It is easy to assert that Jesus rejects all apocalyptic speculation, but it is an ambiguous statement. If by "apocalyptic speculation" is denoted an imaginative description of the varied departments of heaven and hell and their respective inhabitants, then Jesus certainly dissociated himself from it. But can we rightly affirm that the significance of Mark 12:25 is the forbidding to make any picture of the future life? What of the symbol of the messianic feast, used more than once by Jesus (Matt 8:11; Mark 14:25)? More important, the burden of Jewish apocalypses was the passing of this transient age of imperfection and the coming of the new age of eternal glories; that fundamental conviction Jesus shared, and he based his message on it. This coincidence of belief is not surprising, for it was the hope of revealed religion as given in the books of the Old Covenant. The supreme difference between Jesus and his predecessors lies in his connection of the new age with his own

---

[133]Ibid., 125.
[134]Ibid., 128.
[135]Ibid., 67.
[136]Idem, *Jesus and the Word* (ET London, 1935, from the German of 1926), 39.

person and activity: in his person and ministry the kingdom was present, in his parousia it would be consummated. Bultmann's edifice in reality is founded on one consideration: Jesus warned against all calculations—Luke 17:20–21.[137] The great question therefore is: May we rightly describe Mark 13 as "calculation"? We hope to show that it is impermissible to view it as such.

M. Goguel

Maurice Goguel struck out in a new way in his exposition of the thought of Mark 13.[138] He admitted that while the view of the parousia in Luke 17:20ff., instantaneous as a flash of lightning, differed from that in Mark 13, "this fact, taken by itself, would not force us to regard the Synoptic Apocalypse as non-authentic"; the thought of Jesus may have oscillated on this matter. Similarly, the "artificial character" of the connection between 13:1–2 and the discourse proper does not prove the latter unauthentic, for the link may be editorial.[139] For Goguel the decisive consideration lies in the date of Luke's version: Luke 21:24 can have been written only between AD 66 and 70, i.e., from the outbreak of the Jewish revolt to the beginning of the siege, while it was still possible for people inside the city to depart; and Luke's version of the discourse is primitive. The primacy of Luke's version is demonstrated by the following points: (1) the entire setting of the events of the last week in Jerusalem is better in Luke than in Mark: the story of the barren fig tree in Mark is a transformation of an aetiological myth, as Schwartz has shown, so that the division of days by means of it is wrong; Luke 21:37 shows that Jesus spent more than one week in Jerusalem. (2) Luke's version of the discourse is purely Jewish; Mark has altered it to gain a more general significance (cf. the mention of "all flesh" in Mark 13:20). (3) Luke has not the motive, so obvious in Mark, of quieting the impatience of believers, yearning for the parousia; this motive characterizes a late period. (4) The "abomination of desolation" has nothing to do with the events of AD 40, for that crisis was temporary; in Mark it is simply a traditional apocalyptic idea and has no definite reference. "Thus the earliest form of the Synoptic Apocalypse is found in Luke, and this form dates from the period which preceded the siege of Jerusalem."[140] Mark's version appeared in a time when it was realized that the fall of Jerusalem was not the sign which preceded the parousia. Matthew presumably used a copy worked over by Mark. There is

---

[137]Ibid., 40.
[138]Goguel, *The Life of Jesus* (ET 1933, from the French of 1932), 425ff.
[139]Ibid., 425–26.
[140]Ibid., 428.

nothing specifically Christian in the apocalypse; probably it is of Jewish origin.

Goguel is not alone in championing the priority of Luke. Neander had done it a century earlier and others have followed suit since, but we can scarcely be satisfied with the manner of his establishing the point or with the conclusions he draws from it. The employment of Schwartz's reconstruction of the fig tree narrative in Mark 11:12ff. and the parable in Mark 13:28–29 is unfortunate; in our estimate the theory is fantastic.[141] It is quite true that Luke's version is "purely Jewish," but is there a more Jewish phrase than "all flesh" in Mark 13:20? It is a Semitism and is as applicable to Palestine as to the universe; the context must decide its meaning. If it be true that Mark's version has a subsidiary aim to quiet an excessive apocalyptic ardor, does that of necessity prove a late date? Goguel cites Mark 13:32, omitted by Luke, to prove that it does, but most critics think that Luke's omission of Mark 13:32 shows that his version is later than Mark's, being actuated by dogmatic motives. In short, we cannot admit that Goguel has proved his case. That Luke's version was prior to Mark's cannot be established on the basis of the composition of Mark after AD 70. The question of priority rests solely upon what is considered to have been the original form of the "abomination" saying. As it happens, neither version demands a late date and neither is impossible on the lips of Jesus. Once again we see an exegete rejecting as insufficient all the usual reasons for proving the little apocalypse theory, and adducing another which, nevertheless, appears improbable on examination.

G. Hölscher

The OT scholar G. Hölscher took a hand in the debate and produced an article, now widely quoted.[142] Goguel had commented on Jesus' apparent change of attitude toward the temple, in that Jesus one day cleansed the temple and shortly after prophesied its destruction: in the former case he had attempted reform, in the latter he despaired of it.[143] Hölscher began at this point and affirmed that this change of attitude showed the prophecy of destruction to be unauthentic; it played no part in the trial before the Sanhedrin (Mark 14:55–64), the account of which is legendary; Mark 13:1–2 is a *vaticinium ex eventu*.[144] Verses 3–4 are composed to link the public declaration of vv. 1–2 to the discourse in vv. 5ff.: "The fiction of secret instruction . . . corresponds

---

[141]See E. Schwartz, "Der verfluchte Feigenbaum," *ZNW* 5 (1904): 80–84.

[142]Hölscher, "Der Ursprung der Apokalypse Mk. 13," *TBl* 12 (July 1933), 193–202.

[143]Goguel, *Life of Jesus*, 402–3.

[144]Hölscher, "Ursprung," 193.

to the apocalyptic style." Mark 13:14 shows that the text rests on a literary basis. The composite nature of the discourse is revealed in its mixture of "traditional material of Old Testament-apocalyptic eschatology" with references to "the concrete fortunes of the later Christian community"; that means, of course, that the entire discourse is spurious. Hölscher makes this plain in his subsequent exposition. The little apocalypse is vv. 7–8, 12, 14–20, 24–27. Other material is "Christian formation," e.g., vv. 21–23 refer to the many prophets mentioned by Josephus as arising in the years AD 44–66; "all that follows v. 27 is 'rubble' *(Geröll)*, composed by Mark as the conclusion of the discourse. Any specifically Christian element is lacking in the discourse. The whole derives from Daniel."[145]

Like others, Hölscher divided the little apocalypse into three scenes, but after the example of Jewish apocalypses he related them to the three tenses: the first scene, vv. 7–8, lies in the immediate past; the second scene, vv. 14–20, represents the immediate present, for the Danielic prophecy of the "abomination" is about to be fulfilled—the vagueness of the language is due to the danger of the times ("one lays one's finger to the mouth and speaks only in gentle allusions"); the third scene, vv. 24–27, lies in the immediate future. The situation in which one has to speak so discreetly is betrayed by 13:14; one epoch alone in the first century AD suits such language, that of AD 40. In Daniel the "abomination of desolation" is a wordplay on the name Jupiter Olympios, whose statue Antiochus erected in the temple; the reference is manifestly similar in Mark 13—the "abomination" is the statue of Caligula that everyone anticipated was about to be placed in the temple. This is the situation presumed in 2 Thessalonians 2, where the emperor "sits in the temple of God," naturally *in figura*; the prophecy is fully explained by the little apocalypse, "with perhaps certain Christian additions like 13:21–22, 32–37."[146] The date of the Markan apocalypse is thereby demonstrated to be between the winter of 39/40 and that of 40/41, more exactly between spring and autumn, Mark 13:18 (!).

It is apparent that many elements in this exposition depend on perilously subjective criteria. If Hölscher believed that vv. 1–2 are a prophecy after the event, and the account of the trial before the Sanhedrin fictitious, we can but express our disagreement. The idea that the prediction of the ruin of the temple contradicts the attitude of Jesus when he cleansed it is very questionable. The view that passages like vv. 9–13, 21–23 are based on the experiences of the church is also unnecessary; Jesus knew that his disciples could not expect better treatment from the Jews than he himself had received, and he could

---

[145]Ibid., 197.
[146]Ibid., 199–200.

have warned them of what lay ahead. Apart from dogmatic differences, however, Hölscher seems to have been inconsistent in three respects: (1) While he regarded 13:14 as proof that the little apocalypse was originally a written document, he also stated that the offending clause could be a "marginal gloss."[147] If the latter statement be true, the former is not. (2) It is a very subtle use of language to distinguish between an "immediate present" which relates to the setting up of the abomination in a very short time, and an "immediate future" which relates to the time after; most people would describe the former as well as the latter as "immediate future." The only motive for making such a distinction is the a priori view that as the extracted little apocalypse may be divided into three, and many Jewish apocalypses may be divided into past, present, and future sections, this one must also reveal the same structure of thought. This is the Procrustean method in a new guise. (3) It will not have escaped the reader's attention that 2 Thessalonians 2, on Hölscher's view, needs as its presupposition the little apocalypse "with perhaps certain Christian additions like 13:21–22, 32–37." This learned exegete seems to have forgotten that he had earlier stated that 13:21–23 reflects events of the years 44–66; we usually date the Thessalonian letters in the year AD 50! Still worse, he appears to have overlooked that 13:28–37 were described as "rubble," added by Mark to round off the discourse, who *ex hypothesi* wrote after AD 70.

Apart from these instances of forgetfulness, it surely is not without significance for the whole theory we are discussing that Paul is believed to have known, before the year AD 50, the little apocalypse, not in its presumed raw condition but with at least "certain Christian additions like 13:21–23, 33–37." Hölscher has already lumped together vv. 28–37; there is therefore no reasonable objection to Paul's knowing the little apocalypse plus vv. 21–23, 28–37. That leaves only vv. 1–6, 9–13. As v. 6 is closely parallel to vv. 21–23, there is no reason to deny that to the "Christian additions." We know that Hölscher refused the authenticity of vv. 1–2, but the only ground he could adduce for Paul's not knowing it is that Paul did not mention it in 2 Thessalonians 2. We differ from him as to vv. 9–13, and must be allowed to regard these verses as possible to Jesus. If, therefore, Hölscher's view be accepted that 2 Thessalonians 2 presumes the existence of the little apocalypse plus Christian additions, we can see no valid reason for denying the probability that Paul knew a great deal of the material, even if the individual sayings were not in their present contexts.

---

[147]Cf. ibid., 195, 197.

T. F. Glasson

T. F. Glasson raised a significant issue in an article on Mark 13 and the LXX. He acknowledged that Jesus unquestionably cited the OT frequently, but in the eschatological discourse it is the Greek translation that is reflected, and in some instances the renderings differ from the Hebrew text. This would support the view that parts of Mark 13 were drawn up in Greek on the basis of the LXX, so strengthening the conviction that authentic words of Jesus have been expanded with materials from elsewhere.

The first passage to be cited is Mark 13:24–27. The portrayal of cosmic signs in vv. 24–25 does not actually cite specific texts from the OT, but Isa 34:4 (cf. Mark 13:25) reads, "All the host of heaven shall be dissolved . . . and all their host shall fade away." The LXX has, "And all the powers of the heavens shall melt . . . and all the stars shall fall." Thus for "host" the LXX has "powers" (*dynameis*) and "stars" (*astra*), and they are said to "fall" (*peseitai*); but the word "fall" does not occur in the Hebrew text; indeed, "Falling stars do not occur anywhere in the Hebrew Bible."[148] These comments are surprising. I would judge that the LXX translation here is quite acceptable. The Hebrew term "host" (*ṣābā'*) commonly denotes heavenly bodies, i.e., stars, and angels, hence even powers (not least in view of the common belief of stars as living beings). In Isa 34:4 the verb rendered "fade away" is *nābēl*, which in BDB (p. 615) is defined as "sink, or drop down, languish, wither and fall, fade." It is used especially of leaves that wither and fall from a tree, and BDB cites Isa 34:4 for that meaning. It was therefore natural for the LXX translators to render the statement under the imagery of leaves falling from a tree. The author of the book of Revelation developed precisely that understanding of the passage in Rev 6:12–15, and the NIV translators so interpreted the Hebrew text:

> All the starry host will fall,
> like withered leaves from the vine,
> like shriveled figs from the fig tree.

Glasson also draws attention to Mark 13:27: "he shall gather his elect from the four winds, from the end of earth to the end of heaven." The language appears to reflect Zech 2:6 (MT, LXX 10), of which the MT reads, "I have *spread you abroad* as the four winds of heaven" (LXX *ek tōn tessarōn anemōn tou ouranou synaxō hymas*). Glasson acknowledges that some scholars consider that the LXX of Zech 2:6 represents the original Hebrew text, but he believes that the MT is more likely to

---

[148]Glasson, "Mark XIII and the Greek Old Testament," *ExpT* 69 (1957–58): 213.

be original than the LXX. By contrast D. Winton Thomas affirmed, "The LXX rendering is more in accord with the context, where the prophet is thinking of the gathering in of the Jews still outside Palestine, than is the MT, which refers to the spreading abroad of all the Jews all over the world."[149] One should further recognize that Deut 30:4 is closely related to the form of the text in Mark 13:27, along with Deut 13:7. The former reads, "Even if you are exiled to the ends of heaven, from there the Lord your God will gather you" (LXX *ean ē hē diaspora sou ap' akrou tou ouranou heōs akrou tou ouranou ekeithen synaxei se kyrios ho theos sou*). With this Deut 13:7 (LXX 8) should be compared: "from the end of earth to the end of earth" (LXX *ap' akrou tēs gēs heōs akrou tēs gēs*). The two texts have apparently been conflated in Mark 13:27.

The phrase *dei genesthai*, "must happen," in Mark 13:7 represents a different kind of problem. Glasson holds, in common with perhaps the majority of exegetes, that this is a citation from the LXX of Dan 2:28 (*ha dei genesthai*). In his view it is a recognized apocalyptic term, for it occurs in Rev 1:1; 4:1; and 22:6 of "things which must come to pass"; but Dan 2:28 is in the Aramaic section of Daniel, and the Aramaic text reads a simple future; it is the Greek text which supplies the word "must." Now this issue is a cause célèbre, for it is not the only passage in the Gospels in which the term *dei* is found on the lips of Jesus. It occurs in the first "prediction of the passion," Mark 8:31: "The Son of Man must suffer many things . . ." (*dei polla pathein*). The question has been raised how Jesus could have uttered that statement, seeing that there is no term for "must" in Hebrew or Aramaic. Appeal is again frequently made to Dan 2:28 as its inspiration. On that basis it is assumed that the Hellenistic churches viewed the sufferings of Jesus as due to an eschatological, if not apocalyptic, necessity.

A much simpler explanation for this usage, however, can be proposed. Dan 2:28 is not alone in the LXX for the use of *dei* to express a simple future; it occurs in the following sentence, Dan 2:29, and later in the same chapter, v. 45, where, however, the LXX uses a simple future for the same expression, but Symmachus reads *ha dei genesthai*. This is almost certainly a phenomenon of translation, whereby a statement relating to the future is made more emphatic in the light of who uttered it. It is doubtful that Dan 2:28 was at all in the mind of the person who reproduced Mark 8:31, or Mark 13:7, any more than it would have been present to the person who translated Lev 5:17, where *dei* is used for an ordinary future to express the will of God made known, or in the translation of Isa 30:29, where *dei* expresses a future of prophecy.[150]

---

[149]See Winton Thomas, *IB*, 6:1065.

[150]On this issue see further my *Jesus and the Kingdom of God* (Grand Rapids, 1986), 238–39.

One further example of "doubtful" LXX renderings of Hebrew expressions in Mark 13 is the celebrated "abomination of desolation" in v. 14 (*to bdelygma tēs erēmōseōs*). Glasson adheres to the traditional critical opinion that the Hebrew expression signifies "an abomination that horrifies, or appals," whereas the Greek expression is held to mean "the abomination that causes destruction." In reality it is probable that both the Hebrew and the Greek expressions are intended to convey both ideas, i.e., desolation in the sense of horror and destruction. The context of Dan 9:27, the first and determinative occasion of the use of this phrase, tells in favor of this understanding (v. 26: the troops of the coming prince destroy the city and sanctuary). There are also various passages in the OT prophets which include abominations and desolation in a sense related to Dan 9:27, above all Ezek 5:1–15. These associations are significant for the interpretation of Mark 13:14.[151] When, however, Glasson affirmed, "The phrases 'abomination of desolation,' and others, are not such as he [Jesus] normally used,"[152] the question is provoked: How did Jesus characterize the acts of Antiochus Epiphanes when he attended the Feast of the Dedication in the temple of Jerusalem (cf. John 10:22–39), and when he pondered the significance of the feast at home? We do not know, but one thing is certain: he was well acquainted with the phrase in question!

H. A. Guy

H. A. Guy accepted the usual analysis of Mark 13, but he admitted that the incorporated apocalypse has been thoroughly subordinated to the Christian view; all is related to the Christian message and is used as a genuine prophecy in contrast to the work of the "false prophets," of whom the reader is warned, 13:22. "The whole concludes with a prophetic exhortation to watch, 13:37—a genuine instance of *paraklēsis*, found also in Paul (I Thess. 5:6) at the conclusion of a somewhat similar passage."[153] It is difficult to reconcile Guy's adherence to the little apocalypse theory when he follows C. H. Dodd in adducing 13:14–19 along with Luke 17:31, 34–35, 37, as examples of sayings apparently containing an eschatological reference, which nevertheless "were originally intended to relate to the coming political and religious disaster."[154] By classing Mark 13:14–19 with extracts from the Q apocalypse, Guy undoubtedly gives the impression that they are authentic

---

[151]For an exhaustive examination of the meaning of "abomination of desolation" see the monograph by D. Ford, *The Abomination of Desolation in Biblical Eschatology* (Washington, D.C., 1979).

[152]Glasson, *ExpT* 69 (1957–58): 215.

[153]Guy, *New Testament Prophecy* (London, 1947), 108–9.

[154]Idem, *The New Testament Doctrine of the "Last Things"* (London, 1948), 60–61.

sayings of Jesus; are we to presume, then, that the little apocalypse was composed from authentic sayings of Jesus mistakenly applied? It would seem unlikely that this writer has intended this inference.

B. T. D. Smith, G. S. Duncan, S. H. Hooke, and R. Heard

B. T. D. Smith, G. S. Duncan, S. H. Hooke, and R. Heard all regarded Mark 13 as combining genuine sayings of Jesus with unauthentic material, but they all adhered to the confusing habit of referring to the entire discourse of Mark 13 as "the Little Apocalypse."[155] It is desirable that this term be retained for its traditional designation of a group of sayings within Mark 13 regarded as of independent origin, seeing that the vast majority of NT critics have stamped it as a *terminus technicus* in this restricted sense.

Of the critics just named, the most interesting treatment of Mark 13 is that of R. Heard, whose exposition takes us back to the theme of our first chapter. The prime consideration that Heard would have us bear in mind is the nonfulfillment of the parousia promise: "It must either be accepted that Jesus is rightly recorded in the Synoptic Gospels as having taught of his early return in glory and the accompanying judgment—and that he was mistaken, or it must be shown that his teaching was from the earliest days misinterpreted and transformed." Heard adopts the latter alternative.[156] The error dates from the resurrection: "When one misunderstanding—that the Messiah would not die—had been removed, it was replaced by another, that his departure was only for a short while, and that the establishment of the kingdom was to be on lines expected by apocalyptists."[157] In proof of this thesis Acts 1:7 is adduced, with the consideration that the interpretation of the kingdom as present is uncommon in the Epistles generally. Two influences combined to encourage the primitive error: the study of the OT and the rise of Christian prophecy. With the former influence account must be taken of the apocalyptic writings, which exercised a widespread influence in still further adapting Christian teaching on the end to current Jewish conceptions. The latter influence was of great service, but "it was peculiarly fitted to spread in the Church a confusion of ideas about the coming of the end," owing to the freedom of utterance granted to the prophets and their recognized authority. Mark 13 itself represents "an adulteration of Jesus' teaching far beyond that which might be

---

[155]Smith, *The Gospel according to S. Matthew* (London, 1927), 182ff.; Duncan, *Jesus, Son of Man* (London, 1947), 179; Hooke, *The Kingdom of God in the Experience of Jesus* (London, 1949), 62; Heard, *An Introduction to the New Testament* (London, 1950), 249.

[156]Heard, *Introduction*, 247.

[157]Ibid., 250.

expected of Peter"; presumably we are to see the influence of the prophets in this passage. Heard suggests that 13:14–20 (and the rest of the little apocalypse?) is a development of the authentic prophecy of the doom of Jerusalem, amplified in the light of OT prophecy and first-century experience.[158] After dealing thus with Mark 13, pronouncing Matt 10:23 and Mark 14:62 as unauthentic and interpreting Mark 9:1 as the coming of the Spirit, Heard said, "The apocalyptic element in the teaching of Jesus, if such a view of the Gospel evidence is accepted, is reduced to small proportions."[159] Naturally! If such a treatment of the Gospel evidence were meted out generally, the teaching of Jesus on any subject would be reduced to "small proportions."

Among other criticisms that might be made we draw attention to the following: (1) Such a text as Acts 1:7 should not be adduced to prove that the disciples invented the belief in the early coming of the kingdom; it merely shows they cherished it still after the resurrection. The mention of their hopes concerning Israel shows that they had not grasped our Lord's teaching concerning the kingdom of God and the nations, but it should be observed that our knowledge of the teaching of Jesus that militates against their view is due to their preservation of it. This is sound testimony to the faithfulness of the disciples in preserving words of the Lord which they did not really understand and with which they had not come to terms. (2) If "realized eschatology" is not in the Pauline and Johannine writings, it is nowhere in the NT. Of this C. H. Dodd has surely written sufficiently. (3) The sole proof that Jewish apocalypses were read avidly by early Christians is the Epistle of Jude, one of the latest books of the NT. As we know that the OT was authoritative for the church, the burden of proof that the same applied to Enoch, etc., rests on those who assert it. (4) The rejection of all elements in NT eschatology derived from the OT cannot be squared with our Lord's attitude toward and use of the OT. (5) The early church knew the inspiration of the Spirit in fuller measure than most generations since; the proof of that is its production of the NT. It is conceivable that the gift of inspired utterance, in the name of that same Holy Spirit, was the means of the greatest distortion of the teaching of Jesus that ever took place; but there will be a large number of dissentient voices to that proposition.

---

[158]Ibid., 56, 253
[159]Ibid., 249.

3

OTHER THEORIES CONCERNING THE ORIGIN OF MARK 13

DESPITE THE READY AND WIDESPREAD ADOPTION of the little apocalypse theory from the time of its inception, there has been a steadily increasing number of NT critics from the close of the nineteenth century onwards who, while not able to accept the genuineness of the eschatological discourse, have either declined the popular alternative or seriously modified it. Among this group are scholars with the widest range of theological thought and critical attitudes to the Bible. Some of the views proceed from highly individual beliefs about NT origins, but most are products of wrestling with difficulties raised by the little apocalypse theory, and from these we may learn much.

1. From A. Meyer to J. Klausner

A. Meyer

Arnold Meyer, pioneer in Aramaic origins, must be classed with the former group. He thought that the compilation of the NT was a very lengthy process, in which the Gospels underwent drastic modifications. "At the turn of the first century we have to suppose a living movement, a fresh, carefree handling of the transmitted material, which was stamped in ever-new coinage according to the necessities of the time and passed on from hand to hand. . . . Such a time was not minded to distinguish too anxiously between the logia of the Lord walking on earth and of the exalted Lord."[1] In his view, the term *huios tou*

---

[1] Meyer, *Jesu Muttersprache* (Freiburg and Leipzig, 1896), 70–71.

anthrōpou, "Son of man," did not penetrate the Gospel tradition until after AD 170. That was the time when everyone "translated as well as he could," to use Papias's words, the Aramaic Gospel, and that was the time when "Greek-speaking Christians . . . edified themselves with prophecies 'from the Lord' like Matthew 24 and compared them with Daniel."[2] Since the latter reference to Daniel is held to explain the abomination passage, and since the estimate of Jesus as the heavenly Son of man arose together with it at this time, there is no question of an old apocalypse being adopted in Mark 13; the whole structure will be due to a late compilation of materials drawn from various sources. In comparison with this view the little apocalypse theory was rather conservative.

The attitude of Réville to eschatology has been mentioned in the first chapter.[3] It will be recalled that he believed it was impossible for Jesus to have adopted eschatological views without denying his entire teaching. The parousia instruction is said to have arisen through disciples linking the progress of the kingdom with the activity of Christ: "When it became axiomatic for his followers that he was the messiah of God, the triumph of his cause became thereby inseparable from that of his person. . . . The one could be taken, and was taken, for the other."[4] This identification of the triumph of Christ with that of the kingdom is said to have led to the introduction of apocalyptic categories into the teaching of Jesus (why it should have done so is not made clear), and that brought about a modification in the basis of our Lord's conceptions. "It is impossible to make the separation of that which is authentic from that which is not in these apocalypses of the Synoptics. It is only certain that the arrangement, the course, the systematization of these predictions do not belong to Jesus himself and cannot pretend to the same authenticity as his truly original and personal teachings."[5] This, of course, applies equally to the "Q apocalypse" of Luke 17:20ff. as to Mark 13 and every other saying wherein the messianic relation of Jesus to the kingdom appears.

O. Holtzmann

Oscar Holtzmann believed that Jesus agreed with a good deal of contemporary eschatological thought. Consequently, "In its essential features . . . this discourse of Jesus (Mark 13:6–37) may be thoroughly genuine, even though in certain parts it has been very much recast."[6]

---

[2] Ibid., 100.

[3] See above, pp. 25–26.

[4] Réville, *Jésus de Nazareth*, 322.

[5] Ibid., 325.

[6] Holtzmann, *The Life of Jesus* (ET London, 1904, from the German of 1901), 456.

The "recasting" spoken of by Holtzmann concerns vv. 10, 14–18. The former passage cannot be reconciled with the assumptions of Matt 10:23, nor with the behavior of the apostles in the first seventeen years of the church's existence; the latter is too precise to fit the idea of a tribulation during the last days. "If, however, we excise the verses mentioned, as being additions from another hand, all the rest of the discourse would fit in very well with the point of time at which Mark 13:3–5 represents it to have been spoken."[7]

The division of opinion as to Mark 13:10 seems to be unrelated to the question of a little apocalypse, and the attitude of critics to its authenticity is in no way determined by their views of the larger issue. Mark 13:14–20 has certainly provided the biggest stumbling block of the discourse for many, and is usually regarded as the heart of the little apocalypse. David Smith at first found that section, or rather 13:14–19, impossible to accept, but he retracted this view when he came to write *The Disciple's Commentary on the Gospels*.[8] To H. D. A. Major the little apocalypse is 13:14–20. His objections to Mark 13 concern solely this passage.[9] Verses 5–13 are assigned to the earliest stage of Christian history; vv. 24–27 are formed to answer the question as to when Jesus may be expected back again.[10] E. J. Goodspeed adopts a similar position, save that he accepts the authenticity of the situation of Mark 13 and of the whole chapter apart from vv. 9–13, 14–20.[11] Verses 9–13 are held to reflect the experiences of the early believers; vv. 14–20 relate to the circumstances of the Jewish War of AD 66–70. As Goodspeed, like Major, also refers to "the probable presence of a little apocalypse in ch. 13,"[12] we must presume again that vv. 14–20 represent that apocalypse. In view of the great likelihood that Mark 13:15–16 are authentic sayings of Jesus (Luke 17:31), "little" is an appropriate description of the apocalypse that remains! It is impossible to retain the term for such a fragment.

A. Merx

The Syriac scholar A. Merx will be remembered as one who objected to attributing anything savoring of "fanaticism" to Jesus.[13] By "fanaticism" he meant the expectation of a future world sovereignty of

---

[7] Ibid., 457.

[8] Smith, *The Days of His Flesh*, 8th ed. (London, 1910; 1st ed. 1905), xxxi; idem, *The Disciple's Commentary on the Gospels* (London, 1928), 387.

[9] Major, "The Gospel according to St. Mark," in *The Mission and Message of Jesus* (London, 1937), 158–60.

[10] Ibid., 160.

[11] Goodspeed, *A Life of Jesus* (New York, 1950), 186–89.

[12] Ibid., 15.

[13] See above, pp. 26–27.

the Jews. Far from holding such a hope, Jesus taught the disciples to anticipate wars, persecutions, worldwide preaching of the gospel, and above all the destruction of Jerusalem. To the announcement of this destruction vv. 14ff. as truly belong as vv. 1–2; the former passage is clearly Christian: "The Jews sought the place [Jerusalem] as a protecting bulwark, the Christians should forsake it—that was Jesus' previsionary direction."[14] Merx placed v. 14 in a wholly new light by his demonstration that all the Syriac authorities for the text presume the reading *hotan de idēte to sēmeion tou bdelygmatos, to rhēthen Daniēl tou prophētou—ho anaginōskōn noeitō—tote ktl*, "whenever you see the sign of the abomination which was spoken of by Daniel the prophet, let the reader understand, then. . . ." Merx himself believed the original reading to be shorter, viz. *hotan de idēte to sēmeion tou bdelygmatos, tote hoi en tē Ioudaia pheugetōsan*, "Whenever you see the sign of the abomination, then let those in Judea flee." This allows the "abomination" to be viewed in a less rigid way than is usual. Hence Merx felt justified in retaining the "offending" passage. The limits of authenticity in the chapter, so far as he is concerned, are not explicitly declared, but one gathers from the exposition that he accepted vv. 1–22 and refused 24–27, with 28–29 if the parable relates to the parousia. In connection with Merx's view as to the acceptability of 13:14ff. we may notice that of H. J. Schoeps; in his important work on Jewish Christianity he maintains the view that Mark 14:58; 15:29; Acts 6:13, and presumably Mark 13:2 are all falsely reproduced; the primitive form of the logion is Matt 24:15 (= Mark 13:14). He regards the "preserved command of Jesus," Matt 24:15–28; Mark 13:14–23, to be the basis of the oracular command referred to by Eusebius and thus authentic.[15] Evidently, we have not heard the last of Mark 13:14!

M.-J. Lagrange

It may occasion some surprise that the noted Roman Catholic scholar Père M.-J. Lagrange falls to be considered here, but honesty makes it impossible to include him among the defenders of the integrity of Mark 13, honesty on his part, doubtless, as well as on ours. Lagrange wrote a lengthy article on the thought of Mark 13 in which he compared the structure of the discourse with that of OT prophecies. "With them we recognize that the thought follows a kind of rhythm. One stanza is opposed to another stanza, then a third stanza takes up again the thought of the first, while the fourth attaches itself to the second."[16] In

---

[14] Merx, *Das Evangelium Matthäus*, 355.

[15] H.-J. Schoeps, *Theologie und Geschichte des Judenchristentums* (Tübingen, 1949), 262–65, 444.

[16] Lagrange, "L'Avènement du Fils de l'Homme," *RB* 15 (1906): 391–92.

our discourse that parallelism is seen to perfection; read in such a manner it yields two parallel discourses, one dealing with the ruin of the temple (vv. 6–18, 28–31), the other with the coming of the Son of man (vv. 19–27, 32–37). The discourses may be said to follow the same theme, as may be seen in the following table:

Discourse on the Ruin of the Temple			Discourse on the Coming of the Son of Man
1.	6–8	The time of distress	19–20
2.	9–13	How disciples are to behave	21–23
3.	14–18	The catastrophe	24–27
4.	28–31	The parables	32–37

Nobody will maintain that Jesus gave such a discourse in one breath; the arrangement is due to the evangelist, as in the case of the Sermon on the Mount. It is important, nevertheless, to note that the premonitory signs in the world and in the church are wholly concerned with the fall of Jerusalem; the parousia comes without warning.[17] What of the authenticity of these discourses? The agreement among the three Synoptists as to the first discourse is so perfect, and it conforms so well to the theme indicated, that "there is no room for doubting its authenticity."[18] Not so the second. Lagrange had already pointed out that if vv. 24–27, with 19–20, were read separately they would be regarded as a Jewish apocalypse; they are merely a conglomeration of citations.[19] He now adds that these sections at least do not belong to the new and original teaching which Jesus opposed to the old tradition. It resembles the Assumption of Moses rather than the Sermon on the Mount; "from the purely critical point of view it is very doubtful that Jesus pronounced this apocalypse." On the other hand, it is to be admitted that Jesus did speak of his coming and the last judgment somewhat in this manner; it therefore remains possible that Mark "blocked" the varied sayings.[20] The main point that Lagrange is concerned about, however, is not so much the authenticity of these verses as to show that the two discourses are quite separate; in that case Jesus did not set his coming within the contemporary generation; vv. 28–31 refer to the discourse on the ruin of Jerusalem.

One admires the ingenuity of this scheme and the expertness with which it is advocated. The motive, of course, is the commendable one of saving Jesus from predicting an early return, and Lagrange went as far with the critics as a traditional Roman Catholic scholar could. The great obstacle in the way of accepting this interpretation is the diffi-

---

[17] Ibid., 402–3.
[18] Ibid., 408.
[19] Ibid., 388.
[20] Ibid., 409.

culty of making the parable of the Fig Tree, vv. 28–30, refer to the fall
of Jerusalem; the more so in that Mark regarded the parousia as subject
of *engys estin epi thyrais*, whereas Luke viewed it as the kingdom of
God (Luke 21:31). Lagrange is compelled to interpret Luke's language
of the era after AD 70: "What is a chastisement for 'this people,' and
what opens a new period for the nations, is for the disciples a deliverance and even the reign of God." The same interpretation is placed
upon Luke 21:36: the "redemption" that is nigh is the new era of
emancipation from the Jewish tyranny.[21] This is surely desperate exegesis and does not square with the candor Lagrange shows elsewhere.
If the alleged "parallelism" breaks down in the last and most significant
member of the series, it is doubtful if it ever existed. Nevertheless, the
same lines of exposition here outlined are followed in Lagrange's
commentaries on the Gospels.[22] We may note, finally, that the objection
of extreme brevity already brought against the little apocalypse viewed
as 13:14–20 applies equally to the view that it consisted of vv. 19–20,
24–27, the more so because of the doubtful procedure of separating vv.
19–20 from vv. 14, 17–18.

J. Klausner

As a young man the Jewish scholar Joseph Klausner interested
himself in the eschatological ideas of his forebears and wrote a doctoral
thesis on the subject.[23] Since Klausner was a Jew and an expert in
apocalyptic, one would expect that his views on the eschatology of
Jesus would have peculiar value; on examining them, however, one
confesses to a sense of disappointment. Klausner regards Mark 13:1–8
as authentic; of vv. 7–8 he writes, "The description is very like that of
the 'pangs of the Messiah' in various Talmudic baraitas."[24] He asserts
in regard to vv. 9–27: "The majority of scholars incline to the opinion
that these nineteen verses are an apocalyptic document not earlier than
the destruction of the temple; this apocalyptic character is plainly
shown by the words, 'Let him that readeth understand.' " The connec-

---

[21] Ibid., 406–7.

[22] In Lagrange's commentary on Mark (*Evangile selon Saint Marc* [Paris,
1911]), the "unauthenticity" of 13:24ff. is stated with admirable tact. The difference of language used by the three Synoptists enables him to say: "We do not
know exactly the precise terms Jesus used. If it is quite evident that the prophetic
discourse has been written by Luke in a special way and with understanding of
the events that have happened, Mark has been able on his side to adopt traditional terms, useful for describing great catastrophes, for expressing the thought
of Jesus." This statement, it will be noted, carefully sidesteps the question
whether the citations of vv. 24–27 once formed a separate Jewish apocalypse.

[23] Klausner, *Die messianischen Vorstellungen des jüdischen Volkes im
Zeitalter der Tannaiten* (Krakau, 1903).

[24] Idem, *Jesus of Nazareth* (ET London, 1925), 322.

tion of this document with the period of the fall of Jerusalem is inferred
from the "descriptions" of persecutions suffered by the disciples and
in particular to the reference to the flight of the Christians of Jerusalem
to Pella. In addition it is mentioned that the section contains many
details derived from the OT, and apocryphal writings, relating to the
"pangs of the Messiah," similar to those in the baraitas; and there are
traces of primitive Judaistic Christianity, e.g., Matthew's addition concerning Sabbath observation (24:20). "It was impossible in Jesus' mouth;
Jesus only foresaw the 'pangs of the Messiah' without which there
could be no 'Days of the Messiah,' and he saw the kingdom of heaven
'nigh, even at the doors.' . . . The disciples must therefore prepare
themselves to meet the great day, the day of redemption, which was to
come, as the Talmud also declares, 'without the knowledge of men' (b.
Sanh. 97a)."[25]

The force of this argument is not apparent. We will overlook the
curious statement that most scholars regard vv. 9–27 as an apocalyptic
document; there had not been, to our knowledge, a scholar prior to him
who had separated vv. 7–8 as authentic and 9–27 as a solid block of
apocalyptic and unauthentic teaching.[26] But how does similarity to the
description of messianic birth pangs in the Baraitas illustrate the authenticity of vv. 7–8 and demonstrate the unauthenticity of vv. 9–27?
We suspect the calling up of Jewish parallels is not always with the best
of motives; in the case of v. 32, as of the ethical teaching of Jesus
generally, it is to prove that Jesus was not ahead of some of his fellow
Jews in his apparently original statements; in the case of vv. 7–8, which
Klausner must have known are unwelcome to many critics, it brings
Jesus down to ordinary Jewish levels; in the case of vv. 9–27 it shows
that his followers were in the same state. The remark about the Sabbath
is said to have proceeded from Jewish Christians and not from Jesus;
yet Klausner distinctly states elsewhere that Jesus "observed the Sabbath and washing of hands—it was against his disciples that complaints
were made on these scores,"[27] i.e., Jesus was more particular about the
Sabbath than his disciples were. In his chapter on "The Jewishness of
Jesus," Klausner accepts all the elements of Streeter's document M as
genuine, passages which many critics are inclined to attribute to these
same "Jewish Christians" whom, for this one occasion only, Klausner
invokes. If we separate vv. 9–13 from vv. 14–27, as most critics do, the
presumed authenticity of vv. 7–8, and of the parousia hope, will have
repercussions distinctly in favor of the reliability of vv. 14–27.

---

[25] Ibid.

[26] The closest parallel we have found to Klausner's view is that of S. J. Case,
whose work *Jesus, A New Biography* (Chicago, 1927), appeared five years after
the original Hebrew edition of Klausner's book.

[27] Klausner, *Jesus of Nazareth*, 363.

2. From B. W. Bacon to R. H. Lightfoot

B. W. Bacon

Few scholars, apart from those who later wrote monographs on Mark 13, paid such close attention to Mark 13 as B. W. Bacon. The care with which he treated the passage merits a full exposition of his method of analysis. At the outset it is necessary to remember that Bacon's interest in Mark 13 lies not in its eschatological teaching, but solely in its utility as a means for dating the Gospel of Mark; hence he discussed it in a book devoted to the consideration of the composition and date of this Gospel. We may mention in passing that this aspect of Mark 13 causes every book written on the NT documents to reckon with the chapter; it seems to be the one passage in the Gospel offering a clue to its date. The problem is immediately raised as to how one is to use the data of this chapter in such a connection. In a time when Sitz-im-Leben was scarcely reckoned with, the answer depended on one's theological presuppositions. If there is no room within one's *Weltanschauung* for predictive prophecy, reference to events known to have occurred after their utterance in such a chapter as this provides a terminus a quo for its composition.

This was Bacon's position, and he stated it most strongly. "If the foreknowledge of Jesus and the exactitude of the record are placed sufficiently high, no amount of evidence in the record of acquaintance with known events will prove a subsequent date, for no room at all is left for alteration by adjustment to the event. But such dogmatic assumptions are no longer permissible. Either the ordinary rules for predictive utterance and transmission must be followed, as in other documents; or it must be frankly admitted that dates for the gospel record are not established by critical methods, but are assumed without verification."[28] As an illustration of the amount of prescience Bacon will allow, or not allow, to Jesus, we may cite his treatment of Mark 10:35ff., the prophecy of the fortunes of James and John. Bacon states his view thus:

> Let us not deny the abstract possibility that Jesus might have foreseen this martyr fate of the two brothers. . . . The critic must measure relative probabilities. The real question is whether if we found the narrative in any other uncanonical writing, we should not say at once: 'Here is plain evidence that the writer knew of the martyrdom of James in 42 and probably that of John also.' The inference may perhaps be avoided if we make special rules for canonical writings not applicable to others. But the

---

[28] Bacon, *The Gospel of Mark: Its Composition and Date* (New Haven, 1925), 69.

cost is too high. If we claim exemption from the ordinary rules of criticism, we must consent to renounce critical authority for whatever date we finally assume.[29]

The lucidity of the statement is commendable, but for most Christians it is unacceptable. To them, and I number myself with them, the inspiration of the Holy Spirit is not a piece of outworn theological lumber, but a phenomenon to be reckoned with. Link that inspiration with the incarnate Son of God and the situation is even more serious. We do not claim that Jesus possessed omniscience in the days of his flesh, but we refuse to set so narrow a limit to the revelation of God in him as Bacon demanded. We therefore willingly affirm that if the only means of dating the Gospels is by declaring every prediction a *vaticinium ex eventu,* then no means of dating them exists. This may be felt to be a prejudiced way of commencing a review of Bacon's exposition of the growth of Mark 13, but from our point of view we are compelled to protest that this scholar has set out with an attitude that vitiates his whole method: if every prophecy of events that happened is a *vaticinium ex eventu,* then the only task necessary for the investigator of the eschatological discourse is to date its various sections; and that is precisely what Bacon was concerned to do.

In fairness to our author, we must admit that he did devote a few lines to the character of Mark 13. In his view, its unauthenticity is obvious by its blatant use of signs of the end; it is precisely the kind of horoscope against which Jesus warned his disciples, a "Lo here, Lo there" prophecy. Speaking of v. 14 in particular he asserted: "If we were asked to name a passage which, by its contradiction of authentic utterances, as well as by its manifest inferiority to the moral plane of the Master, might be set down as the least worthy of acceptance within the limits of Synoptic tradition, it might well be the section which includes this verse as its climax."[30] This is strong language, but it is mystifying, for if it means what it appears to mean, the reference is to the section leading up to 13:14. Does the reader agree that vv. 9–13 are wholly unworthy of Jesus? Or vv. 5–8? Or vv. 1–2? We imagine that not even Bacon's sympathizers will agree with him in this estimate of the material he dealt with.

The crux of his argument lies in his view of v. 14. It is impossible, so far as he is concerned, to deny that this statement is colored by the events of AD 40; to do so would involve a literary miracle (i.e., a relatively true prediction), yet it would make Jesus responsible for an unfulfilled prophecy, since the temple was destroyed before the "profanation" took place. This argument is circular, for it presumes that a

---

[29] Ibid., 71.
[30] Ibid., 62.

profanation of the kind threatened in AD 40 was originally meant, that therefore the prophecy emerged out of that kind of a situation, and fault is found with the oracle because that profanation did not happen! It is not contemplated that something different may have been intended when the prophecy was spoken. Nevertheless, Bacon took his stand with Torrey, that the oracle of v. 14 emerged from the crisis of AD 40.[31] A witness of this is seen in 2 Thess 2:1–4, which Paul cites as an independent oracle, adding on his own account the exposition which follows.[32] It is to be observed that Paul has no reference here to the destruction of Jerusalem; he has never heard of such a prediction coming from Jesus. It belongs to a later stage of development.[33] Paul is concerned solely with the deeds of antichrist as foreshadowed in the document he cited: "We may accept this result, Antichrist was born under Caligula in A.D. 40. The earliest appearance of the doctrine is in our present Pauline Little Apocalypse."[34] The years passed by without the dreaded profanation taking place. The prophecy continued to circulate among the Christian communities. Mark had to do his best with it. His version is manifestly not the original prophecy, but "an adaptation of the primitive tradition to meet the inconvenient fact that by a second unexpected development (i.e., the burning and subsequent demolition of the temple) it had become forever impossible to experience a literal fulfilment of the expected culmination of the 'mystery of iniquity.' "[35] This presumes Mark to have written after the desolation of the temple, naturally, for 13:1–2 prophesies it! As there was no temple in which the man of lawlessness could sit, Mark had to make him do something else. By interpreting the "profanation" as the destruction of the temple, instead of antichrist's session within it, Mark was able to link the apocalyptic sayings to the prediction of Jesus as to the temple's ruin.

Mark himself was responsible for drawing up the eschatological discourse. His method was exactly the same as in his earlier discourses, that of attaching to a dominant saying a series of loosely connected logia on related themes and representing them to have been delivered to the disciples (cf. 4:10ff.; 7:17ff.).[36] The sources used by Mark in the discourse itself are mainly two, Q and the little apocalypse. To Q are assigned most of vv. 9–13, 15–16; to the apocalypse belong vv. 3–8, 14, 18–27; vv. 14c and 17 are derived from Luke 23:29–31 (!). The mere statement of this analysis gives no idea of the process by which it is

---

[31] Ibid., 61.
[32] Ibid., 85.
[33] Ibid., 88–89.
[34] Ibid., 94.
[35] Ibid., 102.
[36] Ibid., 121.

arrived at. In the Q extracts vv. 9a and 11 = Luke 12:11–12, to which vv. 9b–10 were added in the light of the events of the Christian mission; vv. 12–13 = Luke 12:51–53, but were misapplied by Mark to the delators; v. 13a is from historic events (cf. 1 Pet 5:9), v. 13b from Dan 11:35 and 12:1 (cf. Luke 12:7); vv. 15–16 = Luke 17:31, but it originally applied to the parousia expectation. If it is remembered that v. 14ab is from the little apocalypse, vv. 14c, 17 from Luke 23:29ff., the section Mark 13:9–17 is a most extraordinary mosaic. And that is how the incorporated apocalypse was put together. It is a conglomerate of OT reminiscences, passages of Paul's own composition, and Christian prophecies cited by Paul, themselves often based on the OT. No OT critic ever dissected a passage so minutely as Bacon apportioned out Mark 13. Some passages are provided with a double derivation, e.g., v. 20 is stated to be a quotation from Enoch, cited in Barn 4:3; elsewhere it is a reminiscence of Rom 9:28, itself due to the influence of Isa 28:22.[37] The idea of 13:14–23 is said to have been taken from Luke 12:54ff., but how Bacon's distribution of his material between Q and the apocalyptic source squares with that we are not told. The whole scheme condemns itself by its very complexity. Nobody ever wrote an extended discourse in this way, and we cannot imagine Mark piecing together this jigsaw puzzle out of such minute and unrelated fragments. With this judgment Hölscher is in agreement.[38] If we add to these considerations the unlikelihood that Mark made any use of Q, and the false attitude to prophecy lying at the basis of Bacon's work, it will hardly be claimed that this reconstruction, brilliant though it be, lays serious claim to probability. Though he has impressed many with his linking of Mark 13 with the events of AD 40 and those of AD 70, Bacon has found none to follow him in his analysis of the chapter.[39]

R. Eisler

Robert Eisler made many references to Mark 13 in his lengthy book on Jesus and the Baptist, but he nowhere treated the whole chapter. For him, as for B. W. Bacon, Mark 13:14 is the chief clue to its date, but he

---

[37] Ibid., 131, 122; the reference to Isaiah is presumably to Isa 10:22–23 rather than 28:22. The alleged quotation from Enoch has already been met in Weizsäcker's work; the Paulinism is doubtful.

[38] Hölscher, *TBl* 12 (July 1933): 199.

[39] H. Branscomb has essentially followed Bacon's procedure in taking the Caligula episode and the fall of Jerusalem to be the root of Mark 13, though he declines to assign any specific portion of the chapter to an independent apocalypse (*The Gospel of Mark*, MNTC [London, 1937], 231ff.). A. T. Olmstead walks in the same path, except that he places the composition of the discourse between AD 66 and 70 instead of after the fall of Jerusalem (*Jesus in the Light of History* [New York, 1942], 252ff.).

reverted to patristic interpretation in seeing therein a reference to Pilate's setting up the imperial standards in Jerusalem. The indignation of the Jews at Pilate's action is reflected in the statement of Jerome, evidently based on information from his rabbinic instructors, that Pilate placed in the temple an image of Caesar.[40] Eisler explained that the misunderstanding was due to the fact that small medallions in relief, with portrait-heads of the emperor, were affixed to the soldiers' standards; Pilate had not solemnly erected these medallions in the temple, but simply planted the standards in the ground. It is unlikely that one was placed in the temple itself; the standard concerned would have been that of the unit stationed in the Antonia; but as the Jews regarded the castle as within the sacred precincts of the temple, they would feel that even this measure constituted a profanation.[41] It was on the wave of indignation that swept Palestine that Jesus rose in the year AD 19. To him this act was the sign of the end, hence his preaching began with the clarion call, "The time is fulfilled and the kingdom of God is at hand, repent and believe the good news" (Mark 1:15).[42] Eisler was not prepared to say whether the prophecy as we now have it in Mark 13 goes back to Jesus or whether it was compiled in the similar period of excitement in the days of Caligula. Eisler's view has been neglected, partly because of its position in a book which has not found favor, and partly because of his use of it as a means of putting back the date of the ministry of Jesus. Nevertheless, it illustrates the possibility that the popular application of the Danielic "abomination" to the Roman power reaches back twenty years before the Caligula episode, which alone, in the view of many exegetes, could have occasioned Mark 13:14.

R. Otto

Rudolf Otto gave the theological world some penetrating expositions of leading eschatological utterances of Jesus. Unfortunately, he did not provide us with a full exposition of Mark 13; he merely gave a few hints as to its interpretation. Our starting point must be his opposition to the current interpretation of Luke 17:20, which sees its point "solely in the rejection of calculating omens." Passing over the detail, we note how he relates it to Mark 13:

> In regard to the future kingdom, Here and There, i.e. local determinations, did have their place even for Jesus. The future kingdom had a thoroughly

---

[40] Jerome on Matt 24:15: *to bdelygma tēs erēmōseōs* potest . . . accipi . . . de imagine Caesaris, quam Pilatus posuit in templo.

[41] Eisler, *The Messiah Jesus and John the Baptist* (ET London, 1931), 314–15.

[42] Ibid., 313.

external aspect; it was to come with flaming lightning, with the appearance of the Son of Man, his angels, and the heavenly tribunal. . . . And
even the parateresis, as attention to the signs which indicated his coming
and from which his temporal nearness was to be read, Jesus not only did
not reject but expressly summoned men to it by referring to the blossoming
of the branches of the fig tree, from which the nearness of summer should
be noted (Mark 13:28f.). . . . That is a paratereisthai, i.e. a paying attention
to signs of every kind regarding the future kingdom.[43]

Otto stresses the prophetic element in Jesus' teaching. Jesus spoke
of the messianic woes coming both on the world generally and on his
followers. He prophesied of wars waged by Rome and of a crisis in the
political situation of his own people, as former prophets of Israel
had done. "The gift of prophetic divination known in ancient Israel
emerged anew in Christ. Like them he prophesied the Fall of Jerusalem
and the destruction of the temple. His prophecy like theirs rested on
knowledge of and insight into the politically ominous situation of
Jerusalem and a menacing and aggressive world-power, and yet it was
not based on considerations of probability, nor did it arise from a
rational calculation."[44] What, then, could Otto possibly have against
Mark 13? One point only—that just as the utterances of Israel's prophets
were expanded, so were those of Jesus: "As with the prophecy of the
ancient prophets, so his own prophecy became the instigation and
starting point of later additions; later prophecies were put forth under
his name as had been the case with theirs."[45] If that is intended to apply
to Mark 13, as in the context it must, it requires a careful hand to
separate within the chapter the authentic from the unauthentic elements, at least with Otto's presuppositions in mind. He has asserted
that Jesus prophesied (1) Jerusalem's fall, (2) convulsions in the world
of people and nations, (3) trials for believers, (4) the manifestation of
the Son of man with his angels, (5) the character of the first three points
as signs of the end. The only elements within Mark 13 that cannot come
under these categories are the warnings against false prophets and false
christs, vv. 5–6, 21–23, which Otto would surely have received, and the
warnings of the distress in Judea, vv. 14–20, themselves not forming a
unity. Had this esteemed critic been pressed, it is not impossible that
he would have been ready enough to assent that vv. 15–16 are unexcep-
tionable, and with his views one fails to see how he could have objected
to v. 19. In any case, Otto's contribution to our understanding of Mark
13 is valuable and will be recalled later.

---

[43] Otto, *The Kingdom of God and Son of Man* (ET London, 1938, from the
German of 1934), 132–33.
[44] Ibid., 60, cf. also 357–58.
[45] Ibid.

H. Martin

In a writer like Hugh Martin we see coming to expression a tendency in British writers of the time to view the eschatological discourse as a collection of authentic sayings badly transmitted. He looked on Mark 13 as "a collection of kindred sayings, as for example Matthew collects parables together in ch. 13. Attempts to build up chronological sequences of events on the basis of these verses are, therefore, to say the least of it, precarious."[46]

T. W. Manson

T. W. Manson gave us a similar view more emphatically expressed. The "Little Apocalypse" of Mark 13 (i.e., the whole discourse), he believed, probably circulated before Mark wrote, for the matter contained in it was of vital interest to the churches. "In compiling such a document the writer would naturally incorporate such sayings of Jesus as he supposed to refer to the coming manifestation of the kingdom in power. Any or all of these sayings might well be genuine utterances of the Lord, but by the way in which they were put together a new total effect would be created, which might be quite different from anything which Jesus meant to say. This, as a matter of fact, is what appears to have happened in Mark 13."[47] Manson's chief complaint against the present distribution of sayings in the discourse is that its picture does not square with that given in Q and in Paul; the discourse describes the signs of the end, the other authorities represent it as wholly incalculable, and the two views are irreconcilable. It is noted that 13:32–37 would form a good answer to the question of v. 4; if that was the original connection, the resultant idea would correspond with that of Q and Paul. This is, of course, the mode of argument used by Colani when he separated off vv. 5–31 as an interpolated discourse, but unlike Colani, Manson stated: "Mark 13 is a compilation containing genuine utterances of Jesus, but the way in which the sayings have been arranged is such as to give a wrong impression of his eschatological teaching." To substantiate the authenticity of the material, parallels are adduced from the other teaching of our Lord to passages of the discourse, notably to Mark 13:11–12, 14–20, 27.[48] In practice, however, this position means that the chapter "cannot safely be used as a starting point in an enquiry concerning what our Lord had to say about the consummation of the kingdom."[49]

---

[46] Martin, *The Necessity of the Second Coming* (London, 1928), 40.
[47] Manson, *The Teaching of Jesus* (Cambridge, 1931), 261.
[48] Ibid., 262.
[49] Ibid., 263.

By the time this exegete had written his commentary on the sayings-traditions of the Gospels, his views on Mark 13 had considerably developed; the simplicity of the above representation was abandoned for one much more complicated. After a careful comparison of Mark 13 and Luke 21, he concluded that the latter represents a separate tradition of the discourse, and is not simply Luke's modification of Mark 13. If the little apocalypse (= Mark 13:5–31) was circulated before its incorporation into Mark, it may have influenced the formation of the Lukan material into its present shape: "This would be the more likely if, as Hölscher maintains, the substance of Mark's Little Apocalypse (7f., 12, 14–20, 24–27) was composed in A.D. 40 under stress of the threatened profanation of the temple by Caligula."[50] By considering what sections of the discourse best link together, and on the basis of what is peculiar to Luke, Manson analyzed the discourse into three constituents, which in Mark are as follows:

(1) A Jerusalem prediction: vv. 1–4, 14–20.

(2) Persecution for the disciples: vv. 5–8, 9–13.

(3) A prediction of the end: vv. 24–27, 28–31, (32–37?).

It will be observed that on this scheme each of the three sections of the normal "little apocalypse" is assigned to a different source, a drastic modification of that theory! Manson further agreed with the group of critics that considers Luke's version of the abomination passage to be prior to Mark's; it is presumed that Jesus predicted the distress of Jerusalem as in Luke 21:20–24, and that that prophecy was modified in the light of the Caligula episode of AD 40 so as to include a reference to the expected fulfillment of Daniel's prediction; the result was Mark 13:14ff.[51] On this basis it is reasonable to suppose that the answer of our Lord to the disciple's question as to the time and sign of the temple's ruin is contained in Luke 21:20ff.: "It will happen when you see Jerusalem surrounded by armies." The threefold analysis of the discourse shows that it is a complexity of predictions concerning the fate of Jerusalem, the disciples, and the end of the world. The purpose of its composition will be found in comparing it with 2 Thessalonians 2; the latter utterance explains why the great redemption is delayed; Mark 13 was issued to answer the questionings of the Palestinian disciples, and its burden is "Be ready for the coming of the Lord at any time, but don't expect it yet." Thus the only new feature of the discourse is "not the matter, but the way in which it is put together, the

---

[50] Idem, *The Sayings of Jesus,* book 2 of *The Mission and Message of Jesus* (London, 1937), 617.

[51] Ibid., 621.

way in which persecutions of disciples and tribulations in Judea are used to push the final consummation into the future."[52]

Manson has put us in his debt by his exposition, but it is necessary to note some debatable points in his argument.

(1) Like others before him, this theologian has confused the situations in Palestine and Thessalonica: by his reference to the Palestinian Christians who "had been waiting for the parousia for a matter of twenty years,"[53] he gives the impression that the discourse was composed to allay doubts on the score that the parousia had not happened yet and they need not worry, whereas Paul was writing to show the Thessalonians that the parousia cannot happen yet and they must not worry! If Manson wishes to equate the two situations, as his language undoubtedly demands, then he must retract his earlier view that Mark 13 contradicts Paul's eschatology; the two views are now confessed as identical. The question suggests itself: if Paul could expect a sudden parousia, though preceded by signs, are we sure Jesus could not do the same?

(2) If Manson wishes us to take Hölscher's view seriously, then he himself has given us two different solutions of our problem: on Hölscher's idea, "The substance of Mark's Little Apocalypse (7f., 12, 14–20, 24–27) was composed in A.D. 40 under stress of the threatened profanation of the temple by Caligula."[54] But Manson's own view rejects this link up of paragraphs and works on the basis that Luke's material was composed before AD 40, Mark's being a modification of it. Manson plainly stated that, in his estimation, not only Mark 13:14ff., and Luke 21:20ff. are here involved, but the whole discourse of Luke existed prior to AD 40.[55] We are not merely quibbling with words; on Hölscher's view the little apocalypse is inspired by the events of AD 40; in Manson's view it was modified by that event, and the two positions are very different.

(3) If the version of the eschatological discourse preserved by Luke circulated prior to AD 40 and Mark's version immediately after, then we have two sources of the teaching of Jesus considerably earlier than Q. Both versions circulated while the apostles still worked in Palestine. We are prompted to ask: (a) if the date be so early, is it likely that the disposition of the sayings in the discourse is such as seriously to distort their real meaning: (b) if so, why was it given such prominence with the prime authorities on the spot to correct it?

It is argued that Luke 21:20–24 is authentic and Mark 13:14ff. secondary. This is questionable on one score alone. Luke 21:21bc looks very much like a reproduction of the Q saying Luke 17:31; in Mark (who

---

[52] Ibid., 628–29.
[53] Ibid., 628.
[54] Ibid., 617.
[55] Ibid., 629.

probably did not use Q) it is preserved accurately, but in Luke's discourse it is paraphrased to suit his context better. That implies that Luke 21:20–24, despite its poetic structure, is a sayings group which by no means excludes the possible authenticity of the items in Mark 13:14–20 which it omits. While, therefore, we are grateful to Manson for his positive help, we cannot follow his negative assertions concerning the eschatological discourse.

C. H. Dodd

Probably no writer has influenced contemporary thinking on eschatology, at least in the English-speaking world, so much as C. H. Dodd. It is not easy to gain an overall perspective of the views of this prolific writer regarding our theme, partly because we suspect that some of his earlier views were put forward tentatively, and partly because, like most thinkers, there is discernible in his writings a certain crystallization of thought in the passage of time. His determinative book on the eschatology of Jesus, *The Parables of the Kingdom,* made plain that he regarded the setting of the discourse as unauthentic. Mark's practice, when desiring to explain an important saying, is to introduce a private interview between Jesus and the disciples to elucidate it, and such is the case with Mark 13. The saying requiring elucidation is the temple word; the function of the discourse is to reveal its true meaning. "So far from having threatened to destroy the temple (Mark means), Jesus had predicted that after a long period of tribulation there would be a horrible act of sacrilege in the temple, and then would follow a great tribulation in Judea, and afterwards the final catastrophe in which the whole universe would collapse."[56] It is thus part of his purpose to show that Jesus was not thinking of a merely historical event, an act which could be plotted; rather he prophesied the end of all things.

As to the content of the discourse, Dodd gives three reasons for rejecting it as it stands: (1) it is "inconsistent with the purport of his teaching as a whole"; (2) it "presupposes knowledge of events after his death"; (3) it has been composed to explain the reason for delay in the second coming, just as 2 Thessalonians 2 was written with a similar purpose.[57] The first point presumably refers to the idea that Mark 13 with its relating of signs of the end is irreconcilable with the picture given us in Q of the suddenness of the end: "After all the events forecast in Mark 13:14–25 it is safe to assume that people will no longer be

---

[56] Dodd, *The Parables of the Kingdom,* rev. ed. (London, 1936; 1st ed. 1935), 61–62.

[57] Idem, *The Apostolic Preaching and Its Developments,* 2d ed. (London, 1944; 1st ed. 1936), 38.

eating and drinking, marrying and being married! The two accounts are inconsistent, and of the two we must certainly prefer that of Q."[58] It is also perhaps not unrelated to the view, tentatively proposed, that Jesus conceived the end would come very soon after his death; combining Mark 14:62, the confession before the high priest, with the sayings about the resurrection after three days, the interval would be very short indeed. Perhaps Jesus did not distinguish between his resurrection, ascension, and parousia, but regarded them as "three aspects of one idea." That was probably the view of the primitive church in its earliest history, and it only subsequently distinguished between the three events when the passage of time forced it so to do. Mark 13 would fit in with the developed view, but not the primitive one.[59] The second of the three objections particularly applies to Mark 13:6–14. In this passage references to historical events of the fifties and early sixties of our era are believed to be present: the turbulent international situation, earthquakes and famines of the period, the persecution of Christians within and without Palestine. The abomination passage may well be due to the Caligula scare. There are, however, no references to events after AD 64—the Neronic persecution and the Roman war in Judea. The predicted sacrilege did not occur and the end did not come at the fall of Jerusalem. "On the principles followed in dating apocalypses, the inference would be that the 'Little Apocalypse' belongs to somewhere about the year 60."[60] The third objection need detain us little, beyond noting the belief that 2 Thessalonians 2 represents an afterthought of which Paul had earlier said nothing to this church: "It is clearly the result of reflection upon the fact that the advent had been unexpectedly delayed."[61]

Our views on the three objections raised by Dodd have already been hinted at in earlier discussions, especially in the review of T. W. Manson's work, and need not be repeated. Meanwhile, if this view of the chapter is to be reconciled with what Dodd writes elsewhere about various elements within it, one presumes he must maintain the same distinction as A. E. J. Rawlinson, i.e., between the purpose to which the material has been subjected and the original intention of the sections viewed in isolation. For example, the passage vv. 14–20 is regarded as more or less authentic; it fits well the idea of an invasion of Judea by Roman armies. "The injunction, 'He who is on the housetop must not come down to take up anything from his house, and he who is in the field must not turn to take up his coat,' would admirably suit a supposed situation in which the quick-marching Roman armies are threat-

---

[58] Idem, *Parables*, 84.
[59] Ibid., 96–104; idem, *Apostolic Preaching*, 33–37.
[60] Idem, *Parables*, 52 n. 1 ('Little Apocalypse' = Mark 13 as a whole).
[61] Idem, *Apostolic Preaching*, 31.

ening Jerusalem; and the prayer that it might not happen in winter is appropriate to war conditions. In a purely supernatural 'apocalyptic' tribulation summer or winter would matter little."[62] More than this, it is admitted that Jesus may well have viewed and depicted the coming judgment on Jerusalem in similar fashion as the OT prophets, hence that their use of an eschatological setting for such a judgment may have been employed by our Lord.[63] Even with regard to the fate of the disciples, Dodd elsewhere leaves room for the kind of prediction given us in vv. 9–13, in that he states: "At the last he [Jesus] went open-eyed to death himself, predicting further tribulations for his followers after his death."[64] In a later publication both these sentiments are more strongly expressed: "I cannot resist the evidence that he saw the destined destruction of the temple at Jerusalem in quite special relation to his own coming, since it marked dramatically the close of the old era in religion, to make way for the new. . . . I see no reason to doubt that Jesus did prepare his disciples for a time of troubles and give them guidance how to meet it. Consequently he must have contemplated a further period of history after his departure."[65] This means that the material of Mark 13:9–20, in its gist if not in its wording, is not so wide of the mark after all. A similar view is taken of the parousia pericope, vv. 24–27. In this same work Luke 21:25 and Mark 13:24–26 are cited as an instance of prophetic language as to the day of the Lord in the NT; they are then referred to, apparently as words of Jesus, in the following manner:

> As interpreted by Jesus himself, his total career on earth was the crisis in which the long-awaited kingdom of God came upon men. . . . But that is not the whole truth about what Christ taught. There are some mysterious sayings about the coming of the Son of Man which I have passed over too lightly. There are passages where we are told that before he comes there will be a breakdown of the physical universe. I said before that it would be absurd to take literally the language about the darkened sun and falling stars. All the same, we cannot easily dismiss the impression that the final scene is laid where the world of space, time and matter is no longer in the picture.[66]

One cannot resist the conclusion that these admissions mitigate in no small measure some of the earlier statements made by this scholar. At my request Dodd very kindly clarified my understanding of his views in a private communication, in which he stated:

> I do certainly agree with recent critics who reject the idea that Mark 13 is Jewish apocalypse taken over with certain Christian additions. For the

---

[62] Idem, *Parables,* 64–65.

[63] Ibid., 65–66.

[64] Ibid., 60.

[65] Idem, *The Coming of Christ* (Cambridge, 1951), 19.

[66] Ibid., 4, 16–17.

most part I do not think it is an apocalypse at all. It is a *Mahnrede* [hortatory address] in apocalyptic terms, and I think highly composite. . . . I should not care to draw the line dogmatically between what belongs to the earlier tradition and what the Evangelist (or his authority) has introduced. That a reference to the coming of the Son of Man on the clouds was contained in the earliest tradition of the sayings of Jesus seems to me certain from Mark 14:62. In 13:26 it occurs in a different, and as I think less historical, setting. The apocalyptic colouring given to it in verses 24–25 may have been drawn by the Evangelist himself from Jewish apocalyptic sources, but I do conceive it to be quite possible that Jesus himself did in fact make use of such apocalyptic language: in that case certainly in a symbolic sense. . . .

It has seemed right to incorporate that quotation, for we do not wish to overstate the views held by Dodd. His final judgment on the matter was that while caution is needful in using the wording of Mark 13, "it is an extravagance of criticism to attempt to eliminate the whole of the apocalyptic and eschatological colouring from the primitive tradition of the sayings. . . . It would be as unsafe to leave this kind of material out of account as it would be to press every detail of it." The caution of this statement is comprehensible, but it is probably more sympathetic to the general trend of Mark 13 than some of our distinguished scholar's followers would allow. The conclusion would seem to be from all this that while there is a very considerable amount of authentic material in Mark 13, the detail is not to be unduly pressed and the setting is suspect.[67]

R. H. Lightfoot

R. H. Lightfoot is another example of a leading scholar who does not hesitate to modify his views where it appears to be necessary. Evidently the relation of Mark 13 to the passion narrative is a matter that long exercised his mind. He points out that the importance of the discourse is intensified if the passion narrative existed before it was taken up by Mark into his Gospel, for then the discourse is seen as the climax of all that has gone before. Yet its independence of the passion is instructive: it suggests that "at the time of the composition of this

---

[67] The above was written before I had seen Dodd's discussion of the eschatological discourse, "The Fall of Jerusalem and the 'Abomination of Desolation,'" *JRS* 37 (1947): 47–54. The article is largely devoted to demonstrating the independence of Luke 21:20–24, which is believed to be a unity, while Mark 13:14–20 is viewed as a composite pericope. The Markan discourse is described as "a sequence of warnings, precepts, and predictions, some of which are doublets of passages occurring in other parts of the Gospels, while others readily separate themselves into typical units of tradition" (p. 47). The little apocalypse theory is explicitly denied (ibid.).

gospel the church had not yet found it possible to define satisfactorily the relationship between the crucifixion and the expected final consummation."[68] As evidence of this, it is noted that "the teaching of Mark 13:3–37 has no necessary connection with the facts narrated in the next two chapters. By means perhaps of traditional Jewish material, as well as by reflection on the Church's experience, the teaching set forth in this chapter with regard to what must come to pass before the glory is revealed is already permeated with the thought of suffering. But the climax is still the coming of the Son of Man; and in connection with this, there is no note of suffering."[69] The implications of this statement as to the origins of the material of the discourse will not be overlooked: traditional Jewish material, the church's experiences, and presumably authentic teaching occur in this chapter.

Lightfoot's book on Mark, written fifteen years later, has a chapter devoted to a solution of the problem which he had earlier posed. No attempt is made to analyze the sources; they are not even mentioned. The main desire is to discover the significance of the discourse. Its chief characteristic is that it is "designed by the evangelists as the immediate introduction to the passion narrative"; we are to remember in this story who it is of whom we read. Taking a hint from Hoskyns and Davey, that John enables us to understand Mark better, he calls attention to the Johannine doctrine that the exaltation of the Son of man is his lifting up on the cross, and that at that moment the world is judged and its prince cast out (John 12:31–32). It is suggested that "a comparison of certain passages in Mark 13 with others in Mark 14 and 15 will reveal an unexpected parallelism . . . between the apocalyptic prophecy and the passion narrative."[70] A series of such passages is adduced: the term to *deliver up* or *hand over* is frequent in ch. 13 of the church, in chs. 14–15 of Christ (cf. especially 13:9 with Jesus before the Sanhedrin and Pilate); 13:22–23 tell of attempts to make even the elect go astray, in the passion narrative all went astray, although only one failed completely, and he was not one of the elect; 13:32–33 speak of the uncertainty of the day and hour that is impending, in Gethsemane Christ struggles to be reconciled to the fact that "the hour has come"; the similarity of 13:26 with 14:62 is unique; the possibility that the passion will witness the "judgment of this world" may account for the omission of all reference to the judgment in 13:24–27.[71] It is not suggested that the prophecies of Mark 13 receive their true fulfillment in the passion narrative, but (presumably) that the latter is seen as in some way a prior fulfillment of it; e.g., in reference to Mark 13:30, the passion is felt to

---

[68] Lightfoot, *History and Interpretation in the Gospels* (London, 1935), 94.
[69] Ibid., 104.
[70] Idem, *The Gospel Message of St. Mark* (Oxford, 1950), 51.
[71] Ibid., 51–54.

be "a sign, a seal of assurance, and a sacrament of the ultimate fulfilment"[72] of the parousia. The passion would then be an eschatological event, participating in the finality of the consummation for which it prepares. Without doubt that is good Pauline theology, as well as Johannine; it is worthy of note that it may be Markan also. As to the materials of ch. 13, not much light is thrown on them by these considerations, except that if there is anything specifically Jewish in them it has been very thoroughly subordinated to Christian ends. Mark 13 is Christian—an essential part of the story of the passion of our Lord.

3. From W. G. Kümmel to E. Lohmeyer

W. G. Kümmel

The importance of W. G. Kümmel's work[73] did not appear to have been adequately recognized in the English-speaking world until Cullmann's *Christ and Time* had been translated, for Cullmann manifestly depends a good deal on the careful exegesis provided by Kümmel. Kümmel has perhaps come closer than any other exegete to a genuine synthesis of realized and futurist eschatology in the teaching of our Lord. We can certainly not charge him with an inadequate recognition of the importance of eschatology. Yet this very synthesis has tended to prejudice his view of Mark 13.

He begins his discussion of the chapter by criticizing the position maintained by Busch, that Mark 13 gives us no temporal succession of eschatological events; the frequent occurrence of notices of time in the chapter should dispel that illusion (see vv. 7, 8, 10, 14, 21, 24, 26, 27). "Although Mark cannot in chapter 13 have forgotten his kerygma of the suffering Messiah, yet it is his intention here in the first place to impart a revelation about the eschatological events, their sequence, their meaning, their dangers."[74] This is not to say that this Jewish material ever formed an independent apocalypse: it is too short and colorless; it is difficult to think of its gradual enlargement through Christian additions; no literary connection between its supposed ingredients can be demonstrated; in its midst is contained a fragment of Q (13:15–16). The "little apocalypse" hypothesis is accordingly rejected. The discourse has been put together from isolated sayings or groups of sayings, and each has to be examined for itself.[75] On examination of 13:6, 9, 11, 13, 21ff. it is seen that they presuppose the situation of the Christian

---

[72] Ibid., 54.

[73] Kümmel, *Verheissung und Erfüllung* (3d ed. Zürich, 1956; ET, *Promise and Fulfilment: The Eschatological Message of Jesus* [London, 1957]).

[74] Kümmel, *Promise*, 97.

[75] Ibid., 98.

community; it is not impossible therefore that they may have been influenced by the experiences of the community. And yet, parallels for all these sayings can be adduced from "the other Jesus tradition," so it is equally possible that they may be authentic, even if certainty is not always attainable.[76] In any case, "we are dealing here with presuppositions which do not concern the real eschatological event, but which relate to the entire time before the real end-time occurrences. These sayings, then, have nothing to do with real apocalyptic revelation."[77] Over against this, vv. 7–8, 12, 14–20, 24–27 in no respect reveal the situation of Jesus or of the early church, but give "thoroughly Jewish apocalyptic ideas." Admittedly, this does not in itself prove that they do not go back to Jesus, for "the entire eschatological conceptions of Jesus are naturally of Jewish origin." The two counts against this material are the clause of 13:14, "Let the reader understand," which betrays a literary tradition, and still more its contradiction to Jesus' refusal to give "apocalyptic exposition and signs of the end" (Mark 12:25; Luke 17:20–21). ". . . We are forced to assert that these completely isolated components of the eschatological discourse, Mark 13 and parallels, cannot belong to the oldest Jesus tradition, but represent primitive Jewish-Christian traditional material which has been brought into use by Mark in building up his eschatological discourse. Apart from this no other texts of this nature have penetrated into the Jesus tradition."[78]

The really significant item in Kümmel's indictment of these sayings is the second, which lies at the root of his interpretation of our Lord's eschatological teaching. Kümmel is not averse to eschatology. For example, he regards Mark 13:2 as reflecting the OT-Jewish hope of a new temple in the messianic time, and so must be interpreted eschatologically, not historically. Nevertheless, the great insistence of his book is that Jesus gave eschatological proclamation, not apocalyptic instruction. On this basis the significance of such a saying as Mark 9:1 is not the light it throws on the future, but the fact that that future is determined by the attitude adopted to Jesus in the present—or in the original context of the saying, by the attitude adopted to the historical Jesus. The significance of the proclamation by Jesus of the divine sovereignty accordingly is its present effect—God is at work in Jesus now. As Kümmel puts it in the closing paragraph of his book, ". . . The intrinsic meaning of the eschatological event he proclaims does not lie in the end of the world as such, but in the fact that the approaching eschatological consummation will allow the kingdom of *that* God to become a reality who has already in the present allowed his redemptive

---

[76] Ibid., 99
[77] Ibid.
[78] Ibid., 104.

purpose to be realized in Jesus."[79] There is force in this contention, not to say great insight. Yet it would be happier if Kümmel used his "not . . . but . . ." in a biblical sense and regarded the proclamation of Jesus to have its significance rather in its immediate repercussions on his Person than in its illumination of the end.

Kümmel's thesis leads him to postulate, "In Jesus the kingdom of God came into being and in him it will be consummated."[80] An admirable statement! But does it not contain a statement of eschatological instruction of the utmost importance? It is impossible to make affirmations like Mark 14:62 without implying a whole world of thought; furthermore, affirmations of that kind will mean nothing unless it is believed that their presuppositions as to the future are true, at least fundamentally. If Jesus made claims about his own future and that of the kingdom of God, there would seem to be no reason why he should not have taken care in respect to the manner of his utterance about it, nor why he should not have given the kind of instruction about it which would have corrected the impoverished ideas of his disciples. In that case, the proposition "not apocalyptic instruction but eschatological proclamation" becomes a question of degree rather than a concrete antithesis. If, on the other hand, Kümmel is contrasting our Lord's preaching on the end with the speculations of "Enoch" and his kind, then without hesitation we agree that there is a world of difference between the two, and the proposition we are discussing could express the difference. It would be easy to show that Mark 13, in particular, is not a reproduction of Enoch. But we do not think that Kümmel has this in mind. His contention would carry greater conviction if it could be shown that in the first series of sayings (vv. 6, 9, 11, 13, 21ff.) the slant on the future was negligible, and that the second series (vv. 7–8, 12, 14–20, 24–27) had no practical value, but neither view can be sustained. Admittedly Kümmel did maintain, with regard to the first series, that it has nothing to do with the real eschatological event, but merely describes the entire period before the end. This is an overstatement; it certainly describes the period of the church's testimony, but it is hard to resist the impression that it has in view the present in relation to the conclusion to which the church is heading. In the same way the second series deals not exclusively with the end; if persecutions are the lot of the church in the present era, wars, etc., are the lot of the world through the same period; just as the former are expected to be intensified toward the end, so the latter. Naturally, vv. 14–20, 24–27 stand in a separate category, but their practical value for the church of the first generation cannot be denied; if vv. 1–2 denote an authentic eschatolog-

---

[79] Ibid., 154.
[80] Ibid., 155.

ical event and demand preparedness for it, the same implies to vv. 14–20, 24–27. We conclude that Kümmel's positive contribution is of undoubted importance, but his denials require modification.

V. Taylor

Vincent Taylor provides a further analysis of Mark 13, in which he withdraws his adherence to the theory of a little apocalypse, as popularly enunciated, and replaces it with another. Against the notion of the incorporation of an independent apocalypse in Mark 13 can be urged the fragmentariness of such a document and the diversity of its apparent sources. "Only a very fragmentary apocalypse is suggested, which lacks such distinctive ideas as the casting down of Antichrist, the Judgment, the punishment of sinners, and the blessedness of the righteous. Can we call such a torso an apocalypse?" Of the group usually assigned to the little apocalypse, vv. 14–20 do not belong to 7–8, 24–27, while 30–31 belong to yet another group of material. "On the other hand, Colani's hypothesis is sound in suggesting that a foundation source, apocalyptic in character, lies at the basis of Mark 13, and that it consists of a group of sayings." Colani's mistake lay in not perceiving the complexity of the sayings-groups incorporated in the chapter.[81]

Taylor proceeds to define the sources apparently observable within the discourse as follows: (A) vv. 5–8, 24–27, signs preceding the parousia; (B) vv. 9–13, sayings on persecution; (C) vv. 14–23, the abomination of desolation; (D) vv. 28–37, sayings and parables on watchfulness. "Of these groups A and C have characteristic apocalyptic features, but only A can be called even a rudimentary apocalypse. Both groups may have existed as units of tradition before Mark wrote."[82] Taking the paragraphs in order of appearance, A is felt to be a piece of apocalyptic prophecy with "nothing which could not belong to a Jewish-Christian apocalypse, or to a liturgical poem, or even a nearly Christian sermon"; nothing, that is, except the intrusive phrase of v. 6, "in my name." This latter phrase means "under my authority," or "claiming the power of my name," and so indicates a disciple; but "I am he" is a claim to be Jesus or the Messiah. Would any professed Christian claim to be Jesus or the Messiah? "The phrase is an unsuccessful attempt to explain A as a prophecy of Jesus, and by its incoherence suggests that A is of a different origin."[83] Of group B, vv. 9–13, vv. 9 and 11 are preserved "with relative fidelity," v. 10 is added by Mark, vv. 12–13 reflect the evil conditions of the church. "The group appears to have been com-

---

[81] Taylor, "The Apocalyptic Discourse of Mark 13," *ExpT* 60 (4, Jan. 1949): 95. (The substance of this article appears in his *Gospel according to St. Mark* [London, 1952], 498ff., 636ff.)

[82] Idem, "Apocalyptic Discourse," 95.

[83] Ibid., 97.

piled in the Church at Rome at a time when the danger of a clash with the Imperial authorities grew nearer daily."[84] Group C, vv. 14–23, may not originally have been apocalyptic in character; it suits a description of a military investment. The phrase "abomination of desolation," like the term "Babylon" in 1 Pet 5:13 and Rev 18:2, may refer to Rome as the embodiment of satanic power, i.e., as antichrist (cf. Paul's "Man of Sin"). If we may accept that in this section the words of Jesus shine "through an apocalyptic haze," it is probably, with Luke 21:20–24, our Lord's answer to the question of the disciples (Mark 13:4). Whether Mark replaced what Luke now has in 21:20 by the phrase "abomination of desolation," or whether Jesus himself used it, cannot be known with certainty; either alternative is possible. Group D adds exhortations to extend the relevance of discourse beyond the disciples to the Christians of Rome; it thus represents that church's catechetical teaching.[85]

The origin of the discourse is now apparent: Mark was "attracted by A, which expressed his own convictions, and which he regarded as genuine prophecy. What course, then, was more desirable than to expand A, in line with its apocalyptic character, to insert within it at suitable points B and C, in the interests of the prevailing belief that definite signs would precede the End, and to add the sayings and parables of 28–37 in D?" The implication of this view is that "not a little in Mark 13 is secondary tradition, but on any valid interpretation of the chapter, this result is inescapable." In the view of this theologian the genuine eschatological sayings of Jesus represent the person and ministry of Jesus as the fulfillment of the ancient eschatological hopes; by the process adopted in this interpretation of Mark 13 "we detach from his shoulders . . . the glittering apocalyptic robe with which primitive Christianity clothed him, and with which he is still draped in popular Christian expectation."[86]

Acknowledging the interest and value of this treatment, we must yet confess that the net result is to dismember the original little apocalypse and put its head and legs together, minus its torso; how well it walks, we are not sure. We suspect that the main reason for characterizing section A (vv. 5–8, 24–27) as Jewish-Christian and D as the catechesis of Rome is to be rid of this "apocalyptic robe," but whether the critical grounds are adequate is another matter. No reason is adduced for the Jewishness of vv. 24–27. The one count against vv. 5–8 is the use of the phrase "in my name," an objection urged at least as long ago as by Weiffenbach.[87] The most exhaustive examination of that phrase ever offered, that of Heitmüller, led to the conclusion that the

---

[84] Ibid., 96.

[85] Ibid., 98.

[86] Ibid.

[87] Weiffenbach, *Der Wiederkunftsgedanke Jesu,* 168–69.

translation of *epi to onomati* by "on the ground or authority of my name" is inadmissible, and that in this passage it implies the requisitioning or claiming of the name of Jesus, more briefly "with my name."[88] In that case there is no ground for imagining that a Christian is here thought of as speaker; in fact "with my name" excludes such a possibility on Heitmüller's interpretation.

If Taylor's case in regard to his first source A falls to the ground, the force of his contentions is considerably weakened. Even the analysis is endangered, for presumably vv. 28–32 can be regarded as of different origin from vv. 24–27 only if one regards the latter as unauthentic. It is an obvious and quite legitimate step to isolate vv. 9–13, but it is not so obvious or legitimate to regard them as reflecting the historic situation of the church in Rome under Nero. It is noteworthy that in source C, vv. 21–23 are joined to 14–20; in view of the parallel of 21–23 to the Q apocalypse, Luke 17:23–24, it is likely that it has purely eschatological reference; but such a reference in Mark 13:14–20 is said to be "secondary." That again depends on the view taken of 13:1–2, and of the "glittering robe." To us it is less the analysis that is at fault than the attitude adopted toward the eschatological categories reflected therein. The church of the ages has generally preferred to speak of the "glorious" rather than "glittering" robe, and therein lies the main difference between our reading of Mark 13 and Taylor's, for we are not persuaded that the church has been wrong in this respect.

E. Lohmeyer

In some respects E. Lohmeyer's treatment of Mark 13 seems the most brilliant and provocative that we have met, although we cannot concur with it in toto. It is deeply to be regretted that he did not live to give to his commentary the revision he had planned. We will follow his procedure of apportioning his remarks on the discourse into four sections.

(1) Lohmeyer's fundamental conviction in regard to the discourse is that it is composed out of isolated sayings or sayings groups which in part already lay before Mark in a fixed literary form. There is no possibility of extracting from it a short Jewish apocalypse, but the attempt to do so has revealed that the discourse contains at least in equal proportion apocalyptic teaching and apocalyptic parenesis (exhortation, advice). With this feature is conjoined another significant phenomenon: the chief theme of the discourse, unlike that of apocalypses generally, is the coming of the Son of man not in judgment on the world, but for the "gathering of the saints," i.e., for the formation of the eschatological divine community. To this major theme that of the

---

[88] Heitmüller, *Im Namen Jesu*, FRLANT, ed. W. Bousset and H. Gunkel (Göttingen, 1903), 63.

abomination of desolation is subordinated, as also the related theme of false christs and false prophets, while the third theme of martyrdom is strictly related to the first. From among all the rich diversity of apocalyptic ideas that meet us in other apocalypses a mere fraction is given us: "The point of view that determines this selection is that of the building and continuance of the eschatological community of God. . . . It is therefore comprehensible that the apocalyptic parenesis receives a far greater space than the apocalyptic prophecy."[89]

(2) The occasion of the discourse may be compared with that of many another Jewish apocalypse, e.g., the Testaments of the Twelve Patriarchs: a "man of God" sees his death near, speaks of coming things and gives last exhortations. This one is a farewell speech of Jesus, directed to the heirs of his work and preaching: "The fruitfulness of his [Mark's] purpose is seen from the fact that the three other evangelists, each in his way, have developed the conception of such a farewell discourse more richly."[90] The differentia of this discourse is that, instead of the disciples being spectators of the apocalyptic drama, they are part of it; they are bound up with it through suffering and martyrdom. "The theological significance of this picture, only hinted at, is scarcely to be overestimated; for it makes even the life of the believers in this world era the theme of the apocalyptic event; it overcomes apocalyptic even while it affirms it and knows that it is set in the specific, still continuing historical existence."[91]

(3) The discussion nowhere in ch. 13 centers on antichrist, not even in vv. 14–20. His only significance is that he appears in the holy place, through which act the place of eschatological glory is turned into its opposite. "This prophecy belongs then actually to the series of sayings which speak of the eschatological destruction of the temple and therein break with Jewish tradition and the Jewish people."[92]

(4) The elements of the discourse consist of Jewish tradition, sayings of Jesus, and words of the primitive community. It is difficult to separate them, for they are united through the single conception of the nearness of the eschatological day. Yet it is a true picture of the Christianity of Mark's day: "Its firm ground is 'his words,' its continual affirmation the sacred tradition, its inner condition, 'watch and be ready' for martyrdom."[93]

Despite the confessed difficulty of separating the discourse into its constituent parts, Lohmeyer essays to do it more thoroughly than

---

[89] Lohmeyer, *Das Evangelium des Markus,* 2d ed. (Göttingen, 1951; 1st ed. 1937), 285–86.

[90] Ibid., 286 and 267.

[91] Ibid., 286.

[92] Ibid.

[93] Ibid., 287.

any of his predecessors. The introductory section vv. 1–5a is said to be composed for the purpose: v. 1 is a foil for v. 2; vv. 3–4 follow the conventional notion of the fitness of a mountain for a divine communication. Verses 5b–8 contain three disparate sayings of four lines each: the first, vv. 5–6, is itself not a unity, being an adaptation of a Jewish apocalyptic notion in the light of the experiences of the primitive church; the second, v. 7, is a word of consolation for a helpless yet peaceable people; the third, v. 8, describes apocalyptic signs in the non-Jewish world. Verses 9–13 also contain three strophes of four lines each, but each strophe is concluded by an interpolated prose sentence (vv. 10, 11b, 13): each saying has a different origin and aim, but they are united by the superimposed conception of martyrdom. As to vv. 14–27: v. 14 is from a Jewish apocalypse referring to Jerusalem; the phrase "Let the reader understand" shows that a document is used, but how far it extends we do not know; vv. 15–16 relate to inhabitants of a country town, for there is no reference to craftsmen; vv. 17–18 relate to city dwellers, as their concern for the weather shows; vv. 19–20 are not a prophecy, but a report of an event carried through by God, and are directly from an Aramaic source; vv. 21–23 come here curiously in view of its many pseudochrists—how do they arise after antichrist? Indeed, the contradiction is manifest within this little paragraph, for v. 21 speaks of one anointed who has been seen here and there, but v. 22 says many false christs and false prophets will arise; v. 21 thus gives a false human opinion, what it says does not happen; v. 22 has a real event in view, but it is a deceptive one. In the last section the chief thing to note is that vv. 28–29 answer the question, "What is the sign?" and vv. 30–32 answer "When shall these things be?" The same complexity of composition is discernible in this group.[94]

If readers will check this analysis with the text itself, they will find it difficult not to feel that the genius of Lohmeyer has gone to excess here; it is atomism with a vengeance. The judgment that vv. 5–6 represent a Jewish apocalyptic saying, modified by the experiences of the primitive Christian community, is groundless speculation and produces a needless skepticism, especially if we recall the circumstances of Jesus and his disciples in the midst of a Judaism charged with incipient Zealotism. The entire analysis of vv. 14–23 set forth by Lohmeyer could be debated point by point. In particular, the comparison of vv. 21 and 22 overlooks that v. 21 assumes the Jewish doctrine of the "hidden Messiah" and v. 22 shows at least some ways in which its effects are seen.

---

[94] Lohmeyer provides the analysis of each paragraph at the commencement of his exposition of each section, and so it is scattered throughout the commentary on ch. 13, pp. 267–85.

We would further like to ask: When did it begin to be true of the church that "its firm ground was 'his words,' its continual affirmation the sacred tradition?" Only in Mark's day? If it goes back to early times, would it have been so very natural to confuse the striking warnings and encouragements of Jesus with odd apocalypses and utterances of Christian prophets? The possibility may be reckoned with, but probability points to the opposite conclusion. On Lohmeyer's arguments the key concepts of Mark 13 should indicate not merely a Christian redactor, but a Christian basis of redaction: this confessed emphasis on the rapture of the church and ignoring of lesser matters, this unusual "parenetic" interest, more pronounced than the apocalyptic strain, this rejection of the temple coupled with the severe judgment on the favored people in an eschatological context, does it point to Jewish sources and reflected Christian experience? Theoretically it could be reconciled with such a view, but again the probability does not lie in that direction. Since the discourse of Mark 13, after all, is not on the lips of a Simon Zelotes but on those of Jesus, we have a right to let probability be our guide here.

We are not concerned to deny the view that Mark 13 may be derived from earlier units of tradition, whether shorter or longer, but we do ask for a more reasonable attitude to be taken to the compilers of this discourse. If the discourse goes back to a time prior to the evangelists, then the unknown compiler had the more abundant material from which to select, and we need not presume he lost his powers of judgment when he did so. Lohmeyer's exposition of the significance of the eschatological discourse is consonant with a lofty purpose and no small mind in the person responsible for putting it together; perhaps the great exegete would not have minded our thinking that his theological powers exceeded even his critical judgment! Of one thing we are sure; he has made the little apocalypse theory even more difficult of acceptance than it was before he wrote.

4

ATTEMPTS TO VINDICATE THE ESCHATOLOGICAL DISCOURSE

AS THE LITTLE APOCALYPSE THEORY IS AN ENDEAVOR to explain Mark 13 by resort to critical analysis, the previous chapters have been devoted in large part to critical methods. The defenders of the authenticity of Mark 13 in the main have sought to meet the difficulties by exegetical rather than by analytical methods; consequently it will be necessary in this chapter to pay more attention to questions of interpretation and theology.

The chief cause of perplexity in the eschatological discourse lies in the fact that statements concerning the end of the age are apparently intertwined with an event that for us has been removed to the distant past. No other prophecies of our Lord relating to the hope of his coming are tied in this manner to history. The difficulties of interpretation are unique as far as the Gospels are concerned, and perhaps that accounts for the unique treatment the prophecy has received at the hands of its would-be interpreters. Strauss summarized the efforts of his predecessors and contemporaries to solve the problems of the discourse in terms of this time reference: they held either that the bearing of the discourse is entirely future, or that it is entirely past, or that it is partly past and partly future; in the last case, it was necessary either to deny that the two series of events were placed in immediate chronological succession or to maintain that Jesus took account of the intervening period. The belief that Mark 13 relates solely to the future was held by certain church fathers, such as Irenaeus and Hilary, but they lived near enough the event to be ignorant of their mistake. The past reference involves the notion that the parousia took place at the destruction of Jerusalem, and few are inclined to risk this tour de force. Strauss quite enjoyed recounting the difficulties of those who tried to apportion the discourse between AD 70 and the end of the world.[1] It will be observed that the little apocalypse theory essentially was a revival of the view that the discourse referred solely to the future, for it built on the assumption that it had nothing to do with the fall of Jerusalem and merely portrayed the end of the age. The attempt to refer the discourse to the past also enjoyed a new lease on life, in that not a few serious expositors espoused the view that the parousia took place at the fall of Jerusalem. Most interpreters, however, have wrestled with the problem of how to apportion the chapter between the past and future.

1. The Prophecy of Jerusalem as a Prefiguration of the End

One of the most obvious expedients was to regard the fall of Jerusalem as a foreshadowing of the end of the age. In view of the temper of the last century one would have thought that many exegetes would have adopted that line of interpretation; in reality hardly any did. In his refutation of Strauss, Neander pursued this course, and perhaps succeeded better than his followers. He was one of the first to lay down an important canon of interpretation for Mark 13, viz. that its scope was limited by the practical needs of the disciples: "It was certainly far from Christ's intention to give them a complete view of the course of development of the kingdom of God up to its final consummation. He imparted only so much as was necessary to guard them against deception, to stimulate their watchfulness, and confirm their confidence that the end would come at last."[2] This is a very different estimate of the discourse from that which sees it as a calendar of coming events, as many critics have assumed. In view of the increasing recognition by more recent writers, like Vincent Taylor and Lohmeyer, that Mark 13 omits more apocalyptic themes than it offers, it would seem that Neander had justification for this affirmation. The view of the future is characterized thus:

> When Christ in this discourse speaks of the great import of his coming for the history of the world, of his triumphant self-manifestation, and of the beginning of his kingdom, he betokens thereby partly his triumph in the destruction of the visible Theocracy, and its results in the freer and wider diffusion of his kingdom, and partly his second advent for its consummation. The judgment over the degenerate Theocracy, and the final judgment of the world, the first free development of the kingdom of God, and its final and glorious consummation, correspond to each other; the former, in each case, prefiguring the latter.[3]

---

[1] Strauss, *Life of Jesus,* 3:86ff.
[2] Neander, *The Life of Jesus Christ in Its Historical Connexion and Historical Development* (ET London, 1853, from the 4th ed.; 1st ed. 1837), 406.
[3] Ibid., 406–7.

We have not found this interpretation again until Plummer's commentary on Matthew reproduced it in brief. Commenting on the significance of the Fig Tree parable (Matt 24:32–33 = Mark 13:28–29), he asserted: "If the Day of Judgment is in any way included in it, it is as being symbolised by the judgment on the guilty city."[4] A similar view is adopted by N. Geldenhuys in his exposition of Luke: the judgment of Jerusalem foreshadows the final judgment, so that Luke 21:20 = Mark 13:14 refers first to the Roman army, second to the appearance of antichrist.[5]

This view proceeds from an act of faith; it can be neither demonstrated nor denied from other statements in the Gospels. Its major defect is the presupposition that the discourse was intended to cater for two events separated by a long stretch of time. Neander refuses to contemplate the possibility of Jesus being limited in his knowledge of time, and Geldenhuys thinks Luke 21:24 implies a series of powers occupying Jerusalem. It is difficult, if not impossible, to reconcile such a prospect with the known attitude of Jesus to the future. The interrelation of the two events must be explained by some other means.

2. Two Prophecies Combined in One Discourse

F. Godet

More popular than the foregoing interpretation was the idea that the eschatological discourse is composed of two prophecies, one dealing with the fall of Jerusalem, the other with the final advent, but both authentic. This view, championed by Wendt, was anticipated in principle by a full generation in the expositions of F. Godet. This writer found it difficult to accept the newly propounded theory of the little apocalypse, especially in view of the necessarily widespread adoption of this apocalypse at a time sufficiently early for authoritative denials to be issued against it. To him, the hypothesis is "nothing else than a stroke of desperation."[6] Godet was indignant at the lower views of Jesus that motivated the critics of this chapter:

> Jesus called himself, and consequently either knew or believed himself to be, the future Judge of the Church and the world. In the former case he must be something more than a sinful man—he can only be the God-man; in the latter he is only a fool carried away with pride. In vain will MM.

---

[4] Plummer, *An Exegetical Commentary on the Gospel according to St. Matthew* (London, 1909), 328.

[5] Geldenhuys, *Commentary on the Gospel of Luke,* NICNT (Grand Rapids, 1950), 523, 533.

[6] Godet, *A Commentary on the Gospel of Luke,* Clarke's FTL 15 (ET 1879, from the 2d French ed. of 1870), 274.

Colani, Volkmar, and Keim attempt to escape from this dilemma. Genuine historical criticism and an impartial exegesis will always raise it anew and allow no other choice than between the Christ of the Church and the clever charmer of M. Renan.[7]

As to the interpretation of the discourse, Godet recalls the hints in our Lord's teaching that the parousia may be considerably delayed (e.g., Luke 18:1–2; Mark 13:35; Luke 19:12; Matt 25:5; 24:14), yet this discourse gives a near date for the "end" (Mark 13:30), and Mark 13:32 declares that Jesus has no idea when the advent will be. It is concluded that Mark and Matthew have mingled two discourses together, but that Luke has kept them apart. The confusion is natural, since the OT prophets conjoin the judgment of Israel with that of the Gentiles; to some extent it is justified, for the destruction of Jerusalem is the first act of the world's judgment. "The present epoch is due to a suspension of the judgment already begun—a suspension the aim of which is to make way for the time of grace which is to be granted to the Gentiles."[8]

W. Beyschlag

A similar result was reached by a different path in the case of W. Beyschlag. The analytical solution of the critics had no attraction for him. "That short apocalypse is a mere production of the critical imagination; no evidence of its existence can be found." Like Godet he asked how so recent a Jewish prediction could have been immediately taken up in the circle that possessed a firsthand tradition of the Lord's words and circulated as from Jesus. "The descent of the synoptic prophetic addresses is certified on as good authority as the parables of the kingdom or the Sermon on the Mount."[9] Beyschlag felt that the difficulties of our discourse may be solved if we remember two things: (1) the imperfection of the prophet's view, (2) the imperfection of the hearer's comprehension. With regard to the former, we are to realize that Paul's confession about prophecy and reality being related as a child's thought in comparison to an adult's applies equally to Jesus (1 Cor 13:9ff.). Prophecy does not give the shape of future developments; it only provides ideal truth, and that in emblems, "riddles," as Paul said. Prophecy yields to the seer ideal history "evolved from the idea that the contrasts of good and evil, wheat and tares, must ripen in the world, and that when the opposition to God in the world has reached its climax, the judgment of God must break over it."[10] This is

---

[7] Ibid.

[8] Ibid., 260.

[9] Beyschlag, *New Testament Theology,* 2 vols. (ET Edinburgh, 1895, from the German of 1891), 1:188.

[10] Ibid., 195–96.

an excellent principle, but when we look at Mark 13 we see more than ideal history—we see a very concrete Jerusalem and statements made about various kinds of people.

Here the second of the above-mentioned factors comes in: the reporters did not grasp this aright, hence the discourse mixes up ideal history with what Jesus had prophesied of Jerusalem's fate. The contrast of Mark 13:20 and 32 makes this plain: the concrete statement about the generation that will not pass away naturally refers to what Jesus had predicted of the judgment on Jerusalem; the confession of his prophetic ignorance relates to the wider prophecy. That this is no mere conjecture is shown in the necessity of the gospel to be proclaimed throughout all the world—which is "the one real sign of the end"—and that this is the task of generations after AD 70, as well as before (cf. Mark 12:1–12; Matt 22:7). "According to this the spirit of Jesus clearly saw beyond the near judgment of God on Judaism, not the immediate end of the world, but a growing history both of the world and the Church, the greatest fact of which should be the calling of the nations of the world to the kingdom of God."[11] If it be asked how this is to be reconciled with the statements implying a parousia in the contemporary generation, the answer is given that the advent of Jesus is a historical process (cf. Matt 26:64). "Jesus comprehended the realisation of the kingdom of God, represented by the prophets as momentary (like a flash of lightning), rather as a process of growth, a historical development; and according to the same law he consciously viewed also the future completion of his work as a course of history, achieved not in a single act, but in an advancing series of acts."[12] In seeking to estimate this unrealistic interpretation of the eschatological discourse, it is enough to point out the strange inconsistency of postulating that a prophet can see only ideal history, and that therefore when Jesus prophesies actual history, this must be separated from the ideal history of the discourse, which alone can be the subject of prophecy! If prophecy consists only of "ideal truth . . . in emblem and image, or rather, in a changing series of images," how was Jesus able to speak at all of the overthrow of Jerusalem? Or if this was a case of actualizing prophetic images, why should it be limited to one series only (relating to Jerusalem) and not to that which relates to the wider issues of world history? We suspect that Victorian optimism contributed more to Beyschlag's outlook than Mark 13.[13]

---

[11] Ibid., 198.

[12] Ibid., 200.

[13] G. B. Stevens's exposition of the discourse closely followed that of Beyschlag: see his *Theology of the New Testament*, 2d ed. (Edinburgh, 1906). His ideas in turn were largely repeated by H. A. A. Kennedy in *St. Paul's Conceptions of the Last Things* (London, 1904), 168–69, 172–73.

E. F. K. Müller

E. F. K. Müller, like Godet, dwelt on dominical sayings which imply a period of development before the end; in his estimate these show that sayings relating to an impending coming of Jesus must refer to the judgment on Jerusalem; we are compelled to this conclusion if we compare Matt 10:23 with Mark 13:10, for the latter tells of the worldwide preaching of the gospel before the end, while the former says that not even Palestine will be evangelized before the "coming."[14] Moreover, "it may be that the widely-spread faith of the Church in the immediate nearness of the End has helped to produce the mistaken formulation of these words. This belief perhaps also explains why the judgment on the people of God and then on the entire race, which Jesus had only inwardly joined, is similarly joined together in temporal proximity in the report (Mark 13:14f., 24f.)."[15] While we may not be persuaded by these views, we should not pass over Müller's acute criticism of Weizsäcker's presentation of the little apocalypse theory.

He makes four points: (1) Despite individual parallels with Jewish apocalyptic literature, e.g., in the messianic woes, the "total design" of the discourse shows specifically Christian points which cannot be explained by an external editing of a Jewish basis. (2) Apocalypses of undoubted Jewish origin find it difficult to know how to connect the figure of the Messiah, who originally belonged to the "this-worldly" circle of prophetic ideas, with later transcendent hopes. (3) The theme of the history up to the parousia is the preaching of the gospel of Jesus and personal decision for or against him, with which the predicted struggle stands in closest association; with that corresponds the picture of the end—history is concluded through the judgment of the Messiah and the gathering of the elect about him. (4) No rebuilding of Jerusalem after its destruction is contemplated.

These considerations should show that we cannot be dealing with a Jewish, or even Jewish-Christian, apocalypse in any exclusive sense. May it be a Christian one, pseudonymously attributed to Jesus? "Then we face again the question whether this Christian eschatological system, despite numerous individual parallels to Jewish apocalyptic, does not reveal itself to be a new building on an original foundation which must conclusively be attributed to Jesus himself, even if the parousia discourse may not be regarded exactly as a historical report."[16] This criticism anticipates the kind of approach to Mark 13 made a generation later, yet we have never seen a reference to this article in any publica-

---

[14] Müller, *RE*, 21:264–65.
[15] Ibid., 265.
[16] Ibid., 263–64.

tion that has come our way. That fate is typical of more than one attempt of conservative critics to defend the eschatological discourse: they were ignored by the proponents of the new theory.

A striking variation of the view of two discourses in Mark 13 recognizes a little apocalypse within the chapter, with or without a second discourse, and boldly claims that the entire material is authentic. The two great names associated with this view are the father and son, Bernhard and Johannes Weiss. Bernhard Weiss took over H. A. W. Meyer's commentary and issued the sixth edition of that on the Synoptic Gospels in 1878 (we have used the eighth edition of 1892). Of Mark 13 he wrote: "The parousia discourse is the one greater discourse which Mark had completely repeated from the older source; he provided it with an historical introduction, vv. 1–5, a concluding exhortation, 32–37, as well as lengthened it through two interpolations, 9–13, 21–23." The original source, therefore, must have been vv. 6–8, 14–20, 24–31, the little apocalypse as commonly constructed.[17] Weiss scarcely felt it necessary to discuss in his commentary the opinion of his critical contemporaries that the discourse thus laid bare is unauthentic.

In his *Biblical Theology of the New Testament* he stated what he considered to be the fundamental assumption of the discourse:

> Although the consummation of all things is not brought about in the natural way of historical development, it is nevertheless a condition of its commencement that the time has become ripe for it. As the Messiah could not appear upon the scene until the time was fulfilled (Mark 1:15), so, according to the divinely appointed course of the historical development, certain events must have taken place before he returns; and from these, as its foretokens, men can then discern the nearness of the divinely appointed moment of the consummation. Upon this fundamental thought of apocalyptic prophecy rests also the prophecy of Jesus regarding his return.[18]

As Godet thought that the destruction of Jerusalem was the first act of the world's judgment, so Weiss affirmed of the tribulation of Matt 13:14–20: "Since with this, the last great judgment of God already began, the day of the return must now immediately appear."[19] But how are we to explain the "immediately" (Matt 24:29)? In this matter we fear that Weiss hedged and hovered about in obvious perplexity. As his *Biblical Theology of the New Testament* is his only translated work, it is not apparent to the English reader, but Holtzmann noted it and with evident amusement pointed it out as follows (the references are to the German writings):

---

[17] Weiss, *Die Evangelien des Markus und Lukas*, 8th ed. (Göttingen, 1892), 213.
[18] Idem, *Biblical Theology of the New Testament* (ET Edinburgh, 1882, from the 3d German ed. of 1879), 149–50.
[19] Ibid.

Weiss abstracted from it [the discourse] the compensating judgment, "Jesus set his coming again in prospect for the current generation, even if the point of time remained in the last resort always indefinable."[20] According to Leben Jesu II there lies in Mark 13:30 only a hypothetical prophecy, in Mark 13:32 an absolute prophecy.[21] According to Neutest. Theol. the two sayings cannot possibly have been said one after another, so that the first should be related to the end of Jerusalem, the second to the end of the world.[22] The mixing of the two ends is set, p. 193, to the reckoning of the misunderstanding of the disciples, according to par. 33b, "a peculiar view of the pedagogic wisdom of Jesus."[23]

It is unfortunate when one's writings are subjected to examination by an intellect so acute as Holtzmann's, but this citation will illustrate the difficulty of the time question in Mark 13 and the necessity of candor when dealing with it.

J. Weiss

In the writings of Johannes Weiss one feels the impact of a mastermind. It is unaccountable that so little of his work has been made available for English readers. Moffatt drew attention to the conversion of Muirhead to the little apocalypse theory as "notable."[24] It would have been more to the point if he had called attention to the far more significant conversion of Johannes Weiss from the little apocalypse theory to an acceptance of its general authenticity. The famous Die Predigt Jesu vom Reiche Gottes contains little that bears on our discussion, save an expression of the viewpoint from which this writer never moved and which provided him with the key to Mark 13. In his view, the description of the parousia, Mark 13:24ff., with the parable of the Fig Tree, Mark 13:28–29, supplies for Mark at least the true context for Jesus' prediction of the fall of the temple: the advent brings "the break-up of the old world, which will then bury the temple also beneath its ruins."[25] This was the point of departure for his later investigations of the eschatological discourse.

---

[20] Holtzmann, Lehrbuch, 33, quoting Weiss.

[21] L.J., 2:286, 448–49.

[22] Weiss, Neutestamentliche Theologie, 1:193.

[23] See ibid., 194; Holtzmann, Lehrbuch, 1:328 n. 1.

[24] Moffatt, Introduction to the Literature of the New Testament, 208 n. 3.

[25] Weiss, Predigt Jesu (Göttingen, 1892), 32, ET Jesus' Proclamation of the Kingdom of God (Philadelphia, 1971), 93. The year in which this book was published also saw the publication of the one article Weiss wrote in which he advocated the little apocalypse theory, namely, "Die Komposition der synoptischen Wiederkunftsrede," in Theologische Studien und Kritiken 65 (1892) 246–70. It reflects the same fundamental interpretation of eschatology as in Predigt Jesu, but emphasizes the distinction between the sudden parousia in the

The most elaborate discussion of his views is given in the exposition of Markan theology, *Das älteste Evangelium*. Herein we see the influence of Pfleiderer, noted earlier by us. The purpose of the discourse, like that of 2 Thessalonians, is to quiet feverish expectations of the parousia. "The discourse as a whole does not give the impression that it is a flaming pamphlet of the twelfth hour. The concluding exhortations to watchfulness (vv. 33, 37) . . . rest on and draw their strength from this, that the delay ultimately is incalculable. The day and hour are not known (v. 32), and therefore it is necessary ever to be watchful. An apocalyptic prophet who sees the signs fulfilled and the hour to have come does not speak in this way."[26] This viewpoint is especially noticeable in v. 10, the necessity to preach the gospel in all the world, but it is also contained in such an exhortation as vv. 5–6. Concerning the rise of deceivers Weiss comments: "Even if the community already had experienced something of the kind, the prophetic character of this word nevertheless remains through the 'many,' *polloi*: there certainly had not been a mass appearance of pseudomessiahs hitherto. Watch out then! Do not let such people set you prematurely in an excited condition!"[27] On the other hand, the opposite extreme must not be adopted, for the parousia is expected in the lifetime of the generation of Jesus. The general idea of the discourse excludes the possibility that the "abomination of desolation" refers to the (past) activity of the Romans: "It would be the complete opposite of the guiding purpose of the author if here suddenly the end was stated to be quite near, whereas just now the terminus was set back to the finishing of the mission work."[28] On no account is this interpretation to be reversed by making "Let the reader understand" mean "Let the church realize that the old prophecy is in process of fulfillment or has just been fulfilled"; *noein* can mean "perceive, attend to," but in Mark it is used for "understand," especially of a parable or secret (7:18; 8:17; cf. also Rev 13:18; 17:9). In this passage it implies that the Danielic prophecy is intended in the words of Jesus. Meanwhile the fulfillment is outside the circle of view. Caligula had attempted it, but God had frustrated it. If Caligula had pointed the way of possible fulfillment, the how or the when is yet unknowable. "Just as it is fundamentally false to ask in the

---

Q apocalypse (Luke 17:22–37) and the parousia heralded by signs in Mark 13. Weiss, however, sees both concepts in the Markan discourse; a "firm address of Jesus" in vv. 5–7, 24–25a, 28–37 (from Ur-Markus) conjoined with a little apocalypse in vv. 14, 17, 20, 22, 25b–27, lengthened through additions from Q, namely, vv. 9–13, 15–16, 21. The intention of the total discourse is to warn against an overly early expectation of the parousia (see especially pp. 246–50, 263–64).

[26] Weiss, *Das älteste Evangelium* (Göttingen, 1903), 72.
[27] Ibid., 73–74.
[28] Ibid., 76–77.

exposition of 2 Thessalonians 2 what definite contemporary events Paul had in view with his description, so it is mistaken to ask Mark how he interpreted the *bdelygma erēmōseōs.* He does not interpret it. He only says that a horrible desecration of the temple must have taken place before the end can come. The interpretation is pure apocalyptic theory; he simply imparts here a still unfulfilled prophecy of Jesus."[29]

What shall we then say of the setting of the discourse? More particularly, how do we relate the question of the disciples to what follows? Weiss answers: "There is only one explanation here: only under one presupposition is the answer of Jesus not nonsensical, i.e., if the evangelist tacitly accepts that the temple can be destroyed only at the break-up of the old world, at the coming of the Messiah, at the setting up of the sovereignty of God. The signs of the parousia are then at the same time signs for the ruin of the temple."[30] This, however, does not compel us to the view that the connection is original. Of the authenticity of the temple prediction, Weiss has no doubt, but it could well be an independent saying to which Mark has appended the following discourse. The introduction of the four intimate friends, occurring only in Mark, is probably editorial; they are brought in to give the discourse an appearance of secrecy: "the old text of Mark gives it simply as a discourse to the disciples, i.e., as a piece of teaching for the whole community."[31]

Weiss now proceeds to attempt to define this "old text of Mark." By such considerations as that v. 21 is a doublet of v. 22, coming from Q; v. 7 is a comment on v. 8; vv. 15–16 come from Q, etc., the foundational document is found to be vv. 8, 14, 17–20, 22, 24–25, Matt 24:30ab, 26–27, 30, 33. Weiss makes the further interesting conjecture that the original paragraph vv. 9–13 is better reproduced in Matt 10:17–23, and that Mark took out Matt 10:23, replacing it with the statement about worldwide preaching, 13:10; the whole paragraph would very well fit the document as analyzed above and could have been an integral part of it, particularly if Matt 10:23 be put after Mark 13:13, thus:

> He that endures to the end,
> The same shall be saved.—
> But whenever they persecute you in this city,
> · Flee into the next;
> For truly I tell you, you will not finish the cities of Israel,
> Until the Son of man comes.—
> But whenever you see the "abomination of desolation"
> Standing where it ought not,
> (Let the reader understand)

---

[29] Ibid., 79.
[30] Ibid., 72–73.
[31] Ibid., 274.

Then flee into the mountains.
But woe to pregnant women and suckling mothers
In those days.
But pray that your flight may not happen
In winter or on the Sabbath.[32]

When Weiss came to write his commentary on Mark, he abandoned this suggestion and simply incorporated vv. 9bcd, 11 with v. 8
as preliminary signs of the end.[33] We have mentioned the earlier view
as a good example of the ease with which one can put together a
plausible connection of sayings and then presume that the excellence
of connection proves that it must have once existed!

Whence did this discourse originate? Let Weiss speak for himself:

> Whereas the hypothesis of a "little apocalypse" was earlier very wide-
> spread (I also have represented it), today the grounds for this view have
> become frail. While it was once found surprising that there should be in
> a discourse of Jesus conceptions related to those of Jewish apocalyptic,
> today many people will share my opinion that Jesus could very well have
> thought of the future according to the scheme of the prophecy of Daniel
> and of other apocalyptists. . . . If he spoke of the "coming of the Son of
> Man," then he used an apocalyptic conception generally recognized at
> that time; it is a strong conviction that at the end of the days, "the man on
> the clouds" must come. So also the "abomination of desolation," which is
> taken over by him, is an idea of firm dogmatic strength. It is laid down in
> prophecy and this prophecy must be fulfilled as all others. . . . Or what is
> meant if one demands in this direction "originality" from Jesus? Is it
> wished that he had given on these matters quite new and unheard-of
> explanations? We are thankful that he did not make the attempt to vie with
> the Jewish apocalyptists in depicting the end, but that in this respect he
> simply held to prophecy, or to what was delivered to him as such. He was
> satisfied with the cardinal features of the scheme: utmost concentration
> on the chief matters—that is the signature of this apocalypse.[34]

It is presumed, then, that Mark found this discourse as a Christian
apocalypse and developed it through interpolations from the sayings
source. To this view Weiss adhered in his later writings. In his latest
book, published posthumously, he dealt with the problem of reconciling a view of the end as coming suddenly and as preceded by signs. The
apparently contradictory belief, he points out, is not only to be seen in
the sayings of Jesus—it runs throughout the NT. "It unites two fundamental attitudes of the primitive Christian life: on the one hand, the
continual tension which is maintained and increased through con-

---

[32] Ibid., 278ff.

[33] Idem, *Das Markusevangelium,* Die Schriften des Neuen Testaments, 2d
ed. (Göttingen, 1906).

[34] Ibid., 281.

stantly repeated exhortations to watch at all times, for on this rests in part the intensity of the religious and ethical enthusiasm; on the other hand, the being bound to specified tasks."[35] While it may be felt that Weiss goes too far in some of his assertions, particularly in his relating Jesus so closely to the apocalyptists, there is much of great value in his treatment of our theme. It is hard to understand why critics so frequently confine their quotations of his views to the negative aspects of his approach and overlook his positive contribution.

S. Mathews

The views of Shailer Mathews may be characterized as a fusion of elements from Johannes Weiss and Wendt. He takes over the latter's analysis of Mark 13 into two discourses,[36] except that he removes the paragraph describing the parousia, vv. 24–27, from the Jerusalem discourse and inserts it into that concerning the messianic consummation. Both discourses are authentic. "Despite the objections of Wendt, both may safely be considered as coming from Jesus himself. That he expected the fall of Jerusalem is beyond question, and it has already appeared that he regarded his return as in some way susceptible to interpretation by apocalyptic figures."[37] The great difficulty over this view has always been to explain why these two discourses have been combined in this way. Mathews suggests that a solution may be found in carefully noting the distinction between "these things" of Mark 13:30 and "that day" of 13:32: "The two contrasted pronouns refer respectively to the fate of Jerusalem and the parousia of the Christ, and suggest that the two sets of material are in such a relation that the one gives a basis for confidence in the other." In two respects the predictions of Jesus had proved terribly accurate: those concerning the fall of Jerusalem in the first discourse, which had been completely fulfilled, and those relating to the persecution of the disciples in the second discourse, which were in process of fulfillment through the contemporary policy of the Roman state. Both elements of the Lord's prophecies pointed to an early fulfillment of the rest. "The generation within which all 'these' events—i.e. the political—were to take place had not yet quite passed from the earth, and the woes which . . . were expected to precede the coming of Christ had already begun. Sustained by these fulfilments of Jesus' words as regards Jerusalem and their own persecution, the Christians who 'read' might well 'understand' and rest in

---

[35] Idem, *Das Urchristentum* (Göttingen, 1917), 97.

[36] The discourse on Jerusalem, vv. 7–9a, 14–20, 24–27, 30–32; the discourse on the messianic consummation, vv. 4–6, 9b–13, 21–23, 28–29, 32–37.

[37] Mathews, *The Messianic Hope in the New Testament* (Chicago, 1905), 230.

supreme confidence that Jesus' prophecies of the coming of the kingdom would also be fulfilled."[38] Mathews notes that if Jesus intended
this correlation of the two discourses, then he must have connected in
some way the fall of Jerusalem with his own coming. If he did not, we
must still remember that the limit within which the messianic kingdom
was to be established is expressly set within the contemporary generation (Mark 9:1; 14:62; Matt 10:23). It is in accordance with these
convictions that the apostolic churches ordered their lives and hopes.[39]
Apart from this last statement, it will be noted that Mathews's interpretation rests wholly on the confessed belief that all the evangelists wrote
after AD 70; otherwise it could not be said that the "Jerusalem discourse" serves as a guarantee for the accuracy of the other. This is a
debatable position, especially with regard to Mark, and if the date be
contested the interpretation is the less assured.

H. T. Andrews

H. T. Andrews was more indefinite in his pronouncements on the
discourse, but evidently accepted at least the hypothesis of two sources
for Mark 13. He pointed out the striking fact that "there is only one
definite prediction of the parousia in the synoptics which has been
transmitted in almost identical words by all three Evangelists, viz. the
utterance in Matt 24:30, Mark 13:26, Luke 21:27." This prompts the
question, "If the final discourse of Jesus can be clearly proved to have
been adulterated by a foreign admixture of Jewish eschatological ideas,
why should we hesitate in supposing that other similar elements in the
present records of the teaching of Jesus came from the same source?"[40]
Presuming a general unwillingness to take the latter step, then even if
sources are intermingled in the eschatological discourse, both should
be taken as authentic. "The hypothesis with regard to the Jewish origin
of the 'Little Apocalypse' is not, and cannot, be proved. There is no
tangible evidence which warrants the conclusion that it could not have
been an utterance of Jesus. The supposition that the prediction of the
parousia in Mt. 24.30 (Mk. 13.26) is of Jewish origin is a purely
gratuitous assumption and cannot be substantiated by sound argument."[41] The apparent dogmatism in such a statement is due to our
isolating it from its context. In fact, Andrews provides one of the most
cogent demonstrations of the authenticity of our Lord's eschatological
teaching that can be found in short compass.

---

[38] Ibid., 231.
[39] Ibid., 117.
[40] Andrews, "The Significance of the Eschatological Utterances of Jesus,"
in London Theological Studies (1911), 69–70.
[41] Ibid., 73.

He alludes to a factor that should be obvious enough to us all but which is rarely recognized: affinity with Jewish thought is a quite inadequate ground for rejecting dominical sayings. "If we were to reject every utterance of Jesus which could be paralleled in Jewish Literature, and set up originality as the supreme canon of value, we should reduce his teaching to very small compass. We must not set up one standard for eschatology and another for ethics. Why, for example, should we reject Mt. 26.64 on the ground of its likeness to Dan. 7.13 and accept the teaching of Jesus with regard to forgiveness in spite of the fact that there is a very clear parallel to it in the Testaments of the Patriarchs?"[42]

Two other points that affect our problem are: (1) the fact that our Lord's eschatological teaching represents the climax of his instruction, not an earlier conviction which died as his ministry progressed; (2) that, further, it is bound up with sacred and solemn occasions, such as the transfiguration, the confession at Caesarea, the tense situation when the shadow of the cross was upon him in his closing days, the judgment hall of Caiaphas. "The place which these utterances occupy in the gospel narrative, the sanctity that surrounds the occasions on which they were made, the sense of solemnity that enshrouds them, all go to prove that Jesus himself regarded them as amongst his most important deliverances. We cannot set them on one side without setting on one side what Jesus himself regarded as being of primary significance."[43] Is it not permissible to apply this observation to Mark 13? It should not go unnoticed that even if much of the discourse has been brought from other sources, everything in it presupposes the closing period of the ministry, the period of eschatological instruction. On the whole we must be grateful to Andrews for his contribution, even if we feel the hypothesis of two sources for Mark 13 to be questionable.

3. A Continuous Description of the Christian Era

T. Zahn and W. F. Gess

The view, remarked by Strauss, that Jesus "noticed what is intermediate," between the fall of Jerusalem and the end of the age, is represented by a small group of exegetes, who read the eschatological discourse as a straightforward and continuous prophecy. The most notable of these is Theodor Zahn, but his views were, in measure, anticipated forty years earlier by a little-known writer, W. F. Gess. This scholar protested against the assumption that the evangelists had no compunction in attributing to Jesus words they knew he never said, and

---

[42] Ibid., 80.
[43] Ibid., 82.

that they took undue liberties in editing the Lord's sayings. Having had a special interest in Luke's version of the discourse, he singled out Luke 21:24 for mention:

> Many are now saying that Luke himself, of his own accord, has put these words into the mouth of Jesus. Seeing Jerusalem in ruins, the Jews driven out and waiting in vain for the coming of Jesus, he retouched the saying of Jesus in which the parousia followed immediately on the fall of Jerusalem by this addition. . . . Now Luke certainly in v. 20 has set down another saying in the place of what had been handed on. But while he there explained the meaning of Jesus, here he would have suppressed it. That an evangelist accorded himself such a liberty is improbable in the highest degree.[44]

Investigations of Luke's version of the discourse by B. S. Easton, Vincent Taylor, and T. W. Manson in no small measure support the attitude for which Gess here pleaded. His insistence on the importance of Luke 21:24 further led him to make an observation on Luke's eschatological interests worth pondering in the light of modern opinion on this matter: "We meet in Luke alone the parousia saying of the girded loins (12:35), of the yearning for a day of the Son of man (17:22), of the Nobleman (19:12)—proof enough that what Jesus had said of his coming again was for him a particular object of research (1:3). . . . The most natural view will be that 21:24 is a genuine element of this discourse on the Mount of Olives which was rescued from oblivion through this evangelist's diligence in research."[45] Here, then, according to Gess, is a clue to a right understanding of the discourse: Jesus anticipated a period between Jerusalem's fall and his parousia which he named "the times of the Gentiles"; he also spoke of the universal preaching of the gospel. Now in Matt 22:7–8, 21:43–44, it is assumed that the preaching to the nations does not commence seriously till after the fall of Jerusalem. The times of the Gentiles will accordingly last a long time. Jesus could not possibly have placed his parousia immediately after the events of AD 70; and statements in the discourse which apparently link the two must be interpreted otherwise. In effect, therefore, Gess would solve the problem of Mark 13 by inserting Luke 21:24 at v. 19: an indeterminate period is set between the fall of Jerusalem and the parousia; the discourse in the main runs a straight course through history.

Before commenting on these views, it will be to our advantage to consider Zahn's interpretation. The conservatism of this man of immense learning should not be overemphasized. He argued strongly that Luke's account is secondary, in that it came after the events of AD 70,

---

[44] Gess, *Christi Zeugnis von seiner Person und seinem Werk* (Basel, 1870), 134.
[45] Ibid., 135.

and represents an interpretation of the Lord's words in the light of history rather than a report. Similarly Mark's wording of the abomination passage represents an interpretation of the original, contained in Matthew's account, and reflects the circumstances of Caligula's threat to the temple.[46] The priority of the Markan-Matthean version of the discourse over against that of Luke is established for Zahn by the obvious relation of Paul's eschatology to the former. "The common Christian view of the issue of history, as it appears in II Thess. 2, is historically incomprehensible without a strong support in the prophecy of Jesus, and such it finds in Mt. 24:15–28 = Mk. 13:14–23." Further, it is unthinkable that Matthew and Mark changed the "original" version of Luke "out of love for eschatological ideas which did not originate with Jesus."[47] The little apocalypse theory is dismissed as one which cannot be supported at any point by valid proofs.[48] For the interpretation of the discourse it is imperative to see that the "abomination" passage has nothing to do with the events of the first century.

Commenting on the clause "Let the reader understand," Zahn characteristically writes:

> If the readers of this gospel had followed this exhortation, they would never have reached the idea that the destruction of Jerusalem and of the temple in A.D. 70 was here meant. For Daniel has no such thing. Through the expression taken from Daniel he alludes to definite passages in the book, of which the plainest in expression and thought is Dan. 11:30–39; this says nothing of a conquest and destruction of Jerusalem, but only of a removal of the regular cultus and desecration of the sanctuary through an anti–god world ruler. . . . Thus Jesus speaks not of a destruction of Jerusalem, but of an erection of a desecrating idolatrous abomination in the sanctuary.[49]

Since Zahn writes in the conviction that Jesus here gives a true prophecy, the reference of Mark 13:14ff. is no longer to be regarded as lying in the past, but solely in the future. How is this justified? Like Shailer Mathews, he appeals to the Fig Tree parable, Mark 13:28–29. "All these things" cannot include the parousia, as everyone recognizes; but as little can it apply to the abomination passage.

> The idolatrous abomination, the last distress and the parousia are represented as acts, quickly following on one another, of a single drama, as the three chief moments of the world end, designated in Mt. 24.6, 14 as *to telos*. . . . In Mt. 24.15–31 (Mk. 13.14–27) it is not signs that are in question,

---

[46] Zahn, *Introduction to the New Testament*, vol. 2 (ET Edinburgh, 1909), 500.

[47] Idem, *Das Evangelium des Matthäus*, KNT (Leipzig, 1903), 652–53.

[48] Idem, *Introduction*, 2:588 n. 2.

[49] Idem, *Matthäus*, on 24:15.

but events which were known to the disciples partly from Daniel, partly from the earlier prophecies of Jesus as moments of the *synteleia tou aiōnios*.[50]

"All these things" of the parable accordingly relates to Matt 24:8; the wars and famines, etc., comprehended under the phrase "beginning of sorrows," include the events in Judea in the years AD 66–70. Ultimately the *tauta* of Jesus takes up the *tauta* of the disciples' question, with the difference that "the subjoined *panta* will comprise, in addition to the war leading up to the end of the temple, all that was described in Mt. 24.4–14 (Mark 13.5–13), and in v. 8 was denoted by *archē ōdinōn*."[51]

Zahn seeks to strengthen his interpretation by calling attention, as Gess had done, to the necessity for preaching the gospel in all the world: "According to Mt. 22.7ff. the preaching of the gospel takes a decisive turning to the heathen only after the destruction of Jerusalem. And between the judgment on the temple and the parousia, according to Matt 23.38f., there is to be a time wherein the temple lies desolate, cf. Lk. 21.24."[52] With this in mind, the assertion, "This generation will not pass till all these things happen" (Matt 24:34; Mark 13:30), is thought to have the same reference as the Fig Tree parable and relate to the wars, etc., that include the fall of Jerusalem. Moreover, the phrase "that day" in Matt 24:36; Mark 13:32 is taken over from the OT and denotes the day of the Lord. Thus, there is no inconsistency in the mind of Jesus and no discrepancy in the prophecy. With such a result gained from the consideration of the discourse, we can now understand what Jesus meant when he spoke of his parousia as of an event which some of his contemporaries would experience (Matt 10:23; 16:28; John 21:22): he was referring on these occasions to the fall of Jerusalem.[53]

This is a gallant attempt to maintain the integrity of the eschatological discourse, and it completely won over G. Wohlenberg, who reproduced the view of his master without deviation in his commentary on Mark.[54] One wonders, however, what Zahn would have had to say about this unnatural kind of exegesis had it been put forth in the interests of critical views. His limiting the reference of Mark 13:29 to vv. 7–8 is as arbitrary as the expedient of those who insist that it must refer to vv. 9–13. The "abomination" prophecy is to be interpreted not only in the light of Daniel 11, but also Dan 9:26–27, hence there are good grounds for holding that Mark 13:14–20 include the destruction of Jerusalem as following on the "profanation." If therefore the destruc-

---

[50] Ibid., 660.
[51] Ibid.
[52] Ibid., 663.
[53] Ibid., 663–64.
[54] Wohlenberg, *Das Evangelium des Markus*, KNT (Leipzig, 1910).

tion of the city is to be placed anywhere in the discourse, it is far more likely to be read in that passage than in vv. 7–8. Not even the appeal to a period intervening between the city's ruin and the parousia can obviate this interpretation, for there is no valid ground for making the "times of the Gentiles" extend through unknown centuries. It is possible to make a plausible case for consistently equating the fall of Jerusalem with the coming of Christ and the kingdom of God, but it is hard to know how seasoned expositors in their heart of hearts can adopt that view, still less how they can adopt it for some occasions only. What unprejudiced person would imagine that when our Lord spoke about the coming of the Son of man, or the coming of the kingdom of God with power, he was indicating perpetual "wars and rumors of wars, kingdom against kingdom, earthquakes and famines?" We are compelled to regard this interpretation as a substitute for plain thinking, a failure of courage in the face of awkward facts, and we regret that so great a scholar as Zahn lent his name to it.

4. An Application of "Prophetic Perspective"

J. A. Bengel

It will be evident that the majority of scholars who have wished to retain the eschatological discourse as genuine prophecy of Jesus have resorted to none of the previous views. Their simple answer to the problem of the discourse consisted in an appeal to the old conception of "prophetic perspective." This method appears to have originated with Bengel, long before the rise of modern criticism. He believed that while the disciples asked the Lord concerning the destruction of the temple and the parousia, without making a distinction, his answer treated of the two matters distinctly and separately, yet in order. Taking Mark 13 as our basis (Bengel dealt with Matthew's version), we observe the progression: (1) concerning the temple and city, vv. 5–6, 14; (2) concerning the parousia and end of the world, vv. 24–27; (3) concerning the time of the temple's destruction, vv. 28–29; (4) concerning the time of the end of the world, v. 32. The difficulties of this view are apparent in the parousia passage, Matt 24:29 = Mark 13:24, but Bengel's treatment of this section reveals a candor which many a modern exegete could well emulate.

Four things are noted about this saying: (1) The language of the discourse on the whole is strictly literal; therefore no exception is to be made here. (2) The "tribulation of those days" refers to Matt 24:19, 22 = Mark 13:17, 20, and it is indicated that the tribulation will be brief in duration. (3) This tribulation affects the Jewish nation, and that of a single generation. (4) The expression "immediately," *eutheōs*, implies a very short delay, since *oupō*, "not yet" (Matt 24:6; Mark 13:7) and Luke's *ouk eutheōs* (Luke 21:9) are said of the short delay which must precede that tribulation; indeed, Mark 13:24 excludes delay altogether.[55]

This is bold language from an orthodox theologian of the eighteenth century! Bengel anticipates his objectors: "You will say, it is a great leap from the destruction of Jerusalem to the end of the world, which is represented as coming quickly after it. I reply—A prophecy resembles a landscape painting, which marks distinctly the houses, paths, and bridges in the foreground, but brings together, into a narrow space, the distant valleys and mountains, though they are really far apart. Thus should they who study a prophecy look on the future to which the prophecy refers."[56] Here is the genesis of the constantly repeated comparison of a prophecy with a mountain scene, whose peaks allow no idea of the nature and distance of the valleys between. It is a brave interpretation, but it still involves the theologian in difficulties. Strauss pointed out that this merely shows how easy it was for Jesus to err in questions of time; it does not abolish the error. And Bengel must have realized that, for he weakened and made concessions to contemporary convictions: "The advent of our Lord actually took place (as far as its commencement was concerned, Jn. 21:22) after the destruction of Jerusalem."[57] Still worse, he paraphrased the Lord's words thus: "Concerning these things which will happen after the tribulation of those days of the destruction of Jerusalem, the nearest event which at present it suits my condition to mention, and your capacity to expect, is this, that the sun will be darkened, etc."[58] That comes dangerously near to the view that Jesus knew better, but deliberately withheld the truth. It is unfortunate that Bengel should have lapsed in such a manner after so promising a beginning. Nevertheless, he had sowed a seed from which was to issue a great harvest.

E. de Pressensé

Passing over a complete century we come to E. de Pressensé, whose book on Jesus was written one year after Colani's. He did not directly mention the latter's work, but it is possible that his strictures on the anti–eschatological theologians may have it in mind. He protested against the idealism which restricts the operation of God's justice to the spiritual realm. "Such a theory ignores the fact that evil has not confined itself within these bounds, but has stalked abroad boldly in

---

[55] Bengel, *Gnomon Novi Testamenti*, 2d ed. (1763; ET Edinburgh, 1857, from Steudel's edition of 1855), 1:417, 426.

[56] Ibid., 427.

[57] Ibid.

[58] Ibid., 428.

the external world, as if its triumph there were assured and final; it has laid hold of the springs of natural and social life."[59] Unless human history is to lose its moral character, we must assume that God will work his will within history. The great lesson of the eschatological discourse lies in its revelation that there are lesser as well as final judgments of God, and all are related. "Every period has its own decisive event, and receives its own solemn sentence. These partial judgments foretell the great and final judgment. . . . They are no sudden surprises of fate, or, to speak more correctly, no *coups d'état* of Providence, making violent assaults on liberty. No, nothing can better assure us of the value God sets on human freedom, than to see the history of society and of nature itself so suspended on moral decisions, that heaven and earth may be moved to carry out the awards of divine justice. We know no spiritualism bolder than this so-called materialism."[60] In the discourse we see that the partial judgments lead on to final and decisive judgment, but no line of separation is drawn between the two. "The destruction of the theocracy is confounded with those great final throes out of which will come forth the new earth wherein shall dwell righteousness. Prophecy gives its broad survey without perspective."[61]

Like Bengel, however, de Pressensé cannot leave the matter there. Probably unconscious of his imitation of the former, he asserted that the final judgment really commenced with the destruction of the faithless theocracy; that Jesus avowed subsequently his ignorance of times and seasons; and finally that the disciples applied to the parousia some sayings which referred only to the destruction of Jerusalem.[62] These three propositions are undoubtedly intended to soften the effect of the major contention, but the first and third are sops without taste. If the idea of prophetic perspective is to be taken seriously, considerations of this kind are superfluous.

C. A. Briggs

C. A. Briggs wrote his study of "the Apocalypse of Jesus," as he termed Mark 13, after a prolonged study of the messianic passages of the Old and New Testaments.[63] It is accordingly not without authority that he could write, "The discourse of Jesus . . . is intermediate between

---

[59] De Pressensé, *Jesus Christ: His Times, Life and Work* (ET London, 1879, from the 7th French ed.), 439.

[60] Ibid.

[61] Ibid., 440.

[62] Ibid., 440–41.

[63] This is embodied in three volumes: *Messianic Prophecy* (Edinburgh, 1886), *The Messiah of the Gospels* (Edinburgh, 1894), and *The Messiah of the Apostles* (Edinburgh, 1895).

the apocalypse of Daniel and the apocalypse of John. As it depends upon the former and advances upon the Messianic idea contained therein, so it is the prelude to the latter and the key to its interpretation."[64] There is no cause for wonder that the "apocalyptic" sections of Mark 13 resemble in many respects Jewish apocalypses: "This is because they all depend on the apocalypse of Daniel, and use the language of the judgment scenes of the Old Testament prophets. There is no sufficient reason why Jesus himself should not have used the Old Testament in the same manner. We ought to expect that Jesus in his predictions would bridge the time between the apocalypse of Daniel and the apocalypse of John, and give an intermediate stage in the development of the apocalyptic prophecy, if, as we believe, these apocalypses give us genuine prediction."[65]

Briggs agrees with Weiss that the disciples' question, When shall these things be? implies not one event but a series of events; that is, the ruin of the temple is set in an eschatological context.[66] Mark 13:5–8 supply a negative answer as to the time of their coming to pass: "the end is not yet." The positive answer is contained in vv. 9–13; the gospel is to be preached to the nations and to the whole inhabitable globe, that the nations might be saved and not be condemned in the judgment of the world. "This is the scope of the preaching of the gospel. Until this has been accomplished the second Advent cannot come."[67] This period of gospel preaching (the "times of the gospel") is parallel to Luke's "times of the Gentiles," but the former is spoken of from the point of view of the Jewish Christians, the latter from the point of view of the Gentiles.[68]

How is this related to Matthew's representation that the parousia happens "immediately" after the Jewish tribulation? The prophets of the old dispensation help us. "*Eutheōs* is certainly no stronger than the *qryb* of OT prophecy used in connection with similar advents to judgment. It represents that to the mind of the prophet Jesus, as to the prophets that preceded him, the advent was near. It was near in the prophetic sense—that is, the event was certain, but the time uncertain."[69] This, we fear, is a misuse of the concept of "prophetic perspective." It may be quite permissible to rationalize this phenomenon and relate the sense of immediacy to the feeling of certainty, but this is not to be imported into exegesis. When Briggs attempted to bring his interpretation of "immediacy" into relation with his "times of the

---

64 Idem, *Messiah of the Gospels*, 132.
65 Ibid., 134.
66 Ibid., 138.
67 Ibid., 141, 145.
68 Ibid., 150–51.
69 Ibid., 155–56.

gospel" he involved himself in grave difficulties. "It would seem that while the preaching of the gospel may be to some extent parallel with the tribulation, it cannot be limited by that shortened time, but must extend beyond it and be parallel with the times of the Gentiles, which were certainly subsequent to the destruction of the holy city, and therefore intervene between the tribulation and the parousia, and must be covered by the expression *eutheōs* of Matthew. To take the *eutheōs* strictly, or in any other way than the apocalyptic sense of the Old Testament advent scenes, is to introduce a glaring inconsistency between the two representations."[70] This is asking too much of us. Could Briggs adduce any passage from the OT or Jewish apocalypses which consciously equates the term "immediately" with a period lasting for indefinite ages? It is one thing to show that prophets usually expect the day of the Lord to be "at hand," while history demonstrates that the times are in the Father's authority; it is another thing for them to conceive that it is both at hand and far off. We do Jesus no honor by attributing to him such an impossible attitude, and his language does not require it.

P. Schwartzkopff

Paul Schwartzkopff wrestled with the problem of "prophetic perspective" as none before him did. He agreed with Weiffenbach and his successors that the prophecy of the fall of Jerusalem is quite separate from the exhortations to the disciples, but not that this requires a Jewish apocalypse for its explanation. If the connection between the two strains of prediction is not original, at least it is right in showing us that Jesus had subordinated the catastrophe of Jerusalem to the thought of his coming again: "Thus the Lord's sayings which concern the coming again and the destruction of Jerusalem, apart perhaps from Mark 13:30 and 32–33, originally were never externally bound with each other."[71] The exception made of Mark 13:30 and 32 is significant, for the advocates of the idea of two discourses in the chapter usually regard these two passages as the linchpin of their view. In all conscience Schwartzkopff could not do that, for he was convinced that Mark 13:30 cannot be referred to the fall of Jerusalem; it has to be placed alongside Mark 9:1; 14:62; and Matt 10:23, all of which relate to the parousia.

He seeks to demonstrate his point from the discourse; the disciples had asked concerning the time and signs of the ruin of the temple; all that Jesus relates concerning false prophets, natural phenomena, strife, persecution, distress in Judea, stands under the point of view of preliminary signs, headed up by the coming of the Son of man. "Since the

---

[70] Ibid., 156.
[71] Schwartzkopff, *Die Weissagungen Jesu Christi*, 160.

second question as to the point of time has thus far not been answered at all, then Mark must intend to give this answer in vv. 29 and 30, introduced by the parable."[72] If one objects that this overlooks the admission that two series of sayings are embodied in the discourse, it is observed that as the signs relate to the parousia, it is only natural to refer the statement of time also to the end. Luke shows clearly that the Fig Tree parable can speak only of the kingdom of God; we have no warrant for thinking otherwise of the statement that follows it.[73] A further consideration comes to the fore when we see that in Matt 23:31ff. Jesus alludes to a fearful judgment of God on the murderers of the prophets in similar language as here: "All this shall come upon this generation" (23:36). This looks as though we are dealing here not with a destruction of Jerusalem taken by itself, but with a judgment of the last days.[74] Schwartzkopff does not immediately draw a conclusion from this parallel, but it implies an eschatological setting for the prediction of the temple's overthrow.

Whether this be so or not, it appears that in Mark 13 the destruction of Jerusalem and the coming of Christ have the same signs and same terminus: how is this to be explained? On two grounds, replied Schwartzkopff: the example of the prophets, and the teaching of Jesus concerning his speedy coming. "According to prophetic analogy it is customary for a judgment over the enemies of God without and within Israel to precede the entry of the perfected kingdom, which the prophet as a rule sets in his own age. If now for the first Christians it was plain that Jesus also looked for the setting up of the perfected kingdom in his own time, they also knew, on the other hand, what on the basis of our prophecy Mark 13:2 cannot be doubted, that he had also prophesied the destruction of the temple along with that of Jerusalem. . . . Thus it lay wholly in the line of prophecy if the final judgment took place not long before the entry of the perfected kingdom."[75] The inference from this can only be that the juxtaposition of signs relating to the end of Jerusalem and the end of the age, even if not originally proceeding from Jesus, must approximate to his view. In particular there is no ground for opposing Mark 13:30 and 32 as inconsistent. The prevailing view of the latter verse extracted from it a confession by Jesus as to his absolute ignorance of the time of the end: "This interpretation appears now, in the face of our entire previous discussion, as impossible; this passage in and for itself clearly exhibits, in my opinion, only a relative ignorance of Jesus."[76] In that case the confession of ignorance is consistent

---

[72] Ibid., 166.
[73] Ibid.
[74] Ibid., 166–67.
[75] Ibid., 173.
[76] Ibid., 177–78.

with a conviction that the end would come within a generation. Schwartz-kopff's further discussions as to the psychological and religious problems involved in this interpretation of our Lord's teaching cannot be considered here, since we are dealing with questions of exegesis. His influence on the thinking of his generation was considerable, not the least being that which he evidently had on R. H. Charles.[77]

To return to the British scene from German theological speculation is to step into another world. The clamant voices of the European debate were caught by few ears in Britain. Salmond's exegesis on Mark 13 is simply a reproduction of Bengel's views. Jesus is said to reveal in his teaching the phenomena of OT prophecy. "Events which history shows to have been widely separated are brought together in what is described as prophetic perspective or 'timeless sequence,' or in causal connection, or as if the one formed part of the other. . . . In his eschatological discourses Christ recognises, as Old Testament prophecy did, the partial and preliminary manifestations of the kingdom as involving the final."[78] We believe that this is what is popularly termed having your cake and eating it: the sequence of historical crisis and final end is timeless; the one causes the other, the one is part of the other, the one is a coming of the other—there is not much that can be said after that! If there was excuse for Bengel in the eighteenth century, endeavoring to mollify wounded consciences by his revolutionary contention, the modern critic ought to do better than this.

W. Sanday

William Sanday seems never to have made up his mind finally what to make of the eschatology of Jesus and of Mark 13 in particular. He distinguished six kinds of predictions made by our Lord: they concerned (1) his death and resurrection, (2) the fall of Jerusalem, (3) the end of all things, (4) the coming of the Spirit, (5) the spread of the church, and (6) historical comings of Christ. The last was dubious, the first three certainly authentic. Difficulty arises through the linking in our sources of the second and third kinds, and because it is stated in at least one passage that the third will occur within the contemporary generation. "We know that it has not so taken place, and the great question is what we are to say to this. Is it an error in one who has never been convicted in error in anything else?"[79] A drastic solution of the

---

[77] The views of Schwartzkopff are also reproduced by Arthur Titius in *Jesu Lehre vom Reiche Gottes* (1895).

[78] Salmond, *The Christian Doctrine of Immortality,* 5th ed. (Edinburgh, 1903; 1st ed. 1895), 244–45.

[79] Sanday, *Outlines of the Life of Christ* (1905) (= the article "Jesus Christ," in Hastings's *Dictionary of the Bible* [1899]), 152–53.

difficulty is to reject the apocalyptic element of our Lord's teaching. "The chief means through which this is done has been the supposed discovery that in the discourse of Mark 13 par. there is incorporated a 'Little Apocalypse' of Jewish or Jewish-Christian origin."[80] If this passage is removed, one could account for the other sayings by supposing the disciples to have misunderstood their import, but the theory "has not perhaps as yet been brought to any final solution."[81]

Meanwhile, an attractive interpretation would make passages like Mark 9:1, which speak of the imminent kingdom, refer to the coming of the Spirit at Pentecost.[82] In an article written on the subject in 1911 Sanday despairs of a solution of the problem ever being reached. In regard to eschatology we must confess, "It is impossible to say exactly what belongs to the Master and what to the disciple."[83] This uncertainty reaches its peak in respect of Mark 13. Of the little apocalypse theory he writes:

> It would make not a little difference if we could be sure that this hypothesis was true. The verses under discussion concentrate in themselves all the more striking features of Jewish apocalypse; apart from them we should have but little evidence that our Lord adopted the more extreme and fantastic features of this branch of Judaism. When it seemed that these features could be thus got rid of, the hypothesis by means of which the amputation was performed was eagerly welcomed, and from that time onward has been a generally accepted part of the liberal tradition.

A candid confession of the kind of motive which made the little apocalypse theory so popular! He continues:

> But we must distinctly recognise that it is nothing more than a hypothesis. The proof of it is very far from being stringent. It is one thing to say that certain verses are detachable from their context, and another thing to infer that therefore they ought to be detached. For myself I fail to see how the decision can ever be final; if we accept the verses as an integral part of the discourse, we still cannot be sure that they are not an interpolation, but on the other hand, if we reject them as an interpolation, we can have no guarantee that they may not after all be genuine.[84]

The same indefiniteness, and yet perception of the issues, characterized Sanday's discussion of the prophetic consciousness. "What measure are we to apply to it? Are we to measure it strictly by what was

---

[80] Ibid., 156.

[81] Ibid.

[82] These views are reproduced unchanged in Sanday's *Life of Christ in Recent Research* (Oxford, 1907), 53–54.

[83] Idem, "The Apocalyptic Element in the Gospels," *Hibbert Journal* 10 (1, 1911): 94.

[84] Ibid., 94–95.

in the mind of the speaker? If we do that, then we have to allow that not a little Old Testament prophecy came far short of the reality. If we are to measure prediction by what it meant for the hearers, then the gap between prediction and reality would be greater still. If we measure prediction by that which the Spirit of God intended when it inspired the prophet, then history itself becomes the key to prophecy. But in the case of our Lord we know that he referred all things to the Father. To all his acts he annexed the condition: 'Nevertheless, not my will, but thine, be done.' "[85] This is excellently stated and has bearing on our subject, but Sanday hesitates to apply it. In regard to what the Spirit inspires as to the end of the age, of course, the historical canon is scarcely adequate; it will be too late to pass any judgment on the prophet when that comes to pass. But to say that our Lord referred all things to the Father with the prayer, "Thy will be done," has bearing only if that prayer stands in the background of his actual predictions of the future. Jesus prophesied as he prayed—subject to the Father's will. It so happens that the only explicit statement of our Lord, in the days of his flesh, that the consummation lies in the Father's hands is contained in Mark 13. Instead of putting Mark 13:32 over against the rest of the chapter, what is there to prevent our reading the discourse with this as the silent presupposition of the whole?

W. C. Allen

W. C. Allen strangely neglected the critical problems of the eschatological discourse in his commentary on Matthew, but he gave them careful treatment in his commentary on Mark. He rejected the little apocalypse theory as a "serious indictment" of Mark, which would have repercussions on our view of the general reliability of his Gospel. The major difficulty of Mark 13 appears to be the likeness of its ideas to those of Jewish apocalyptic: but such parallels are not confined to Mark 13. Conceptions like the kingdom of God, the Son of man, the coming of the Son of man in glory, life, the world to come, the resurrection, inheriting eternal life, the nearness of the kingdom, are all apocalyptic ideas, and yet form an integral part of our Lord's message and appear in the body of Mark's Gospel.[86] The much-loved Q also has genuine eschatological teachings, such as Luke 17:22–23; 10:12; 11:31–32; 22:30, which imply the whole cycle of Gospel apocalyptic teaching; hence "we have no right to question or deny that he who spake these words can have uttered the sayings recorded in Mk. 13."[87] Allen deals

---

[85] Ibid., 108.

[86] Allen, *The Gospel according to Saint Mark*, Oxford Church Biblical Commentary (London, 1915), 163.

[87] Ibid., 164.

very strongly with Streeter's contention of a double evolution in eschatology within the church, one away from futurism, the other developing it.

> This extraordinary theory, that the tendency in the Gospel literature of the Church was exactly the reverse of the movement in its theology, can be nothing else but a perversion of the truth. It is only arrived at by constructing, by uncritical methods, as a first source of Gospel tradition a source Q which contains comparatively little eschatological material, and underestimating the value and significance of even that. The truth is that there are two aspects of religion which are present throughout the whole New Testament side by side, the thought of eternal life or of the kingdom as present, and the conception of it as future. . . . The ingenious manipulation of Gospel sources by which it is proposed to show that there has been an increasing fabrication of eschatological material in successive Gospel documents is unsound in method, and leads to a result so absurd that it must necessarily be untrue, viz. that the Gospel writers were heading a counter-movement to the general drift of the Church's theology.[88]

How, then, are we to interpret Mark 13? Partly as a conscious use of technical apocalyptic language, the consummation of history. "If we are faced with the difficulty that he [Jesus] seems to have said that this coming would be immediate, we can but say that that is no reason for denying that he uttered the words in question. Better to say that upon this point he did not think well to reveal more than a prophet's insight into the development of the future, or to say that he wished each generation of men to watch and wait for him, than to tamper with historical evidence because it causes us difficulty and we cannot wholly understand it."[89] With language like this constantly meeting us, it looks as though conservative critics were becoming increasingly courageous in their thinking about this problem.

C. H. Turner

C. H. Turner gave typical expression to a modern conservative critic's view of Mark 13. He noted that the discourse was not part of our Lord's public teaching; it was a private talk with his most intimate friends. "There had been in more general discourse references to the Return—e.g. 8:38, 9:1—and our Lord did not hesitate to proclaim it before Caiaphas (14:62); but details about the indications which would precede it were not part of the Gospel, and he only discussed them in confidence with some few of those who were to be his most trusted representatives, and at the very close of his ministry."[90] Turner adopted the simplest analysis of the chapter: (1) the signs before the end, vv.

---

[88] Ibid., 165–66.

[89] Ibid., 167.

[90] Turner, *The Gospel according to St. Mark,* ed. C. Gore, H. L. Goudge, A. Guillaume (London, 1928), part 3, p. 102.

5–23; (2) the end, vv. 24–27; (3) the moral, vv. 28–37. He rejected any idea of modification of the discourse through the church's experience and apparent fulfillment of our Lord's words: "It cannot be said that there is any evidence of this."[91] If the time perspective is wrong, that is part of the consequences of the incarnation; in that respect, "no Christian critic can speak more than tentatively and with reverent caution, and always with the recollection that the *ultima ratio* is the guidance of the Spirit in the Body of Christ. But it does not seem that we can exclude consideration of the possibility that the ignorance which our Lord attributed to himself was not merely academic, but a real ignorance with real results."[92] That conviction of Turner is shared by perhaps a majority of critics since his time, and there is no necessity to trace it in their writings.

5. A Composition of Isolated Fragments

C. H. Weisse

The idea that the eschatological discourse was constructed from originally separate sayings was advocated, it will be remembered, by C. H. Weisse.[93] This view had been forgotten in the two generations that had elapsed since his time, but D. E. Haupt revived it, duly acknowledging his debt to Weisse. He began by criticizing Wendt's recent exposition of the little apocalypse, the two discourse theory. If Mark had taken over two separate discourses, it was a puzzle to know why he had mixed them so confusingly instead of reproducing them independently. It is not as though Mark had placed related items together; e.g., he has separated the two passages concerning false messiahs and false prophets (vv. 6, 21–23), and the position of the Fig Tree parable is ambiguous; it cannot possibly relate to its immediate antecedent. Pfleiderer's view, that the ingredients of the one discourse have been separated by the insertion of parenetic sayings, is also unsatisfactory; for the chief feature of the distress is supposed to be the events of the Jewish War, yet the warning against false christs precedes the distress instead of following it, and we know there was no crowd of messiahs before AD 66. Haupt accordingly proposes the hypothesis that "this discourse is in the fullest sense a mosaic work, composed from little pieces."[94] The method adopted is that which we have seen in our account of Lohmeyer's exposition: each verse is examined and a demonstration provided that it does not suit its context.

---

[91] Ibid.

[92] Ibid.

[93] See above, pp. 6–8.

[94] Haupt, *Die eschatologischen Aussagen Jesu in den synoptischen Evangelien*, 22–24.

Mark 13:6 gives the impression of being "an erratic block"; it owes its present position to a verbal contact with v. 5, the *blepete mē tis hymas planēsē* of v. 5 is balanced by the *pollous planēsousin* of v. 6. Verse 8 with its *gar* should offer a ground for the statement of v. 7, but it simply repeats its substance. It is noted that Luke separates the two verses with the expression *tote elegen autois*, which points to a fresh source for the second statement. Verses 9–13 need not be regarded as eschatological in nature; Matthew gives them in a different kind of context, showing that he found them elsewhere. The paragraph contains two parallel sections, each having a climax: vv. 9b–11 tell of persecutions through governing powers, vv. 12–13 of the same through relatives, and so generally; the former section gives the encouraging thought that persecution will not hinder God's kingdom; the latter is concerned only with the personal destiny of the disciples. Verses 15–16 are repeated by Luke in a different context, Luke 17:31, but neither evangelist has preserved the true context; Luke found the saying with the addition "remember Lot's wife," and that occasioned the context in which he placed it, while in Mark it disturbs the flow of thought in 13:17–18. Verses 19–20, unlike Mark 13:14, 17–18, relate to a general catastrophe which none can escape, not a Judean invasion from which one should fly; cf. the *pasa sarx* of v. 20. Verses 21–23 come from another context, for v. 24 harks back to vv. 19–20, while Luke gives the passage (in part) in the Q apocalypse (Luke 17:23). Mark 13:24–27 are allowed to remain; Luke 21:26a could well be inserted in the midst of Mark 13:25, while Luke 21:28 would well round off the passage. That Mark 13:28–29 comes from another source is shown in Luke's introductory clause *kai eipen parabolēn autois*, and in any case it does not suit the discourse. The softening of the fig tree's branches shows the kindly power of summer; a better parallel to the distresses that herald the kingdom would be the storms of spring! It is possible that this parable provides the answer to the disciples' question, v. 4; Jesus meant to say, "When you see the counterpart of this natural phenomenon happening in the realm of history, that is, the summer-like powers of the kingdom taking effect among humanity, then the temple and the covenant it symbolizes are *engys aphanismou*." These "summer-like powers" are the effects of the ministry of Jesus and the founding of the Christian church. Mark 13:32, on the other hand, comes from a context which speaks of the "day" of the Lord.[95] An incidental conclusion from the above analysis will be that "That presumed apocalypse breaks in one's hands when it is examined more closely."[96]

---

[95] Ibid., 27–39.
[96] Ibid., 33.

Not all this discussion carries equal conviction, but it is admittedly less arbitrary than Lohmeyer's analysis. Had Haupt been more reasonable in his application of this result, he would probably have gained an immediate following. In reality, his purpose in conducting this analysis was akin to that of Weisse who first propounded it, viz. to rid Jesus of a "materialistic" eschatology. The impossible interpretation of the Fig Tree parable, reproduced above, hints of what is in Haupt's mind.[97] He wishes to extend the parabolic method of Jesus' instruction to his eschatology. Insisting that it is impossible to express the supersensuous through sensuous, conceptual material, he maintains that Jesus did not attempt it; for the first time he reached the thought of the supernatural life in all its purity and in sharp distinction from everything relating to this world.[98] The only coming of which Jesus spoke is a continual coming; cf. Matt 18:20; 28:20. Inevitably this view provoked opposition among Haupt's contemporaries, and in rejecting his eschatology they rejected his criticism.[99]

F. C. Burkitt

F. C. Burkitt seems to have undergone a development in his views on the significance of our Lord's eschatology and of Mark 13 in particular. Not that he ever embraced the little apocalypse theory. "Both the general purport of the discourse and most of the single sayings seem to me, if I may venture to give an opinion, perfectly to harmonise with what we otherwise know of the teaching of Jesus." But the literary form is different from the rest of Mark; it was probably not a composition of his own. "The hypothesis that the eschatological discourse in Mark 13 once circulated, very much in its present form, as a separate fly-sheet, explains the allusion to 'him that readeth.' "[100] We gather that Burkitt at this time did not greatly desire to "read." "The hope of the Second Coming of the Son of Man has faded with us into an unsubstantial dream. We are not expecting a new heaven and new earth—at least, not in our time." Our best recourse is "to accept the Coming of Messiah upon the clouds of heaven to gather together his elect from every quarter as the natural picture, the natural way of expressing faith and

---

[97] Haupt went astray in trying to make the *tauta* of the application, v. 29, relate to something within the parable, an inexcusable procedure. Cf. Schwartzkopff: "Logically it is absolutely demanded to understand by 'this,' since it signifies the compared object, something other than that with which it is compared" (*Weissagungen*, 172).

[98] Haupt, *Aussagen*, 117ff.

[99] See Schwartzkopff, *Weissagungen*, 172–75; Titius, *Jesu Lehre*, 141–45.

[100] Burkitt, *The Gospel History and Its Transmission*, 3d ed. (Edinburgh, 1911; 1st ed. 1906), 63.

hope in the triumph of the good over evil, all that people mean nowadays by the vague word Progress."[101]

We hazard a guess that Burkitt, after writing this, was shaken not a little when reading Schweitzer. In another essay the emphasis is wholly changed. It is stressed that the modern doctrine of progress is the precise opposite of the convictions of the Gospels, and that that doctrine is less defensible than it used to be: "There are not wanting indications that our race, like the ruling race in the time of the Antonines, is beginning to get tired." While declining to enter upon apocalyptic prophecy on his own account, he urges, "If we really are confronted with disquieting signs of great and fundamental changes in the social and political system that has lasted so long, it is the Gospel above all things that can reassure us."[102] Burkitt had begun to "read!" Indeed, he had gone to another extreme. Believing the fundamental idea of apocalyptic to be the hope of a future kingdom of God, he writes: "Without the belief in the Good Time Coming I do not see how we can be Christians at all. The belief in the Good Time Coming as the most important thing in the world, and therewith the duty of preparing ourselves and our fellow-men to be ready as the first duty and privilege of humanity—this is the foundation of the Gospel."[103]

In an article published in 1929 Burkitt gave his maturest thoughts on the eschatological discourse. The setting of the discourse seems to him singularly appropriate. "What Mark puts down in Ch. 13 is in some of its main characteristics historical reminiscence and not literary invention."[104] This is so unlike the usual critical account that some explanation is required. "I regard Mk. 13.3–37 as a literary composition, the literary composition of the Evangelist. In it he has put together the Sayings of Jesus which he had about the future, just as in 4.2–32 he has put together his store of Galilean Parables. I do not think that Mk. 13.3–37, or the portions of it which are often called 'the Little Apocalypse,' ever had a separate literary existence before incorporation in the Gospel of Mark. Some of the single sayings may be genuine utterances of Jesus belonging to other occasions, others may be sayings never really said by Jesus."[105] To this last class the word about the "abomination" belongs, probably originating in the Caligula episode. "But I am

---

[101] Ibid., 179.

[102] Idem, "The Eschatological Idea in the Gospel," in *Essays on Some Biblical Questions of the Day by Members of the University of Cambridge*, ed. H. B. Swete (London, 1909), 208.

[103] Ibid., 209–10.

[104] Idem, "Jesus Christ, An Historical Outline," in *A History of Christianity in the Light of Modern Knowledge* (London, 1929). The article was reissued separately with additions in 1932; the citations are taken from the later edition, p. 49.

[105] Ibid.

not thinking of these details. What I have in mind is the difference in tone between Mark 13 and the Galilean gospel which began and ended with 'the kingdom of God is at hand.' The burden of Mark 13 is, 'Wait: do not be always imagining that the End is just coming. It will seem a long time to you, and you will have a hard time of it; but be firm and patient, and above all things be ready, and you will not lose your reward.' "[106]

Burkitt observes, "These ideas fit curiously well with what we might fancy to be in the mind of a Prophet who had come up to Jerusalem to hasten the coming of the kingdom of God—and it had not come! It is just in this interval, between the action of Jesus and the action of the chief priests, when Jesus had abandoned Jerusalem, that this new conviction, that the End was not so near after all, would show itself."[107] The background of this interpretation is the view that Jesus started with the belief that "the kingdom of God should immediately appear"; the Gospel story is the narration of how Jesus came to realize that the time was not yet ripe and that he must die at Jerusalem as the condition for the coming of the new age. "Jesus was fully persuaded that unless he did of his own initiative court failure and a violent death the new state of things, so ardently expected and longed for, would not arrive." There follow the famous words of Schweitzer about Jesus taking hold of the wheel of the world to end history and being crushed by it.[108]

It is clear, even without this quotation, that Burkitt has capitulated to Schweitzer, despite the modifications he has made in the latter's construction. In contrast to the advocates of the little apocalypse theory, Burkitt has accepted Mark 13 at the cost of giving up the relevance of the earlier eschatology of Jesus, a position as unsatisfactory as the other. It is extraordinary that it should be thought that Jesus had adopted this new view about the delay of the end during the last week of his life. What of the sayings like Matt 10:23 and Mark 9:1, which assume an interval between the death of Jesus and his parousia, the former also presuming a time of mission preaching for the disciples? What are we to make of the policy of Jesus in calling out and preparing for the building of the church, if no thought had been taken of an interval between his death and coming again? In this matter it very much looks as though this most careful and competent scholar had not exercised his gift of incisive thinking in his customary manner.[109]

---

[106]Ibid., 49–50.

[107]Ibid., 50.

[108]Ibid., 18, 37–38.

[109]The view that Mark 13 contains sayings uttered on more than one occasion appears also in Swete's commentary on the Apocalypse of John. David Smith, in *The Disciple's Commentary on the Gospels*, 390–91, makes the alternative suggestion that in Mark 13 we have only fragments of the discourse given

6. Approaches Toward a Synthesis

It will have become apparent that certain exegetes whose work we have considered combine more than one viewpoint in their interpretation of our discourse, although we have attempted to make clear their distinctive approach in each case. From about the year 1930, however, distinctions break down and a fair measure of agreement becomes manifest among the critics and theologians who reject the little apocalypse theory. It is more usually assumed than denied that Mark 13 is composed of related material, some at least of which is drawn from other occasions than the situation presumed in the chapter. Most incline to accept the shortened perspective of Jesus as a factor to be reckoned with, however it is to be explained. On that basis there is a tendency to believe that Jesus in some way associated the fall of Jerusalem with his parousia. It then becomes easier to read the discourse as a fairly straightforward prophecy, even if it is expanded by other elements, and it is often felt that the discourse offers aspects of things to come rather than an unveiling of the future in quasi–historical order. One is tempted to make a division of expositions and characterize them as theological and critical, but that would be unfair to the theologians and critics alike. Nevertheless, we have come to a period when scholars have become more interested in the teaching of our Gospels than in their analysis, and this is reflected in the treatment of Mark 13.

G. Gloege

We begin with a writer whose work on eschatology is generally considered to be of first importance, Gerhard Gloege.[110] Here we are confronted with a strictly theological treatment of our subject. Gloege does not once mention the little apocalypse, but his use of Mark 13 shows beyond doubt that he accepts the discourse as authentic teaching of Jesus. He approaches it from the angle of his fundamental belief that to Jesus "the conception of the sovereignty of God is thoroughly dynamic." God is central to his thinking, revealing himself as "the royally working world-will."[111] " 'God ruled, rules, and will rule.' That is the theme which perpetually sounds out in the most varied sayings-com-

---

on the Mount of Olives, the scattered nature of which inevitably has created difficulties for us which did not exist originally.

[110]The book by which Gloege is generally known is his *Reich Gottes und Kirche im Neuen Testament* (Gütersloh, 1929). The eschatological views expounded therein are conveniently summarized in a doctoral thesis published in the previous year, *Das Reich Gottes im Neuen Testament* (Borna-Leipzig, 1928).

[111]Idem, *Reich Gottes und Kirche*, 56, 57.

positions of Jesus."[112] Here is to be found the long-sought unity of present and futurist eschatology: "If the conception of God is set with deliberate decision in the center of the entire preaching, then that alternative in fact is surpassed and therewith antiquated; present and future completely concur on the ground of the NT view of the kingdom."[113] In the present the in-breaking of the future is already given; the future is only the working out of what is already begun in the present. "Neither is thinkable without the other, both moments are indissolubly bound with one another."[114]

With this clue in our hands, several characteristics of the eschatological discourse receive illumination. (1) The emphasis in the discourse falls on the final event, to which the whole leads. "The parousia itself is . . . introduced or prepared for through terrestrial-cosmic signs and catastrophes (Mark 13:5–37 par.) of such proportions, that all statements about it must be looked on as hints of an intervention of God far surpassing the forms of expression."[115] It is suggested that as the cloud at the ascension (Acts 1:9) signifies a veiling of the event, rather than a vehicle, so the description of the coming in the clouds denotes the "sudden becoming-again-unveiled" of the invisible Kurios. Any exact prediction is lacking.[116]

(2) No detailed description of preliminary signs is afforded. "Because the dynamic conception of God stands in the foreground and expresses itself in the unconditioned working of the Christ, Jesus' proclamation contains no particular information as to the individual stages of the powerful 'unconditioned' event." If the discourse be compared with Judaistic eschatology we see "a modest silence as to all that could excite human curiosity." And the same consideration applies to what follows the parousia. "It is a plain mark of the prophecy of Jesus, that it ends at that point when he makes himself visible again to the community."[117]

(3) The parousia is linked with the catastrophe falling upon Jerusalem, but not with the intention of affording a date for the disciples. This interrelation of historical catastrophe and the end of history is due to something more than the nature of prophecy, which pushes temporally separated events on and into one another; it is part of that "dynamic conception of the reign of God, which comprises present and future, historical and final event, and causes the end time to break in

---

[112]Idem, *Reich Gottes im Neuen Testament,* 11.
[113]Idem, *Reich Gottes und Kirche,* 109.
[114]Ibid., 110.
[115]Ibid., 178.
[116]Ibid., 190.
[117]Ibid. The last saying comes from Schlatter's *Die Geschichte des Christus* (Stuttgart, 1923), 469.

with the crucifixion and resurrection of Christ."[118] A most important principle is involved here, not explicitly brought out by Gloege: the present era is an eschatological present, wherein the reign of God is manifest not alone in sovereign blessing, but in the exercise of sovereign judgment. The judgments of God belong not only to the end; they belong to the administration of God throughout the entire period between the resurrection and parousia. Otherwise expressed, this era is necessarily characterized by signs; the manifestation will be more apparent at the end, because that is the time of a special unveiling of the invisible God. In the same way, the "eschatological" sufferings of the church, if we may so term them, belong to the whole period as well as to the end, and to the end more than to the rest of the era. The reign of God is one, but the climax, as the initiation, particularly manifests it.

H. D. Wendland

A not dissimilar outlook may be discerned in the work of H. D. Wendland. He also does not provide a critical discussion of the discourse of Mark 13, yet his unreserved use of it for our Lord's teaching on eschatology leaves no doubt as to his acceptance of its authenticity. Curiously enough, he always cites the discourse in its Matthean version, perhaps because he often wishes to allude to Matthew 25 together with Matthew 24. In Wendland's view it is necessary to recall that the idea of the consummation contains a "double polarity." It reveals final salvation and final judgment on the one hand, and it is personal and cosmic-universal on the other.[119] On the former antithesis Wendland does not dwell; Matt 25:46 is cited, but we have already seen how it has frequently been a matter of wonder that Mark 13 should contain no hint as to the lot of the reprobate. The second is more relevant to the discourse for it has bearing on the question of signs. "If Jesus had given up the forms of expression for the universal-cosmic eschatology, the pictures of the catastrophes affecting humankind and the universe (Matt 24:6–8, 29–30 = Mark 13:7–8, 24–26), then the universal horizon of the coming sovereignty of God would have been lost, to which the world is contrasted as a unity and to which it is subordinated as a unity, and it would have threatened the omnipotent character of the God who comes to us."[120]

If Jesus held to the character of the messianic office respecting humankind, he must have held also to this universal-eschatological

---

[118]Gloege, *Reich Gottes und Kirche* (Gütersloh, 1929), 191.

[119]Wendland, *Die Eschatologie des Reiches Gottes bei Jesus* (Gütersloh, 1931), 245.

[120]Ibid., 245–46. The last phrase, *Zu-uns-kommen Gott,* is a play on *Zukunft,* the term for the coming of Christ.

view; and he must have equally maintained the personal aspect, for the messianic community is gathered to him.

> This indivisible unity of personal and universal eschatology in equal absoluteness of conception denotes the dividing line over against a groundless apocalyptic speculation as to the form of the coming world and the appearance of God. It is characteristic that these two questions remain completely in the background in the discourse in Matthew. No single declaration as to the new world is given, and only the dealing of God himself. The personal-soteriological eschatology is the central thing. The abundance of related questions and conceptions of Jewish eschatology is and remains excluded. All expectation is directed to the ethical decision: the coming of the Messiah, the judgment and the gift of life.[121]

In this connection Wendland cites Lütgert: "Eschatology is only an object of the prophecy of Jesus insofar as it is the prophecy of redemption and should be a motive of behavior"; he adds, "In all these fundamental points the eschatology of Matthew 24 and 25 is completely one with the kingdom proclamation of Jesus."[122] Like Gloege, Wendland stresses the view of the church in the discourse. The apostolic commission is to gather the church, not to set up the kingdom. It is a work of preparation. The consummation takes place "when all peoples are gathered around the throne of the Son of man, the elect are brought together from all four quarters of the wind and the righteous go into life (Matt 24:31; 25:32, 46)."[123] The church of the present era must be distinguished from the perfected community of the discourse: "The former can only be a preparation of the latter, in the same sense as we have spoken of a beginning of the end time, a beginning of this end as the eschatological present. The kingdom of God gathers the people who belong to it through the word and work of Jesus and the disciples, but it only perfects the community through the judgment of the world."[124]

J. Mackinnon

J. Mackinnon rejected the little apocalypse theory on the basis of one consideration, generally neglected by critics: the discourse in the main echoes what Jesus had repeatedly taught in his instruction of the disciples, especially following upon Peter's confession at Caesarea Philippi.[125] From that time on Jesus dwells on the sufferings of the Son of man, the persecutions of his disciples, and the coming of the Son of

---

[121]Ibid., 246.
[122]Ibid., 247.
[123]Ibid., 160.
[124]Ibid., 161.
[125]Mackinnon, *The Historic Jesus* (London, New York, and Toronto, 1931), 193–94.

man in glory (Mark 8:31ff.). By an extraordinary coincidence the one monograph on Mark 13 written prior to the mid-twentieth century appeared not long after this book and announced as its major premise the similarity between Mark 8:34ff. and the discourse.

F. Busch

The volume issued by F. Busch has exercised considerable influence in Germany and must be given careful consideration. This author first lays down the affirmation that Mark 13 possesses a train of thought. The question of its originality and whether the individual sayings permit of being separated can be settled only if this prior fact is recognized. It is further to be acknowledged that "the evangelist, when he wrote down the discourse, must have seen in its connection an unambiguous sense, even if he had welded together ingredients that were originally diverse."[126] If we ask what this "train of thought" is, we are told that it "proceeds from the construction of the entire Gospel."[127] Peter's confession of Jesus' messiahship is closely connected with the first announcement of the passion, and with the transference of the proclamation of suffering to the disciples also. Following Jesus now means carrying a cross. Confession of his name and proclamation of the gospel amidst persecution are part of the renunciation of life which gains the life of the age to come. On this discipleship amidst suffering rests the issue of the judgment which takes place at the coming of the Son of man in glory (Mark 8:27–9:1). The same conception is to be seen in the conversations following the scene at Caesarea (9:30–32, 33–37; 10:32–34, 35–45): the Lord's proclamations of suffering are not isolated preparations of the passion story, but form a whole with the exhortations to the disciples; they, too, must drink the cup of suffering with Jesus (10:38).

Looking at Mark 13 from this angle, one will observe that the discourse beginning at v. 5 corresponds to the whole of the Gospel: "As truly as the confession of messiahship could not occur without proclamation of suffering, so little can the announcement of the parousia stand without developing the proclamation of suffering for the band of disciples. Mark 13 is an explication of Mark 8:34."[128] The chapter, coming as it does between Mark 8–12 and 14–15, is to be understood, like Luke 22 and John 14–16, as the "Farewell Discourse" of Jesus, not in a biographical-historical sense, but as "a factual construction which arranges in this place sayings relating to the significance of the cross

---

[126]Busch, *Verständnis*, 38–39. (The book was written several years before its publication.)
[127]Ibid., 39.
[128]Ibid., 48.

for the disciples who remain behind, and to the confession and suffering of the community."[129]

On this basis the section vv. 5–23 may be interpreted in the light of such a saying as John 16:33, "In the world you have *thlipsis*." "There is no question here of premonitory signs which can be objectively established as symptoms of the end. . . . Here are meant temptations, which rob the disciples of the patience required for 'watching.' "[130] Consequently the reference of v. 29, "Whenever you see these things happen . . ." is to the whole description of *thlipsis* in vv. 5–23, as v. 23 itself shows. Verses 28 and 30 speak of conditions which are daily fulfilled for the church since Easter and Pentecost. Clearly, then, the parousia passage, vv. 24–27, must be separated from the foregoing as something new: "after the tribulation" of v. 24 will answer the question as to "When." Matthew's *eutheōs* has nothing to do with the fall of Jerusalem. "In all that precedes and follows any calculation is refused, because the parousia comes in a flash, like lightning, surprising, contrary to expectation, in a sudden act, without a long drama such as Judaism knew. . . . The parousia and world-judgment take place without many stages and preliminary periods preceding the *thlipsis*, they come *eutheōs*" (i.e., speedily).[131]

Busch believes that the supreme motive of the little apocalypse theory is a weakened Christology. "The first presupposition for the grounding of that hypothesis is the construction of a Christ who in every respect was adapted to the colorless features of a century whose representatives must perpetually call the artless, magnificent view of Mark 13 'bizarre.' If this presupposition, this prejudice, is renounced, then all the reasons for the hypothesis tumble down."[132] By assuming that v. 4 does not fit 5 and that 30 and 32 contradict each other, 5–31 are removed as a disturbing interruption: "That is, one removes the roots from the tree and marvels then at its dryness!" No agreement exists as to where the little apocalypse begins, where it ends, and what lies between. But an even graver mistake is the low estimate of Jewish apocalyptic thought subsumed in this hypothesis. Schniewind is cited as saying, "We must free ourselves from the fancy that Jewish eschatology is a collection of absurdities."[133] Yet such an exegete as Wellhausen looses Jesus from the world of his day and even distances him from OT prophecy. "The thesis of the little apocalypse in this its root is false."[134]

---

[129]Ibid., 44.
[130]Ibid., 50.
[131]Ibid., 52.
[132]Ibid., 54.
[133]Ibid., 59. The quotation is from the introduction to A. Schneider's *Gesammelte Aufsätzen*, x.
[134]Busch, *Verständnis*, 59.

We must surely be grateful to Busch for calling our attention to the parallel between Mark 8:34–9:1 and the eschatological discourse: the association of the impending passion of Jesus, sufferings for disciples, and the heavenly kingdom that dawns with the parousia is fundamental to all that we know of the mind of our Lord in this closing period of his life. This remains, even if we admit that 8:34–9:1 is a compilation, for the context of the sayings, whatever the historical order of their utterance, must be the post-Caesarea period. It is probably healthy, too, to link the thought of the disciples' sufferings with those of the world in Mark 13, since they together characterize the period between the resurrection and the parousia. Nevertheless, we are not convinced that it is a just reading of Mark 13 to deny that vv. 5–23 partake of the nature of "signs" of the end. The endeavor to do so leads to the virtual interpretation of Matthew's *eutheōs* as "suddenly," a procedure which is not open to us, while it makes impossible Mark's *en ekeinais tais hēmerais.* If these expressions be regarded as interpolations of the evangelists or their sources, at least it must be postulated that they regarded Mark 13:5–23 as signs of the end; yet part of Busch's thesis lies in the appeal to take seriously the interpretation placed by Mark on the sayings! We shall probably pursue a sounder course if we regard the "signs" of ch. 13 as relating to the eschatological present, and to the end in particular. The denial of either aspect is of doubtful validity.

C. C. Torrey

Our study is not without its lighter moments, as when one contrasts the attitudes toward the little apocalypse theory on the part of such critics as Holtzmann ("Few hypotheses have proved so unavoidable") and Muirhead ("If certainty belongs to any literary theory in the Gospels it may be claimed for this") with that of C. C. Torrey ("No scientific basis for it exists!"). Never has Mark 13 been dealt with so trenchantly and confidently as by the last-named critic, perhaps because the issues had simmered in his mind for so long a time. Torrey's views on the little apocalypse were known as long ago as 1925 through B. W. Bacon, who modified them for his own purpose.[135] They were incidentally referred to in Torrey's *The Four Gospels,*[136] but not until the publication of his *Documents of the Primitive Church* in 1941 did he give a full-scale treatment of the chapter, at which time it was difficult for British scholars to procure the book owing to the progress of the war.

---

[135]In *The Gospel of Mark: Its Composition and Date,* Bacon referred to unpublished communications given by Torrey to the Society of Biblical Literature in 1919 and elsewhere.

[136]Torrey, *The Four Gospels* (London, 1933), especially 261–62.

Torrey is always emphatic, but the explosiveness of a lifetime's indignation comes to expression in this article. He first endeavors to demonstrate that Mark 13 is not an apocalypse at all. Referring to the expression "little apocalypse" he writes, "The use of this term applied to some part of the eschatological discourse contained in Mark 13 and its parallels is one of the *curiosa* of Synoptic criticism."[137] Technically, the word *apokalypsis* does not cover any or every statement of eschatological beliefs; it is a literary term connoting certain characteristic features of a well-defined type of writing. An apocalypse purports to contain a direct revelation of truths or coming events, disclosed by God through a vision or dream, usually by the mediation of angels, occasionally by the voice of the Most High himself. By the very nature of the scene and its accessories an atmosphere of mystery is created. "In the thirteenth chapter of Mark there is no indication of any special revelation, no mystery in the language (except in v. 14), none of the characteristic apparatus of the vision, nothing even to suggest knowledge received from heaven for the purpose in hand. Whatever may be thought of the material of the chapter, or conjectured as to its composition, there is nothing in any part of it that can justify the use of the term 'apocalyptic.' "[138] It should be noted that the features characteristic of apocalyptic literature in Mark 13 enumerated by Colani all derive from half a verse—the abomination passage. Of that there is more to be said.

Torrey rightly challenges Moffatt's characterization of the little apocalypse as "an intelligible unity": "No one ever reconstructed the supposed apocalypse, or succeeded in exhibiting anything else than a mere fragment. And this most impressive body of early Christian prediction is 'an intelligible unity' only when it stands in the place which it now occupies, as an integral part of the great discourse. Without such a framework as this it is perfectly incomprehensible. It would be necessary to suppose another chapter, exactly like Ch. 13, from which this great section was transferred!"[139] This assertion, of course, proceeds on the assumption that the little apocalypse is incomplete. It will be recalled that several critics realized its inadequacy as a document; that which Charles postulated in his commentary on Revelation comes very near what Torrey regards as the reductio ad absurdum of the theory. It is further maintained that the method of excising a coherent passage from a text, as Colani did, is fundamentally false. "If any and every passage which can be excised from a document without leaving an obvious gap is therefore liable to be pronounced an interpolation, there is an end of sane criticism of authorship and composition."

---

[137]Idem, *Documents of the Primitive Church* (New York and London, 1941), 13.
[138]Ibid., 14–15.
[139]Ibid., 16.

Consequently Torrey makes bold to affirm, "No scientific basis exists for supposing Mark 13 to have been expanded by interpolation after it left the hands of the Evangelist, nor for regarding the great discourse as anything else than an original unity. . . . Every portion of this material is needed in its present place, no word of it could be omitted."[140]

This last sentence introduces us to Torrey's own reading of the chapter. The background presumed is that of OT prophecy. There was an outline of events of the end familiar to all Jews through their reading of the prophets; a hostile army is to capture Jerusalem, and half of its inhabitants will be transported (Zech 14:2); tribulations will follow for "a time, times, and a half" (Dan 12:7); this interval will witness great missionary activity, to Israel and all the world, that scriptures like Isa 45:14; 49:22–23; 66:19–20 may be fulfilled; a final onslaught on Jerusalem will occur, accompanied by portents in heaven (Joel 2:30–31; 3:4) and the coming of the Messiah (Dan 7:13–14), but by the hand of Yahweh Israel's enemies will be destroyed (Isa 41:12; 45:1; Hab 3:13). This background will have been in the disciples' minds when they asked, "When will these things be?" They did not want new information; they simply wished to know how it could be realized that the day is near and how long they had to wait. The request is partly answered, partly denied. Jesus confirms the program of the prophets and applies it in many details, but declines to fix a date.

The only element in the discourse that is unsuitable to Jesus is Mark 13:14a; this is due to the Caligula episode. If Jesus accepted the prophetic program of the end, he will have uttered the prediction given in Luke 21:20–21, but we must have sympathy with the situation of the earliest believers.

> To the already numerous Christian communities in Judea and Galilee it is easy to see what the events of the years 39 and 40 and especially the edict of Caligula must have meant. Here at last was the realisation of their great hope and the triumph of their faith. . . . The Nazarenes saw before their eyes not merely the royal blasphemer desecrating the sanctuary, but the very thing, the "Abomination bringing Devastation," foretold as the beginning of the mysteriously numbered "days" or "times" which must elapse before the coming of the Messiah in the clouds of heaven. If ever in the world fulfilment of prophecy was recognised with certainty, this was the time. When all the circumstances are taken into account, it would be difficult to find in history, with all its astonishing coincidences, anything to match this instance.[141]

Jesus had given the indefinite sign from Zechariah about the surrounding of Jerusalem by armies. Mark, followed by Matthew, was impelled to insert the far more definite sign, the erection of Caligula's

140 Ibid., 17.
141 Ibid., 33.

statue on the altar in the temple. "Should not the fulfilment of Daniel's prophecy be mentioned? This must have seemed most important, for every reason. The evangelist gives a plain hint that he is editing: Jesus did not say to Peter, James, John and Andrew, 'Let him who reads understand!' "[142] This event, therefore, occasioned not the writing of the eschatological discourse but its modification in the one point of the great sign. The Gospel of Mark was compiled for the purpose of evangelism and issued immediately—in Aramaic for Jews and in a Greek translation for Gentiles. When the expected clash was averted the work of evangelization was postponed.

It may be freely admitted that this is the most persuasive presentation of the case for the influence of the Caligula affair on Mark 13 that we have read. The distinction so plainly drawn between prophecy and apocalyptic, as it affects this chapter, can be overlooked by no one. The criticisms of the little apocalypse theory have no small weight. Yet the major premise of Torrey's view leaves us with grave doubts: it presumes an interpretation of OT prophecy which has to be read into Mark 13; it is not there on the surface, and we are not at all sure that it reflects our Lord's usual manner of dealing with the OT. This is illustrated by Torrey's interpretation of Mark 13:2, which closely follows that of Johannes Weiss: "The conception of 'new heavens and new earth' meant either a totally different world or at least the present world greatly changed in its physical features. Earthquakes will shatter and refashion it, Is. 13:13, 24:19f. Mic. 1:4 . . . Jerusalem and the temple hill in particular will have a new form, Is. 2:2, Joel 4:18, Zech. 14:8, Ezk. 47:1f. . . . This, of course, involved the wiping out of the present city of Jerusalem, and could have nothing to do with the impending conquest by the Romans."[143] We cannot dogmatically affirm that Jesus did not hold this belief, but at least it will be granted that it reads a great deal into the language of Mark 13:2, more than we are warranted in doing. Torrey has viewed the whole discourse in similar light.

We must urge, as we have done before, that Mark 13 is silent about any blotting out of multitudes in Jerusalem, and where silence is maintained we are not at liberty to fill in according to our own ideas as to the mind of the Author. In particular, this interpretation depends on the assumption that Luke's version is more original than Mark's as concerning the fate of Jerusalem: it is maintained that Luke 21:20 is less definite than Mark 13:14. On the contrary, most exegetes have felt that Luke 21:20 is more definite than Mark 13:14 and bears marks of interpretation—whether innocent or otherwise is irrelevant for the moment. Our last word on this cannot be said without a detailed

---

[142]Ibid., 35.
[143]Ibid., 20.

consideration of Mark 13:14, but meanwhile we have to admit that Torrey's interpretation in this respect is questionable.

C. J. Cadoux

The careful and exhaustive study of our Lord's eschatological teaching by C. J. Cadoux appeared in the same year as Torrey's work. The measure of agreement between the two scholars is surprising, although their approaches differed widely. Cadoux did not find it easy to imagine how Mark, writing at Rome, either could or would have incorporated in his book "an alien document produced (ex hypothesi) in Judea, possibly within a few years of the time at which he himself was writing." Neither was it plausible to imagine that the document was embodied in the Gospel after Mark had finished it. The parallels with the little apocalypse in other Gospel passages have also to be taken into account. "It seems on the whole preferable to explain such discrepancies as the chapter contains partly by the natural tendency of Mark (as of the other evangelists) to put in close proximity to one another sayings originally spoken on different occasions, and partly to the tendency of the early Church to modify radically certain remembered sayings of Jesus and even to ascribe to him (without any dishonest intent) some sayings which in point of fact he never actually uttered."[144] Although Cadoux recognized the latter possibility, in practice he scarcely appealed to it in individual statements of the chapter. He admitted that critical uncertainty as to the origin and relation of the contents of Mark 13 makes its use difficult; nevertheless, he employed it in constructing our Lord's eschatological teaching in the conviction that "on the main point, its evidence is in line with that which is abundantly provided elsewhere."[145]

A possible modification of the original utterance is seen in Mark 13:14, where Luke may be following a more authentic tradition; if otherwise, Luke in any case "is only making explicit what Mark expresses less concretely, and his operations cannot rightly be taken as discrediting his reports when no Markan parallel is in question."[146] As against Streeter's view that Mark was referring in 13:14 to the temple's desecration by antichrist, rather than its destruction in AD 70, Cadoux asks whether Mark would clearly distinguish between the two calamities if he was writing before AD 70. The persecution of disciples was a natural expectation for Jesus to hold, both in view of his own experience and the description of the sufferings of the saints in Daniel's vision of the Son of man.[147] Such a persecution, as he probably foresaw, was

---

[144]Cadoux, *The Historic Mission of Jesus* (London, 1941), 11–12.
[145]Ibid., 292.
[146]Ibid., 275 n. 3.
[147]Ibid., 101, 302ff.

to become the opportunity for wider missionary activity. While it is doubtful whether Jesus placed the fall of Jerusalem and his advent in such close temporal proximity as we see them in the discourse, "In the nature of things, we should expect some positive and definite relationship to have existed between the two anticipations, seeing that both arose out of Jesus' certainty that his enemies would encompass his death, and both were expected to materialise before the generation then living had died out."[148] Even the element of privacy in the instruction of the disciples by Jesus fits in with the consistent phenomenon that almost all the Son of man sayings concern Christ's redemptive mission and were spoken to the disciples, not to the public.[149] On the whole we feel that C. J. Cadoux had no great quarrel with Mark 13 as a representation of the teaching of Jesus.

H. H. Rowley

H. H. Rowley provided a valuable discussion on Mark 13 in his review of Jewish and Christian apocalyptic literature. He approached the problems of the chapter from the angle of the phenomena of apocalypse generally. For example, he viewed the question of authenticity in the light of the pseudonymity adopted in almost all these writings: "If it [the discourse] does not really represent the teaching of Jesus, then it shares the pseudonymous character of so much apocalyptic work, while if it does represent His teaching, we have here at last a clear breach with that tradition."[150] The discourse is not to be refused on account of the element of secrecy, since this feature is characteristic of apocalyptic, and does not necessarily entail the authenticity of its contents.[151] The unity of the chapter is to be viewed in a similar light, for apocalyptic writings are notoriously inharmonious, a fact which has often led to complicated analyses where they are not required: "It seems wiser to recognize that the strictly logical integration of the elements into a whole is not characteristic of apocalyptic, and is not to be sought here."[152] Rowley therefore concludes: "I find no reason to deny that most of the material of this chapter consists of genuine utterances of Jesus, and if we had these utterances in their original setting, the transitions might be less baffling. Even the linking together of the fall of Jerusalem and the end of the age may be due to Him, who expressly disclaimed omniscience on the matter."[153] It is precisely this confessed limitation of knowledge which distinguishes the discourse from apoca-

---

[148]Ibid., 318.
[149]Ibid., 96–97.
[150]Rowley, *The Relevance of Apocalyptic* (London, 1944), 109–10.
[151]Ibid., 110 n. 1.
[152]Ibid., 138.
[153]Ibid., 139.

lypses generally; for while Daniel endeavored to indicate the time of the end exactly, Jesus declared that it was unknown to him.

It will be noted that Rowley did not commit himself to accept the chapter as authentic in every respect. He found one clear exception to the general reliability of the discourse in the abomination passage, Mark 13:14. That verse must be relegated to a later age since it relates to the fears inspired by the Caligula episode. Like B. W. Bacon, Rowley found it difficult to believe that Jesus could foresee that Caligula would command his statue to be placed in the temple, but not foresee that it would not happen. Nevertheless, insofar as the discourse contains the utterance of Jesus, "it may be understood to proclaim His certainty that a time of dire tribulation for Jerusalem lay in the not distant future, that a time of bitter persecution for His followers was before them, and that the glorious kingdom to which the Book of Daniel had looked forward was to come with divine power. He believed these things to be associated with one another, but expressly disclaimed any precise knowledge."[154]

It would be difficult to find a more striking illustration of the recent change of attitude to Mark 13 than this defense of its essential authenticity on the basis of its relation to Jewish apocalyptic. The similarities and divergencies alike shed light on its problems and are believed to ease them rather than increase them. The interpretation of the abomination of desolation may be found to be questionable, for we have already seen reason to believe that the connection with Caligula may not be so strong as was formerly thought, but to that we shall return later. Meanwhile we note the positive contribution to our study that we have found here.

A. Schlatter

Adolf Schlatter evidently regarded the discourse as an original unity, delivered on one occasion, though perhaps not retained in its completeness. The destruction of the temple, and of Israel, is linked with an end as "a real member in the judgments of God which precede his kingdom." The two events concerning Jerusalem and the world are not to be confounded, however; there is a clear distinction between them in the discourse: "He does not come at the destruction of Jerusalem, nor to bring the time of distress upon Israel. He does not appear as avenger of the sins committed against him. Their consequence must certainly be manifested, but that belongs to the course of earthly history and precedes his coming. Only after the time when Israel is trodden down does he put his appearing, but at the same time after it."[155]

---

[154]Ibid., 113.
[155]Schlatter, *Das Evangelium nach Matthäus*, 354.

The nature of the signs of this chapter is hinted at in the parable of the Fig Tree: whereas the disciples wanted an external definition, a calendar date, Jesus speaks on a different plane. "He makes them consider that the course of history has its inner conditions. . . . They should not wish to define Jesus' coming with outward calculations, but pay attention to what God's providential rule creates before their eyes."[156] Herein is given a clue for the time perspective of the chapter. Jesus had taken conjointly the disciples' lifetime with that of the world, for he was considering not them alone but the entire community that was to be. "Those, however, whom Jesus has strengthened with the word, that this generation will experience all this, assuredly do not lament that Jesus' word has deceived them . . . God's providential rule is the sole true exposition for every prophecy, even for those of Jesus."[157] Such a conclusion is in line with much else that we have considered, and indicates perhaps the direction in which a right solution of this problem is to be found.

O. Cullmann

Oscar Cullmann apparently takes for granted the authenticity of the eschatological discourse. His use of it and discussion of its problems are confined to the same two points of the nearness of the end and the nature of the signs.[158] The preaching of the proximity of the kingdom indicates that this nearness is bound up with Christ himself, with his person and action. If the kingdom is near, it is because it has been brought near (ēngiken, Mark 1:15). The announcement of the nearness of the end, therefore, affects the nature of the present rather than the future. Its special insistence toward the close of the ministry of Jesus points to a relationship with his prospective death. Cullmann affirms, "The essential element in the proximity of the kingdom is not the final date, but rather the certitude that the expiatory work of Christ on the cross constitutes the decisive event in the approach of the kingdom of God."[159] In that case the entire time which elapses after the death and resurrection is the time of the end, and this conclusion cannot be affected by the delay of the parousia. It inevitably affects our reading of the signs of the end of which Mark 13 speaks so much: "Because the present time, admittedly extended over many generations, constitutes an eschatological unity, all these signs, which will be produced at the extreme limit of the present, belong already to the last phase in which

---

[156]Ibid., 361.

[157]Ibid., 363.

[158]See Cullmann, *Le Retour du Christ* (Neuchâtel, 1948), 22ff.; idem, *Christ and Time* (ET 1951), 84ff.

[159]Idem, *Retour*, 27.

we find ourselves since the resurrection of Christ."[160] That is, since signs characterize the time of the end, they characterize the whole of this present era, for the whole is eschatological. Events which before Christ might have been deemed of no significance take on a new value; "they bind together faith in the present and that in the future, without wishing to create opportunity for an illegitimate calculation."[161] In this way the preaching of the gospel to pagans becomes significant of the end; in each generation it is announced by the church as a sign of the end which approaches.

P. Althaus

In his most impressive treatment of eschatology, Paul Althaus declined to discuss the critical questions raised in our discourse. "It has been desired to deny this 'little apocalypse' to Jesus, the community is said to have taken it over from Judaism. But this distinction between Jesus and the first community, even if it were surer than it is, could have no significance theologically, i.e., for the comprehension of the primitive Christian gospel."[162] Presumably Althaus trusted the primitive community to have handed on the teaching in the discourse reasonably well, for he used it without qualification in his subsequent review of our Lord's eschatology. He believed that it is not possible to remove apocalyptic features from the tradition of Jesus' teaching, yet they acquire therein a different aspect from what we see in Jewish apocalyptic. "Despite its apocalyptic features, Jesus' eschatological message in its fundamental points is completely unapocalyptic. The decisive thing is not what Jesus takes over from the apocalyptic material of Judaism, but the particular character of his eschatological message, which gives to everything a quite other tone." The peculiar characteristics in mind are the emphasis on the nearness of the end, and the attitude toward signs.

> Everything apocalyptic in Jesus, and then in Paul, remains wholly in the bounds of the near expectation. It is true that Judaism also, in the succession of prophetism, in general expected the great turning point to be quite near. But the near expectation gains an earnestness unheard-of in Judaism in the case of Jesus and primitive Christianity: "This generation will not pass . . ." (Mark 13:30). Therewith all eschatological utterances gain the highest actuality. They give no plan of the coming end-history; they prepare the living for the magnitude of the distress, the severity of the temptation. The stress lies alone on this preparation, not on a theoretical picture of the coming course of the world.[163]

---

[160]Ibid., 30.
[161]Ibid., 31.
[162]Althaus, *Die Letzten Dinge,* 5th ed. (Gütersloh, 1949), 271.
[163]Ibid.

The aspect under which "signs" are viewed brings home a similar lesson: the community must observe signs of the times (Mark 13:28f.), yet the end cannot be reckoned from such signs; it comes with incalculable suddenness (Luke 17:20ff.); it has portents, but only the Father knows when it comes (Mark 13:32); believers must watch for signs, yet be prepared for it at every moment (Mark 13:35). "Hence the near expectation is no dogma. It is limited through the secret of the Father, it stands under the precondition of his free decision. The livingness of God is above all portents. Alongside the predominating near expectation, therefore, the possibility can also be considered that the end will yet be protracted."[164] This is why the primitive church was able to surmount the lack of fulfillment of the hope of the immediate nearness of the end without shock: "They were not so sunk in the near expectation that they did not recognize at all times in respect of it the living God and the decisiveness of his freedom."[165] It is because of this stress on the "actuality" of the various elements of our Lord's teaching on the end that Althaus makes the startling assertion: "Eschatology must refuse to treat of the last epoch of history."[166] As a definition of the limits of eschatology that is extreme, but as a corrective to point us to the ethical intention of Christian teaching on the end it is salutary.

J. Schniewind

A similar view to that of Althaus is expressed in the commentaries of Julius Schniewind. He approached in the same way the question whether it is possible or necessary to distinguish a Jewish apocalypse within Mark 13. "It is more probable that the same thing applies here as in everything hitherto: a rich possession of Jewish hope is presupposed in the Gospel tradition, but it receives a new determination from Jesus. And the question which then arises, whether Jesus himself speaks here or his earliest community is not otherwise resolved as in former cases: each single word has such a stamp as is only possible from the reality 'Jesus,' and therewith the question of 'genuineness' becomes a question of secondary importance."[167] In practice Schniewind sought to show the "Jesus" stamp on the contents of the discourse by noting sayings in other strata of the Gospel tradition parallel to those of Mark 13; while therefore the above statement could have been equally made by a scholar like Lightfoot, who hesitated to draw a line between what comes from Jesus and what comes from the community, in the case of

---

[164] Ibid., 272.
[165] Ibid.
[166] Ibid., 296.
[167] Schniewind, *Das Evangelium nach Markus,* 5th ed., NTD (Göttingen, 1949), 166.

Schniewind it is consonant with an attitude of practical acceptance of the authenticity of the discourse. He recognized that the chapter is as little unified as Mark 4, and that therefore each saying has to be investigated on its own merits. From that an important conclusion is to be drawn in regard to the discourse: "There is no question of looking on it as a program of future individual events in their necessary sequence; rather something fundamental, something typical, is said about the events of the world's end, and it will generally be seen that with that a comprehension and estimation of these sayings is immediately given."[168] Like Althaus, Schniewind recognizes the presence in Jesus of the expectation of signs together with the hope of a speedy end; his reconciliation of them is fundamentally the same: "Both correspond to the fact that the end solely depends on God's plan. He causes the times, and what happens in them, to be developed and fulfilled; and he alone knows the time and season."[169]

K. H. Rengstorf, P. Feine, J. Behm, and J. Schmid

As examples of the all but complete victory gained among the more cautious critical scholars by the view that Mark 13 is a compilation of sayings, we may note that it is advocated by K. H. Rengstorf in his commentary on Luke, P. Feine and J. Behm in their introduction to the NT, and the Roman Catholic scholar Josef Schmid in his commentary on Mark.[170] The views of the last-named writer are interesting as showing how modern opinions on Mark 13 are reflected in the Roman Church as elsewhere. But while it is recognized that the question of the disciples shows that they had in mind both the destruction of the temple and the end of the age, it is not admitted that Jesus held the same view. The discourse is divided into general warnings (vv. 5–13), the judgment on Jerusalem (vv. 14–23, 30), the parousia and the end of the world (vv. 24–27, 32), with exhortations to the disciples (vv. 33–37), and an assurance as to the truth of Christ's words (v. 31). The Holy See could not complain about that analysis.

---

[168]Ibid.

[169]Idem, *Das Evangelium nach Matthäus*, 5th ed., NTD (Göttingen, 1950), 239.

[170]Rengstorf, *Das Evangelium nach Lukas*, 5th ed., NTD (Göttingen, 1949); Feine and Behm, *Einleitung in das neue Testament* (Heidelberg, 1950); Schmid, *Das Evangelium nach Markus* (1950). A further revision of the Feine-Behm *Introduction to the New Testament* was undertaken by W. G. Kümmel, published in 1963 (Heidelberg), ET 1966, revised 1973 (Nashville). No discussion of Mark 13 is contained in Kümmel's revision, but his publications show his adherence to the view that the discourse is a compilation of sayings without a ready-made apocalypse. See pp. 101–2.

Lest we be allowed to conclude this section of the review on an optimistic note, providence has decreed that we should be called on to deal with a puzzle—Austin Farrer's *A Study in St. Mark* (London, 1951). The perspective of the study, insofar as it affects Mark 13, is declared to be that of "Christ and his disciples, and St. Mark in the Holy Ghost."[171] It is insisted that the first is to be taken seriously. The prophecy is authentic, being presupposed in 1 and 2 Thessalonians. "Christ proclaimed himself Son of Man, and supported the prophecy of his advent with that context in which Daniel has set it. According to Daniel, to be the Son of Man is to be supplanter of Antichrist. The roles are inseparable. Christ made no special apocalyptic predictions. He simply affirmed the old prophetic images as they stood, and left the decoding of them to the action of God in future events."[172] The purpose of this discourse, with its "shadowy mysteries," its "painted pictures on the clouds of prophecy," was to set out the relation between Christ's passion and the end, and to show that "the destiny of the Church was the reenactment of his passion and resurrection."[173] It will be recalled that R. H. Lightfoot had treated of the relation between the eschatological discourse and the passion narrative; in his view the latter was represented as in some sense a prior fulfillment of the former, so that the passion is regarded as an eschatological event. Farrer's contention works in the reverse direction: the discourse is a type of the passion, the tyranny of antichrist sets forth the historic sufferings of the Messiah. No doubt this appears to be topsy-turvy, but, it is pointed out:

> In the history of our faith, the image of Antichrist came first and the passion of Christ came afterwards. Long before Israel had heard of a suffering Messiah it had been accepted that Israel would go through great sufferings, a sort of national martyrdom, before the glorious days of Messiah come. The prophecy of Daniel is largely devoted to such a theme, and it is the prophecy of Daniel which gives its decisive shape to Christ's prediction on the Mount of Olives. When Christ began to speak of the sufferings of the Son of Man he appeared to be talking not of what Caiaphas or Pilate did, for they had not yet done it, but about the figures of prophecy. He was saying that the Messiah would be first in the sufferings, as he would be first in the deliverance of Israel. From the point of view of Jesus before his death it was more natural to think of his sufferings as a summing-up of those which his church would meet in the end time than to think of the latter as a second "Calvary." That is the same thing as saying that "the images foreshadowing the tyranny of Antichrist were once the natural images of Christ's passion."[174]

---

[171]Farrer, *A Study in St. Mark* (1951), 361.
[172]Ibid.
[173]Ibid.
[174]Ibid.

In what ways does the discourse foreshadow the passion? The following are noted: (1) Mark's story of the death of Jesus runs from the Wednesday evening when Judas betrayed him till the Sunday morning of the resurrection, i.e., three and a half days! The sufferings of Jesus epitomize the future sufferings of his church. (2) This "apocalyptic half-week" ends with the empty tomb; the discourse ends with the appearance of the Son of man; the silence of the evangelist on the joy of the resurrection appearances is matched by the silence of Jesus concerning the resurrection of the church, the judgment, the consummated kingdom, etc. "The apocalyptic prediction breaks off at the same point as the Gospel does, that is, with the end of the half-week." (3) The last words of the discourse seem to draw a parallel between the disciples facing the imminence of Christ's passion and Christians facing the imminence of antichrist's persecution: "What I say unto you, I say unto all, Watch." (4) The events preceding the passion reflect the conceptions of the discourse:

> On Wednesday evening betrayal, the desolating abomination, was set up in the true and spiritual temple of Christ's company. On Thursday at midnight the Eleven saw it standing where it ought not, within the very garden of Christ's prayer. "When ye see the abomination stand where he ought not," Christ had said, "then let them that are in Judea flee to the mountains, . . . and let not him that is in the field turn back to fetch his coat." When the disciples saw the abomination they were in the field, and they fled fast enough. And one of them, a young man, feeling the hands of the enemy upon his coat, left it to them, and fled without it. . . . The young man puts off his sindon and escapes alive. Christ is destined at this season to wear his sindon alone. The Arimathaean wraps him in it: it is his shroud.[175]

So much for the relation of passion and apocalyptic. What of the precedents of the discourse? Farrer had said at the beginning of his discussion on Mark 13 that its authenticity is demonstrated if he can show that it "results from the imaginative process which produced the whole book, that it builds on what precedes and is built into what follows, and that is the very stuff of the author's mind."[176] We have seen in what manner the discourse is "built into what follows"; we must now look at the material on which it is built. The relevant section of Mark is the parabolic discourse of 3:20–4:34. Farrer's contention is, "The evangelist started with the Lord's predictive utterances in mind, shaped as they were in Danielic figures, and passing over the parabolic discourses in 3:20–4:34 took from them such points as could be applied to the matter of Christ's predictions."[177] Compare, e.g., 3:22–26 with 13:8:

175Ibid., 141.
176Ibid., 261.
177Ibid., 165.

"His disciples will live to see ungodly power rising against itself, nation against nation, and kingship against kingship. They might well think that this is the end (v. 26), but it is not, it is only the beginning-pains of the world's travail." Mark 3:28–30 speak of resistance to and blasphemy against the Holy Spirit by opponents of the gospel; 13:9–11 tell of the inspiration the Holy Spirit will give to the disciples facing opponents of the gospel. Mark 3:31–35 narrate a family division; 13:12–13 predict a more terrible condition of the same. In 4:1–20 (especially vv. 16–17) we read of those who break down through oppression and persecution, 13:13–20 describe antichrist's oppression. Mark 4:26–29 speak of one harvest, 13:24–27 another. Mark 4:35–41 tell of a time when Jesus slept and the disciples were awake, fretfully; 13:32–37 reveal a time when it will be right to keep watch and awake. It will thus be seen that the topics of the parabolic discourse are taken up into the eschatological discourse, so that they have one set of applications to the present and another to the future. "Because both sets of applications can be made, it is possible to compose an apocalyptic discourse by running over the topics of the parabolic discourses with the pattern of Christ's prophetic doctrine in one's head."[178]

If this be a true account of the origin of Mark 13, then the "imaginative process" by which it came into being certainly needed the Holy Ghost to bring it through. To us it seems more ingenious than convincing. The exposition of the discourse in relation to the passion is too allegorical to be possible; the last point in particular would have made even Origen uneasy. The comparisons between the parabolic discourse and Mark 13 admittedly contain some striking features, but they are insufficient to demonstrate the desired thesis.

Insofar as Mark 3:20ff. and Mark 13 speak of antagonism between the Christ and the forces of evil, there is bound to be some coincidence of topic and even of language. In lesser measure the same will apply to the narrative of the passion, except that here perhaps we have more justification for seeing a general parallel; the Son of man in Daniel 7 suffers tribulation, it is echoed in Mark 13, and the supreme instance of it is described in Mark 14–16. It may be true that the eschatological discourse and the passion illuminate each other, but it is going beyond the evidence to make either the exposition of the other.

---

[178]Ibid., 167.

5

CONTRIBUTIONS SINCE THE RISE OF REDACTION CRITICISM

IT IS DIFFICULT TO GET A PRECISE DATE FOR THE RISE of redaction criticism of the Gospels. Schlatter's emphasis on the church of Matthew, manifest in his commentary on the Gospel of Matthew, has been seen as an anticipation of the method.[1] R. H. Lightfoot's *History and Interpretation in the Gospel,* reproducing the Bampton Lectures of 1934, is an early example of preoccupation with the theology of an evangelist and its effect upon his Gospel (primarily that of Mark). The method became explicit in the work of Bornkamm about the year 1950, and in that of Marxsen and Conzelmann a little later in that decade.[2] Thereafter, mounting interest in the "third *Sitz im Leben*" became manifest in writings on the Gospels.[3] In the early part of the period the transition to the newer mode of approach was gradual: in some writers

---

[1] See J. Rohde, *Rediscovering the Teaching of the Evangelists* (London, 1968), 42–46.

[2] See Bornkamm, "Die Sturmstillung im Matthäusevangelium," in *Wort und Dienst,* Jahrbuch der Theologischen Schule Bethel, NT 1 (1948), 49ff.; ET in *Tradition and Interpretation in Matthew* (1963); idem, "Matthäus als Interpret der Herrenworte," *TLZ* 79 (1954): 341ff.; idem, "Enderwartung und Kirche im Matthäusevangelium," in *The Background of the New Testament and Its Eschatology,* Festschrift C. H. Dodd, ed. W. D. Davies and D. Daube (Cambridge, 1956), 222–23; W. Marxsen, *Der Evangelist Markus* (Göttingen, 1956; ET *Mark the Evangelist* [Nashville, 1969]); H. Conzelmann, *Die Mitte der Zeit* (Tübingen, 1953; ET *The Theology of St. Luke* [London, 1960]).

[3] The third *Sitz im Leben* is Marxsen's characterization of the evangelist's frame of reference set in relation to the church he served; this is in contrast to the unique situation of the ministry of Jesus (the first *Sitz im Leben*) and the situation of the primitive church (the second *Sitz im Leben*), which was the prime concern of the form critics.

it is not manifest at all; in others it is beginning to become operative; and in yet others it is explicit. Somewhat arbitrarily we shall place some essays on the eschatological discourse under the rubric on transitional critical treatment of the discourse; others will be recognized as plainly exemplifying redaction-critical approaches to it; some contributions from more traditional positions will then be reviewed, after which monographs on the discourse will be considered, and finally the treatment of the discourse in the commentaries on Mark will be examined.

1. Transitional Critical Treatment of the Eschatological Discourse

G. Harder

A careful discussion of the discourse along the older critical lines was penned by G. Harder the same year that I wrote *Jesus and the Future* (1952, published 1954). Harder begins his review by observing that Mark 13 is presented as a secret revelation to four disciples; in the context of the Gospel this hints of the appearance of prophecy in connection with the apostolic kerygma; Mark recognizes that the discourse is post-Easter.[4] The discourse is composed of sections of late Jewish apocalyptic (at least vv. 8, 14–20, 24–27), words of Jesus, and prophecies of Christian prophets; but the discourse as a whole is "a Christian composition with use of late Jewish material."

The prophecy of v. 2 is seen as a prophetic threat against the temple, such as appears more than once in the OT; in the prophets the destruction of Jerusalem is followed by prophecies of a new Jerusalem, and a like belief will have been cherished among certain pre-Christian Jewish groups. Mark himself will have so understood the prophecy; for him the utterance intimates an eschatological rather than a political catastrophe, "a piece of the end-time drama."[5] This controls the evangelist's understanding of the discourse. The apocalyptic elements in it indicate that the temple will be destroyed by God, and the cosmos will be drawn into the destruction. So the Christ will come from heaven and gather his elect from the high point of earth to the high point of heaven, i.e., from the earthly Jerusalem to the heavenly Jerusalem.[6]

The discourse is a farewell discourse rather than a typical apocalypse. "It has a center which apocalypses elsewhere do not have: Jesus Christ. He sets in motion the apocalyptic event. God's people are

---

[4] Harder, "Das eschatologische Geschichtsbild der sogenannten kleinen Apokalypse Markus 13," in *Theologia Viatorum* 4, *Beiträge zur Eschatologie, Jahrbuch der kirchlichen Hochschule Berlin, 1952* (Berlin, 1953), 71.

[5] Ibid., 73.

[6] Ibid., 92.

persecuted for his sake, false prophets and christs come forward in his name, and the working of his Spirit is promised to the churches."[7] The emphasis entailing a concentration on the final act is due to the appearance of the Messiah in hiddenness and to his death and resurrection, which signify a partial realization of the apocalyptic prophecy; clearly this reflects the Christian reworking of Jewish apocalyptic materials. The discourse is not inharmonious with the Synoptic framework, for the total construction of the Synoptic Gospels is set on the background of Jewish apocalyptic thought: "The eschatological view of history determines not only Mark 13 but the entire Gospel of Mark."[8]

The recognition of Christ as center of the discourse is significant and welcome, and in this Harder concurs with Busch (explicitly); it serves as a reminder that the Christ and Son of man within the discourse is the Jesus in whom the kingdom of God has already appeared. On the other hand the contrast between historical and eschatological is overdrawn and wrongly conceived; alike in prophecy and in apocalyptic, God is presented as one who can use human agents to accomplish his judgments (e.g., in Dan 11:40–45 Antiochus Epiphanes is expected to come to his end in a war campaign; in Revelation 17 the Harlot City is to be destroyed by antichrist, aided by kings who support him; in Luke 13:1ff. judgment threatened is set in the context of natural calamity); further, it is false to deduce from theophanic descriptive language the notion of the end of the cosmos (cf. e.g., Habakkuk 3).

E. Grässer

This writer's consideration of the discourse in his work on the delay of the parousia not unnaturally reflects his preoccupation with this theme. Like Harder, Grässer views Mark 13 as a composition out of three elements, namely, fragments of Jewish apocalyptic tradition (vv. 7–8, 14–20a, 24–27), words of the Lord (e.g., vv. 28–29), and pieces framed by the church for its consolation and exhortation (e.g., vv. 9–11, 13, 20–32, 33–37).[9] The introductory paragraph (vv. 1–4) is plainly redactional; the question of v. 4 suffices to show that for Mark the temple's destruction and the end of the world fall together.[10] The opening utterance of the discourse, "See that no one leads you astray" (v. 5), indicates the *theme* of the discourse: "It defines its real interest; its intention is to give the parenetic direction rather than apocalyptic instruction. It is concerned to preserve the church from disappoint-

---

[7] Ibid., 97.

[8] Ibid., 99.

[9] Grässer, *Das Problem der Parusieverzögerung in den synoptischen Evangelien und in der Apostelgeschichte* (Berlin, 1957), 152.

[10] Ibid., 154–55.

ments and fears."[11] Mark's *tendency* within the discourse is revealed in vv. 7–8: correction of the primitive near expectation is made in the sense of postponement of the end. The like is to be observed at various points in the discourse, e.g., in v. 10, the function of which is to provide a retarding moment in the course of the saving events; vv. 21–23, coming after the description of antichrist in v. 14, extends the time further by making room for more false prophets; the Fig Tree parable of vv. 28–29, originally referring to the hour of decision brought by Jesus' ministry, is related to the near approach of the end, so justifying its delay; v. 30 is a *Trostwort*—a saying to provide encouragement—assuring that though the parousia had not yet occurred it will yet do so in this generation; v. 32 is similarly fashioned in the light of the delayed parousia; the parabolic utterances of vv. 33–37 reflect the same view, for the Master may return in the third watch, or even in the fourth! Grässer commented, "Here in my view the problem of the delay of the parousia is shown. But whether that remains in the frame of the teaching of Jesus is questionable."[12]

Grässer's eagle eye for motifs indicating the theme of the delayed parousia sometimes perceives notions which are not apparent, and distorts those which are. Undoubtedly the opening *blepete* relates to false prophets, but its immediate application is to false claimants to messiahship, just as vv. 21–22 allude to the Jewish doctrine of the hidden Messiah, who is made known in secret places, and pseudo-christs and pseudoprophets who seek to lead the elect astray. It may well be, as Grässer maintains, that this element in the discourse is parallel to the teaching of 2 Thessalonians 2; the claims that the Messiah has arrived would suit the notion, spread by some in Thessalonica, that the day of the Lord had begun; but in the epistle this idea is repudiated as a perversion of Christian eschatological teaching, as it is in Mark 13:5–6, 21–22. Verse 10 certainly puts a brake on eschatological fever, but its intention is to draw attention to a task to be performed rather than the postponement of hope. It is implausible to read out of vv. 28–29 the delay of the parousia; in Mark's context the opposite would be understood by his readers. Grässer can make of v. 30 a *Trostwort* because he views it as inspired by Mark 9:1; it is more plausible to see it as reproducing the thought of Matt 23:36, which signifies the opposed notion of overwhelming judgment of the people of God.

Verse 32 will be considered later, but what of the allegedly "great difficulty" of the parable in vv. 34–36? To read the notion of delayed parousia into the third watch of the night, or the fourth, is unnatural.

---

[11] Ibid., 156.
[12] Ibid., 88; see also 128–31, 158–69.

Mark has replaced Luke's Jewish division of the night watches into three by the Roman division of four (cf. Luke 12:38); but in Luke's version of the parable the master has gone to a wedding, from which he may return at any hour of the night—the thought of a postponed parousia is foreign to such a depiction. Mark's version may have been influenced by the tradition of the parable of the Talents/Pounds (in v. 34a), but the possible nearness of the master's return is alluded to in the command to the doorkeeper that he should "watch," which is the duty of all. Few will be convinced that this watchword of the Jesus tradition and of the primitive catechesis was due to the church's experience of the delayed parousia. Grässer has exaggerated the nature of Jesus' near expectation through his failure to acknowledge and weigh the significance of Jesus' proclamation of the advent of the kingdom of God in his word and works, and of the Lord's conscious submission to the Father's will in relation to the end.

J. A. T. Robinson

In a series of Harvard lectures J. A. T. Robinson sought to delineate the hope of Jesus regarding the future and to trace the development of the parousia doctrine from the early traditions of our Lord's teaching. As to the discourse of Mark 13 he makes two preliminary observations: first, Mark's eschatology is dominated by the discourse and must be interpreted by it; second, the eschatology of ch. 13 is dominated by the paragraph on the parousia, vv. 24–27, and must be interpreted by it.[13]

The most striking feature of the latter is said to be its lack of connection with the attested teaching of Jesus. It is "a pastiche of Old Testament allusions . . . a secondary compilation on which it is impossible to rely for any fresh evidence on how Jesus himself thought."[14] Moreover, the rest of the discourse, both before and after vv. 24–27, is given in the second person, whereas the paragraph in question is in the third person, in the style of apocalypse, and appears to be inserted into a spoken discourse. When the passage is omitted we have a connected discourse which predicts a period of suffering, culminating in the destruction of Jerusalem (vv. 5–23), followed by a series of isolated sayings and parables, the main thrust of which also relates to the historical crisis coming upon Israel in the near future.[15] The discourse owes its structure to the church rather than to Jesus; despite v. 14 it is

---

[13] Robinson, *Jesus and His Coming: The Emergence of a Doctrine* (London, 1957), 118.

[14] Ibid., 56–57; see also 118–20.

[15] Ibid., 120. This applies to the parable of the Fig Tree, as also to the statements of vv. 30 and 32 (though with hesitation as to the latter) and to the hortatory material of vv. 33–37 in its original intent.

not an apocalypse, but a warning in the manner of the prophets concerning the historical consequences of Israel's rejection of the word of God through Jesus and of the attitude the faithful must take.[16] The discourse bears a fundamental similarity to that of Luke 17:22–37, which also concerns the historical consequences of unbelief, but which later became conflated with other material and so related to the parousia. Mark 13:5–23 circulated as "a sort of broadsheet to provide guidance and warning to Christians in Palestine as the political situation came to a head."[17]

That the discourse comprises diverse materials, including some having in view a historical crisis for Israel, is not to be doubted; that vv. 24–27 can rightly be separated off as an alien element in the discourse is questionable. Robinson's view of the parousia passage is inevitably influenced by his interpretation of Mark 14:62 as denoting the ascent of the Son of man to God, hence a prophecy of vindication fulfilled from Easter onwards. In our judgment this is mistaken. Daniel 7:9–13, on which Mark 14:62 depends, describes a theophany of the Ancient of Days for judgment and deliverance (cf. Dan 7:21–22), and the appearance of one like a son of man must also be so viewed (in the myth reflected in the vision the victory over the monster of the deep is wrought by the Rider on the clouds). Mark 14:62 in like vein speaks of the revelation ("you shall see") of the Son of man raised to the right hand of God. The significance of Mark 13:24–27 is its depiction of the parousia as a theophany of the Son of man. The same holds good of the representation of the day of the Son of man in Luke 17:22–37; the delineation of "the Son of man in his day" in Luke 17:23–24 is a theophany, exactly like Mark 13:24–27. Such teaching is not derived from Jewish apocalyptic; there is no parousia representation in Jewish apocalyptic prior to Jesus.

It is misleading to speak of the discourse in Mark 13:5–23 as narrated in the second person while vv. 24–27 are written in the third person; an oscillation is observable throughout the discourse. Note for example that v. 9 gives an address in the second person, v. 10 an implicit exhortation in the third person, v. 11 another in the second person, v. 12 an observation in the third person, v. 13a an observation in the second person, and v. 13b a statement in the third person. Similarly in vv. 14–20 we find v. 14 addressed in the second person, vv. 15–16 giving a third person imperative, v. 17 a third person comment, v. 18 a second person exhortation, vv. 19–20 prophetic declarations in the third person, precisely as in vv. 24–27.

---

[16] Robinson considered that the reference to the abomination of desolation represents an apocalypticizing of the more primitive tradition which is embodied in Luke 21:10 (ibid., 121–22).

[17] Ibid., 126.

More important, vv. 5–23 should not be contrasted in an unqualified manner as prophecy relating to history over against vv. 24–27 as
apocalypse in the language of myth, even though there is some justification for it. The whole discourse of Mark 13 is composed of diverse
materials which share a common background. We recognize without
hesitation that the paragraph vv. 14–20 has the tribulation of Israel in
view, and that it was linked from earliest times with the prophecy of v.
2; but the passage describes the day of the Lord upon Jerusalem, which,
by definition at least, anticipates the parousia and final kingdom of
God. Verses 9–13 bear no relation with the tribulation of Israel, but tell
rather of the tribulation of the followers of Jesus as they witness to Jesus
and pursue their mission in the world; but the eschatological nature of
the mission is hinted at in v. 10 (cf. *prōton!*), and is plainly indicated
in vv. 12–13. The parallel noted between vv. 24–26 and Luke 17:23–24
extends, in fact, to vv. 21 and 24–26, which earlier may well have been
a unit; in view of the link between vv. 6 and 22 it may well be that at
an early time vv. 5–6, 21–23, and 24–27 were grouped together under
the theme of pseudomessiahs and the true Messiah. Indeed, it is likely
that in very early days the parousia passage was linked on the one hand
with sayings on Israel's tribulation and on the other with those relating
to the church's tribulation in mission, for it forms the horizon of both,
and the goal of history which Israel and the church subserve.[18]

We conclude that Robinson is justified in recognizing the historical dimensions in Mark 13:5–23, but not in isolating vv. 24–27, as
though the history has no eschatological goal or the apocalyptic prophecy has no relation to history. The whole discourse, from beginning to
end, stands related to the Son of man whose ministry and mission is
one from Jordan's bank to the parousia.

S. G. F. Brandon

In a series of books and articles S. G. F. Brandon discussed the
origin of the Gospel of Mark and drew attention to the importance of
the discourse in ch. 13 for the solution of the problem. As the first
literary Gospel Mark's work "constituted a novel creation," and so
required a powerful reason for its production. Since it is generally
agreed that the Gospel appeared in the period AD 65–75, the most likely
stimulus for its composition was the catastrophe of Jerusalem; and
since Rome is the probable place of its origin, the "triumph" of Vespasian and Titus in AD 71, celebrating the conquest of Jerusalem, will have
elicited the reaction which led Mark to write his Gospel, for on that
occasion scenes from the Jewish War were vividly depicted in the

---

[18] On the development of the elements of tradition from which Mark 13 was
composed see below, pp. 350–63.

parade, and spoils from the Jerusalem temple were displayed. All this would have made a great impression on the Christians in Rome.[19]

In such a situation, Brandon urged, it will have been apparent that the primitive traditions concerning Jesus received from the Christians of Judea should be preserved, for the church of Jerusalem was annihilated with the rest of the populace of the city.[20] It was further necessary for Christians to be dissociated from suspicion of complicity or even sympathy with the Jewish rebellion; to this end Mark stresses throughout his Gospel the opposition of the Jews to Jesus, and of Jesus to the nationalist aspirations of his people and of his disciples; admittedly in this respect Mark was unhistorical, for he greatly exaggerated the Jewish opposition to Jesus, and he wholly covered up the involvement of Jesus and the disciples and the Jewish church in the Zealot movement.[21] Equally important as the foregoing, the overthrow of Jerusalem, coupled with some convulsive events in the empire (e.g., Nero's persecution of the church and the civil wars that followed his death) led to mounting eschatological expectation among the Christians in Rome; Mark will have written to control the excitement of his fellow believers and to dissuade them from extravagant actions.[22]

In Brandon's view the prophecy of Jerusalem's fall in Mark 13:2 was composed in the light of the event. It contradicts Mark's representation of the accusation that Jesus threatened the temple as false witness (Mark 14:58–59); Mark must have felt it suitable that Jesus should appear to have shown knowledge of so significant an event, but he omitted reference to the mention of Jesus as the destroyer of the temple.[23] Similarly the prophecy concerning the abomination of desolation in v. 14 is deemed to have been written in the light of what actually happened in AD 70. In this case, however, a precedent existed: the oracle of the abomination (vv. 14–22) arose in the agitated period when Caligula sought to erect his image in the Jerusalem temple; subsequently the prophecy was attributed to Jesus, and its fulfillment was seen in a twofold action of Titus and his troops; when the temple fire became beyond control, Titus and officers entered the most holy place to view it, and his soldiers set up imperial standards in the temple

---

[19] See Brandon, *The Fall of Jerusalem and the Christian Church* (London, 1951), 185–86; idem, "The Date of the Markan Gospel," *NTS* 7 (1960–61): 126–28; idem, *Jesus and the Zealots* (Manchester, 1967), 242. Cf. also idem, "The Apologetical Factor in the Markan Gospel," in *SE* 2, ed. F. L. Cross (Berlin, 1964), 34–46.

[20] Brandon, *Fall*, 199–201. Brandon considers that the reports mentioned by Eusebius and Epiphanius concerning the flight of the Jerusalem church to Pella at the bidding of an oracle are without historical worth; see especially the lengthy discussion in *Jesus and the Zealots*, 108–21.

[21] Idem, *Jesus and the Zealots*, 14–15.

[22] Idem, *Date*, 128–30.

[23] Idem, *Fall*, 201–2; idem, *Jesus and the Zealots*, 233–35.

area and sacrificed to the images thereon.[24] Mark accordingly built on the foundation of this earlier apocalypse; he began by repeating in vv. 5ff. the warning of vv. 21–22, in order to check at once the apocalyptic fever; he owned that the era of the birth pangs had arrived (v. 8), but emphasized the necessity of taking the gospel to the nations before the end came (vv. 9–13). Since the events of vv. 5–23 were already fulfilled, the Fig Tree parable indicates that the end is not far off (vv. 28ff.); indeed, it is to come within the present generation (v. 30), but v. 32 forbids attempts to reckon the date of the end; and so the discourse concludes with an appeal to remain ever wakeful (vv. 33–37).[25]

This interpretation of the origin of Mark's Gospel, and of ch. 13 in particular, in the light of the triumphs of Vespasian and Titus, is an ingenious speculation, but it is burdened with difficulties and improbabilities. For Brandon it is bound up with the belief that Jesus and the Palestinian church were in full sympathy with the Zealot movement, and that Mark was therefore compelled to dissociate Jesus from his nation, his disciples, and the church which sprang from them; scholars have rightly repudiated this as an implausible and unprovable hypothesis.[26] It is equally questionable to make Mark 13:2, 14 points of departure for the date of the discourse (and the Gospel) on the assumption that they are *ex eventu* statements. The culpability of the Jewish contemporaries of Jesus in their rejection of the word of God brought through him lies deep in his proclamation (cf. Luke 12:8–9 as an example, and such passages as Luke 10:13–16; 11:29–32, 49–51; 12:49–52). From this conviction of Jesus the prophetic oracles of doom upon Jerusalem and its people flow naturally (cf. Luke 13:1ff.; 19:41ff.; 23:27ff.).

Granting the likelihood that the abomination prophecy found eager circulation in the Caligula crisis, it is wholly improbable that Mark 13:14 reflects the actions of Titus and his soldiers after the city had fallen, for the call therein is for Jews to flee from the city to the hills when the abomination "stands where it [or *he*] ought not"; the whole paragraph assumes that the abomination marks the beginning of the Jewish agony, not its end. The concept of "the abomination of desolation" originated in the blasphemous acts perpetrated by Antiochus Epiphanes; the Feast of Dedication ensured its continuance in the memory of the Jews, and it is reflected in the representations of antichrist in 2 Thessalonians 2 and Revelation 13; its presence as a symbol

---

[24] Idem, *Jesus and the Zealots*, 231–32.

[25] Ibid., 237–42.

[26] See, e.g., M. Hengel's review of *Jesus and the Zealots* in *JSS* 14 (1969): 231–40, and his book, *Was Jesus a Revolutionist?* (ET Philadelphia, 1971); O. Cullmann, *Jesus and the Revolutionaries* (ET New York, 1970); C. F. D. Moule and E. Bammel, eds., *Jesus and the Politics of His Day* (Cambridge, 1977).

in the doom prophecies of Jesus is in harmony with the context of his ministry, and is certainly less open to objection than alleged recollections of the acts of Titus and his men. Above all, the echoes of major elements of Mark 13 in 1 and 2 Thessalonians rule out an origin of the content of the discourse after AD 70.[27] That the evangelist could have utilized the material of the discourse after that date is, of course, a perfectly possible notion; there is nothing in the discourse, however, which demands the conclusion that he did so.[28]

H. J Schoeps

H. J. Schoeps sought to justify the thesis that the core of the discourse of Mark 13 was a flyleaf which originated among Jewish Christians of the Ebionite sect.[29] He pointed out that the older Tübingens (Baur and his associates) viewed the Synoptic apocalypse en bloc as an Ebionite product. This, Schoeps acknowledged, went beyond the evidence, as the Synoptic parallels to Mark 13:2 show; nevertheless, there are elements within Mark 13 which came from an apocalyptic flyleaf, especially vv. 14–20, and possibly also vv. 24–27. This flyleaf was derived from a word of Jesus used by Jewish Christians in relation to the time of distress and affliction in the winter of AD 66–67 (cf. Mark. 13:18, and the Matthean *mēde sabbatō*, Matt 24:20); it was probably brought to light by a prophet of doom in the style of Agabus (Acts 11:28; 21:10). The call for flight to the mountains would have in view the east Jordan plateau. The prophecy was the "oracle" reported on by Eusebius, to which Epiphanius gave independent testimony, though the latter described it as a "command of Christ," and elsewhere as a divine warning brought by an angel.[30] Schoeps further draws attention to a reference to the flight to Pella in the Pseudo-Clementine literature, *Rec.* 1:37, 39, which clearly reflects the self-understanding of the Ebionite group. In an address by Peter it is stated that the True Prophet, Jesus, spoke of the destruction of the temple and that baptism would take its place: "Everyone who, believing in this prophet who had been foretold by Moses, is baptised to his name, shall be kept unhurt from the destruction of the war, which impends over the unbelieving nation, and

---

[27] See below, p. 383, n. 24.

[28] On the relation of the discourse in Mark 13 to the date of Mark see the discussion of J. A. T. Robinson, *Redating the New Testament* (London, 1976), 15–19; but also the reviews in this book of other writers, e.g., W. Marxsen, R. Pesch, W. Kelber, K. Grayston, F. Hahn.

[29] Schoeps, "Ebionitische Apokalyptik im Neuen Testament," *ZNW* 51 (1960): 101–11.

[30] Eusebius, *Hist Eccl* 3.5.3; Epiphanius, *Haer.* 29.7; 30.2; *De Mens* 15. Schoeps urged that the rejection of the historicity of the report of the exodus to Pella, maintained, e.g., by Brandon, "lacks any foundation" ("Apokalyptik," 105 n. 11).

the place itself [i.e., the temple]." In addition, the Syriac of *Rec.* 1:37 states that this war does not come unexpectedly, but that it is to occur prior to the parousia of the prophet. Thus the war and its tragic consequences were viewed as prophesied by Jesus, and the parousia was awaited for the period after AD 70, when the prophecy of the temple's ruin and the ending of sacrifice, which the Ebionite Jesus had taught, had been fulfilled.[31] Schoeps also sees in Rev 12:4–17 another reflection of the flight to Pella, and maintains that Mark 14:28 and 16:7 have in view the prospect of the parousia taking place in "Galilee of the nations," east of the Jordan.[32]

This thesis of Schoeps is hardly to be accepted. The evidence he adduces shows no more than that Ebionites claimed that their forebears had fled from Palestine on the basis of a command from Christ; it does not demonstrate that Mark 13:14–20, 24–27 originated with Ebionite prophets and that the discourse was an expansion of an Ebionite flyleaf. The endeavor to support the thesis by appealing to Rev 12:4–17 as a reflection of the flight to Pella belongs to an outmoded way of interpreting the book of Revelation; the appeal to Mark 14:28 and 16:7 as evidence for the expectation of the parousia for followers of Jesus east of the Jordan is even more improbable.

N. Perrin

Norman Perrin's review of modern discussions about the kingdom of God in the teaching of Jesus does not concern itself greatly with the eschatological discourse.[33] In that volume Perrin's treatment of the discourse is confined to a critical review of the position outlined in my *Jesus and the Future.* For Perrin two considerations sufficed to demonstrate the unauthenticity of the content of the discourse: the high concentration of non-Markan vocabulary within it, and its use of the LXX.

As to the former, Perrin reckoned that of the 165 words in the Nestle text of Mark 13:5–27, no less than 35 do not occur elsewhere within the Gospel (i.e., 21.2%), and of these 35 words, 15 are found in the book of Revelation. By contrast, in Mark 13:28–37, of the 79 words, 13 (i.e., 16.4%) are not found elsewhere in the Gospel and only 2 are in the book of Revelation.[34] This is held to point to the secondary nature

---

[31] Schoeps, "Apokalyptik," 105–7.

[32] Ibid., 110. This position was maintained on the basis that the phrases "beyond the Jordan, Galilee of the nations" in Matt 4:15 denote the area east of the Jordan where Pella was situated. Jerome is cited for the belief of the "Hebrews," i.e., Ebionites, that Jesus first preached the gospel in the land designated in Isa 8:23, which was "the land where they now dwelt" (Jerome on Isa 8:23).

[33] Perrin, *The Kingdom of God in the Teaching of Jesus* (London, 1963).

[34] These figures are compared by Perrin with statistics relating to the longer ending of Mark's Gospel, 16:9–20, where 17.2% of the words do not occur in

of the material in the discourse—i.e., secondary to Mark, and to the authentic teaching of Jesus. As to the use of the OT in the discourse, Perrin affirmed that prior to ch. 13 in Mark there is no case of dependence on the LXX in the recorded teaching of Jesus, where that version differs from the Hebrew or does not yield the same point as the Hebrew text. In Mark 13, on the contrary, there is a series of quotations from the LXX that are different from the Hebrew (or Aramaic), and there is no instance of necessary dependence on any text other than the Greek.[35]

I confess to perplexity at the first element in Perrin's demonstration of the secondary nature of the discourse. In *Jesus and the Future* I argued that a form of the discourse was current in the church prior to Mark, known also in some fashion to Paul, to the author of Revelation in an independent version, and to Luke in a version possibly related to that reflected in Revelation; it was to be expected accordingly that much of the discourse should reflect non-Markan vocabulary and style. Since the early appearance of the book I have had opportunity to study Mark's style more closely, and I now recognize that the discourse has more affinity with Mark's writing than I had realized. We shall see that J. Lambrecht's meticulous investigation into the vocabulary, style, and composition of Mark 13 led him to believe that no one other than Mark could have composed the discourse. Lambrecht has perhaps been too ambitious in his endeavor to demonstrate that every phrase and clause in the discourse is due to Mark; nevertheless, it is difficult to resist his conclusion that Mark's hand is evident throughout the whole. A mediating position between these two writers is not unjustified; the material of the discourse reflects pre-Markan origin, but it is stamped throughout with Mark's impress.

Perrin's statements regarding the relation of the OT citations in Mark 13 to the Hebrew and LXX texts are largely dependent on T. F. Glasson's representation of the issue.[36] R. T. France has submitted Glasson's treatment to a critical examination and has come to quite different conclusions.[37] In his view it is only in Mark 13:14 that the wording is an exact quotation of the LXX (the familiar *to bdelygma tēs erēmōseōs*); in general the citations in Mark 13:24–25 support the MT against the LXX; the difference in meaning between the LXX and the MT in most cases is nonexistent, or discernible only by one who demands

---

Mark; so also of John 7:53–8:11, again 17.2% of the words do not occur elsewhere in the Fourth Gospel.

[35] Ibid., 133.

[36] See Glasson, "Mark 13 and the Greek Old Testament," *ExpT* 69 (1957–58): 213–15.

[37] France, *Jesus and the Old Testament* (London, 1971), 35–36, 254–58, the latter set in an appendix on "The Detailed Study of the Text-Form of the Old Testament Quotations in the Teaching of Jesus," 240–58.

a highly literal translation; and the use of the LXX is to be expected in a rendering of the teaching of Jesus for Greek-speaking communities.[38] We shall deal with this issue later (pp. 319–21), meanwhile, we should observe that it is not always possible to be confident that an LXX phrase is intended as a citation. For example, most exegetes regard the phrase *dei genesthai* in Mark 13:7 as cited from Dan 2:28 LXX, where the Aramaic text has a simple future ("things that will be"), but this is quite doubtful; its pertinence is as an example of the translation of an Aramaic future by *dei* with infinitive in order to convey the assurance of the fulfillment of that which is spoken in a divine revelation; such a phenomenon will have arisen in a bilingual community, such as existed in Jerusalem and many parts of north Palestine.[39]

Perrin cannot be said to have devoted the same care to the elucidation of the discourse of Mark 13 as he applied to the understanding of the eschatological instruction of Jesus generally. In his later work, *Rediscovering the Teaching of Jesus,* he manifested a greater hesitation to accept the authenticity of any elements within the sayings traditions of the Gospels, finding the approach of E. Käsemann particularly congenial. The eschatological discourse received even less attention than it had in the earlier work; concerning the chapter Perrin was content to state: "We omit Mark 13 and its parallels, because this is, at best, a version of something which Jesus taught that has been so severely apocalypticized that we have no present means of recovering any authentic teaching directly from it."[40]

In an edited collection of essays, *A Modern Pilgrimage in New Testament Christology,* Perrin is impressed with the work of L. Hartman, who sought to show that the discourse has much in common with similar discourses in Jewish apocalyptic, and with that of Marxsen, Weeden, and Kelber, who emphasized the reflection of Mark's own situation, interests, and concerns in the discourse. His view of the origin of the discourse is summarized in the statement: "My own working hypothesis is that 13:1–5a form an introduction to the discourse, giving it a setting in the Gospel and composed by the evangelist; 13:5b–27 are the discourse proper, and 13:28–37 are a parenthetical conclusion composed by the evangelist. Within the discourse itself we have to reckon with considerable Markan redaction, especially in vv. 9 and 26 and perhaps in other places also."[41]

---

[38] Ibid., 35–36.

[39] See the remarks of R. Pesch in "Die Passion des Menschensohnes," in *Jesus und der Menschensohn,* Festschrift A. Vögtle, ed. R. Pesch and R. Schnackenburg (Freiburg, 1975), 168.

[40] Perrin, *Rediscovering,* 155.

[41] Perrin, *Pilgrimage,* 131. For further comments by Perrin on Mark 13 see idem, *The New Testament: An Introduction* (New York, 1974), 79, 149, 159; and

The one element within the discourse to which Perrin devoted detailed attention was the parousia passage, Mark 13:26 with its parallel in 14:62.[42] He postulated that the idea embodied in these sayings was the product of early Christians viewing the resurrection of Jesus in the light of Ps 110:1; with this text Dan 7:13 became linked, interpreted as the ascension of the Son of man to heaven, and finally Zech 12:10ff., with its statement, "they shall look on him whom they pierced" (cf. Rev 1:7). It was the element from Zechariah, the "seeing" of the Son of man, which made of the saying a visible parousia instead of an ascension. The thesis is ingenious but needless. The linking of Ps 110:1 with Dan 7:13 is attested in the Midrash on Ps 2:7, which was certainly not influenced by belief in the resurrection of Jesus; the idea of "seeing" is rooted in the text of Dan 7:13 ("I *saw* in the night visions, and *look*, with the clouds of heaven there came. . ."); the interpretation of Dan 7:13 as coming from heaven rather than going to heaven was standard in Judaism and in accord with its original intention.[43]

2. Early Redaction-Critical Approaches to the Eschatological Discourse

W. Marxsen

Willi Marxsen's treatment of Mark 13 is set forth as an illustration of the method of redaction criticism applied to a single Gospel text.[44] In accordance with his insistence that the object of interest in this mode of study is the situation of the evangelist and his church, rather than that of Jesus in his ministry or the first-generation church, he states: "It is not possible to keep in mind both the unity of Mark 13 and the historical Jesus. We must rather be clear about the situation in life against whose background we intend to exegete."[45] In Marxsen's view, failure to grasp this distinction doomed earlier attempts to understand the chapter.[46]

---

idem, *Jesus and the Language of the Kingdom* (London, 1976), 59–60.

[42] See Perrin, "Mark 14.62: The End Product of a Christian Pesher Tradition?" *NTS* 12 (1965–66): 150–55; the thesis of the article was developed in *Rediscovering,* 173–85, and was reproduced with further reflections in *Pilgrimage,* 10–23.

[43] See K. Müller, "Der Menschensohn im Danielzyklus," in *Jesus und der Menschensohn,* ed. R. Pesch and R. Schnackenburg (Freiburg, 1975), 45; F. H. Borsch, "Mark XIV.62 and 1 Enoch LXII.5," *NTS* 14 (1968): 556–57; D. Flusser, *Jesus* (New York, 1969), 102ff.; G. Vermes, *Jesus the Jew* (New York, 1973), 171–72, 187.

[44] Accordingly, no less than a quarter of Marxsen's book, *Mark the Evangelist,* is devoted to the consideration of Mark 13 (151–206).

[45] Ibid., 156.

[46] For example, Marxsen writes of Schniewind's exposition in his commen-

In analyzing the discourse, Marxsen distinguishes four groups of sayings: (1) An apocalyptic leaflet, or at least apocalyptic material, vv. 7, 8, 12, 14–22, 24–27; whether an originally Jewish apocalypse can be constructed from these verses is uncertain. (2) A "Christian piece," which Mark found already connected, vv. 5–6, 9, 13a, 11, 23, 30–32; following J. Sundwall, Marxsen thinks that these verses (in the order given) may well show an original coherence. (3) An individual saying, v. 2, to which the geographical and temporal frame of v. 1 was prefixed. (4) Further individual sayings from the tradition, vv. 10, 13b, 28–29, 32?, 33–37. The idea that Mark came upon the discourse as a unified whole is rejected, since this postulate ignores alterations made by the evangelist and the contradictions within the chapter (e.g., between vv. 30 and 31, or v. 14 with its interest in Jerusalem and vv. 15–16, which assume rural conditions).[47]

Verse 2 is important, since its anticipation of the imminent destruction of the temple provides a clue to the time of the composition of the discourse. It is assumed that Mark altered the logion of Mark 14:58 to its present form in v. 2, so that a saying which earlier expressed the church's self-understanding became a prophecy of the destruction of the temple. Similarly v. 14 has had its meaning transformed: originally it spoke of a desecration of the temple, reflecting the apocalyptic expectation in the time of the Caligula crisis; but instead of the temple's desecration as the prelude to the end, Mark has made the temple's destruction to be the sign. Verses 5–13 depict the situation of the primitive community in the light of the turbulent events of the years AD 66–70, and Mark stands in that time; the war that has begun is not the end (*oupō to telos*), the events thus far are simply *archē tōn ōdinōn*. Verse 14 therefore is the hinge of the discourse. The conjunction of vv. 2 and 14 shows that Mark looks for the capture of the city and the destruction of the temple, when the antichrist will take his place there: "the world catastrophe will then begin from the temple." Christians should then "flee to the mountains," which for Mark means Galilee. Following Lohmeyer, Marxsen sees in v. 27 a prediction that the elect are to be united at the world's summit and center. He asks, "Does Mark think of Galilee as the center of the earth? Do heaven and earth meet at Galilee?" The question evidently is to be answered in the affirmative.[48]

On this understanding of the chapter, the discourse is organized by Marxsen as follows. The question in v. 4 is a kind of title which is

---

tary on Mark, and the monograph of Busch on Mark 13: "Schniewind and Busch never come to grips with Mark 13 itself. This is possible only when we regard the unity of this chapter strictly as the Evangelist's own work" (ibid., 158).

[47] Ibid., 162–65. Sundwall's cited work is *Die Zusammensetzung des Markusevangeliums* (Abo, 1934).

[48] Ibid., 166–86.

developed in a threefold way: the answer is given in vv. 5–13, which qualify the present moment as the *archē* of the end; next a concrete event at the temple is the subject, vv. 14ff.; finally the end event in the narrower sense is described in vv. 24ff. Mark stands in the midst of the *thlipsis*; hence present and future stand under its sign. But since ch. 13 is followed at once by the passion narrative, this line is extended into the past also. Accordingly "the community endures the *thlipsis* of its Lord; through it leads the way to glory at the *parousia*. The 'way of Jesus' becomes a kind of paradigm for the Christians." Hence Mark transforms apocalyptic into eschatology.[49] From the last paragraph of ch. 13 "a great arc can be described toward 1:14–15 . . . Jesus proclaims the nearness of the *parousia*." Accordingly, both in the summary of Jesus' preaching in Mark 1:15 and in the discourse of Mark 13, the risen Lord is the speaker, using Mark for the interpretation of his proclamation.[50]

It is not our intention to scrutinize all Marxsen's views on Mark 13. His fundamental postulate, shared by his successors, however, does call for comment. A concern for the *Sitz im Leben* of the evangelist is clearly right, including the raising of questions concerning it prior to those relative to the primitive church and Jesus. For Marxsen, however, the goal of such investigation is to comprehend Mark, not Jesus; the latter concern falls outside the task of the redaction critic. Indeed, Perrin, when adopting redaction criticism as a method of studying the Gospels, came close to abandoning the quest for the teaching of Jesus; for him this was no great loss, since the locus of revelation is not the historical Jesus but the present experience of Jesus. He reached the conclusion: "Redaction criticism is teaching us that the content of a Gospel is as much a product of the present experience of the men who transmitted the tradition and of the evangelist as apocalyptic literature is a product of the seer's vision."[51]

When one contemplates the greatest of all apocalypses, that of John in the NT, and recalls that it describes itself as witness to "the word of God and the testimony of Jesus Christ, even all that he saw" (Rev 1:2), and yet there is hardly a solitary citation of (as distinct from allusion to) the OT or of words of Jesus in the book, it is evident that such a view totally rules out the Gospels as sources for the words and works of Jesus. But does the distinguishing between the three life situations—of the evangelist, of the primitive church, and of Jesus—really lead us to such a position? And do we have to concur with Marxsen that it is impossible to bear in mind both the unity of Mark 13 and the historical Jesus? May we not penetrate through the redaction-critical work and the form-

---

[49] Ibid., 189.

[50] Ibid., 187; also 133–34, 170–71.

[51] Perrin, *What is Redaction Criticism?* (Philadelphia, 1969), 69 and 79. See the whole chapter entitled "The Significance of the Discipline," 64–79.

critical labors to the historical-critical questions? To fail to show interest in Jesus himself is surely to fail the people of God in that service for which they look to their theologians. In the judgment of many, they who feel compelled to admit that failure, on the ground that the Gospels do not yield the needful data about Jesus, are failing to recall the uniqueness and solitary power of the teaching of Jesus on the kingdom of God, its coherence with his action in his life, death, and resurrection, and the implausibility of crediting it all to his followers and evangelists rather than primarily to Jesus himself. In reality scholars who apply the redaction-critical method to the exposition of the Gospels generally do so with more hopeful intent than these pessimistic reflections would suggest.

Marxsen's actual discussion of the problems of Mark 13 is highly stimulating. His finding the unity of the discourse in the subject present in v. 2—the destruction of the temple and its relation to the end of the age—is perhaps better described as its frame of reference, for the parenetic emphasis of the discourse, which commences in its first word and continues to its last line, finds its ultimate explanation in the sovereign action of God in the Son of man, alike in his ministry to Israel and in the end which approaches (hence the judgment and the salvation, the *via dolorosa* and the glory). The belief that the evangelist recognizes his own time in vv. 5–13 and the imminent fulfillment of vv. 14ff. is to be taken with seriousness; it explains the significance of the chapter to Mark's community and why he included so long a discourse in his Gospel. The origin and history of vv. 2, 5–13, and 14 are another matter; the urgency of these statements to Mark's contemporaries in no wise rules out their pertinence for the first-generation church, especially in the time of Caligula's madness over the temple, and neither is incompatible with the situation of Jesus in relation to a nation which had rejected the *kairos* for which its history had prepared it.

Marxsen's observations on the relation of the discourse to apocalyptic thought and to the eschatological sayings of the rest of Mark's Gospel call for further reflection. For "apocalyptic" is an ambiguous term. We saw how J. A. T. Robinson separated out Mark 13:24–27 as apocalyptic, over against the rest of the chapter; yet with equal justice we may recognize v. 32, which proscribes all apocalyptic reckoning, as apocalyptic at its core, for the hour which is known to God alone is the end which is determined by God alone, the hour wherein he brings to pass his purpose for creation through the one he has ordained as his instrument of judgment and redemption.[52] The thought that Mark 13 is related to the passion narrative, and therefore to the church as a body of suffering disciples, following in the way of Jesus by the *via dolorosa*

---

[52] See the discussion on Mark 13:32 in relation to apocalyptic by A. Strobel, *Kerygma und Apokalyptik* (Göttingen, 1967), 85.

to the parousia, is not new; whether it is rightly described as entailing a transformation of apocalyptic into eschatology is a moot point. And the question as to who initiated this train of thought is not without interest. It was the merit of F. Busch to emphasize the close relation between Mark 13 and 8:34ff., and this Marxsen acknowledged. Mark 8:34–37 culminates in the apocalyptic utterance in 8:38, as 13:9–13 anticipates 13:24–27. Apocalyptic was born in the crucible of suffering, and from the beginning went hand in hand with it; did they not go together with Jesus to Jerusalem?

H. Conzelmann

In an article on the theme "History and *Eschaton* in Mark 13," Conzelmann endeavored to determine Mark's stance in the discourse, set as Mark was between the primitive Synoptic tradition and the more developed writings of Matthew and Luke. Conzelmann stated that in the primitive church Christology and eschatology existed side by side without relation; the kerygmatic declarations about Christ's death and resurrection do not mention the parousia, and the parousia proclamations do not mention the content of the "credo." Mark took the step of integrating Christology into eschatology, though without expressly relating the exalted Lord to the time between the resurrection and the parousia (the time is characterized negatively as the period of the Bridegroom's absence, Mark 2:18ff.). His positive achievement was to link the christological utterances about the past with those concerning the future. With this synthesis of Christology and eschatology Mark seeks to show the relation of the near expectation and the nonoccurrence of the parousia; the former is not to be given up, but the problem is how it may be retained in face of the delay of the parousia. The construction of the discourse enables the question to be answered.[53]

The opening scene (Mark 13:1–4) is composed on the basis of a logion received in the tradition (v. 2). While in itself the form of the disciples' question accords with Jewish apocalyptic, in Mark's context it is thought of in relation to Jesus; the real interest is not in the apocalyptic representation but in the right attitude to the one who is to come, and thus in the eschatological parenesis which instantly follows. The wording of the question, with its *tauta panta* and the singular *sēmeion*, reflects a concern to correct a current eschatological error, which affirms a false connection between the fate of the temple and the end of the world.[54] The new thing in Mark's outworking of the discourse is that for the first time future events are consciously separated into two

---

[53] Conzelmann, "Geschichte und *Eschaton* nach Mc 13," *ZNW* 50 (1959): 210–11.

[54] Conzelmann holds that Mark wrote his Gospel after AD 70 (ibid., 214 n. 27).

groups, which are related but fundamentally to be distinguished. The last epoch of world history, namely, the great tribulation, remains basically in the frame of history to that time; it is divided from the final cosmic catastrophe, which forms the true sign of the parousia, but in such a fashion that sign and event fall together.[55]

Contrary to Marxsen, who sees the transition from present to future in v. 14, with the expectation of one single last act in the future, Conzelmann stresses the importance of v. 24 (the end comes after that tribulation) and Mark's reflection thereon. In apocalyptic generally (e.g., Daniel) the transition into the future takes place smoothly, so that historical and supernatural flow together; in Mark there is a clear distinction. This is due to the binding of faith to the historical person of Jesus. Though the parousia may be described in dependence on Daniel, the expectation is changed, since the Coming One is already known as a historical figure—the discourse must not be loosed from the preceding report about his work. No longer therefore is it necessary to have assurance of the future by awaited events which make up the apocalyptic course of the world, for the continuity is given in the person of him who is awaited.[56] The motif of suddenness receives fullest expression in vv. 24–27; the cosmic catastrophe alone will be the immediate sign of the parousia, but when it happens none can prepare any more, for before one can do anything about it the Son of man is present. Thus Mark finds a balance between the two motifs which belong to the firm content of eschatology: the observation of signs, in which what is coming is made known, and the expectation of a sudden and unexpected in-breaking.[57]

The problem of delay in the coming of the Lord is dealt with through the significance of the Markan insertion at v. 10: the delay is explained as necessary, and as in accordance with the divine plan (*dei*), for between the present and the end the era of the Christian mission to the world has to be fulfilled.

This is not systematized into a concept of the era of the church, as in Luke; it suffices to recognize the necessity of mission prior to the end.[58] With this recognition, however, the final paragraph provides a balance: exhortation is given for preparedness in face of both the delay and the possible sudden coming of the Son of man. So the question with which Mark began receives its answer.

Acknowledging the interesting and helpful insights of Conzelmann's article, it is doubtful that his main thesis concerning Mark's purpose in the discourse is correct, for there is no evidence that Mark

---

[55] Ibid., 215.
[56] Ibid., 216–17.
[57] Ibid., 219–20.
[58] Ibid., 219.

was preoccupied with the problems posed on his behalf by Conzelmann. The relation of history to the end and the role of the risen Lord in both would not have been a matter of perplexity for the primitive church, or for Mark. The idea that the "credo" and the parousia were not brought together in the primitive Christian kerygma is negated by 1 Thess 1:9–10, commonly recognized as a pre-Pauline citation. Moreover, the early Christians saw the resurrection of Jesus as an apocalyptic event in the truest sense: the exaltation of the Lord to the place of power with God, the beginning of the resurrection of the dead, and so the intersection of this age and the age to come (cf. Rom 1:3–4; Phil 2:9ff., etc.). Mark's repeated predictions of the resurrection of Jesus after three days indicate that he shared the same theology. To cite Mark 2:18ff. as evidence of Mark's lack of reflection on the activity of the risen Lord is as doubtful as citing 2 Cor 5:9–11 as evidence that Paul held a similar view. I am persuaded that as Mark 14:62 presupposes the resurrection of Jesus to the right hand of God, so Phil 2:9ff. presupposes the parousia of the risen Lord, as the related vision of Revelation 5 suggests. As to the notion that the "cosmic catastrophe" of Mark 13:24–25 serves as a *sēmeion* of the parousia, but too late to allow for repentance, the description is, on the contrary, not a cosmic catastrophe at all, but the characterization of a theophany, given in time-honored picture language (cf. Isa 13:9–10; Hab 3:3–13). Mark looks for the revelation of the glory of the Lord in the parousia.

It is similarly doubtful that Mark inserted v. 10 into vv. 9–13 in order to explain the delay of the parousia. Christian witness is already implied in vv. 9 and 11, and v. 10 emphasizes its extent. If v. 10 matches the *oupō to telos* of v. 7 and the *archē ōdinōn* of v. 8, and so supplies a "retarding moment" in the discourse, this is to counter those who see the parousia as immediately impending in the light of the signs that are occurring (especially in vv. 7–8 and 14ff.). The *prōton* of v. 10 defines an urgent task to be performed prior to the parousia. Mark recalls his fellow Christians to forsake the stargazers and to declare the good news to a world for which redemption was achieved, even if it entails a like fate as that of the Lord whom they preach. He who endures to the end will share his salvation (Mark 13:13).

A. Suhl

In his investigation into the use of the OT in Mark, A. Suhl paid brief attention to Mark 13. He followed Hölscher in holding that Mark used a Jewish apocalyptic flyleaf, which arose in connection with the Caligula uproar ca. AD 40 (vv. 7–8, 12, 13–22, 24–27), and observed that the OT allusions are found in these sections only.[59] The statement of

---

[59] Suhl, *Die Funktion der alttestamentlichen Zitate und Anspielungen im*

time in v. 24 he attributed to the source; consequently no great weight should be laid upon it, as though it were an important redactional addition; with Marxsen he held that the important insertion is found in v. 14. While the signs of vv. 5–13 are described in a succession, they do not announce an order of eschatological events; they are all seen by the evangelist as present. These happenings, war and earthquakes, etc., are understood as end-time events, but the character of calculability is taken from them.[60]

As to the date of the composition, it is laid down that Mark 13:10 is not to be taken as setting the parousia in the distance. The delay of the parousia was perceived before Mark, and v. 10 could have come out of an earlier situation. Mark writes after Paul, and Paul has taken the gospel far and wide by the time Mark's Gospel was written. Verse 10 is thus reconcilable with a genuine near expectation; indeed, it can be viewed as a command now fulfilled.[61] Mark 9:1 was formed by Mark because many of the first generation had died out. But the hope was still strong that the parousia would come before the contemporary generation had passed. Mark 9:1 and 13:30 tell against a date for the composition of the discourse after AD 70: "A composition of the Gospel of Mark after the destruction of Jerusalem, with a prospect of a parousia temporally far removed, is utterly improbable."[62]

On the position taken regarding the apocalyptic *Vorlage* we need not comment. The argument as to the date of the discourse and of Mark is worthy of careful consideration.

N. Walter

In an article devoted to the theme of the destruction of the temple in the eschatological discourse, Walter returns to the traditional critical theory of an apocalyptic flyleaf at the base of Mark's discourse (vv. 7–8, 12, 14–20, 22, 24–27). Since this document is free from specifically Christian elements it may be assigned to a Jewish origin. In contrast to J. A. T. Robinson, Walter states that the flyleaf is given in descriptive form, and speaks to the readers only indirectly; the direct address in vv. 7 and 14 is through Mark's redaction. With the apocalyptic document Mark has conjoined parenetic material, occasioned through the notion that the end of the temple leads to the end of history and the parousia of the Son of man.[63]

Markusevangelium (Gütersloh, 1965), 152. The observation would be more significant if vv. 12 and 21–22 were not included in the Jewish source.

[60] Ibid., 153.

[61] Ibid., 21–22.

[62] Ibid., 25.

[63] Walter, "Tempelzerstörung und synoptische Apokalypse," *ZNW* 57 (1966): 39–40.

Walter agrees with Conzelmann therefore that Mark desires to tear apart the traditionally held connection between the destruction of Jerusalem and the final event. The prophecy of v. 2 is the precipitate of apocalyptic expectations during the Jewish War; since it was so well fulfilled it is to be seen as a *vaticinium ex eventu*. In v. 14 Mark does not speak of the temple. Whereas the flyleaf had it in view, as in Dan 9:27; 12:11, Mark disengages the prophecy from it; neither temple, nor altar, nor image is in view in the *bdelygma*, but the antichrist in person. Hence the *synteleia* is not through a sign in the temple, but through the appearance of antichrist in a mysterious place which is not defined. This change has been necessitated through the destruction of the temple as a past event without the end of history taking place; the expectation of the end and the fate of the temple therefore have to be separated. In this way Mark corrects the flyleaf. He teaches his church that the events that have occurred in Palestine do not belong to the end (v. 7c), but at most signify the beginning of the end (v. 8c); those who proclaim the immediate coming of the Messiah on the basis of their occurrence are false prophets and deceivers.[64] The destruction of the temple accordingly is eschatologically irrelevant; in its place the appearance of antichrist in a mythical future is set as the transition to the last period of history.[65]

The seeking of the basis of Mark 13 in a Jewish apocalyptic flyleaf is doubtful. We have already mentioned our conviction that the parousia of the Son of man is not a Jewish doctrine. The notion that the prophecy of Mark 13:2 is a *vaticinium ex eventu* following on the Jewish War is also needless, although some admittedly see it as a saying of Jesus given greater precision; the expectations and warning of Jesus regarding the impending judgment upon the Jewish nation for their rejection of the word of God and the abundant precedent for such warnings in the OT prophets is clear. Nor is it plausible that the *bdelygma* prophecy of v. 14 is divorced by Mark from Jerusalem and the temple and reinterpreted of a personal antichrist; both before the prophecy in the discourse (v. 6) and after it (vv. 21–22) Mark refers to a multiplicity of pseudochrists appearing on the scene to deceive the people. In view of his lack of reticence to speak of such agents, it would have been simple for Mark to make his intention clear in the appearance

---

[64] Ibid., 43–44.

[65] Ibid., 44–45. In Walter's view Matthew and Luke diverge from Mark's interpretation. Matthew interprets the abomination of desolation as taking place "in the holy place," i.e., on the hill of Zion, where the temple formerly was; but this is the place, according to apocalyptic thought, where the heathen gather for the final battle against the Messiah; Matthew therefore totally separates the temple's destruction from the end events. On the contrary, Luke has historicized the prophecy of the abomination (Luke 21:20–24) (ibid., 48).

at the end of an antichrist par excellence, as Paul has done in 2 Thess 2:4–10. Accordingly, this element in Walter's interpretation is implausible. His emphasis on Mark's direction of polemic against those who exploit contemporary events in Palestine to arouse fervent eschatological expectations has much to commend it.

J. Schreiber

In the reflections of J. Schreiber on Mark 13 we see a highly individual application of the principles of redaction criticism.[66] Schreiber approaches the discourse with two postulates in mind. First, in his account of the ministry of Jesus, Mark consciously exploits the verbal agreement of apocalyptic formulae with everyday speech regarding hours (e.g., "that hour") and days ("that day," "in those days"); in this way Mark expresses eschatology under the form of historiography.[67] Second, Mark 13 is set before, and thus subordinated, to Mark 14; hence eschatology is interpreted in the light of the cross event.[68] These two principles are manifest from the beginning of the Gospel onwards. John the Baptist appears as the forerunner of the Messiah and as Elijah redivivus; accordingly, "The apocalyptic event of Mark 13 began in Mark 1 and reached its conclusion in Mark 15, insofar as judgment and salvation (thus the eschaton) took place in the cross."[69] Jesus was baptized "in those days" (Mark 1:9); it is deduced, "If the baptism of Jesus is in a quite special way identical with the eschatological event of the cross, so in Mark's view the formula of the days ('in those days') is to be understood in connection with the similarly sounding apocalyptic formula in Mark 13:17, 24, as an expression of his hellenistic eschatology."[70] More clearly, in Mark 2:20 it is said that "days will come" when the Bridegroom will be taken from his friends, and "in that day" they will fast; thus "those days" of the apocalyptic event are identified with "that day" on which Jesus dies.[71]

Coming to Mark 13, Schreiber holds that the introduction poses the question as to the "when" of the eschaton (v. 4). That is a typical late Jewish question; in v. 32 it is set aside as not worth knowing for the Christian. It is understandable therefore why no answer is given to the question in the discourse, but rather exhortations. The many notices of time within it (vv. 7–8, 10, 14, 21, 24, 28–29, 30) provide no date for the parousia, but state something about the discipleship of the cross,

---

[66] Schreiber, *Theologie des Vertrauens* (Hamburg, 1967), especially pp. 120–45.
[67] Ibid., 122.
[68] Ibid., 127.
[69] Ibid., 123–24.
[70] Ibid., 125–26.
[71] Ibid., 124.

and that the parousia will be a long time coming (v. 10). Verse 32 indicates that the knowledge of Jesus about the eschatological hour is that he does not know when it comes, but he commits himself entirely to God (cf. 14:36: "not what I will, but what you will"). The same paradoxical interpretation of 13:32 is given in 15:34: the eschatological hour consists in the fact that the Son on the cross is forsaken by the Father; of its end he knows nothing, but he holds firmly to the Father in unconditioned trust.[72]

In 13:9–13 the insertion of v. 10 not only indicates a reaction to the delay of the parousia but alludes to the hellenizing of apocalyptic, for the proclamation of the gospel is itself already an apocalyptic end event. Inasmuch as Christians are handed over, as Jesus was in his passion, "that hour" of vv. 32 and 35 is fulfilled in hiddenness here and now.[73]

The description of the parousia in vv. 24–27 is to be compared with 8:38 and 14:62; none of these three passages speaks expressly of a judgment at the parousia; for Mark the thought is inconceivable, because the judgment took place long before in the death of Jesus on the cross and in the decision of faith or unbelief at the proclamation of the gospel. The parable that follows is more important. For Mark it is bound up with the fig tree episode of 11:12–25, and calls to mind OT passages which link Israel with the fig tree (cf. Jer. 8:13, where the unfruitful fig tree is compared with Israel). If one views the parable in the light of the action of Jesus in 11:12ff., it is evident that Judaism, with its adherence to law and apocalyptic, has not reckoned with the presence of the Son of God in the form of one who hungers; it offers only "fig leaves"—i.e., long prayers and devouring widows' houses! Jesus answers this hypocritical piety with a curse. The addition "to you also" of v. 29 indicates that Jewish Christians who cherish the same piety as the Jews face the same judgment.[74] The oracle of v. 14 conveys a related idea: the "abomination of desolation" takes place through the piety of the high priests and scribes, who seek the life of Jesus in the temple; so, in apocalyptic language, the "son of perdition," the antichrist, sets himself in the place of God and stands where he ought not (cf. 2 Thess 2:3–4). Jewish Christians are bidden to "flee" from this, i.e., to distance themselves from Judaism with its Torah and temple piety.[75]

Mark 13:30 is not intended to express an acute near expectation, any more than v. 35. It states that all will happen before this generation of unbelievers passes away (cf. 8:12, 38; 9:19); i.e., in the cross of Christ decision has already been made over the eschaton.[76] Schreiber draws

---

[72] Ibid., 128–30.
[73] Ibid., 131.
[74] Ibid., 135–40.
[75] Ibid., 142–44.
[76] Ibid., 141.

the conclusion: "From the standpoint of his kerygma of the passion the evangelist rejects the near expectation, insofar as this kerygma already declares and fulfills the eschaton in this time of the world and sets people in the decision between faith and unbelief. The parousia, which temporally lies in the distance, only confirms this eschatological event which is already fulfilled in the present."[77]

One has sympathy with what Schreiber is endeavoring to do in all this, namely, to establish the unity of Mark 13 with the eschatology of Mark's Gospel in its wholeness. He is surely right in maintaining that for Mark the ministry of Jesus initiates the *kairos* of the kingdom of God (1:15), and that it reaches its climax in the death and resurrection of Jesus. Presumably Mark wished his readers to perceive the unity of this eschatology with that of the discourse on the end, but it is doubtful that he would have recognized Schreiber's attempt to do it. If the kingdom of God was manifest in the deeds as well as the words of Jesus, it is conceivable that eschatology can be set forth in terms of history, but not by equating marks of time, however general, with the last day; that is surely a fanciful procedure of Schreiber. Similarly the eschatological significance of the cross is plain in Mark's Gospel, above all in his Last Supper narrative; but there is no indication that Mark wished to downgrade the significance of the parousia in the interests of emphasizing the significance of the cross. The attempt to make Mark 13 render that function entails doing violence to the text.[78] It is right to recognize the polemic in Mark 13 against those who misuse apocalyptic and thereby endanger the faith of the church (as in vv. 6, 21–22); this should not, however, lead to the notion that Mark rejects all forms of apocalyptic. On the contrary, the faith which sees the eschatological intervention of God in the action of Jesus—his ministry, death, resurrection, and parousia—is apocalyptic in the truest sense (in the sense that v. 32 is apocalyptic!). Bath water is for babies; babies should not be lost when the water gets unclean!

M. Hooker

The interest of Morna Hooker in the Son of man in Mark led her to consider the nature of Mark 13 as the context for vv. 24–27. To her the character of the material in Mark 13 is of greater moment than its authenticity. Contrary to prevailing opinion, she adjudged the discourse to be closer to the form of OT prophecy than to apocalyptic. Granting that Mark 13 resembles apocalyptic in various ways, she held that it lacks many of the normal characteristics of apocalyptic litera-

---

[77] Ibid., 145.

[78] As in Schreiber's exegesis of vv. 14 (which is not related at all to v. 2), 24–27, 28–29, 30, 31; even v. 32 is not satisfactorily expounded.

ture, e.g., it is not an account of visionary experience, nor is it a revelation of an apocalyptic timetable (cf. vv. 32–37).

One of the problems bearing on this question is the juxtaposition of "historical" and "supernatural" elements; we have what seems to be a prophecy of the fall of Jerusalem along with anticipations of the parousia. The distinction, however, between "historical" and "supernatural" events is foreign to the biblical writers generally. "The whole Hebrew understanding of God is grounded in the belief that he is a God who acts in history. . . . It was therefore not incongruous to link together the activities of men and what today are termed 'acts of God'; Roman armies were as much God's tools as were thunderbolts and falling stars."[79]

This mixture of historical and supernatural events in Mark 13 is in many ways closer to OT prophecy than it is to later apocalyptic. So also is the element of judgment on Israel for its rejection of the Messiah, a theme which dominates the discourse and links the latter with OT prophetic teaching. The prophecy against the temple in Mark 13:2 is to be read against the background of its preceding context (Jesus' actions against the temple, the cursing of the fig tree, and the religious authorities' hostility toward Jesus, chs. 11–12) and in the light of the chapters that follow (the Jews' handing of Jesus over to the Roman authorities, chs. 14–15). The disciples' assumption, revealed in their question, that the fate of the temple and of Jerusalem is bound up with other eschatological events, puts the prediction in the category of prophecy, as related passages like Mic 3:6–12; Jer 7:14–34; Isa 63:15—64:13 illustrate. The connection between the rejection of Jesus and coming judgment is in harmony with the teaching of the OT prophets, for they, too, regarded their nation's rejection of their message as connected with the judgment of God (e.g., Isa 1:19–20; Jer 7:1–15). But it is also linked with that of Jesus, as Mark 8:38 attests. Apart from this general connection with Mark 8:38, the travail of the disciples in 13:9–13 is an elaboration of the theme of 8:34–38; and the climax of the discourse in 13:24–27 implies that the revelation of the Son of man is synonymous with judgment—disaster for those who have rejected Jesus, vindication for those who have been faithful to him.[80]

Admittedly, in comparison with Mark 14:62 the saying in 13:26 has several secondary features;[81] yet it is felt to be significant that the

---

[79] Hooker, *The Son of Man in Mark: A Study of the Background of the Term "Son of Man" and Its Use in St. Mark's Gospel* (London, 1967), 149–50.

[80] Ibid., 156–57.

[81] The secondary features are the use of *opsontai* instead of *opsesthe*, of *en nephelais* for *meta tōn nephelōn*, a generalizing summary of *meta dynameōs pollēs kai doxēs*, and that Mark represents the "coming" as a parousia from heaven, whereas 14:62 is more faithful to Dan 7:13.

"arrival" of the Son of man is connected, as in Daniel, with the theme of present suffering and future vindication; by contrast the Son of man in Enoch and 4 Ezra has been detached from this theme, and the emphasis there falls on his judgment of the wicked. Mark has, of course, interpreted the event of the parousia, and in this his faithfulness to Jesus is questioned; it is possible that "behind Mark's interpretation there may well lie a stage in the tradition in which the coming of the Son of man was understood, as in Daniel, of a judgment before God rather than of a parousia to earth."[82]

In a lecture delivered fifteen years after the publication of *The Son of Man in Mark,* Morna Hooker returned to the subject of Mark 13.[83] Convictions earlier expressed as to the nature of the discourse are freshly stated, not least that Mark 13 is not strictly an apocalypse, but rather is midway between prophecy and apocalyptic.[84] The element to which she particularly directs attention in the lecture is the relation between signs and the parousia.

The discourse divides itself into five sections (vv. 5–8, 9–13, 14–20, 21–23, 24–27), followed by two parables (the Fig Tree, vv. 28–29) and the Watchman (vv. 34–36), plus a few sayings concerning the time of the end (vv. 30–32). The chief lesson of the first six sections appears to be, "Do not be alarmed by these events . . . the end is not yet; but when the event occurs—then watch out!" But the last section of the discourse appears to contradict this mood by urging the need for constant watchfulness, since the time of the parousia is unknown. Yet it is this last section that is closest to the authentic teaching of Jesus, which may be summarized: "Watch, for the kingdom of God may come at any moment." That encouraged the earliest Christians to expect an imminent end to the world, and it led to the necessity for a new warning: "Don't get too excited; the end is near, but not as near as all that!"

This is the kind of situation reflected in the letters to the Thessalonian church, a situation Paul had to correct. It seems to have been duplicated in Mark's church, and he had to adapt the eschatological teaching to fit it. He modified the original warning regarding the end coming at any time to suggest that it may be later than that; Christians need to serve the Lord faithfully and face trials, however long they may have to wait. The question is how to reconcile these conflicting attitudes.[85] The inconcinnity is lessened by the observation that in the three sections where a sign is mentioned emphasis is laid on the speed with which the signs are followed by the event they herald: "When the temple is invaded by antichrist, then it will be destroyed; when the

---

[82] Ibid., 158–59.
[83] Idem, "Trial and Tribulation in Mark XIII," *BJRL* 65 (1982): 78–99.
[84] Ibid., 78.
[85] Ibid., 79–81.

heavens break up, the end is here; when the leaves unfold, summer has come. There is no time for anything." The signs are not detached phenomena, but rather the beginning of the disaster itself. In this situation the message of the final paragraph is appropriate; if things happen so suddenly, the disciples must always be on the alert.[86]

Among the likenesses and differences between the situation in Thessalonica and Mark's church it is noteworthy that the great sign in the former was the appearance of the man of lawlessness, who sits in the temple and proclaims himself as God and performs signs and wonders. In Mark 13 the activities of the antichrist are divided among three groups of figures: those who usurp Jesus' name and say, "I am"; the abomination of desolation; and the pseudomessiahs and pseudo-prophets who do signs and wonders. Mark's three groups seem to represent different parts of the tradition about the rebellion of the last times. The tradition preserved in 2 Thessalonians 2 may have led to the kind of misinterpretation to which Mark is opposed, namely, the hunting for signs. Hence "Mark's message is a warning against looking for false signs . . . [his] readers must not be misled by talk about the signs of the End. This is why he adapts the final parable. They need to wait patiently and work as well as watch."[87]

The caveat at categorizing Mark 13 as purely and simply an apocalypse is timely.[88] If with Hooker we are to view the discourse as midway between prophetic and apocalyptic, it would perhaps be just to think of it as prophetic-apocalyptic.

As to the notion that behind Mark 13:26 stands an earlier tradition of an ascent of the Son of man to a judgment scene in heaven, I have given reason elsewhere in this book to believe that Dan 7:13; Mark 13:26; and 14:62 are to be understood in terms of theophany, and that always denotes a coming from heaven to earth, not vice versa.[89]

The relation between signs and suddenness of the end is a problem not confined to the discourse, but it is particularly apparent in it. Hooker's solution is intriguing and helpful, but calls for some modification. The cosmic upheavals of vv. 24–25 are strictly not preliminary signs announcing the parousia but accompaniments of it, in no way related to the end as the abomination is to the destruction of the temple. Moreover, the parable of the Fig Tree assumes that the end is in some way preceded by signs, which excludes the notion of an imminent coming of the kingdom. Indeed, I do not believe that it can be demonstrated that Jesus taught a coming of the kingdom of God in the imminent future. A near expectation in his teaching is plain, but that is

---

[86] Ibid., 95–96.
[87] Ibid., 97.
[88] Ibid., 99.
[89] See 507–11.

different from the idea that the kingdom of God is likely to come tonight or tomorrow. We must bear in mind the implications of the prophecy with which the discourse opens in v. 2; that presumes some period between the anticipated death of Jesus and the event declared. Verse 32 leaves room for a near expectation and the possibility of one more remote. Mark's ordering of the discourse is compatible with that scheme.

G. Minette de Tillesse

De Tillesse precedes his treatment of Mark 13 by drawing attention to a feature of apocalyptic writings that could be of significance for the discourse.[90] In such literature the present situation is depicted as seen long beforehand by God and announced as a prophecy. Of this feature Daniel is the classic example. The precision in descriptions of past history and present tribulations contrasts with the imprecise character of the promised future salvation. And so it is with Mark 13. The *tauta panta* which are to occur in the contemporary generation (v. 30) refer to the content of the disciples' question in v. 4; the chronological precision suggests that the *tauta panta* had been accomplished when Mark wrote. Similarly the *tauta* of v. 29 relates to things which the readers have seen happening, and Mark invites them to draw the consequences: the Lord is at the door and will not delay. In v. 23 "I have told you all things" indicates that the description has finished at this point; everything that has gone before is past history. This is confirmed in the redactional elements: the *oupō* of v. 7; the *archē ōdinōn* of v. 8 (they have started!); the observation in v. 14, "Let the reader understand," for the reader is in the midst of the situation; "I have told you all" in v. 23, for the parousia alone is to come to pass.[91] What is said of the "abomination" is instructive; in both 2 Thessalonians and Mark 13 a fresh violation of the sanctuary of God is to occur before the parousia, but Paul tells Christians to be calm because the adversary has not yet come, whereas Mark says that they must watch and be on the guard because he has come![92]

Accordingly the date of Mark's composition is to be set after the fall of Jerusalem, perhaps after the triumph of Vespasian and Titus in Rome, as Brandon suggested. Both Christians and Jews had experienced persecutions at that time, as in the Jewish War; Mark judged it necessary to write his Gospel in this period to give the church at Rome a new foundation.[93] In composing the discourse Mark built on a Christian

---

[90] Minette de Tillesse, *Le Secret Messianique dans l'Evangile de Marc* (Paris, 1968), especially pp. 421–38.

[91] Ibid., 421–27.

[92] Ibid., 428–29.

[93] Ibid., 434–37.

apocalyptic tradition, which is solidly attested in 2 Thessalonians and in Revelation. This tradition in all likelihood drew its origin from the "word of the Lord" (1 Thess 4:15), and so enjoyed great authority; Mark therefore puts the apocalypse on the lips of Jesus.[94]

This is an unusual mode of expounding the relation between Mark 13 and contemporary apocalypses. The closeness of similarity has perhaps been overstated. Mark 13 does not portray a march of events through history to AD 71–72, nor is there any such precision in prophetic declaration such as is observable in Daniel 11. Admittedly it is as feasible, theoretically, that Mark stands at a point after the appearance of the abomination of desolation as the author of Daniel did in the prophecies of Dan 9:26–27 and 11:31, and there is no objection to it on principle. The difficulties arise from a precise identification of the abomination prophecy with the destruction of the city and temple and the other data of the discourse. In the former case, as we pointed out in reference to Brandon's interpretation (to which Minette de Tillesse approximates), the directions given in vv. 14ff. are incomprehensible, for these assume that the appearance of the abomination heralds the outbreak of Israel's distress, hence the call given to flee from the city and for those in the country not to take refuge within it; such advice is inapplicable if the abomination denotes the destruction of the city and temple which has already taken place. Admittedly the date of the composition of the discourse is difficult to determine, but Minette de Tillesse builds on the assumption that the whole prophecy, apart from the parousia, has been fulfilled; yet there is no clear intimation that the fall of Jerusalem has actually taken place; if we are to invoke the example of apocalypses we may contrast the distinction between Dan 11:1–39 and 11:40–41, which has no counterpart in Mark's discourse.

That the evangelist made an independent use of traditions current in the church about Jesus' teaching on Jerusalem's judgment and the end of the age, as did Paul and the Seer of Revelation, is wholly plausible. It is possible, however, that the "word of the Lord" may have taken firmer shape before Mark's redaction than Minette de Tillesse has allowed for.

C. B. Cousar

Occasionally a writer is drawn to subordinate the problems of the origin of Mark 13 to a consideration of its theology. While not neglecting the former, C. B. Cousar pays special attention to the latter. In an article on the discourse[95] he sets the following statement as a preface:

---

[94] Ibid., 438.

[95] Cousar, "Eschatology and Mark's *Theologia Crucis:* A Critical Analysis of Mark 13," *Int* 24 (1970): 321–35.

"Mark's whole understanding of the gospel, what it does for believers, and what believers must do in response, points to an eschatology understood in mission, not in withdrawal. The Son of Man who is to come recognizes as his own those who through proclamation and suffering have identified with his redemptive activity in the world. No moment is incidental, because in view of the cross and resurrection the history and life of the people of God have become thoroughly eschatological."[96] This reflection on what Mark sought to convey in the discourse is followed by a summary statement of Cousar's thesis, that ch. 13 is an integral part of Mark's announcement of the gospel of Jesus Christ, summoning the church to "a mission of bondage to the suffering Son of Man" and at the same time opposing "a distorted *theologia gloriae* in which overly enthusiastic adherents neglected the call to cross-bearing and discipleship."[97]

Cousar operates on the basis that the discourse is a Markan composition, containing Jewish or Jewish-Christian apocalyptic material, traditional sayings, and redactional comments, and that it is these last which enable us to trace Mark's message in the discourse. In them a note of warning sounds throughout the chapter. These are directed, however, not to one danger but to several. They have in view (1) pretenders and false prophets (vv. 5–7, 21–23), (2) the need of the community to take heart in face of trials provoked by witness to the gospel, and (3) the need for watchfulness on the part of believers in face of the suddenness and unknown time of the end (vv. 33–37).

The warnings against pseudomessiahs and false prophets are bound up with a call not to be alarmed at the wars, earthquakes, famines, etc., which could be mistaken as evidence that the end has come. The same thought controls vv. 14–20. These events may be preliminary to the parousia, but they are not signs of the end itself. "By attributing to the events recorded in vv. 5–23 the character of *Vorzeichen,* Mark indicates that they are to be understood eschatologically but not apocalyptically. . . . The parousia alone remains exclusively an apocalyptic hope."[98] Indeed, the parousia stands on the opposite side of the line from the events of the sixties that impressed the enthusiasts, for the time of the parousia cannot be calculated; one can only watch and wait. This attitude which Mark would inculcate is one with the message of the parable of the Seed growing secretly (4:26–29): the farmer can neither hasten nor deter the growth of the seed he has planted; he does not understand how it happens; he can only be ready for the harvest when it comes. Neither Matthew nor Luke has reproduced this parable, but

---

[96] Ibid., 321.
[97] Ibid., 322.
[98] Ibid., 326–27.

significantly Mark has embodied its lesson again in his discourse. Therein Mark is guided by an apocalyptic perspective which sees history moving toward its goal according to God's plan, but he takes an anti–apocalyptic attitude toward speculation and unwarranted enthusiasm. Both perspectives are present in the discourse. Mark affirms "the divine order and the eschatological necessity of what is happening," and at the same time directs the community away from a preoccupation with apocalyptic calculations to an immediate and urgent discipleship.[99]

The section vv. 9–13 has a relation both to 8:31–38 and to the passion narrative, which immediately follows the chapter. Accordingly it may be said: "Behind and before the delivering over of the community into the hands of its persecutors stands the suffering Lord of the community, falsely accused before councils, hated, beaten, yet through endurance to the end bringing salvation. In the way of discipleship he leaves to his followers a no less difficult road to travel than he himself walked."[100] Mark's redactional addition of v. 10 declares the mission of this eschatological community and at the same time suggests a delay in the appearance of the Son of man. The community therefore discovers its eschatological dimension not through poring over apocalyptic timetables but by engaging in its mission to the nations, which has to be fulfilled before the parousia takes place. The directing of the gaze of the community forward to the parousia as well as back to the passion of the Son of man gives hope to an otherwise hopeless predicament. Mark's *theologia crucis* is not "a morbid masochism bordering on suicidal mania," for the way of discipleship is the path by which true life is found (8:35) and by which one is saved (13:13).[101]

The emphasis on watchfulness, which concludes the discourse in vv. 33ff., is noteworthy, for the false prophets would have found that agreeable to their views: that was precisely their call to the church! The difference between their emphasis and Mark's is apparent in the relation between ch. 13 and the passion narrative: 13:33–37 serve as a transition to the latter and have a clear relation to the Gethsemane pericope in 14:33–42. The demand on the disciples in the garden to "watch" is symbolic of a deeper demand: they were expected to share in the messianic suffering, to identify with Jesus in drinking the cup of sorrow and in enduring the cross. Their prayer in the hour of temptation was intended to unite them with Jesus in the final struggle against Satan. Thus the *theologia crucis* comes to the fore again.[102]

---

[99] The first quotation is a citation from N. A. Dahl's comments on the parable of the Seed growing secretly, in "The Parables of Growth," *ST* 5 (1952): 149–50; see Cousar, "Eschatology," 327.

[100] Ibid., 329.

[101] Ibid., 329–32.

[102] Ibid., 333.

A further question arises from a consideration of v. 37: Why does Mark bracket the discourse between a private beginning and a public ending? The answer is twofold: on the one hand the fact that disciples are addressed shows that the eschatological instruction in the discourse can be understood only by the Christian community (cf. 4:11: "to you the secret of the kingdom of God has been given"); on the other hand Mark breaks the traditional apocalyptic pattern in which secrets of the future are revealed to a select few. The enthusiasts may well have maintained the tradition, but Mark makes it clear that what he has written is intended for the whole community.[103]

Cousar's article is exceedingly stimulating and illuminating. It exemplifies a mode of dealing with the text of the Gospels that one could wish were more frequently followed. It is particularly valuable to have the discourse of Mark 13 linked with Mark's message in the Gospel as a whole. The connection between the situation of the church in Mark 13 and the call to discipleship to the suffering Son of man in 8:31ff. and the passion narrative is important for understanding 13:9ff.; mission in the midst of *thlipsis* is characteristic of the apostolic view of the church on the way to the parousia via tribulation. In setting this out Mark will have been motivated less by apocalyptic dogma than by recognition and acceptance of the vocation of the community of the Son of man.

It is right also to emphasize Mark's concern to put a brake on apocalyptic expectations of enthusiasts, and to distinguish between the fate of Jerusalem and the hope of the church in the parousia, as Cousar does. Nevertheless it is important also to acknowledge in the discourse a concern for Jerusalem and Israel. Mark 13:14–18 clearly reflect apocalyptic expectations, but they are not an exposition of those expectations so much as an exhortation in face of their anticipated realization. The apocalyptic enthusiasts will have been concerned only to identify the calamity of the Jews with the last day and then to proclaim their apocalyptic conclusions; the passage itself has a different emphasis, reflecting a pity for those involved in the dread situation, and Mark has not eliminated this note, even though he was not responsible for it.

The call to watchfulness may perhaps be interpreted too narrowly if it is understood exclusively in the light of the Gethsemane narrative. If the *blepete* in v. 33 is a Markan redaction, strengthening the call in *agrypneite*, it evidently anticipates the parable of the Porter in vv. 34ff. In harmony with the use of *blepete* earlier in the discourse, it calls on believers to be awake to what is happening around them in the world, so that they may not be led astray (vv. 5ff.) and may seize with courage the opportunities presented for testimony before the opponents of the

---

[103]Ibid., 334.

gospel (vv. 9ff.). As such it denotes a spiritual alertness which is to be expressed in all areas of life. Hence it finds a variety of application in the parables of Jesus, and was taken up by the primitive church in its parenesis.[104]

F. Flückiger

In the same year that Cousar's article on Mark 13 was published a very different one on the same theme appeared from the Swiss theologian F. Flückiger, who had earlier written a book giving a critique of the "thoroughgoing eschatology" of A. Schweitzer and M. Werner.[105] In his article Flückiger pointed out what an unusual phenomenon the discourse of Mark 13 is in Mark's Gospel; the only other discourse in the book, that of ch. 4, is not comparable, since the parables retain their independence in a series and are not worked together into an address on the kingdom of God. Further, the discourse of ch. 13 is not a consistent composition; it contains many unresolved statements and contradictions, such as the early expectation of the parousia and the long period wherein the gospel goes to all the nations, or the proclamation of the catastrophic end of the world, which is yet preceded by a local disaster in Judea. Moreover, the leading theological viewpoints of Mark are missing from the discourse; the eschatology is unrelated to the death of Jesus, and the salvation of the elect is due to the shortening of the tribulation before the final catastrophe can overtake them. Flückiger concluded that Mark must have received the discourse and integrated it into his Gospel without essential change.[106]

In examining the discourse to discover its original elements, Flückiger found three groups of sayings which reveal thematic and linguistic connections: (1) apocalyptic sayings concerning the final catastrophe of history, vv. 8, 12, 17, 19–20, 24–27; (2) mission sayings which presuppose the Christian mission, vv. 5–6, 21–23, 7, 9–11, 13; (3) a temple prophecy, vv. 1–4, 14–16, 18, 28–32.[107]

---

[104]See, e.g., the parables of the Watchful Servants, Luke 12:35–38; the Burglar, Luke 12:35–38 par.; the Widow and Judge, Luke 18:1–8; the three parables of Matthew 25. Matthew's understanding of these last is well reflected in Bonnard's comment: "To make provision of oil [in the parable of the Maidens] is faithfully to accomplish a mission received (Matt 25:14–30) and to go to the aid of the least of the brothers of the Son of man (Matt 25:31–46)" (*Matthieu*, 358–59). On the early church's parenesis cf. 1 Thess 5:1–11; 2 Thess 1:5; 1 Pet 1:13, 4:7, 5:8.

[105]Flückiger, "Die Redaktion der Zukunftsrede in Markus 13," *TZ* 26 (1970): 395–409; idem, *Der Ursprung des christlichen Dogmas, Eine Auseinandersetzung mit Albert Schweitzer und Martin Werner* (Zürich, 1955).

[106]Flückiger, "Redaktion," 396–97.

[107]Ibid., 397–98.

The first group is an impersonal description of the events of the end, given in the third person. Its content and language indicate that it belongs to a late Jewish apocalypse which theologically stands near to the book of Enoch. It contains nothing Christian. There is no hint that the Son of man is Jesus, and that he lived and suffered and achieved salvation for humankind. Its description of the coming of the Son of man is derived from Dan 7:13; originally it will have indicated a coming to God, as in Daniel, but the redactor (and Mark) will have thought of Jesus coming to the world.[108]

The mission sayings stem from a connected text having common presuppositions and formal similarities. It is presupposed that Jesus is the speaker, and all believers who bear witness for him are addressed. The rejection of near expectation is plain, both from the attitude to the alleged signs of the end (v. 7) and from the necessity of proclaiming the gospel to all nations. Probably we have here sayings of a Christian prophet that were viewed as revelations received from Jesus and that circulated in the church as words of Jesus, perhaps in the time of Nero's persecution.[109]

The temple prophecy takes its rise from the prediction of v. 2. But the comprehensive expression "all these things" in v. 4 hints that something more than the temple destruction was originally in view; an earlier version would have included the announcement of a new house of God replacing the temple, as in 14:58 and 15:29. The background of this prophecy is that of Nathan to David: God is to raise a successor to David who will be called God's Son, and he will build a house that will stand for ever (2 Sam 7:13); thus the new house that Jesus will build is the messianic kingdom of David. The unknown redactor of the discourse omitted the second part of the original saying, since he belonged to those Christian groups who no longer looked for the conversion of Israel (cf. Stephen's speech in Acts 7) and who believed that the end of all things was near. The temple prophecy probably went back to Jesus; it could have been an independently formed story, intended for reading in worship, perhaps even a pericope from a Gospel no longer extant.[110]

In composing the discourse the redactor did not attempt to modify the wording of its individual sections; he simply joined them together and allowed the contradictions and roughnesses to remain. His work must be looked on as a preliminary to the making of the Gospels, for it is much more primitive than the procedures of the evangelists.

Flückiger's article represents independent thinking about the discourse and warrants careful evaluation by scholars. There is no doubt

---

[108]Ibid., 400.
[109]Ibid., 401–2.
[110]Ibid., 403–8.

as to the uniqueness of ch. 13 in Mark's Gospel. But the contradictions of the chapter have been overdrawn. Flückiger seems to have overlooked that characterizations of a local catastrophe in terms of the (or a) day of the Lord are common in OT prophecy.[111] It is also to be remembered, as we earlier pointed out, that Paul found no difficulty in conjoining a near expectation with a commission to take the gospel to the whole world. The same applies to the lack of expression within the discourse of Mark's own theological viewpoints. It is hardly just to the discourse to maintain that the salvation of the Son of man is wrought simply by his shortening the great distress; he manifests the kingdom of God in his parousia and gathers his elect into it (cf. vv. 20 and 27). But was Cousar mistaken in reading Mark's theology of suffering in the discourse? No, for while Mark works with the materials handed on to him, he links them by his redaction to the theology of the cross expressed before and after the discourse. Flückiger has taken insufficient account of the significance of *Mark's* redaction for the theology of the discourse.

The analysis of the discourse into three groups and their delimitation is important. The moot question is how extensive they were, and whether the sayings have been assigned to the right groups. In this, of course, probability has to be our guide.

As to the first group of "apocalyptic sayings," it is unclear why v. 7 has been separated from v. 8, v. 17 from vv. 14–16 and 18, and why vv. 19–20 have been divorced from v. 14, since both v. 14 and v. 19 are derived from the Danielic descriptions of Israel's distress. The parousia passage of vv. 24–27 admittedly can be linked with this group, but not necessarily so originally; contrary to Flückiger, there is no ground at all for viewing it as Jewish rather than Christian, least of all in Mark's Gospel, where in the parousia the Son of man is of prime importance.

It is surprising to see vv. 5–7 and 21–23 conjoined with vv. 9–11, 13 as betokening the Christian mission. Presumably Flückiger is impressed with the motif of delay manifest in vv. 5ff. and 9ff., and the use of the link word *blepete* in all the passages. No doubt unity can be found among them within their context in the discourse, but there are closer connections between them and other groups in the chapter.

---

[111] See, e.g., Amos 5:16–27, where the day of the Lord is said to be a darkness wherein God will drive the people into exile beyond Damascus. In Isaiah 13 the oracle against Babylon is pronounced as the day of the Lord upon the city, accompanied by cosmic signs, but the instruments of its destruction are the armies of the Medes (vv. 4, 17), and there is no indication that the end of the age is then reached. Similar descriptions of judgment upon cities and peoples, with or without mention of a (or the) day of the Lord may be seen in Nahum 2–3; Isaiah 15–16; 17; 19; 23–24; Jeremiah 25; 26; 46; 47; 48; 49; 50–51; and with equal frequency in Ezekiel (25; 26–28; 29–30).

The temple prophecy truly links vv. 1–4 with v. 14, but is it likely that an early redactor reduced a saying on the temple in the form of 14:58 to that of 13:2 by reason of his belief in the hopelessness of Israel's conversion? The redactor is thought to share Stephen's opinion regarding the Jews; curiously, in the charge cited against Stephen (Acts 6:13) his polemic against "the holy place" contains no reference to a spiritual temple replacing the material one, which Jesus is said to be about to destroy; but in Stephen's address there is a likely echo of the thought of Mark 14:58: "The Most High does not live in places made by hands" (*cheiropoiētoi*, Acts 7:48). In the context of the address the contrast between the material temple, which cannot contain God, and the spiritual temple of believers wherein he dwells, now that the Christ has wrought his work, may well be in mind.[112] But the judgment of God on the temple does not, in fact, carry with it the corollary that Israel's doom is irretrievable, as the books of the prophets illustrate, and as the NT similarly attests. The condemnation of the Jews and their doom sounds final enough in 1 Thess 2:14–16, but Rom 11:25ff. presents a happier picture by Paul of Israel's final destiny. So also the condemnation of the Jews expressed in Matt 23:34–36, followed by the judgment on the temple in vv. 37–38, is very strong, yet v. 39 contains a ray of hope for the nation facing wrath.

If Flückiger's exposition of the solution to the problem of Mark's sources is questionable, it is nevertheless our conviction that he points toward the direction in which we need to travel. The earlier conjunctions of sayings in the discourse require more thought, as also the motives that led to their eventual union. In this process, however, recognition must be given to the role of the evangelist in the final redaction.

3. Later Redaction-Critical Discussions of the Discourse

A. M. Ambrozic

The investigation by Ambrozic of Mark 13 was undertaken in the context of Mark's view of the kingdom of God as reflected in Mark 9:1. This caused him to be especially interested in the expectations of the time of the end set forth in Mark 13, and it led him to make an unusual approach to the discourse. He postulated that the evangelist's aim is most clearly revealed in the last paragraph of the discourse, indeed, in

---

[112]Especially in Luke's mind! His omission of Mark 14:58 from his passion narrative may well be influenced by his desire to reserve the concept for inclusion in Stephen's address. On its place in Acts 7:48–50 see F. F. Bruce, *The Book of the Acts*, NICNT (Grand Rapids, 1954), 158–60; and W. Neil, *The Acts of the Apostles*, NCBC (Grand Rapids, 1981), 114.

the final short sentence, "What I say to you, I say to all: Watch!" On this Ambrozic comments: "This last verse, undoubtedly redactional, bursting as it does the framework of esoteric instruction imposed upon the discourse by Mark in v. 3, insists that the watchfulness urged upon the disciples is also the attitude demanded of all Christians."[113] From this point one is inevitably led backwards into the discourse. The key term in v. 37 *grēgoreite* is also the opening word of vv. 35–36, and this unit forms the application of the parable in v. 34; v. 33 enunciates the same message as vv. 35–36. This close-knit final paragraph of the discourse, however, spells out the message of v. 32, which in turn qualifies the preceding vv. 28–31. The unit vv. 28–32 fulfills an important function in the discourse, since it answers the question posed in v. 4. Thus the exhortation to watchfulness reveals Mark's fundamental intention in the composition of the discourse. The parenetic emphasis of the closing paragraph runs through the entire discourse, as is seen in the appearance of the characteristic Markan *blepete* at salient points within the discourse (vv. 5, 9, 23, 33).[114]

What, then, does Mark think about the time of the end? That can be gathered from the introduction in vv. 1–4, with its prophecy of the ruin of the temple and the disciples' question provoked by it, and vv. 28–32, which form the reply to the question. These two passages form the redactional clasps of the discourse. In v. 4 the question as to the destruction of the temple broadens into one about the sign of the end, and the weight of the question falls on the latter aspect. The section of the discourse which lies between the inclusion formed by vv. 6 and 21–23 is evidently intended to be understood as a unity; it contains a clear delineation of the history from the time of Jesus to the fall of Jerusalem. Invoking the parallel drawn by Minette de Tillesse between the detailed predictions in Daniel up to the time of the temple's profanation under Antiochus as compared with the vague prophecy of the end, and the detailed historical predictions in Mark 13:5–23 followed by the prophecy of the parousia, Ambrozic concludes that Mark wrote after the fall of Jerusalem; historical events are described in vv. 5–23 and the parousia anticipated in vv. 24–27. A connection between the destruction of the temple and the end of the age is recognized, but while this destruction is viewed as a sign of the end (v. 29), the historical event is separated from the coming of the Son of man (vv. 24–27); the latter is looked for within the life span of the contemporary generation (v. 30), but is declared to be incalculable (v. 32). The destruction of the temple therefore is acknowledged to be a sign of the end but

---

[113] Ambrozic, *The Hidden Kingdom: A Redaction-Critical Study of the References to the Kingdom of God in Mark's Gospel,* CBQMS 2 (Washington, D.C., 1972), 222–23.

[114] Ibid., 224.

not a reckoning device, and it serves as the basis of the ethical exhortations contained in vv. 33–37.[115]

Ambrozic has performed a useful service in calling attention to the importance of the final paragraph of the discourse, which is commonly viewed as an insignificant Markan appendix. He observes that Hartman and Conzelmann have pointed out the presence of a similar parenetic tendency in early Christian eschatological and apocalyptic teaching before Mark's time;[116] he could have added other names to the list of those who have recognized the importance of this feature in the catechesis of the primitive church; we shall consider it in some detail later, and its significance for the formation of the discourse. Ambrozic's adherence to the views of Minette de Tillesse and R. Pesch on the relation of vv. 5–23 to vv. 24–27 as a means for dating Mark's redaction of the discourse is more problematic; we refer the reader to our comments made elsewhere on this issue.[117]

T. J. Weeden

Weeden's exposition of Mark 13 takes its place in the context of an unusual thesis: Mark wrote his Gospel to counter a false Christology in the church of his day; the heresy viewed Jesus as a *theios-anēr*, a superhuman figure who authenticated his status through his superhuman powers, and it originated with and was promulgated by the apostles of Jesus; so Mark's account of the ministry of Jesus is dominated by an increasingly violent conflict between Jesus and the disciples on this issue. Weeden holds that Mark represents the disciples as passing through three stages in their pilgrimage in Christology: (1) a lack of perception on their part as to who Jesus is; (2) a misconception as to the nature of his messiahship; (3) a downright rejection of his teaching on the messiahship.[118] Peter's confession of Jesus as the Messiah is a confession to a *theios-anēr* Christ; this characterization Jesus rejects, and he sets forth instead his own understanding of the Messiah's vocation in terms of the Son of man who must suffer; Peter rebukes Jesus for such a representation of the Messiah, whereupon Jesus declares Peter's views to be satanic. Thus two Christologies are set in vivid contrast over against each other. From then on Jesus and the disciples are locked in continuous conflict over the nature of authentic messiahship. The apostles' total rejection of the instruction of Jesus on this matter reaches its climax in Judas' delivering Jesus to his enemies, the

---

[115] Ibid., 226–31.

[116] See Hartman, *Prophecy Interpreted,* ConBNT 1 (Lund, 1966), 145–226; Conzelmann, "Geschichte und *Eschaton* nach Mc 13," 213–15.

[117] On the view of Minette de Tellesse see above, 190–91; on that of R. Pesch see below, 273–83.

[118] Weeden, *Mark: Traditions in Conflict* (Philadelphia, 1971), 26–40.

disciples' forsaking Jesus in the garden, and Peter's disowning Jesus in the high priest's courtyard. So the relations between Jesus and the apostles end in an irremediable rupture: Mark records no resurrection appearances to the apostles, no rehabilitation of them, and no commissioning of them. Peter's tears after the denial are appropriate: as he was ashamed of Jesus, so the Son of man will be ashamed of him at his parousia (Mark 8:38).[119]

The pertinence of Mark 13 to this interpretation of Mark's intention in his Gospel lies in the relation between the false teachers in the discourse and the disciples in the rest of the Gospel. The redactional features in the discourse, especially the interpolations of *blepete,* emphasize the dangerous activity of the impostors in the church. Verse 22 states that they perform "signs and wonders," actions which are characteristic of *theios-anēr* claimants. They are Christian charismatic leaders, who in their visionary ecstasy feel one with the exalted Lord.[120] Mark opposes their claims by emphasizing two characteristics of the present period of the church. First, it is marked by the absence of the risen Lord from his community (cf. vv. 9–13, where the persecuted believers are promised the aid of the Holy Spirit, not of the risen Lord as in Luke 21:17); since the church in this time has to function without the guidance of its Lord, the falsity of the claims of these charismatic teachers is clear.[121] Second, the activity of pseudomessiahs and pseudoprophets is a feature of the whole period from Easter to the parousia, including Mark's time.[122] The predicament of Mark's church is mirrored in the parable about the absent Master, Mark 13:34–36: the resurrected Lord is absent from his people, and they are concerned about his failure to return; Mark encourages them with the assurance that the Lord will come in their lifetime (v. 30), but they must refuse the apocalyptic timetables of the false teachers (v. 32). Here the relevance of the apocalyptic source incorporated by Mark is seen: Mark cites vv. 7–8 and 14–20, with corrections, to warn against attempts to calendarize the last times (note especially vv. 7b and 8d), and vv. 24–27 to show that the parousia of Jesus will not take place till after this world has passed away.[123]

So Mark endeavors to make it plain that the church's situation, endangered by the proponents of a false Christology, is similar to that of Jesus, who was opposed by uncomprehending and intractable disci-

---

[119]Ibid., 34–51, 52–69.

[120]"As the plenipotentiaries of Christ, they understood themselves to be not only the mouthpieces of the exalted Lord, but also to a certain extent the incarnate vehicles of the Lord's Spirit" (ibid., 80).

[121]Ibid., 85–87.

[122]Ibid., 89.

[123]Ibid., 90–97.

ples; the christological controversy is one and the same, alike for Jesus and his church! Mark writes to ensure that his community will not reject the authentic faith taught by Jesus and succumb to the heresy of his enemies.[124]

Reading Weeden's book brought to mind a remark of a British scholar: "How Mark does hate the Twelve!"[125] Weeden has provided an exposition of that notion and involved himself in exaggerations as evident as that of the exclamation. These are seen in the interpretation of Mark's emphasis on the miracles of Jesus, in virtue of which Jesus in the first half of Mark's Gospel appears as the *theios-anēr:* "If the only portion of Mark's Gospel one possessed was 1:1—8:29, one would have to assume that Mark understood Jesus to be a *theios-anēr* and that his messiahship was to be interpreted only within that perspective. There is absolutely no hint in the first half of the Gospel that authentic messiahship should contain any other christological dimension."[126] This reads strangely in the light of Mark's introduction to the ministry of Jesus, which culminates in the presentation of Jesus as the Proclaimer of the good news of God (1:14–15). The "good news" is that the promise of God's saving sovereignty is now in process of fulfillment, and Mark proceeds to show that this takes place in the word and deed of Jesus, and not least in his table fellowship with sinners, which anticipated the fellowship of God with humankind in the perfected kingdom (2:19–20); the divine saving sovereignty thus is experienced in the fellowship of Jesus. The key to Mark's account of the ministry of Jesus, even in the first half of his Gospel, is not the category of the divine man, but eschatological hope fulfilled in Jesus, the representative of the divine saving sovereignty.

The blindness of the disciples in Mark's account is also exaggerated by Weeden. It is, after all, Mark alone who enables us to see the "imperfect" miracle of the opening of a blind man's eyes as representative of Peter's experience (8:22ff.); at Caesarea Philippi Peter sees Jesus only imperfectly, but through the succeeding events of Jesus' ministry he is enabled to see properly. The notion that Mark depicts the apostles as ending in total apostasy, leading to irreparable separation from Jesus, is possible only on the basis of an improbable interpretation of 14:28 and 16:7, and moreover it is ruled out by ch. 13 itself. For the address is expressly stated by Mark to be given to Peter and the other leading apostles; they are the ones addressed in vv. 9–13, whose sufferings in the service of Christ are described, who are told that the gospel must be preached to all nations, and who are assured of the Spirit's aid

---

[124]Ibid., 98.

[125]Cited by A. E. J. Rawlinson as from an unnamed friend (*Mark* [1927], xxviii).

[126]Weeden, *Mark,* 56.

as they faithfully continue their witness. There is not a hint of apostasy of the apostles here. Similarly they are the recipients of warnings about false prophets and false messiahs; these warnings are handed on by them through Mark to the church; how then can Mark have equated the beliefs and activities of the false teachers with the instruction of the Twelve? On the contrary, it is through giving heed to the word of Jesus conveyed through the apostles that the troublers of the church are overcome and the authentic faith is preserved.

W. Kelber

Werner Kelber found Weeden's thesis not uncongenial, but the leading idea in his interpretation of Mark 13 is quite independent and equally original. Kelber's primary concern is Mark's intention in the discourse, for he believes that the motivation for producing the address is that which led Mark to write his Gospel.

Manifestly the point of departure of the discourse is the prophecy of the temple's destruction (vv. 1–2). To Kelber this indicates that the event in question had already taken place, since in apocalypses "predictions" of events that occur in history are reflections of what happened. But further, the close relation of the address with the prophecy suggests that the ruin of the temple had precipitated an eschatological crisis of the greatest magnitude for the Christian community.

The warnings of vv. 5–6 and 21–22 draw attention to the activity of false messiahs and false prophets. They come in the name of Jesus and declare *egō eimi*; the latter is a formula of theophany and implies that the persons concerned are Christian prophets who take to themselves the authority and identity of the Messiah-Jesus. For them the death and resurrection of Jesus are without soteriological significance, and the parousia is all that matters; it is of greatest moment therefore that they claim in effect that the parousia has been realized in them.[127] It is because these individuals have gained a hearing and wield powerful influence on Christians that Mark lays such emphasis on the necessity of recognizing them to be false prophets. Kelber suggests that the situation is illuminated by the importance attached to the prophecies of Daniel in the discourse.[128] In the era of the Roman war the Jews were greatly occupied with these same prophecies; it is wholly probable that

---

[127]Cf. Kelber's statement: "Anyone who approximately forty years after Jesus' death claimed Jesus' presence must have claimed the reappearance of the crucified Jesus of the past. This brings us to the very core of the opposition eschatology. It decreed the fulfillment of the *eschaton* by enacting the parousia of Jesus!" (*The Kingdom in Mark: A New Place and a New Time* [Philadelphia, 1974], 115).

[128]Kelber cites with approval Hartman's conviction that the basis of the discourse is a Midrash on Danielic texts (ibid., 135).

the Christians of Jerusalem were one with their fellow Jews in believing
that Daniel's prophecies of the deliverance of their nation were about
to be fulfilled. They therefore threw in their lot with those who resisted
the Romans. Their faith, however, was fearfully discredited: the "abomination of desolation" appeared. The apocalyptic cipher is used to categorize the shocking nature of what took place; it was none other than the
epiphany of Satan, a parousia of the Evil One. So the temple was desecrated and destroyed, and the church along with the rest of the defenders
of the city was annihilated. This caused the crisis of faith and eschatology
among the Christians; the church of Jerusalem had looked for the parousia and kingdom of Jesus, and instead there took place the parousia
and kingdom of Satan, and the Jerusalem community was no more.

Mark's response to this crisis is his Gospel, but in ch. 13 he took
the apocalyptic instruction of the Jerusalem prophets and corrected its
errors. He first laid stress on the falsity of the notion that in these men
the parousia of Jesus took place. He then cited the abomination prophecy, with the appeal that when Christians "see" the abomination they
should flee from Judea to "the mountains"; this apocalyptic speech has
to be translated to a call to recognize the meaning of the disaster as a
satanic action, and to flee to the mountains of Galilee, for there the
kingdom was proclaimed and manifested in Jesus, and there it is to be
perfected. Herein lies the importance of the parousia prophecy in vv.
24–27: "The Christians have already seen the epiphany of the Evil One.
They are called to go the way to the parousia, away from the site of
judgment, and they look forward to the consolidation of the eschatological people of God."[129]

In this respect the discourse is one with the Gospel of Mark in its
entirety, for the error of the false prophets is traceable to the apostles
themselves. They never heard the message of the women at the tomb to
depart from Jerusalem to Galilee (16:7–8), and they failed to grasp the
logic of the kingdom gospel preached by Jesus; so they mistook Jerusalem for the place of promise, forfeited entrance into the kingdom, and
perished in the fall of the city.[130] Mark instructs the church to recognize
that the authentic future lies in the new Jerusalem, i.e., in Galilee.
Christians are to look to the Son of man, back in history to his labors
and his suffering and resurrection, and forward to his parousia. They
are to grasp that while the present is the time between the parousia of
Satan and the parousia of the Son of man, the kingdom continues as a
living reality. "The gospel is the unfinished gospel and its Christ not
fully revealed because the Kingdom is a Kingdom-in-the-making."[131]

---

[129]Ibid., 124.
[130]Ibid., 146.
[131]Ibid., 142.

In Kelber a number of lines of earlier investigations come together to form a striking interpretation of the discourse. Nevertheless, its cogency depends on a cluster of questionable postulates. The prophecy of v. 2 is viewed as a *vaticinium ex eventu,* as is most of the discourse; we have seen reason to query that strongly. It is further assumed that the pseudomessiahs claim to fulfill the parousia of Jesus and are prophets of the Jerusalem church; that many members of that church followed them; that these joined forces with the Zealots in their struggle against Rome; that some imbibed their spirit sufficiently to kill fellow Christians (13:12); that the church in Jerusalem was annihilated in the fall of Jerusalem; that this led to a crisis of faith among the Palestinian churches; that Mark produced his Gospel for the churches of that area; that the apocalyptic passage of v. 14 appeals to those Christians after the fall of Jerusalem to forsake Judea and look to the "mountains" of Galilee, where Jesus in his glory and kingdom will shortly be manifested. Every one of these assumptions is doubtful, and most of them are improbable. Even if one admits that the false messiahs could be viewed as apostate Christians, it is unlikely, despite Weeden, that their claims were due to experiences of the Spirit, or that they were the spiritual heirs of the apostles. If, as many scholars believe, the prophecy of 13:2 circulated in the Gospel traditions with other warnings of Jesus to his people about impending judgment, it is conceivable that the fall of Jerusalem was viewed not as a stumbling block to the faith of many Christians but rather as a confirmation of the word of Jesus, as it undoubtedly was so for Matthew and Luke, and would have been for Paul, had he lived to see the event (cf. 1 Thess 2:16). There are many helpful insights of Kelber in his exposition of Markan thought, but his interpretation of Mark 13 fails to convince.

K. Grayston

An analysis of the discourse on yet another basis was proposed by Kenneth Grayston. Like Flückiger, he is impressed with the solitariness of Mark 13 within the Gospel. He can find no other continuous speech in Mark of more than six sentences;[132] that suggests to him that Mark lacked the ability to write continuous addresses, and so the discourse of ch. 13 must have been received by the evangelist from earlier tradition. Grayston finds a clue to the original core of the discourse in the appearance of the term *hotan* in vv. 7, 11, 14, together with the equivalent *tote ean* in v. 21; here we have four temporal clauses which relate to the outbreak of war (v. 7), when Christians would be de-

---

[132]Grayston maintains that Mark 4 consists of a series of parables, isolated logia, and short passages loosely strung together ("The Study of Mark XIII," *BJRL* 56 [1974]: 375).

nounced as traitors (vv. 9ff.), the gentile invader would defile the
temple as Antiochus had done earlier (vv. 14ff.), and a Jewish guerilla
leader would set himself up as war leader and messiah (vv. 21–22). The
intent of the four clauses would appear to be that in their critical
situation Christians are to preserve an attitude of detachment: "When
you hear of fighting, do not be disturbed" (v. 7); "When you are
denounced, do not worry about the defense" (v. 11); "When you see the
gentile sacrilege, clear out" (v. 14); "When messianic claimants appear,
remain uninvolved" (v. 21). That does not correspond to the situation
in the lifetime of Jesus, or to the demand that he made on the disciples.[133] But neither does it belong to the apocalyptic tradition; if K.
Koch's list of eight motifs found in apocalyptic literature is used to test
Mark 13, it is seen that the marks of apocalyptic are scarce in the
chapter.[134]

Since the solutions of the problems of Mark 13 offered by the
experts are all unsatisfactory,[135] the clue to the composition of the
discourse is best seen in the four passages mentioned: a situation of the
church is presupposed with the prospect of war, of peril for Christians,
of a sacrilege in Jerusalem, and the appearance of a messianic war
leader. The document will have consisted of vv. 7, 9, 11, 14–16, 18, 21,
23. These instructions received a conclusion in the reassurances given
in the parable of the Fig Tree (vv. 28–29) and exhortations to watch (vv.
33–35). This leaflet was expanded later, largely from the apocalyptic
tradition, and between the instructions and the assurances the passage
about the parousia was inserted (vv. 24–27).[136]

This mode of dealing with challenges is dangerous if it is not set
in the larger context of the Gospel. Mark therefore took the pamphlet
with its apocalyptic supplement and inserted it in the most suitable
context—between the temple cleansing, with the controversies that
followed it, and the passion narrative. Mark tied it especially with the

---

[133] Ibid., 376–78.

[134] See Koch's *The Rediscovery of Apocalyptic*, SBT 2/22 (ET London,
1972), 28–33.

[135] Pesch's reconstruction of an apocalyptic flyleaf at the base of Mark 13 is
dismissed as improbable: "It is difficult to see why anyone should have gone to
the trouble of taking this pamphlet, dividing it up, partly rearranging it, supple-
menting it with sayings of Jesus and experiences of the Church, and intruding it
into the lively and moving narrative of the last days of Jesus." On Hartman's
proposals for deriving the heart of the discourse from the OT Grayston comments:
"It is difficult to see the principle on which the nucleus was organized or the
process by which it received the various accretions." As to Lambrecht: "The same
objections must be made to the work of Lambrecht. . . . Why use the material
organized in this manner and not in some other? And what reason have we for
thinking that the nucleus was this kind rather than that?" ("Study of Mark XIII,"
381–82).

[136] Ibid., 383–85.

latter: e.g., the reports of war (v. 7) have an echo in the centurion at the cross; the sufferings of the disciples (vv. 9ff.) with Jesus before the Sanhedrin (the aid of the Spirit being parallel with Jesus citing the scriptures); the call to flee in v. 14 with the flight of the disciples (14:50); the cosmic eruptions of 13:24 with the darkness at the crucifixion; and the call to watch with the Gethsemane narrative. "By these means the crucifixion is seen in its full eschatological significance; and at the same time the eschatological expectations of the church are controlled by the crucifixion."[137]

Grayston's statement as to the unusual nature of Mark 13 is impressive, but it is possible that he has exaggerated its difference from the parables chapter. It is not the case that ch. 4 is composed of isolated segments and ch. 13 is a continuous whole; the former reflects an earlier collection of parables, and the latter is a discourse consisting of many fragments.[138] The unity which has been imposed on the sayings in ch. 13 has been aided by earlier groupings, and some of Mark's handiwork in this respect is plainly observable. The linking of sections through *blepete* in vv. 5, 9, 23, 33 is more or less universally acknowledged as Markan redaction; the binding of the disparate logia in vv. 9–13 through the use of *paradidomi* is an example of the linking of sayings within a single section; and the connection of unrelated logia in the tradition through the particle *de* is to be seen in the joining of v. 32 to vv. 30–31.[139]

More importantly, it is questionable whether the four adverbial clauses should be separated out and linked as the nucleus of an earlier document on the basis of the use of *hotan* and *tote ean*. Grayston has singled out the appearance of *hotan* in vv. 7, 11, 14, but curiously omitted its appearance in vv. 28 and 29. This omission is the more surprising when it is acknowledged that v. 28a is likely to be redactional, so that in the tradition the parable could well have begun: *hotan ēdē ho klados tēs sykēs hapalos genētai*, and the *hotan* in v. 29 echoes its use again. The pertinence of the observation is that the appearances of *hotan* in vv. 7, 11, 14, 28–29 clearly take up the *hotan* of the disciples' question in v. 4, and so are planned by Mark![140] Moreover, instead of

---

[137]Ibid., 386–87.

[138]For example, vv. 5a and 5b are Markan redaction; v. 6 is isolated in its present context; vv. 7 and 8 are distinguished from v. 6 in source, and perhaps from each other; vv. 9 and 11 are likely to be originally linked as one statement (cf. the Q version in Luke 12:11–12), but vv. 10, 12–13a, and 13b are all separate sayings; vv. 14–18 are probably a compilation, since vv. 15–16 appear to have parallels in Q (Luke 17:31); vv. 19 and 20 are not necessarily originally bound together, and so on. For our discussion on the origin of the discourse and its development see below pp. 350–65.

[139]The like may be seen in vv. 13b, 23, 37. The particle is used to link different sections in vv. 5, 9, 14, 28.

[140]Neirynck sees the uses of *hotan* in ch. 13 (including the equivalent in v.

connecting the *tote ean* of v. 21 with the *hotan* in the rest of the chapter, we should observe that v. 21 begins with *kai tote*, and this invites comparison with the appearance of the phrase in vv. 14, 26, 27.

A further objection to the linking of vv. 7, 11, 14, 21 as the basis of an earlier document is the notion of detachment which is thereby extracted from them. Admittedly the rejection of the idea that wars proclaim the end of the age could be viewed as calling for an attitude of "detachment," but that is due not to laissez-faire, but to a different concept of the end. The refusal of zealotic messianic claims likewise is bound up with a totally different notion of the Messiah, his calling, and the salvation he introduces. More important still, the implications of vv. 9 and 11 are the reverse of a call to take it easy and let the Holy Spirit do the work; rather it is an appeal to turn to good account the dangerous situations in which the disciples will find themselves, and to use them for the furtherance of the mission to the nations which the church must fulfill in this age. That is how Matthew and Luke read Mark, as their variants testify (Matt 24:14; Luke 21:13). It is particularly interesting to see how Luke rewords the reference to the Spirit's aid in Luke 21:17, for thereby he intends the reader to see the process illustrated in the courageous and powerful witness of Stephen in such circumstances (Acts 6:10; 7:55). If Cousar's judgment is right: "Mark's whole understanding of the gospel . . . points to an eschatology understood in mission, not in withdrawal,"[141] Mark must be seen as a redactor who was by no means incapable of weaving his materials into a powerful and unified discourse of Jesus.

E. Trocmé

Trocmé gave a brief but stimulating treatment of Mark 13 in his work on the Gospel of Mark. His discussion of the chapter was inevitably affected by his conviction that Mark's Gospel was composed of two major sources, chs. 1–13 and 14–16, the former written for Palestinian churches about AD 50. The discourse is seen as bringing to a conclusion the evangelist's exposition of the ecclesiological intentions of Jesus. The author's purpose in the discourse is said to be "to arm Christians against the manifold temptations of apocalyptic."[142] The two chief evils in view are timidity in proclaiming the gospel and attachment to certain holy places. To the evangelist "the Master offers a much wider, and,

---

30) as characteristic of the Markan "correspondence in discourse," manifest elsewhere in the Gospel; see his *Duality in Mark: Contributions to the Study of the Markan Redaction*, BETL 31 [Louvain, 1972], 129–30).

[141] See pp. 191–95.

[142] Trocmé, *La formation de l'Evangile selon Marc* (Paris, 1963; ET *The Formation of the Gospel according to Mark* [London, 1975]), 208.

above all, more active future than certain other Christians would have them believe."[143] This is demonstrated by a series of tableaux, in which various apocalyptic ideas are refuted.

The first of these tableaux is in vv. 5–8; the events mentioned therein are seen as part of the eschatological drama, but by Mark's comments are reduced to the level of curtain raisers (vv. 7b and 8c). The deceivers of v. 6, in the evangelist's view, are the heads of the church; they boast of being the successors of Jesus and of having assumed after his death his role of Davidic Messiah. The second tableau (vv. 9–13) warns the disciples to watch themselves; they must not avoid persecution by soft-pedaling the proclamation of the good news; the authorities are certain to resist their revolutionary message, but the preachers must not retreat into cowardly caution. The third tableau (vv. 14–23) is an attack on all apocalyptic geography, and in particular on any attempt to locate the parousia in Jerusalem. God is to bring disaster upon the city, and those who persist in their attachment to the temple will not escape it. "The author of Mark certainly meant this as a thrust at the church of Jerusalem, so entrenched on its holy hill."[144] The fourth tableau (vv. 24–29) describes the parousia, which, though it follows the catastrophe described in vv. 14–23, is seen as further in the future. The author stresses neither the suddenness of the end nor a prolonged delay, though he does emphasize the progressive character of the parousia ("in those days . . . and then . . . and then . . ."). The parousia is not so much the end as a sign to its approach, as the parable of the Fig Tree shows (the *tauta* of v. 29 refers back to vv. 24–27, if not to vv. 5–27).[145] The answer to the disciples' question in v. 4 accordingly is that the final crisis has already begun (tableaux 1–3), hence the call to wakefulness *now*.

Two further points made by Trocmé call for notice. In Mark's view the catastrophe on Jerusalem, referred to in vv. 2 and 14ff., signifies neither the end of the world (cf. vv. 19–20) nor a long-drawn-out period of war, but rather a sudden and relatively brief disaster that will fall upon Judea (v. 18).[146] The discourse therefore was not composed with the Roman-Jewish War in mind: "We do not believe that the Jewish war of A.D. 66–70 has left any visible imprint on Mark, nor that it was the cause of its composition."[147] Further, while vv. 24–27 are apocalyptic in nature, there is no ground for attributing them to a Jewish apocalyptic document; the passage could as well have come from a Christian who wished to give a context for the saying recorded in Mark 14:62. Had Mark desired he could have built up a real "little apocalypse" on

---

143 Ibid., 208–9.
144 Ibid., 212.
145 Ibid., 213 n. 3.
146 Ibid., 204 n. 2.
147 Ibid., 245.

the basis of words of Jesus, OT texts, and Jewish or Christian models. "If he did not do so, and was satisfied with a few separate tableaux, it is because his aim was to exhort and warn, even where his text borders on pure description."[148]

Trocmé's interpretation of the discourse as a warning against apocalyptic views which obstruct the church's mission to the world and bind believers to Jerusalem is well stated. His understanding of the latter point, however, is affected by his view of the date and provenance of chs. 1–13. The belief that "Mark" wrote for churches in Palestine about the year AD 50 enabled Trocmé to hold that the evangelist regarded James and his associates in Jerusalem as the pseudomessiahs and false prophets of vv. 6 and 21–22. This is difficult to accept. Both the stylistic unity of Mark's Gospel and its relationship to the kerygma render the notion unlikely that chs. 1–13 were composed as a separate Gospel apart from chs. 14–16; nor does the evidence of chs. 1–13 establish that the evangelist looked on James and his followers as playing the role of antichrists. It is also questionable to relate the parable of the Fig Tree so closely to its context so as to include the parousia within the signs of the end. This is yet another instance of the failure of an exegete to recognize in vv. 24ff. a theophany, and thus the advent of the Lord as the occasion of judgment and revelation of the final kingdom of God.

F. Hahn

With the contribution on Mark 13 by Hahn we return to the main line of critical studies on the eschatological discourse, with certain significant differences. Hahn begins with the generally agreed position that the introduction to the discourse (vv. 1–4) and the conclusion (vv. 33–37) are from Mark, irrespective of the extent of traditions which Mark used. The conclusion is viewed as "an appendix which stands in direct connection with the Markan estimate of eschatology,"[149] so no further consideration is given to it. The connections of the address are stated in accordance with generally accepted views: vv. 7–8, 14–20, 24–27 are a description of eschatological events leading to the parousia, vv. 5–6 give warnings against deception, vv. 9–13 an exhortation to endurance, and vv. 28–31 a clear conclusion to the discourse; v. 32 is a pre-Markan logion set here by Mark to limit the near expectation in vv. 28–31 and to form a bridge to vv. 33–37.[150]

---

[148]Ibid., 214.

[149]Hahn, "Die Rede von der Parusie des Menschensohnes Markus 13," in *Jesus und der Menschensohn,* Festschrift A. Vögtle, ed. R. Pesch and R. Schnackenburg (Freiburg, 1975), 242.

[150]Ibid., 242–44.

It is in the relations of these sections that Hahn diverges from earlier writers. First, he agrees with Vögtle, in whose honor the article was written, that the parousia passage is "a testimony of primitive Christian parousia proclamation"; hence the ground document is Jewish-Christian, not simply Jewish. Then vv. 21–22 are seen as closely bound to vv. 19–20: the "elect" may be led astray by false messiahs (v. 21), and for their preservation the days are shortened (v. 20). Verses 5–6 are regarded as written in a style different from that of vv. 21–22 and are formed by Mark on the analogy of the latter. The structure of vv. 28–29 contains balanced clauses with *hotan* in both sentences, which link them with vv. 7 and 14; this suggests that vv. 28–31 belonged to the main document prior to Mark. The pre-Markan discourse therefore will have consisted of vv. 7–8, 14–22, 24–31. But while vv. 9–13 are styled in a parenetic manner and represent a little collection of words of the Lord, the possibility is not to be excluded that this passage also, including v. 10, may have been incorporated into the address prior to Mark.[151] The concern in this tradition is to work out the events which immediately precede and lead to the parousia.[152]

Mark's setting of the discourse in vv. 1–4 represents *his* exposition of the discourse. The twofold question of v. 4 therefore is to be carefully observed: "When?" concerns the *tauta* of v. 4a, "What signs?" the *tauta panta* of v. 4b. The former has in view the prophecy of the temple's destruction, the latter the *sēmeion* of the end events. This distinction divides the discourse into two, certainly from Mark's viewpoint. In the source the events of vv. 7–8 relate to the beginning of the eschatological process and are assumed to have commenced, but those of vv. 14ff. belong to the (impending) future. It is otherwise with Mark. The key words of v. 4 reappear in vv. 28–30, but in a significant manner: the *tauta* in v. 29 clearly includes the events of vv. 14ff., while in v. 30 the *tauta panta* embraces the entire description of the eschatological process, including the parousia passage of vv. 24–27. This leads to the conclusion that the "wars" referred to in vv. 7–8, and which must happen according to God's plan, have primarily in view the Jewish War with Rome in 66–70, including its culmination in the destruction of Jerusalem. In that case the description in vv. 14ff. of the sign of the end, the appearance of the "abomination," in Mark's view has nothing to do with the ruin of the temple, but anticipates an event which still lies in the future; in view of the masculine term *hestēkota* in v. 14 that event must refer to the appearance of the antichrist.[153]

---

[151]Ibid., 244–46. For Hahn's views on Mark 13:10 see p. 257, and also the discussion in his book *Das Verständnis der Mission im Neuen Testament* (1963), 57–62; ET *Mission in the New Testament,* SBT 47 (London, 1965), 70–75.

[152]Idem, "Rede," 247.

[153]Ibid., 254–55.

The source which Mark employed accordingly will have been inspired by the report of the Roman-Jewish War, which began in Galilee. It will have been written in a Jewish area, probably in Jerusalem, at the beginning of the war, and was expected to lead to the desecration of the temple, followed by the deliverance through the parousia of the Son of man Jesus. It had nothing to do with the Caligula episode of a generation earlier. From the beginning it was a Christian address regarding the parousia of the Son of man. In it the parable of the Fig Tree retains at least one element of the intention of Jesus in the parable: it anticipates the completion of the salvation promised in his word and completed at his coming as Son of man for his own. Admittedly the Jewish element in the discourse is strong, but we have here a Jewish-Christian church, heavily indebted to apocalyptic thinking, interpreting the parable of Jesus with the help of traditional motifs in relation to its own situation prior to the beginning of the final tribulation. Mark has the destruction of the temple behind him as he writes. The persecutions of the church continue, hence the call for endurance till the parousia. There is no decrease of hope, despite the delay of the parousia, for the whole time from the resurrection to the parousia is seen as the time of the already begun and continuing eschatological process; it witnesses both the "beginning of the woes" and the in-breaking kingdom of God which came with Jesus; further eschatological events therefore lead to the perfection of salvation. Hence there is a real correspondence between chs. 4 and 13. The parable in vv. 28–29 is the kernel and angle point of the discourse; through relating the whole discourse to the time between Easter and the parousia Mark comes close to the original meaning of the parable and is enabled to bind together Christology and eschatology.[154]

Hahn's article is very perceptive and very persuasively argued. Pesch was one of the two editors of the Festschrift in which the article appeared, and as we shall see, it was a major factor in his change of mind concerning the nature and extent of the original discourse, not least in the conviction that the discourse was Christian. It is surprising, however, that Hahn did not discuss where the elements of the tradition came from and how they came to be combined in this manner before Mark received them. The question needs to be raised, since Hahn assumes, for example, that vv. 14–20 and 24–27 belong together as apocalyptic instruction. This judgment may be more indebted to an automatic acceptance of a critical tradition than to a consideration of the content of the passages. We have called attention to the possibility that the parousia passage may have closer links with the immediately

---

[154]Ibid., 263–64.

preceding warning against pseudomessiahs than with the abomination passage, as in Luke 17:23–24.

The importance of the parable of the Fig Tree is rightly recognized: in Hahn's view it was the "crystallization" element of the discourse round which the rest of the elements clustered. But questions need to be raised about its interpretation. In our judgment it is doubtful that the *tauta* of v. 29 can be pressed to correspond with the *tauta* of v. 4a in the manner advocated by Hahn and with the results he produces. Did Mark really intend to make so clear a distinction between the significance of *tauta* and *tauta panta* in v. 4, and to relate the *tauta* of v. 29 to the *tauta* of v. 4a so subtly and decisively as to transform the meaning of vv. 14ff.? That is difficult to accept. The admission that Mark came close to the original meaning of the parable through his positive estimate of its relation to the Easter-parousia period is welcome. Are we sure, however, that the parable in its intention did not from the beginning have the future prospects in view? That decision is bound up with one's judgment on the origin of v. 29 (whether or not it is due to a redactor), for the most natural interpretation of *hotan idēte* in v. 29 is its relation to the future, not the present. One may therefore be even more positive than Hahn and affirm that in its present form the parable accords wholly with the basic concept of the discourse, which is history under the hand of God and ministry of the kingdom of God thrusting forward in face of opposition till the revelation of the kingdom in the intervention of the Son of man Jesus.

Hahn's belief as to the date of the source document and Mark's redaction of it should be viewed in the light of another item of evidence neglected by him, namely, the relation of the discourse to the eschatological teaching of 1 and 2 Thessalonians. These letters display a striking number of parallels with leading elements in the discourse, and they include links not only with the body of the discourse but with its final paragraph, which Hahn regards as a Markan appendix. These parallels raise questions as to whether the discourse was indeed fashioned long before the Jewish War, or whether its elements circulated among the churches, not entirely in isolation, and if so who gathered them and presented them in the coherent form we now find them in Mark, and the extent of Mark's redaction in the process. Hahn's solution, which we saw reason to question, is very much bound up with an understanding of the relation between vv. 4 and 28–29, and accordingly his reasoning as to the date of the discourse is less acceptable. The decision must remain open for consideration in the light of other evidence.

D. A. Koch

The relation of Mark 13 to the Markan theology of redemption and the role of the church, so differently interpreted by Cousar and Grayston,

is the subject of a study by D. A. Koch in the Festschrift for Conzelmann.[155] Koch begins by pointing out the disproportionate amount
of space given to the eschatological material in Mark 13 in comparison
with its place in the Gospel as a whole: "The concentration of eschatological material in Mark 13 corresponds inversely to the small role it
plays in the rest of the presentation of the Markan Gospel." Nevertheless there is one passage in which eschatology features prominently,
and in a manner significant for the whole Gospel, namely, in the section
8:27—9:1, which provides a kind of contents list for the second half of
Mark's Gospel. The composition of this section is not accidental. It
displays the sequence of dogmatic foundation and parenesis characteristic of the Pauline and sub-Pauline letters. Moreover, the pattern of
concluding instruction with eschatology is widespread in early Christianity; it is met in Q, the discourses of Matthew, the Didache, and the
Letters of the NT, and has its origin in the homiletic or catechetical
praxis of the primitive church.[156] Mark has manifestly followed it both
in the construction of the passage 8:27—9:1 and in the plan of the whole
Gospel—hence the eschatological discourse is set directly before the
passion narrative.[157]

In 8:27—9:1 Mark seeks to set out a direct relation between Christology and eschatology, i.e., between 8:27–33 and 8:38—9:1. This connection he achieves by the use of the title *ho huios tou anthrōpou* in
vv. 31 and 38; the employment of the two distinctive meanings of the
expression in the passage has the consequence of bringing together the
passion and resurrection of the Son of man and the parousia of the Son
of man as Judge.[158] This juxtaposition of the two concepts of *huios tou
anthrōpou*, along with the corresponding appearance of the apocalyptic
Son of man in 13:26, shows that Mark does not wish one meaning of
the title to be ousted by the other. On the contrary he desires to indicate

---

[155]Koch, "Zum Verhältnis von Christologie und Eschatologie im Markusevangelium," in *Jesus Christus in Historie und Theologie*, Festschrift H. Conzelmann, ed. G. Strecker (Tübingen, 1975), 395–408.

[156]Koch refers to Bornkamm's exposition of this theme in *Enderwartung
und Kirche im Matthäusevangelium* in *The Background of the New Testament
and its Eschatology*, Festschrift C. H. Dodd, ed. W. D. Davies and D. Daube
(Cambridge, 1956), 222ff. (later found in *End-Expectation and Church in Matthew* by G. Bornkamm, G. Barth, H. J. Held, 5th ed. [1968], 13–21), and to
Conzelmann, *Der erste Brief an die Korinther* (Göttingen, 1969), 18 n. 51. For
more complete references see below, pp. 350–52.

[157]Koch, "Verhältnis," 397–99. In an extended footnote (p. 399 n. 15) Koch
considers and criticizes the view of R. Pesch that Mark constructed his Gospel
without reference to ch. 13, and that he interpolated the discourse into its present
position after completing the Gospel.

[158]The significance of this procedure is heightened for Koch by his belief
that this use of the title Son of man in the predictions of the passion was not given
in the pre-Markan tradition but was due to Mark himself (ibid., 400–402).

the identity of the Crucified with the Judge.[159] The discipleship logia of 8:34–37 occupy a middle position between the christological beginning and the eschatological prospect, and so are framed by them. In this way the sayings relating to the present existence of the church are given a double foundation, through the retrospect on the suffering of the Son of man and through the prospect of the coming of the Son of man as Judge. The sufferings of disciples are no accidental or passing phenomenon, but are a possibility always and insofar as they are oriented to the suffering Son of man. At the same time, the continuation of the discipleship logia through to 8:38 makes it plain that the prospect of the parousia of the Son of man does not enable disciples to escape present suffering; rather, the Son of man judges in accordance with the yardstick given in his own passion.[160]

Mark 13, then, does not represent a step back with respect to this theme. On the contrary, the agreement of ch. 13 with Mark 8:27—9:1 is manifest in what is said concerning the present existence of the church. In his editing of the apocalyptic traditions in ch. 13, Mark consciously carries through a distinction between historical and final events. This distinction opens the possibility of reflecting (in 13:9–13) on the existence of the church before the end as an independent question. In content Mark characterizes the present, so marked off from the end time, as a period of affliction and of confession. The identity of the coming Son of man with the present Son of man, explicitly represented in 8:38—9:1, is also operative in the editing of the apocalyptic traditions in ch. 13. In the time before the end, a time of (inner-historical) afflictions, the orienting to the Son of man as the Crucified and the Judge has the effect of enabling disciples not to withdraw from this situation, but to accept it as in accord with the nature and calling of the church.[161]

This contribution of Koch is, to adapt his own language, in inverse proportion to its length. The parallelism between 8:34—9:1 in relation to 8:27–33 and ch. 13 to the Gospel as a whole is a significant insight, and it accords with the basic studies of Bornkamm, Conzelmann, and Dodd on the primitive Christian catechesis.[162] Similarly, the common presuppositions of 8:34—9:1 and 13:9–13, with their implication for the understanding of ch. 13 as a whole, accord with the position

---

[159]Ibid., 405.

[160]Ibid., 406.

[161]Ibid., 407–8.

[162]These studies appear to have been carried out independently by the scholars named. On the link between the primitive Christian catechesis and the preservation of the eschatological teaching of Jesus, see the discussion on this theme and the contributions of these and other scholars to its significance in chapter 6, especially pp. 350–63.

maintained by Busch in an earlier generation and now set forth by Koch in the context of more recent Gospel studies.[163] In dependence on Conzelmann, Koch resorts to the distinction made by Mark between "inner-historical" and eschatological in order to make room for a church with a role to play in the present age;[164] and similarly he maintains that the use of the concept "Son of man" in relation to the suffering and resurrection of Jesus was due to Mark's reflection, and was not a datum of tradition. There is room for difference of opinions in both these respects, but the major thesis does not stand or fall according to decisions on these issues. The recognition of a positive relation between 8:27—9:1 and ch. 13 is of no little importance. With respect to the latter it confirms the conviction, given in its relation to the Gospel as a whole, that the true context of the discourse is the redemptive action of the Son of man in his death and resurrection on the one hand and his parousia on the other, and that the way of the church in the time between is the *via dolorosa* of its Lord, illumined by the Easter resurrection and the prospect of the parousia glory.

J. Dupont

This veteran scholar was requested to consider the significance attributed to the destruction of the temple of Jerusalem in Mark 13. In a lucid and lengthy treatment of the theme, which takes into account all the important current literature on the subject, Dupont set out to deal with three problems raised by the discourse: (1) the relation of the destruction of the temple to the events of the end time; (2) the relation of these events to the people concerned, whether Israel under judgment or Christians to be encouraged; (3) the relation of the future events to the exhortations concerning the present.[165]

The first issue has the lion's share of attention. It is observed at once that whereas the prophecy of v. 2 dominates the chapter, the rest of the chapter makes explicit mention neither of the temple nor of the destruction prophesied. Dupont considers this puzzling feature at length. First, however, he clarifies the question of v. 4. The double question has a parallel in 11:28: "By what authority are you doing these things, or who gave you this authority to do them?" In this question the two parts are practically equivalent, but the second is more precise than the first; so in v. 4 the second part is not only more specific than the first; it enlarges the question ("all these things" instead of "these

---

[163]See F. Busch, *Zum Verständnis der synoptischen Eschatologie: Markus 13 neu untersucht* (1938), passim.

[164]See above, pp. 179–81.

[165]Dupont, "La ruine du temple et la fin des temps dans le discours de Marc 13," in *Apocalypses et Théologie de l'ésperance,* LD 95 (Paris, 1977), 207–70.

things"), and it introduces a strongly eschatological note (*estai* is replaced by *mellei synteleisthai*). The question thus assumes that the destruction of the temple will be part of the vaster catastrophes of the end of the world.[166]

The discourse in reply to the questions divides itself into vv. 5–27 and 28–37. As to the former, vv. 5–23 form a section complete in itself; v. 5 begins, "Jesus commenced to say to them," and v. 23 states, "I have told you all"; that ends the answer to the question concerning a sign; vv. 24–27 do not form part of the answer, but go beyond it. Verses 28–37 again divide into two sections, vv. 28–31 and 32–37. Whereas vv. 28–29 speak of knowing the approach of the end, vv. 32ff. stress ignorance relating to it. The *hotan* in vv. 28–29 refers to knowing that an event is near and corresponds to the *hotan* in v. 4b, continuing also the series in vv. 7 and 14; but the *pote* of vv. 33ff. refers to the moment of the event in view, and it corresponds to the *pote* in v. 4a. This has the effect of relating the question to the parousia; v. 29 indeed refers to the signs heralding the appearing of the Son of man, and v. 30 embraces the parousia as well as the tribulation of vv. 14–20. Verses 32–37 are occupied with the time of the end (*pote*), so returning to the question of v. 4a, but without retaining the scope which its proximity to the prophecy of v. 2 appears to give it. The reply to the two parts of the question of v. 4 therefore gives the impression that the occasion which provoked the question has been lost to view.[167]

From Mark's viewpoint, of course, the discourse has the purpose of replying to the question of the sign in v. 4b; yet the substance of the discourse is concerned with the events of the *end*. Verses 5b–6 and 21–23 form the frame of the reply, yet they have nothing to do with the fall of Jerusalem, but rather with the parousia. So also the apocalyptic unit vv. 7–8, 14–20, 24–27 concerns the events of the end of the age. Verses 9–13 likewise are oriented to the parousia, not to the destruction of Jerusalem. The discourse in its totality thus concerns the end of time, not the ruin of the temple. Its varied appeals and observations do not provide instruction on the significance of the temple's ruin, because that is not the subject in view. It is the introduction, vv. 1–4, which poses that question.

The representation of the "sign" as the abomination of desolation alone provides a clue as to the relation of the destruction of the temple to the end.[168] But this is equivocal. The abomination of desolation denotes a profanation rather than a destruction. The phrase "standing where he ought not" relates to a holy place; in Daniel the scene of the

---

[166]Ibid., 211–12.
[167]Ibid., 217–18.
[168]Ibid., 233–34.

profanation is the temple; in Mark the profaner must similarly occupy the temple. It is to be observed that v. 14 recalls 11:17: the priests have profaned the temple and made it a den of robbers; in Josephus the term *lēstai* ("robbers") denotes the Zealots; it is therefore possible that Mark in this statement had in mind the profanation of the temple by the Zealots.[169] It is by no means certain that v. 14 speaks of the destruction of the temple; rather, the announcement of the temple's destruction appears to be practically replaced by the announcement of a sacrilegious profanation. At all events the accent in v. 14 lies on the profanation of the temple, not its devastation, and the event is envisaged in an eschatological perspective, in relation to the end of the world. It is this perspective which permits the passage from v. 2 to v. 4, and the line from v. 14 to the events of the end; that which happens to the temple sets in motion the crisis which leads to the tribulation and ends in the coming of the Son of man.[170]

The second of Dupont's questions raises the issue whether Mark 13 announces a judgment or proclaims a hope. In opposition to Pesch, who considers that vv. 24–25 provide a setting in judgment for the parousia, Dupont views the theophany description as simply providing the context for the coming of the Son of man; it is not a symbolic representation of a massacre. In v. 27 the sole purpose of the parousia appears to be that of gathering the elect. The chapter accordingly is intended for the encouragement of believers; it is "a pure message of hope."[171]

The third question relates to the function of the parenetic elements in the discourse. These are of equal importance as, if not more important than, the elements of eschatological expectation. Admittedly most of the nineteen imperatives are apocalyptic in tone; the really significant ones are seven in number, chiefly the repeated *blepete* ("watch") and *grēgoreite* ("be on the alert"). Matthew in his parallel section has fewer imperatives than Mark, though he is longer, and he keeps the revelations separate from the exhortations (Matt 23:37—25:46). Mark, on the contrary, sets the apocalyptic revelations and parenetic sections in continual alternation; they begin and end with parenesis (vv. 5–6, 33–37), and *blepete* runs all the way through the discourse. While the apocalyptic sections relate to the question of the sign, the question of the "when" has a different slant: the affirmation of ignorance leads to exhortations to vigilance. This mode of reply is consonant with the way Jesus answers questions elsewhere, especially apocalyptic ones (cf. Luke 13:23; 17:20–21). So in Mark 13, while Jesus gives some answers

---

[169]Ibid., 224, 234–35.
[170]Ibid., 242–43.
[171]Ibid., 250–54.

to satisfy the disciples' desire to learn of the future, the exhortations go beyond what was asked; these latter are not addenda, but are accentuated by their place in the discourse and by their repetition.[172]

Dupont's essay is an outstanding contribution to the elucidation of Mark 13. Our comments will be confined to the major issue with which he wrestles, namely, the relation of the temple destruction to the end of the age. Dupont's contention that in the Markan perspective the ruin of the temple is viewed as an eschatological phenomenon which finally leads to the denouement is not to be denied (he fully recognizes the "braking" elements in vv. 7, 8, 10, 24a); his virtual elimination of the destruction of the temple from the discourse, however, is dubious. Dupont maintains that (1) the discourse proper does not mention the temple; (2) it has in view the profanation of the temple rather than its destruction; (3) the occasion which provoked the disciples' question, the prophecy of v. 2, appears to be lost to view in the discourse. Strictly speaking, the first point is correct, the second is doubtful, and the third is contradicted by the second. In fact, the inconcinnity points to a feature which accounts for all three points, namely, the indirectness of the discourse, and the ambiguity of v. 14 in particular. The temple is not mentioned in the discourse, but Dupont states that in the phrase "standing where he ought not" (v. 14) Mark had the temple in view, in accordance with the Danielic understanding of the abomination of desolation.

What then does Mark wish to convey as to its fate through the enigmatic v. 14? In Daniel a profanation of the temple is certainly in view. Every Jew of Mark's day knew about Antiochus Epiphanes and his blasphemous acts; the Festival of Dedication ensured that. Equally certainly the memory of Caligula's mad attempt to do something just as blasphemous was strong in Mark's time, with a full understanding of the bloody conflict which would have ensued had Caligula succeeded. Mark will also have known that the first mention of the abomination of desolation in Daniel is set in a context of destructive war (Dan 9:26–27). That he viewed the abomination prophecy in Mark 13:14 in a comparable manner is indicated by his use of the flight motif in vv. 14–18. Dupont's suggestion that vv. 15–16 in the tradition referred to the circumstances of the parousia is implausible; Luke admittedly did so apply the passage in the apocalypse of 17:22ff. (i.e., v. 31), but in so doing he interpreted the language in a purely symbolic sense. Mark's interpretation of the statement in relation to flight from a threatening power is in harmony with its primary intention.[173] It is therefore

---

[172]Ibid., 254–68.

[173]So V. Taylor, *Mark,* 512–13; Schmid, *Markus,* 243; Marxsen, *Mark,* 164–65, 184–85; L. Gaston, *No Stone on Another,* 28; Schweizer, *Mark,* 272–73; Pesch, *Naherwartungen,* 147; idem, *Markus* 2:293; Zmijewski, *Eschatologiereden,* 199–

altogether likely that in vv. 14–18 Mark had in view the notion of destruction no less than profanation, a destruction which would entail great suffering for the Jewish nation; the prophecy then will have been essentially related to that of v. 2, and so formed a key element in the reply to the question of v. 4. It is therefore strictly incorrect to maintain that the announcement of the destruction of the temple in v. 2 is replaced by the announcement of a sacrilegious profanation. Nor is there any likelihood of Mark losing from view the temple prophecy of v. 2 as the discourse unfolded. Mark himself was responsible for the shape of the discourse; by setting the abomination prophecy in its present place he accorded it a centrality in significance as well as position in the chapter; it is therefore impossible for him to have forgotten that at any point in the discourse.

M. E. Boring

Boring saw in the discourse of Mark 13 an unusually suitable opportunity to test his thesis that the traditions of the sayings of Jesus in the Gospels were in large measure mediated through the ministry of Christian prophets in the early church (hence the title of his work, *Sayings of the Risen Jesus*).[174] Boring sought to set on a firm foundation Bultmann's belief that a large number of the sayings of Jesus in the Synoptic Gospels were produced by the first-generation church, and that this creativity within the tradition was due to the work of the Christian prophets.[175] Bultmann never attempted a critical justification for this view of the prophets' role in the church; Boring endeavored to supply the lack through a detailed examination of the evidence for it.

He began by the reminder that in the primitive church Jesus of Nazareth was now the risen Lord, still active in the world, and so such phrases as "word(s) of Jesus" and "saying(s) of the Lord" had a potential ambiguity from the beginning. The church's prophets were spokespersons of the Lord, and were active both in worship and in the process of transmitting the teaching of the Lord. They had, accordingly, a positive relation to the Christian tradition and were not only partners with the church's teachers but often were themselves also teachers. It is comprehensible therefore that when the prophets spoke in the name of the Lord they sometimes took up and re-presented words of Jesus from the tradition and sometimes spoke fresh words of revelation in his name.

200; Marshall, *Luke,* 664. See further our discussion below, pp. 408–11, 416–17, and above all D. Ford, *The Abomination of Desolation in Biblical Eschatology* (Washington, D.C., 1979).

[174]Boring, *Sayings of the Risen Jesus. Christian Prophecy in the Synoptic Tradition,* SNTSMS 46 (Cambridge, 1982).

[175]Bultmann, *History of the Synoptic Tradition,* 40, 56, 368.

In such circumstances variations in the relationship of their utterances to original sayings of the earthly Jesus were clearly possible.

The examination of the problems entailed in this theme and its application to the text of the Gospels was Boring's self-appointed task. His method was first to establish the characteristics of early Christian prophecy, then to demonstrate in detail the contribution of the prophets to individual sayings within the Jesus tradition.[176] In order to achieve this latter aim two criteria had to come into operation. First, only those sayings could be viewed as falling within the orbit of the prophets' activity which could be seen as having existed independently of a narrative context, i.e., they must be shown to have been originally independent sayings. Second, there must be grounds for considering the sayings to be secondary for reasons other than their similarity to Christian prophecy.

It does not fall within the purview of this study to review and evaluate Boring's work relating to the entire Jesus tradition, for we are concerned only with the discourse of Mark 13. From the outset, however, I would query Boring's assumption that the prophets of the church were the primary bearers of the traditions relating to the works and words of Jesus. Granting that the prophets and the teachers of the early church were partners in the church's ministry, there are references in the NT to the *instruction* given to converts—the *paradosis* (2 Thess 3:6), which undergirds a great deal of the epistolary literature of the NT, and which assuredly will have fallen primarily within the responsibility of the church's teachers. There are reasons for believing that the catechesis fashioned by the teachers will have provided the structure for preserving the traditions of sayings of Jesus given in his earthly ministry. Admittedly that does not rule out the possibility of the prophets' exerting an influence on those traditions, but it certainly suggests limits to the range of their influence.

There is, of course, one book in the NT which transparently exemplifies the work of a prophet, namely, the book of Revelation; to this writing Boring makes constant appeal in order to illustrate the nature of prophetic activity in the primitive church. It is indeed a significant work, and its self-description is very impressive. It is described as "the revelation of Jesus Christ which God gave him," and John the Seer declares that he "bore witness to the word of God and the witness of Jesus Christ." The book therefore claims to be a "word of the risen Lord." But how vastly different is this "prophecy" (Rev 1:3) from the Gospels, which also bear witness to "the word of God and the witness of Jesus Christ!" Quite apart from the form of the book of Revelation, with its visions and luxurious apocalyptic imagery, there are very few

---

[176]Boring, *Sayings,* 58–136, 137–229, respectively.

echoes of words of the earthly Jesus within it, despite the inclusion of seven letters from the risen Christ to the churches. It is evident that this prophetic work not only belongs to a different genre from the Gospels; it reflects a totally different mode of thinking from that of any evangelist, and a wholly different way of setting forth the gospel of Jesus Christ. What, then, of Mark 13? Is that not positively related to the book of Revelation? Yes, of course, and we must now proceed to consider Boring's discussion of the eschatological discourse.

Two matters are made plain at the outset. Boring's interest in the discourse is confined in two issues: (1) What points of contact with early Christian prophecy are to be seen in it? (2) Can the theory of a pre-Markan apocalyptic document be reasserted and strengthened by seeing it as Christian prophecy? No less than twelve points are adduced to give a positive answer to the first question. We shall consider four of them.

First, "The most obvious prophetic feature in Mark 13 is its claim to reveal the events of the end time and of the eschatological future."[177] True; no one will disagree with that. Boring is also right in pointing out that we should not designate its eschatological character as simply "apocalyptic," for while it shares some features with Jewish apocalyptic literature it lacks many typical features of it.

Second, a related feature both distinguishes Mark 13 from Jewish apocalyptic and associates it with Christian prophecy, namely, its hortatory character. And this characterizes the whole discourse, not simply a part. "The only real parallels to the hortatory apocalyptic of Mark 13 are found in Christian prophecy, above all in the Book of Revelation."[178] Essentially I think that this is correct, although E. Brandenburger has protested against the common opposition between "eschatological parenesis" and "apocalyptic instruction," maintaining that parenesis is a firm constituent of apocalyptic theology.[179] The protest is justified, but I believe it remains true that no other apocalyptic writing has so complete a balance between prophetic expectation and prophetic parenesis as the discourse of Mark 13.

Third, the Christian prophet speaks directly to his hearers/readers, using second person imperatives and first person address because he speaks with the ego of the risen Christ. This is manifest in Mark 13 in (a) the many imperatives of the discourse, (b) the first person declarations of vv. 6, 9, 13, 23, 30, 31, and (c) the claim to speak in the name of Jesus and the utterance "I am" of v. 6, which is a prophetic formula by which Christian prophets authenticated their oracles. The

---

[177]Ibid., 188.

[178]Ibid.

[179]Brandenburger, *Markus 13 und die Apokalyptik*, FRLANT 134 (Göttingen, 1984), 91.

discourse therefore is not pseudonymous, nor does it make appeal to
Jesus as a figure of the past, but is a message of the contemporary
Christic.[180]

This understanding of the discourse is bound up with a fourth
observation: the author of the discourse opposes the prophets mentioned in vv. 5–6 and 21–22, not because they claim to be the returned
Messiah Jesus but because they speak in the name or by the authority
of Jesus Messiah. These "false prophets" are within the church, not
outside it. There is revealed here, says Boring, Mark's suspicion of a
prophetism which looses itself from the earthly Jesus and too freely
claims to speak in the name of the risen Lord. This is why Mark does
not use Q; it too obviously contains post-Easter revelations of the risen
Lord. Mark countered this form of prophetism by binding the message
of the risen Lord within the traditions of Jesus of Nazareth, within a
pre-Easter framework. So Mark created the Gospel form.[181]

This seems to me a highly questionable interpretation of the
discourse. The "false prophets" of v. 6 "lead many astray"; their error
is described in vv. 21–22 as proclaiming that the Messiah is "here" or
"there," a plain allusion to the Jewish doctrine of the Messiah who is
hidden from public eyes until the set time of his manifestation. The
only way of maintaining that the prophets of v. 6 are Christian is to
assume that they had adopted this Jewish teaching of the hidden
Messiah and that vv. 21–22 explicitly rebut their doctrine; but that
makes Boring's interpretation of the rationale of Mark's Gospel collapse. It is better to assume that the prophets of v. 6 come forward
"under the name" of the Messiah, i.e., falsely using his name and
claiming to be the Messiah. The prophetic aspect of the discourse is due
to prophetic words *within the Jesus tradition* being assembled to
form a discourse on the future as it relates to Israel and the church.
Mark, who redacts the whole, has no doubt that it goes back to the
historical Jesus.

Noting points of contact between the discourse and forms associated with Christian prophecy, Boring observes that nearly all these
occur outside the verses usually assigned to the "little apocalypse" (vv.
7–8, 14–20, 24–27). Does this indicate after all that an apocalyptic
fragment has been taken over and expanded in the pre-Markan tradition? Boring answers no. He suggests that the history of investigation
into Mark 13 has played a trick on us. In searching for the Jewish
apocalyptic core, scholars excluded everything in the discourse except
that which was specifically apocalyptic in the Jewish sense. This
entailed excluding all the peculiarly prophetic elements, which were

---

[180]Boring, *Sayings,* 188–89.
[181]Ibid., 199–200.

considered secondary accretions, and so the "little apocalypse" was reduced to the minimal section. But on the understanding of the discourse as prophecy this reduction is unnecessary, for vv. 5–6, 9–11, 21–23, 28–30 should not be excised, and the discourse retains its coherence, which it lost in the reductionism of the little apocalypse theory. In the light of Hartman's studies, vv. 7–8, 14–20, 24–27 may be viewed as the work of the Christian prophet on the basis of his interpretation of the OT; they with the rest of vv. 5b–31 form a single unit.[182]

This is an interesting and novel suggestion, and has much to commend it. Boring's work is highly stimulating, but his conclusions appear to require modification in the light of a more sober estimate of the work of the prophets in relation to other servants of the risen Lord in the church, and in the light of the fact that the message of Jesus centered on the kingdom of God. For him that meant the divine saving sovereignty mediated through his total ministry, from his baptism to his cross and resurrection and ultimate parousia. That is prophecy par excellence—in the Jesus way!

R. E. Clements

Research into the origin and meaning of Mark 13 yields surprises. The oracle relating to the "abomination of desolation" in v. 14 interjects a brief appeal that interrupts the flow of the statement: "Let the reader understand." It was one of the indications that led Colani to postulate an apocalyptic source for the chapter: the author thereby showed that the discourse was from the beginning a literary composition. Others, like myself, have viewed it as a comment interposed by the evangelist, drawing attention to the importance of a right understanding of the saying. The OT scholar R. E. Clements, however, devoted an article to the consideration of this clause of three words, and shed no little light on its implications for the discourse.[183]

Clements observes that the intention of the clause is presumably to help the reader to perceive the special import of the message in the verse and the allusions it contains to Daniel and other writings of the OT (note that both aspects are held to be in view, not simply one, as is frequently maintained). But there is more. It also raises two issues of concern to biblical scholarship: the first is the importance of literacy and its implications for the understanding of the Bible; the second is the relevance of the expression to "canon criticism."

---

[182]Ibid., 192–93.

[183]Clements, "Apocalyptic, Literacy, and the Canonical Tradition," in *Eschatology and the New Testament*, Festschrift G. R. Beasley-Murray, ed. W. H. Gloer (Peabody, Mass., 1988), 15–27.

As to the first issue, we are to recall that the members of the early churches were only semiliterate, and needed the help that skilled and literate teachers could give. The call for the reader to "understand" is not a pointer to the existence of a source document, but a witness to the differences of understanding available to the literate person. The full significance of the reference to "the sacrilege that makes desolate" will be understood only by the person who can read the OT scriptures. The development of Jewish apocalyptic was, in fact, a markedly scribal activity, developed with the aid of written texts, and dependent on the ability of interpreters to recognize allusions and make verbal connections that would not be obvious to the nonliterate person. "What is being conveyed by the eschatological discourse of Jesus is not simply a prophecy about forthcoming events, but at the same time a vitally significant evaluation of the import and meaning of those events for all who look to the Hebrew scriptures as the ground and guide of their hope."[184]

The rise of apocalyptic literature was the outcome of the oral traditions of the prophets being set down in writing. This led to the formation of paradigms or patterns, so that prophecy relating to one set of historical circumstances could be adapted to others. If that led to the abandonment of the uniqueness of a particular historical context, a prophetic theme nevertheless could become part of a much wider scheme of divine revelation. In this sense it became truly "apocalyptic," i.e., revelatory of a wide segment of the divine purpose. Scripture was interpreted with the aid of other scriptures, and scribal interpretation gave rise to harmonizations and even more intricate literary connections. This process drew together apocalyptic speculation and wisdom. "Both depended on the elaboration of subtle literary techniques, such as the scribes had developed, for an adequate appreciation of their meaning. Apocalyptic became a form of prophecy intelligible to scribes."[185]

The pertinence of canon criticism to our theme, according to Clements, is its emphasis on understanding and recognizing the extant form of the biblical books, as over against the common emphasis on defining and dating sources within the biblical materials. Further, the collection of texts into a corpus and the elevation of the corpus to the status of a "canon" implies that one passage may and should be read in conjunction with another. Whereas the historical method seeks to uncover the original circumstances, intentions, and ideas of the author, the canonical approach ignores this in favor of regarding the remainder of the canonical scriptures as forming the true spiritual context. Of

---

[184]Ibid., 18–19.
[185]Ibid., 20–22.

course, the two methods require correction and supplementation by each other: "Each does in its own way express something of the dialogue between the text and its interpreters which is very important to the rich and extensive task of hearing the word of God."[186]

Drawing together his observations on the two strands of literacy and canonicity, Clements expresses a conviction worthy of note:

> Apocalyptic patterns of biblical interpretation are to be seen not simply narrowly confined to the biblical books of Daniel and Revelation, but quite extensively spread throughout the prophetic literature of the Old Testament, widely present in the biblical interpretations of St. Paul and, most centrally of all, present in the teaching of Jesus. It may then be hoped that the seeming vagaries and excesses of the biblical apocalyptists, which have so often in the history of the Christian church been the target of heavy criticism and even outright rejection by theologians, may be seen not to be so repulsive as they at first appear. They belong by a kind of theological necessity to the processes by which the word of God, originally proclaimed orally, came to be preserved and disseminated for the benefit of later generations.[187]

Returning finally to the note in Mark 13:14, "Let the reader understand," Clements affirms, "Whatever the source of its entrance into Mark 13:14, it undoubtedly represents a very illuminating comment on the complexities of biblical apocalyptic and on the demands that its interpretation places upon the Christian scholar."[188]

Clearly these reflections on the parenthetic clause of Mark 13:14 are offered not as an exegesis of the words, but rather as a consideration of their background and their implications for understanding the mode of thought represented in the discourse of Mark 13. Clements has shown that this is part of a long and widespread movement in the process of interpreting the biblical revelation, and one which is not only comprehensible but justified in its endeavor to hear the word of God in one's own generation. He does not hesitate to acknowledge that Jesus and Paul participated in this mode of interpreting the OT, and he calls on modern biblical scholars to treat it with due seriousness. It is not the first time that an OT scholar has called on NT scholars and theologians to take more seriously apocalyptic thought and literature *theologically,* rather than viewing it as an antiquarian phenomenon that has no relevance for Christian faith. Klaus Koch did the same in his provocative work, *Ratlos vor Apokalyptik!* (a much more compelling title than the ET *The Rediscovery of Apocalyptic!*), in which he called attention to the contribution of earlier British biblical scholars to the

---

[186]Ibid., 25–26.
[187]Ibid., 26.
[188]Ibid., 27.

understanding of apocalyptic literature and their positive evaluation of its significance, an attitude that Koch himself wished to see contemporary scholarship recovering. To pursue this mode of study of apocalyptic in the NT could produce a more sympathetic treatment of the eschatological discourse and a regard for it as more pertinent to Christian theology than a walk through the halls of the British Museum.

R. Guelich

In a seminar on the Gospel of Mark at the SNTS meeting in Cambridge, 1988, Robert Guelich presented a comprehensive paper on Mark 13.[189] During that year the first volume of his commentary on Mark appeared,[190] but his sudden death deprived us of a completed second volume, which doubtless would have contained his maturest thoughts on the form, origin, and interpretation of the discourse.

Guelich first considers the form of the discourse. He points out that while the discourse has apocalyptic elements, it can be apocalyptic without being an apocalypse. The lack of a revelatory or visionary setting in the material, and the absence of a final judgment of sinners and vindication of God's elect, are major obstacles for finding here an apocalypse. So also the classification of the discourse as a Testament assumes the present literary setting at the end of Jesus' ministry; there is no basis for that within the discourse itself, and in any case the Last Supper would have been a far more appropriate setting for a Testament. Nor does the discourse correspond formally to a catechetical schema, despite the opening questions. It is concluded that no one form adequately fits the discourse, either in the tradition or in Mark's Gospel. When one compares the discourse with other extensive passages of teaching in Mark (notably with chs. 4 and 7), it is observable that Mark worked almost exclusively with traditional material; it is likely that he did the same in ch. 13.

Mark's redactional role in the chapter is generally acknowledged in the settings of vv. 1 and 3, as also in the exhortations to watch in vv. 23, 33, 37. By developing the contexts provided in vv. 1 and 3, Mark both located the discourse in the events of holy week which centered on the temple (cf. also chs. 11 and 12) and introduced the motif of the destruction of the temple at this point, thereby placing the discourse in close association with it. In Mark's mind the final discourse clearly has something to do with the temple's destruction.

The emphasis on watchfulness, and v. 32, combined with the assumption that most of the events in the discourse had already taken

---

[189]Guelich, "Mark 13: A Text under Scrutiny," Paper for SNTS Seminar on Mark (Cambridge 1988).

[190]Idem, *Mark 1–8:26*, WBC (1988).

place, has led to the view that the evangelist had an imminent end expectation. The summons to watchfulness, however, runs throughout the discourse. The alertness called for applies especially to the absence of the home owner (vv. 34–36), which holds good of the whole period following Jesus' death and resurrection. It is noted that these summonses to alertness correspond to Jesus' own way in Mark's story (cf. 3:20–35; 6:1–6) and the emphasis on the cost of discipleship (8:34–38; 10:29–31).

If Mark added to his source vv. 5–6, 9–13, 34–36, the core of the tradition received would be vv. 7–8, 14–22, 24–32, perhaps in a written form (cf. v. 14b). Since Danielic formulations are seen throughout this traditional core (vv. 7, 14, 22, 26), the Danielic ring of v. 4b probably indicates an underlying traditional introduction to the collection of sayings.

As to the historical referents of the discourse, advocates of the little apocalypse theory have made much of vv. 14–20, many being inclined to see a first reference to the Caligula episode, and a later application to Jerusalem in the Roman war. Contrary to those who interpret the call to "flee" the city, whether viewed as under siege or under threat of it, the sign of the abomination of desolation could not have referred to events surrounding the destruction of the temple in August of AD 70, for by the time the abomination appeared, it would have been too late to flee to the mountains. "The details of Mark 13:14 do not correspond to the situation surrounding the destruction of the temple." In the source v. 14 will have alluded to the coming of a sacrilege that challenges God Almighty, which may nor may not have involved the temple; for Mark it will have been interpreted in the light of the gathering storm over Palestine, and he related it to the prophecy of v. 2; this accounts for the lack of direct correspondence with the circumstances of AD 70.

The key to Mark's use of the discourse lies in its location and its relationship with the discourse of chapter 4. Both discourses are applied to the disciples, and both expound Jesus' ministry of the kingdom of God. Mark 4 emphasizes the presence and the future of the kingdom; Mark 13 focuses on the future consummation, but develops the nature of the intervening period as the "beginning of sorrows." The messianic triumphalism which distorted the disciples' perception of Jesus during his ministry continues to haunt believers in Mark's church, hence the warnings which run through the discourse. For Mark the destruction of the temple belonged to foreboding future events which appear to deny God's power in history, especially his sovereign intervention through Jesus. For Mark's readers the discourse addressed the present by describing life as they knew it. If the immediate future threatened worse, it nevertheless offered hope by pointing to the ultimate deliverance through the coming of the Son of man in power and glory.

The value of Guelich's contribution is clear, despite its loss through my abbreviated summary. I content myself with one or two observations.

The limits of form-critical methods applied to the discourse are clear. It is right to point to the lack of formal correspondence of the discourse to a catechetical schema, but that does not preclude the likelihood that elements of the discourse were preserved in the primitive catechesis, as were many other items of the teaching of Jesus which were later brought together to form discourses. In the light of the Pauline epistles it is probable that some units of the discourse were already linked in the catechesis prior to Mark, and that could have included the conjunction of the prophecies of vv. 2 and 14, not least in the light of the connection between the abomination and destructive warfare in Daniel 9. Guelich's observations as to the difficulty of applying Mark 13:14 to the circumstances of the Roman war, however, demand careful note.

The call to relate Mark 13 to the rest of Mark's Gospel is important. The proclamation of Jesus is represented in 1:15 as the breaking into history of the kingdom of God. This is expounded in the parables of ch. 4, including that of the Sower, which represents the triumph of the mission of the kingdom initiated through Jesus, despite all the obstacles it meets in this world. So also the emphasis on the predictions of the passion, with their corollary of cross bearing by disciples, is paralleled in ch. 13 with the proclamation of the gospel to all nations in face of their dire opposition. But history's last word is not with the powers of this world but with the Son of man. All of this indicates the realism and optimism of faith, set forth alike in Mark's Gospel and in his eschatological discourse.

Conference on the Relationships of the Gospels

In 1984 a conference was held in Jerusalem which brought to a climax a series of conferences to examine afresh the relations of the Synoptic Gospels, along with other issues that have to do with all four Gospels. The result was a symposium which appeared in 1990, under the leadership of W. R. Farmer, M.-E. Boismard, and F. Neirynck, bearing the title *The Interrelationships of the Gospels*, edited by D. L. Dungan.[191]

Three contemporary approaches to the theme were expounded and evaluated by respondents. The first was the so-called Two Document Hypothesis (referred to as 2DH), commonly accepted for the past century and a half, maintaining that Matthew and Luke used Mark, together with another source generally denominated Q. The second was the Two Gospel Hypothesis (2GH), generally associated with Augustine, namely, that Matthew was utilized by Mark and Luke. Whereas

---

[191]Dungan, ed., *The Interrelations of the Gospels*, BETL 95 (Louvain, 1990).

Augustine considered that Mark abbreviated Matthew and "holds a course in conjunction with Luke," those representing this solution in the conference primarily support the notion that Matthew was followed by Luke, and Mark used and abbreviated both (hence the name "Two Gospel Hypothesis"). A third solution of the Synoptic problem proposed in the symposium is called the "Multiple-Stage Hypothesis." M.-E. Boismard elaborates the thesis of an original Proto-Mark, Proto-Matthew, and Proto-Luke, that Matthew and Luke depend on Proto-Mark, and that Mark was influenced by Proto-Matthew and Proto-Luke.

The pertinence of these expositions to our concern is that each hypothesis was tested by reference to the eschatological discourse in the Synoptic Gospels, together with that in Luke 17. No less than five papers on the discourse appear in the symposium. We shall attempt briefly to review their contributions.

A. J. McNichol. A lengthy paper was contributed by McNichol from the viewpoint of the Two-Gospel Hypothesis, entitled "The Composition of the Synoptic Eschatological Discourse."[192] McNichol sets out to demonstrate how Luke drew material from Matt 24:1–51 to compose the three eschatological units Luke 12:35–48; 17:20–37; 21:5–36, and that Mark had before him both Matthew 24 and Luke 21. Linguistic and stylistic analysis is held to show that Mark followed the *common* testimony of Matthew and Luke, and omitted material which was in one Gospel only. McNichol emphasized this point. Mark's adherence to the principle of brevity is seen in his omission of nearly all of Matt 24:37–25:46, much of Matt 24:1–36 not in Luke, and all of Luke 21:5–36 which is not in Matthew 24. "Mark (13:1–37) overwhelmingly limits himself to source material common to Matthew 24 and Luke 21 . . . Mark composed primarily by using those materials which Matthew and Luke shared."[193] At the same time it is noted that Mark tends to follow the wording of Matthew closely: "But on several occasions Mark will copy material from Matthew which is not in Luke. For example, see Mark 13:19b–23, 27, 32."[194] The lesson is drawn that Mark has great respect for Matthew, and that he wished to combine the texts of Matthew 24 and Luke 21, while closely following the wording of Matthew; at the same time he sought to avoid contradicting the meaning and sense of Luke. "These are Mark's two basic compositional principles throughout his gospel."[195]

Before we proceed further it would seem needful to comment on those two observations, for they are ambiguous and even tend to contradiction. Both C. M. Tuckett and Boismard comment on the claim

---

[192]Ibid., 157–200.
[193]Ibid., 183.
[194]Ibid.
[195]Ibid.

that Mark "overwhelmingly limits himself" to what is in *both* his sources, yet shows respect for Matthew by sometimes copying material from Matthew not in Luke.[196] Moreover, Tuckett rightly points out that Matt 24:26–28, omitted by Mark, has a parallel in Luke 17:23–24, and that Matt 24:43–51, also omitted by Mark, has parallels in Luke 12 and 17. McNichol himself acknowledges that Mark may have used Luke 12:35–38 in Mark 13:35–37.[197] Tuckett asks, "If Luke 12:35–38 is in Mark's mind, why does Mark not include the further material in Matthew 24:43–51 which has such a close parallel in Luke 12:39–46? No very satisfactory explanation seems to be implied here."[198]

Evidence for Mark's use of Matthew 24 and Luke 21 is declared to be the shared order of pericopes, examples of conflation of Matthew and Luke by Mark, common omissions (of Matt 24:10–12, 26–28, 30a, not in Luke, and of Luke 21:12, 14a, 16b, etc., not in Matthew), and shared literary details, i.e., words and phrases and literary structure; most words and phrases in Mark which differ from Matthew and Luke are Markan linguistic characteristics.

Let us consider two instances of conflation cited by McNichol. Mark 13:1 speaks of *potapoi lithoi kai potapai oikodomai*: Matthew has *tas oikodomas*, Luke has *lithois*. This is hardly a convincing example of conflation; neither Matthew nor Luke uses *potapos*, and their statements are quite different, rather like paraphrases of Mark. In Mark 13:4 the second question runs, *kai ti to sēmeion hotan mellē tauta synteleisthai panta* ("What will be the sign when all these things are about to be accomplished?"). It is urged that Mark follows *kai ti to sēmeion* in both his sources; like Luke, he does not use Matthew's term *parousia* at all in his Gospel; rather he here copies the Lukan clause, but takes up Matthew's *synteleias* in his *synteleisthai* instead of Luke's *ginesthai*, and so conflates.[199] This, too, appears to be doubtful conflation. It is true that Mark and Luke employ almost identical language, other than Luke's omission of *panta* and use of *ginesthai*, but Mark's term *synteleisthai* almost certainly is not a modification of Matthew's *synteleias* but is derived straight from Dan 12:6–7: "When the power of the holy people ceases to be dispersed *syntelesthēsetai panta tauta* (all these things shall be accomplished)."

Commenting on Mark 13:9–13 McNichol points out that, assuming the correctness of the 2GH, Mark had several accounts of persecution of the disciples, notably Matt 24:9–14/Luke 21:12–19; Matt 10:17–22/Luke 12:11–12. He states, "One would expect Mark to conflate his

---

[196]Tuckett, "The Eschatological Discourse," 70; Boismard, "La 'Two-Gospel Hypothesis': Le discours eschatologique de Matthieu 24 et parallèles," 266–67.

[197]McNichol, "Composition," 198.

[198]Tuckett, "Eschatological Discourse," 71.

[199]McNichol, "Composition," 187.

two sources in this literary context (Mt. 24:9–14/Lk. 21:12–19), instead he chose to follow the two closest texts, Matthew 10:17–22 / Luke 21:12–19."[200] It is further suggested that Mark copied Matt 10:23a/Luke 21:20 rather than Matt 24:15a to form his 13:14a.[201] Such judgments are perplexing. With regard to the former suggestion, Luke is very paraphrastic in this section; it is more plausible to suggest his dependence on Mark 13:10 for his 21:13 than vice versa. As to Mark 13:14a, all three evangelists begin with the same expression, *hotan de idēte*, after which Matthew and Mark have an identical opening clause, whereas Luke departs from both drastically. McNichol nevertheless continues: "Mark drops *to rēthen dia Daniēl tou prophētou* from Matthew as Luke did. This is a clear case of Mark omitting where Luke omits because Mark no longer has two sources to unite. . . . The 'weakening' of Mark 13:14a *vis-à-vis* Matthew 24:15b may represent Mark's attempt to bring the content of Matthew 24:15 and Luke 21:20 closer together, or may be a reflection of Mark's eschatological agenda (cf. 2 Thess. 2:3f)."[202] I should have thought that something much more drastic was needed to bring Matt 24:15 and Luke 21:20 together than Mark's omission of a reference to Daniel. On the contrary, the addition of the reference to Daniel by Matthew would appear to be distinctly more plausible than this particular suggestion.

Regarding Mark 13:33–37, McNichol suggests that Mark 13:33 is a summary of Luke 21:34–36, and Mark 13:34–37 a summary of Matt 24:37–25:46; Mark 13:33b, *ouk oidate gar pote ho kairos estin* ("You do not know when the time is") conflates Luke 21:36 (*kairos*, "time") with Matt 25:13 (*ouk oidate tēn hēmeran oude tēn hōran*, "You do not know the day or the hour").[203] The content of Mark 13:34–37 is considered to be supplied by a paraphrase of the common theme of the parables in Matt 24:37—25:30, namely, the departure of a prominent man and his sudden return. One acknowledges that all these suggestions could follow on the basis of Mark's use of Matthew and Luke, but they do not appear to me to be likely solutions of the problems presented by the texts. For example, the thought of a prominent man's departure and sudden return is certainly present in the passages mentioned, but a far closer parallel to Mark 13:35–36 is the parable of Luke 12:36–38 (to which McNichol also draws attention, of which the core parable in Mark 13:35–36 is surely a variant).[204]

---

[200]Ibid., 188.

[201]Ibid., 193.

[202]Ibid.

[203]Ibid., 197.

[204]See ibid., 198. On the relations between the Markan parable and the Q parable of the Talents/Pounds see our commentary below on Mark 13:34–36, pp. 470–74.

McNichol summarizes Mark's procedure in 13:33–37 thus: "Mark sets out to give a summary of the eschatological material in his sources, Matthew 24:37–25:30 and Luke 21:34–36. Mark accomplishes this through the literary technique of juxtaposition. First Luke 21:34–36 is condensed into Mark 13:33a, then Matthew 25:13 and Luke 21:36 conflated, resulting in 13:33b; Matthew 25:14–15 is condensed to Mark 13:34, Matthew 24:42–43 to Mark 13:35, Matthew 25:5, 12 condensed and supplemented to form Mark 13:36–37."[205] On this the comment of Neirynck is to be pondered: "The description of evidence is one thing. To give it probative force against the priority of Mark is quite another task. The main point in McNichol's analysis is perhaps the emphasis he gives to 'Markan linguistic characteristics.' But is it Mark who, copying and conflating his two sources, 'utilizes a favorite literary device,' or was this Markan expression already present in the common source of Matthew and Luke? The last alternative cannot be denied without serious examination."[206] Most of us would add that it is much simpler and more plausible than the former alternative.

M.-E. Boismard. Boismard, approaching the eschatological discourse from the "Multiple-Stage Hypothesis," deals first with the discourse in Luke 17, since it has parallels with that in Matthew 24 (Luke 17:22–24, 26–35 / Matt 24:26–28, 37–41). These sections are acknowledged to have come from Q, but Boismard endeavors to prove that their language is Lukan, hence that they actually belong to Proto-Luke (not, of course, in the sense defined by B. H. Streeter as Q + L). Among the examples of the vocabulary referred to we select two: the frequent appearance of verbs for eating and drinking; in the common tradition and in passages special to Luke they are always *esthiō* and *pinō*, but in Matt 24:38 Matthew has *trōgō*, while Luke 17:27 has the usual *esthiō*, hence Matthew is viewed as secondary here. In the same passage the expression *achri hēs hēmeras* appears; *achri* is a Lukan term; everywhere else Matthew uses *heōs*. Boismard comments on these and many other examples: "The Lukan color of all these expressions is undeniable; a Matthean origin of these texts is impossible."[207] He adds the unusual suggestion that the discourse of Luke 17 originally ended with Luke 21:34–36. His reason? "The double theme of remaining sober and of watching suits much better a discourse on the return of the Son of Man (Lk. 17:22–30) than a discourse on the destruction of Jerusalem (i.e. Lk. 21)."[208]

On Boismard's general procedure Neirynck raises a question: "Can we declare a source used by Luke 'Proto-Lukan' because of the presence

---

[205]Ibid., 199.
[206]Neirynck, "Note on the Eschatological Discourse," 80.
[207]Boismard, "Discours eschatologique," 272.
[208]Ibid., 286.

of some words and phrases which are attested as 'Lukanisms' elsewhere in Luke and in Acts? Is it not rather their relative frequency in Luke and in Acts which allows us to speak of a word or phrase characteristic of Luke? A more or less isolated use of the same word in another gospel or in a source of Luke is not necessarily Lukan usage."[209]

In his discussion on the discourse of Matthew 24, Mark 13, and Luke 21, Boismard notes the variety of vocabulary and content of their introductions (Mark 13:1–4; Matt 24:1–3; Luke 21:5–7), and he concludes that they are all independent. If it were otherwise, and Matthew was the source of Mark and Luke, he asks why they avoided the terms *parousia* and *synteleia*, which Matthew alone has. Or if Mark was prior, why did Matthew and Luke omit reference to the four disciples named in Mark 13:3, the seating of Jesus opposite the temple, and the imperfect *epērōta*, which occurs fifteen times in Mark, not at all in Matthew, and only five times in Luke? "The text of Mark contains too many expressions exclusively Markan, or quasi–exclusively Markan, to be considered as the source of Matthew and Luke."[210]

Advancing further into the discourse Boismard characterizes three passages as a triplet: (a) Mark 13:5b–6/Matt 24:4–5/Luke 21:8–9; (b) Mark 13:21–23/Matt 24:23–25; and (c) Matt 24:26/Luke 17:23; in the first the language is said to be Markan, in the second it is claimed to be Matthean, and in the third it is viewed as Lukan. From this Boismard states: "The theories of multiple sources permit us to propose a thesis: the first variant of the triplet comes from a Proto-Mark, the second a Proto-Matthew, the third a Proto-Luke. It is on the plane of the ultimate Matthean, Markan, and Lukan redactions that these diverse traditions influence one another."[211]

The observations on the section concerning the witness and persecution of the church are interesting. Mark 13:9–13/Matt 10:17–22/Luke 21:12–19 are said to be "not homogeneous," for Matt 10:17–20 and Mark 13:9–11 are in the second person plural, Matt 10:21 and Mark 13:12 in the third person, Matt 10:22a and Mark 13:13a in the second person again, and Matt 10:22b and Mark 13:13b in the third person, but Luke puts them all in the second person. Boismard suggests that the second person plural is better in a mission discourse than in a discourse on the ruin of the temple, and there the vocabulary indicates a Matthean origin, whereas a third person plural is better in the situation of Mark's discourse. A harmonization has taken place: the second person sections have passed from the mission discourse to that on the temple, the third person sections from the temple discourse to the mission discourse.

---

[209]Neirynck, "Eschatological Discourse," 108.
[210]Boismard, "Discours eschatologique," 276.
[211]Ibid., 277.

Accordingly, "it is impossible to hold that Matt 10:17–22 is the source of Mark 13:9–13, as the 2GH would have it, or that Mark 13:9–13 is the source for Matt 10:17–22, as the 2DH would wish it. The problem is far too complex and cannot be resolved by making appeal to the conditions of the earlier discourses as to the actual redactions of Matthew and Mark."[212]

Surprisingly, Boismard maintains that the parousia description in Mark 13:24–27 is dependent on Matt 24:29–31, primarily on the ground of Matthew's interest in the parousia (see, e.g., ch. 13), his use of the term *parousia* in the discourse, and the references in Matt 24:30a to the sign of the Son of man and to the trumpet sound in 24:31. To this one must object: Mark can hardly be said to be without interest in the parousia—far from it; the Matthean features in Matt 24:30–31 are more simply explained as interpolations into the Markan text, probably on the basis of other traditions besides Mark's. Boismard further suggests that Mark 13:30 depends on Matt 24:34, since the perspective is that of Matthew (cf. 10:23; 16:27–28), and that Mark 13:32 is dependent on Matt 24:36, since the thought is expressed in terms found elsewhere in Matthew but not in Mark (e.g., Matt 24:50, "day and hour"; 25:13, "You do not know the hour"; 24:44, "at an hour you do not suppose"; 11:27, "Nobody knows . . . except the Father"; and the absolute use of the terms "the Father . . . the Son"). These considerations are by no means equal, but Boismard himself acknowledges, "There were reciprocal influences of Matthean and Markan traditions which must be borne in mind on the level of actual redactions."[213]

There remains a consideration of Luke 21. Luke 21:20–28 is viewed as the heart of the discourse. The section is said to contain two elements, one original and the other of texts more or less identical with Matthew and Mark. The original passage consists of vv. 20, 21b–22, 23b–25, 28 and was derived from Proto-Luke. The introduction to this little discourse is suggested to have been originally Luke 19:41–44, since in this discourse Luke is concerned with the destruction of Jerusalem, not of the temple, and the style of 19:41–44 is very Lukan.[214]

Boismard's approach to these issues is highly ingenious, particularly his postulate of a Proto-Mark, Proto-Matthew, and Proto-Luke. Its tentative nature, however, is illustrated in an admission of Boismard himself: "It is almost impossible to distinguish the vocabulary and the style of Proto-Luke from those of the ultimate Lukan redaction, and the one and the other being closely connected to the vocabulary and style of Acts."[215] On this Neirynck comments: "In these conditions the

---

[212]Ibid., 280.

[213]Ibid., 283.

[214]Ibid., 284.

[215]Boismard, *Synopse,* 2:469, cited by Neirynck, "Eschatological Discourse," 115.

vocabulary argument can be of no direct utility in the discussion on the alternatives, Lukan *rewriting* of Mark or *Proto-Lukan source*."[216]

4. Contributions from More Traditional Positions

C. E. B. Cranfield

Cranfield wrote a series of articles on Mark for the *Scottish Journal of Theology,* presumably by way of preparation for his commentary on Mark for the Cambridge Greek Testament Commentary.[217] From the outset he made it clear that he was not impressed with the objections commonly voiced to the authenticity of the discourse of Mark 13. The main objection appeared to be the alleged inconsistency between the discourse and other traditions of the eschatological teaching of Jesus, especially the representation of a parousia heralded by signs in contrast with a sudden parousia as depicted in the source Q. This difficulty, Cranfield urged, is due to failure to take into account the undoubted fact that Mark 13 is not a typical apocalypse, and also the place of paradox in the teaching of Jesus. "To see that the apparent contradictions here may be not inconsistencies due to unintelligent compilation but intentional paradox is, we would suggest, to hold a key to the understanding of the discourse."[218]

Cranfield has especially in mind the tension between v. 32, on the unknowability of the time of the end, and the concern with signs of the end in vv. 5–23, 28–29, and a second tension between the caution that the end is not yet, expressed in vv. 7–8 and implied in v. 10, and the intimation in v. 29 of the nearness of the end when the signs come to pass. He urged that these tensions must be held together, so that each may control and help to interpret the other. Curiously, the former tension exhibits within the discourse the contrast which exegetes have drawn between Mark 13 and the Q apocalypse, Luke 17:22–37. Cranfield affirms that the signs in Mark 13 are not to provide data for reckoning the date of the end; rather they have an ethical intention, encouraging the faith and obedience of Christians in the midst of their trials, and they serve as reminders of the coming Lord in the midst of history.[219]

A major problem raised in the discourse is the relation of history to the end of the age, notably as it applies to the prophecy of the ruin

---

[216]Neirynck, "Eschatological Discourse," 115.
[217]Cranfield, "St. Mark 13," *SJT* 6 (1953): 189–96, 287–303; 7 (1954): 284–303. The introductory material in the articles is very briefly reproduced in his commentary, *Gospel of Mark,* CGTC, 3d ed. (Cambridge, 1966), 387–91.
[218]Idem, *SJT* 6:299–300.
[219]Ibid., 300–301.

of the temple (and implied fall of Jerusalem) and the parousia for judgment and the coming of the kingdom of God. Here Cranfield sets forth varied considerations. The temple belonged to an order that was being superseded, at once fulfilled and abrogated by Jesus. H. Roux is cited: "The announcement of the destruction of the temple is directly connected with the advent of the kingdom of God, of which it is the first act."[220] Further, the destruction of the temple is linked with the sin of the nation which rejected God's Messiah, Jesus; Schrenk's view is adduced that the destruction of the temple would be "a token *(Zeichen)* of judgment as well as foretoken *(Vorzeichen)* of the parousia."[221] There is therefore a correspondence between the ruin of Jerusalem with its temple and the end of the age: "The eschatological is seen as it were through the medium of an approaching historical crisis, the historical catastrophe being regarded as foreshadowing the final convulsion."[222] Another theologian, Karl Heim, is cited to illustrate the point: "All this is for him [Jesus] only a *Transparent* [i.e., transparency] standing in the foreground, through which he beholds the last events before the end of the world, in which all this will at last come to its real fulfilment."[223] In dealing with the question therefore as to whether the prophecy of the abomination of desolation in Mark 13:14 is to be given an exclusively historical or exclusively eschatological interpretation, it is replied that we must allow for a double reference, since the historical and eschatological are mingled together.[224]

On the question as to the time of the end in the discourse, Cranfield appeals once more to the notion of paradox: "The fact that Mark apparently sees no inconsistency in including in one discourse vv. 7, 29, and 32 is surely significant."[225] More importantly, the problem requires a more theological understanding of the imminence of the end: "The clue to the meaning of the nearness of the end is the realization of the essential unity of God's Saving Acts in Christ—the realization that the events of the Incarnation, Crucifixion, Resurrection, Ascension and Parousia are in a real sense one Event."[226] This is the significance of representing the period from the incarnation to the parousia as "the last days." However long the time between the ascension and the parousia may be, theologically speaking the parousia is always near;

---

[220]Ibid., 191. The citation is from Roux, *L'Evangile du Royaume* (Geneva, 1965), 279–80.

[221]Cranfield, *SJT* 6:191. The citation is from Schrenk's article, *TDNT*, 3:245, Cranfield's translation.

[222]Cranfield, *SJT* 6:297.

[223]Ibid., 300, citing Heim, *Die Königsherrschaft Gottes* (Stuttgart, 1948), 55–56.

[224]Cranfield, *SJT* 6:298.

[225]Ibid., 7:288.

[226]Ibid.

the two moments are "drawn together by an overwhelming magnetism, and yet for a time are held apart." The unity is no impersonal principle but Jesus Christ himself. Here Karl Barth is brought forward as witness: "Strictly speaking there are no 'last things,' no abstract independent 'last things' beside and apart from Him who is *the* Last. . . . If one understands this, then one also understands that, and why, the NT hope could only be the hope of the imminent coming of the kingdom."[227]

Cranfield concludes that the discourse gives us substantially the teaching of Jesus—not his precise words, nor an address uttered on one occasion, but "authentic sayings of Jesus which have been brought together intelligently, so that the resulting discourse does not misrepresent the teaching of Jesus."[228] The disparagement of the chapter by scholars has led to its neglect by preachers, to the impoverishment and weakening of the church's life. Mark 13 has a special contribution through its reminder that eschatology is more than a matter for academic reflection: "Our gaze that is so easily diverted from the Lord who is coming to us is thus again and again directed back to its proper Object, and the events of the present become for us God's summons to renewed penitence, trust, love, obedience, joy."[229]

It will be appreciated that I have no little sympathy with Cranfield's viewpoint. The paradoxes of the discourse are inherent in eschatological thinking, as may be seen in the eschatological passages of Q, of Paul, and in the book of Revelation. The point that signs serve as reminders of the coming Lord in the midst of history is important alike for faith and for life. Cranfield has struggled hard to express a positive relation between history and eschatology as set forth in the discourse. Whether it is adequate to the source to represent the relation between the prophecy of Israel's tribulation and the end of history by Karl Heim's ingenious image of a transparency through which the events of the end are viewed is doubtful. Its truth is the consistency of God in his judgments in history, but it is important to recognize that the biblical writers maintain a tradition in depicting them, and that this tradition is reproduced in Mark 13. The OT descriptions of the day of the Lord on peoples and cities reproduce a pattern, based on Israel's ancient traditions of the theophanies of Yahweh for the "wars of the Lord," in the conviction that he who so acted in the past does so still, and will do so in the end (the second exodus motif is important here).[230] The

---

[227]Ibid., 289; the citation is from Barth's *Kirchliche Dogmatik* III/2, pp. 589–90, Cranfield's translation.

[228]Cranfield, *SJT* 7:302.

[229]Ibid.

[230]On this see G. von Rad, "The Origin of the Concept of the Day of Yahweh," *JSS* 4 (1959), 101; idem, *Old Testament Theology*, 2 vols. (ET New York, 1962–65), 2:119–25.

days of the Lord in the past therefore serve as models for the days of the Lord in the immediate future and for the ultimate day of the Lord. It was natural for prophets to employ the cosmic language of the final day of the Lord in describing judgments on contemporary powers, including lesser peoples like Edom (Isaiah 34) or Israel judged by a plague of locusts (Joel 2). It was equally comprehensible that the prophets, in anticipating a day of the Lord on their generations, should at times expect a climactic day of the Lord to lead to the great deliverance for which they looked, the kingdom of God. All this suggests that Mark 13 does not so much view the end through the spectrum of Israel's tribulation as Israel's judgment in the light of the prophetic-apocalyptic tradition of the day of the Lord. We need perhaps an image from the communications world—beaming a picture to a country by means of a satellite beyond earth's orbit! The essential point is that Mark 13 gives a typical prophetic-apocalyptic representation of the future relating to Israel and the church, and depicts a judgment to fall on Israel in terms of the day of the Lord on Jerusalem. Its relation to the time of the end (nearness or distance) is determined less by that fact than by the nature of the warnings and exhortations which accompany the prophecy, particularly those in the concluding section, vv. 28–37.

A. L. Moore

The investigation by Moore of the NT teaching on the parousia centers upon the nature of the near expectation held by Jesus and the early church; the consideration of Mark 13 concentrates on those elements in it which attest a near expectation. Moore sees two elements in the self-consciousness of Jesus which stood in tension: the eschatological significance which Jesus attached to his own person and work, attested, e.g., in Matt 12:28, and a "grace character," expressed especially in his healing miracles. The former motif presses toward the final revelation of the divine rule; the latter strives to veil and to give people time and opportunity for repentance and response to the call of God. To the former element are due the sayings expressing a conviction that the end is near, to the latter those sayings which express an element of delay.[231] A near expectation in the teaching of Jesus is thus freely acknowledged, as also in the primitive church, but Moore is emphatic that the expectation is not "delimited," i.e., not set within a defined time limit; sayings which appear to suggest the contrary are susceptible of a different interpretation.

Mark 13:30 is one of the utterances which appear to attest an expectation of the end coming within a specific time limit. The decisive

---

[231]Moore, *The Parousia in the New Testament,* NovTSup 13 (Leiden, 1966), 202.

issue is the reference of *tauta panta* in the statement; if it is an isolated saying in the tradition we do not know to what it refers, but it is urged that in Mark's context it must be the same as the *tauta* of v. 29, which clearly refers to the events preceding the end and not the end itself; in that case the *tauta panta* of v. 30 emphasizes that all the signs of the end in vv. 5–23 will come upon the contemporary generation. Moore, however, enters a caveat: "It is not here suggested that Mark 13:30 refers to specific events, but rather to the entire complex of events which may be termed 'signs of the end' and which are to be experienced, though not necessarily exhausted, by the contemporary generation."[232]

This interpretation is supported by an analysis of the discourse. Verses 1–4 provide an introduction, culminating in the question of v. 4, which leads to a discourse on the end and its date, and the signs of the end and their dates; vv. 5–23 describe the signs of the end; vv. 24–27 portray the end itself; vv. 28–31 have in view the time of the signs of the end, vv. 32–37 the time of the end event. The signs therefore are given a specific time reference—they are to occur within the immediate future, but the end itself is not so limited. Mark 13:30 accordingly does not provide a delimited expectation of the parousia.[233] The conclusion is drawn: "It appears that Jesus may well have predicted here that the contemporary generation must experience all the preliminary signs and therefore could expect the end at any moment. But this does not mean that he held to a delimited expectation, only rather that he had that undelimited near-expectation which we have seen to have characterized the early church."[234] With this interpretation the allied sayings Mark 9:1 and Matt 10:23 are correlated. The former is believed to find a "real fulfillment" in the transfiguration, viewed as an anticipation of the parousia, while the latter speaks of a conceptual, not chronological, limitation of time; hence "You will not finish this work until," rather than, "On or before the year 'X' the Son of Man will come."[235]

Moore's main contention that a distinction should be drawn between a near expectation in general terms and a specifically "delimited" near expectation, and that it is the former which Jesus possessed, is justified. It represents an application of a concern, long maintained by scholars, to distinguish between Jesus and those apocalyptists who

---

[232]Ibid., 133.

[233]Ibid., 134–35.

[234]Ibid., 189. Observe that the passage is attributed to Jesus. On the authenticity of the discourse Moore is cautiously affirmative: "There seems good reason for the judgment 'that 13:5–37 does give us substantially our Lord's teaching' (citation from Cranfield, *Mark* p. 390). . . . If we are not able to treat the chapter as an authentic discourse, we certainly are justified in weighing each pericope on its own merits, allowing at least the possibility of authenticity" (Moore, *Parousia*, 179–80).

[235]Ibid., 125–31.

claimed to be able to calculate the time of the end. On this issue the declarations of Jesus in Luke 17:20–21 and Mark 13:32 are unambiguously plain. Moore has sought to give a clear definition of the distinction. The difficulty, of course, is precisely how to relate sayings like Mark 13:30 to this kind of expectation,[236] and in particular whether Moore's solution of the problem is satisfactory.

Moore acknowledges that Mark 13:30 is an isolated saying, and therefore may not originally have referred to the end of the age, but he is convinced that in the discourse it refers to the signs of the end, rather than the end itself. Moore, however, proceeds to qualify this understanding in two ways: first, by stating that Mark 13:30 does not refer to specific events, but to the whole complex of "signs of the end"; second, by hinting that the signs may be fulfilled again in some remoter future (they are "experienced, though not necessarily exhausted, by the contemporary generation").[237] In this he appears temporarily to have overlooked that whereas some signs are general, like "wars and rumors of war," and some constant, like the opposition to and the witness of the church, one major sign is very specific, namely, the appearance of the desolating abomination and the event to which it leads. In the Markan redaction this is not a peripheral event, but one related to the primary concern of the disciples. Their "What sign?" was called forth by the statement of Jesus, "Not a stone [of the temple structures] shall be left on a stone, all are to be thrown down." The primary answer to that question is supplied in vv. 14ff.: "When you see the desolating sacrilege," then those in Judea must flee, woe is pronounced on those who cannot hasten (pregnant women and nursing mothers), for those shall be days of unparalleled and unrepeatable distress. How does this sign, and the calamity to which it leads, relate to Moore's characterization of signs "experienced, though not necessarily exhausted, by the contemporary generation?" Is it contemplated that the "abomination" may arise again, and Jerusalem and its inhabitants be engulfed in further calamities? If so, some quite explicit explanation is demanded on that issue—which indeed has exercised the minds of exegetes through generations (see, e.g., the discussion of Cranfield). In reality, when Moore states that according to Mark 13:30 the signs of vv. 5–23 find

---

[236]To this question A. Vögtle devoted an extended discussion, "Exegetische Erwägungen über das Wissen und Selbstbewusstsein Jesu," in *Gott in Welt,* Festschrift K. Rahner, 2 vols. (Freiburg, 1964), 1:608–67. Vögtle's position was in close agreement with that of B. Rigaux, "La seconde venue de Jésus," in E. Massaux et al., *La Venue du Messie,* RechBib 6 (1962), 173–216.

[237]This is not an expression thoughtlessly dropped. Moore adds a footnote adducing this as a correction of the view that if the signs are to happen within the generation, the end must also fall in the same period (Moore, *Parousia,* 133 n. 4).

fulfillment in the contemporary generation, in such a way that the end can be expected at any moment, that should mean that no further signs of consequence are to be expected than signs of the kingdom of God in action and consequences of resistance to the kingdom. That would be in complete harmony with Moore's fundamental position about no "delimited" expectation of the end in the Lord's teaching. But if he believed that the period between the resurrection and the parousia of Jesus is necessarily characterized by signs of that order it would have been helpful for him to have stated that in his interpretation of Mark 13.

The notion that eschatology and grace existed in tension in the consciousness of Jesus calls for a further comment. That grace was to the fore in his mind is not to be doubted, but it was manifested precisely in the operation of the kingdom of God in and through him. The healing miracles were themselves manifestations of the saving sovereignty of God in action in Jesus. It is that self-same sovereignty revealed in the grace of the death and resurrection of Jesus, in the gift of the Holy Spirit, and the consummation of the kingdom at the parousia. Admittedly the last entails also a manifestation of the divine sovereignty in judgment, but the entire NT, including even the book of Revelation, makes plain that the future consummation of the saving sovereignty of God is for the completion of that gracious action manifest in the works of Jesus, and that is why the message of Jesus can be described as good news of God (Mark 1:14).[238] There is not a word in the proclamation of Jesus about the kingdom of God which suggests that the grace of the kingdom acts as a deterrent to its ultimate revelation. That is a notion imported from 2 Pet 3:9, and is due to reflection on other elements of the OT scriptures. Moore's recognition of the christological unity of the eschatological events is much more to the point in the matter under review: "The nearness of the end is bound up with the person of Jesus Christ, in whom the events of the end, including their open, unambiguous manifestation, coinhere. In him death, resurrection, ascension, and parousia belong together. They do not belong together as a general principle, but as a matter of theological, or more exactly of Christological fact. The Christological unity of the end events is thus the mainspring of the end's nearness."[239] That is well stated and well worth stating.

J. K. Howard

In an article concluding a series on eschatology for the *Evangelical Quarterly*, J. K. Howard firmly identified himself with the view advo-

---

[238]Curiously this is in line with the emphasis of Mark 13:24–27, which contains no explicit mention of judgment but only of the gathering of the elect at the parousia.

[239]Moore, *Parousia*, 172.

cated by E. Haupt, that the discourse of Mark 13 is "of composite origin, consisting of a collection of various sayings relating to the future, spoken originally at different times, and now incorporated by Mark into the framework of a single discourse."[240] The material of the discourse is acknowledged to have been ordered with two questions in mind, stated in Mark 13:4: the one relating to the destruction of the temple and the other to the end of time; the answers, however, since they are drawn from various sources, are scattered through the discourse and require to be disentangled. The question concerning the fall of Jerusalem is answered in vv. 14–20; material concerning the approaching end can be divided into three: warnings of persecution during the interim, vv. 9–13; dangers of the last days, vv. 5–6, 21, 22; sayings concerning the parousia, vv. 7–8, 24–27; finally, the discourse is closed by the parable of the Watchman, vv. 28–37.[241]

It is emphasized that there is no doubt that vv. 14–20 relate to the imminent desecration and destruction of the temple by the Romans; the "profanation that appals" probably has in view the ensigns of the Roman legions.[242] Nevertheless, the historical situation of AD 70 has elements of the ultimate eschaton: "In the same way that the Old Testament prophets had seen in the various judgments which had come upon Israel through her enemies a portrayal of the final day of judgment, the great Day of the Lord (Amos 5:18–20), so also the fall of Jerusalem was a shadow of the catastrophic events which would mark the end of the age."[243] By contrast, the interim persecutions of the church do not refer to a single period of tribulation but characterize the difficult way which the church must tread. This period would also be marked by the appearance of false christs who seek to lead astray Christians; Paul combines this picture with that of the "appalling horror," to produce his portrait of the one final antichrist. The description in vv. 7–8 has in view a society which begins to crumble, the collapse of human government in the time immediately prior to the parousia, which is described in vv. 24–27. The final parable, a variant of that of the Waiting Servants (Luke 12:35–38), inculcates the necessity of wakefulness. So the parousia is presented as an event preceded by clearly defined signs, yet an imminent and sudden possibility.[244]

This is an honest and commendable attempt to deal with the material of the discourse, and in its essentials proceeds along generally

---

[240]Howard, "Our Lord's Teaching concerning his *Parousia:* A Study in the Gospel of Mark," *EvQ* 38 (1966): 150–57; citation p. 150.

[241]Ibid., 151–52.

[242]Ibid., 153, following a suggestion of mine in an earlier *Commentary on Mark Thirteen,* 59–60.

[243]Howard, "Our Lord's Teaching," 153.

[244]Ibid., 155.

approved lines. It is not entirely clear why the appearance of false christs is distinguished from the phenomena of vv. 7–8, as though the former relate to the whole period prior to the end but the latter to the last time itself; we have noted how frequently attention is called to the significance of the comments in vv. 7 and 8 that warn against identifying the signs therein portrayed as indicating the immediately impending end. It is likely that the evangelist viewed all the events described in vv. 6–13 as characteristic of the time of the church, and thus all as relating to the "last" times. Howard also seems to find it needful to detach vv. 28–30 from that which follows and view the parable of the Fig Tree, along with v. 30, as relating to the fall of Jerusalem (contrast Luke's interpretation of the parable in Luke 21:31, which is probably closer to Mark's). On the inadequacy of viewing the events of AD 70 as a "shadow of the catastrophic events of the end time," and so requiring a double fulfillment, we would refer the reader to our thoughts already expressed on this issue.[245]

G. E. Ladd

Ladd's discussions of the eschatological discourse have been set in contexts of wider treatment of the eschatological teaching of Jesus.[246] His interest has been in the teaching of the discourse rather than its formation. He assumed that Jesus gave a discourse on the Mount of Olives, but that the three reports of the sermon are the result of editorial work by the evangelists, drawing on available traditions.[247] The teaching of Jesus generally and the Olivet discourse in particular show that Jesus was closer to the prophets than the apocalyptists, especially in relation to the form of his teaching (the discourse is not apocalyptic in form, its symbolism is akin to that of the prophets, and Jesus refrains from picturing eschatological conditions). In one respect, however, Jesus stood closer to the apocalyptists, in that he shared the dualistic eschatology which looked for the kingdom of God to be established by the in-breaking of God into history; on the other hand Jesus stands with

---

[245] See above, pp. 238–39.

[246] Ladd's two best-known works, on which we have drawn, are *The Presence of the Future: The Eschatology of Biblical Realism* (Grand Rapids, 1974), which is a revision of *Jesus and the Kingdom* (Grand Rapids, 1964), and *A Theology of the New Testament* (Grand Rapids, 1974).

[247] Ladd writes: "It is evident from a comparative study that the form the discourse has assumed in the three Gospels is due to tradition and to the authors. The original form of the discourse is lost to us. . . . In the original discourse the historical event of the fall of Jerusalem and the eschatological consummation were blended in a form impossible for us to recover" (*Presence*, 310). Ladd sees evidence of editorial work illustrated in the absence of Mark 13:9b–12 from Matthew 24 and the appearance of the section in Matt 10:17–21 (*Theology*, 196).

the prophets in his recovery of the tension between history and eschatology, and that in a more dynamic form.[248]

Ladd calls for recognition of two tensions in the eschatological teaching of Jesus which are especially plain in the Olivet discourse: (1) the anticipation of certain historical events and the eschatological consummation, (2) the presence of a historical perspective and a note of imminence. As to the first, the anticipation of the destruction of the temple and that of the end of the age in Mark's report of the discourse appear to be inextricably interwoven; while that holds good also of the reports of Matthew and Luke, the eschatological stands out more clearly in Matthew and the historical in Luke. The problem is not to be solved by preferring one tradition to another. The discourse sets out from a question which raises both issues: When will the temple be destroyed, and what will be the sign of the end? Despite the efforts of form critics, we cannot recover the ipsissima verba of Jesus, but from the totality of his teaching it is clear that Jesus spoke both of the fall of Jerusalem and of his own parousia. Ladd approves of Cranfield's suggestion that in the view of Jesus the historical and the eschatological fields are mingled, and the final eschatological event is seen through the "transparency" of the immediate historical. This is comparable to the outlook of the prophets, who viewed the immediate future in terms of the ultimate future without strict chronological differentiation, and so proclaimed the ultimate will of God for his people in the here and now.[249]

The juxtaposition of a historical perspective with imminent expectation is also observable in the discourse, as in the rest of the teaching of Jesus. Here Ladd distinguishes three types of sayings on the end: those which appear to speak of an end in the immediate future, of which Mark 13:30 is most conspicuous (cf. also Matt 10:23; Mark 9:1); those which emphasize delay, such as the comments in Mark 13:7 ("the end is not yet") and 13:8 ("these are the beginning of sorrows"), and the declaration that the gospel must be preached to all nations (v. 10; cf. further Luke 17:22; 18:1–8; 19:11, and the parables of Matt 25); but the strongest note in the discourse is that of uncertainty as to the time of the end, observable above all in Mark 13:32 and in vv. 33, 34–36, 37 (cf. also Matt 24:30, 42, 44). The contradictory nature of these three kinds of sayings is more apparent than real, and the solution would doubtless be clearer if we had the full contexts of their original utterance. As to Mark 13:30, Ladd has the same view as A. L. Moore: the immediate context in v. 29 shows to what it refers: "When you see these things take

---

[248]Ladd suggests that it is better to speak of prophetic and nonprophetic apocalyptic rather than sharply contrast the prophetic and apocalyptic eschatologies (*Presence*, 319, referring to his article "Why not prophetic-apocalyptic?" *JBL* 76 [1957]: 192–200).

[249]Idem, *Theology*, 198–99; idem, *Presence*, 65–69.

place, you know that he is near" obviously relates to the signs described
in the discourse, hence "all these things" in v. 30 should be given the
same reference. "What Jesus appears to be saying is that the signs that
presage the end are not to be confined to a remote future; his hearers
would themselves experience them."[250] With this understanding the
elements of delay and uncertainty are in accord. Jesus teaches that a
great manifestation of the kingdom would be seen by some of his
followers, that the signs that point to the coming of the kingdom would
be seen by his own generation, and other sayings point to a delay of the
kingdom to an "indeterminate future." But "the predominating emphasis is upon the uncertainty of the time, in the light of which men must
be ready."[251]

The tensions of which Ladd speaks are certainly present in the
teaching of Jesus, and he is right in seeing analogies to them in the
prophetic writings, intensified in the utterances of Jesus through his
consciousness of being the bearer of the kingdom of God and the agent
of its action in the world. "Historical" and "eschatological" were already experienced realities in Jesus' service of the kingdom of God; in
the closing stages of his ministry he must have been conscious of the
intensification of their interaction in the forces, human and suprahu-
man, bringing about his death, and in their continuance in the period
leading to the ultimate end. The tension of historical perspective and
imminent expectation is, however, more complex than Ladd has represented. He emphasizes the element of "uncertainty" as to the time of
the end in the teaching of Jesus, but does not sufficiently call attention
to the element of imminence in many of the sayings expressive of
uncertainty, such as Mark 13:33–37. Moreover, Ladd fully recognizes
the element of misunderstanding of the disciples as to the time of the
end, reflected especially in the question of Mark 13:4. On this Ladd
comments:

> There can be little doubt but that the disciples thought of the destruction
> of the temple as one of the events accompanying the end of the age and
> the coming of the eschatological kingdom of God. Matthew interprets the
> disciples' question to involve these two events: "When will this be (i.e.,
> the destruction of the temple), and what will be the sign of your coming
> and of the close of the age?" The question is: Did Jesus, like the disciples,
> expect the destruction of the temple and the end of the age both to occur
> in the near future? [252]

Therein, however, the issues of redaction are involved, for Mark and
Matthew alike fashion the discourse in accordance with the twofold

---

[250]Idem, *Theology*, 209.
[251]Ibid., 210.
[252]Ibid., 196–97.

question. Ladd is well aware of these issues, and he could have exploited them more in his exegesis of the discourse.

Ladd's exposition of the eschatological teaching of Jesus beyond the confines of the discourse is very insightful. His most useful service with respect to the discourse is his relating it to its prophetic and apocalyptic predecessors and to the other eschatological instruction of Jesus.

R. T. France

France has sought, with vigor and confidence, to rehabilitate and set on a firm foundation the once popular view that the substance of the discourse in Mark 13 relates to the fall of Jerusalem.[253] In his estimate the question of the disciples in Mark 13:4 is concerned solely with the destruction of the temple, announced in v. 2. The paragraph vv. 5–13 describes the situation prior to the catastrophe; the whole section is couched in terms of what the disciples are to witness and experience, the use of the second person running straight into the next section, beginning at v. 14, "When *you* see." The events of vv. 5–13 therefore are the immediate prelude to those described in vv. 14ff., which have in view the events of AD 66–70. It is important to observe that while vv. 14–23 describe circumstances connected with the siege of Jerusalem, the fall of the city is not described. It is significant then that v. 24 begins, "But *in those days, after that tribulation.*" France comments, "The impression is virtually irresistible that one is about to be introduced to the catastrophe to which vv. 14–22 have been leading up." In his view the impression is correct. The imagery of vv. 24–25 is part of the stock-in-trade of OT prophecy, used especially in relation to political disasters and the destruction of cities and nations. The language of these verses is directly drawn from Isa 13:10 and 34:4; the former predicts the judgment of Babylon, the latter the doom of Edom. It is natural to apply such language to the impending judgment of Jerusalem. The traditional application of v. 26 to the parousia is due to a misunderstanding of Dan 7:13, which describes the vindication of the Son of man and his exaltation to everlasting dominion, hence a coming to God, not a coming to earth. Such is the primary intent of Mark 14:62. Admittedly the latter saying contains a secondary reference to a manifestation of that power in the near future ("you shall see"), but that is explained in Mark 13:24–26: "Jesus is using Daniel 7:13 as a prediction of that authority which he exercised when in AD 70 the Jewish nation

---

[253] *Jesus and the Old Testament: His Application of Old Testament Passages to Himself and His Mission* (London, 1971). While many references to Mark 13 occur in the book, the interpretation of the discourse is the subject of Appendix A, pp. 227–39.

and its leaders, who had condemned him, were overthrown, and Jesus was vindicated as the recipient of all power from the Ancient of Days."[254] Verse 27 takes up the language of Deut 30:4 and Zech 2:10 to describe the gathering of (the new) Israel by the "messengers" (*angeloi*) of God, i.e., through the proclamation of the gospel.

The parable of the Fig Tree, vv. 28–29, and the saying that follows in v. 30 answer the disciples' question as to the time of these events. But v. 32 introduces a new subject. Instead of the *tauta* of v. 29 and *tauta panta* of v. 30, which echo the disciples' question in v. 4, Jesus speaks of "that day," an expression frequent in the OT of the final judgment; the time of "that day," namely, the parousia, Jesus does not know, and this is the theme of the final paragraph, vv. 33–37.[255]

This is a valiant attempt to give new life to an old solution to Mark 13, but it will not do. The question of v. 4 is worded on the assumption that the prophecy of v. 2 has an eschatological setting, hence the use of the verb *synteleisthai*, which Matthew paraphrases in the expression *synteleia tou aiōnos*; that accurately expresses the evangelists' interpretation of the disciples' thought. More important is the interpretation of vv. 24–25; it is true that the cosmic imagery of this passage is frequent in OT prophetic descriptions of God's judgment of the nations, but one cannot simply say that it symbolizes political disasters. It is due to the OT view of the day(s) of the Lord as theophanies for judgment and deliverance, when Yahweh steps forth in his power, and nature goes into confusion and dread before his presence.[256] The theophanies of history, such as the exodus and the victory over Sisera (Judg 5:4–5), become the pattern for the Lord's anticipated action in the future, as may be seen in the classic theophany description of Habakkuk 3. Lesser "days" anticipate the great "day," and the context must make clear when the latter is in view. Daniel 7:9ff. is to be classed with the latter, which is a theophany for judgment and salvation; the one like a son of man comes to the Ancient of Days, who has "come" precisely for the judgment of the antigod power and the giving of his kingdom to another; "the one like a son of man" participates in this theophany. This is how the Jewish teachers understood the passage, and it is evident that Jesus so interpreted it also. France acknowledges that the Q passage Luke 17:23–24/Matt 24:26–27 relates to the parousia; it has the same fundamental view as Mark 13:24–26, for theophany is described in terms of the coming of the Lord of the storm; Matthew has seen this, hence he places the passage immediately prior to his version of Mark

---

[254]Ibid., 236.

[255]Ibid., 232–33.

[256]On the nature of theophany in the OT and its relation to the day of the Lord, see Jörg Jeremias, *Theophanie: Die Geschichte einer alttestamentlichen Gattung* (Neukirchen-Vluyn, 1965).

13:24–27. That the language is highly pictorial is not to be disputed; the same applies to the stepping forth of the Son of man in the glory of God, by which his parousia is represented as partaking of the nature of a theophany.

It is of secondary importance that one observes how strange it would be for the discourse to be so explicit concerning the events of the judgment of Jerusalem as far as Mark 13:31, and then so indirect in its allusion to the parousia in v. 32. It is altogether more likely that v. 32 explicitly relates to the description of the coming of the Lord in vv. 24–27, to which the parabolic conclusion then relates.

R. Schnackenburg

This great contemporary Roman Catholic exegete of the NT defies classification; nevertheless, Schnackenburg's initial work on eschatology, *God's Rule and Kingdom,* manifested considerable critical caution and rejected positions commonly associated with some of the more fashionable critical schools. His treatment of the discourse forms only a minor part of the whole, but his findings require to be recounted here. It will be found that in subsequent works Schnackenburg, like Perrin, has had a "pilgrimage in Christology," but as a maturer scholar, older in years and from a very different tradition, his "pilgrimage" is of a profounder order than that of his younger contemporary.

Schnackenburg observes that Roman Catholic approaches to the eschatological discourse have been of three kinds: a logical explanation in terms of the final judgment, an interpretation in terms of the destruction of Jerusalem, and a combination of both in a balance between historical and eschatological passages, appealing to the "prophetic perspective" that sees the immediate and the remote in one vision. None of these is regarded as satisfactory; rather, the discourse should be seen as "a purely eschatological vision," partly colored with historical elements, but wholly concerned with the last things.[257] "If this be accepted," comments Schnackenburg, "could not Jesus have made these future events appear near in the prophetic manner? He could have taken the language of prophets and apocalyptists and enriched it, as in another way the seer of Patmos did in the New Testament apocalypse."[258] With respect to the logia that speak of an end in relation to the contemporary generation (Mark 9:1; 13:30; Matt 10:23), it is urged that resort should not be made to interpreting them as concerning the resurrection of Christ, or Pentecost, or the spread of the church through history, or the destruction of Jerusalem. "There is no evidence in the

---

[257] Schnackenburg, *God's Rule and Kingdom* (ET London, 1963; originally published under the title *Gottes Herrschaft und Reich* [Freiburg, 1959]), 202.
[258] Ibid., 202–3.

gospels that Jesus taught such a progressive coming of the *basileia*, that he ever understood the advent of the *basileia* and of the Son of man as anything other than the final eschatological manifestation."[259] It may well be that Mark 13:30 in its original form and context related to the destruction of Jerusalem; in its present context it is related to the parousia as well as the events which precede it.[260]

One thing is certain: Jesus repudiated any calculation and knowledge of the time of the end (Mark 13:32). Luke 17:20 makes it clear that Jesus was not and had no desire to be an apocalyptist; he deliberately kept clear of apocalyptic questions, including that of prophetic calculation. The signs of the discourse do not militate against this view, for they are stated for the purpose of preparing the disciples for the difficult times ahead of them. The Fig Tree parable alone appears to present the events as "portents," but originally the parable will have related to the signs of the kingdom in the ministry of Jesus; the application of v. 29 gives the impression of being secondary.[261] Mark 13:32 declares the absolute, not relative, ignorance of Jesus with respect to the time of the end; this is in harmony with other passages which describe the end as absolutely uncertain, such as Matt 24:44/Luke 12:40; Matt 24:50/Luke 12:46, and it corresponds with representations of the sudden and unexpected onset of the events of the last days (Luke 17:26–30, 34–35 par.). Jesus, then, left the time of the parousia in complete obscurity; the day and hour are not merely indefinite within a certain period of time; knowledge of them is reserved wholly to God.[262] If it be asked whether Mark, by placing 13:32 closely after v. 30, understood the former as a relative ignorance of the time, the likely solution is that the tradition brought together these two divergent sayings and so created a dialectical antithesis.[263]

Schnackenburg concludes by affirming that a broad stream of tradition shows that Jesus announced the coming of God's reign and of the Son of man for a near future, but without specification of the time; a few passages contain a definite time reference to the generation then alive, and the church was uncertain how to fit these "awkward" pieces into the discourse of Jesus. It is deduced: "This attitude of the Church may well point to the best method for ourselves: namely, to nourish a living eschatological hope from the urgent prophetic preaching of Jesus without drawing false conclusions about that prophecy from individual passages. The early Church did not admit any mistake on the part of Jesus. Nor need we do so, if we adopt a careful attitude towards

---

[259]Ibid., 203.
[260]Ibid., 208.
[261]Ibid., 209–10.
[262]Ibid., 210–11.
[263]Ibid., 211–12.

tradition as a whole and pay attention to the manner, the significance and the purpose of Jesus' preaching."[264]

In an article on "near expectation" Schnackenburg referred to the doubts of form critics regarding sayings of Jesus which appear to announce the end within the contemporary generation (Mark 13:30, etc.), but he affirmed his conviction that the near expectation cannot be removed from the preaching of Jesus by critical methods.[265] Nor is the Protestant solution acceptable, that Jesus was mistaken as to the date of the end, while the significance of his eschatological message remains unimpaired. The key to the problem is the prophetic nature of Jesus' proclamation, which addresses people in their actual situation and calls for their decision; the events of the future thereby are moved to a temporal nearness, and so a "shortened perspective" comes about. "Ultimately Jesus reveals only the God of salvation, who will lead to its end that work begun in the acts of Jesus—whether earlier or later (according to man's reckoning) is unessential, since the certainty of the completion remains. To that extent the near-expectation of Jesus is 'a continual expectation' (H. Schürmann)."[266]

Later Schnackenburg contributed an article on the church and the parousia for the Rahner Festschrift.[267] In this he affirmed that Jesus made frequent reference to the parousia, but in a manner characteristic of his reserve in speaking of himself. It is therefore idle to fight over whether individual expressions go back to him, or to the primitive church or the evangelists: "If Jesus himself had the fact in mind, the primitive Church after Easter had the right to clarify and illustrate many an idea."[268] So with regard to Mark 13, the extent to which an application is made to the situation of the primitive church is of secondary moment: "Under the cover of a strongly apocalyptic representation, the kerygmatic-parenetic concern is very powerful, and firmly holds and preserves the intention of Jesus."[269] Once again the prophetic nature of the message therein embodied is emphasized; Jesus wished less to give revelations about the future than to prepare his hearers for the future. The certainty of real future events is included, but Jesus does not convey that in the form of a teaching, but through sayings that warn and console, through exhortation and promise.[270]

---

[264]Ibid., 212.

[265]Idem, *LTK,* 7:777–79.

[266]Ibid., 778.

[267]Idem, "Kirche und Parusie," in *Gott in Welt,* Festschrift K. Rahner, 2 vols. (1964), 1:551–57.

[268]Ibid., 567.

[269]Ibid., 568.

[270]Ibid.

In these contributions the discourse of Mark 13 is considered only as it has bearing on problems under review. In his popular commentary on Mark, Schnackenburg had opportunity to expound the discourse, but inasmuch as the work is part of the series "The New Testament for Spiritual Reading," discussion of critical problems and finer points of exegesis is necessarily limited.[271]

Mark, it is stated, brought together sayings and teaching of Jesus about the future. The question is posed: "Why should he not have transposed these sayings of Jesus, who had always preached very urgently, prophetically, in a way that came home to his contemporaries, into the present situation of the Church community and applied them to an already different state of affairs?"[272] These sayings are appropriately placed immediately prior to the passion, for the church which is called to follow its Lord's way of suffering has to hear his predictions, warnings, and reassurances addressed to it, that it may have a better understanding of itself and cope with the situation in which it finds itself.[273]

The prophecy of v. 2 is thought to be shaped by Mark from the larger saying cited in 14:58. Possibly Mark was looking back on the event prophesied; if so, both the questions of the community and the answers to them in the discourse are more easily explained. The double question of v. 4 itself matches the queries of the community, above all as to the relation of the temple's destruction and the eschatological fulfillment. The first part of the answer (vv. 5–13) recounts events which are not signs of the imminent end; the second section (vv. 14–23) is in the stylistic form of a prediction of events which have taken place, hence the comment in v. 14: "Let the reader understand"—it has been *fulfilled!* Not till vv. 24ff. is the reader's gaze actually turned to the future. The cosmic signs (or "drama," as Schnackenburg prefers to call them) in vv. 24–25 do not so much depict a judgment as focus attention on the event to which all else leads—the parousia. The latter is described through a reinterpretation of Dan 7:13: the Son of man, instead of being led to the throne of God, comes from God, for he is the risen Lord on whom power and glory have been bestowed, and who at his coming will manifest himself as ruler. The symbol is retained to express the transcendental nature of the event; for the parousia is, as it were, "a Christological reinterpretation of the actions of God which bring about the consummation."[274]

---

[271]First published as *Das Evangelium nach Markus, Geistliche Schrift-lesung* (Düsseldorf, 1966); ET *Mark*, New Testament for Spiritual Reading, 2 vols. (London, 1971). The exposition of ch. 13 is in vol. 2.

[272]Ibid., 2:90–91.

[273]Ibid., 91.

[274]Ibid., 101.

The parable of the Fig Tree shows signs of a fresh application: in the ministry of Jesus the hypocrites were reproached for being unable to read the signs of "the present time," which pointed to the presence of the kingdom in Jesus' ministry and called for decision; for Mark and his community, awaiting the parousia, the intermediate period is the present moment and time of decision. The saying of 13:30 is akin to 9:1, and perhaps developed from it, and is in any case of identical meaning. Yet v. 32 declares that none knows the day or hour, for knowledge of the last things is reserved to God alone. So the discourse ends with a call to the whole church to be as the porter, and maintain vigilance for the coming of its Lord (vv. 33–37).[275]

One is embarrassingly aware of the difficulty of doing justice to Schnackenburg's thinking on Mark 13 through such compression as has been exercised in this review. In the absence of statements from him which explicitly modify previously held views, one can make only tentative observations. I am not sure that Schnackenburg would any longer describe the discourse as "a *purely* eschatological vision," in view of the concern attributed to Mark to make plain the relationship between the fall of Jerusalem and the parousia, which was being confounded by false prophets. His view regarding contemporary application of eschatological sayings of Jesus to the situation of Mark's church, with inevitable modification of their form at times, is in line with earlier thought, though more developed. As a principle it is to be recognized, but differences in the extent of its application are bound to arise (e.g., as to the interpretation of the Fig Tree parable).

Schnackenburg has consistently maintained an interest in the problem of the near expectation of Jesus; whereas earlier he found other explanations of sayings anticipating the end within the contemporary generation, these are now viewed as truly reflecting that expectation, but the emphasis is still laid on the prophetic and therefore parenetic nature of these sayings—we recall the plea to understand the message of Jesus as "prophecy" rather than "teaching." This is akin to the viewpoint of his fellow Catholic B. Rigaux, who called for a distinction to be drawn between an expectation of the future, defined as a personal bearing *(comportement)* and feeling, and a teaching concerning the future; the sayings of Jesus under review should be withdrawn from the domain of the true and the false, of teaching and illusion, and be set in the category of exhortation, desire, hope, and vigilance.[276] The distinc-

---

[275]Ibid., 102–4.

[276]Rigaux, "La seconde venue de Jésus," in E. Massaux et al., *Messianisme et Eschatologie,* RechBib 6 (1962), 173–216. Rigaux's position was adopted and developed with modifications by A. Vögtle in his article "Exegetische Erwägungen über das Wissen und Selbstbewusstsein Jesu," in *Gott in Welt,* Festschrift K. Rahner, 2 vols. (1964), 1:608–67.

tion is a valid one, especially if the position be held, as Rigaux strongly does, that Mark 13:32 is the key to Jesus' eschatological understanding. Again, however, care is required in applying this interpretation. Whereas Matt 10:23 may be justly viewed as expectation with parenetic implications, Mark 13:30 has no such overtones; but there is reason for viewing the latter more in the nature of an apostrophe over Israel's doom rather than an utterance with parenetic intent.[277] While Schnackenburg no longer speaks, as Rigaux and Vögtle did, of the "absolute" ignorance of Jesus as to the time of the end expressed in Mark 13:32, he still sees it as expressing a fundamental element in the prophetic proclamation of Jesus: apocalyptic reckoning is excluded from his message, since the end is in the hand of God. That principle is rigorously to be applied in the interpretation of the discourse.

J. R. Michaels

Michaels read a paper on Mark 13 at the spring meeting of the Jesus Seminar, 1989, in Sonoma, California. He began by citing an observation by Burton Mack, made at an earlier meeting of the Seminar: "Read as the Christian myth of origin, the Gospel of Mark traditionally has not been thought of as an apocalypse, but only as containing an apocalypse (Mark 13). By treating the question of the 'little apocalypse' differently than the question of the gospel itself, the 'eschatological' beginnings of the gospel have been retained even while dismissing or discounting the apocalyptic endings. *But both go together.*"[278]

Michaels agreed with the sentiment of the statement, but disagreed with its application. Mack was arguing that because the apocalyptic chapter Mark 13 is suspect, the Markan presentation of Jesus and the kingdom of God is suspect as well. Michaels reversed the logic to affirm that if the Markan presentation of Jesus and the kingdom is to be taken seriously, then ch. 13 deserves to be taken equally seriously.[279]

The uniqueness of ch. 13, in Michaels's view, is its concentration on events that lie outside the Markan story, i.e., on what will happen after Mark 16:8. It describes a time on earth when Jesus will be absent. But so far as Mark's Gospel is concerned this is a matter of degree, not of kind, for there are many passages in the Gospel that look beyond 16:8 to the absence of Jesus. For example, Jesus promises that he will lead

---

[277]Mark 9:1 is in another category; for its relation to Mark 13:30, see the commentary below on the latter passage.

[278]Mack, "The Kingdom Sayings in Mark," *Forum* 3 (1987): 6, cited by Michaels, "An Intemperate Case for an Eschatological Jesus?" unpublished. (The title relates to an article by M. J. Borg, "A Temperate Case for a Non-eschatological Jesus," *Forum* 2 [1986]: 81–102.)

[279]Michaels, "Intemperate Case," 1.

his disciples into Galilee after his resurrection (14:28), something not recorded by Mark. In 14:62 he tells the high priest, "You will see the Son of man sitting at the right hand of the Power." John the Baptist declares that the Mightier One will baptize with the Holy Spirit (1:8). The gospel is to be preached in all the world, when the anointing of Jesus by a woman for his burial will be recounted (14:9). Jesus' disciples will one day fast (2:20); they will deny themselves and follow Jesus in the way of the cross, and must not be ashamed of him, whatever the cost (8:35–38). Their leadership is not to be one of lording it over believers but exercised in the Jesus way of sacrifice (10:43–45). If Mark 13 is to be viewed as a little apocalypse, 8:34–9:1 is yet "littler!" And the viewpoint of 9:1 is similar to that of 13:30. Mark 13, accordingly, is thoroughly at home in its Markan setting.[280]

Michaels points out two surprising features of Mark 13. (1) Although it presupposes the absence of Jesus, it reveals nothing of how the absence came about. It is a farewell speech, yet gives no clear signal that Jesus is shortly to die. (2) The expression "kingdom of God" is not once used. If it is assumed that the kingdom announced in 1:15 comes in power in 13:24–27, it is not stated in so many words. The real link between Mark 13 and the opening of Jesus' ministry is the word "gospel" (cf. 1:14–15 and 13:10). The gospel is to continue in proclamation till the time when "they see the Son of man coming in clouds with power and great glory."[281]

The most obvious difficulty about Mark 13 is that while it begins with a prediction that the Jerusalem temple will be destroyed (v. 2), it does not explicitly return to this theme. Jesus takes the disciples' questions in v. 4 seriously, yet his answer, punctuated with calls to "watch out," "don't be in dread," "don't be anxious," and warnings against deceivers who try to exploit the desire for signs of the end, is not a conventional apocalyptic answer. The sufferings of the disciples, described in vv. 9–13, are in form parallel to the signs in vv. 5–8, so that turmoil in the natural world is paralleled with turmoil in the experiences of Jesus' disciples, and both fall under the divine necessity (cf. the "must" of vv. 7, 10 and the "must" of Jesus' sufferings, 8:31); even so, they are not decisive signs of the end.

The real sign is given in v. 14. To what does it refer? Not the destruction of the temple, in contrast to Matthew's and Luke's redaction, in both of which the calamity on Jerusalem lies in the past. In Mark the "abomination of desolation" retains its Danielic obscurity, and like Daniel refers to a person ("standing where he ought not"). Presumably he is an antichrist figure. Paul's statement about the "man of lawless-

---

[280]Ibid., 2–5.
[281]Ibid., 5–7.

ness" in 2 Thess 2:3–10 is based on Mark 13:14; as Paul's prophecy is part of an unfulfilled oracle based on Mark's "abomination of desolation," it is likely that Mark 13:14 is also unfulfilled so far as Mark is concerned. The link between the sign of the abomination in v. 14 and v. 32 as both constituting an answer to the disciples' question as to the time and the sign of the destruction of the temple suggests that the prophecy of v. 2 refers "not to the destruction wrought by Roman armies but to the dissolution of the present world order brought about by the coming of the Son of Man. The temple is simply a convenient visible reminder of that world order, appropriate to the setting because Jesus has been teaching there and because the temple will be the scene of the antichrist's activity."[282] Hence the only possible fulfillment of the prediction of the temple's destruction is in vv. 24–25 and 31. The time of this event is indicated in v. 32: God alone knows it!

This is a very perceptive review of the teaching of Mark 13, with much more that I have had to leave unnoticed. We are grateful for the demonstration that Mark 13 is thoroughly harmonious with the rest of Mark's Gospel, for the note on the absence of "kingdom of God" from the discourse (though the reality is there without the word), for the link up of the "gospel" in 13:10 with "gospel" in 1:15, and the relating of 13:5–8 with 9–13 as different kinds of signs, yet not of the immediate end. Michaels's discussion and interpretation of 13:14 will find approval with not a few scholars. The understanding of the abomination of desolation as the antichrist is an ancient tradition and is still widely accepted. But the text alike of Mark and of Daniel, from which the abomination figure derives, hardly supports the restriction of the abomination to a solitary figure. The first use of the desolating abomination, in Dan 9:26–27, speaks of an invading prince working havoc on the city and sanctuary, "and in the train of these abominations will come the perpetrator of desolation" (REB). An antigod figure with an army is here in view, producing alike blasphemy and destruction. Consonant with this the hurried flight enjoined in Mark 13:15–16 and the sympathy expressed in vv. 17–18 for pregnant and nursing mothers who cannot hurry strongly suggest that flight from an army after the crucial sign is perceived is in mind. It is therefore natural to see in vv. 14–20 the fulfillment of the prophecy of v. 2, expressed in terms of the Danielic prophecy. The cosmic signs of vv. 24–25 do not denote the collapse of the universe and the world, entailing in particular the destruction of the temple; the signs described are the traditional accompaniments of theophany, the appearance of God in his glory; of such an order is the parousia.

---

[282]Ibid., 21–22.

5. Monographs on Mark 13

During the decade 1960–70 an unprecedented concentration of attention on the eschatological discourse took place. Apart from the contributions which we have reviewed, no less than seven monographs on the discourse appeared in these years, and others were to follow. The works grew longer as the years progressed! Most of the writers concerned employed redaction-critical methods in their investigations. Our review of them will, of necessity, be brief. We freely acknowledge that with the brevity it is difficult to do justice to the labors of their authors. We shall, however, endeavor rightly to highlight the emphases which they sought to make.

G. Neville

Neville announced in the introduction to his book the foundation on which he built his work, namely, the distinction between prophecy and apocalyptic. The former he characterized in three assertions: God's working respects human freedom; God achieves his purpose in and through history; God's prime concern is with a people, not simply with individuals. By contrast, apocalyptic thought presupposes that God has predetermined his actions; God negates history to bring his purpose to an end; God is primarily concerned with individuals. The Gospels show that Jesus grounded his appeal on the ancient tradition of the Law and the Prophets; he thus stood in the tradition of the prophets. His picture of the future was one with that which the prophets had given; in this we find a foreground of immediate expectations arising from a prophetic judgment on the contemporary generation, and a background of ultimate events which belong to the real eschaton, the final consummation which lies beyond the horizon.[283]

Approaching Mark 13 from this viewpoint, Neville begins with the observation that the discourse is not an apocalypse; rather, its structure is what might be expected in the prophetic tradition; it has the double horizon which the nature of prophetic vision demands.[284] The heart of the chapter is in vv. 5–27, which consists of two sections of unequal length: vv. 5–23 deal with the immediate future and contain moral instruction rather than prediction; vv. 24–27 describe the parousia. Between these two sections there is no temporal connection. The phrases "in those days, after that tribulation" in v. 24 effect the transition out of the immediate future into the undatable time of the end.[285]

---

[283]Neville, *The Advent Hope: A Study of the Context of Mark 13* (London, 1961), 42.

[284]Ibid., 45–46.

[285]Ibid., 48. Neville later suggests that Mark's source simply read "in those

Hence it is affirmed, "The prophetic imagination of Jesus takes flight. It overleaps the gap between the immediate and the ultimate and declares the certainty of God's triumph in the end."[286] The teaching of the discourse relates well to the eschatological instruction of Jesus elsewhere attested in the Gospels. In the latter, while the presence of the kingdom of God in the ministry of Jesus is plain, the picture of the future given by him contains three chief moments: his death, which will release the powers of the kingdom of God in the world; the experience of his followers of that redemptive power, and at the same time their endurance of sufferings like those of Jesus, culminating in the appearance of the abomination of desolation; and finally the revelation of the kingdom of God in power and glory at the parousia.[287] The discourse, however, reveals a tendency of the church's teachers, under the stress of suffering and persecution, to apply words of Jesus which originally referred to the earlier phases of the eschatological drama to the final stage. This is observable with particular clarity in Mark 9:1, which first referred to the release of power in the church through the death of Jesus, but which subsequently became related to the eschaton; the same holds good of the parable of the Fig Tree in 13:28–29, and of v. 30;[288] v. 31 has been given an eschatological application instead of the ethical one which was originally intended; and vv. 33–37 are related to the parousia instead of to the crisis which confronted the Jews through the ministry of Jesus, and especially through their rejection of his message.[289]

This is a brave attempt on Neville's part to demonstrate the prophetic character of the eschatology of Jesus. Unfortunately it is marred by a tendency to exaggeration in order to establish the position maintained. The contrast between prophecy and apocalyptic is undeniable, but it is unjustified to denigrate the apocalyptic writers in the cause of magnifying the worth of the prophets. This is done when Neville writes: "The hope of apocalyptic is not ethically conditioned, nor concerned with history, nor centred upon a visible community. It is the hope of God's capricious action, negating all antecedent historical development and gathering a number of elect individuals into a better age."[290] While one appreciates an author's motivation in making a statement of this

---

days"—"a form nearer to the characteristic wording with which in the Old Testament prophets we find ourselves brought face to face with the End" (ibid., 64).

[286]Ibid., 48.

[287]Ibid., 58–59.

[288]Of v. 30 Neville writes, "In adapting for his own purposes a saying of Jesus which referred to the imminence of the era of power and suffering, Mark has eliminated the unbridgeable gap between proximate and ultimate, and made Jesus a false prophet" (ibid., 63).

[289]Ibid., 60–63.

[290]Ibid., 31.

kind, it is unjust to apocalyptic thought generally. It is manifestly inapplicable to the book of Daniel and the book of Revelation, to the ethical tone of such a work as the Testaments of the Twelve Patriarchs, and to the Qumran movement, which was inspired by apocalyptic theology through its two centuries of history.

In agreement with this emphasis, however, Neville affirms, prior to examining the teaching of Jesus, that if Jesus held the adventist views attributed to him he was a false prophet; if he did not understand the relative chronology of history, he misconceived the nature of God; if he was an adventist, he was not God.[291] Assertions of this kind, preceding examination of the text, make objective study of the text all but impossible. They certainly make difficult a sober assessment of the phenomenon of apocalyptic in Israel and the primitive church, and still more an impartial weighing of the possibility that in Jesus prophecy and apocalyptic come together to form a synthesis greater than either. It will not do to dismiss the near expectation of Jesus; it is a characteristic of prophecy and apocalyptic alike,[292] but in Jesus it is unique, because it is bound up with his consciousness of vocation to be the mediator of the kingdom of God in the present and in the future, and is tempered with the recognition that God is the Lord of history and of the end to which it leads. One may, if one will, distinguish between events worked out on the plane of history and the end of history brought about by God, but it is the one God who works in all history and at the end for the achievement of his purpose. This conviction is plain in the teaching of Jesus, attested outside the eschatological discourse, in Mark 13 itself and in the book of Revelation.

In sum, Neville's endeavor to emphasize the prophetic nature of Mark 13 is good, and it produces some helpful insights; his mistake is to divorce the prophetic and apocalyptic elements too sharply, and to fail to see the significance of their coalescence in such sayings as Mark 13:32.

F. Mussner

The work of F. Mussner on Mark 13 differs from those of his predecessors and successors by its being addressed to the Christian public rather than to scholars. This naturally controls the nature of the discussion and its presentation. Mussner's conviction as to the compos-

---

[291]Ibid., 10, 12.

[292]The fact that the day of the Lord upon a city or nation need not coincide with the advent of the kingdom of God does not justify the idea that a prophet—or Jesus—when proclaiming God's judgment on a nation overleaps in thought intervening ages. Hab 2:3 applies to many a vision of weal as well as woe, as the writer to the Hebrews assumes (Heb 10:36–39).

ite nature of the discourse is revealed in the statement: "Everything essential which he [Jesus] taught on this subject has been gathered and combined in the so-called synoptic apocalypse."[293] The "subject" is the last things, and this is strictly what is treated in the discourse. While Jesus speaks at the outset of the destruction of the temple, the disciples ask about the "when" and the "sign" in apocalyptic terms, and so of eschatological events, of the end; it is this apocalyptic question to which Jesus addresses himself, and accordingly he ceases to speak about the temple and of its destruction. The signs of vv. 7–8 are described as "the beginning of sorrows"—that, and no more: "They are merely a beginning, pointing to that end which is sure to come some day, but nothing more."[294] The persecutions mentioned in vv. 9–13 are also not signs of the approaching end; as their position in Matt 10:17ff. indicates, the sayings were spoken in another context; persecutions belong to the interim period.[295] The paragraph which follows (vv. 14–23) directly continues the theme of vv. 9–13; the tribulations therein described are to be experienced by the community of Jesus, not by the Jewish nation. The abomination of desolation is not envisaged as sitting in the temple of Jerusalem, for that will no longer exist; rather, he represents the antichrist, as Paul makes plain in 2 Thessalonians 2.[296]

The character of Mark 13:24–27 is in line with all this. The purpose of all apocalypses is to explain to the persecuted people of God how they are to view their sufferings, and to let them know that they are not abandoned: "That is why the coming of the Son of Man is primarily proclaimed as the day of the Church's deliverance."[297] Precisely because the Synoptic apocalypse was intended to be a consolatory writing it gives no description of the destruction of the rebellious world. The cosmic collisions portrayed in vv. 24–25 do not signify the destruction of the world; rather, they depict the effect of the advent of the Son of man on the "firmament," and so illustrate the tremendous power with which the Son of man will come (cf. Hag 2:6). "The parousia therefore is an epiphany, a manifestation of the heavenly world in the centre of which the radiant Son of Man appears, shining with divine glory and surrounded by a host of angels."[298] The passage does not say that Christ comes to the earth; he gathers his dispersed elect in an unnamed place and leads them to his heavenly home.

---

[293]Mussner, *Was lehrt Jesus über das Ende der Welt? Eine Auslegung von Markus 13*, 2d ed. (Freiburg, 1963); ET *Christ and the End of the World*, Contemporary Catechetics (Notre Dame, 1965), 11.
[294]Ibid., 26.
[295]Ibid., 28–30.
[296]Ibid., 36–38.
[297]Ibid., 48.
[298]Ibid., 51.

As to the time when these things will happen, the parable of the Fig Tree draws attention not to the nearness of the summer when the fig tree blossoms, but to the certainty of its coming when that occurs; such is the application to the relation of signs and end.[299] The "generation" which will not pass away before all these things happen (v. 30) is the Jewish race, which will persist until the end.[300] Verse 31 is a conditional statement: "Even if heaven and earth pass away, my words will not do so." The parable inculcating watchfulness in vv. 34–36 is to be interpreted as an allegory: Jesus is the Lord of the house; he goes on a journey—at his ascension; he leaves his house—his church—to his servants, the apostles, and he gives them the same authority as that committed to him; the doorkeeper has a special task—he represents Peter, the prince of the apostles.[301]

An evaluation of this exposition of the discourse should begin with a word of commendation that a scholar should endeavor to mediate to members of the church the teaching of Mark 13; the task is rarely attempted, and the endeavor ought to be emulated. In our judgment, however, the approach to the chapter has been compromised through interpreting the discourse in the light of 2 Thessalonians 2 instead of the reverse; it is always doubtful to approach Jesus through Paul rather than Paul through Jesus, as the history of the interpretation of the Sermon on the Mount illustrates. That the abomination of desolation represents the antichrist is questionable, that the place of his appearing should be divorced from the Jerusalem temple is yet more doubtful, and that the persecuted people of God in vv. 15–20 are the Christian church rather than the Jewish nation in Palestine is entirely implausible. The counsel to flight in vv. 15–16 and the compassion on the unfortunate expressed in vv. 17–18 indicate that Jews in Judea are in mind. Similarly the warnings about pseudochrists and false prophets in vv. 21–22 plainly reflect Jewish expectations of the Messiah's anticipated appearance. By contrast, the reference of v. 30 to the Jewish race through the course of history and not to the contemporary generation of Jewish rejectors of Jesus is hardly to be accepted. And the interpretation of vv. 33–37 is too plainly allegorical; the passage is open to a much simpler exegesis, in harmony with the nature of Jesus' parables generally.

It must nevertheless be recognized that the interpretation of the parousia in vv. 24–27 and its significance for the church, of which we have given the barest outline, is very helpful, not least through its recognition of the representation of the parousia in terms of theophany, which has been so rarely acknowledged.

---

[299]Ibid., 61.
[300]Ibid., 57.
[301]Ibid., 66–67.

L. Hartman

In Lars Hartman's work on the eschatological discourse we have a thorough and original attempt to investigate the text in the light of apocalyptic literature generally. Prior to examining Mark 13, the author investigates Jewish apocalyptic texts whose content resembles that of Mark 13.[302] Hartman studies patterns of thought rather than eschatological dogma, because apocalyptic texts for the most part consist of hymns and prophecies which do not represent a dogmatic system; moreover, these books consist of small units which have a relatively independent content, and some at least existed prior to inclusion in the books. Sixty-five pericopae are selected for examination. They are of two basic kinds: the main form is one in which God intervenes or comes, and no mention is made of the Messiah; the second form is one in which the Messiah is given a place in the end times with God. In both types a predominant pattern is observable, wherein five points are featured: the onset of evil times, God's intervention, God's judgment, the punishment of sinners, and the joy of the righteous in their vindication.[303] When comparing this structure with that of Mark 13, Hartman recognizes that the latter is simpler; the "evil times" are concentrated in the antichrist phenomena, and then the parousia is described in the gathering of the elect.[304]

As to the discourse itself the thesis is maintained that the text is basically "an exposition on the basis of Daniel, a kind of 'midrash' which is on the way to becoming a 'mishna,' in that its connections with the original text are no longer clear and the traces of exegetical work may have been largely effaced."[305] The origin and development of this "midrash" is traced as follows:

(1) The basis of the midrash is Dan 2:31–45; 7:7–27; 8:9–26; 9:24–27; 11:21–12:4. The limits of the midrash in Mark 13 are vv. 5b–8, 12–16, 19–22, 24–27. This midrash is interwoven with OT associations which derive from the text interpreted. It contains material partly apocalyptic and eschatological and partly parenetic. The apocalyptic and eschatological field has two poles, namely, the activity of the antichrist and the parousia of the Son of man.

(2) Logia on watchfulness were added at the end of the discourse.

(3) An incipient historicization took place, in that the antichrist motifs became linked with the churches' experience of false prophets

---

[302]Hartman, *Prophecy Interpreted: The Formation of Some Jewish Apocalyptic Texts and of the Eschatological Discourse Mark 13 Par.*, ConBNT 1 (Lund, 1966), part 1, pp. 23–141.
[303]Ibid., 55–70.
[304]Ibid., 239.
[305]Ibid., 174.

(Mark 13:6, 21–22; cf. 1 John 2:18ff.; 4:1ff.). This was subsequent to the stage of development reflected in 1 and 2 Thessalonians.

(4) The persecution logia of Mark 13:9–11 were incorporated at a later date; they express the churches' experience of strained relations with the outside world and show reflection on the prospect of distress.

(5) The framework in Mark was supplied through vv. 1–4 and 28–32. The discourse then became the answer to a question as to the fall of the temple, and this fall was brought into the events at the end of time.

(6) Mark 13:10 was inserted in the persecution logia in one of the closing stages of the development of the tradition. It was occasioned by the churches' experience of missionary work in the midst of persecutions and so fitted into the eschatological picture.[306]

As to the *Sitz im Leben* of the discourse, the combination of parenetic midrash and material of a different kind reflects the need of teaching in the early church in the light of its history. The *Sitz im Leben* of the original midrash is difficult to determine; it must be the work of one man (in contrast to its later expansion by others). Paul in 1 Thess 4:15 links it with Jesus.[307] The form of parenetic midrash is that of a teaching and not that of a community, nor of an inspired prophet (an alleged mouthpiece of the risen Lord). The "word of the Lord" to which Paul refers could relate to a "teaching" of the Lord equally as to an isolated saying. Jesus was a teacher, and he will have used teaching methods of his time. Other Gospel texts indicate that he sometimes based his teaching on the scriptures. The concept of the kingdom of God is fundamental to the preaching and teaching of Jesus, bound up with his person and work, and set also in a positive relation to his disciples. This holds good of the discourse also; satanic resistance to God is depicted in Danielic terms, with its emphasis on the kingdom of God, and the disciples are portrayed as in the same situation of conflict as Jesus was in his ministry.[308]

Of the value of Hartman's work there is no question. The eschatological discourse undoubtedly reflects OT prophetic teaching, and particularly that of Daniel. It is good to be reminded that the use of the OT is not foreign to Jesus. It is also salutary to recall that the hope of Israel as transmitted in the contemporary apocalyptic tradition is of importance in considering the tradition of Jesus' words. Hartman's examination of significant apocalyptic texts is important in its own right. The general outlook of Mark 13 has much in common with apocalyptic expectations. Yet it is noteworthy that elements of the patterns of expectation are lacking from the discourse, especially messianic judg-

---

[306]Ibid., 235–41.
[307]Ibid., 212–13.
[308]Ibid., 246–48.

ments and the punishment of the rebellious at the end. In addition, the parousia concept of the discourse lies beyond the horizon of contemporary apocalyptic. If the eschatological discourse is to be classed as apocalyptic, it must be recognized as a special form of apocalyptic, modified by concepts of the eschatological community and the Son of man such as are characteristic of the Gospel traditions rather than of purely Jewish thought.

The great question, of course, is whether Hartman's thesis of a midrash on Daniel lies at the base of Mark 13. The influence of Daniel on the discourse is incontrovertible. It is possible, however, that Hartman has taken a valid point and overextended its application to the discourse as a whole.

The sections thought to have been based on Daniel and forming the original midrash are vv. 5b–8, 12–16, 19–22, 24–27. The only plausible citation of Daniel in vv. 5–8 is the phrase *dei genesthai* in v. 7, which occurs twice in Dan 2:28–29 (and in Dan 2:45 Theodotion) for the Aramaic "what shall be." The reference of this phrase in the Danielic passages is to the purpose of God in the latter days, when the kingdoms of this world have to give place to the kingdom of God, whereas in Mark 13:7 it is to the occurrence of wars and rumors of wars. In our judgment it is wholly unlikely that Dan 2:28–29 is in mind in Mark 13:7; the phrase in question in all probability reflects current usage in the early Christian community.[309] The feature of wars in the latter times is constant in prophetic and apocalyptic works, and so one should not insist that vv. 7–8 have in mind Danielic passages; Jer 4:13–20 and 6:22–26 among other passages form clear parallels to the wars and rumors of wars in Mark 13:7; v. 8a echoes 2 Chron 15:6 and Isa 19:2; and the rest of the sentence can be related to many OT passages (for earthquakes cf. Isa 24:18–19; 29:6, etc.; famines, Jer 14:12; Ezek 14:13; travail pangs, Isa 13:8; 21:3, etc.). On the whole Daniel gets little attention in Mark 13:5–8.

In Mark 13:9 it is again unlikely that the key term *paradōsousin* is derived from Dan 7:25, where the saints are said to be "delivered" into the hands of the antigod emperor. Hartman himself points out that the use of *paradidōmi* in Mark 13:12 probably reflects the tradition embodied in the Targum of Jonathan on Mic 7:22ff. ("A man delivers up his brother to destruction").[310] It is a likely guess that the employment of *paradidōmi* in Mark 13:12 has inspired the adoption of the term in vv. 9 and 11.[311] There is no ground to postulate a link with Daniel in any of the three instances of its use in vv. 9–13.

---

[309]See pp. 396–97.
[310]Hartman, *Prophecy Interpreted*, 168–69.
[311]Ibid.

By contrast, Mark 13:14 certainly relates to the Danielic passages which speak of the abomination of desolation in connection with the temple of Jerusalem (Dan 9:27; 11:31; 12:11). Oddly enough there is no further OT reference in the verses which immediately follow (Mark 13:15–18). It is an interesting possibility, taken up by Hartman and others, that the last clause of v. 14 ("those who are in Judea must flee to the hills") reflects the injunction to Lot and his family to flee to the hills (Gen 19:17). The further suggestion, however, that the Markan and Danielic abomination passages are linked with Genesis 19 via Lam 4:6; Dan 7:11 and 8:11, revealing a typology that an ungodly or blasphemous place or thing will be destroyed by fire, is tenuous.

Mark 13:19 harks back to Dan 12:1 in describing the unique nature of Israel's distress in language which itself was becoming proverbial (cf. Joel 2:2), but no further clear references to Daniel occur in Mark 13:20–23.

Mark 13:24–27 have at their center the description of the Son of man coming in the clouds, inspired by Dan 7:13–14, which is the source of the Son of man parousia sayings in the Gospels. The verses which surround Mark 13:26 reflect passages from other OT prophets relating to the final theophany and day of the Lord, and the regathering of the scattered people of God (see especially Isa 13:10; Joel 2:10; 4:15; Isa 34:4; Zech 12:12ff.; 14:5; 2:10; Isa 27:13; Deut 30:3–4).

In the discourse, accordingly, we find important references to Daniel in vv. 14, 19, 26. The first and last of these certainly form "pivotal points" in the discourse. While they may be said, in Hartman's words, to form its two poles, they can hardly be justly described as forming the core of the discourse. One of the curious features of the discourse is that so little is said of the abomination, so that it is difficult to know how to interpret its precise meaning in the passage. So also nothing is said of the outcome of the parousia, beyond the gathering of the elect. The thesis of a Danielic midrash as the basis of the discourse appears to me to be a pardonable exaggeration of a highly significant feature of the discourse, namely, the important role of OT and apocalyptic concepts, above all of certain ones from the book of Daniel.

One should perhaps further point out the dubiety of characterizing Mark 13:5–23 as clustering around antichrist's activity. Verses 15–18 do not directly refer to an antichrist figure, nor vv. 19–20, and vv. 7–8 are general prophecies of woe in the world. By contrast, vv. 6 and 21–22 relate to pseudochrists and pseudoprophets; if their presence in the discourse reflects the churches' experience of such figures, which is highly probable, their origin in the evangelic tradition is earlier, and almost certainly independent of the idea in v. 14 (cf. Luke 17:23–24 = Matt 24:26–27). Moreover, if we are to speak of origins, we may not assume without further ado that the description of the parousia answers to the activity of the abomination of desolation; the parousia is more

closely linked to the pseudochrists of vv. 21–22, and scarcely less
closely to the parenesis on watchfulness in vv. 28–29, 33ff. When the
basis of the discourse is not assumed to be a Danielic midrash, the
relations within the varied elements of the discourse may be seen as
more varied and more complex than the midrash hypothesis suggests.

J. Lambrecht

In the work of J. Lambrecht we encounter the most detailed
analytical study of Mark 13 which had appeared to the time of its
publication, and in many respects it remains unique. The secondary
element of the title of the book is to be observed: "A literary analysis
and investigation of structure," for the author strictly adheres to the
intention therein defined: he abjures the attempt to provide an exegesis
of the eschatological discourse, and confines himself to an examination
of the chapter with respect to its redactional character, its structure,
and its use of sources.[312] The method pursued is chiefly literary-critical. The author tests the vocabulary, analyzes the style, and tries to
discover elements of composition by the evangelist in each statement
of the discourse, and so he searches for sources and traditions behind
the text. Working on the hypothesis that the form of the text may be due
to the redactor, he continually raises the question as to what is Markan
in the text. The major part of this volume therefore is given to a
painstaking literary analysis of the discourse, verse by verse and phrase
by phrase. An unusual element of Lambrecht's critical assumptions is
the conviction that Mark used Q extensively. To this subject he devoted
a separate article, in which he maintains that in ch. 13 Mark utilized Q
in vv. 2, 5b–6, 21–23, 9–11, 12, 15–16, 30–31, 32–37; the source
included a compendious mission charge on which Mark drew in various parts of his Gospel, namely, in 4:21–25; 6:7–13; 8:34–9:1; 13:9–
13.[313] This understanding of Mark's relation to Q naturally influences
Lambrecht's treatment of the text of Mark 13 considerably.

To summarize Lambrecht's treatment of Mark 13 is difficult, since
his work is not concerned with the themes of the discourse, the circumstances which led to its composition, or the purpose in view. He
plunges immediately into an analysis of the context of the chapter, then
of the chapter itself, and finally he considers its structure. Considerable
space is required to set forth his analyses of each segment of the text.
We must content ourselves with illustrating Lambrecht's work by adducing some of his more interesting and unusual findings.

---

[312]Lambrecht, *Die Redaktion der Markus-Apokalypse: Literarische Analyse und Strukturuntersuchung*, AnBib 28 (Rome, 1967), 67.
[313]Idem, "Die Logia-Quellen von Markus 13," *Bib* 47 (1966): 377.

In the wider context of Mark 13, the passage which centers on the question about the authority of Jesus, Mark 11:27–12:1, is viewed as especially significant. It is held to show many indications of Mark's redaction and to be a composition of little units; comparison with John 2:13–22 confirms this point. Although the Fourth Evangelist sets the temple cleansing at a different point in time, he has set in succession the account of the cleansing (2:13ff.), a question about a sign (2:18), and the temple prophecy (2:19ff.). Mark's source probably had a similar order. Mark appears to have taken apart a section of tradition and separated its elements. In his source also the question of a sign followed the cleansing and then the prophecy about the temple. But Mark has interpreted and changed the material; the temple cleansing is given another point; the request made of Jesus for a sign (John 2:18) is made a question about authority (Mark 11:28); and the resurrection prediction, veiled in a picture (John 2:19), has become a prophecy of destruction (Mark 13:2), although a reminiscence of the original appears in the passion narrative—twice (Mark 14:58; 15:29).[314]

Lambrecht returns to this issue in his analysis of Mark 13:2. He points out that two explanations for the origin of the prophecy are possible. The first is that the saying embodied in John 2:19 was known to Mark, but he left it till the trial (Mark 14:58), and omitted the idea of the temple as a symbol of the body; he also knew from his version of Q the saying in Matt 23:38/Luke 13:35 (*idou aphietai hymin ho oikos hymōn*); Mark therefore combined the logion of John 2:19 and Matt 23:38 and from them produced a new saying, Mark 13:2. The other possibility is that Mark created 13:2 simply on the basis of Matt 23:38. Lambrecht leaves the question open, but appears to favor the former alternative. The conclusion of the matter is that the two strands of allusion to resurrection and to the destruction of Jerusalem go back to Jesus, but Mark 13:1–2 is wholly due to Mark. Nevertheless, concludes Lambrecht, "in the nature of the case this way of thinking has a certain degree of uncertainty in itself. Mark can indeed also have written down or redacted a reminiscence preserved in the tradition."[315]

Mark 13:3 is seen as a link statement, presupposing vv. 1–2 and v. 4 and providing a transition between them. The vocabulary and structure indicate that Mark has created the saying. Lambrecht observes that in vv. 1–3a we have an example of the *a b c—c′ b′ a′* scheme which is exemplified elsewhere in the discourse: the terms *hieron*, *lithos*, and *oikodomē* of v. 1 recur in reverse order in vv. 2–3a.[316] Verse 4 is purely redactional.[317]

---

[314]Idem, *Redaktion*, 37–43.
[315]Ibid., 79.
[316]Ibid., 80–85.
[317]Ibid., 88.

The warning of vv. 5b–6 relates to the many who will come *epi tō onomati mou*. This is explained by the immediately following phrase: the pretenders will say, *ego eimi*, affirming, "I am it," i.e., the returning Messiah. The interest of the passage lies in its origin: it stems from the Q logion, preserved in Matt 24:26/Luke 17:23. The Q saying is even more closely related to Mark 13:21; Mark has clearly modified the Q saying in v. 21 and further modified it to suit his intention in vv. 5b–6; but while v. 21 forms a bridge between Q and vv. 5b–6, it is also true that vv. 5b–6 have influenced vv. 21–23. The repetition of the passage in Mark is quite deliberate; it is not a mere doublet, but has to be viewed in terms of the structure of the discourse as an inclusion, the second balancing the first.[318]

The paragraph Mark 13:9–13 is complicated. The link between v. 11 with the Q saying Luke 12:11–12 raises the question of the relation between the passage and Q. Two possible explanations of the Markan text are offered. Mark could have had a Q logion like Luke 12:11–12; if so he has reproduced it faithfully in 13:11, anticipated it with great freedom in v. 9, and expanded in v. 10 the concept of witness which is contained in the original saying. It is also possible that a fuller form of Q existed, which Matthew used in Matt 10:17–23 (= Q^{mt}), and on which Mark drew in his 13:9–13 (= Q^{mk}). Lambrecht finds indications confirming the latter alternative. If Matt 10:23 stood in Q^{mk} as well as Q^{mt}, Mark's text is easier to understand: the *eis telos* of v. 13 stands close to the *telein* of Matt 10:23 (*ou mē telesēte tas poleis tou Israēl*); the reference to the coming of the Son of man prompted the setting of the pericope in the discourse; the *hotan de* construction of Matt 10:23 (*hotan de diōkōsin hymas*) with the command to flee (*pheugete eis tēn heteran*) is repeated in Mark 13:14; Matthew speaks of fleeing to various cities of Israel; Mark names Judea in v. 14. Moreover, the statement that the gospel must be proclaimed *eis panta ta ethnē* in Mark 13:10 is adequately motivated: it is a correction of Matt 10:23. The missionary thought was already contained in the Q statement (*stathēsesthe . . . eis martyrion autois kai tois ethnesin*), but Mark carried it further: his *eis panta ta ethnē* creates a dynamic dimension; with *panta* he stressed the universality of the testimony; with *prōton* he gave to the proclamation of the gospel its place in the saving history; with *dei* he related it to the divine plan of salvation; and with *kērychthēnai* he overlooked the setting of trials; he was concerned with positively intended missionary activity.[319]

Passing over the treatment of the immediately following verses, we note Lambrecht's dealing with the parousia passage, vv. 24–27. The

---

[318]Ibid., 91–105.
[319]Ibid., 114–36.

cosmic disorders portrayed in vv. 24–25 form the prelude to the coming described in v. 26. From the viewpoint both of the structure of v. 26 and its content the statement has a central place in the discourse: "The tone is purely positive; the appearance is that of a theophany. It is concerned with the power and glory of the Son of man; he finally gathers together his elect."[320] No less than five indications show that Mark is the composer of the pericope: (1) the influence of the LXX within it; (2) the editing of the biblical material to make it fit the discourse; (3) the redactional "hooks" which link the paragraph to the discourse ("in those days, after that distress," v. 24, and the reference to the elect, v. 27); (4) vv. 26–27 have parallels in wording and content with Mark 8:38–9:1 and 14:62; the three passages are so similar that it is improbable that they all go back to Jesus, and vv. 24–25 lose their right to exist apart from v. 26; (5) the double definitions given at the beginning of v. 24 and end of v. 27 are Markan, as also the periphrasis in v. 25a and the change from *meta* to *en* (*nephelais*) in v. 26. Nevertheless, despite all this, Lambrecht is at pains to state that Mark is the composer of the paragraph, but not the creator of each segment of it: "It is quite unthinkable that the content of this pericope does not go back finally to an authentic teaching of Jesus. But it is another question whether, e.g., Mark 13:26 is a genuine saying of Jesus."[321]

The similarity of Mark 13:30 to Matt 23:36 suggests that it may have given Mark the notion in the saying, but its relation to Mark 9:1 intimates that Mark structured the saying in line with the latter. A different possibility is the influence of Matt 5:18, which reads: *amēn gar legō hymin, heōs an parelthē ho ouranos kai hē gē, iōta hen ē mia keraia ou mē parelthē apo tou nomou heōs an panta genētai.* Lambrecht suggests that Mark made from the first clause the affirmation, "This generation will not pass away," and to it joined the final phrase "till all happens." He then used the first line again to produce, "Heaven and earth will pass away," but replaced the reference to the law by reference to words of Jesus: "my words will not pass away." Thus at a stroke two sayings which have caused great perplexity to the church are accounted for.[322]

Reviewing the results of his analysis, Lambrecht is led to the conviction that the whole frame of the discourse is artificially produced and redactionally ordered.[323] Few logia can be shown as unedited and unaltered tradition. "This compels us to the conclusion that little in this address . . . bears the marks of authenticity." Characteristically, however, Lambrecht adds: "Whether Jesus delivered an apocalyptic

---

[320]Ibid., 191.
[321]Ibid., 193.
[322]Ibid., 202–26.
[323]Ibid., 228–50.

address (cf., e.g., Luke 17), whether the Markan content essentially agrees with a declaration and parenesis of Jesus in relation to the destiny of Jerusalem and the parousia, whether indeed something of the stylized frame (place and time) goes back to reliable reminiscence and tradition remains nevertheless a justifiable question." Whatever the answer to that question, however, it has to be stated: "In our modern concern for historical truth no norms can be set for the freedom in which Mark took up his task as an author."[324]

Lambrecht finally considers the structure of Mark 13. Its most important characteristic is believed to be its concentric or cyclic nature, which shows itself in repeated A B A or a b c c' b' a' schemes. This appears in its most simple form in the fundamental structure of the discourse, which (after its introduction in vv. 1–4) divides itself conveniently into three:

vv. 5–23—Apocalyptic warning section

vv. 24–27—Coming of the Son of man

vv. 28–37—Parable section

The beginning and the end of the discourse (i.e., vv. 4–5a and 29–37) are believed to be constructed to form inclusions, and striking parallels are observed between the beginning and the end of the first section of the discourse, vv. 4–23.[325] As well as the phenomenon of inclusion, the use of link words which bind the different sections of the discourse together may be observed.[326] After recounting these and other examples of such procedure, Lambrecht concludes that Mark structured his ch. 13 with utmost thoroughness. The evangelist shows himself to be a skilled author in the fullest sense of the term: "Self-evidently he used material, the great part of which surely goes back to the tradition or (as regards content) to Jesus himself; nevertheless, the discourse in its construction, form, and concept, the intended and achieved structural effect, the fine and artistically executed linking up—in a word, the 'structured' unity must in all probability be provided with the name of the evangelist as its author."[327]

The erudition and patience which went into Lambrecht's study of the discourse elicit unbounded admiration. If his aim was to establish the presence of Mark's hand throughout the discourse he has surely succeeded. In this respect his work represents the antithesis of Perrin's belief, based on a brief count of words in Mark 13, that the language of the discourse is non-Markan.[328] Such a position is henceforth possible

---

[324]Ibid., 259.

[325]Ibid., 272, 273–74.

[326]Ibid., 275.

[327]Ibid., 293.

[328]Perrin, *Kingdom of God and Teaching of Jesus*, 113.

only on the basis of a detailed rebuttal of Lambrecht's analysis of each verse in the chapter, and that will be a formidable task. Yet one cannot refrain from voicing the impression that Lambrecht has driven his method to excess, and that despite his striving for objectivity he has at times given expression to a high degree of subjectivity. Of this an example or two must suffice, related to our review of Lambrecht's analysis.

Many exegetes have viewed Mark 13:2 as an abbreviation of the logion in 14:58; Lambrecht's suggested history of the saying, however, is much more complicated. He suggests that Mark knew the logion reproduced in John 2:19 in the context of the cleansing of the temple, but that Mark rewrote the sequel to the cleansing in order to hold back that saying, combined it with another, quite different in meaning (viz., Matt 23:18) in order to produce out of both a saying different from both, which then became the fount of a discourse he was composing on the end of the age, and that later he reproduced the original twice in the passion narrative. All things are possible, but this is much less plausible than the simple postulate that Mark found in the tradition of Jesus' sayings one which spoke of the impending destruction of the temple. The presence in more than one strand of tradition of other sayings about the temple, relating its future to God's acts of judgment and redemption, as well as related sayings about Jerusalem's fate, also in more than one strand of tradition, strengthen rather than weaken the likelihood that Jesus gave an utterance with a content similar to that of Mark 13:2.[329]

The relation of 13:6 and 13:21–22 will be discussed in the commentary. Here it suffices to observe that the similarity of v. 21 to the Q saying Luke 17:23/Matt 24:26 is apparent; in both Luke and Matthew the saying is followed by one relating to the Son of man appearing as the lightning, and Mark 13:21 is followed by the parousia-theophany saying of vv. 24–26. Have we not here a straightforward case of sayings handed down in two different traditions, that of Mark and that of Q?

Lambrecht's treatment of vv. 9–13 is again unnecessarily complex. Self-evidently vv. 9 and 11 are parallel to the Q saying Luke 12:11–12/Matt 10:17–20. It is not plausible, however, that the whole block Matt 10:17–23 comes from Q and that Mark took his version from it. Schürmann's suggestion that Matthew's Q source contained the parallel to Luke 12:11–12 plus the logion Matt 10:23 has more to commend it,[330] but that does not carry the corollary that Mark knew and extensively modified Matthew's Q passage. The idea that the structure and content of the *bdelygma* saying in Mark 13:14 was inspired by Matt 10:23 is

---

[329]See below, pp. 377–82.

[330]Schürmann, "Zur Traditions-und Redaktionsgeschichte von Mt 10:23," *BZ* 3 (1959): 82–88; repr. in *Traditionsgeschichtliche Untersuchungen zu den synoptischen Evangelien* (Düsseldorf, 1968), 150–56.

unreasonable. The suggestion has this amount of interest: it illustrates how contact of structure and vocabulary between different sayings can lead to the framing of a hypothesis as to their relationship which on its own merits is improbable. That surely supplies a warning with regard to the application of this method of comparative study.

The presence of redactional elements in Mark 13:24–27 is clear, especially in the "double definition" at the beginning of v. 24 ("in those days, after that distress"). The possibility should not be excluded, however, that one of those phrases existed in Mark's source, and that he amplified it.[331] The similar example at the end of v. 27 is not so clear, since it brings together reminiscences of OT language to emphasize the universality of the gathering of the elect by the Son of man; it is therefore more than a stylistic device.[332] More serious is the suggestion that Mark 13:26–27; 8:38—9:1; and 14:62 are all Mark's creation from a single tradition.[333] Each of these passages has an emphasis of its own; the similarity lies in their common reference to the Son of man coming on the clouds, echoing the vision of Dan 7:13–14. But is this a compelling objection to their substantial authenticity? Daniel 7:13 is the passage in the OT above all which has inspired the concept of a parousia from heaven, and virtually every reference in the Gospels to the parousia is indebted to it. Since the same Danielic passage is the prime source for the key concept of the Son of man in the Gospels, it is hardly surprising that statements about the parousia should echo its description of the Son of man coming on clouds of theophany. To raise objections to passages which are mutually contradictory is understandable, but to do it when they employ a figure in a consistent manner in a variety of settings is doubtful criticism.

Similarly, Lambrecht's suggested derivation of Mark 13:30–31 from Matt 5:18/Luke 16:17 is ingenious but unlikely. One understands the possibility of confusion in the tradition relating to sayings of Jesus, but that is quite different from the complex modification suggested by Lambrecht. Moreover, the scope of the two passages is not the same. Lambrecht himself points out that Mark 13:31 does not assert simply the continuance of words of Jesus through all times, but "the passing into fulfilment of that which they declare. . . . Jesus says, 'My prophecies will not pass away, they will remain and will be fulfilled.' "[334] On that interpretation the two sayings have different emphases, the one asserting the abiding obligation and authority of the law, the other the fulfillment through divine action of that which Jesus proclaimed. The

---

[331]See below, pp. 422–23.

[332]See Lambrecht's discussion of this, which can hardly be improved on (*Redaktion*, 186–89).

[333]Ibid., 193.

[334]Ibid., 221.

burden of the words of Jesus is the kingdom of God; Mark 13:31 looks beyond its immediate context and anticipates the realization of those words in the eternal kingdom.

In some respects the final section of Lambrecht's work, dealing with the structure of Mark 13, is the most impressive. We are called on to recognize a detailed structuring of the discourse beyond anything most critics had perceived. Impressive as the presentation is, however, we are again compelled to acknowledge that the elaboration of the structuring at times evokes more admiration for Lambrecht's ingenuity than assurance that Mark intended it.[335] Nonetheless, it remains that Lambrecht has clearly shown the presence of a careful structure in Mark 13, for which the evangelist himself is responsible.

Lambrecht has performed a valuable service, demonstrating in both his analytic and synthetic treatment of the discourse that an adequate treatment of Mark 13 must take into account the hand of the evangelist. Mark has not inserted into his Gospel a fully fashioned and articulated address; Lambrecht has made that clearer than any of his predecessors. Nevertheless he seems to have insufficiently weighed the implications of admissions he makes at various points throughout his book, that Mark has worked on traditions of the teaching of Jesus in producing the discourse. Some of Lambrecht's suggestions about the origins of sayings in the discourse convey the impression that Mark used sayings of Jesus virtually as lexica out of which to create statements embodying notions of his own, wholly different from the known teaching of Jesus. We do not gather the impression from the rest of Mark's Gospel that Markan redaction denotes Markan new creation. If the reverse seems self-evident to some in relation to ch. 13, to others it appears neither likely nor proven.

R. Pesch

With the work of Pesch on Mark 13 we reach a high point in our review of literature on the discourse. If Lambrecht has given us a most detailed linguistic analysis of the discourse, Pesch has provided a most closely reasoned examination of its content. He passes in review stud-

---

[335]This may be illustrated from the scheme of inclusion believed to bracket the beginning and end of the discourse, vv. 4–5a and 29–37. It is a curious selection of materials on which to base a comparison. The first passage consists of a few lines of text, taking in one and a half sentences, and the second embraces a comparatively lengthy section, including the second half of a short parable (v. 29—why only half of it?), three disparate sayings (vv. 30–32), a complex parable (vv. 33–36), and the concluding sentence of the discourse (v. 37). Moreover, some items selected include common terms which can hardly fail to appear in a discourse of any sort; and to balance *eipon hēmin* and *ērxato legein autois* in vv. 4a and 5a with *legō hymin* of v. 37 strikes one as of small significance.

ies of Mark 13 that appeared subsequent to my *Jesus and the Future*. Recognizing the impasse which had been reached in research on the chapter, Pesch seeks to resolve the problems by more thoroughly applying redaction criticism to it, and by setting the chapter within the context of Mark's Gospel.

The latter issue is dealt with first. On examining the structure of Mark, Pesch proposes a sixfold division of the Gospel: 1:2—3:6; 3:7—6:29; 6:30—8:26; 8:27—10:52; 11:1—12:44; 14:1—16:8. It will be observed that he omits ch. 13 from this analysis. On stoichiometric grounds Pesch holds that the balance of these divisions precludes ch. 13 from the original structure of the Gospel.[336] The chapter must have been inserted by Mark in its present position after he had completed the Gospel, and this he was led to do by the urgent situation which had developed in his church. After the fall of Jerusalem Jewish-Christian prophets had come to Mark's church, declaring that the last times had set in and the parousia had occurred. For their authority they appealed to an apocalyptic flyleaf, viewed as coming from Jesus. Mark took this flyleaf and conjoined with it dominical sayings from the tradition; by this means he composed a discourse which corrected the errors of the false teachers and provided the church with a balanced near expectation.[337]

With regard to the structure of the discourse itself, Pesch concurs with Lambrecht (whose work appeared too late for his use): (1) vv. 5b–23, preliminary signs of the end; (2) vv. 24–27, the parousia; (3) vv. 28–37, parenesis inculcating watchfulness.[338]

The prophecy of the fall of the temple in v. 2c is viewed as a redacted form of the more enigmatic saying in Mark 14:58; vv. 1–2ab were composed by Mark as a setting for the prophecy.[339] The question of the disciples in v. 4 is framed so as to indicate both a link between the destruction of the temple and the end of the age and the possibility of correcting the notion of that link; the false teachers asserted an indissoluble connection between the end of the temple and the end of the age, and the discourse will set that error right. Herein Pesch sees an indication of the date of the discourse: "Since he [Mark] clearly holds fast to a near expectation colored by a sober eschatology, he will have written after the year AD 70, for otherwise he could hardly deny so decisively the connection of the destruction of the temple and the final end."[340]

---

[336]Pesch, *Naherwartungen: Tradition und Redaktion in Markus 13* (Düsseldorf, 1968), 48–50.
[337]Ibid., 218–22.
[338]Ibid., 74–82.
[339]Ibid., 83–96.
[340]Ibid., 105.

Importance is attached to the inclusion which Mark has made in vv. 6 and 22. This the evangelist achieved by dividing into two an originally single saying. To speak "in the name of the Lord" is a common OT claim, hence those in v. 6 who "speak in my name" are false prophets; Mark himself added the interpretative clause, "saying that I am (he)," as he also added the mention of false messiahs in v. 22. The original sentence in the source therefore ran:

Many will come in my name
and will deceive many.
And false prophets will arise
and will perform signs and portents
in order to deceive the elect.

The transfer of the warning about pseudomessiahs and pseudo-prophets to a place after v. 20 has the effect of putting a brake on apocalyptic calculation. In the source the account of the tribulation in vv. 14–20 was followed by that of the parousia; Mark teaches that not the parousia but false prophets teaching a false near expectation follow the distress of Jerusalem![341]

The statements in vv. 7–8 concentrate on the incidence of war prior to the end; such must happen, but "the end is not yet" (Mark's addition). In this context the "war" which must happen, but is not the end, can be none other than the Jewish War of AD 70.[342]

This is the situation portrayed in vv. 14–20. The passage refers not only to a desecration of the temple but to its destruction also. In v. 14 Mark has modified his source in one significant respect: since Judea is already in hill country, and the temple is in Jerusalem, it is likely that the original reference was a command to flee from Jerusalem; that has little relevance to Mark's congregation, so he changed "Jerusalem" to "Judea," which he viewed symbolically: on the temple's destruction Christians should flee from *Judaism*. This is strengthened by allusion to Lot's escaping from Sodom to the hills (Gen 19:17); Jerusalem has become as Sodom in the sight of God.[343]

In the source vv. 14–20 were followed by the parousia description, vv. 24–27. Pesch suggested that the introduction to v. 24 began, "In those days the sun will be darkened," so intimating that the high point of the tribulation will be the coming of the Son of man. Mark adds the phrase "after that tribulation" to mark the disjunction between the present and the future. The cosmic symbolism in vv. 24–25 reproduces OT descriptions of the day of the Lord; that suggests that the event will be for the purpose of judgment. Contrary to most exegetes, therefore,

---

[341]Ibid., 108–18.
[342]Ibid., 118–25.
[343]Ibid., 139–49.

Pesch holds that v. 26 describes the coming of the Son of man primarily for judgment and not simply for the gathering of the elect mentioned in v. 27.[344]

As to the parable of the Fig Tree, the heart of the comparison in v. 28bc may well be a reminiscence of the teaching of Jesus, relating to the nearness of the kingdom of God (cf. 1:15); the introduction in v. 28a and the application in v. 29 are, however, Markan redaction, by which Mark teaches that the signs described in the discourse indicate the nearness of the end (though not the completion of the end).[345]

Verses 30–32 give three sayings, of which v. 31 forms a kind of fulcrum. Verse 30 has no claim for an origin from an older saying, nor can it relate to the fall of Jerusalem, since this would depend on the authenticity of vv. 1–4, which has been ruled out; the saying affirms an intensive near expectation, yet at the same time gives no handhold for apocalyptic reckoning. Verse 31 serves to affirm alike the near expectation of v. 30 and the incalculability of the end in v. 32; it binds together the expectation of a speedy end and a warning against fanaticism. Verse 32 is an earlier logion edited by Mark, asserting the ignorance of Jesus about "that day" (the "hour" reflects the parable of vv. 34–35); the phrase "neither the Son, only the Father" is a Markan replacement of an original, which may have run, "only one, that is, God," as in 10:18.[346]

The final paragraph has as its nucleus an authentic parable in v. 34, allegorized through Mark's addition of *tēn exousian*, indicating the bestowal of authority on the church for its service in the latter time. The remaining sentences stress the need for watchfulness in view of the unknowable time of the end, but the conscious parallels with the Gethsemane scene in vv. 35–36 hint that the way of the disciples is a way in suffering discipleship to the Son of man. Hence v. 37 leads straight into the passion narrative.[347]

As to vv. 9–13, Pesch believes that Mark received connected persecution logia, represented in vv. 9, 13a, 11 (in that order). These can hardly be attributed to Jesus, since the situation of disciples being handed over to sanhedrins, synagogues, governors, and kings is not that of the earthly days of Jesus; they are *vaticinia* belonging to the time of the church. Verse 10 was added by Mark; v. 12 comes from the apocalyptic flyleaf.[348]

In Pesch's view the postulate of a flyleaf must be accepted. It will have been in three divisions: the first describing signs of the end, vv. 6,

---

[344]"The meaning of vv. 24b–25d therefore is: 'In those days after the great tribulation the day of judgment comes' " (ibid., 160–61).

[345]Ibid., 175–81.

[346]Ibid., 181–95.

[347]Ibid., 195–202.

[348]Ibid., 204–5.

22, 7b, 8, 12, 13b; the second the tribulation connected with Jerusalem and its temple, vv. 14–20a (v. 18 is uncertain); the third portraying the parousia, vv. 24–27. So short a passage is better called a "flyleaf" rather than an apocalypse; its length would correspond with the two sides of a papyrus sheet of medium size. Since there is no clear reflection of the Jewish War in the document, it is most plausibly set in the crisis precipitated by Caligula. Since the author of the flyleaf looked for the speedy intervention of God for his temple and his people, it is likely that he was a Jew, voicing the hopes of his people, and not a Jewish Christian. It is understandable that such a document gained a fresh pertinence in the Jewish War of AD 66–70.[349]

Prior to the destruction of the temple the division between the present and the future would lie between vv. 13 and 14; the fulfillment of the prophecy was awaited, and with it the immediate coming of the Son of man. Such a belief would have been shared by Jewish Christians along with their non-Christian compatriots. Mark's redaction indicates that the flyleaf was subsequently misused in the church; Jewish-Christian prophets proclaimed: "The temple is destroyed and therefore the end must now come about, as Jesus taught in the apocalyptic discourse." This impelled Mark to compose the full discourse of ch. 13. He took up the flyleaf, accepted as from the Lord, and worked it into a discourse of Jesus; by his use of the inclusion of vv. 6 and 22 he brings it about that Jesus predicted that deceiving agitation of false teachers should occur after the destruction of the temple. Thus a fanatical apocalyptic exposition of the flyleaf in the church is condemned and out of the document is made an anti–apocalyptic discourse.[350]

Mark still reflects a near expectation, but it is flexible, and its presentation has the parenetic purpose of encouraging watchfulness. It is more sharply expressed than elsewhere, for the emphasis in Mark's writing is rather on the present as the time when the risen Lord comes in the proclamation to the gentile world. The nearness in Mark's message is that of the kingdom of God, as expressed in 1:15, but this is not apocalyptic, and so it is not directed to the coming of the Son of man. In ch. 13 Mark is compelled to enter into debate with an extreme apocalyptic near expectation, and so to develop a form of near expectation of his own to counter it. In so doing Mark does not fall away again into apocalyptic; rather he moves toward viewing the future christologically; it is that future in which he is to come who has come and is present in the proclamation. On that foundation a form of near expectation is laid which is unapocalyptic, an eschatological attitude not

---

[349]Ibid., 207–18.
[350]Ibid., 218–23.

exposed to disintegration through tradition, but one capable of continuing renewal.[351]

It is no surprise that this work was greeted as an outstanding
contribution to the study of Mark 13.[352] It has an abundance of illuminating suggestions on the origin and interpretation of passages in the
chapter; for example, the discussion and exegesis of the parousia passage
in vv. 24–27 is of unusual worth. Nevertheless, misgivings arise with
regard to a number of positions adopted which are of significance to Pesch.

The sixfold division of Mark's Gospel is a plausible view of its
structure, and Pesch works it out with extraordinary precision. The
idea that ch. 13 is an afterthought of Mark, due to a crisis precipitated
by apocalyptic fanatics, is in itself not at all repugnant; it simply is not
likely. The stoichiometric balance of the divisions of the Gospel, on
which the view is based, leads to some doubtful dealings with the text
to make it conform to the pattern imposed upon it. For example, Mark
4:10–23 has to be viewed as a single paragraph, which is frankly pre-
posterous; 9:30–50 is divided into three paragraphs, instead of four at
least; and 11:1—12:44 is shorter by far than the other five divisions of the
book, but becomes of similar length when ch. 13 is included with it!

More doubtful is Pesch's way of using redaction criticism, which
to him is the key to the discourse. A few examples will illustrate the
point. In the prophecy of v. 2c, certain characteristics of the speech of
Jesus are observable (e.g., the double negative [ou mē] twice over, often
seen in prophetic words of Jesus comparable to that in v. 2c); this is
declared to be "a sign for its formation through the evangelist . . . who
even in freshly formulating a saying took note of the structure of
comparable sayings of Jesus (as the tradition generally did), and so to a
certain extent stood under a 'compulsion of form.' "[353] One may perhaps be forgiven for regarding this as an example of the procedure
known as "Heads I win, tails you lose," for if a saying is given in the
vocabulary and style of the evangelist, it is attributed to his composition; if a saying reflects the mode of speech of acknowledged sayings of
Jesus, this suggests the handiwork of the evangelist who reproduces
them! A different example of this mode of criticism is seen in the
treatment of v. 21. Pesch effectively shows the Markan style of the
saying;[354] that encourages him to view it as an independent Markan
construction, derived neither from the Jewish flyleaf nor from sayings

---

[351]"It can be described as the merit of Mark that he has fundamentally
solved the problem of near expectation . . . in the discussion with a false
apocalyptic form of expectation in Mark 13" (ibid., 243).

[352]See, e.g., the review article by J. Gnilka relating to the contributions of
Hartman, Lambrecht, and Pesch: "Markus 13 in der Diskussion," BZ 13 (1969): 134.

[353]Pesch, Naherwartungen, 92.

[354]See the linguistic evidence given on p. 114.

of Jesus. But a comparison of v. 21 with the Q logion Luke 17:23/Matt 24:26 surely indicates that few examples of doublets of Mark and Q are so obvious as this one; it would appear to be a clear instance of Mark reproducing in his own idiom a word from the tradition of Jesus' sayings, and in spite of all keeping close to the alternative tradition of the saying.

We have noted that Pesch attaches importance to the presence of an inclusion in vv. 6 and 22, which he viewed as originally a single sentence, divided and redacted by Mark so as to create the inclusion.[355] The recognition that vv. 5b–6 and 21–23 form an inclusion is undoubtedly important, and Pesch's deduction as to its purpose is illuminating. That by no means demands, however, that the two passages be viewed as identical in meaning or that they originally formed a single saying. It is commonly acknowledged that in v. 6 the "many" who come "in my name" are represented as "using" or "claiming" the name, hence that the following clause, "saying that I am (he)," is a justifiable exposition of the former phrase. It describes the claims of pseudomessiahs. By contrast, vv. 21–22 refer to the claims of false prophets as to the messianic status of others whom they view as Messiah (so, clearly, v. 21), as well as the appearance of false claimants to the messiahship (assumed in v. 21, explicitly mentioned in v. 22). Verses 5b–6 accordingly should be acknowledged as closely related to vv. 21–22, but neither passage means the same nor renders the other superfluous.

We have already discussed the date of Mark's Gospel and recognized the difficulties involved in its determination. Pesch, however, sees no complexities here. Mark looks back on the fall of Jerusalem and inserts between the descriptions of the tribulation and the parousia the activity of false prophets who declare that the parousia has occurred; this post-ruin-of-Jerusalem situation is plainly indicated in v. 23: "You, beware, I have told you all things." How this is a "plain indication" that all prior to v. 23 has come to pass is far from clear to this plain reader. The argument that Mark's correction of the alleged indissoluble link between the city's destruction and the parousia presupposes the fall of the city is admittedly strong; but Pesch nowhere recognizes that a concern to defuse apocalyptic fanaticism would hold good if the chapter were composed during the Jewish War, especially in its later stages.

The discussion on the composition of the supposed flyleaf makes its existence more, rather than less, difficult to accept. The linking of vv. 6 and 22, proposed by Pesch, makes it unlikely that either saying originally belonged to a Jewish document (note the connection with v. 21). The sole remnant of v. 7 assigned by Pesch to the Jewish source is *dei genesthai*, which is unmotivated when vv. 6–7 are ruled out. The

---

[355]Ibid., 139.

statement in v. 8 relates to wars, earthquakes, and famines, and v. 12 to
the mutual hostility of parents and children; but what curious oddities
with which to begin a Jewish apocalyptic document! The original form
of v. 14 is uncertain; Pesch reproduces it from Mark's rendering as "the
abomination of desolation, standing where it ought not, then those in
Jerusalem should flee to the mountain." The statement is both incomplete and unclear, and the mention of Jerusalem is speculative (it
replaces Mark's "Judea"). Verses 15–16 are clearly Christian tradition
(cf. Luke 17:31). Verse 18 is admitted to be of uncertain origin. Thus the
supposed Jewish paragraph consists of part of v. 14, vv. 17, 19–20a, plus
possibly v. 18; this is surely a feeble fragment to inspire a Jewish
apocalyptic document. But, of course, there remains the parousia passage in vv. 24–27! Or does there? We have asked before where in Jewish
apocalyptic literature prior to AD 40 a theophany of the Son of man for
judgment and salvation is described; we know of none. The Jewish
flyleaf then shrinks to small proportions—so small as to make its
existence as a separate source no longer credible.

The acceptance of a Jewish apocalyptic flyleaf is not, in fact,
integral to the leading notion of Pesch, that Mark's concern was to
correct a false near expectation with one more truly in harmony with
the teaching of Jesus. It is right to call attention, as Pesch does, to the
"brakes" on apocalyptic enthusiasm in vv. 7 and 8 and to recognize that
the doom which threatens Jerusalem is judgment in tribulation, not the
end itself; for the end is not the abomination of desolation, but the
saving sovereignty of God in the intervention of the Son of man. Now
the calamity does not have to take place in order to teach this lesson. It
takes no more than war clouds to rouse apocalyptic enthusiasm, as the
history of the church through the centuries, including our own, bears
witness. If vv. 14–20 had urgent relevance to Jews of Palestine, there is
little doubt that believers everywhere in the later sixties of the first
century AD would also be concerned about their content in relation to
contemporary history. For them Mark's message of watchfulness, issu-
ing in mission and faithful discipleship to the suffering Savior, would
have been of intense pertinence. It is not impossible that such parenetic
concerns may have been shared by Jesus also.

It has seemed right to include an evaluation of Pesch's *Naherwartungen* on its own merits in view of the importance of the work, the
attention it has evoked, and the influence it has had on other writers,
and because not all are aware of the profound changes which Pesch's
views on the discourse have undergone since the book's publication. It
must be admitted, nevertheless, that this review in some senses has
been a work of supererogation. For ten years after the completion of
Naherwartungen the second volume of Pesch's commentary on the
Gospel of Mark appeared, wherein significant modifications of his
earlier convictions are made known, not a few of which concur with

our evaluation.[356] He has himself given an account of the changes in a lecture later included in a volume of essays on apocalyptic in the NT, issued by Louvain University.[357] They may be indicated as follows.

(1) The idea that the basis of Mark 13 was a Jewish apocalyptic flyleaf is abandoned in favor of the belief, following Hahn's suggestion,[358] that Mark used a Christian apocalypse, stemming from the time of the Jewish War. Pesch now believes that the source comprised vv. 7–8, 9, possibly 10, 11–13, 14–22, 24–31, and that the introduction in vv. 3–5 may well have been included in it. Thus the only verses omitted from the basic document of vv. 3–31 are vv. 6 and 23 (v. 10 being uncertain). This address is considered to have been constructed from the tradition of Jesus' words and a topical exposition of Daniel set in the contemporary context;[359] probably it was the oracle referred to by Eusebius, which prompted the Jewish-Christian community to emigrate to the east Jordan country.[360]

(2) The prophecy of v. 2, with its introduction in vv. 1–2ab, is now believed to have been derived by Mark from the passion narrative which he received. Mark reproduced it at this point since it offered him the place for inserting the discourse. The prophecy has not been derived from 14:58, as was formerly maintained, since it is a simple prediction in the passive of the destruction of the temple, not a prophecy of its destruction through Jesus. The real parallel to v. 2c is Luke 19:44, a text independent of Mark 13:2 and possibly, like it, to be attributed to Jesus himself.[361]

(3) Pesch still places emphasis on the inclusion formed by vv. 6 and 21–22; but whereas he earlier considered that vv. 6 and 22 were originally one saying, he now follows V. Howard in holding that Mark formed v. 6 by means of v. 22.[362]

---

[356]Pesch, *Das Markusevangelium,* 2 vols., HTKNT (Freiburg, Basel, Vienna, 1976–77).

[357]Idem, "Markus 13," in *L'Apocalypse johannique et l'Apocalyptique dans le Nouveau Testament,* ed. J. Lambrecht, BETL 53 (1979), 355–68.

[358]See his article "Die Rede von der Parusie des Menschensohnes, Markus 13," in *Jesus und der Menschensohn,* Festschrift A. Vögtle, ed. R. Pesch and R. Schnackenburg (Freiburg, 1975), 240–66.

[359]Here Pesch accords recognition to the work of Hartman; see his essay "Markus 13," 356.

[360]Pesch, *Markus,* 2:266–67.

[361]In these conclusions Pesch has followed Dupont's exposition in "Il n'en sera pas laissé pierre sur pierre (Marc 13,2; Luc 19,44)," *Bib* 52 (1971): 301–20.

[362]The *egō eimi* of v. 6 is a proclamation of identity, not of authority, as Pesch formerly asserted; and v. 22 tells of false prophets and false christs who claim to be the returned Messiah (*Markus,* 2:278–79). See V. Howard, *Das Ego Jesu in den synoptischen Evangelien, Untersuchungen zum Sprachgebrauch Jesu,* Markinische Theologische Studien 14 (Marburg, 1975), 116–23.

(4) The double expression in v. 24, "in those days, after that distress," is held to suit the tendency of the source. "Those days" are not those of the great distress but the time immediately before the end, whose cosmic signs make any further question as to "when" superfluous. Both in the source and in Mark's discourse the answer to the question as to the sign of the end is given in vv. 24–25: the cosmic signs show that the arrival of the Son of man follows with the unmediated suddenness of a lightning flash. Sign and completion of the end therefore fall together.[363]

(5) In the conclusion of the discourse the core of the final parable is seen as vv. 34–36, redacted by Mark, not in v. 34 only.[364]

(6) Most surprising of all is Pesch's conclusion relating to Mark's mode of redaction in the chapter: "On the whole Mark shows himself also in the most topical chapter of his work . . . as *the conservative redactor which the whole Gospel shows him to be.*"[365] Pesch himself, in his account of his present convictions relating to the discourse, cites the comment of J. Blank in his review of the Markan commentary: "If one compares the commentary on Mark with Pesch's work on Mark 13, *Naherwartungen*, then one must without doubt speak of a 180 degree turn which Pesch has made."[366] This Pesch does not deny. Rather he admits that the results of his dissertation on the discourse no longer held up to his own criticism; and the basis of this was the estimate of Mark, to which his studies on the Gospel increasingly led him, as the "conservative redactor."[367]

Despite these changes, neither Pesch's understanding of the purpose of Mark's incorporation of the discourse nor the conviction as to the date of Mark's writing has changed; it is the origins of the discourse and the nature of Mark's redaction on which the changes of opinion have been most marked. The questions of the extent to which the "Jesus tradition" can be traced in the discourse and the origin and extent of the "topical exposition of Daniel" embodied in the discourse are clearly open for discussion. In the commentary Pesch appears to assign to the latter the apocalyptic passages vv. 7–8, 14, 19, 24–27. In our judgment the Danielic allusions in vv. 7–8 are less clear than in vv. 14, 19, 24–27. Moreover, the last passage raises the acute question as to the relation of the "exposition" to a word or words of the Lord (1 Thess 4:15). Pesch has never conceded the significance of Paul's reflection of these passages in the Thessalonian correspondence. To do so would lead to the

---

[363]Pesch, *Markus*, 2:302–3.

[364]Ibid., 313, following A. Weiser, *Die Knechtsgleichnisse der synoptischen Evangelien* (Munich, 1971), 139–44.

[365]Pesch, *Markus*, 2:267.

[366]Blank, *BZ* 23 (1979): 130; cited by Pesch in "Markus 13," 361.

[367]Pesch, "Markus 13," 355 and 362.

recognition that the allusions to Daniel in the discourse, including the parousia hope in vv. 24–27, could be topical not only in the ferment of the Jewish War, but in the time when the inevitability of doom upon the sinful nation was perceived.

Again, one is compelled to state that the work of Pesch in his commentary is of unexampled value in its brevity, its comprehensive use of sources ancient and modern, and its penetrating exegesis. Whether he will continue to stress the relation between the discourse and the Eusebian oracle, as he has throughout the exegesis of the discourse in his commentary, will be a point of interest in view of the debate engendered on the issue.[368]

L. Gaston

The work by Gaston, taking its title from the prophecy of Mark 13:2, is massive, learned, and at many points highly original. It treats not only the discourse of Mark 13 but many other related subjects such as the concern of Jesus about the political future of Israel, his thought about the temple, and with it that of the Qumran community and the early church concerning the temple, the relation of Jesus to prophecy and its role in the early church, and so on. A reading of Gaston's book reveals convictions which determine to no small extent his view of Mark 13. They may be summarized as follows.

(1) Jesus maintained an interest in the political situation of Israel and therefore in the fate of the nation under Roman rule. The reflections of this interest appear especially in Luke and should not be rejected.[369]

(2) Jesus stood in the tradition of the prophets rather than of apocalyptists. He did not give predictions, but he did issue warnings or threats of calamity upon Israel if repentance were not forthcoming. This does not, however, justify a sharp severance between historical and apocalyptic, as though they were mutually exclusive.[370]

(3) The theme of the preaching of Jesus was the kingdom of God. "This concept in itself excludes all Christology from his teaching," comments Gaston. Why this should follow is not explained; a reference is given to Vielhauer in support of the view, but Vielhauer's understanding of the issue is highly questionable. Gaston does believe that Jesus spoke of the destiny of the Son of man, but that is regarded as a

---

[368] See especially the strong criticism of Pesch's appeal to the oracle in the contribution of F. Neirynck, "Marc 13. Examen critique de l'interprétation de R. Pesch," in *L'Apocalypse johannique,* 369–401.

[369] Gaston, *No Stone on Another: Studies in the Significance of the Fall of Jerusalem in the Synoptic Gospels,* NovTSup 23 (Leiden, 1970), 358–59, 423–24.

[370] Ibid., 423–28.

corporate figure, indicating Israel's vocation to suffer and experience vindication at the hand of God.[371]

(4) Schweitzer was correct in maintaining that Jesus did not distinguish between resurrection and parousia, and that Jesus looked simply for a divine vindication of the "Son of man" after "three days," i.e., a short time. To Jesus Dan 7:13 will have conveyed the notion of the exaltation of the people of God to rule; the concept of the parousia accordingly is foreign to Jesus and was the product of later Christian prophets.[372]

(5) The whole setting for apocalyptic teaching in the life of Jesus is in the mouth of the risen Christ. This is indicated by Acts 1:6–12, which contains a summary of tradition parallel to Mark 13, and the book of Revelation, which is a vision of the risen Christ. There is no need therefore to invoke Jewish apocalypse to explain the production of Mark 13; attempts to restore a Jewish apocalypse at the base of the discourse have signally failed; early Christian prophets working on the traditions of the contemporary church suffice to explain the origin and composition of the discourse.[373]

(6) Proto-Luke is a source of prime importance for the ministry of Jesus; in particular it provides an independent version of the eschatological discourse besides Mark 13.[374]

Approaching Mark 13 with these convictions, Gaston urges that Mark 13:2 is no *vaticinium ex eventu*. Apart from the independent tradition of Luke 21:6, there is a third variant in Luke 19:44. In Proto-Luke the last named is immediately followed by the eschatological discourse; this confirms that the saying was spoken in public, as in Luke 21:6, and not in private, as in Mark 13:2; more importantly, it shows that the saying originally related to the city, and not to the temple of Jerusalem. In applying it to the temple Mark has created a point of departure for the discourse and transformed the meaning of the abomination passage in v. 14.

In the discourse itself there exists a close interweaving of "eschatological parenesis grounded in apocalyptic instruction."[375] This may be seen in the opening paragraph, vv. 5–8:

paraclesis (v. 5b)

gar—the ground of it (v. 6)

paraclesis (v. 7a)

gar—the ground of it (v. 7b)

---

[371]Ibid., 408–9.
[372]Ibid., 31–35, 141–42.
[373]Ibid., 9, 42–47.
[374]Ibid., 10, 355–65.
[375]Ibid., 15.

paraclesis (v. 8b)

gar—the ground of it (v. 8a)

The phenomenon runs through the length of the discourse. The hortatory elements are found in vv. 5b, 7a, 8b, 9a, 13b, 21, 23, 28–29, 33–37, the apocalyptic elements in vv. 6, 7b, 8a, 14–20, 22, 24–27. It will be observed that the term gar occurs at the beginning of vv. 6, 7b, 8, 9b, 11b, 19, 22, 33, 35: "With the exception therefore of the longer sections of 14–18 and 24–27 every apocalyptic element is attached to its context by a gar. The apocalyptic is therefore not an independent element in our text, but exists here only to provide the ground for the exhortation."[376] Passages similarly structured may be seen in Acts, the letters of Paul, and in other NT writers.[377] Mark 13 is a particularly good example of this tradition of eschatological exhortation, but it should be recognized that the framework is provided by the exhortation, not by the apocalyptic instruction.

Attempts to isolate Jewish apocalyptic elements within the discourse, in order to fashion an earlier form of the discourse, are to be rejected.[378] If it be asked how the discourse came into being we have to begin with v. 14. The core of the discourse is in vv. 14–19. This did not originate in Jewish apocalyptic, since vv. 15–16 come from the Christian tradition of words of Jesus. The oracle reflects the crisis precipitated by Caligula, ca. AD 40. To this core vv. 20 and 24–27 were early joined, the latter coming not from Jesus but from Christian prophets. The next stage was the combination of these passages with a hortatory sermon of a Christian prophet, vv. 5–13, 21–23, and perhaps vv. 33–36. When the discourse was believed to have come from Jesus the sayings of vv. 28–37 were added, though not necessarily at the same time. Mark's contribution may be seen in various minor additions, such as vv. 23 and 37, but above all in setting the discourse as an answer to the question concerning the destruction of the temple; he thereby gave a new interpretation to the prophecy of v. 2 and to the oracle of the "appalling sacrilege" of v. 14.[379]

Several factors may have contributed to the composition of the discourse: the experience of persecution, which encouraged belief in a

---

[376] Ibid., 52.

[377] For example, 1 Thess 5:1–11; 2 Thess 2:1–15; Rom 13:11–14; Eph 6:10–18; 1 Pet 4:7; Jas 5:7ff.

[378] "The procedure of removing all sayings which refer to some specific characteristic of Christianity and saying that the remainder must be Jewish is not one to be scientifically recommended. Anyone proceeding in such a way would reflect his own dislike of apocalyptic and prejudice against Judaism, and he would also, of course, beg the whole question" (ibid., 47).

[379] Ibid., 61–64.

near parousia; the conviction that the messianic age should follow on Jerusalem's destruction; and the notion that the messianic age should last forty years (the period from the end of the ministry of Jesus to the end of the Jewish War was forty years!).[380]

One's first reaction to Gaston's researches must be appreciation for their range and their multitudinous insights. His discussions—for example, concerning the significance of the temple in the teaching of Jesus, set in the light of the thought of the Qumran community and that of the primitive church—are particularly valuable. The insistence on the interrelatedness of eschatological paraclesis and apocalyptic instruction in the discourse is of first importance. Conzelmann's belief that the key to the discourse is the opposition between historical and apocalyptic is rejected as a relapse into older categories. Instead, the description given by Busch is adopted: "An exhortation to hypomonē in thlipsis."[381] While this is incontestable, and insufficiently recognized by contemporary scholarship, Gaston's endeavor to demonstrate a structure in the discourse by the use of gar is insufficiently grounded, since five out of the nine instances of the particle mentioned by him are not present in the better texts of Mark.[382] But the contention that eschatological paraclesis and apocalyptic instruction are intertwined in the discourse, with emphasis on the former, remains without that linguistic support.

It is also important to be reminded that Jesus was interested not simply in the salvation of individual Jews but in the welfare of his nation, including what for want of a better word we should call its political future. Negatively, however, it may be doubted that Mark 13:2 related originally to the ruin of the city rather than the temple, and that such importance attaches to the issue as Gaston has implied, since neither city nor temple could be destroyed without the other. It is worth observing, nevertheless, that both Luke and Mark explicitly relate the word of Jesus to the stones of the temple, and Gaston is insistent that Luke is independent of Mark in this respect. In the light of Luke 19:44ff., is it out of the question that Jesus applied to the temple, with

---

[380]Ibid., 449–67.

[381]Busch, Zum Verständnis der synoptischen Eschatologie: Markus 13 neu untersucht (1938), 48. Gaston observes that the definition is close to Dodd's: "A Mahnrede in apocalyptic terms," and Lohmeyer's, "It is not only apocalyptic teaching, but in at least the same measure apocalyptic parenesis" (Lohmeyer, Markus, 237).

[382]C. H. Turner called attention to the absence of particles as a feature of Mark's style, and in particular discussed the pertinent passages in Mark 13; the lack is made up alike in Matthew's and Luke's versions of the discourse, and also in later mss. of Mark. See Turner, "On Marcan Usage, Particles," JTS 27 (1926): 58–59. Similarly, M. Zerwick, Untersuchungen zum Markus-Stil (Rome, 1937), 21; and Lambrecht, Redaktion, 95 n. 2.

deliberate emphasis, what he also said of the city? The issue is not easy to decide, but the OT precedents relating to Yahweh abandoning his house in judgment on the people, and therefore the city, favor the former as prior to the latter.[383]

Moreover, if the declaration of 13:2 be viewed as authentic reminiscence, it is unclear why the so-called core of the discourse, vv. 14ff., has to be viewed as emanating from a post-resurrection era, for in the context of Judaism a desolating sacrilege relating to the temple could not but issue in a conflict to the death, and the desolating sacrilege was a given factor of prophecy (as Daniel would be viewed). For any who, like Gaston, believe that Jesus was a prophet who warned his nation of impending doom, there is no valid reason for declaring that Jesus could not have employed Daniel's symbol of the abomination of desolation to indicate the nature of the disaster, especially since its context in Dan 9:26–27 is one of destructive warfare.

If Jesus did declare the onset of war that should bring destruction to Jerusalem and its temple, when did he conceive of its happening? Assuredly not contemporaneously with his own death. The prophetic warnings Jesus addressed to the nation presume a history to follow on his suffering. This adds to the difficulty of believing that Jesus viewed the vindication God would give him as a resurrection in anticipation of a visitation upon Jerusalem. Contrary to Gaston's interpretation of Dan 7:13, the implications of his own assertion that there is only one parousia, that of the theophany of God, require further reflection; for Dan 7:13 speaks of the one like a son of man "coming" to the Ancient of Days when *he* "comes" to judgment (Dan 7:22), implying that the manlike one participates in the theophany. The insistence therefore that the concept of a parousia could not arise till after Easter is unjustified. The Jesus who went to his death in the service of the kingdom of God, and who saw in Daniel 7 a theophany wherein the dominion and glory and kingdom are given to the one like a son of man, would naturally view the coming of the manlike one on the clouds as a theophany of like order to and bound up with that of God. That possibility becomes strong probability when the destiny of the kingdom is related to him who manifests it in history and acts as its instrument among human beings, and when we observe that confession and denial of the Son of man in judgment is related by Jesus to himself in a context reminiscent of Dan 7:13–14 (see Luke 12:8–9 par.). Gaston acknowledges that the idea that the kingdom of God excludes a Christology has to be modified in the light of the role of the one like a son of man in Daniel and in the Gospels. We must go further and affirm that the teaching on the kingdom of God and the Son of man in the Gospels

---

[383] See the commentary below on Mark 13:1–2, pp. 379–81.

demands a Christology shot through with eschatology; or, if you will, an eschatological Christology which entails a christological eschatology.[384] That is one of the least ambiguous results of research into the teaching of Jesus on the kingdom of God.

J. Zmijewski

The volumes grow ever larger. Mussner's book is eighty pages long, Neville's a little over one hundred, those by Hartman, Lambrecht, and Pesch extend to about three hundred pages—but large pages, and much fine print! Gaston's book is five hundred such pages. J. Zmijewski continues the upward spiral in producing a weighty volume of six hundred pages on the same theme. The focus of his interest is different from that of his predecessors, however, inasmuch as he is concerned about the Lukan eschatology. He writes on Luke's version of the eschatological discourse and provides a similar study of the Q apocalypse, Luke 17:20–37. In the light of his conviction that Luke's sole source for the discourse in ch. 21 of his Gospel is Mark 13, Zmijewski feels obliged to examine in detail Mark's discourse and thus to evaluate Luke's redaction and exposition in the light of Mark's writing and intention. In his consideration of Mark 13 Zmijewski leans heavily on the researches of Pesch, but he takes his own way on various issues. Our interest in this review is primarily on what he writes about Mark.

Zmijewski calls attention to the significance which the Mount of Olives has, not only for Mark, but for the eschatological traditions of the Jews. Zech 14:4 is of importance here, for a theophany of Yahweh is described as taking place on the Mount of Olives, when "the Lord your God will come and all the holy ones with him." That Jesus is represented in Mark 13:3 as sitting on the Mount of Olives when giving the eschatological address is believed to make it an eschatological revelation discourse.[385] Its esoteric nature (addressed to four disciples only) enables Mark to incorporate in the discourse apocalyptic texts, which he freshly interprets and corrects.

These texts come from more than one source. One group consists of vv. 7a, 8ab, 12, 24–27; this is viewed as a Christian, not a purely Jewish, apocalypse, since the description of the parousia reflects Christian concepts (e.g., "seeing" the Son of man coming on the clouds, and his sending angels to gather the elect). The theme of this apocalypse is the end of the age and its premonitory signs. By contrast, vv. 14–20 have

---

[384] So H. D. Wendland: "Christology is eschatology. Eschatology is Christology" (*Die Eschatologie des Reiches Gottes bei Jesus* [Gütersloh, 1931], 247–48).

[385] Zmijewski, *Die Eschatologiereden des Lukas-Evangeliums: Eine traditions- und redaktionsgeschichtliche Untersuchung zu Lk 21,5–36 und Lk 17,20–37*, BBB (Bonn, 1972), 84–85.

in view concrete events relating to the fate of the Jerusalem temple. The Christian apocalypse is poetical in form, but this one is more prosaic in language; note the commands given in the third person, the circumstantial detail of vv. 19–20, and the lack of OT allusions, apart from vv. 14 and 19. The phrase in v. 14, "he who reads," suggests that Mark had this section in written form, whereas the other group of sayings is likely to represent oral tradition (cf. the *legontes* of v. 6). It is not known whether vv. 14–20 are of Jewish or Christian origin, or what situation was originally in view. Zmijewski considers that the question in v. 4 is framed so as to cover both sources incorporated by Mark; the first clause refers to the prophesied destruction of the temple, the plural *tauta* being due to an adjustment to the *tauta panta* of v. 4b; the second clause relates to the apocalyptic tradition, with its interest in the end of the age.[386] The distinguishing of the two sources in this way leads to a rejection of the hypothesis of a pre-Markan "flyleaf."[387]

Mark's prime concern in the discourse is revealed in its opening sentence, v. 5: *blepete* establishes the parenetic nature of the discourse; *mē tis hymas planēsē* shows Mark's desire to warn the church against being led astray by false prophets and teachers. Contrary to Pesch, Zmijewski regards vv. 6 and 22 as belonging to different contexts; v. 22 speaks of miraculous *deeds* of false christs and false prophets, v. 6 of what the pseudomessiahs *say*. Verse 22 belongs to the section vv. 14–20, while v. 6 clearly relates to Christian deceivers, who use the formula which belongs to Jesus alone—*egō eimi*. The *Sitz im Leben* of v. 6 is the confusion in the period following on the destruction of the temple, when Christian apocalyptists claimed to possess secret teaching from Jesus that the end was now imminent. The views of these teachers are reflected in vv. 7–8, 12, 24–27. In warning against them Mark warns against apocalyptic.[388] As to the signs of vv. 7–8, Mark acknowledges that wars, etc., belong to the apocalyptic scheme, and that he and his contemporaries stand in an "apocalyptic situation"; but he warns against misinterpreting the war in the Holy Land as though it portended the end, for it belongs only to the *archē ōdinōn* (v. 8).[389]

A Synoptic persecution tradition is seen to provide the source of vv. 9b, 11, 13. The situation of the years 66–70 forms its context, itself an apocalyptic time by reason of the danger of apostasy through the persecutions inflicted by Jewish and gentile authorities. For Mark v. 9b is significant because of the mention of gentile authorities. He himself has added the phrase *eis martyrion autois* to explain *heneken emou*, and to point to v. 10, which is a Markan formulation, having the

---

[386]Ibid., 85–87.
[387]Ibid., 85, 192–93, 235.
[388]Ibid., 107–10.
[389]Ibid., 111–13.

intention of interpreting the current situation in a positive manner: the church, even in tribulation, has the task of preaching the gospel to all peoples. The *prōton* of v. 10 both marks the present from the end and relates the present to the end.[390]

It is unlikely that the "abomination" in v. 14 represents the antichrist. The destruction of Jerusalem is in prospect in the context, and a plurality of antichrists are mentioned in vv. 21–22. The term *hestēkota*, which qualifies *to bdelygma tēs erēmōseōs*, underscores the active sense of *erēmōseōs*; whether a destructive person or power, or a Roman commander or his army, is in view is uncertain. The flight from Jerusalem commanded in the text is viewed, after Pesch, as calling for a forsaking of Judaism.[391]

In the parousia passage of vv. 24–27 both phrases of the introductory clause are thought to have come from Mark's pen (*en ekeinais tais hēmerais, meta tēn thlipsin ekeinēn*), not one alone; by this means Mark brings together the two sources, for vv. 7–8, etc. have in view the last days ("*those* days"), and vv. 14ff. the distress of the Jews ("after that distress"), though both phrases, it is observed, occur in v. 19. In agreement with Pesch, Zmijewski acknowledges that vv. 24–25 should be interpreted symbolically and not realistically, but in contrast to Pesch he interprets the coming of the Son of man in v. 26 as primarily connoting a universal judgment, when all see the Son of man, whether for their salvation or their condemnation. For Mark the parousia is a universal event; to the universality of the judgment corresponds the universality of the gathering of the elect, mentioned in v. 27. The elect are, of course, in Mark's understanding the worldwide church, for whose encouragement he is writing; it is comprehensible that he is more interested in the destiny of the Christians than of unbelievers.[392]

The parable of the Fig Tree was taken by Mark from the tradition of Jesus' words, but he lengthened it by adding an introduction (v. 28a) and the application, of which v. 29 consists. In formulating the parable Mark takes up the language of the discourse: the *hotan* of v. 28 harks back to vv. 4 and 14 and anticipates the *hotan* of v. 29; the *tauta* similarly echoes v. 4 and anticipates vv. 29 and 30. But while the question of v. 4 insinuates that the destruction of the temple and the end of the age are bound together, vv. 5–23 repudiate such deceptive apocalyptic notions; the parable continues in this strain and implies that there are signs for the nearness of the end but no sign for the end itself; thus the destruction of the temple is not one with the end, but an indication that the end is near to come. The parable relates primarily

---

[390]Ibid., 142–45.
[391]Ibid., 192–99.
[392]Ibid., 238–40.

not to the parousia, of which there is no mention in v. 4, but simply to the end of the age, of which v. 4 hints (*synteleisthai panta*). There is no question of Mark countering a delay of the parousia; rather, his desire is to clarify for his readers an authentic near expectation.[393]

Verse 30 also harks back to the introduction, and has in view first of all the concrete event of the temple's destruction (v. 2), or at least the fall of Jerusalem (cf. Matt 23:36). Yet, as in Mark 13:4, the phrase *tauta panta* embraces the ruin of the temple and the end of the age, of which the discourse has spoken. Of this v. 32 serves as a kind of correction: despite the near expectation, which must be adhered to, the incalculability of the end is stressed against apocalyptic notions.[394] The saying leads directly into the parenetic conclusion of vv. 33–37, which is framed by appeals to "watch" (vv. 33 and 38). Because Christians do not know when the time is, but do know that it comes soon, it is their part in the comparatively short time before the end to be ever "watchful," i.e., ready for the coming of the exalted Lord.[395] The concluding verse emphasizes this, with its *legō pasin*: the appeal to the esoteric group is thereby applied to all, and the *legō* stresses that the Lord himself has revealed these things; the speedy coming of the Lord is part of the gospel of Jesus Christ which goes to the whole world.[396]

In all this exposition Zmijewski prepares the way for an understanding of Luke's presentation of the discourse; in this respect we have to be satisfied with indicating the main lines of his interpretation of Luke's work. It is stressed that Luke, unlike Mark, does not make of the address a farewell discourse to the disciples, but a last public utterance in the temple, hence the conclusion of Jesus' instruction of the people (Luke 21:6). Luke's concern is quite different from Mark's. Luke is not obliged to counter contemporary apocalyptists, who stress the nearness of the end; rather, his desire is, as Conzelmann put it, "to interpret in a cogent manner the continuity of history which has resulted from the delay of the parousia." Consonant with this situation Luke stresses the mission of the church more than Mark does, for since the fall of Jerusalem the *kairoi* of the nations have come (v. 24), i.e., their opportunity for conversion. All that has taken place from the ministry of Jesus to Luke's own time is viewed in the light of the salvation history. Jerusalem played a crucial role in this, for there the salvation of the world was wrought, and so Jerusalem was the place of salvation; but there also the salvation wrought by the Christ was rejected, and so Jerusalem became also the place of judgment. The purpose of God in

---

[393] Ibid., 261–64.
[394] Ibid., 276–78.
[395] Ibid., 294–95.
[396] Ibid., 300.

history is realized in and through both aspects, and the gentile nations now take the place of the Jews as the new Israel.[397]

A comparison of Luke's address with Mark's has both negative and positive aspects. Luke 21 is not an apocalyptic address, any more than Mark's is; but neither is Luke's discourse an anti–apocalyptic address, which Mark designed his to be. Luke has taken over the three apocalyptic sections of Mark (vv. 7–8, 14–22, 24–27) and avoided, or at least reduced, their apocalyptic features. For example, Luke 21:8ff. warns not of apocalyptic deception, but of falling away from true discipleship to Christ through a false estimate of the *kairos*; vv. 20–24 omit the reference to the abomination of desolation, replace the *thlipsis* of Israel by the great *ananke* and wrath upon the people, omit the shortening of the days in God's mercy, and follow Jerusalem's judgment by the *kairoi* of the nations; in vv. 25–28 the emphasis falls not on the cosmic signs but on their effect on humankind, and the parousia is presented as the revelation of the exalted Son of man, whose exaltation *apo tou nyn* is wholly foreign to apocalyptic notions. Positively it is recognized that historical events, such as the destruction of Jerusalem, have the character of a certain nearness to the end; while the delay of the end is plain, the suddenness with which it can come is emphasized, and therefore the demand for constant orientation to it. This entails not a division between history and the eschaton, but the recognition that history is eschatologically determined, for it runs its course according to the divine plan of salvation.

It may be said that Mark and Luke have the same fundamental eschatological understanding. Both operate in the scheme of promise and fulfillment (Mark 13:23; Luke 21:22); both recognize the incalculability of the end (Mark 13:32; Luke 21:34–36); and both stress the demands of the present time prior to the end as testimony for Christ to the nations, and both emphasize "watchfulness," i.e., life in the light of the end. Luke, standing at a later date, develops Mark's insights in various ways. Mark interprets the present eschatologically, Luke extends this to the entire *Heilsgeschichte.* The parenetic concerns of Mark and Luke converge in their emphasis on watchfulness, but Luke does not have in view a defined situation like Mark; he rather provides directions for any conceivable situation (cf. *en panti kairō*, Luke 21:36). For Luke all situations are conditioned by two moments: the long duration of the time to the end and the suddenness of its coming. Hence the call to hold to true discipleship (v. 8), for endurance in the time that is lengthening out (v. 19b), and for watchfulness in prayer (v. 36a). Such emphases are significant for the church of all times.[398]

---

[397] Ibid., 313–18.
[398] Ibid., 319–25.

The value of Zmijewski's labors, so briefly described in these pages, will be immediately apparent. Their greatest contribution lies in the exhaustive redactional analysis and exegesis of the Markan and the Lukan texts, which Zmijewski provides. Whether he is right in adopting the view that Luke's sole source for his discourse was Mark 13 is not certain, strong though the case may be.[399] The conviction that a variety of sources, rather than one only, lie behind Mark's discourse is surely a pointer in the right direction. Yet Zmijewski presses Mark's opposition to fanatical apocalyptic teachers as though the evangelist rejected apocalyptic thought as such. This can be maintained only if one narrowly prescribes apocalyptic as connoting a system of calculating the end through premonitory signs, but that would be an unacceptable understanding of apocalyptic. Mark 13:24–27 is transparently apocalyptic, and there is no suggestion that Mark wished to modify its description of the parousia, still less to polemicize against it, but only to caution against the insistence on its immediacy (hence the insertion *meta tēn thlipsin ekeinēn*). The utterance of Jesus in Mark 14:62 forms the climax of Jesus' self-revelation in Mark, again an apocalyptic statement but with a difference, by which apocalyptic becomes a unique revelation in Jesus. Even the celebrated Mark 13:32 has at the heart of its rejection of apocalyptic calculations of the "day" or "hour" the apocalyptic understanding of history under the hand of God, moving toward its divinely appointed end.[400]

With respect to Zmijewski's interpretation of Luke we would make one observation only, apart from appreciation for his guidance generally in this sphere. He has felt it right to adopt Conzelmann's view, which has become a *sententia praecepta* in Lukan studies, that Luke rejected the near expectation of Mark and the primitive church, and wrote his Gospel on the assumption that the parousia was far off. Despite the popularity of this view it must be pronounced an exaggeration of Luke's interpretation of Jesus in his church.[401] In Conzelmann's case it is bound up with a serious misunderstanding of the eschatology of Jesus, which Zmijewski does not share. Luke has in no way modified Mark 13:30 in his version of the discourse, nor is his slight editing of Mark 9:1 of great significance. Zmijewski acknowledges that Luke 21:32 must be recognized as extending beyond the destruction of the temple

---

[399]See the summary statement of current opinion in I. H. Marshall, *The Gospel of Luke*, NIGTC (Grand Rapids, 1978), 754–57.

[400]On this point see the spirited remarks of A. Strobel, *Kerygma und Apokalyptik, ein religionsgeschichtlicher und theologischer Beitrag zur Christusfrage* (Göttingen, 1967), 85–87.

[401]A. J. Mattil has a lengthy consideration of this issue in *Luke and the Last Things: A Perspective for the Understanding of Lukan Thought* (Dillsboro, N.C., 1979), chs. 4–6.

to the end itself. On the assumption that Luke writes later than Mark, what does that signify for Luke's expectation of the time of the end? How can it be reconciled with the idea of a far-off parousia? Is there any passage in the Gospels which expresses a near expectation more vividly than Luke 12:35–36? "Let your loins be girded and your lamps burning, and be like men who are waiting for their master to come home from the marriage feast." It suggests that Luke's inclusion of the parable of the Burglar, which immediately follows the parable of 12:35ff., must connote not only the suddenness of the parousia but its possible nearness also (Luke 12:39–40).

The same passage continues with another parable, setting forth the danger of saying, "My lord delays his coming" (Luke 12:45–46). In Luke's version of the eschatological discourse no hint is contained in v. 24 that the *kairoi* of the nations are to last for a lengthy period. Did Luke not know, or did he reject the notion, that in the apocalyptic tradition, including that of the Bible (Daniel), the *kairoi* in which the nations exercise oppressive power over Israel are always viewed as lasting for a short time? Dan 7:25; 8:13; 12:6–7 must have continued to impress not only Jews but Christians also, as the use of the symbol in the book of Revelation (including the curious *kairos kairoi kai hēmisy kairou*, Rev 12:14) shows. It is an extraordinary fact that the Danielic "time, times, and half a time," i.e., three and a half years, corresponds with a usage which apparently established itself among the Jews, whereby three and a half became a mode of expression for a limited number; it represented a half of seven, in a similar manner as we speak of half a dozen. Luke himself reflects this usage in no less a passage than his summary of Jesus' sermon in Nazareth, wherein the period of Elijah's drought is said to have lasted for three and a half years (Luke 4:25), a tradition which is repeated in Jas 5:17, although the Hebrew text appears to indicate three years.[402] We have no desire to press this issue and to insist that Luke viewed the *kairoi* of the nations as lasting a short time, but the context of thought hardly favors the opposed view, that he must have viewed the *kairoi* as lasting a long time. Nor do we call into question or minimize Luke's concept of *Heilsgeschichte*. Zmijewski is surely right in emphasizing its importance to Luke and the significance of its embracing past, present, and future. But Luke should be interpreted by Luke; this concept must not be allowed to set aside his own indications of a persisting near expectation. Our own developments of the implications of his theological insights should be distin-

---

[402]The Jews assumed on the basis of the mention of the "third year" in 1 Kgs 18:1 (cf. 1 Kgs 17:1) that the famine lasted "three years" (so Seder Olam Rab. 17), or at least part of the first year, the whole of the second, and part of the third. For examples of the "round" figure (!) three and a half, see Str-B, 3:760–61; and the discussion by Dibelius, *Der Brief des Jakobus* (Göttingen, 1964), 237.

guished from those of Luke himself, the bounds of whose horizons were assuredly no more distant than those of his contemporaries.

These remarks, however, are caveats entered on a notable contribution to the eschatological discourses of Luke and Mark, of which future scholars will doubtless make full use.

R. Geiger

A reversal in the trend to lengthy works on the eschatological discourse is seen in that of R. Geiger.[403] In much shorter compass than that of Zmijewski he provides an elucidation of the two Lukan eschatological discourses, Luke 17:20–37 and 21:5–36. While Zmijewski's volume appeared a year earlier than Geiger's, the latter must have been written prior to the appearance of the former, since there is no reference to Zmijewski's findings in Geiger's discussions and exegesis of the Lukan material. Like Zmijewski, however, Geiger sets the discourse of Luke 21 in the light of Mark 13; he first considers the origin and nature of the Markan discourse and then discusses each Markan pericope and expounds the Lukan parallel in comparison with it.

For a reason not altogether apparent, Geiger selects Bultmann's delimitation of the little apocalypse in Mark 13 as definitive. He rightly declares Marxsen's study of the chapter to be the first thoroughgoing application of redaction criticism to the discourse and summarizes Marxsen's findings for the reader. He then describes at length the interpretation of Mark 13 given by Pesch in his monograph. In both his general understanding of the Markan discourse and in his exegesis of its content, Geiger is heavily indebted to Pesch. The value of his work lies primarily in its assessment of the Lukan eschatology, which, of course, is precisely in accord with Geiger's intention.

F. Keck

Yet a third work to appear within a comparatively short time on Luke's version of the eschatological discourse was presented by F. Keck. His contribution owes much to his concentration on the linguistic, stylistic, and structural features of the discourse and his constant relating its content to the Acts of the Apostles.

The first characteristic of Luke's account to which Keck draws attention is indicated in the title of his work: "The Public Farewell Discourse of Jesus in Luke 20:45—21:36." "Farewell Discourse" is its *Gattung;* it is delivered in public to the disciples of Jesus (not privately

---

[403]Geiger, *Die Lukanische Endzeitreden: Studien zur Eschatologie des Lukas-Evangeliums,* Europäische Hochschulschriften, Reihe XXIII, Theologie 16 (Bern-Frankfurt a.M., 1973).

to a selected few); and it commences at Luke 20:45, not 21:5 as is usually assumed. This is justified on the basis of the two summaries in 19:47–48 and 21:37–38; these bind together the public teaching of Jesus in the temple as a continuing activity; the first part is delivered mainly to the Jewish leaders in the presence of the people (19:47—29:44), the second to the disciples, also in the presence of the people (20:45—21:36); hence, in contrast to Mark, Jesus is depicted as giving this instruction within the temple, not overlooking it on the Mount of Olives.[404]

Throughout his work Keck examines the Lukan style and terminology of each passage, and concludes that Luke had no source other than Mark for the discourse; the differences from Mark are all due to Luke's redaction. The major contribution of Luke's version of the discourse is believed to be in the section vv. 10–28, wherein vv. 10b–11 and 25–28 are viewed as forming an inclusion. In this passage Luke consciously employs the Deuteronomic understanding of history, which was maintained as a living tradition in the literature of late Judaism. In the tradition, stress was laid on Israel's constant disobedience to God, its continual rejection of the ministry of the prophets, and the consequent judgment of God on Jerusalem and the nation. It is observed that the tribulations of Israel in the period of Antiochus Epiphanes and in the Roman war, climaxing in the catastrophe of AD 70, were integrated by later apocalyptic writers with the overthrow of Jerusalem and the deportation of the people in 587 BC; the later events were understood *as* the earlier judgment.[405] That led Luke to interpret the destruction of Jerusalem in AD 70 as the day of the Lord on the city and people, and therefore as the judgment of God on Israel, as is clearly stated in vv. 20–24 ("These are days of *vengeance,* a fulfillment of all that is written. . . . There will be great distress on the earth and *wrath* against this people"). It is emphasized, however, that Luke, for whom the destruction of Jerusalem lay in the past, did not regard this as an eschatological act of God, nor did he set it in immediate relation to the eschaton. Just as the catastrophe of 587 BC was seen by at least some of the prophets as the day of the Lord on Israel (e.g., Lam 1:12; 2:1, 21, 22; Ezek 13:5; 34:12), so Luke viewed that of AD 70, and that underscored its nature as divine judgment on Israel for its rejection of the gospel of Christ.[406] The significance of the "times of the Gentiles" in 20:24 is not in anticipation of Israel's conversion (cf. Rom. 11:25–26), nor primarily as the time of the gentile mission, but simply the times of the rule of the Gentiles

---

[404]Keck, *Die öffentliche Abschiedsrede Jesu in Lk 20,45–21,36. Eine redaktions-und motivgeschichtliche Untersuchung,* FB 25 (Stuttgart, 1976), 18–25, 317–18.

[405]Ibid., 190–91.

[406]See especially pp. 21–24.

over Israel. Self-evidently these "times" have a limit appointed by God. Their length, however, is not hinted at; they represent the last epoch before the end-time judgment, which is determined solely by God.[407]

It is instructive to observe that Luke follows Mark again in portraying the coming of the end-time "judgment" (i.e., the parousia) in terms of the day of the Lord. This time it is viewed as strictly eschatological— the event of universal judgment and the precursor of the kingdom of God. Luke's adoption and extension of this interpretation are in complete harmony with the apocalyptic writings of the OT and of late Judaism.[408] Again, his concern in this application of the day of the Lord imagery is due to his desire to emphasize the reality of judgment, both on the impenitent of Israel and the impenitent of the other nations.

In Keck's estimate Luke wrote at a time when Judaism had rejected the gospel, and the break between the synagogue and the church had long since taken place. He desired therefore to strengthen the church's self-consciousness and identity as the true Israel, standing in the continuity of the salvation history and destined to inherit the salvation of the kingdom of God. The destruction of Jerusalem, it is to be noted, is not the result of killing Jesus, but punishment for the rejection of the gospel proclaimed by the church's preachers. The logical consequence of all this is that no hope is entertained for the conversion of Israel or of its entrance into the kingdom of God.[409]

The discourse ends with parenesis (21:34–36), which clearly echoes Isa 24:17 but is still more closely connected with the early Christian catechesis. Its purpose is that Christians may "escape" from the final judgment (i.e., secure in it the divine approval) and "stand" before the Son of man (i.e., share in his fellowship in the kingdom of God), for such alone may inherit the saving sovereignty.[410]

Keck's work is a masterly handling of the problems of the Lukan discourse; this brief summary gives little indication of the wealth of linguistic and exegetical labor that has gone into its production. While it does not provide a consistent review of the parallel teaching in the Markan discourse, as Zmijewski has done, much of the exposition of the Lukan version is relevant to Mark 13, not least the twofold application of the day of the Lord concept to the destruction of Jerusalem and the parousia of the Lord and the distinction between them, based on Luke's use of the Deuteronomic interpretation of Israel's history.

Of one conclusion I am not persuaded. Keck's frequent attention to Luke's emphasis on Israel's rejection of the gospel and its consequent judgment leads him to affirm that Luke thereby wished to show that

---

[407]Ibid., 224–25, 228.
[408]Ibid., 231–32.
[409]Ibid., 251–59.
[410]Ibid., 297–316.

Israel had forever forfeited its relation to God as his covenant people. Is it really so that the recognition that the destruction of Jerusalem constitutes the day of the Lord on Israel "logically" means that God has cancelled his covenant with the nation and withdrawn the promise of their part in the kingdom of God? That is no part of the Deuteronomic view of Israel's history; the possibility of the nation's restoration is implied in the demand for repentance. And if the apocalyptic development of this view led to a division of the nation between its repentant and impenitent members (the former only being heirs of the kingdom), it is still Israelites who are expected to repent. Paul found it impossible to believe that when the "fullness of the Gentiles" came to God, the only nation that would miss the kingdom would be Israel; on the contrary he affirmed that Israel's repentance would mean "life from the dead" for the nations. Was Luke less hopeful than Paul? The concern for the Jewish people, expressed in "beginning at Jerusalem" (Acts 1:18) and the success of the mission to Israel, alluded to in Acts 21:20 ("You see how many *tens of thousands* of believers there are among the Jews, all zealous for the law"), could lead to a more positive answer.

D. Wenham

David Wenham has pursued an intensive study of the eschatological discourse over many years. His first contribution to the subject consisted of two articles in which the major monographs on Mark 13 were reviewed.[411] A subsequent discussion on Paul and the Synoptic apocalypse investigated parallels between the forms of the eschatological discourse in the Synoptic Gospels and the eschatological teaching in 1 and 2 Thessalonians.[412] In this Wenham maintained that Paul knew a form of the eschatological discourse that included the parable of the Thief, and that Paul's links with the Synoptics included all three Gospels and all the main Gospel traditions (Mark, Q, M, and L).

In an article on Mark 13:30 and its relation to the discourse, Wenham concurred with recent opinion that Mark 13:5–23 is a single section, describing "normal" aspects of the whole period, whereas vv. 14ff. have in view the disaster of the desolating sacrilege, with its evident reference to calamity upon Jerusalem, followed by unparalleled tribulation in the world (vv. 19–20) and finally by the parousia (vv. 24–27).[413] The Fig Tree parable and the logion of v. 30 relate to every-

---

[411]Wenham, "Recent Study of Mark 13," *TSF Bulletin* 71 (Spring 1975): 6–15; 72 (Summer 1975): 1–9.

[412]Idem, "Paul and the Synoptic Apocalypse," in *Gospel Perspectives: Studies of History and Tradition in the Four Gospels*, ed. R. T. France and D. Wenham (Sheffield, 1981), 2:345–75.

[413]Idem, " 'This Generation will not Pass . . .' A Study of Jesus' Future Expectation in Mark 13," in *Christ the Lord*, Festschrift D. Guthrie, ed. H. Row-

thing in vv. 5–23, whereas v. 32 refers to the time of the parousia, which is unknown.

Wenham's earlier labors on the discourse culminated in a volume which, by its painstaking attention to detail of the text, reminds one of the thoroughness of Lambrecht's study. This investigation sought to demonstrate that there existed an elaborate pre-Synoptic form of the eschatological discourse, known to and independently used by Matthew, Mark, and Luke. "Matthew appears as the evangelist who most often and most fully reproduces the pre-synoptic form of the tradition, Mark abbreviates it substantially, Luke is the most free, so far as order is concerned."[414] Wenham's method is to work from the end of the discourse, in which he believes that this thesis is most plainly discernible, and to consider the sections of the discourse seriatim back to the beginning. As an example of this work we shall look at Wenham's treatment of the conclusion of Mark's version of the discourse, Mark 13:33–37.

Verse 33 ("Watch, keep awake . . .") is parallel to Matt 25:13, set at the end of the parable of the Virgins. In reality Matt 25:13 is more suitable to conclude the parable of the Watchman (Mark 13:34–36 = Luke 12:36–38), and so it is postulated that in the early tradition it did stand there. Luke 12:35 forms an admirable conclusion to the parable of the Virgins; it is considered that originally it stood there. Mark 13:34–36 has a close parallel to the parable of the Watchman in Luke 12:36–38; but Mark's opening sentence echoes Matt 25:14, the beginning of the parable of the Talents; it would appear then that Mark took over that sentence and ignored the rest of the parable. Mark 13:37 forms an excellent answer to Peter's question in Luke 12:41, which introduces the parable of the Faithful Steward (Luke 12:42–44); it is therefore proposed that in the source Mark 13:37 was that answer. Mark 13:33–37 accordingly consists largely of applications of parables which, apart from the Watchman, Mark does not reproduce. It is clear, however, that his text draws upon a great deal of eschatological material. This material, it is urged, points to the existence of a pre-Synoptic tradition which formed the conclusion of an eschatological discourse, and that in the following order: the parable of the Virgins (Matt 25:1–12), "gird up loins, keep lamps burning" (Luke 12:35), the parable of the Watchman (Mark 13:34–35 = Luke 12:36–38), "Keep awake . . ." (Matt 24:42), the parable of the Thief (Matt 24:43), "So be ready" (Matt 24:44), "Do you say this to us . . . ?" (Luke 12:41), "To all I say, Keep awake" (Mark 13:37), the parable of the Steward (Luke 12:42–44), "Keep awake . . ."

---

don (London, 1982), 127–50.

[414]Idem, *The Rediscovery of Jesus' Eschatological Discourse,* Gospel Perspectives 4 (Sheffield, 1984), 365.

(Matt 25:13), the parable of the Talents (Matt 25:14–30), the parable of the Disobedient Servants (Luke 12:45–46).

Matthew's continuation of the discourse at the point where Mark ceases begins with a comparison of Noah's flood with the parousia (Matt 24:37–39), which appears in Luke 17:26–27. That leads Wenham to believe that Luke 17:22–37 is an extract from the pre-Synoptic eschatological discourse. This is supported by the overlap between Luke 12:34–36 and 17:26–37, as also between Luke 17:20–23 and Mark 13:19–22. Matthew has rightly kept the material together in his ch. 24, but Luke used some of it in ch. 17 to illustrate the theme of the unpredictability of the coming of the kingdom, stated in Luke 17:20–21.

As to the desolating sacrilege, Mark 13:14–20 par., Wenham considers that we are not to choose between the Lukan redaction of what is in Matthew/Mark and the independence of Luke's tradition but to recognize both as true: Luke has adapted that which is in Matthew/Mark in the light of another tradition. Originally it ran, "When you see Jerusalem surrounded by armies, and the desolating sacrilege that was spoken of by Daniel the prophet standing in the holy place . . . then let those in Judea flee . . . Jerusalem will be trodden down by Gentiles until the times of the Gentiles are fulfilled." The tribulation described in Mark 13:19–20 is believed to refer to tribulations that affect all humanity ("all flesh"), not Israel alone. The obscurity of Matthew/Mark could be due to the sensitivity of the subject in their particular historical situations.

In the warnings of persecution (Mark 13:9ff. par.) agreements of Matthew and Luke against Mark are believed to indicate a common non-Markan tradition, best preserved in Matthew (10:17–23), and originally belonging to a mission discourse. Matt 10:17–19 and 23 link on with v. 5; the Lukan account of the sending of the Seventy provides an excellent context for these sayings. The Seventy are sent to every place to which Jesus was about to "come"; accordingly the logion in Matt 10:23, "You will not have gone through the towns of Israel before the Son of man comes," relates to that "coming" of Jesus (though it is admitted that it could refer to the fall of Jerusalem). Mark 13:9–11 accordingly is not rightly situated in an eschatological discourse, though Mark 13:12–13 certainly reflects an eschatological-apocalyptic context.

The pre-Synoptic tradition will have contained the introduction in Mark 13:1–4 par. The conclusion of the discourse is likely to have been the parable of the Sheep and the Goats (Matt 25:31–46), preceded by Matt 19:28.

Wenham concludes by pointing out that this investigation entails placing a question mark against the received view that the discourses of the Gospels are compilations of separate traditions that came together over a long period of time; on the contrary, the Gospels indicate a process of extracting materials from more elaborate pre-Synoptic forms. The existence of such a pre-Synoptic tradition points to something like an Ur-Gospel. It is admitted, however, that these findings do not prove the authenticity of the traditions in the eschatological discourse, for they could have been put together by the church; but they do suggest that the onus of proof must be on those who deny the teaching to Jesus, not on those who affirm it.

Wenham's basic conclusion is not impossible, however unlikely it may appear at first sight. It would mean that the process of editing the gospel traditions goes back a good deal further in the past than the time of the evangelists. The moot question is whether the evidence justifies the conclusions adopted. It should not be overlooked that on Wenham's hypothesis the reconstruction of the pre-Synoptic tradition would apply to other discourses than Mark 13, notably to the Sermon on the Mount, the mission discourse of Matthew 10, the parables discourse of Matthew 13. These must all be viewed not as Matthean constructions but as redacted pre-Matthean discourses.

We saw how Wenham explained the construction of Mark 13:33–37. Without doubt Mark 13:33 is parallel to Matt 25:13; it is precarious, however, to argue that the parable plus the logion were in a pre-Synoptic discourse known to Mark, that he took this sentence from it, then adopted the first two clauses from the Talents parable, which stood later in the discourse, conjoined with them the parable of the Watchman, which stood earlier in the discourse, and finished his form of the discourse with the answer to Peter's question, now found in Luke 12:41, which *ex hypothesi* introduced the parable of the Faithful Steward. It is altogether more likely that Matt 25:13, as Mark 13:33, is an *Einzelwort*, one of the many isolated sayings found in the Gospel traditions, and that Matthew deemed it suitable to round off the parable of the Virgins, whereas Mark used it to introduce his parenetic conclusion to the discourse. Similarly, it is probable that the parable of the Watchman, better preserved in Luke 12:36–38 than in Mark 13:34–36, gained features from the parable of the Talents in the oral stage of tradition, rather than that Mark took a couple of short clauses from that parable and thereby complicated the parable he was narrating. If Mark was acquainted with all that stands now in Matthew 24–25, why did he omit the gems of eschatological material like the parable of the Thief, the comparisons of Noah and Lot with the parousia, and the like, which are all short, easily assimilable, and wholly in line with his aims in the discourse?

Even more difficult than this is the postulate that the pre-Synoptic discourse included the Q apocalypse, Luke 17:22–37, and Luke 12:35–48, a belief that led Wenham to describe the former passage as "an extract from the eschatological discourse." Luke's motivation to transfer this "extract" is suggested to be its suitability to follow Luke 17:21, understood as affirming the suddenness of the coming of the kingdom of God. Certainly it is suitable. But most contemporary scholars see in Luke 17:21 an affirmation of the presence of the kingdom, in line with other related sayings of Luke.[415] Luke's motivation for setting his two eschatological passages in chs. 12 and 17 is very similar. Both groups of sayings are predominantly from Q, and both follow a striking saying on the kingdom of God. In 12:28 Jesus issues a call to "seek his kingdom," to rejoice that God has given the kingdom to his little flock, and so to lay up treasure in heaven (12:22–34). Thereupon Luke relates the eschatological teaching of 12:35–48. Similarly, in 17:20–21 he cites Jesus' rejection of typical Jewish preoccupation with calculating the date of the kingdom's coming and his striking utterance, "The kingdom of God is within your grasp!" implying, "Receive the word of the kingdom, and open life to it now!" Then follows the Q apocalypse. Luke used the Q source throughout his Gospel; it is completely comprehensible that he should set its conclusion at this point, and reserve the other eschatological discourse for the context where Mark and Matthew placed it—immediately prior to the passion of Jesus.

Wenham's treatment of the passages relating to the "desolating sacrilege" (Mark 13:14–20 par.) is unusually interesting, not least in his relating the Synoptic material to Daniel and Revelation. The suggestion, however, that Mark 13:19–20 par. describe a worldwide tribulation, distinct from Israel's calamities, and leading to the parousia, is questionable. The reference to "all flesh" in Mark 13:20 is strictly in relation to Israel's tribulation, just as the *anankē* ("calamity") in the parallel passage, Luke 21:23, concerns the Jews and their land, and Luke 21:24 describes the putting of the Jews to the sword and treading down of Jerusalem. It is unjustifiable to evade the clear reference of Mark 13:14–20 to Israel's doom on the ground of the expansion and application of the discourse in the book of Revelation; that author's concern is no longer Jerusalem, but the Roman Empire and the world of nations.

Despite the negative tone of this assessment of Wenham's thesis I would acknowledge in strongest terms the value of a great deal of his exposition of the discourse and its related material in Q and elsewhere. The book is described in its blurb as a "painstaking analysis," and so it is of everything that comes under scrutiny. Wenham has an independent mind, and his investigation is consistently patient and thorough; no one can read it without profit. In my judgment he has carried to excess an idea which warrants serious consideration, namely, that elements of the Synoptic discourses on the doom of Jerusalem, the trials of the church, and the end of the age circulated and gravitated together in the pre-Synoptic tradition from a quite early date. Paul's use of such

---

[415]See the discussion of this issue in my *Jesus and the Kingdom of God* (Grand Rapids, 1986), 97–102.

eschatological traditions in the Thessalonian correspondence supports that view. The extension of this highly probable thesis, however, to the hypothesis of a discourse in the early tradition consisting of everything in Mark 13; Luke 12:35–48; 17:22–37; 21:5–36; and Matthew 24–25 appears to exceed the evidence.

E. Brandenburger

Brandenburger, in his work on Mark 13, has given a highly concentrated study of considerable significance. The volume distinguishes itself from many earlier studies by its emphasis on the apocalyptic nature of the discourse as a whole. "Mark 13 can, indeed, must, be called through and through an apocalypse."[416] The author insists that marks of the apocalyptic *Gattung* and pattern of thought are observable throughout and determine the whole.

The chapter is viewed as consisting of two scenes, vv. 1–2 and 3–37. Verses 1–2 are an apophthegm, with its high point in the prophecy; vv. 3–37 are an apocalypse. An apocalyptic "school question" is asked in vv. 3–4 and an answer is given in the form of a revelation of end-time mysteries in vv. 5–37. Otherwise expressed, the apocalypse is framed as a "school discourse" in response to a "school question." In context we have a little apocalypse in the form of a testamentary school discourse.[417]

The discourse itself is in two parts: (1) vv. 5–27, (2) vv. 28–36. The first answers the question as to the "when" of the temple destruction and the "what" of signs; the answer is an apocalyptic description of the final events from beginning to end. The end is in three stages: the beginning of woes, vv. 7–8; the high point of final distress, vv. 14–20; the decisive turning, vv. 24–27. The whole is a unity, linked together by time signals. Into these three parenetic pieces are inserted: vv. 5b–6, 9–13, 21–23, all indicated by *blepete*. They do not determine the structure but are important elements within the apocalyptic structure. Contrary to popular view, they do not overcome or remove the apocalyptic structure. Verses 28–36 give another answer to v. 4, but in another form and from another perspective. The theme has changed. Verses 28–32 reflect on the temporal relation of future signs and the salvation turning point and the time of the turning point itself.

It is well to state Brandenburger's view of the source and Mark's redaction. Verses 7–8, 14–20, 24–27 constitute the source; vv. 1b–2, 9b–13, 21 (22) are traditional materials used by Mark; vv. 28–32 are traditional logia material; vv. 33–36 are from primitive Christian parenesis; vv. 1a, 3–6, 9a, 23, 33 (in part), 35a, 37 are Markan redaction.[418]

---

[416]Brandenburger, *Markus 13 und die Apokalyptik*, FRLANT 134 (Göttingen, 1984), 13.
[417]Ibid., 15.
[418]Ibid., 41.

The time and the place of the source are considered to be the time when Jerusalem is threatened in the Roman war. The standing ground of the author of the source is fear of the war, and so prior to vv. 14–20. The present is the beginning of woes which must happen; one is in the end time. And present troubles are not the worst—the events of vv. 14–20 lie ahead. The source therefore is not to be divided too schematically into past, present, and future. Remembrance of the events of AD 40 are present in writing v. 14, but the determining orientation to Daniel is also clear. A desecration of the temple by the Roman Caesar as tyrant of the end time is meant and leads on to the distress of the end. A personal antichrist is not present in the source, nor in Mark's mind.[419]

Brandenburger affirms that vv. 24–27 cannot be explained by Daniel 7, 1 Enoch 62, or 4 Ezra 13. Characteristic for the unity of the text is the *Gattung* of theophany. A dependence of vv. 24–27 on a text complex is not provable; it is simply a knowledge of the structural meaning of the theophany concept. Verses 24–25 depict the decisive signs that show the immediately impending coming of the Son of man. Since the theophany concept usually presupposes the accomplishment of salvation, salvation primacy is to be seen in v. 26, but also other motives; "seeing" is a first preliminary act in the course of annihilating judgment. But v. 27 is a salvation utterance (cf. Matt 24:30).[420]

The source is from a Christian group with strong Jewish traditions—the Jerusalem church. The Son of man concept in this form cannot be proved in Jewish texts. The development of the Son of man view, with its concept of eschatological theophany, is a primitive Christian characteristic. Not even the Similitudes of Enoch know of a coming of the Son of man.

As to the function and meaning of v. 23: both utterances are elements of the *Gattung* of "Testament." The prophecies relate to present problems—the situation at the time of the historical writer (i.e., not of the source). It appears that the "now" of vv. 7–8, 14–20 is past history; the insertions of vv. 5b–6, 9–13, 21–22 are of present events. So the future can now be told—vv. 24–27. Verse 23 shows that vv. 5b–22 are a *vaticinium ex eventu*. Mark himself is now standing in the present, and the end of history is now taking place. The temple destruction has just happened. The *bdelygma*, with its masculine and neuter expressions, will have been interpreted of Titus. Luke's localizing of the prophecy in Jerusalem was none other than Mark's! That Mark did not have the antichrist figure in view is seen in his addition of vv. 21–22 after vv. 14–20.[421]

---

[419]Ibid., 46–51.
[420]Ibid., 61–63.
[421]Ibid., 83–85.

Prevailing exegesis sees warnings in vv. 5–6 and 21–22 as having a dominant theme of guarding against apocalyptic extremists. Brandenburger urges that this overlooks the *Gattung* "school discourse," and the *Gattung* elements of v. 4. The alternative "eschatological parenesis" and "apocalyptic instruction" is fundamentally false. Parenesis is a firm constituent of apocalyptic theology. A comparable critical concern to rescue addressees from false ideas may be seen in apocalyptic literature, e.g., 4 Ezra 4:33–37—even the whole book! There is no basis for the idea that the situation of 2 Thess 2:2 is in view in vv. 5–6, 21–22. In v. 30 Mark himself affirms the nearness of the end. Mark 13 has to do with school discourse, not controversial discourse (*Schulgespräch*, not *Streitgespräch*).

The double question of vv. 3–4 is occasioned by the special problem which Mark here introduces. The first question is clear: when is the temple to be destroyed? The second shows the real intention of the first. In the horizon of the problem the first question of v. 4 is at the same time the question of the temple destruction as a sign of the end. The question is formulated in the light of the Markan exposition—not a continuation of vv. 1–2 but the opening of the apocalyptic school discourse. The church stands at the same point of time as Mark—after the temple's destruction—and needs to know wherein the decisive sign for the final salvation consists. Since vv. 14–20 lie in the past and vv. 21–22 do not give a clear sign, the answer to the question as to the decisive sign is in vv. 24–27.[422]

Mark's special conception of apocalyptic signs is his concentration on one decisive sign, viz., its identification with cosmic accompanying appearances which announce beforehand the theophany on earth. Hence there are two stages in the theophanic manifestations: (1) cosmic manifestations beforehand—the preparing of the manifestation of God or the Son of man; (2) the coming itself. This interpretation of Mark frees the hope from forecasts of historical-cosmic tribulation of this world time; it is a fundamentally critical way of thinking, won under actual circumstances, and releases Christian hope from Daniel's pattern of thought.

In harmony with this the sign referred to in the parable of vv. 28–29 is the cosmic manifestations of vv. 24–25. The parable is not from Jesus. Verses 28a–29 are Markan redaction, and v. 28b could not be handed on in tradition alone. Accordingly Hahn's view that the parable is the germ cell for the address is to be rejected as false.[423]

Brandenburger has certainly given the reader cause for reflection. His insistence on acknowledging the entire discourse as an apocalypse

---

[422]Ibid., 95–100.
[423]Ibid., 119 n. 240.

should be compared with C. C. Torrey's spirited rejection of this claim.[424] Granting that the employment of the Danielic "abomination of desolation" figure and the parousia of the Son of man are apocalyptic representations, we should nevertheless observe that these are combined with traditional prophetic expectations of the end—there is nothing more "prophetic" than the concept of theophany!—along with typical Christian parenesis relating to the church's witness in the world. The discourse contains both prophetic and apocalyptic eschatology.

Separating vv. 3–37 from 1–2 and viewing the former as a "school discourse" answering a "school question" are plausible, but require examination. There have been and are multitudes of ordinary people who have never heard of an apocalypse but who have asked the question "When" of the judgment and deliverance of God (cf. "How long, O Lord?"), and virtually as many who have little acquaintance of the Bible and none of apocalyptic literature but who ask, "How shall we know?" These questions are natural for Jews and Christians who believe in God and hope. (I've heard them ask them!) More importantly, the point of departure of the discourse is the prophecy of v. 2. Typically Brandenburger denies its dominical origin and apparently views it as a *vaticinium ex eventu*.[425] But we will not argue the point just now. The disciples' question in v. 4 appears to assume that the destruction of the temple can be envisaged only as an eschatological event. Mark himself will have known that; indeed, he probably formulated the question in its present form—in order to deny the axiom! The discourse takes its shape from his desire to show that the tribulation of Israel is not the end, nor an integral element of it, as the disciples apparently supposed; on the contrary it was false prophets who in his time were maintaining that, and Mark sought to correct the error. To deny Mark's purpose in putting a brake on apocalyptic enthusiasts by appeal to the *Gattung* "school discourse" can have a reverse effect, i.e., in diminishing its plausibility. The warning in v. 6 against claimants to be the Messiah naturally includes the notion that the end is near—as Luke interprets with his addition, "and the time has drawn near!" (Luke 21:8). Contrary to Brandenburger, the connection of thought between Mark 13:6–7 and 2 Thess 2:2 is highly illuminating, especially in the light of the presence of the unusual verb *mē throeisthe* in both passages.

Brandenburger attributes the integrating link between the destruction of Jerusalem and the end of the age to the source, i.e., vv. 7–8, 14–20, 24–27. We have given reasons for doubting that that source ever existed, not least through observing that the equivalent saying to vv. 15–16, namely, Luke 17:31, is much more plausibly explained as being

---

[424]See above, pp. 148–51.
[425]Brandenburger, *Markus 13*, 75 n. 153.

from Q than a borrowing from Mark,[426] which makes the idea that Mark 13:15–16 originated in a Jewish-Christian apocalypse difficult. Similarly the notion that vv. 24–27 are essentially bound up with vv. 14–20 is set in question by the connection of thought between vv. 24–27 and v. 21, as Luke 17:23–24 illustrate.[427] On these and other grounds the "little apocalypse" source disintegrates.

Perhaps the most significant contribution made by Brandenburger in his work on Mark 13 is his recognition of the theophany concept in vv. 24–27, and that its application to the parousia of the Son of man is uniquely Christian. These two features of primitive Christian eschatology I have long maintained, and it is good to have the support of so expert a writer in the field of apocalyptic. In one major respect, however, I beg leave to question Brandenburger's interpretation of the concept in vv. 24–27. He regards the cosmic manifestations in vv. 24–25 as the real sign of the end, for which the disciples asked in v. 4, and that Mark has divorced the parousia from all earthly signs and concentrated attention on the theophanic manifestations which prepare for the supreme manifestation of the Son of man at his coming. Now this appears to me a misunderstanding of the fundamental notion of theophany in the OT, as indeed in the ancient religions of the Middle East which shared the concept. Consistently in representations of the coming of God, the quaking of earth, moving or shaking of mountains, waters in heaven and earth pouring out in terror, sun and moon failing to shine, and stars falling from their places are all expressions of the fear and confusion caused by the appearance of the mighty (storm) God. Observe: they are *consequences* of the stepping forth of God into his creation, not *precedents* of his appearing. If they are represented as *accompaniments* of his coming they are understood as manifestations of his presence.[428]

The fundamental pattern of theophany is seen with all clarity in Judg 5:4–5:

---

[426] So T. W. Manson, *Sayings of Jesus*, 144; L. Gaston, *No Stone on Another*, 25; Kümmel, *Promise and Fulfillment*, 101; J. Lambrecht, *Redaktion*, 157–58; I. H. Marshall, *Luke*, 664–65; A. Polag, *Die Christologie der Logienquelle* (Neukirchen-Vluyn, 1977), 99–100; Beasley-Murray, *Jesus and the Kingdom of God*, 318–19. H. Schürmann assigns it to L or Q (*Traditionsgeschichtliche Untersuchungen zu den synoptischen Evangelien*, 280–81); J. A. Fitzmyer to L (*Luke*, AB 2:1165), L. Hartman simply to a non-Markan source (*Prophecy Interpreted*, 162). J. Zmijewski is uncertain whether the saying comes from Mark or Q or a source common to Mark and Q (*Eschatologiereden*, 474–78).

[427] See the commentary below on Mark 13:24–27.

[428] For a thorough exposition of the concept of theophany in the OT and the religions of Israel's neighbors see Jörg Jeremias, *Theophanie: Die Geschichte einer alttestamentliche Gattung* (Neukirchen-Vluyn, 1965).

O Lord, when you set forth from Seir,
when you came marching out of the plains of Edom,
earth trembled, heaven quaked,
the clouds streamed down in torrents.
Mountains shook in fear before the Lord, the Lord of Sinai,
Before the Lord God of Israel.

This same pattern is observable elsewhere in the OT and in later Jewish literature, e.g., Ps 18:3–19; 77:16–18; Amos 1:2; Mic 1:3–4; Nah 1:2–6; Hab 3:3–13; Sir 16:18–19. The first century AD Assumption of Moses, 10:3, gives a particularly clear picture of contemporary apocalyptic representation of a theophany:

The Heavenly One will arise from his kingly throne . . .
And the earth will tremble, even to its ends shall it be shaken.
And the high mountains will be made low. . . .
The sun will not give its light,
and in darkness the horns of the moon will flee.
Yea, they will be broken in pieces.
It will be turned wholly into blood,
Yea, even the circle of the stars will be thrown into disarray.
And the sea all the way to the abyss will retire . . .
Yea, the rivers will vanish away.
For God Most High will surge forth, the Eternal One alone.
In full view he will come to work vengeance on the nations.

Similarly clear representations of theophany in relation to the coming of the Lord will be found in 1 Enoch 1:4–7; T Levi 3:9; 4 Ezra 3:17–19; 1QH 3:34–36; Rev 6:12–14; 20:11. It is to be noted that the references to thunders, voices, lightnings, and earthquakes at the end of the three descriptions of the messianic judgments in Rev 8:5; 11:19; 16:18 are all veiled allusions to the parousia then taking place, as the cry "It is done" in 16:17 and the fleeing of the mountains and islands in 16:20 show.[429]

Matthew, after repeating Mark 13:24–25 almost verbatim, adds, "And then the sign of the Son of man will appear in heaven." The most likely explanation of the sign of the Son of man is that it represents the shekinah glory with which he appears. Luke's interpretation does not fundamentally differ from that of Mark and Matthew. He anticipates the heavenly portents in 21:11, but their real place is in vv. 25–26; the terror of humankind at the events in the heavens and on the earth is integral to descriptions of theophany and harmonious with the fundamental meaning of theophany: the universe goes into terror before the coming of the Lord.

---

[429]See my commentary *Revelation*, NCB (Grand Rapids, 1974), 30–31, 150–51, 188–91, 246–47.

The upshot of this discussion is that Mark 13:24–26 depicts the coming of the Son of man in terms of a revelation of the divine glory. The cosmic signs are an ancient delineation of the overwhelming and overpowering manifestation of the divine being who steps into creation to accomplish his purpose of judgment and salvation. They are not a sign of the impending coming of the Lord but the accompaniment of the event itself. Accordingly the parable of the Fig Tree in vv. 28–29 cannot refer to the cosmic manifestation of vv. 24–25, but must refer to events that precede the advent of the Lord in his glory.

T. J. Geddert

The work on Mark 13 by T. J. Geddert was written in the conviction that there was an urgent need to examine the chapter from Mark's own perspective, i.e., in the context provided by the Gospel of Mark. This called for a study of the Gospel with a view to grasping Mark's understanding of the issues raised in the discourse. Geddert affirmed: "What is needed is not a more powerful microscope focusing on ever smaller details within Mark 13. What is needed is a network of floodlights illuminating this chapter from all over the rest of the Gospel."[430]

To achieve this understanding Geddert supplied a series of studies to examine Mark's views on (1) signs, (2) his use of the term *blepō* ("watch") , and (3) *grēgoreō* ("keep awake"), (4) Mark's temple theology, (5) suffering and persecution in Mark's Gospel. These studies take up more than half the book. The second half deals with Mark's literary method, his doctrine of the secret kingdom, and the time of the end, especially the relation between the destruction of the temple and the end of the age.

As to "signs" in Mark, it is pointed out that the term occurs in Mark in two passages only—in the request of the Pharisees that Jesus show them a sign from heaven (8:11–13) and in ch. 13. These two passages show that Mark has a negative judgment on sign seeking. The Pharisees' request is emphatically rejected ("No sign at all will be given to this generation"), and the disciples of Jesus are warned against sign givers (13:22). Mark's primary concern is the relation between signs, including the miracles of Jesus, and the apprehension of their truth and meaning. The controversy passage of 2:1—3:6 shows that miracles are ineffective in persuading Jewish leaders to side with Jesus. "What is important about these stories is not the substance of the miracles but the implicit epistemology: for Mark, understanding of reality is achieved not by availability of evidence but by revelatory insight."[431]

---

[430]Geddert, *Watchwords: Mark 13 in Markan Eschatology,* JSNTSup 26 (Sheffield, 1989), 24.

[431]Ibid., 52.

On this basis it is suggested that the disciples' request for a sign (in 13:4) was misguided; that within Mark 13 there are no valid signs at all; that the discourse is more concerned with understanding what is happening than with providing predictions about the future; that the so-called ambiguities and inconsistencies in Mark 13 are devices by which Mark reveals a message more subtle than has been suspected.[432]

This "subtlety" of Mark is seen in his taking the ordinary term *blepō*, "to see, to look," and using it as part of a call to perceive what is below the surface of events, discourses, and texts. "Every usage of the term in Mark appears intended by the author to contribute to a carefully devised call concerning realities which lie beyond the observations of the physical senses."[433] The primary content in the use of the term is an appeal for discernment, as in 13:2, "Don't be misled by external appearances," and in vv. 5, 23, "Don't be deceived by false words and misleading deeds." By contrast, *grēgoreō*, "keep awake," has a different connotation from *blepō*. If the latter relates to correct discernment, the former has in view correct behavior in the waiting period before the parousia. Neither term has any connection with sign seeking or timetables. It is particularly important to note the link between the use of *grēgoreō* in 13:33–37 and 14:32–42: the connection indicates that the eschatology of Mark 13 is highly infused with Mark's passion theology, not an eschatology on the lookout for signs and apocalyptic phenomena. So also Mark's passion narrative is itself suffused with eschatological features, as allusions to OT representations of the day of the Lord indicate (e.g., 15:33).[434]

Three passages outside Mark 13 feature the temple, namely, the cleansing of the temple (11:15–17), the allegation that Jesus will destroy the temple and raise another (14:58; 15:29), and the tearing of the veil of the temple (15:38). The temple cleansing is plainly a condemnation of the Jewish religious rulers, as the citation from Jer 7:11 and the parable of the Vineyard show. In the latter the Son becomes the cornerstone of a new temple. Mark 14:58 indicates that the new temple is Jesus and his church; he is God's replacement of the rejected leadership, and the church acknowledges his lordship. Mark 13 accordingly is to be interpreted from the perspective of temple replacement. The discourse is not simply about the destruction of the temple but about its replacement by a new temple, that of Jesus and his community.[435] The rending of the veil illustrates Mark's understanding of the death of Jesus as replacing the cult as means of access to God; the blessings of the kingdom of God are available because Jesus' death signifies the

---

[432] Ibid., 57–58.
[433] Ibid., 60.
[434] Ibid., 104–7.
[435] Ibid., 128.

arrival of "that day" and "that hour" (Mark 13:32), the judgment of the
Jewish leaders, and the redundancy of the temple, hence its eventual
destruction.[436]

Persecution and vindication are a two-beat theme in Mark's Gospel, wherein a consistent pattern emerges: the passion of John the
Baptist, the passion of Jesus, and the passion of the disciples and the
church. Mark's theology of the kingdom is like a relay race in which
persecution for the gospel is the baton passed on from each runner to
the next as they make their way round the track. After the resurrection
Galilee is the scene of discipleship renewal, the starting point for the
discipleship road. The new beginning is marked by Mark 13.[437]

Mark has modeled himself after Jesus in terms of the means by
which the gospel is communicated. The Markan Jesus spoke in parables
and riddles with hidden meanings; so too Mark wrote his Gospel with
considerable conscious ambiguity. The entire Gospel is an extended
parable. This has to be borne in mind when considering the relation
between the judgment on the temple and the parousia. Geddert views
the former as the intermediate vindication of Jesus and his followers,
prior to that which will occur at the parousia. The primary period of
mission and discipleship is between the tribulation linked with the
temple and the final tribulation leading to the parousia, but the issue
is left ambiguous by Mark. Mark 13:24a ("In that day, after that tribulation") affirms neither continuity nor discontinuity between the events;
the ambiguity is deliberate on Mark's part. So also in 13:30 *hē genea* is
distinctly equivocal; it may or may not denote the contemporaries of
Jesus—and of Mark. But that suits Mark's purpose: Jesus also was
ambiguous!

With this Mark 13:32 comports. The feature of the end which
neither human being nor angel nor the Son knows is the final event
itself, or rather "the final eschatological events." Verses 33–37 apply
the saying to the time of the end. "Mark does not know how many
generations will take up the baton and run the course before the race is
declared finished and won."[438]

In the light of these observations it is urged that the Fig Tree
parable (vv. 28–29) should not be construed as affirming that "signs of
the times" will indicate the nearness of the end. The parable speaks of
awareness of the fig tree's greening; it does not depict a cause and effect
relationship between two objective events or their temporal proximity,
but rather the relationship between seeing something and knowing
something. In the Markan context the nearness is a reality before it is

---

[436]Ibid., 140–45.
[437]Ibid., 150–78.
[438]Ibid., 247.

recognized, but the actual arrival may have to be awaited for a long time. Linking up the cursing of the fig tree with the parable of the Fig Tree it would appear that "these things" of the parable (v. 29) refer not simply to the destruction of the temple, but also to its replacement by the new temple, the locus of God's eschatological fulfillment.[439]

Geddert sums up the message of Mark 13, as of Mark's Gospel as a whole, that collecting information is insufficient; there must be understanding, and the prerequisite for that is faithful discipleship: "Without both discernment and discipleship the secret kingdom cannot be experienced, the Lord cannot be followed, and the Gospel cannot be apprehended. That is the challenge. The example and the victory of Jesus make both discernment and discipleship a possibility. That is the good news."[440]

Geddert's work, while highly provocative, has an abundance of insights which challenge common critical positions on Mark 13 and which call for careful reflection. The attempt to determine Mark's intention and meaning in the discourse was right, even when it is acknowledged that one cannot stop with Mark himself. Geddert has performed a valuable service in examining the concepts central to the discourse as they appear in the Gospel of Mark and then interpreting their meaning in ch. 13. This especially applies to the consideration of the significance of *blepō* and *grēgoreō* in the discourse, but Geddert's treatment of the other leading concepts in Mark 13 is also very perceptive. The frequent concentration of attention on the apocalyptic elements in the discourse, interpreted in the light of late Jewish rather than biblical apocalyptic, has resulted not only in a doubtful understanding of the apocalyptic concepts themselves but also in a diminution of the positive relation of the discourse to the teaching of Jesus and the theology of the evangelist. Through Geddert's constant viewing of the content of the discourse in the light of the Gospel as a whole he has, for example, been able to affirm that the hermeneutical key to Mark 13 is the theology of the secret kingdom, and to show that the "passion of the disciples," related to the passion of Jesus, is present in the whole discourse.

It is likely, however, that some of Geddert's readers will find difficulty in the way in which he presses certain of his views. For example, the undoubtedly close relation of the discourse with the rest of Mark's Gospel has led Geddert to postulate a parallelism between the structure of the discourse and that of the Gospel which is frequently far from plausible.[441] More seriously, the author's justified opposition to the belief that Mark 13 provides an eschatological timetable has caused

---

[439]Ibid., 250–51.
[440]Ibid., 258.
[441]Ibid., 193.

him to deny that there are any signs in the discourse relating to the future consummation, and to an implausible interpretation of the Fig Tree parable.[442] Curiously enough, although Geddert denies that the parable relates to signs of the end, he concludes that the parable "assures the discerning reader that when the temple has fallen the Son of man may arrive at any time,"[443] which is exactly what most scholars have thought it meant in its present context!

The stress on Mark's studied ambiguity, which frequently includes multiple meanings of passages, has also led to some questionable exegesis, especially in utterances concerning the time of the end. Mark 13:32 is interpreted primarily not as referring to the unknowability of the time of the end but of the events which are to constitute the end time, a dubious notion when it is realized that it is the ignorance of Jesus, not of human beings and angels, which is chiefly in view. Geddert acknowledges that v. 33 shows that this ignorance includes the incalculability of the time of the end—but also of various intermediate applications of the saying, including the end of Jesus himself; accordingly the first fulfillment of Mark 13:32 occurred within a few days (in Gethsemane), the second in his own death, the third in the passion of the disciples; presumably one could continue with other unnamed fulfillments in history until the final end. That is not inharmonious with Geddert's conviction that Mark 13 was written both in order to prevent the reader from concluding that the ultimate end follows immediately the destruction of the temple and at the same time to leave the possibility open that it will: "The End would be 'imminent' after that event, but could remain so for generations."[444] That appears to be judging the situation of Mark and his contemporaries from the standpoint of a couple of millennia later; such hindsight was not available to the primitive church, and in any case near expectation according to the will of God is not to be so expressed.

One must concede, however, that such caveats are but flaws in a most stimulating discussion on the eschatological discourse. It will set scholars thinking for many a year.

K. D. Dyer

It is appropriate that this review of monographs on Mark 13 should conclude with an examination of K. D. Dyer's work, for it is one of outstanding worth.[445] The author has sought to understand the chapter

---

[442] Ibid., 247–53.

[443] Ibid., 253.

[444] Ibid., 254.

[445] " 'Reader Note Well,' Intertextuality and Interpretation in Mark 13," a dissertation for the Melbourne College of Divinity, unpublished at the time of writing this review. Page numbers relate to the typescript.

in a "wholistic" manner, i.e., by "making use of a range of analytical approaches from both the traditional historical-critical methodologies and some of the new literary ones."[446] Dyer classifies the works of scholars on Mark 13 according to their methodological approaches to the discourse and offsets their findings with his own convictions as to the problems they have raised. In evaluating the varied modes of dealing with the pre-Markan traditions and the Markan redaction Dyer lays heavy emphasis on the vocabulary and syntax of the discourse; in the determination of the latter, computer aids and charts are freely used.

The grouping of scholarly discussions on the discourse is achieved by characterizing the way the chapter is regarded by the various writers, thus: (1) A Jewish Apocalypse (Source and Form Analysis); (2) Jesus' Eschatological Discourse (New Testament Traditio-Historical Analysis); (3) A Danielic "Midrash" (Old Testament Traditio-Analysis); (4) Markan Anti–Apocalyptic Discourse (Redaction Analysis I); (5) A Christian Prophetic Oracle (Redaction Analysis II); (6) A Markan Apocalypse (Religio-Historical Analysis); (7) A Parenesis for the Markan Community (Socio-Political Analysis); (8) The Teacher's Farewell Discourse (Literary Analysis). The review concludes with the author's own assessment of the context and intent of the discourse in light of his evaluations of the scholarly works he has examined.

Already in his critique of the notion that Mark 13 is an elaboration of a Jewish apocalypse Dyer brings to light a conviction which is for him the key to the discourse, and which finds constant mention throughout his work: the central paragraph, vv. 14–21, manifests considerable Semitic influence, whereas vv. 24–27, while also showing Semitic influence, are marked by a consistently Septuagintal style, which suggests that they come from a tradition different from that of vv. 14–21.[447] This, together with other links in the discourse (e.g., vv. 7–8, 11d–13a, 22), raises serious questions as to the likelihood that a Jewish apocalypse formed the basis of the pre-Markan tradition.

The distinction between vv. 14–21 and 24–27 is strengthened through an analysis of the syntax of the discourse. An examination of three word sequences in Mark 13 is held to demonstrate that the chapter has the most distinctive syntax in Mark's Gospel, apart from vv. 24–27, where the three word sequences do not appear. This confirms Dyer's belief that vv. 14–21 and 24–27 could not have belonged together and that, whereas vv. 24–27 are at home in the Gospel, vv. 14–21 are not. This latter passage is characterized as the most likely unit of distinctive pre-Markan tradition, not only in the discourse but in the whole Gospel of Mark. Conversely an examination of six word sequences in Mark 13

---

[446]P. 13.
[447]Pp. 74–75, 104.

shows that vv. 24–27 are most in keeping with the syntax of the Gospel as a whole.[448]

Accordingly, Dyer's investigations lead him to formulate the pre-Markan traditions as follows:

(i) The prophecy of v. 2, together with vv. 30–31, which may have formed the conclusion to the prophecy, v. 32 in an earlier form, and the part parable of v. 34.

(ii) Palestinian (Targumic?) traditions, vv. 7, 8, 11a, b, d, 12, 13a, 22.

(iii) A distinctive pre-Markan source, vv. 14–21.

(iv) A Markan pastiche of Septuagintal references, vv. 24–27.

(v) Editorial comments or compilations of smaller units, vv. 3–6, 9–10, 13b, 23, 28–29, 33, 35–37.[449]

Turning to the content of the chapter, Dyer points to certain theological principles of the Gospel of Mark which aid in reconstructing the process of composition of chapter 13.

1. The anti–temple stance of Jesus in Mark (e.g., the cursing of the fig-tree and the cleansing of the temple) finds expression both in the pre-Markan traditions and in Mark's redaction in chapter 13. The fulfillment of the prophecy of v. 2 therefore can hardly be viewed as a devastating event for the Markan community and a sign for the fulfillment of all things.

2. The inappropriateness of seeking signs, reflected in Mark 8:11–13, is strongly represented in the discourse. The other Gospels use the concept of "signs" positively, but not Mark.

3. The ambiguity of time references within the Gospel, referring both to historical and eschatological events, links the discourse with the Gospel. The "hour" (13:32) and the four watches of the night (13:35) appear in the passion narrative (14:41; see also 14:17, 37, 72), indicating that the four watches of the eschatological night are lived out in the passion of Jesus. So also distinction is maintained between "in those days" and "in that day" in the Gospel and in the discourse: the former is related to the baptism and temptation of Jesus (1:9), the feeding of the multitude (8:1), the tribulation of Jerusalem (13:17), and the vindication of Jesus (13:24–27); the latter appears in relation to the taking of the bridegroom (2:20), the disciples' testing (4:35), the "telos" (13:32), the eschatological banquet (14:25). The former passages indicate a process, the latter an event; that means that vv. 24–27 portray a process and v. 32 an event.

---

[448]Pp. 171–74.
[449]Pp. 139–40, 214.

4. The inappropriateness of the disciples' questions and comments, conveyed frequently in the Gospel, applies to those of v. 4. The discourse is intended less to provide an answer to the question of signs than a correction of that kind of inadequate perception of the fulfillment of all things.

5. There is a nexus between the judgment of the temple state and the mission to the Gentiles in both the Gospel and the discourse: the former occurs three times in Mark (11:22; 13:1–2; 15:38), each time with a corresponding reference to the Gentile mission (11:1; 13:10; 15:39).

6. There are three references to the coming of the Son of Man in the Gospel—8:38, 13:26, 14:62. All are related to Dan 7:13, where the one like a son of man is said to return to the Ancient of Days in heaven. Such is the meaning in Mark. The three statements stand in relation to opponents of the Son of Man, and so are more appropriately described as setting forth the *vindication* of the Son of Man rather than his *parousia*.[450] The emphasis in vv. 24–27, accordingly, is not on final salvation, but on the gathering together of a new community drawn from all nations, a process accomplished by the mission of the church.[451]

Dyer finds support for this understanding of the discourse from proponents of socio-political analysis of Mark 13, notably in the works of F. Belo,[452] Ched Myers,[453] and H. Waetjen.[454] It leads him to propose his own socio-political context for the discourse, the clue to which is in the oracle of vv. 14–21. The "abomination of desolation" will be the coins issued by Vespasian in A.D. 69, after his crushing military campaign against the Jews in A.D. 68 and his proclamation in Rome as emperor. A prophetic word was sent to the Christians in Judea to flee the impending completion of the destruction of Jerusalem by the Romans. They did so, and brought the oracle with them to the Markan community. By the addition of vv. 24–27 to 14–21 the Christian communities were called to recognize that the gathering of God's elect would involve people from all nations and would occur in another place and another time. The composition of the discourse assumes that the destruction of Jerusalem has taken place, it is viewed as a "post-war reflection on the nature of the Christian hope and the emergence of a new multi–ethnic Christian community."[455]

On this basis the subsidiary prophecies of the chapter find their place, and a new outline of the chapter becomes possible:

---

[450]Pp. 202–13.

[451]P. 232.

[452]*A Materialist Reading of the Gospel of Mark* (Maryknoll, 1981).

[453]*Binding the Strong Man* (Maryknoll, 1988).

[454]*A Reordering of Power: A Socio-Political Reading of Mark's Gospel* (Minneapolis, 1989).

[455]P. 281.

vv. 1–2: The closing scene of the anti–temple stories, providing the occasion and setting for the discourse.

vv. 3–4: The temple and the end—the eschatological question, "When and what sign?"

vv. 5b–13: The future which is past (and still present for the Markan community)—the faithful planting of the seed, at great cost and by the aid of the Spirit.

vv. 14–23: The future which is recent (and still present for the Judean refugees)—the awful tribulation, and assurance that all was foreseen by Jesus.

vv. 24–30: The future which is present and still coming. The opposing powers will witness that vindication of the Son of Man and gathering of the new community—the sign that the harvest is breaking in and the kingdom is coming with power.

vv. 31–37: The future which is to come (and may occur at any time!)—The ultimate end, when heaven and earth pass away, is in the Father's hand, yet because it may be encountered existentially at any time, it calls for alertness.

The discourse thus is a Markan compilation. It functions as a farewell discourse, but placed before the passion narrative it ensures that nothing detracts from the overriding theme of the Gospel—faithful discipleship and mission through suffering.[456]

There can be no gainsaying that Dyer's investigation into the eschatological discourse is one of the most comprehensive and insightful works on Mark 13 that has appeared. Whatever one's judgment of its conclusions, one cannot fail to be impressed by the sheer scope of the study and its penetrating observations. Nevertheless, the feature of the work to which Dyer himself attaches greatest importance, and which he emphasizes time and again, may prove to be the Achilles' heel of his interpretation, namely, his insistence that the syntactical phenomena of vv. 14–21 show it to be unique, and that vv. 24–27 are a Markan pastiche of citations from the LXX.

Dyer's presentation of the syntactical data of Mark 13 is impressive, but on reflection its pertinence is unclear. His list of syntactical features unique to the chapter shows that vv. 14–21 (note—not simply 14–20) contain twenty-two examples of three word groupings in the Greek text, but none in vv. 24–27. That is a striking phenomenon, but Dyer does not comment on the significance of the fact that these same three word groupings are scattered *throughout the chapter*, irrespective of the sources of the sayings. These include the prophetic sayings which Dyer ascribes to Jesus (vv. 2, 30–31 and part of 32), early Palestinian sayings (7–8, 11–13a), and Mark's redaction (4, 23, 33, 37).

---

[456]Pp. 335–36.

Moreover the greatest concentration of these "unique syntactical features" occurs in vv. 11, 15–16 and 21: verse 11 has six examples, 15–16 have seven, and 21 six (seven if the transition to 22 be included), whereas the saying relating to the abomination of desolation (v. 14) has four only, 17 has two, 18–19 one between them, and 20 has two. Now the remarkable feature about vv. 11, 15–16 and 21 is that they are generally acknowledged to be Markan parallels to the Q tradition: v. 11 is parallel to Luke 12:11–12 = Matt 10:19–20, vv. 15–16 to Luke 17:31, v. 21 to Luke 17:23 = Matt 24:26. Dyer appears not to have faced this issue and its implications, but the evidence is too strong to be lightly dismissed. That Luke 12:11–12 came from the Q source is little contested; J. S. Kloppenborg, in his *Q Parallels,* tersely writes of it: "In Q: (so) most authors."[457] Similarly the majority of critics concur that the parallel to v. 21 in Luke 17:23 (= Matt 24:26) is a Q passage.[458] Unless one is prepared to assign all vv. 14–20 to Q one must surely dissociate v. 21 from it in the early traditions. Its reference is forwards, not backwards; the answer to contemporary claims about the hidden Messiah is the revelation of the Son of Man from heaven (vv. 24–27), as in the Q version (Luke 17:24 = Matt 24:27).

In the nature of the case there is less unanimity as to the Q origin of the Lukan parallel to Mark 13:15–16 (Luke 17:31), since the only Matthean parallel is in Matthew's version of the eschatological discourse. But Luke also reproduces the substance of Mark 13:15–16 in his own version of the discourse (Luke 21:21), whereas Luke 17:31 is set in a predominantly Q context (just as Luke 17:33 is a Q doublet of Mark 8:35, and is also reproduced by Luke [9:24] in a Markan context). Luke 17:31 is interpreted by Luke in relation to the parousia, as demanded by the Q context, but its parallel in 21:21 is interpreted of flight from impending danger, as in Mark 13:15–16. The difference of standpoint between Mark 13:15–16 and that of v. 14 (the former is concerned

---

[457] *Q Parallels: Synopsis, Critical Notes, Concordances* (Sonoma, California, 1987) 126–27. Of those who concur one may note S. Schulz, Q, *Die Spruchquelle der Evangelisten* (Zürich, 1972) 442–43; A. Polag, *Die Christologie der Logienquelle* (Neukirchen-Vluyn, 1979) 96; Zmijewski, *Die Eschatologiereden des Lukasevangeliums,* 146, n. 107. E. Schweizer views the Q version as more original than that in Mark and considers that this saying is the only one on the Spirit in Matthew and Mark that may certainly be traced back to Jesus, *TDNT 6,* 398 n. 413, 402–3

[458] See, e.g., Polag, *Fragmenta Q, Textheft zur Logienquelle* (Neukirchen-Vluyn, 1979) 98, and *Christologie,* 99, 101; Schulz, *Spruchquelle,* 278; Kloppenborg, *Q Parallels,* 190–91; Bultmann, *History of the Synoptic Tradition,* 128; V. Taylor, *Mark,* 515; P. Vielhauer, "Gottesreich und Menschensohn in der Verkündigung Jesu," *Aufsätze zum N.T.* (Munich, 1965) 75; Lambrecht, *Markusapokalypse,* 101; Marshall, *Luke* 659; Zmiejewski, *Eschatologiereden,* 410–11; Nineham, *Mark,* 355.

especially for people in the country, the latter for those in the city)
favors its independence in the early tradition, and therefore its possible
circulation also in Q.[459]

The syntactical phenomena of Mark 13 may conceivably be linked
with the existence of pre-Markan traditions in the discourse, but Dyer
has misrepresented the significance of that link. As we have seen, the
parallels to Q in vv. 11 and 21 manifest the phenomena even more than
vv. 14–20, and neither passage can on that ground be integrated with
vv. 14–20 as a separate source. The original unity of vv. 14–20 is
questionable if vv. 15–16 are from Q. The linguistic peculiarities are
observable throughout most of the chapter, including the Markan redactions. They cannot be adduced as indicating specific sources or as a
criterion of authenticity. If they are held to betray the work of a single
hand, then virtually all the sources of the chapter have been worked
over by that hand, including those assigned to Markan redaction. That
would, indeed, be a radical solution!

Similar qualifications arise concerning Dyer's judgment of the
composition and interpretation of Mark 13:24–27. His discussion of the
relation of the passage to the Old Testament is detailed and illuminating, but by no means supports the deductions drawn from it. In v. 24,
for example, the darkening of sun and moon echoes various passages—
Isa 13:10, Ezek 32:7–8, Joel 3:4 (= 2:31); on these Dyer comments, "The
Massoretic text of Isa 13:10 suffices, but there is also substantial agreement
with the LXX of Isa 13:10 and the Joel texts."[460] The observation is correct,
but this is not grounds for later insisting on *dependence* on the LXX here.

As to v. 25, Dyer cites Kee, Hartman, and France as maintaining
that it reflects the MT, and Glasson and Perrin holding that it is
dependent on the LXX. Dyer admits that Glasson's three points of
Mark-LXX agreement against the MT (*hai dynameis hai en tois ouranois,
hoi asteres* and *esontai piptontes*) do not agree exactly with the LXX and
can be seen as independent translations of the MT, but he adds, "However the coincidence in root words indicates clearly that there has been
more dependence on some form of the LXX text (Isa 34:4) than the
MT."[461] In this last assertion Dyer is more emphatic than is warranted.
The Hebrew text represents:

---

[459]Among the criteria that P. Vassiliadis listed for assigning to Q passages
in Matthew and Luke with no parallels in either Gospel he included those which
"accord with the country-life language of Q," "The Nature and Extent of the Q
Document," *NovT* 20 (1978), 67, cited by Kloppenborg, *Q Parallels*, 64. The Q
origin of Luke 17:31 is affirmed by H. Schürmann, *Traditionsgeschichtliche
Untersuchungen*, 280–81; Polag, *Fragmenta Q*, 98, *Christologie*, 100 n. 313;
Grundmann, *Lukas*, 342; Lambrecht, *Markusapokalypse*, 157–79; Marshall, *Luke*,
664–65; Crossan, *In Fragments: The Aphorisms of Jesus* (San Francisco, 1983) 92.
   [460]P. 128.
   [461]P. 129.

All the host will wither,
and the heavens will roll up like a scroll,
and all their host will fall.

The primary image is of leaves on a tree that wither and so fall to the ground. Mark's text omits reference to the disappearance of the heavens like a rolled up scroll: the term "host" is interpreted (as often in the Old Testament) as stars (LXX *dynameis*), and "wither" as "fall" (LXX has *takēsontai*, used in 2 Pet 3:12 of the elements dissolving through fire). In Mark's further statement, "the powers in the heavens will be shaken," the term *saleuthēsontai* frequently appears in the LXX for the "shaking" of the mountains and hills before the Lord in a theophany (see e.g., Jud 5:4–5, Mic 1:4, Hab 3:6). In Mark 13:25 it is less a translation of the Hebrew text than an interpretation in light of similar passages in the Old Testament, and so it represents a departure from the LXX text rather than a dependence on it.

Verse 26 is commonly acknowledged to reproduce the thought and language of Dan 7:13–14, as other parousia passages in Mark. Dyer briefly comments: "Distinctively LXX or MT. Not Theodotian."[462] He's correct, there is no ground for preference, other than the preservation of a reference to "seeing" the Son of Man in Mark's v. 26, which the MT has, but the LXX omits.

Verse 27 is more problematic. It appears to conflate the LXX of Zech 2:6 with Deut 30:3–4. The MT of Zech 2:6 [MT = 2:10] may be translated, "Up, Up! Flee from the land of the north, says the LORD; for I *have spread you abroad* like the four winds of heaven." The LXX reads, *ek tōn tessarōn anemōn tou ouranou synaxō hymas*, closely similar to Mark's rendering, leading Dyer naturally to affirm that the LXX is here being followed. Old Testament scholars have discussed how the LXX translation arose, and many have concluded that it has rendered an earlier Hebrew text than the MT. Kittel's critical edition of the Hebrew Old Testament recommends that the Hebrew text be amended to accord with the LXX, reading *me'ar^eba'* instead of *k^e'ar^eba'*, and *'āsap^etî* instead of *pāraś^etî*, a solution adopted by a number of commentators on Zechariah.[463] It so happens that Dyer himself observed, "Even if Jesus knew no Greek, he may still have been aware of the exegetical tradition embedded in the LXX or Theodotian," citing W. W. Combs' observation, "A number of manuscripts from Qumran have been seen to display varying degrees of affinity with the kind of Hebrew text behind the Septuagint."[464]

462Ibid.

463See J. Wellhausen, *Die kleinen Propheten übersetzt und erklärt* (Berlin, ³1898), 180; W. Nowack, *Die kleinen Propheten* (Göttingen, 1922); E. Sellin, *Das Zwölfprophetenbuch*, KAT, ed. E. Sellin, 12:2 (Leipzig, 1930), 491; Winton Thomas, *IB* 6, 1065.

464Pp. 114–15. The citation from Combs is from his article, "The Transmis-

In light of Dyer's own statements about the relation between Mark 13:24–27 and the Old Testament, and our own occasional qualifications, his repeated unqualified assertions that vv. 24–27 are "a pastiche of LXX references" is an exaggeration. His interpretation of the passage is even less acceptable, namely, that the cosmic phenomena of vv. 24–25 depict figuratively the dismay of "the powers that be" (Rom 13:1), Jewish and others, as they see the "vindication," i.e., exaltation, of the Son of Man and the gathering of his elect from all directions into a new community of Jews and Gentiles—the sign that the "harvest" is taking place (vv. 28–29) and the kingdom coming in power (v. 30). However well intentioned this may be, in my judgment it is a wholly illegitimate way of interpreting theophanic texts, both in the prophets of the Old Testament, including Daniel, the Gospels, the Epistles of the New Testament and the book of Revelation.

This negative critique of Dyer's work concerns his own solution to the problems of Mark 13 on which he has laid most emphasis; in no way is it intended to minimize the immense contributions he has made to contemporary studies of the discourse. They remain invaluable. I admit to feeling less enthusiastic about his evaluation of my own work on Mark 13. I fail to comprehend how he should group David Wenham's investigation of the discourse with mine, as though we shared essentially the same approach. It is difficult to understand how he can maintain that Paul's letters to the church in Thessalonica reflect no acquaintance with the material embodied in Mark 13 or what ground he has for the assertion that my argument for "the historicity of the discourse" depends more on "perceived links with the content of Thessalonians than with the rest of the gospels or Revelation," not least in view of his having read my later work *Jesus and the Kingdom of God* and (possibly) my commentary on the book of Revelation. Perhaps the revision of my work on this theme in the present volume may encourage him to have "Second Thoughts on the Eschatological Discourse of Mark 13," as I have been compelled to have!

6. Commentaries on Mark

W. Grundmann

W. Grundmann sees in the Markan eschatological discourse a counterpart to the farewell discourses of great leaders, recounted in Jewish apocalyptic literature, such as the speeches of the patriarchs in the Testaments, or of Moses in the *Assumption,* and his words from Mount Nebo in the Qumran literature.[465] The theme of Mark's Gospel

---

sion History of the Septuagint," *BSac* 146 (1898): 257–58.

[465]Grundmann, *Das Evangelium nach Markus,* 2 vols., THKNT (Berlin,

is the accession of Jesus Christ to sovereignty; as the one designated to be the Son of man, Jesus had exercised this sovereignty during his ministry in the capacity of a servant; now he advances to his passion, and the discourse shows the end of the process in the unveiling of the sovereignty of the Son of man. The discourse and the passion narrative alike show that the way to that goal is through catastrophe and suffering; as their Lord, so the disciples must attain the destined sovereignty through enduring suffering—the parallel with Mark 8:27–9:1 is plain.[466] Varied sources flow into the discourse, notably from Jewish apocalyptic tradition and the words of Jesus, but in the latter a distinction has to be made between those from the historical Jesus and others from the risen Lord declared through Christian prophets.

Three groups of sayings may be traced in the discourse: an apocalyptic flyleaf (vv. 14–27); isolated sayings, such as vv. 10, 28–29, 31, 32; and sayings linked up for didactic purposes, e.g., vv. 5–6, 9, 11, 13.[467] Grundmann follows Lohmeyer in emphasizing that the discourse is to be regarded as apocalyptic parenesis; it is marked by a surprising lack of features common to apocalypses generally, and a concern for the preservation and building up of the eschatological community. The *Sitz im Leben* of the discourse is difficult to determine, for elements drawn from varied temporal settings have been taken by Mark and given a new reference. The *bdelygma* prophecy of vv. 14–18 is likely to have originated in the Caligula crisis, but in the discourse it has become the vehicle of an expectation of antichrist in the early stages of the Jewish War; in this new crisis the prophecy urges flight, and it could well have been that which led to the migration of the church to Pella, reported by Eusebius.[468] The date of the discourse, and therefore the Gospel itself, is likely to be after AD 66 but before 70, since there is no trace in the work of the end of the war or the fall of Jerusalem.[469]

The exposition of the discourse reflects in no small measure the influence of Marxsen and especially Lohmeyer. Verses 5–13 are viewed as a single section, exhibiting warnings and exhortations to disciples as they seek to discharge their mission. The persecutions described in vv. 9ff. reflect the situation of the Diaspora. Originally v. 10 had in mind a proclamation to all nations through the angels of the victory of Christ (cf. Rev 14:6–12); Mark has applied it to the mission as it is advanced through Christians dragged before Jewish and pagan authorities; the mission is fulfilled through martyrdom.[470] The flyleaf of vv. 14ff.

1959), 2:259.
    [466]Ibid., 261.
    [467]Ibid., 260, 266.
    [468]Ibid., 260, 267.
    [469]Ibid., 19.
    [470]Ibid., 264.

manifestly contains Christian elements, i.e., words of Jesus; it may well have come from an early Christian prophet like Agabus.[471] The parousia of the Son of man is represented as signifying the end and dissolution of all things (vv. 24ff.); the church is gathered to the topmost part of earth, i.e., Galilee, for removal to the highest heaven.[472] The final paragraph, vv. 28–37, deals with the question of the "When" of the end event.[473]

Comment is scarcely needed on these individual items of interpretation. Grundmann does not treat of the relationship of the apocalyptic thought in the discourse to the tradition of Jesus' instruction on the kingdom of God in Mark, other than noting the similarity of theme in vv. 9–13 to that of 8:27ff.

D. E. Nineham

In his commentary D. E. Nineham laid down that to understand Mark 13 one needs to recognize that many of the things therein described were already known to the earliest readers of the Gospel, and that the fall of Jerusalem also lay in the past; moreover, the readers were familiar with the kind of speech here attributed to Jesus through current apocalypses and farewell discourses, both from the Bible and of contemporary origin.[474] By its position the Markan discourse points to the significance of the ministry of Jesus already recorded—it is so momentous as to lead to the end of the world and the coming of God's kingdom—and it sets in perspective the passion about to be recorded—the passion leads to the glory of the kingdom. Not that the connection between the suffering and the glory is explained; that is a feature which apparently the church of Mark's time had not yet grasped.[475]

The discourse proper is stated to consist of vv. 5–27; vv. 5–13 describe miseries which precede the last days, vv. 14–23 portray those last days, and vv. 24–27 the end. Verses 5–8 and 24–27 are viewed as derived from a Jewish or Jewish-Christian apocalypse; vv. 14–23 represent a pre-Markan document, distinct from that apocalypse, with interspersed sayings from the Jesus tradition; vv. 28–37 are a supplement of independent sayings which set forth the time of the end as unpredictable and sudden.[476]

Coming to particulars, Nineham thinks the introduction of vv. 1–4 is a construction of the evangelist, providing a setting for the saying of

---

[471]Ibid., 266.

[472]Ibid., 268–69.

[473]Ibid., 270.

[474]Nineham, *The Gospel of St. Mark,* Pelican Gospel Commentaries (London, 1963), 339–40.

[475]Ibid., 341.

[476]Ibid., 343, 358–59.

v. 2, which has an uncertain relation to that in 14:58, and a question from which the discourse can start. The portrayal of the discourse as delivered to a group of disciples is a typical Markan device; it provides a revelation whereby the teaching of Jesus may be applied to the contemporary needs of the church.[477] An answer to the teaching of fanatics current in the church is provided in vv. 6–8, closely related to the answer to a similar situation in 2 Thessalonians 2. Mark 13:9–13 reflect the experience of the early church, especially in the Neronian persecution; an example of this is seen in v. 13, where words of Jesus have been transposed into another key for Christians who are hated for the sake of the Name (cf. 1 Pet 4:14). The suggestion of Lohmeyer is approved that an early poetic structure in vv. 9–13 has been disturbed by vv. 10, 11b, and 13, which provide encouragement for Christians who are beset by the troubles described in the interpolated verses.[478] In vv. 14ff. we see an early apocalyptic oracle, originating in the events of the year AD 40, subsequently incorporated into the tradition of Jesus' words; it is difficult to know how many, if any, authentic sayings of Jesus can now be traced in the passage.[479] Since the temple had been destroyed, Mark gave the prophecy a more general reference, seeing in the abomination a reference to antichrist.

The outlook in the "supplement" to the discourse, vv. 28–37, is radically different from that in vv. 5–27; in it the parousia appears to be only a preliminary sign, and the time of the end is beyond human knowledge, so human beings have to be continually on the watch for it. This is akin to the view attributed to Jesus in other traditions of his sayings (cf., e.g., Luke 17:22ff.). It is possible that v. 30 originally followed on v. 27, so bringing the discourse to a conclusion; v. 31 is an early Christian claim made on behalf of Jesus, adapting Matt 5:18; Mark 13:32 is an independent saying relating to the day of judgment and could have been framed by Christians to explain the nonfulfillment of prophecies of Jesus regarding the end.[480] The situation reflected in vv. 33ff. assumes the delay of the parousia, hence the call to be on the alert.[481]

In viewing the discourse as written after the fall of Jerusalem, Nineham concurs with many other writers; not all, however, who hold that view assume that the tradition of the sayings of Jesus has been so drastically affected as Nineham thinks. Most recent discussions on the

---

[477]Ibid., 348.

[478]Ibid., 350.

[479]"Jesus is nowhere else reported as having given detailed instructions of this sort about what his followers were to do in situations of the remote future" (ibid., 350).

[480]Ibid., 359–61.

[481]Ibid., 361–62.

structure of the discourse view vv. 28–37 as an integral part of the discourse, the fulcrum of which is vv. 24–27; that makes it plain that Mark in forming the discourse saw no inconcinnity between a parousia preceded by signs and one incalculable and sudden; for him the two representations were complementary—as they were for Paul (2 Thess 5:1ff.) and the author of Revelation (16:15). And is it really so that the church of Mark's day had not grasped the relation between the suffering of Jesus and the glory of the kingdom? That is inharmonious with the significance of the predictions of the passion of the Son of man (Mark 8:31, etc.), Mark 10:45, and the accounts of the Last Supper (14:22–25) on which 10:45 depends.[482] The parallels between 8:27—9:1 and ch. 13 suggest that Mark, who drew up both passages and recorded the Last Supper narrative, assumed the theology of suffering service for the kingdom in ch. 13 as in the other narratives.

E. Haenchen

Ernst Haenchen wrote a compendious commentary on Mark, which took account also of the parallels in Matthew and Luke. Even more than Nineham, he drew a radical distinction between the prophecy of Mark 13:2 and the discourse. In his introduction (vv. 1–4), Mark brought together two quite different and unrelated expectations of the future. If vv. 3–4 assume that the destruction of the temple is connected with the end of the age, the discourse itself relates solely to the latter. The question in v. 4 ("When?") expects an answer not in terms of a date, but of events by which the nearness of the end can be known. This is answered in the discourse, in contrast to the tradition embodied in Luke 17:20ff.[483]

The problem of sources behind Mark 13 interests Haenchen little, not only because he sees the exegete's task as that of bringing to light what the text says, but also because he is not impressed with the *Flugblatt* hypothesis. In his view vv. 14–20 relate to Mark's congregation rather than to churches in Judea; but more importantly, the framers of theories concerning apocalyptic documents behind Mark 13 appear to overlook that early Christians were capable of shaping their views with the aid of the OT and apocalyptic traditions without resorting to apocalyptic documents that allegedly were in circulation. It may be

---

[482] See, e.g., Joachim Jeremias, *Eucharistic Words of Jesus*, passim; H. Patsch, *Abendmahl und historischer Jesus* (Stuttgart, 1972), 89–149; H. Schürmann, *Jesu ureigener Tod*, 2d ed. (Freiburg, 1976), 16–65; R. Pesch, "Das Abendmahl und Jesu Todesverständnis," in *Der Tod Jesu*, ed. K. Kertelge (Freiburg, 1976), 137–87; and briefly in idem, *Markus*, 2:357.

[483] Haenchen, *Der Weg Jesu: Eine Erklärung des Markus-Evangeliums und der kanonischen Parallelen* (Berlin, 1966), 436–37.

assumed that Mark himself put together the discourse from sayings of
Jesus and from OT or late Jewish citations.[484]

The representation of pseudomessiahs in v. 6 reflects the expectations of the appearance of the Messiah in the wilderness, attested in
accounts of Josephus concerning episodes when Jews went into the
wilderness in hope of meeting the Messiah.[485] The mention of wars in
v. 7 is too general to discover therein a reference to the Jewish War of
AD 66–70. The prophecy in v. 8 has a different content, and its affinity
is with the parousia prophecy in vv. 24–27. The experience of Christians in the first half of the century after Jesus is mirrored in vv. 9–13.
There is no ground for viewing vv. 14–20 as the oracle which caused
the church of Jerusalem to flee to Pella, or for seeing in it an oracle
directed to any church in Judea; if an "abomination of desolation"
stands in Jerusalem, it will be too late for churches in Judea to flee, for
the whole area will be overrun by the Roman forces. The injunction
"Let the reader understand" indicates a message for Mark's own readers. It has a significance comparable to the appeal of the Seer of
Revelation that his readers understand his references to the "Beast" in
a time when it was dangerous to speak openly of such things (Rev 13:9,
18; 17:9); as John bids Christians to refuse to worship the image of the
beast, so Mark prepares his readers to anticipate a worldwide demand
to worship Caesar, but he draws his images from Daniel and the
Maccabean struggle.[486]

The parousia description in vv. 24–27 is formed from OT prophecies of the end, when the heavens are expected to break up. The Fig
Tree parable is not well placed from the viewpoint of the progress of
the passage, but it gives the meaning of the preliminary signs, and it
leads on to a section in which the readers are directly addressed.[487]
Verse 30 relates the prophecy to Mark's contemporaries, but the term
"generation" is not a "strongly defined temporal concept," unlike Mark
9:1, which is fashioned in dependence on v. 30. Possibly v. 32 earlier
followed on v. 30; it reflects the thought of the early church rather than

---

[484]Ibid., 437, 441, 449.

[485]Ibid., 438–39.

[486]Haenchen elucidates: "As soon as the Christians see that preparations
are setting in for sacrifice for the Caesar (an image of Caesar being set up, an altar
erected or the like) and the 'abomination of desolation' stands where he ought
not, then 'those in Judea,' i.e., the Christians, must 'flee into the mountains,' as
once the priest Mattathias and his sons fled into the mountains when they slew
the king's commissioner. Judea is named because the representation remains in
the frame of the book of Daniel, but any quarter of the Roman Empire is meant.
As soon as 'Day X' breaks in, when all Christians will be compelled to worship
the Caesar, then every Christian should flee as fast as possible from the place
where he lives" (ibid., 447).

[487]Ibid., 451.

of Jesus (cf. Matt 11:25–27), and it was formulated because the Christian tradition had no statement from Jesus about the "day or hour" of the parousia.[488]

Haenchen's exposition of the discourse is interestingly indepen-dent. His views on sources behind the discourse are worth pondering, but his interpretation of vv. 14–20 is doubtful. Contrary to Haenchen, the destruction of Jerusalem and its temple, threatened or accom-plished, would be far from irrelevant to Christians in Rome or anywhere else in the empire, partly by reason of the many Jewish Christians in the churches of that time, and partly through the enhanced expecta-tions of the end that the war inevitably aroused. The passage most naturally relates to Christians in Judea. By way of corollary that indi-cates that Mark found the passage in the traditions handed on to him; not everything that he reproduced for his church was framed with direct reference to its circumstances.

W. L. Lane

The exposition of Mark 13 by W. L. Lane is based on a wide-rang-ing investigation of scholarly literature on the discourse and is highly stimulating, even when controversial. Lane begins by pointing out that the discourse forms a bridge between the public ministry of Jesus, concluded in the conflict with authorities in the temple (chs. 11–12), and the passion narrative, when the authorities procure his death; by this positioning and further allusions to Jesus' prophecy of the temple's ruin (14:58, etc.) Mark points to the relationship between the death of Jesus and the destruction of the temple.[489] In form the address is a farewell discourse, containing, as is usual in this genre, prophecy and exhortation (Gaston's view of the relation between the two features in the discourse is recounted with approval); its primary function is to promote faith and obedience to the call of Jesus to cross bearing and witness in the light of his sure parousia.[490] As to the origin of the discourse, Lane accepts Hartman's thesis that the foundation of the discourse is an exposition of texts from Daniel, supplemented by other related OT texts, to which words of Jesus on watchfulness were added; this discourse, known to Paul as a "discourse of the Lord" (*logos kyriou*, 1 Thess 4:15), Mark reproduced without substantial alteration. As a connected address it contrasts with ch. 4, which is a collection of parables and sayings, not a discourse on the kingdom of God.[491]

---

[488]Ibid., 452–53. The same possibility is entertained by J. Bowman, *The Gospel of Mark* (Leiden, 1965), 250; E. Schweizer, *The Good News according to Mark,* 279; H. Anderson, *Mark,* NCBC (London, 1976), 301.

[489]Lane, *The Gospel of Mark,* NICNT (Grand Rapids, 1974), 444.

[490]Ibid., 445–47.

[491]Ibid., 449–50.

Lane urges that an analysis of the structure of the discourse must take into account the key phrase "these things" in v. 4, lengthened to "all these things" in v. 4b; it finds an echo in v. 23, which indicates that all that the disciples need to know about the signs for which they asked is recounted in vv. 5–22, and in vv. 29–30, which also relate to the signs described in that passage; when this is recognized there is no tension between vv. 5–31 and the concluding section concerning the parousia, vv. 32–37.[492] This distinction is fundamental for Lane's understanding of the content of the discourse, but it is not without its difficulties. It is acknowledged that the *tauta synteleisthai panta* of v. 4b echoes Dan 12:7, which assures that after the period of tribulation, "all these things will be accomplished," i.e., the "wonders" of history and of the resurrection of the dead; Lane affirms that vv. 4a and 4b have the same intention; the *tauta* and *tauta panta* have an identical reference, and so he sees that if the disciples had this scripture in mind they assumed that the fall of Jerusalem and its temple is the prelude to the consummation. One would have thought that "*integral to* the consummation" would be a more fitting expression for that conviction, and the contention that "these things" and "all these things" of vv. 29–30 be dissociated from the consummation was illegitimate.

In point of fact the reference of "these things" in v. 29 becomes unexpectedly restricted through Lane's understanding of v. 14. He follows the suggestion of S. Sowers that the abomination of desolation is to be understood of the profanations of the temple by the Zealots which culminated in a mocking investiture of the clown Phanni as high priest (*he* undoubtedly stood "where he ought not!").[493] This act of profanation, in Lane's view, led to the abandonment of the temple by God and to its destruction. The Fig Tree parable then conveys the message: "When you see this appalling sacrilege taking place in the temple, then know that the destruction of the temple is at hand." Lane insists that such is Mark's intention in his structuring of the discourse.[494]

The interpretation of v. 14 in relation to the episode of Phanni the clown is implausible. One should recall the protest of Schlatter against the demand for seeing in the prophecies of Jesus detailed predictions of historical happenings.[495] Is it to be taken seriously that Jesus envis-

---

[492] Ibid., 447–48.

[493] The event is recorded by Josephus, *War* 4.3.6–8, and is discussed by Sowers in his article, "The Circumstances and Recollections of the Pella Flight," *TZ* 26 (1970): 305–30.

[494] Lane, *Mark*, 478 and n. 99.

[495] Schlatter, *Matthäus*, 702–3.

aged the abandonment of the temple by God and the consequent destruction of Jerusalem to be God's judgment for that event? The Danielic prophecy has in view the actions of an antigod world power which defied the Lord of Hosts; Paul understood the "discourse of the Lord," as Hartman has it, in precisely that manner; Luke's rendering is in harmony with it, as also that of the Seer of Revelation, in his own development of the concept; it would be strange if Jesus, and Mark, were so out of harmony with Daniel and the interpreters of Jesus.

If Lane's exposition in this particular is questionable, it should be stated that his exegesis of the rest of the discourse is of a superior order, notably of the paragraph vv. 9–13, while his exposition of the parousia passage, vv. 24–27, is nothing short of excellent in its lucidity and penetration.

J. Ernst

The commentary of J. Ernst, following in the tradition of Joseph Schmidt, is very concentrated, in both its introduction to and exposition of Mark 13. Acknowledging that the discourse can formally be compared with the farewell discourses of Jewish men of God, Ernst affirms that the strictly eschatological orientation to the coming of the Son of man gives it a special quality. Mark, at the conclusion of his work, has yet once more very plainly accentuated the future perspectives of the message of Jesus that run through the Gospel. The eschatological discourse is to be seen as a consolatory and hortatory address to Mark's community in order that it should better understand the promise of the Lord which it had long ago received.[496]

A thematic structure of the discourse runs against difficulties on account of the interweaving of elements of apocalyptic tradition, reflections of contemporary events, parables with parenetic intentions, and sayings of Jesus. Linguistic and stylistic "signals" (e.g., "when you . . . ," "watch out," "then," "be on the alert," future and imperative verb forms, emphasis on the speaker through the first person singular) have significance for the address as a whole, but they yield no clear criteria of structure.[497]

Recent works of exegesis reveal two basic critical types, namely, redaction-critical and tradition-historical procedures. The critical and exegetical work of such scholars as R. Pesch, J. Gnilka, W. Schmithals, and F. Hahn confirm the fundamental rightness of the second position. The threatening situation at the beginning of the Jewish War provides

---

[496]Ernst, *Das Evangelium nach Markus,* RNT (Regensburg, 1981), 266–67.
[497]Ibid., 367.

the background of the source. For the composer of that source the impending tribulation and the time of the end flow into one another, and the parousia of the Son of man is expected immediately. Mark's intentions are evident through his editorial activity, e.g., his warnings against false prophets, and the extension of the parenetic emphasis already present in the source. For the evangelist, the Jewish War, which the source had coordinated with the eschatological expectations, lay in the past. His supreme goal is the maintenance in the church of preparedness for the parousia, along with a correction of unhealthy speculation over the arrival of the events in the immediate future. In its present form the discourse mirrors the burning concerns of the Christian community; beyond this, however, it has, through the relatively certain dominical sayings, preserved the intention of the proclamation of Jesus, above all the orientation to God's future, and set it as an essential norm of faith before every time.[498]

It is hardly necessary to comment on the above summary of Ernst's views on the composition and intention of the discourse. The exegesis of the text is terse, and a commendable effort is made at the end of each section to relate the passage to the life of the church today. One of the most interesting of such applications of the text falls at the end of the chapter. The question is asked whether the call to "remain awake" for the coming of the Son of man and the kingdom of God has any sense today. The following possibilities are offered to give actuality to the appeal:

(1) "To be awake" for the call of God here and now. Every hour sets us in decision *(Krisis);* the judgment of the Son of man relates to present attitude and conduct toward one's fellow human beings (cf. Matt 25:31–46). False or right decisions in the present can mean judgment, but also grace.

(2) "To be awake" for a future which stands beyond all human planning.

(3) "To be awake" for the coming of God, who will consummate human history sublimely, and in Jesus, the coming Son of man, will recompense each person according to his action (Rev 22:12) and then create everything new (Rev 21:5).

(4) "To be awake" for the personal encounter with God in one's own death. The Synoptic apocalypse reveals to us the authority to which we are referred in that meeting with God: Jesus, the Son of man, to whom we have to make our confession in this present time (Luke 12:8). In the presence of God our nearness to Christ or distance from him will become our reward or judgment.[499]

---

[498]Ibid., 367–68.
[499]Ibid., 393–94.

So to reflect on the message of Mark 13 brings the study of the eschatological discourse out of the purely academic realm into the ultimate concerns of life—which is surely the ultimate purpose of biblical exegesis.

E. Schweizer

E. Schweizer has his own way of writing a commentary; after reviewing the critical issues of a passage he seeks to provide an exegesis of it and then to expose its significance for the church today. This suits Mark 13 well. The chapter is divided into six sections: an introduction (vv. 1–4), signs (vv. 5–13), events in Judea (vv. 14–20), warnings (vv. 21–23), parousia (vv. 24–27), and concluding parables (vv. 28–37).[500] The introduction embodies the prophecy of v. 2, but it appears no more thereafter, for the question in v. 4 relates to what is described in vv. 5ff. The same theme as in vv. 5–6 appears in vv. 21–23, which shows that it had a firm place in the tradition received by Mark. Verses 7, 8, 12 recount seven signs of the end which the church found in its Bible: war (v. 7), imperialism (v. 8a), earthquake (v. 8b), famine (v. 8c), pestilence (Luke 21:11, accidentally omitted in Mark's discourse), internecine rebellion (v. 12), cosmic signs (vv. 24–25); the sixth feature (v. 12) was interpreted in the light of the church's experience of persecution for Jesus' sake within families. Verses 9–11 were handed down as a unit, though v. 10 was perhaps an expansion of the last phrase in Matt 10:18 (it is actually a reflection of post-Pauline ideas and terminology). Mark 13:14–20 are a separate segment, having in view the inhabitants of a war zone; they reflect the circumstances of the Caligula crisis and the later Jewish War. Verses 26–27 come from a Greek-speaking church, not from Jesus, since v. 27 reflects a reading of Zech 2:6 only in the LXX. It is therefore concluded that the discourse in vv. 5–27 arose from the church's reading of the Bible; a prophecy of Jesus concerning the end of the temple was augmented by a prophecy of a Jewish or Christian prophet. The exhortations added to it are theologically significant in that they portray the contemporary church as standing before the end and address the church there.[501]

In the exposition of the chapter Schweizer sees in v. 6 a warning against a danger threatening the church: men within its fellowship claim to be either Christ who has reappeared or a reincarnation of Christ; this is evidence of an extreme fanaticism within the church which had to be combated.[502] In vv. 14ff. it seems that the seer expected a sacrilege similar to that planned by Caligula, possibly in expectation

---

[500]Schweizer, *The Good News according to Mark* (ET Richmond, 1970), 261.
[501]Ibid., 262–67.
[502]Ibid., 268.

of the antichrist appearing in the temple; the prophecy was formulated before the anticipated tribulation began (v. 18) and may have been included by Mark to show that the troubles of the Judean war did not signify the end of the world, but were simply signs. From a historical perspective we have to recognize that in a particular time of emergency in Judea, which to us was an obscure event, like the suppression of the revolt of an Arab sheikh, a prophet arose and with his apocalyptic convictions interpreted the situation as a coming of God. Mark took up the prophecy without referring to any concrete event, teaching us to acknowledge that behind those experiences of apocalyptic horror God stands as the God who accomplishes his objective, and we are called to put faith in him and in his future, despite every appearance to the contrary.[503] In accordance with his use of vv. 14–20 Mark introduces the parousia description with a characteristic phrase of his, "in those days"; no relation is intended between the "Awful Horror" of v. 14 and the parousia; the latter is simply represented as happening later. Nor is any mention made of the many features prominent in apocalyptic descriptions of the end, only that the parousia issues in the ultimate fellowship of God's people with their Lord.[504]

On reviewing the discourse Schweizer affirms: (1) it provides nothing resembling a travel guide for the events of the last time to enable a traveler to plot his position on the journey; (2) the goal in view is not the annihilation of enemies and the like, but the power and glory of the Son of man and the homecoming of the dispersed to fellowship with God; (3) the account is constantly interspersed with appeals to the church in reference to its situation—in this respect the discourse is truly prophetic; (4) all suffering in the present time is subject to God's sovereignty, and is a part of a history over which he is Lord and which he will bring to fulfillment; (5) it is God in his glory who matters above all, and when he meets us in his triumph he will have the appearance of the Son of man, in whose ministry he revealed himself in Galilee and Judea; (6) the events of the present are not insignificant, but are signs of the final coming of God. So the church is enabled to endure through the strength supplied in the Son of man and to experience the power and glory of God in its common life.[505]

This exposition of Mark 13 is refreshingly invigorating. With certain of its details we are compelled to disagree. For example, the idea that the prophecy of v. 2 disappears wholly from view in the discourse is possible only by divorcing the representation of the "abomination of desolation" from the Danielic source, where the sacrilege is introduced

---

[503]Ibid., 274.
[504]Ibid., 275–76.
[505]Ibid., 276–78.

in time of war (Dan 9:26–27). That the discourse is due to the *church's* reading of the Bible is not self-evident. To contend that the parousia passage of vv. 26–27 came from a Greek-speaking church because of its dependence on the LXX of Zech 2:6 is disputable, for this latter point is uncertain (see the commentary ad loc.). It is, moreover, highly unlikely that Mark divorced vv. 14–20 from their setting in Judea and applied them generally; this admittedly was maintained by Pesch and Haenchen also, but it led them to an unnatural exegesis of the passage; we should rather see the injunctions to the church in Judea as having lessons for the church generally, which is a different matter.

These points, nevertheless, do not diminish the significance of Schweizer's lessons for the church today, drawn from the discourse; they reflect the operation of a mind that is alert to what God speaks to his people through the Scriptures, and we ungrudgingly express gratitude for his insights.

H. Anderson

In the estimate of Hugh Anderson, whose exposition of the eschatological discourse has clearly benefited from that of Schweizer, we enter a world of thought and expression in Mark 13 different from that of the rest of Mark's Gospel. "Elsewhere the stress is on the hiddenness of God's kingdom in Jesus' word and deed, discernible only to faith. Here the stress is apparently on the visible and cosmic events of the last days leading up to the end."[506] Anderson regards the chapter as consisting mainly of echoes from apocalyptic sections of the OT (thus in vv. 7–8, 14–20, 24–27). Despite the alien nature of this material, however, Mark's redactional work enables us to discern in this chapter the situation of his church more clearly than anywhere else in his Gospel. The church is seen to be in a crisis of great suffering through persecution from without and troubled by apocalyptic fanatics from within; Mark therefore directs his readers away from this apocalyptic fervor to renewed faith in Christ, who remains at all times Lord of all, and to steadfastness in its trials.[507]

The extent to which the materials of the chapter go back to Jesus is acknowledged to be a controverted matter. On the one hand the basic view of the whole is not necessarily incompatible with the attitude of Jesus, who could have affirmed the world and at the same time subordinated all in it to God's future; on the other hand "it is not in character for Jesus to string together OT quotations or to indulge in apocalyptic timetabling, even as sketchily as here in Mk 13."[508] Some elements of

---

[506]Anderson, *The Gospel of Mark*, NCBC (London, 1976), 287.
[507]Ibid., 289.
[508]Ibid., 290.

the discourse can be discerned as from Jesus, e.g., the prophecy of v. 2 and possibly the saying in v. 32;[509] but the perspective of the latter is fundamentally different from that in the rest of the discourse. Accordingly the chapter is to be viewed as an amalgam of (a few) authentic sayings of Jesus and pronouncements of a Jewish or Jewish-Christian prophet(s), worked together and developed in the church and finally edited by Mark.[510]

Anderson's exposition of the chapter is lucid and proceeds along the lines observable in the commentaries we have reviewed. One is constrained to remark, however, that the attitude to the discourse maintained in his discussion is characteristic of the inherent distaste of British NT scholars for apocalyptic thought, in distinction, one may add, from the positive attitude taken to it in the British tradition of OT scholarship.[511] The claim that elsewhere in Mark the stress is on the hiddenness of God's kingdom, which is discernible only to faith, is an inadequate representation of the proclamation of the kingdom of God by Jesus, as set forth not alone by Mark but by Matthew and Luke also. The good news of the kingdom of God preached by Jesus (Mark 1:15) certainly includes the staggering news that the saving sovereignty has entered into the present; but, as the parables proclaim, that which is present in his ministry is none other than the kingdom of glory which belongs to God's future; and as that sovereignty is operative in the words and deeds of the Son of man, it is to become operative with peculiar decisiveness and power in his redemptive suffering and resurrection, and it is destined for total triumph in the revelation of the Son of man at his parousia. To eliminate the expectation of the end of that process in the works of the Son of man is to misrepresent alike the teaching of Jesus and the gospel of the evangelists. There is in Mark a direct line of connection between 1:15; 8:31–38; and 14:62, and in that frame the eschatological theology of Mark 13 is not alien. It is disturbing that Anderson's exposition of the discourse makes no real advance on that of Colani, who worked from the presuppositions of a mid-nineteenth-century philosophy and theology in which there was no room for biblical eschatology. Such a view is not that of Anderson, but he fails to observe that the eschatology of Mark 13, despite the entanglements of the sayings within it, is manifestly closer to the proclamation

---

[509]In the exposition Anderson is uncertain as to the authenticity of v. 32; he considers that it could be a wholly church formation (ibid., 301).

[510]Ibid., 290.

[511]Klaus Koch contrasted the negative attitude to apocalyptic in German OT scholarship with the positive attitude manifest in the writings of British OT scholars, and wrote of the "agonized" attempt to save Jesus from apocalyptic, manifest in European Continental NT scholarship. See *The Rediscovery of Apocalyptic*, SBT 2/22 (ET London, 1972), chs. 4–6.

of Jesus, as we can gain it from Mark and his fellow evangelists, than the bloodless eschatology with which Colani and his successors sought to replace it. Jesus no more rejected apocalyptic than he rejected law and prophecy; he fulfilled and transcended all three. That is part, at least, of the lesson to be drawn from the setting of Mark 13 between Mark 11–12 and 14–16.

J. Gnilka

J. Gnilka has contributed a major two-volume work on Mark for the Evangelical-Catholic commentary on the NT, and so had space to provide a full discussion on the problems of Mark 13. Gnilka views the introduction to the chapter, vv. 1–4, as Markan; the apophthegm of vv. 1–2 is traditional, but the prophecy in v. 2 is not from Jesus, since its formulation approximates too closely the destruction of the temple by the Romans, and it provides no statement as to why the destruction should take place.[512] In the discourse of vv. 5–27 the existence of a pre-Markan apocalypse can be discerned from the connectedness of vv. 6, 22, 7–8, 12, 13b, 14, 17–20, 24–27. Its *Sitz im Leben* is Judea in the period immediately prior to the Jewish War, or in its early stages. It is not to be viewed as a flyleaf, for which contemporary parallels are lacking, but simply as a little apocalypse. It contains no specifically Christian features, but neither does it have many of the elements characteristic of Jewish apocalypses; hence it is likely to have come from a Jewish Christian who was acquainted with Jewish apocalypses.[513]

As to the content of the apocalypse, the "I am" of v. 6 is parallel to the OT revelation formula and indicates a claim to be the messianic Savior; this roots it in the Christian church and signifies that final salvation is present. Verses 7–8 suggest that a Roman war is in mind, the "reports" that are heard point to AD 66 as the time. Gnilka observes that the two temporal statements of vv. 7b and 8c express both eschatological distance and expectation together.[514] In vv. 9–11 Mark has combined two sources, vv. 9, 11, 13a embodying a persecution tradition, and vv. 12 and 13b, which go with v. 7; to these sayings Mark added vv. 9a and 10. The punishment of Christians through Jewish "sanhedrin" and in synagogues points to a Palestinian background and to a time when Christians had not become separate from Jews. The passage does not derive from Jesus, but from a Christian prophet.[515]

The paragraph vv. 14–20 consists of ingredients of various kinds. The "abomination" is still expected; the memory of the Caligula epi-

---

[512]Gnilka, *Das Evangelium nach Markus*, EKKNT, II/2 (Neukirchen, 1979), 184–85.
[513]Ibid., 211–12.
[514]Ibid., 186–88.
[515]Ibid., 189–92.

sode could have inspired the source to anticipate that a similar "abomination" would appear in the last time; since Mark looks back on the
destruction of Jerusalem, the personal reference will be to the Antichrist, whose appearance (not the destruction of Jerusalem) will be the
sign of the end.[516]

There are no traces of Mark's hand in vv. 24–27, other than the
second phrase in the opening clause of v. 24 ("after that tribulation");
the first phrase ("in that day") emphasizes the link between the appearance of the Antichrist and the parousia of the Christ. The traditional
day of the Lord features in vv. 24–25 have the function of illustrating
the judgment of the wicked in that event; they thus suggest, what in any
case is clear in vv. 26–27, that the parousia is both for judgment and for
deliverance.[517]

The celebrated v. 30 includes in its scope the parousia as well as
the signs prior to it, as the allusion of *tauta panta* to v. 4b and the
differentiation from the *tauta* of v. 29 show; its meaning is similar to
that of 9:1, but its wider reference suggests a later date than that saying.
Verse 31 has a more extensive application than simply to v. 30, or to the
discourse itself, and could go back to Jesus. Verse 32 is not to be
understood as giving precision to v. 30; Mark has deliberately set the
uncertain utterance alongside the certain one in tension. Since v. 32
will have arisen in a situation of pressing expectation of the parousia,
and as its correction, it cannot be attributed to Jesus; this judgment is
confirmed by the absolute title "the Son" accorded to Jesus. The passage
vv. 28–32 forms Mark's answer to the question "When?"; it teaches that
the present yields only signs for the nearness of the end, whereas the
actual sign of the end will be the Antichrist; nevertheless, the bitter
experiences of the present and the Jewish War offer a foretaste of the
final tribulation, hence the necessity to be ready, to build on the words
of Jesus alone, and to trust in the leading of the Father.[518] The final
paragraph exhorts readers to allow themselves to be determined by the
end; in the light of the parable that means "to follow the events of the
present attentively, to exercise the authority given by the Lord, and to
remain aware of the reckoning which he will ask for."[519]

In our judgment Gnilka has attributed to the church logia within
the discourse more frequently than is warranted; this is especially
evident with respect to vv. 2, 9–13, 32. His reasons for assigning them
to later hands are not compelling. Possibly this restricted view of the
words of Jesus in the chapter contributes to his belief that there is
nothing specifically Christian in the "little apocalypse" (though Gnilka

---

[516]Ibid., 193–96.
[517]Ibid., 199–202.
[518]Ibid., 203–7.
[519]Ibid., 210.

tentatively ascribes it to a Christian apocalyptist). This is contestable above all in relation to the parousia passage, which forms the climax of the "apocalypse." Admittedly the opening clauses are drawn from the OT, but this makes evident the nature of the parousia as a theophany. Yet the parousia of the Son of man is a Christian doctrine and in the context of the Gospel should be seen as truly Christian as the resurrection of the crucified Son of man. That it has analogies in the OT, and is dependent for its imagery on Dan 7:13, is not to be wondered at, since Jesus in his message of the kingdom of God was heir to the prophetic and apocalyptic traditions.

Gnilka subscribes to the view that Mark 13:26 is indebted to 1 Enoch 62 rather than Dan 7:13; on the contrary, there is no clear evidence that the Similitudes of Enoch were in circulation in the *first*-generation church; nor is there a doctrine of a parousia in the Similitudes, only descriptions of his exaltation to the throne of judgment, the terror of the wicked before him, and the consolation of the righteous through him.

It should be added that Gnilka concludes his exposition of Mark 13 with a review of its interpretation in the church and with an illuminating discussion of the meaning of "near expectation" in the discourse, in the NT, and for the modern Christian.[520]

W. Schmithals

In his exposition of Mark 13, W. Schmithals contrives some highly ingenious variations on themes from earlier writers. He distinguishes three strands of traditions in Mark 13: (1) The *Grundschrift*, i.e., foundation document, of the Gospel, from which come vv. 1–2, 30–31, 10. (2) A little apocalypse, preserved in the Q tradition, consisting of vv. 7–8, 12, 22, 28–29, 13b, 14–20, 24–27. (3) Other sayings from Q, considerably edited: vv. 9b, 11, 21, 34–36. To these are to be added redactional elements from Mark: vv. 3–4, (5–6), 9a, 9c, 13a, 23, 32–33, 37. The text is expounded in this grouping, and we shall follow it in our comments.

Schmithals understands the prophecy of v. 2 as setting forth the definitive end of the temple worship and its replacement by the eternal worship of Christ's community. The worship that cannot save is replaced by the eschatological worship of the new aeon. The prophecy looks back to chs. 11 and 12, and still more to the destruction of the temple by the Romans. It is therefore a *vaticinium ex eventu*, a prophecy after the event. Verse 30 underscores the *vaticinium ex eventu* of v. 2, and v. 31 the reality of the new order implied in the prophecy. The "words" of Jesus that will not pass away are not particular words, but

---

[520]Ibid., 212–16.

his "Word," therefore Jesus himself, insofar as he meets humanity in his Word. With that Word the new age, "the imperishable sovereignty of God," has broken in.[521]

Contrary to Kümmel, who has stated that a literary association between the elements of the supposed little apocalypse cannot be demonstrated, Schmithals affirms that that is easily shown; in fact, the apocalypse embodied in Mark 13 is "an excellent literary unit," "a classic document of apocalyptic thought." There is, however, no basis for viewing it as a "flyleaf"; rather it was constructed for the instruction of the elect. Since it has no frame it is doubtful that it ever circulated independently.[522]

The signs of vv. 7–8 are the "beginnings" of the woes; they lead therefore to a sure expectation of their high point, the impending end of this world and the birth of the next. Accordingly the phrases "not yet the end" in v. 7 and "the beginning of the woes" in v. 8 do not push the end to a far distance, but on the contrary bring it to a close proximity, as one would expect in an apocalypse, and as vv. 28–29 expressly state. The little apocalypse thus is no mission tract, but is addressed to the circle of the elect, who wait for the end and are encouraged to hold on till then.[523]

The warning regarding the abomination of desolation in v. 14a is the decisive statement in the apocalypse. In v. 14b readers are called on to note this sign of the in-breaking of the end, so that when the statue of Caligula is set up in the temple they can draw the consequences.[524] Mark took over vv. 14–20 without change, but in view of vv. 2 and 4a he related it to the fall of Jerusalem. His addition "after that tribulation" in v. 24 changed the original thrust of the passage; in the little apocalypse the parousia was expected not *after* the tribulation but as the high point of "those days," and so the beginning of the new age.[525]

In Schmithals's estimate it is evident that there is nothing Christian in this apocalypse; it is purely Jewish. But it does conclude with the coming of the Son of man. Mark transposed this teaching into one of his esoteric disciple discourses (vv. 3–4), and by this means Jesus is made to identify himself with the coming Son of man. So the theory of the messianic secret, which dominates this Gospel, is met again, as also the attempt to christologize, or kerygmatize, the apocalyptic Son of

---

[521]Schmithals, *Das Evangelium nach Markus, Kapitel 9,2–16,18*, Ökumenischer Taschenbuchkommentar zum Neuen Testament 22 (Gütersloh, 1979), 557–59.

[522]Ibid., 568–69.

[523]Ibid., 562–64.

[524]Ibid., 565.

[525]Ibid., 567.

man. From this it is further to be concluded that the little apocalypse was preserved in the logia tradition, i.e., Q.[526]

Mark's editing of the apocalyptic material is especially characterized by the elimination of all calculations of the time of the end. By this means he disarms apocalyptic expectation. In its stead he joins exhortation to watchfulness to the frequent allusions to ignorance of the time of the end. But this watchfulness is to be an active one. It is to be carried out in the exercise of the authority given to Christians and in the works assigned to them (vv. 34–36), which in vv. 9–13 is above all witness to the gospel to all the world. Through Mark's placing v. 10 in the apocalyptic address, the near expectation which Mark adopted is relativized. In the pre-Markan kerygmatic tradition of the *Grundschrift* there were no apocalyptic ideas, but the sovereignty of God set up in the midst of the old aeon. Through Mark the apocalyptic picture of hope is itself relativized, since it was abrogated in the gospel. Thus "the apocalypticizing of the kerygma in Mark is accompanied by a kerygmatizing of apocalyptic."[527]

This is, without doubt, a stimulating interpretation of Mark 13, which challenges readers to consider afresh their own understanding of the discourse. I cannot but think, however, that the contrasts believed to inhere in the materials of the chapter are overdrawn.

Schmithals's interpretation of v. 2 is impressive, but it would accord more with John 2:19 than with Mark 13:2. The latter is presented by the evangelist as an oracle of judgment, without the slightest hint of a new order of worship to be inaugurated through the destruction of the temple. The exegete has no warrant to read into such a statement meanings imported from elsewhere. So also the notion that the saying is a *vaticinium ex eventu,* however popular, is purely subjective; it would entail a similar verdict on a number of related sayings in the four Gospels, which many would question.

The little apocalypse has been considerably expanded through Schmithals's appropriating for it other sayings in the discourse. Little wonder that its "connections" are deemed to be "excellent!" I still remain unconvinced of the likelihood that an independent apocalypse would begin as v. 7 does. It is also a doubtful procedure to assign vv. 28–29 to a non-Christian source; these verses are obviously akin to the parables of the kingdom which Jesus spoke. Above all it remains true, as we have earlier stated, that there is no clear testimony to the parousia of the Son of man in any pre-Christian Jewish apocalypse. It is the erroneous assumption that this concept was current in Jewish apocalyptic that enabled Schmithals on the one hand to declare that the little

---

[526]Ibid., 569, 582.
[527]Ibid., 585.

apocalypse was non-Christian and on the other hand to suggest that it was handed on in the (unkerygmatic) Q tradition. Admittedly the latter idea is an intriguing suggestion; if it were true it would surely vindicate the Christian character of this material (cf. the "Q apocalypse" in Luke 17:22–37!). But the belief that Mark was acquainted with and utilized the Q material is very debatable, and I greatly doubt that he did use it.

The mission concept embodied in v. 10 is rightly regarded by Schmithals as of first importance in the Markan redaction and as informing the whole discourse. I would further suggest that it is fundamentally at one with its immediate context, namely, vv. 9 and 11 (which are parallel to Q and not drawn from it), as well as with vv. 12 and 13, on account of their evident relation to the mission of the followers of Jesus. So also the rejection of the word of the kingdom by the people to whom it was sent, first through the Bearer of the kingdom and then through his representatives, is undoubtedly viewed by Mark as the background of the judgment announced in v. 2 and of the day of the Lord on the temple, city, and nation declared in vv. 14–20 (cf. 11:12–14, 17–18; 12:9).

That there has been a transformation of apocalyptic in the discourse of Mark 13 is indisputable, and we are indebted to Schmithals for his emphasis on this. He is justified in stressing Mark's elimination of all calculations of the end, to which Jewish apocalyptists were prone; in this sense Mark "disarmed" apocalyptic expectation and stressed instead the necessity for watchfulness. There is, however, one supreme "expectation" of the future in Mark 13, and that is the coming of the Son of man at the end of the age; but that expectation was integral to the teaching of Jesus (as we see, e.g., in Mark 14:62; Luke 17:24, 30). The transformation of apocalyptic through its relation to Jesus and the gospel was not really Mark's achievement, but went back to the source of the Christian revelation in Jesus, the Mediator of the kingdom of God.

It should be added that Schmithals's exposition of the discourse ends with a notable appreciation of the importance of apocalyptic. It is set forth in a series of contrasting propositions, calculated to show that the understanding of the Christian faith requires the balance which apocalyptic thought supplies, and without which it suffers distortion. The last assertion indicates the tone of the rest: "Against all nihilistic hopelessness and against all utopian self-exaltation of humanity the apocalyptic elements of the Christian tradition remind us of the God of all hope and of hope in God as the central element of faith"[528]—a suitable conclusion of an exposition of Mark 13 which affirms the evangelist's achievement in "disarming" apocalyptic expectation!

---

[528]Ibid., 586.

C. S. Mann

C. S. Mann's treatment of Mark 13 is characterized by several uncommon (though by no means solitary) features. First, he rejects the priority of Mark and the two document hypothesis which goes with it. "Mark exhibits all the classical signs commonly accepted as evidence of conflation."[529] Of that judgment ch. 13 is considered to be a conspicuous example: "If one had to make a demonstration of conflation and digest, Mark 13 would serve as an admirable example of an economy of words in choosing between Matthew and Luke."[530] Second, the composition of the discourse is viewed as possibly beyond solution. The core of the work is prior to Jesus, and dominical sayings within it are minimal. "In our view the apocalypse . . . was a whole body of material inspired in part by Daniel, and compiled to encourage Palestinian Jews facing the certainty of Roman imperial vengeance. It was ready at hand for Christians to use, but with the significant and decisive interpretation that the ministry of Jesus had indeed been the manifestation of The Man."[531]

The third feature is hinted at in the last sentence of the citation: the primary function of the discourse is to introduce the passion narrative as "the eschatological/apocalyptic event by which all human actions are and will be weighed."[532] Various factors led to this interpretation: there is the link between Mark 13 and 9:1, both passages apparently anticipating the kingdom to be revealed within the contemporary generation; the connection between the emphasis in the discourse on "wakefulness" and the Gethsemane narrative; and the clue provided by Dan 7:13 as to the real context of the gospel sayings about the "coming" of The Man, namely, that The Man's coming is to the Father.[533] The depiction of The-Man-in-Glory in Mark 13:24–27 is part and parcel of Mark's portrait of The-Man-in-Suffering. Moreover, 13:26, "They shall see The Man coming in clouds," is closely parallel to 14:62, "You shall see The Man . . . coming with the clouds." The parable of the blossoming Fig Tree applies its lesson, "When you see these things happening . . . ," and v. 30 underscores the contemporaneity of the event. Mann writes,

> For this commentator the conclusion is irresistible that attention is being called to the passion narrative and all that this implies as the eschatological revelation of the purpose of God. The contrast in this apocalypse, as

---

[529]Mann, *Mark,* AB 27 (Garden City, 1986), 66.
[530]Ibid., 504.
[531]Ibid., 531.
[532]Ibid., 505.
[533]So already in W. F. Albright and C. S. Mann, *Matthew,* AB 26 (Garden City, 1971), 287.

framed by Mark, between 'when you hear' and 'when you see' is in our view too pointed to be missed. Mark's community might in distress hear many things and be tempted by many rumors, but there was a distinction to be made by members of that suffering community between rumor and the definitive revelation of God's purpose in the Passion.[534]

The first two features of Mann's treatment of the discourse need not detain us in view of our earlier reviews of these positions. The third feature is much more interesting, but hardly more tenable in the form put forward in the commentary. The significance of the setting of Mark 13 as both providing a context for the passion narrative and receiving light from it has long been recognized and is an important datum. But that does not warrant interpreting the parousia as the revelation of the kingdom come in the death of Jesus. Mann states, "Search as we will, we can find no tradition in the Judaism of Jesus' time of a messiah coming from God: on the contrary the common view was that the identity of the messiah would not be known until he was taken up by God."[535] The latter observation is mistaken; some Jews expected the unknown Messiah to be revealed by Elijah (Midr. Ruth 2:14); many more anticipated that, like Moses "the first redeemer," the "second redeemer" would reveal himself to the people after hiding himself from them many days (part of the elaborate typology of the messianic redemption as a second exodus).[536] The first observation is strictly correct but misleading. The Judaism of Jesus' time does not provide us with a tradition of the Messiah coming from heaven, but neither does it provide us with an exegesis of Dan 7:13 that depicts it as a representation of the Messiah ascending to heaven. Daniel 7 describes a theophany, and a theophany is always from heaven to earth. The rabbis admittedly were frequently perplexed by Dan 7:13. That is illustrated by the endeavor of the third-century rabbi, Joshua ben Levi, to reconcile its picture of the Messiah coming on the clouds with that in Zech 9:9 as one mounted on a donkey: his solution was that if the people are worthy the Messiah will come on the clouds of heaven; if they are unworthy he will come on a donkey (b. *Sanh.* 98a). By contrast, the representation of the messianic kingdom in 2 Bar 29:3 and 30:1–2 indicates that the apocalyptic writer interpreted Dan 7:13 in the same way as the Christians, and in this he may have been influenced by the depiction of the Son of man in the Similitudes of Enoch.[537]

---

[534]Mann, *Mark,* 530.

[535]Ibid., 528.

[536]See Str-B, 1:86–87.

[537]See the discussion on 2 Baruch and the messianic kingdom in my *Jesus and the Kingdom of God,* 48–49; for Dan 7:13, 28–29, and the related issue in Mark 14:62, see ibid., 300–302.

Mann's exposition of Mark 13 contains many noteworthy insights and is particularly helpful in its relating of the discourse to the OT.

D. Lührmann

Lührmann sees in Mark 13 the clearest indication in the Gospel of the time and situation within which it was written. Not only does the chapter begin with the prophecy of the destruction of the temple in Jerusalem at the end of the Jewish War, but that theme and its relation to the end of the age dominate the chapter. Whether the destruction of the temple has already taken place or is immediately impending (the latter having long been obvious in the later stages of the war), in any case the Gospel itself will have been composed about AD 70. The time cannot be determined on the basis of 13:14, but v. 2 could indicate that the temple was already destroyed.[538] As the last great discourse of Jesus before his passion the chapter has the character of a Testament; it looks onward to what the disciples will experience as men guided by his word and as his followers.[539]

The division of the discourse accords with the questions of the disciples in v. 4: the first question as to the time of the temple's destruction is answered in vv. 5–23, that concerning the sign of the end of the age, formulated according to Dan 12:1, is answered in vv. 24–27. That means that the time of the great *thlipsis* and the time following it are separated from each other; hence the time of the Jewish War, including the destruction of the temple, and the time of the coming of the Son of man are similarly separated.[540]

Lührmann emphasizes that the prophets against whom warning is given in vv. 5–6 and 21–22 are Christian prophets, inasmuch as they speak in the name of Jesus. They interpret the situation of the Jewish War as the time of the parousia of the Messiah Jesus, but Mark views them and their teaching as false. He seeks to enable his readers to understand their situation through the word of Jesus as one of tribulation, but also of proclamation of the gospel among all nations and of temptation and testing of the prophets, but not as the time in which Jesus the Son of man will come from heaven.

In this connection Mark's linking of the situation with the book of Daniel is noteworthy, for allusions are made to key texts, but each time with corrections. The citation in 13:7, "these things must happen," in

---

[538]Lührmann, *Das Markusevangelium*, HNT 3 (Tübingen, 1987), 222. See also idem, "Markus 14,55–64: Christologie und Zerstörung des Tempels im Markusevangelium," *NTS* 27 (1981): 457–74, in which certain positions assumed in the commentary are expounded at greater length.

[539]Idem, *Markusevangelium*, 215.

[540]Idem, "Markus 14,55–64," 466.

Daniel (2:28) refers to what will happen at the end, but according to Mark it is precisely not the end. In 13:14 the abomination of desolation belongs for Daniel among the events of the end time, but for Mark the desolation of the city and temple is not the end event. Mark 13:19 speaks of a distress such as has not been "from the beginning of creation until now," using language drawn from Dan 12:1. For Daniel the time of the "tribulation" is the end time itself, after which there can be no more historical time; for Mark, on the contrary, there is a time afterward: ". . . and will not be again." Clearly it was possible on the basis of Daniel to qualify the time of the Jewish War as the end, culminating in the coming of the Son of man, but according to Mark, Jesus opposed just such an estimate; for Mark that teaching was due to false prophets, and he corrected it by what Jesus "really" said.[541]

Lührmann makes some interesting observations on the origin of the discourse. The lack of external literary-critical evidence and the thoroughgoing redactional composition of the discourse, unique in the Gospel, make the search for Mark's sources difficult. Sayings like vv. 9 and 11 are certainly recognizable as traditional, but the alternation with other interpretations of the present suggests the reference back to "paroles." Admittedly this does not lead to the acceptance of an apocalyptic flyleaf, whether of Jewish or Christian origin. It is more prudent to start with the remarkable association with key texts of the book of Daniel (note above all Hartman's contribution here); the postulated "paroles" can then be reconstructed from vv. 7–8, 12, 14, 19, and 24–27; these interpret the war events as fulfillments of the statements in Daniel about the immediately impending time of the end; in addition there is the conjectured version of the temple saying which interprets this event as the work of the Son of man.[542]

In any case we would then have to do with a Christian tradition, and the question may remain open whether the concept "paroles" actually had reference to a verbally fixed source. The complex of apocalyptic is well enough anchored in the Christian tradition and in the tradition of sayings of Jesus without having to resort to a Jewish origin. It is not to be doubted that Mark edited the tradition before him. The strong revision may well indicate the great interest the evangelist had in this complex, as also the emphatic mode in which the situation of the readers is addressed. In this very situation he binds his readers to the word of Jesus as the word of the Son who must be heard, as the word of the Righteous One set in the right by God, whose word cannot be overtaken by the events of history, and from which the readers

---

[541]Ibid., 467.

[542]Lührmann posits that Mark 14:58 is closer to the original form of the logion than Mark 13:2; see "Markus 14,55–64": 465–66, 469.

cannot withdraw themselves in favor of other words declared in his name. This discourse therefore is an integral part of the Christology of Mark. The impossibility of the words of Jesus being outstripped by the circumstances of the readers, who live by his word, turns out to be the fundamental motif of the discourse. This motif rules not only the address but the entire Gospel.[543]

Lührmann's interpretation of the setting of the discourse in the Jewish War with Rome, with the intention of correcting fanatical apocalyptic "prophets" who maintained that this was the end spoken of by Jesus, is surely right. The suggestion that these prophets supported their beliefs with the aid of the book of Daniel is interesting and plausible. On Lührmann's grounds, however, I do not see why Mark 13:2 indicates that the discourse should be dated after the fall of Jerusalem, since the address to the readers in v. 14, "when you see the abomination . . . flee to the hills," would appear to locate that event in the future, and the references to flight in vv. 14–18 after the destruction of the city would no longer be relevant (Lührmann relates v. 14 to the Roman forces and their leader and views the instructions in vv. 14–18 as literally intended, so rejecting the idea that the flight to the hills denotes either departure to Galilee or forsaking of Judaism). I also find it difficult to believe that Mark wished us to understand that the false prophets claimed the authority of Jesus to declare, "I am Jesus (returned)" (v. 6), and that "many" were to do just that! If v. 6 is linked with vv. 21–22, as is likely, since Mark used them to form an inclusio for vv. 5–23, then we have to do in both passages with pseudomessiahs and pseudoprophets *outside* the church.

More interesting is Lührmann's interpretation of Mark's use of Daniel. He believes that the three allusions to Daniel in vv. 7, 14, and 19 are made in order to correct Daniel, who on each occasion has the end in view, a notion which Mark is compelled to correct. It is evident that the "false prophets" of Mark's time could have misused these passages, but it is also possible that Mark had a different purpose in view. First, despite the exegetes, I am doubtful that the *dei genesthai* of v. 7 is a citation of Dan 2:28. In the latter passage the *dei* simply represents an emphatic future; it occurs in the same sense in Dan 2:29 (LXX), but in v. 45 ("A mighty God has made known to your majesty what is to be hereafter") the LXX renders with a simple future *ta esomena*, while Symmachus reads *ha dei genesthai*. One may observe that in Mark 13:10 Mark again uses *dei*, whereas Matt 24:14 has a simple future. The use of Danielic language in Mark 13:14 and 19 is undoubtedly deliberate, and the desecration (and destruction) of the temple, with the appalling tribulation thereby entailed for Israel, is emphasized

---

[543]Idem, *Markusevangelium*, 226.

by Mark (so vv. 17–19). In Daniel, as in earlier comparable passages of the prophets that predict the destruction of Jerusalem, it is thought of in terms of the judgment of God on the city and nation, hence the day of the Lord on Israel. Mark similarly viewed the calamity of Jerusalem as due to the judgment of God. His use of the Danielic passages could well have been due to his seeing the destruction of the temple and city and the tribulation of the nation as the day of the Lord on Israel, and his insistence that that was not the end will have been consonant with many prophetic descriptions of the day of the Lord on nations, even if he wrote prior to the fall of the temple and city. That this identification of the destruction of Jerusalem entailed a correction relating to the time of the end, since history was to continue between the catastrophe in Israel and the parousia, is clear, but the indebtedness to Daniel is yet more important than the correction. Both Matthew and Luke had to resort to the same understanding; the utterance of Matt 23:37–39 is peculiarly instructive in this connection.

Lührmann's insight that Mark wished to impress on his readers the impossibility of the words of Jesus being outstripped by the events through which they were passing, or which might come to pass, is excellent. It remains a lesson for the church of all ages.

E. Drewermann

The massive commentary by E. Drewermann on the Gospel of Mark has a lengthy treatment of Mark 13, the significance of which lies not in its critical treatment of the passage but in its unusual exegesis.[544] In the author's view the value of this apocalyptic passage lies not in its representations of the future but in the light that these representations throw on the psychological and moral problems of humanity.

As to the origin of the chapter, Drewermann is content to follow Hölscher and Pesch in viewing the "flyleaf," which formed the core of the discourse, as composed in the light of Caligula's attempt to install his image in the Jerusalem temple, and its subsequent use, shortly after AD 70, by certain who saw in the destruction of the temple the sign of the end of the age. Mark took up this little apocalypse, recognizing the events portrayed therein as the prelude of the coming universal catastrophe, but warning his contemporaries against false prophets who interpreted the present situation as the onset of the day of the Lord (cf. 2 Thess 2:1–2). In Mark's understanding the Lord calls his people through the prophecy to look for the new humanity which will be revealed in the parousia, in fulfillment of Dan 7:13. The coming of the

---

[544]Drewermann, *Das Markusevangelium, Zweiter Teil: Mk 9,14 bis 16,20* (Olten and Freiburg im Breisgau, 1988), 330–411.

Son of man on the clouds is an ancient mythical symbol which can be understood with the help of psychological categories.[545]

To this feature of apocalyptic writings the author returns again and again in his exposition of the discourse. He points out that in Mark's day, as through later centuries to our own time, people have interpreted the discourse in a literal fashion, as though the darkening of the sun and moon and the falling of the stars were a description of the physical or astronomical destruction of the world. But religiously it has nothing to do with the fate of the heavenly bodies. On the contrary, it is essentially unreligious to speculate on the point of time when the world will be destroyed, as though the destruction of the world were an outward event instead of a spiritual experience of faith. In the apocalyptic texts of Judaism and the NT all talk of the end of the world is to be understood in a purely symbolic manner, as a projection of human ideas, anxieties, and hopes. These pictures are not to be understood as something that is to happen to our earth in a distant future, but as something that can fashion our human life here and now between salvation and ruin. In other words, the symbolism employed has to do not with the external circumstances of our existence, but with the question as to what could and should cease in order that we might begin a life that looks up to the clouds of heaven and brings us nearer to the vision of genuine humanity.[546]

Drewermann urges that if the Bible can do no other than describe God or the "Son of man" on the "day of judgment" with the help of ancient mythical symbols, then these images must be understood first through psychological means before it is possible to understand how far they say anything of abiding validity about the "Messiah." An example of this is seen in the coming of God in or on the "cloud." The latter is the classic image of the appearance of God, the veil of the divine. It is viewed as the vehicle not only of God but of believers at the parousia (1 Thess 4:17). The symbolism of the cloud is to be perceived in terms of psychical experience, a concern which is ignored in historical-critical exegesis. How widespread the symbol of the cloud in relation to humankind can be is seen in Chinese mythology: in the latter the cloud which dissolves itself in heaven becomes "a symbol for the necessary transformation which the wise man must undergo in order to extinguish his earthly personality and to be able to pass into the infinite."[547] In Mark 13 the vision of the breakup of the universe is followed by that of "Son of man" coming on the clouds of heaven; the picture represents the utter hopelessness of human existence, the "end"

---

[545]Ibid., 333–45.

[546]Ibid., 348–49, 376–77.

[547]Ibid., 344–45 n. 31, citing M. Oesterreicher-Mollwo, *Lexikon Symbole* (Freiburg, 2d ed., 1979), 185.

of every human world, the yawning emptiness for the individual—or a new beginning beyond all imagining, not from this world but from a new "heaven" that comes down in the form of the Son of man.

So the question arises how much must be destroyed before the world begins for which we have been made, how much of our worth must collapse that we may more deeply comprehend God.

> When the rubble falls away and we with quaking steps make our way across this quaking earth, God will be with us with the protection of his love. . . . That world for which we wait and in which alone we can live as human beings must be born by the effort to understand one another and by a universal willingness to help every human distress wherever we may meet it. How much we could give up of our normal habits in order to win humanness! The church since its early days has believed and known that such a world of understanding, of trust and of peace among all people has in principle begun in the form [Gestalt] of Jesus, and the form of the coming "Son of man" is identical with him.[548]

Other examples of this psychological approach to Mark 13 are seen in the warning of impending famines, wars, and earthquakes (vv. 7–8). Drewermann observes that in ancient and in modern times wars and famines form a unity. But "hunger" and "earthquake" are acknowledged psychological symbols, and in this sense they belong regularly to the obstetricians of any deeper knowledge (cf. "hunger" for truth) and the collapse of all previously existing viewpoints.[549] In Mark 13:20 the days are shortened because of the elect—not merely for their sakes, but through them. The saints recognize and repudiate the chaos that human organizations and ideals bring about and instead seek God's way.[550] The theme of "wakefulness," with which the discourse ends, shows that the coming of Christ is not a distant future, but an experience which becomes reality when one is awakened to the potentialities of one's own life that are personified in the form of the Son of man. Watchfulness represents the in-breaking of hope, the setting free of the individual for undreamed-of powers, the grasping of real life, the opening of eyes to see what we are, and to be rid of illusions that prevent us from living. "To be awake and to wait—that we can do in the consciousness that from eternity God has waited for our little life. He waits solely and exclusively that we truly live. And everywhere, where we do that, a fragment of God enters into this world; there God comes to us as he showed himself in Jesus; there the arrival of the Son of man draws near."[551]

---

[548]Ibid., 344, 390–92, 395–96.
[549]Ibid., 368–69.
[550]Ibid., 389–90.
[551]Ibid., 399–405.

Drewermann's views on the origin of Mark 13 have been sufficiently discussed earlier in this work and do not need repetition. The interest lies in his interpretation of the chapter. The insistence on the symbolic nature of apocalyptic language, and therefore of the imagery of the eschatological discourse, is entirely justified. The roots of this pictorial speech are seen in the OT and go back yet further to ancient Semitic religious thought and expression. The moot question is what is imaged in these pictures. Of one thing we may be sure: the primary purpose of the cosmic signs and the portrayal of the coming of the Son of man on the clouds of heaven in Mark 13:24–27 is not to depict the psychological conditions or needs of humankind but to set forth the action of the Son of man in the power and glory of God. We have to do with theophany, with action of God for humanity, not with the interior condition of the human soul. More specifically, the action of the Son of man is for the kingdom of God, i.e., God's saving sovereignty, to complete his redemptive purpose for humanity. That purpose was manifest in the ministry of Jesus and in his death and resurrection for the reconciliation and re-creation of humankind. The parousia of the Son of man represents action in the service of the kingdom of God as objective as that of his ministry in Israel and death on the cross. Its reality is conveyed in symbolic language, not only because it could not be otherwise represented, but in the consciousness of its fulfillment of the pictures of salvation and judgment handed down from ancient times. That such representations have profound moral and spiritual implications for human life is obvious, and that their language can provide equally profound symbols for the pyschological well-being of people is also plain. But the latter must be acknowledged as derivative from the primary intention of the message they embody, and not be allowed to diminish the reality of the divine activity which they are intended to portray.

6

A FRESH APPROACH TO THE DISCOURSE OF MARK 13

---

1. The Origin and Development of Mark 13

The instruction given in the primitive church, and the relation of this instruction to the teaching of Jesus, has been a matter of no little interest in the central decades of the twentieth century. C. H. Dodd drew attention to one aspect of this study in which progress has been conspicuous, namely the instruction of candidates for admission to the church, the so-called Christian catechesis. Basing his conclusions on the researches of Philip Carrington and E. G. Selwyn,[1] Dodd sought to investigate the relation that may have existed between the catechesis and the channels through which the sayings of Jesus were transmitted. Noting the references in the Thessalonian letters to the "tradition" which Paul handed on to the church (1 Thess 2:13; 4:1–8; 2 Thess 2:15; 3:6), he observed that it conveyed theological dogmas on the one hand (e.g., monotheism and the repudiation of idolatry, the resurrection and parousia of Jesus, the Son of God, salvation from wrath, the calling of the church into the kingdom and glory of God) and ethical precepts on the other (e.g., the holiness of the Christian calling, repudiation of pagan vices, the law of charity, the order and discipline of the church, eschatological motives).[2] A feature of this "pattern of teaching" (so

---

[1] Carrington, *The Primitive Christian Catechism* (Cambridge, 1940); Selwyn, *First Epistle of St. Peter* (London, 1946), 363–466.

[2] Dodd, "The 'Primitive Catechism' and the Sayings of Jesus," in *New Testament Essays: Studies in Memory of T. W. Manson* (Manchester, 1959); reprinted and revised in Dodd, *More New Testament Studies* (Manchester, 1968), 12–13.

called by Paul in Rom 6:17) is that it commonly includes a passage appealing to eschatological motives for Christian conduct, which almost always is placed at the end, and, remarkably enough, eschatological parenesis holds a similar place in the Gospels. The Sermon on the Mount is an example of this, since it ends with eschatological warnings (Matt 7:15–27); that led Dodd to conclude that the structure of the Sermon has been influenced by a form of catechetical instruction, if not based directly upon it. It would appear that the catechetical scheme provided a kind of schedule, defining the order in which topics in the sayings of Jesus might be treated.[3]

Bornkamm commented on this feature of the Gospel traditions, and also on its appearance in connection with teaching contained in the epistles of the NT.[4] Whereas Dodd had been concerned primarily with the application of eschatological motives, seen in such passages as 1 Thessalonians 4—5; Rom 13:11–12; Jas 5:1–11; 1 Pet 5:6ff.; Eph 6:10ff., Bornkamm was interested in the frequent appearance of warnings against false teachings in the conclusions of epistles, e.g., in Gal 6:11–12; Rom 16:17ff.; 1 Cor 16:22; Phil 3:2ff., 18–19; 1 Pet 5:5ff.; Jude 17ff.; 2 Pet 3:2ff.; Rev 2:9ff.; Did 16:3. This gave him a clue to the puzzling order of the chapters of 2 Corinthians: by placing the polemic against Paul's opponents at the end of the collection of the apostle's communications with Corinth the redactor characterized these teachers as false prophets of the last times, and at the same time set on this collection of letters the apocalyptic seal of inviolable validity.[5]

The custom of setting eschatological instruction at the end of a writing is adhered to with remarkable consistency in Matthew's Gospel. Each of the discourses manifests this arrangement. The Sermon on the Mount ends with warnings about false prophets and miracle workers and with a parable of judgment on the basis of response to the words of Jesus (7:15ff.); the missionary discourse ends with declarations of persecution in the service of the gospel, of judgment according to confession of Jesus, the apocalyptic division of humanity, and rewards at the judgment on the same basis (10:17–39); the parables discourse

---

[3] Dodd, *More New Testament Studies,* 16ff.

[4] For his treatment of the Gospel traditions, see Bornkamm, "Enderwartung und Kirche im Matthäusevangelium," in *The Background of the New Testament and Its Eschatology,* Festschrift C. H. Dodd, ed. W. D. Davies and D. Daube (Cambridge, 1956), pp. 222ff., then in revised form in "End-Expectation and Church in Matthew," in G. Bornkamm, G. Barth, and H. J. Held, *Tradition and Interpretation in Matthew* (ET Philadelphia, 1963), 15ff.; for the Epistles, see Bornkamm, "Die Vorgeschichte des sogenannten zweiten Korintherbriefes," reprinted in *Geschichte und Glaube,* part 2, *Gesammelte Aufsätze,* 4:162–94, and reproduced in abbreviated form in "The History of the Origin of the So-called Second Letter to the Corinthians," *NTS* 8 (1962): 258–64.

[5] Bornkamm, *Geschichte und Glaube,* 4:180–82; idem, *NTS* 8 (1962): 261–62.

has in its latter section the parable of the Darnel, with an interpretation, and concludes with the parable of the Drag-net (13:24ff., 36ff., 47ff.); the discourse to the congregation concludes with the parable of the Unmerciful Servant, with its stern warning of judgment (18:23–35); the discourse against the Pharisees contains sevenfold woes, burdened with warnings of judgment, and concludes with a passionate declaration of retribution and lamentation in 23:31–39; finally, the apocalyptic discourse is lengthened in ch. 24 with the inclusion of the so-called Q apocalypse and the three parables of judgment in ch. 25.[6] The setting of this teaching in Matthew 24—25 as the last of these major discourses itself conforms to the pattern observable within each separate discourse. In this the evangelist had before him the precedent of the compiler of Q, who also concluded his collection of the Lord's words with an "apocalypse" (Luke 17:22ff.), and above all Mark, in his ordering of the eschatological discourse at the conclusion of his account of the ministry of Jesus.

It is noteworthy that Mark's adherence to this pattern is manifest, even apart from the discourse in ch. 13. D. A. Koch noted its presence in the supremely important collection of teaching in Mark 8:27—9:1. The passage contains a section on Christology, 8:27–33, followed by sayings on discipleship, vv. 34–37, and utterances relating to the parousia and the revelation of the final kingdom, 8:38—9:1, in accordance with the catechetical praxis of the church.[7] Koch's statement as to the character of this passage clearly pertains to Mark 13:

> The conclusion of 8:27–9:1 through its prospect of the coming judgment does not bring any new accents, from the point of view of content, which modify the statements regarding the present existence of the church. Rather it effects a final sharpening of the parenetic exhortations. . . . At the same time the continuation of the discipleship logia through v. 38 makes it plain that the prospect of the parousia of the Son of man does not bring about a leap over the present suffering. The Son of man judges in accord with the yardstick which is given through his own passion.[8]

From this point of view Koch sees a parallel between the central "discourse" and Mark 13: both are concerned with the present existence of the church before the end, and both represent this present as a time of affliction and of confession, wherein the church is called faithfully to follow Christ.[9] On this account Koch rejects the notion of

---

[6] See the treatment of this theme in Bornkamm, *Tradition and Interpretation in Matthew,* 16–24.

[7] Koch, "Zum Verhältnis von Christologie und Eschatologie im Markusevangelium," in *Jesus Christus in Historie und Theologie,* Festschrift H. Conzelmann, ed. G. Strecker (Tübingen, 1975), 396–98.

[8] Ibid., 406–7.

[9] Ibid., 408.

Pesch that Mark 13 is an afterthought, injected into the Gospel after its completion; the pattern of catechesis confirms that the eschatological discourse was fashioned by Mark to form the climax of his presentation of the teaching of Jesus.[10]

This same principle sheds light on two matters: (1) the relation of the discourse to the rest of Mark's Gospel; (2) the nature and disposition of the material within it.

(1) We have long been familiar with the idea that Mark 13 partakes of the character of a *discours d'adieu,* of which the Bible and late Jewish literature contain numerous examples.[11] Munck pointed out that while these "testaments" are strongly parenetic, most of them are not concerned with the destiny of God's people in the latter days; that is, they are not strictly eschatological (As. Mos. 7; Testaments of the Twelve Patriarchs; Jub 45:14 are recognized as exceptions, to which may be added the "Words of Moses" in 1QDM). The Markan farewell discourse, on the other hand, contains a distinctly eschatological emphasis, together with parenetic instruction, in accordance with the tradition of the early Christian catechesis.[12] This in no way detracts from the fact that Mark has taken pains to tie the discourse closely to the context in which he has placed it. Lambrecht would take that context back as far as Mark 10:32, the third prediction of the passion, but chs. 11—12 form a more obvious setting.[13] It is not merely that Jesus is then found in Jerusalem, but that most of this section provides an account of Jesus in the temple—first his act of "cleansing," with its strong note of judgment (cf. 11:17) sharpened by Mark's insertion of it into his account of the withering of the fig tree (11:12–14, 20–21); then the parable of the Wicked Husbandmen (12:1–12), and the series of controversies between Jesus and Jewish leaders in the temple, wherein attempts are made to trap Jesus with a view to securing his condemnation. The prophecy of the doom of the temple in 13:1–2 comes as the climax of this series of confrontations of Jesus with the Jewish leaders. Mark's setting of the prophecy at this point inevitably confirms the impression that the ruin

---

[10] Ibid., 399.

[11] So J. Munck, "Discours d'adieu dans le Nouveau Testament et dans la littérature biblique," in *Aux Sources de la Tradition Chrétienne,* Festschrift M. Goguel (Paris, 1950), 155ff. See further, in agreement with Munck, Lohmeyer, *Markus,* 286; Grundmann, *Markus,* 259; N. Walter, "Tempelzerstörung und synoptische Apokalypse," *ZNW* 57 (1966): 40 n. 2.

[12] This has long been acknowledged in studies on Mark 13. See my *Jesus and the Future,* 212–16, and for more recent works cf. H. Conzelmann, "Geschichte und Eschaton," *ZNW* 50 (1959): 214; N. Walter, "Tempelzerstörung," 40; A. M. Ambrozic, *The Hidden Kingdom,* 224; L. Gaston, *No Stone on Another,* 51–60.

[13] Lambrecht, *Die Redaktion des Markus-Apokalypse: Literärische Analyse und Strukturuntersuchung,* AnBib 28 (Rome, 1967), 21ff.; see F. Neirynck, "Le Discourse Anti–Apocalyptique de Mc. XIII," *ETL* 45 (1969): 158–59.

of the temple is the divinely ordained judgment upon Israel for its rejection of the word of God brought by Jesus.

The prophecy in turn becomes the occasion for the discourse that follows, which can be viewed as an eschatological exposition of the prophecy, wherein the doom of the temple, city, and people of God is related to the accomplishment of God's ultimate purpose in history and to the vocation of the followers of the Son of man.

The relation of the discourse to the passion narrative in chs. 14—16 is not so easily defined. The theological aspects of this issue are reserved for the immediately following section on the themes of the discourse. Meanwhile it should be said that attempts to show that the discourse is constructed as an introduction to the passion narrative, with a point by point parallelism with the latter, tend to endeavor to prove too much.[14] Nevertheless, that certain fundamental points of contact between the discourse and the passion narrative exist is inherent in the nature of both. R. H. Lightfoot, in summarizing the content of Mark 13, emphasizes the chief one: "In ch. 13 the Lord upon the Mount of Olives, using language taken from the book of Daniel, tells four disciples of the final triumph, after unspeakable horrors, of good over evil, of salvation over destruction; and in one way or another it is all connected with and hangs upon the person and manifestation of the Son of Man."[15] Despite the small space occupied by Jesus in the earlier part of Mark 13, that is a correct assessment of the chapter; for the temple prophecy is regarded as due to the Jewish rejection of God's word through him; the pseudochrists and pseudoprophets usurp his role and pervert his message; the persecutions are occasioned through association with and proclamation of his name; the climax of history is brought about by his parousia; and the end of the discourse is a call to be on the alert for his coming.

The discourse also provides the context for understanding the passion of Jesus: he treads the path, traced by Israel's apocalyptic faith before him, through suffering to glory, as he will acknowledge before his judges (14:62), so that the outcome of his rejection will be the revelation of heaven's glory in the theophany and the gathering of the elect into the eternal kingdom. This path his followers must also tread; that is underlined by Mark by his redactional repetition of a term already in the tradition, applied both to Jesus and to his disciples: they will be "handed over" to authorities, to suffer and to die, just as Jesus was to be handed over by Judas, by the Jewish leaders, by Pilate, and by God himself (13:9, 11, 12–13; cf. 9:31; 14:10, 18, 21; 15:1, 15). Such

---

[14] See, e.g., R. H. Lightfoot, *The Gospel Message of St. Mark* (Oxford, 1950), 50ff.

[15] Ibid., 12.

is the context of the church's mission (13:10), as it was for Jesus in his mission till his trial and crucifixion. The end of the discourse emphasizes the call to "watch," which sounds throughout its length; the necessity of the call is illustrated for Mark through the disciples' experience in Gethsemane, wherein their failure to "watch" with Jesus resulted in their failure to stand firm in his dread hour (14:34, 37–38).[16]

(2) The nature of the discourse accords with the catechesis from which its materials are taken, in that from first to last it is both eschatological and parenetic; i.e., it is parenetic eschatology or eschatological parenesis. It provides anticipations of the end of the present age in order to warn Christians to be on their guard against a perverted eschatology and to inspire endurance in suffering witness after the order of Christ's own passion, with faith and hope in the victory of Christ. Conzelmann sees the basic structure of the discourse, including its relation to the double question of v. 4, to be formulated in dependence on the catechesis, for if (as he believed) the question itself is dictated by Jewish apocalyptic, it is interpreted by Mark in a Christian way, as Paul's treatment of the same issue illustrates: "How early the scheme is developed in the church is seen in 1 Thess 4:13—5:11. Significantly the line does not directly run from the question to the answer. The prevailing interest does not lie, as the question could lead one to suppose, with the apocalyptic representation, but with the right attitude to what is coming, thus with eschatological parenesis. . . . This deflection from the question to the answer manifestly is present also in our passage [i.e., Mark 13]. Here also the answer does not commence with apocalyptic representation but with exhortation or warning."[17]

It is to be observed that most of the elements within the discourse of Mark 13 can be traced in the catechetical tradition.[18] The emphasis on warnings against false christs and false prophets is frequently made (cf. Matt 7:22ff.; 1 Thess 5:3; 2 Thess 2:2ff.; and cf. the later 1 Tim 4:1ff.; 2 Tim 4:1ff.; 2 Pet 3:3ff.; the theme finds special application in Rev 13; 16:12ff.; and 17:1ff.). Persecutions and sufferings of the people of God are often mentioned (1 Thess 1:6; 3:1–4; 2 Thess 1:4–7; 1 Pet 4:12–19; cf. Rev 11:3–13; 13:11–13). While the judgment upon Jerusalem and its people does not figure prominently in the Epistles, it is represented in Q (Matt 23:34–36; Luke 11:49–51), is a major theme of Luke (13:1–5; 19:41–4; 23:27–31), and is alluded to by Paul (1 Thess 2:16), while Mark 13:14 finds a clear echo in 2 Thess 2:4ff. The call to watchfulness in the

---

[16] Note, however, that this Gethsemane reference is an illustration of the demand in Mark 13:33–37 to maintain spiritual alertness, not its fulfillment, contra C. S. Mann, *Mark*, 540–41.

[17] Conzelmann, "Geschichte und Eschaton," 214.

[18] See Dodd's treatment of this theme in "The 'Primitive Catechism' and the Sayings of Jesus," in *More New Testament Studies*, 18ff.

light of the near but incalculable parousia is characteristic of the catechesis (e.g., 1 Thess 5:1–11; 2 Thess 1:5; 1 Pet 1:13; 4:7; 5:8; Rev 3:2ff.; 16:15).

If then Mark found the constituents of his discourse in the Christian catechesis, we must ask in what form the materials existed, whether they were wholly disparate, or whether they had in any manner already become combined in the tradition. In doing so we would beg no questions as to the existence of an apocalypse fully formulated and ready to Mark's hand; we shall examine the elements themselves and endeavor to discover what links suggest themselves by virtue of their form and content.

We remind ourselves that the chief parallel in Mark to ch. 13 is the parable collection of ch. 4. The theme of that discourse, significantly, is the kingdom of God in the proclamation of Jesus, with explanations given in private to his disciples. The situation described in 4:1–2 is uncertainly related to the contents of the chapter; the language is Mark's, yet the introduction could reflect knowledge of a situation in the ministry of Jesus. It is commonly believed that the tradition had already brought together the three parables of the Sower, the Seed growing secretly, and the Mustard Seed,[19] and that Mark brought to them other material, including the statement on the *parabolai* of vv. 11–12 framed in vv. 10 and 13, the interpretation of the Sower in vv. 14–20, the material of vv. 21–25, and the concluding observations in vv. 33–34.

In ch. 13 the situation is set by the prophecy of v. 2, reproduced in the form of a pronouncement story,[20] followed by the question of vv. 3–4. But, as has been frequently recognized, many elements in the discourse do not appear to be immediately related to the prophecy. This is particularly clear with respect to vv. 9–13, which have no immediate reference to the doom of Jerusalem, and vv. 32 and 33–37, which refer to the end of the age, in all probability to the parousia. Verses 28–29 are of uncertain reference, but they appear to relate to the advent of the kingdom of God. The one passage which has unmistakable connection with v. 2 is the paragraph vv. 14–20. The cement which binds all these discrete elements together is the redactor's conviction that they all participate in the process leading to the end of the age, but in different ways, for he is at pains to point out that some of the events described do not portend the end itself (e.g., vv. 7–8).

---

[19] See Bultmann, *History of the Synoptic Tradition*, 325; A. E. J. Rawlinson, *Mark*, 47; V. Taylor, *Mark*, 93–94; and especially the instructive note by Jeremias, *The Parables of Jesus*, 14 n. 11.

[20] For Bultmann it is a biographical apophthegm (*History of the Synoptic Tradition*, 36, 60); V. Taylor speaks of it as a pronouncement story (*Mark*, 500).

Even more than the parable discourse the elements of ch. 13 give the impression of having once circulated as units of tradition. For example, there is no necessary connection between vv. 6, 7, and 8. Verses 9 and 11 have a parallel in Q, Luke 12:11–12, set in a different context, but consisting of one sentence; v. 10 accordingly appears to have been interpolated between vv. 9 and 11. Verse 12 looks like an independent saying; nevertheless, it is so closely bound with v. 13a that the clauses could have been formulated as a unity, but v. 13b is an isolated saying.

The paragraph in vv. 14–20 is often considered as a unity, yet it is likely that it is comprised of originally separate sayings. In Luke's Gospel vv. 15–16 appear in a different context, Luke 17:31; while Luke could have transferred them from the Markan apocalypse into the so-called Q apocalypse, the passage also appears in his version of the eschatological discourse (Luke 21:21); it is altogether likely that he found the sayings elsewhere in the (Q) tradition and set them in his second "apocalypse," in relation to the flight from Sodom and the warning about Lot's wife. One is encouraged in this view in that Mark 13:21 also appears in the Q apocalypse, Luke 17:23; it is apparent that the latter is a Q doublet of Mark 13:21 (Matthew reproduces both versions, Matt 24:23–24, 26–27) and thus illustrates that a saying of the discourse circulated in a floating tradition.

While vv. 24–27 are a closely woven unity, its constituents could have circulated also in more than one grouping, particularly vv. 26 and 27. Verses 28–29 are a parable, set in its present position almost certainly by Mark. Few dispute that vv. 30, 31, and 32 are independent sayings, linked in part in the tradition and in part by Mark. Verse 33b is possibly an original introduction to the parable of vv. 34–36, itself enlarged in the tradition or by Mark, and v. 37 is an independent conclusion furnished by Mark. While, then, there are good reasons for regarding the discourse as composed of units of tradition, there are also signs of rudimentary groupings of sayings which themselves attracted related sayings to form clusters in the tradition.

First, in view of the firm place in the tradition of the prophecy of vv. 1–2, it is likely that vv. 14 and 19 were very early associated with it to indicate the teaching of Jesus on the tribulation of Israel. These two sayings, and these alone in the paragraph vv. 14–20, are inspired by the book of Daniel, the former relating to the abomination of desolation in Dan 9:27; 11:31; 12:11, and the latter citing the description of Israel's tribulation in Dan 12:1. The *bdelygma* in v. 14 connotes both profanation and destruction, recalling the deeds of Antiochus Epiphanes, when he transformed the temple of Jerusalem into a heathen temple; such actions inevitably provoked resistance, war, and ruin. The first appearance of the expression "abomination of desolation" appears precisely in such a context in Daniel (9:26–27), where it is set in a description of the destruction of the city and sanctuary. The importance of Mark 13:14 and 19 is that they characterize the tribulation of Israel, linked with the ruin of the temple, as having eschatological import, indeed, as signifying the day of the Lord on Jerusalem and its people. It is comprehensible that vv. 17 and 18 were attracted to this nucleus of sayings, as also vv. 15–16, with their reminiscence of the flight from Sodom, and v. 20, declaring yet more emphatically the eschatological nature of the distress of Jerusalem. We may, indeed, perhaps go further: if the introductory vv. 3–4 convey an early tradition of the disciples' asking Jesus for further information about his prophecy of the temple's destruction (they must have been bursting with questions about it!), then it is plausible that in some circles the prophecy of v. 2 circulated with a reminiscence of the question in vv. 3–4 plus the essence of the answer in vv. 14–20. That could have served as a nucleus for the construction of the discourse at a later time.

Quite independent of this grouping are sayings relating to the tribulation of the disciples of Jesus, set forth in vv. 9 and 11. That these sayings circulated together is indicated by Luke 12:11–12. There is no need to postulate a borrowing by Mark of the Q version or the dependence of the Q version on Mark; we may assume that Mark's source contained a version of its own, which was fuller in its opening clauses than the form of the saying in Luke 12:11a. Two factors probably caused Mark 13:10 to become linked with the passage; on the one hand the witness activity of the disciples would have been a major cause of persecution by authorities, and on the other hand the mission of the church was viewed in an eschatological light, as v. 10 attests in one way and Matt 10:23 in another. And so in turn vv. 12–13a also were brought to this point, since the opposition from within the family and from those without was viewed as occasioned for the sake of Christ's name.

Within the discourse the opposition between false christs and the true Christ is an important feature. It is strikingly expressed in vv. 21 and 24–26, which set forth the contrast between the Jewish notion of the Messiah appearing in secret (cf. the more primitive expression of v. 21 in Matt 24:26) and the Christian representation of the parousia of the Son of man in power and glory. This contrast appears without ambiguity in Luke 17:23–24, where the equivalent of v. 21 is followed without a break by the equivalent of vv. 24–26: "They will say to you, 'Look! There!' and 'Look! Here!' Do not go running off in pursuit. For like the lightning-flash that lights up the earth from end to end, will the Son of Man be when his day comes." In view of the constant assumption that vv. 24–27 are related to vv. 14–20, it must be pointed out that the appearance of false claimants to messiahship and false prophets by no means requires the onset of the day of the Lord on Israel for its formulation (in the sense of vv. 14 and 19); the concept had roots as deep as the contrast between true and false prophecy in Israel's history (cf. Deut 13:1–5), and it is naturally taken up and developed both in the apocalyptic tradition and in the Christian catechesis. Nor is there any likelihood that the representation of the parousia in vv. 24–27 was framed in the light of the tribulation of Israel; there is no reference in this description to the deliverance of Israel from its oppressors in Judea, nor to judgment upon the destroyers; in this respect the portrayal of the parousia in vv. 24–27 differs markedly from the descriptions of the parousia in 2 Thess 1:6–10; 2:8–12; and Rev 19:11—20:3; the parousia of the Christ for his faithful people, on the other hand, is a constant theme in the Christian catechesis (cf. especially 2 Thess 4:15–18), and the appearance of the Christ of God is frequently set over against the appearance of false christs and false prophets in the catechesis (cf. 2 Thess 2:4–12; Phil 3:18–21; 2 Tim 4:1–8; 2 Pet 3:3–7; Rev 13; 19:11–21).

How early vv. 6 and 22 were conjoined with v. 21 in Mark 13 it is impossible to say, but it is likely that vv. 6 and 22 were found conjoined by Mark, and that he separated them for the purpose of inclusion (i.e., to bind the section on "signs" through vv. 5b–6, 22–23). The activity of false messiahs and false prophets called for emphatic warning.[21]

Finally it is to be observed that the theme of the parousia and watchfulness, contained in vv. 26 and (33) 34–36, is common in the Gospels and in early Christian instruction. Here we need not concern ourselves unduly with how much of vv. 24–27 was joined with vv. 33ff. (the whole of it is presumed in 1 Thess 4:15—5:11); it is sufficient to recognize it as a theme common to Mark 13 and Christian catechesis. It is a quite separate issue from the third subject (in vv. 21 and 24–26) and equally distinct from the first (in vv. 14ff.). Due to preoccupation with the little apocalypse, thought to be embodied in Mark 13, scholars have tended to view vv. 33–37 as an appendix, not actually belonging to the discourse. That is a mistake; if vv. 24–27 form the climax of the eschatological drama, vv. 33–37 form the climax of the parenetic appeal, and for Mark the latter is every bit as important as the eschatological doctrine, and indeed is integral to it. Matthew and Luke have their own representations of the same theme, with Matthew replacing Mark's brief conclusion with an expansion of the appeal for watchfulness that extends to double the length of the original discourse.

Presuming that some such natural groupings of the units of Mark 13 did occur, is it possible to suggest how the groups became firmer, and whether any came together in the tradition? Here the ground is not very firm beneath our feet, but there are not lacking indications to suggest some of the factors which may have caused the coalescence of the sayings in their groups and between the groups themselves.

---

[21] So, e.g., Pesch, *Naherwartungen,* 108–17; cf. idem, *Markus,* 2:278–79.

We take it that the *Sitz im Leben* of the differing groups of sayings
in Mark 13 (note *groups,* not the discourse itself) was on the one hand
the instruction of converts who had received the gospel, and on the
other the experience of the early church as a company of believers,
suffering hostility to their message just as their Lord experienced at the
hands of Jewish and gentile authorities.[22] This is particularly applicable to the second and fourth groups of sayings. The catechesis at times
associates the call to "watch" with an appeal for prayer and resistance
to the hostile powers in the world, including the spiritual powers (see,
e.g., 1 Thess 5:6–8; 1 Pet 4:7; 5:8–9; Rom 13:11–13). This is most
strongly developed in Eph 6:10–18, which, while it is not set in an
eschatological context like the related 2 Thess 2:15, is nevertheless
rooted in the magnificent eschatological vision of Isa 59:15–20 and has
a related intent in the concept of the conflict with the cosmic powers
that rule this dark world (Eph 6:11–12). Is not this idea close to that of
suffering witness before hostile powers, with endurance to the end, in
Mark 13:9–13? And is that not sufficient cause for the church's mission
to a hostile world to be linked with the call for spiritual watchfulness
in the light of the coming of Christ and the kingdom, and so for the
second and fourth groups of sayings to be associated in the discourse,
as in the catechesis? This perspective would have strengthened the
eschatological consciousness reflected in the section on the tribulation
of the church, both in the sufferings and in the concept of the mission
(with Mark's *prōton,* "first," in v. 10 cf. Rom 11:25ff., which could well
be an echo of the tradition in Mark 13:10).[23] On this ground it is possible
that Mark 13:10 found its place in its present grouping prior to Mark's
Gospel, although it is more likely to have circulated as an independent
tradition till Mark placed it in its present position.

The prophecies of the day of the Lord on Israel and its city and
temple needed no external crisis to stimulate their remembrance among
early Christians; the Christ of the kerygma was the rejected and crucified Lord, and Christians early experienced the continuance of opposition from Jewish leaders to their proclamation of the message of Jesus.
Nevertheless, the Caligula episode of AD 39–40 must have shocked the
Jewish Christians of Palestine as deeply as it did non-Christian Jews. It
would have prompted an urgent interest in the sayings of Jesus relating
to the desecration and destruction of the temple, hence the early
circulation of vv. 14 and 19 with the rest of the paragraph, vv. 14–20,
and with the prophecy of v. 2. But the same crisis would have encouraged the combination of this group of sayings with that relating to the
appearance of false christs and the true Christ, for eschatological expec-

---

[22] Cf. Hartman's discussion, *Prophecy Interpreted,* 211–12.

[23] So E. Käsemann, *An die Römer,* HNT (Tübingen, 1973), 300.

tation would have run high in Jewry at that time, giving rise to dire expression of belief as to the imminence of Israel's final distress and deliverance, according to Dan 12:1ff. Jewish Christians would have shared the fears and hopes of their contemporaries; their hopes, however, were more concrete through their faith in Jesus as the Messiah-Son of man who had already wrought redemption and was to complete the establishment in power of God's sovereignty over the earth and cosmos. So the first and third groups of sayings could have become associated under the pressure of Caligula's threat to Jerusalem. There is no need to extend the influence of this event to the second and fourth groups; Jewish opposition to the Christians was older than the danger from Caligula, while the call to be on the alert was already firm in the Christian catechesis. It is of interest that groups one and three (the tribulation of Israel and appearance of false christs and the true) are reflected in 2 Thess 2:1–9, while groups two and four (endurance in suffering witness and watchfulness in the light of the parousia) are echoed in 1 Thess 1—3; 4:15—5:11. This suggests the conjunction of at least some of these elements of Christian catechesis in the period of Paul's early ministry.[24]

It may be mentioned in passing that the conjunction of these units of tradition, and their coming together in a manner such as is here postulated, renders superfluous the notion of an independent apocalypse at the root of the discourse. The combination of vv. 7–8, 14–20, 24–27, which is constantly maintained by advocates of this theory, is much less plausible than the linking of the appearance of false christs and the true Christ (vv. 21–22 and 24–27) and the parousia with witness and watchfulness (vv. 24–27 and 33–36), supported as these are by other Gospel traditions and the primitive catechesis. The origin of the elements of the discourse is a separate issue; each saying is to be judged on its merits, not least in the light of other attested elements in the traditions of the teaching of Jesus.

One general question, however, is pertinent in considering the more debated elements of the eschatological discourse: Is it likely that Jesus anticipated the coming of a day of the Lord on his nation? If he

---

[24] The reflections of the eschatological discourse in Paul's writings have been underestimated in recent years. On a fresh examination of the evidence the following contacts appear to me to be highly probable: v. 5 reflected in 2 Thess 2:3a; v. 6 in 2 Thess 2:2 and 9; v. 7 in 2 Thess 2:2 (*mēde throeisthai*); v. 14 in 2 Thess 2:3–4; v. 22 in 2 Thess 2:9; vv. 24–27 in 1 Thess 4:15–17; 2 Thess 2:1; Luke 21:34–36 in 1 Thess 5:3, 6; 2 Thess 1:5. Less certain echoes may be seen of v. 10 in Rom 11:25; Col 1:23; v. 13 in 1 Thess 5:9; 2 Thess 2:13; v. 17 in 1 Cor 7:28; v. 19 in 1 Thess 2:16 (cf. Luke 21:23b); v. 20 in 1 Cor 7:29; v. 32 in 1 Thess 5:1ff.; vv. 33ff. in 1 Thess 5:4ff. With vv. 9, 11, 12 cf. Col 1:23–29; 2 Cor 4:5; 2 Tim 2:12–13; 4:1–5; these show similar viewpoints as Mark 13:9ff. without apparent citation.

did, is it conceivable that he employed in any measure the language of the prophets before him when alluding to that day, as also to the final theophany? In the light of the eschatological orientation of his message (Mark 1:14–15), the importance he attached to giving heed to his message of the kingdom (Luke 12:8–9), the existence of other traditions of his warnings to his people (Luke 13:1–5; 19:41–44; 23:27–31), and the difficulty of speaking of the day of the Lord and theophany without reflecting traditional language relating to them (cf. Mark 8:38; Luke 17:24, 26–30), a positive answer to both aspects of the question is not to be excluded. Of one thing, however, we may be confident: there is neither evidence nor likelihood that the groups of sayings which we have described were brought together to form a single discourse prior to Mark.

What then are we to say of Mark's role in the composition of the discourse? The variety of answers to this question is illustrated by the two scholars who have worked most painstakingly on the discourse, and in whom the two poles of critical judgment on this issue are evident. On the one hand, J. Lambrecht, applying rigorously the redactional-critical method to Mark 13, concluded that every sentence of the discourse was fashioned by Mark. "Little in this address . . . bears the marks of authenticity. . . . So much has become plain: in our modern concern for historical truth no norms can be set for the freedom in which Mark took up his task as author."[25] On the other hand, R. Pesch, equally enthusiastic for the redactional-critical method, when writing his commentary on Mark concluded that in this chapter "Mark shows himself . . . as the conservative redactor which the whole Gospel shows him to be."[26] On his present view Mark embodied in the discourse a Christian apocalypse (vv. 5, 7–8, 9, 11–13, 14–20, 21–22, 24–27, 28–31); the only statements within the discourse not in the pre-Markan apocalypse are vv. 6, 10, 23, but v. 10 could have been part of the source. Beyond these limits vv. 1–2 are considered to have belonged to the pre-Markan passion narrative, vv. 3–4 were probably received with the apocalypse, vv. 34–36 were from the Christian tradition, with v. 33a possibly conjoined as introduction to the parable; but v. 37 is Mark's conclusion to the whole. The discourse itself shows evidence of Mark's redaction, but in a "conservative" way. The majority of exegetes and critics range themselves at varied points on the line between these two extremes.

One can but confess one's own convictions on this issue. The consistency of Mark's style throughout his Gospel has been emphasized by those who have most carefully investigated it. So impressed were

---

[25] Lambrecht, *Redaktion*, 259.
[26] Pesch, *Markus*, 2:267.

C. H. Turner, M. Zerwick, N. Turner, and F. Neirynck by this phenomenon that they tended to minimize the influences of Mark's sources in
the composition of his Gospel.[27] Lambrecht, on the contrary, while
agreeing with the evidence of the evangelist's uniform style in the
Gospel, is convinced that Mark utilized sources in ch. 13, above all a
version of Q which he designated Q^{mk}. After working carefully through
Lambrecht's treatment of Mark 13 and the works by the writers mentioned earlier in this paragraph, it was difficult for me not to acknowledge Mark's hand throughout the length of the discourse. "Conservative
redactor" he may have been, but the whole discourse bears the imprint
of his style. This does not, however, impel one to adopt the position of
Lambrecht, that Mark has transformed beyond recovery what he has
reproduced in the discourse. The closest parallel in Mark's Gospel to
ch. 13 is, as we have seen, the parables discourse of ch. 4. The latter
"discourse" evidences Mark's redaction of material delivered to him;
the entire chapter bears evidence of Mark's style, as truly as ch. 13, but
the parables he has reproduced are one in their message with parables
of Jesus in other gospel traditions, and the same applies to the connective material he has added. There is no a priori reason why Mark should
have dealt in a different fashion with the material which came to him
in the eschatological parenesis of ch. 13.

It is reasonable to assume that Mark's prime function, in the
composition of this discourse as in ch. 4 and 8:27—9:1, was to bring
together the varied elements available to him and to fashion them into
a unitary whole in the light of the contemporary situation and needs of
the church in his area. Precisely when that was is extremely difficult
to determine. It is generally acknowledged that it was related in some
way to the circumstances of the Roman-Jewish War, whether to its
beginning, or to its middle, when a lull in the Roman pressure on
Jerusalem took place, or to its conclusion, after the devastation of the
city and the Jewish people had suffered their terrible fate. It so happens
that Mark gives no hint in the discourse or anywhere else that the city
had suffered destruction,[28] unlike Luke, whose "translation" of Mark

---

[27] See C. H. Turner, "Marcan Usage: Notes, Critical and Exegetical on the
Second Gospel," *JTS* 25–29 (1924–28). Zerwick, *Untersuchungen zum Markus-
Stil* (Rome, 1937). Observations are scattered throughout this work, see, e.g., pp.
42, 73. N. Turner, *A Grammar of New Testament Greek*, vol. 4, *Style*. On p. 11
Turner writes: "It seems that, although there may have been literary sources to
begin with, a final redactor has so obliterated all traces of them that Mark is in
the main a literary unity from the beginnings to 16.8." Neirynck, *Duality in
Mark: Contributions to the Study of the Markan Redaction*, BETL 31 (Louvain,
1972), 14–72.

[28] This is emphasized by a number of writers. Grayston is convinced that
the placing of Mark 13 between chs. 11–12 and 14, the former showing hostility
to the temple and the latter to the priesthood, suggests that at the time of

13:14 in 21:20 at least suggests that he has been "taught by the event," and Matthew (cf. 21:30 with Mark 12:8), and yet more plainly Rev 11:1–2.

The period in the middle of the war is a more plausible setting, both by reason of the temporary cessation of the war while Vespasian awaited orders owing to Nero's death and by virtue of the chaotic situation that then developed, when three emperors in succession arose and were murdered—a perfect situation for the publication of an apocalypse! The difficulty for this solution is that even before Nero's death Vespasian had overrun Judea and isolated Jerusalem, and there was little possibility of its inhabitants fleeing from it.[29] Of course, it is possible that Mark did not know exactly what the situation was in Palestine at that time, but that would nullify the suggestion that knowledge of it impelled him to write the Gospel at that time! It is perhaps best to be content with recognizing the immense effect that the outbreak of the Jewish War would have had on the eschatological expectations of Jews—in Palestine and throughout the world, as also on the Christian churches, many of which had a nucleus of Jewish members, not least the churches in Rome. It would have occasioned a great dread on the part of many, with clear realization that only God could deliver from the peril that now confronted them, and at the same time a conviction of many that now was the time when God would surely act for their deliverance—an ideal time for the arising of false prophets and false messiahs!

In such a setting Mark will have had good reason to warn Christians against the activities of such persons and to inspire them to continue in faith and hope in Christ and to encourage them to faithful witness and conduct. This situation would have provided a needful impetus to gather into one context the sayings in the tradition that related to the judgment upon Israel and the vocation of the church, the coming of the Lord and the call to maintain alertness of spirit. The balance of eschatological anticipation and parenetic statement in part inheres in the material at Mark's hand, but the maintenance of the balance from the first word of the discourse to its last sentence in no small measure is due to Mark's redactional work. In addition the welding of available groups of sayings and individual logia into the form now exhibited in the discourse is due to Mark's structuring of the material. For this aspect of Mark's work the reader is referred to the detailed discussions of Lambrecht and Pesch.[30] While concurring with the threefold division of the discourse that both advocate (namely vv. 5–23, the Tribulation; vv. 24–27, the Parousia; vv. 28–37, the Time), I think it is desirable to provide a more complete analysis of the chapter:

---

composition of the Gospel the temple and priesthood were still seen as a threat to Christians ("The Study of Mark XIII," *BJRL* 56 [1974]: 377).

[29] So M. Hengel, *Studies in the Gospel of Mark* (ET London, 1985), 10.

[30] Lambrecht, *Redaktion*, 261–94; Pesch, *Naherwartungen*, 74–82.

1–4 Introduction
  1–2 Prophecy of the Temple's Destruction
  3–4 Questions as to Time and Sign
5–23 Tribulation
  5–6 Appearance of Pseudomessiahs
  7–8 Tribulation in the World
  9–13 Tribulation in the Church
  14–20 Tribulation in Israel
  21–23 Appearance of Pseudomessiahs and Pseudoprophets
24–27 Parousia
28–37 Times of Fulfillment
  28–29 Signs and the Kingdom of God
  30–32 Time, Day of the Lord, and the Parousia
  33–37 Exhortations to Watchfulness

2. Leading Theological Issues in Mark 13

The *Gattung* of the eschatological discourse: is it an apocalypse? From Colani onward the majority of critical scholars have entertained no doubt about this question. Colani himself viewed the eschatological discourse as an apocalypse complete in itself. Proponents of the little apocalypse theory see the discourse as an apocalyptic expansion of an earlier apocalyptic fragment. Brandenburger strongly affirms that this must be acknowledged without reservation: "Mark 13 can, indeed, must be called through and through an apocalypse."[31] His definition of the discourse will be recalled: an apocalyptic "school discourse" in answer to a "school question."[32] Interestingly, Burton Mack, in an article in the journal of the Jesus Seminar, advanced from this position to categorizing the Gospel of Mark as not merely containing an apocalypse but as being an apocalypse, and he urged that scholars have generally failed to take this into account: "By treating the question of the 'little apocalypse' differently than the question of the Gospel itself, the 'eschatological' beginnings of the Gospel have been retained even while dismissing or discounting the apocalyptic endings. *But both go together.*"[33] It is, of course, an illegitimate use of technical language to call the Gospel of Mark an apocalypse, but Mack was concerned to divorce Jesus from Jewish apocalyptic eschatology. Ramsey Michaels, in response to Mack's position, affirmed in a meeting of the Jesus Seminar his willingness to accept the proposition that Mark 13 and Mark's Gospel "go together," but he reversed Mack's argument: if Mark's presentation of Jesus and

---

[31] Brandenburger, *Markus 13 und die Apokalyptik*, FRLANT 134 (Göttingen: 1984), 13.

[32] Ibid., 15.

[33] Mack, "The Kingdom Sayings in Mark," *Forum* 3 (1987): 6.

the kingdom of God is to be taken seriously, then ch. 13 deserves to be taken with equal seriousness.[34]

Anyone who has had the charity and patience to read the review of scholarly opinion on Mark 13 in the earlier pages of this volume will recall that not all critics have agreed that the eschatological discourse is to be classified as an apocalypse. C. C. Torrey, whose acquaintance with apocalyptic writings is demonstrated in his work *The Apocryphal Literature,* is an outstanding example of such writers. He observed that apocalyptic writings commonly purport to contain revelations from God through visions, usually by means of an angel, and he asserted that in Mark 13 there is no indication of any special revelation, none of visions, no suggestion of knowledge from heaven, no mystery in language (apart from the well-known expression "abomination of desolation" in v. 14, cited from the book of Daniel). "Whatever may be thought of the material of the chapter, or conjectured as to its composition, there is nothing in any part of it that can justify the use of the term 'apocalyptic.' "[35]

The discussion has not always been clear, since the distinctions among the varied meanings of "apocalyptic," familiar to Torrey, are not always recognized. Paul Hanson defined these as (1) apocalyptic literature, developed mainly in the last two centuries BC and the first century AD; (2) apocalyptic eschatology, concerned especially with the kingdom of God, the judgment, and the resurrection of the dead; (3) apocalyptic symbolism, called by Hanson apocalypticism, drawn from the traditions of centuries and even millennia, through which the apocalyptic message is represented.[36] It is clear that the second meaning of "apocalyptic," namely apocalyptic eschatology, has been the focal point of interest in the discussion about Mark 13. It should never be forgotten, however, that the eschatological thought of later apocalyptic literature has close affinity with the later prophetic works of the OT, notably Ezekiel, Deutero-Isaiah, Zechariah, and Isaiah 24—27 and 65—66, while the first truly apocalyptic work, the book of Daniel, has much in common with the prophetic outlook, particularly on the relation of God to history; and scholars still debate whether the book of Revelation is to be classed as apocalyptic or prophetic! There is much to be said in favor of Morna Hooker's view that Mark 13 is not strictly an apocalypse, but rather is midway between prophecy and apocalyptic, having affinities with both genres.[37]

---

[34] Michaels, "An Intemperate Case for an Eschatological Jesus," unpublished at the time of writing, p. 1.

[35] Torrey, *Documents of the Primitive Church* (New York, 1941), 14–15; cf. idem, *The Apocryphal Literature* (New Haven, 1945).

[36] Hanson, "Apocalypticism," *IDBSup,* 29–34.

[37] Hooker, *The Son of Man in Mark* (London, 1967), 149; idem, "Trial and Tribulation in Mark XIII," *BJRL* 65 (1982): 78.

With that position R. E. Clements would be in full agreement. We recall his affirmation: "What is being conveyed by the eschatological discourse of Jesus is not simply a prophecy about forthcoming events, but at the same time a vitally significant evaluation of the import and meaning of those events for all who look to the Hebrew scriptures as the ground and guide of their hope."[38] He sees the apocalyptic patterns of biblical interpretation as not confined to the biblical books of Daniel and Revelation, but as widespread in the prophetic literature of the OT, in the writings of Paul, and "most centrally of all, present in the teaching of Jesus."[39]

If one asks why there is such a concentration of concern with apocalyptic expectations in Mark 13, the answer must lie primarily in the critical time in which the discourse was composed, namely the Jewish war with Rome. This consideration holds good whether the author stood at the beginning of the war, or in its middle when the outlook for the Jews was grim, or at its end when Jerusalem lay in ruins and its people decimated. Eschatological fever was possible at all these points, as the twentieth century, with its experiences of wars, abundantly illustrates.

It may be noted in passing that the so-called apocalyptic cipher of Mark 13:14, "the abomination of desolation," was no cipher to the Jews of our Lord's day. The memory of Antiochus Epiphanes and the deliverance from his blasphemous oppression were kept fresh in the people's mind through the annual celebration of the Festival of Dedication, just as the oppression of the Egyptian Pharaoh and the deliverance at the exodus were recalled through the annual celebration of the Festival of Passover. To a people under the heel of an imperium far more powerful than that of Antiochus, the possibility of a repetition of that history, prior to the ultimate deliverance described in Daniel, was evident; how much more so for one who declared that not a stone of the temple would be left on a stone? And how very clear it was to a generation which, but a few years later, experienced the attempt of a mad emperor to repeat the acts of Antiochus!

Several purposes of the eschatological discourse have been put forward.

(1) To inspire faith, endurance, and hope in face of the impending sufferings of the church and of the Jewish nation. It seems right to place this object first, in view of the frequent habit of stressing the negative objects of the discourse. Warnings of Jesus to his followers concerning the inescapability of suffering are frequent in the Gospels. One such is

---

[38] Clements, "Apocalyptic, Literacy and Canonical Tradition," in *Eschatology and the New Testament,* Festschrift G. R. Beasley-Murray, ed. W. H. Gloer (Peabody, Mass., 1988), 18–19.

[39] Ibid., 27.

included in the Beatitudes of the Sermon on the Mount: "Blessed are you when men revile you and persecute you and utter every kind of calumny against you, lying as they do so, on my account" (Matt 5:11; Luke reads, "on account of the Son of man," Luke 6:22). Doubtless that beatitude belongs to a later period in the ministry of Jesus, when the opposition to him by Jewish authorities was becoming more intense. It reflects a foreboding of the impending rejection and suffering to death of the Son of man, described in the prophecies of the passion (Mark 8:31, etc.), and its consequences for his followers, alluded to in Mark 8:34. When disciples of Jesus become proclaimers of his message of the kingdom of God, and still more when, after his death, they proclaimed the crucified and risen Jesus as the Messiah and Lord of the kingdom, it was impossible for them to avoid sharing his passion (as 13:9–13, with its threefold repetition of *paradidonai*, makes plain; cf. 9:31 and the frequent appearance of the term in the passion narrative, e.g., 14:10, 41; 15:1, 10, 15). The experience of suffering had become daily bread for the Christians in Rome during and after the terrible persecution of the church under Nero.

But the concern of Jesus extended also to his people, and Mark included his warnings to them that they should not perish in the holocaust of Jerusalem to which the nation was heading. The point, nevertheless, to which the discourse moves is not the abomination of desolation but the parousia of the Son of man. That is the ground of hope, on account of which Christians can endure all things and abound in the service of the Lord and his kingdom, and for which Jews who do not confess his name should make themselves ready.

(2) To warn Christians against false teaching concerning the end. There is now virtually a consensus among exegetes that the warnings against pseudoprophets and pseudomessiahs, which occur in vv. 5–6 and 21–22, have been set by Mark at the beginning and the end of the narration of "signs" to draw attention to the danger of listening to such people. The position of these warnings most probably indicates that there were prophets both within and without the Christian church who proclaimed teachings viewed by Mark as highly dangerous.

The primary illusion is that the end of the age is immediately at hand, indeed, that the process has begun already, and Mark counters it at points throughout the discourse. While this is often thought to be a modern interpretation, it goes back to the very early years of critical study of the eschatological discourse. It may be seen, for example, in Pfleiderer's essay in 1868 on the composition of the eschatological discourse in Matthew 24, and it was staunchly maintained by Johannes Weiss.[40] Hauck's statement would gain the assent of most critical scholars

---

[40] Pfleiderer, *Jahrbücher für Deutsche Theologie* (1868): 144–46; Weiss, e.g., *Das älteste Evangelium* (Göttingen, 1908), 72–74.

today: "The tendency of Mark 13, despite all tension of thoughts as to the great hope of the end, is directed more to holding back extravagant views as to the near expectation of the end."[41]

The motif appears in the warning that opens the discourse: "Watch out . . . many will come in my name, saying, 'I am he' " (vv. 5–6). That is not intended to represent a Christian utterance, claiming the authority of Jesus for the statement "I am he," namely the risen Lord. It cites rather the claim of a non-Christian Jew to be "the Coming One," i.e., the Messiah. In v. 21 the claim is made on behalf of others in terms of the notion of the "hidden" Messiah, whose presence and identity are unknown till the time of his appearing. The followers of such are viewed as saying, "He's arrived! I know where he is! Come, and I will show you!" Needless to say, if the Messiah has appeared, the deliverance is about to take place. Despite the denials of some, the comparison with the teaching in the church at Thessalonica, which Paul had to counter, that the day of the Lord had set in (2 Thess 2:2), is pertinent.

The immediately following statements in vv. 7–8 relating to wars, "They must happen, but the end is not yet . . . These are the beginning of the birth-pangs," rebut the notion that the end has come upon the world and the new age is at the birth. To represent the latter statement, "These are *only* the beginning of the pangs," is, however, an over-statement. J. Gnilka is right in observing, "The two temporal statements of 7b and 8c express both eschatological distance and expectation together."[42]

The paragraph vv. 9–13 refers to quite different kinds of sufferings, namely those occasioned through confession of faith in Christ. The statement of v. 10, "The gospel must first be proclaimed to all the nations," is significant for our discussion: first, it is Mark who inserted it between vv. 9 and 11 (the two sentences occur in Luke 12:11–12 without any break); second, v. 10 is entirely traditional (from the catechesis?) with the possible exception of the term "first": "the gospel must first be preached to all nations." That is, it must be preached to all before the end comes! That emphasis of Mark not merely corrects apocalyptic excitement; it calls for devotion to the apocalyptic task of taking the good news to all humankind, for such is the divine purpose before the end comes. Matthew spells out the implication plainly: "Then the end shall come!" (24:14). On this Schmithals observed, "Verse 10 thus is a key to the understanding of the intentions which the evangelist combines with ch. 13."[43]

---

[41] Hauck, *Das Evangelium des Markus,* THKNT (Leipzig, 1931), 154.

[42] Gnilka, *Das Evangelium nach Markus,* EKKNT (Neukirchen, 1979), 186–88.

[43] Schmithals, *Das Evangelium des Markus,* Ökumenischer Taschenbuch-kommentar zum Neuen Testament II/2 (Gütersloh, 1979), 574.

A corollary of this correction of an extreme near expectation is an implicit denial that the parousia will take place in order to prevent the temple from falling into the hands of the "heathen." Mark's composition of the discourse is set as an exposition of the prophecy of Jesus in v. 2: the temple will be completely overthrown. The disciples' question as to the premonitory sign that will herald this shocking event is given in v. 14: "When you see the abomination of desolation standing where it ought not . . . then let those who are in Judea escape to the hills." Whatever the precise meaning of these words may be, it is plain that God has no intention of saving the temple. On the contrary, its destruction is assumed to be due to a divine decree of judgment (cf. Mark 11:12–14, 15–18, 20–21; Matt 23:34–36, 37–39; Luke 13:1–5; 19:41–44). The abomination of desolation will herald the execution of that judgment. Accordingly the instinctive resort of every Jew to flee for refuge to Jerusalem, and in particular to the temple, when disaster threatens, is reversed; the command is given that all who are outside the city should flee from it, for the day of its judgment has come.

This entails a corollary to the corollary: the employment of the Danielic language for the anticipated destruction of the temple, and its kinship with other prophetic proclamations of the judgment of God on Jerusalem, indicate that the end does not fall with that event. "Day of the Lord" for Jerusalem it may be, but not every "day" of the Lord signifies the last day. God has something more to accomplish before the final end (e.g., the sending of the gospel to all). That is strangely suggested by the proverbial language of v. 19 concerning the tribulation—"such tribulation has not been . . . nor ever shall be!"[97]and the (probably) Markan insertion in v. 24: the cosmic signs of the parousia will take place "after that tribulation." It is likely that the description of the parousia in vv. 24b–27 circulated independently without v. 24a, and that the expression "in those days" was added with a strictly eschatological meaning: "those days that end the old age and introduce the new." But if Mark received the passage with that introduction, the context which he now provided it was highly misleading, for it was capable of yielding a meaning opposite to that which he wished to convey; hence he added the phrase "after that tribulation," so effectively separating the parousia from the ruin of the temple.

3. The Eschatological Discourse and the Passion Narrative

That the discourse on the judgments and the deliverance of the Lord should take place at the end of the public ministry of Jesus is entirely in accord with the catechetical tradition. But its position as immediately preceding the passion narrative has long intrigued students of the Gospels. We have already noted that R. H. Lightfoot saw a

great deal of parallelism between the discourse and the passion narrative. This convinced him that Mark viewed the passion narrative as a
first fulfillment of the eschatological discourse, "a sign, a seal of
assurance, and a sacrament of the ultimate fulfillment" of the parousia.
On this understanding the passion is an eschatological event, participating in the finality of the consummation for which it prepares.[44]
K. Grayston reached a similar conclusion. Reviewing the connections
between the discourse and the passion narrative, he wrote, "By these
means the crucifixion is seen in its full eschatological significance; and
at the same time the eschatological expectations of the Church are
controlled by the crucifixion."[45]

To what extent Mark was conscious of the connections pointed out
by Lightfoot and Grayston I am not sure, but of the close link in Mark's
mind between the death, resurrection, and parousia of Christ there can
be no doubt. That is demonstrated by the little "discourse" of Mark
8:27—9:1, which is of central importance to the evangelist and his
Gospel. The passage includes Peter's confession of Jesus as the Messiah,
the first prediction of the passion, a group of sayings on discipleship in
relation to the sufferings of the Christ, and two sayings on the parousia
in relation to the disciples. It was the merit of F. Busch to grasp the
importance of the connection between 8:27—9:1 and ch. 13. He saw that
so surely as messiahship and suffering belong together, so proclamation
of the gospel and suffering of the proclaimers are inseparable, hence
"Mark 13 is an explication of Mark 8:34."[46] His book is virtually an
expansion of that thesis.

D. A. Koch developed this insight in an essay on Christology and
eschatology in Mark. He observed that the Christology of 8:27–33 and
the eschatology of 8:38—9:1 are linked through the use of the title "the
Son of man," so bringing together the passion and resurrection of the
Son of man and the parousia of the Son of man, and indicating the
identity of the Crucified with the Judge. The discipleship sayings of
8:34–37 are framed between the christological beginning and the eschatological prospect. Hence the sayings on the present existence of the
church are given a double foundation, through retrospect on the suffering of the Son of man and prospect of the coming of the Son of man.
Mark 13 is constructed on the same theological basis. The present is a
period of afflictions, but the orienting to the Son of man as the Crucified
and as the Judge has the effect of encouraging disciples to accept this
situation as in accord with the nature and calling of the church.[47]

---

[44] Lightfoot, *The Gospel Message of St. Mark* (Oxford, 1950), 51–54.

[45] Grayston, "Study of Mark XIII," 386–87.

[46] Busch, *Zum Verständnis der synoptischen Eschatologie: Markus 13 neu
Untersucht* (Gütersloh, 1938), 48.

[47] Koch, "Zum Verhältnis," 400–408.

This recognition of the relation between 8:27—9:1 and ch. 13 is significant in emphasizing the relation of the discourse to the redemptive action of the Son of man in his death and resurrection on the one hand and in the parousia on the other, and the way of the church in the time between as a *via dolorosa* illumined by the Easter resurrection and the parousia glory.

4. Signs and the Incalculability of the End

This theme is a perennial problem in studies of Mark 13. The discourse depicts a succession of events leading to the parousia in answer to questions as to the time when the temple will be destroyed and the sign when it will happen, on the apparent presupposition that the ruin of the temple and the parousia will occur together. By contrast the Q tradition represents the parousia as taking place suddenly and without warning (e.g., Luke 17:24, 26–30). Pharisees are told that the kingdom of God does not come "with observation" (Luke 17:20–21), and Mark 8:11–12 reports Jesus as emphatically rejecting a demand that he should give a sign "from heaven" to authenticate his mission ("No sign will be given to this generation"). Strangely enough, these two representations of the future appear side by side in Mark 13 itself: the parable of the Fig Tree (vv. 28–29) appears to sum up the function of the discourse as indicating signs by which the nearness of the end may be known ("When you see these things happening know that he is near"), yet v. 32 declares in strongest terms the unknowability of the time of the end ("Of that day or hour nobody knows"), and the parabolic sayings that follow emphasize the need for watchfulness in the light of that fact. It could be maintained that Mark has presented a contradictory picture of the end of the age. Inasmuch, however, as he himself fashioned the elements of the discourse into one, that is not very likely. Some preliminary observations may help to dispel some of the fog.

The "evil and adulterous generation" which demanded from Jesus a sign from heaven is rebuked by him for failing to discern signs of the kingdom present in his ministry (Luke 12:54–56), and he warned them of coming wrath for their failure to repent in face of such signs (Matt 11:20–24). His message to John the Baptist conveys the same fundamental idea, although couched in gentler language (Matt 11:5–6). The emphasis in Mark 8:11 is probably on the demand for a sign "from heaven," since the Pharisees alleged that the signs of Jesus on earth were inspired by Satan (Mark 3:22); they evidently wanted a sign that was unmistakably from God, like the fire from heaven that consumed Elijah's sacrifice.

Luke 17:20–21 must be understood in the light of these sayings. The term *paratērēsis* (observation) is used in secular literature by physicians for the observing of signs and symptoms of the body, and by astronomers and astrologers of the movements of stars and the planets. Jewish priests regularly pursued the latter kind of observation in order to fix the dates of their religious festivals. If, with W. Bauer, we understand *meta paratērōseōs* in Luke 17:20 as "so that its approach can be observed," we need to qualify "observed" with such some term as "accurately" or "precisely."

Most apocalyptists believed that God works in history according to a timetable. Consider, e.g., 4 Ezra 4:36–37: "He has weighed the age in a balance, and measured the times by measure, and numbered the times by number; and he will not move or arouse them until that measure is fulfilled." With this goes the belief that God has revealed this timetable to certain elect souls (see, e.g., 2 Baruch 54:1–5), and that a comparison of such revelations with events in history will show where one is at any given time in the divine plan. The process is simpler than it may appear, since it is always assumed by apocalyptists that the close of history is at hand, and it is not difficult to construe current events as signs of the end. (For examples of this viewpoint see the Apocalypse of Weeks in 1 Enoch 91—93, and the more detailed Apocalypse of the Clouds in 2 Baruch 53—74). We know that many rabbis after the fall of Jerusalem busied themselves with calculations of the time when the kingdom of God should come; according to one system of reckoning it should have arrived in AD 70, and those who so believed strove to explain why it failed to come at that time. It is unlikely that this kind of calculation on the basis of signs started only after AD 70. In Luke 17:20–21 Jesus apparently called on his Pharisaic interlocutors to abandon such futile apocalyptic arithmetic and to recognize the truth, "The kingdom of God is within your grasp," thus, by implication, to experience its grace by receiving the word of the kingdom that he brought.[48]

Anyone who reads the portrayals of the divine revelations of the course of history in such works as 1 Enoch 91—93 or 2 Baruch 53—74 will readily acknowledge that they are far removed from the picture of the future in Mark 13. There is no timetable in Mark's discourse. The warnings regarding false messiahs and false prophets, wars far and near, persecutions for witnessing to the gospel of Christ, are not stated in a chronological order, neither are they datable. Rather they characterize the entire period between the resurrection and the parousia, which is the eschatological time, "these last times," as the writer to the Hebrews terms it (Heb 1:2). The one apocalyptic sign in Mark 13 which refers to a specific event in history is the appearance of the abomination of desolation, and that is stated in answer to a question concerning the prophecy of the ruin of the temple in 13:2.

---

[48] On the interpretation of Luke 17:20–21 see my *Jesus and the Kingdom of God,* 97–103.

What, then, are we to say of the parable of the Fig Tree, vv. 28–29, with its application, "When you see these things taking place, know that he is near, at the doors?" What things are in mind here? They are happenings future to the time of speaking but prior to the end. In Mark's setting they must include the events described in vv. 5–23, but not all in the same manner. It is said of the wars in v. 7, "the end is not yet," and in v. 8 that they are the beginning of birth pangs; while therefore they belong to the "last" times, they are not to be emphasized as heralding an immediate end. Curiously, the same thing applies to the one clear sign of a historical and geographically locatable event, the appearance of the "abomination of desolation"; while described by means of Danielic language relating to the day of the Lord which immediately precedes the end, it is not viewed by Mark as integral to the end—the parousia comes after, not with the catastrophe upon Jerusalem. The remaining events in vv. 5–23, viewed as premonitory signs of the nearness of the end, are the activities of pseudomessiahs and pseudoprophets (vv. 5–6, 21–22) and the suffering witness of disciples (vv. 9–13). The importance of the former is emphasized by Mark's enclosing all other signs between their mention, doubtless because individuals of this sort were creating mischief by their claims about the immediacy of the end. It is ironical that a sign of the end can become a means of deception through misleading people to think that the end is nearer than it is! The suffering witness of the disciples is manifestly a sign perpetuated through the whole era of the church; its nature as a sign of the end is peculiarly in harmony with the Fig Tree parable, for believers who share in the sufferings of Christ through their witness to his message of the kingdom are encouraged to know that the end of their labors is none other than the event which will consummate the kingdom he initiated, namely his parousia in glory.

On no account, however, should the so-called cosmic signs described in vv. 24–25 be viewed as premonitory signs of the parousia. Brandenburger, following Conzelmann, maintains that Mark looks back on the whole portrayal of signs in vv. 5–23, including the catastrophe on Jerusalem and its people, as lying in the past; consequently the only signs referred to in the Fig Tree parable are the cosmic signs that herald the parousia; when they occur, however, it is too late to do anything about it! Brandenburger considers that thereby Mark has released the expectation of the parousia from the typical apocalyptic projection of historical-cosmic tribulation of this world time: "It is a fundamentally critical way of thinking, won under actual circumstances, and releases hope from Daniel's pattern of thought."[49] This I view as a questionable interpretation of Mark's intention. The notion of cosmic signs of the

---

[49] Brandenburger, *Markus und die Apokalyptik*, 96–102.

coming of God belongs, as Brandenburger himself emphasizes, to the ancient concept of theophany. But the fundamental idea of signs in heaven and on earth is the reaction of creation to the stepping forth of the awesome and terrible Creator. The elements of creation go into confusion and fear *because* he appears, not as a sign that he is about to do so (see, e.g., Judg 5:4–5; Amos 1:2; Hab 3:3–6, 10–11; Ps 77:14–16; 114:1–8). The cosmic signs mentioned in Mark 13:24–26 are accompaniments of the appearing of the Lord in his advent, manifestations of his glory rather than heralds of his coming; they characterize the parousia as a theophany, the revelation of the divine Son of God.

All this bears significantly on the nature of signs in Mark 13. Like the other evangelists, Mark recognizes that the kingdom of God is present in and through Jesus—his ministry, death, and resurrection, and that it presses on to his parousia. The whole period between the Christ event and the parousia is kingdom-of-God time, for it is characterized by continuing signs of the in-breaking kingdom which comes in its fullness at the parousia. All the events described in 13:5–23 have to be viewed as falling under the sovereign rule of God, for the judgments of God are as truly manifestations of the rule of God as his acts of salvation. This includes the appearance and works of the abomination of desolation, just as, in the book of Revelation, the Antichrist is given authority by God to open his mouth in blasphemies and to "act" for forty-two months, the period of the great distress (see Rev 13:5); the enemies of God have to subserve the purposes of God!

There is, accordingly, some justification for the recent trend to view the Fig Tree parable as the key to understanding the eschatological discourse.[50] The signs of Mark 13 show God at work in and through the processes of history under the lordship of Christ and through the Spirit in the church, leading the world and the church to their destined end in the consummated kingdom of God. Hence the suitability of the conclusion of the discourse in exhortations to remain on the alert, ready for the final manifestation of the kingdom in the parousia of Christ. This preparedness for the end includes serving the Lord till the end, as the parable of vv. 34–36 suggests, and not least in serving Christ in mission and sufferings for the kingdom, as vv. 9–11 show. Signs and suddenness are reconcilable when they relate to the Lord of the cross and resurrection and parousia.

5. Personal and Cosmic-Universal Eschatology

In an earlier work on the eschatology of Jesus, H. D. Wendland drew attention to the double polarity contained in the idea of the

---

[50] Hahn, "Die Rede von der Parusie des Menschensohnes Markus 13," in *Jesus und der Menschensohn,* Festschrift A. Vögtle, ed. R. Pesch and R. Schnackenburg (Freiburg, 1975), 263–64.

consummation: it has to do with final salvation and final judgment on
the one hand, and it is personal and cosmic-universal on the other.[51]
That is a generally acknowledged feature of mainline apocalyptic thought.
When we apply it to the eschatological discourse, final salvation is
plainly set forth, whereas judgment, declared at the outset (13:2), is
simply assumed in the latter part (its reality is reflected in the repeated
calls for watchfulness in vv. 33–37); by contrast cosmic-universal eschatology is assumed in the early part of the discourse (vv. 7–8) but fills
the horizon at the parousia; and throughout the whole, the messianic
function of Jesus includes the personal aspect.

Wendland, however, saw the emphasis within the discourse as
falling on a combination of the first and last of the double-polarity
features: "No single declaration as to the new world is given, and only
the dealing of the Son of man with humankind is depicted, not the
dealing of God himself. The personal-soteriological eschatology is the
central thing. . . . All expectation is directed to the ethical decision: the
coming of the Messiah, the judgment, and the gift of life."[52]

It is well that Mark has provided us with a discourse that maintains the balance which the apocalyptic dimension supplies; without it
our understanding of the eschatology of Jesus would be incomplete. By
the same token the representation of the eschatology of Jesus in Mark
13, if divorced from that which Mark himself and the other three
evangelists have set forth, would be unbalanced. But not even Mark
intended it to be read in isolation; it forms the climax of his presentation of our Lord's instruction on the kingdom of God, and the same
applies to Matthew and Luke in their versions of the discourse. A
full-orbed understanding of the teaching of Jesus, in eschatology as in
all other aspects of the revelation of God through him, requires the total
witness of all four evangelists, illuminated by the Spirit.

---

[51] Wendland, *Die Eschatologie des Reiches Gottes bei Jesus* (Gütersloh,
1931), 245.

[52] Ibid., 246. The comment is just. Mark's restraint in the discourse has
often been commented on. Apocalyptic works frequently describe the heavenly
world and the world to come, the appearance of God, the judgment of the wicked,
and the reward of the righteous. In these respects the book of Revelation is typical
of apocalypses, whereas the discourse of Mark 13 is atypical, yet it preserves the
elements of hope which are essential to a full-orbed eschatology.

7

A COMMENTARY ON MARK 13

Mark 13:1–2

The prophecy of the destruction of the temple—the point of departure of the eschatological discourse—is itself deeply significant, but its origin and significance, like many other elements of the discourse, are strongly contested, and there is no little confusion about them.

The suggestion made by Colani[1] has been widely taken up, that 13:2 is the negative half of the saying reproduced in 14:58: "We heard him say: 'I will pull down (*katalysō*) this temple, made with human hands, and in three days I will build another, not made with hands.' " In his dissertation on the discourse, Pesch hazarded the view that the double form of the logion would be more likely to be preserved in the tradition than the single form, and so Mark himself probably fashioned 13:2.[2] By contrast, J. Schlosser maintains that the dual members of the saying could have developed from one, and that the first part is more firmly anchored in the tradition than the second.[3] A. Loisy described v. 2 as a lifeless version of the more brilliant oracle of 14:58 that was never fulfilled.[4] G. Theissen (perhaps unwittingly) complemented this

---

[1] Colani, *Jésus Christ et les croyances messianiques* (Stuttgart, 1864), 180.

[2] R. Pesch, *Naherwartungen: Tradition und Redaktion in Mk 13* (Düsseldorf, 1968), 91; followed by J. Zmijewski, *Die Eschatologiereden des Lukas-Evangeliums: Ein traditions- und redaktionsgeschichtliche Untersuchung zu Lk. 21.5–36 und Lk. 17.20–37*, BBB 40 (Bonn, 1972), 81–83. Similarly, D. Lührmann, "Markus 14:55–64: Christologie und Zerstörung des Tempels im Markusevangelium," *NTS* 27 (1981): 463–69; idem, *Das Markusevangelium*, HNT (Tübingen, 1987), 217–18.

[3] J. Schlosser, "La Parole de Jésus sur la Fin du Temple," *NTS* 36 (1990): 409.

[4] A. Loisy, *L'Evangile selon Marc* (Paris, 1912), 365.

notion by suggesting that the negative half of the saying was isolated precisely because it was so plainly fulfilled in the Jewish War; that makes the prophecy a *vaticinium ex eventu*, although it goes back to a saying which could have emanated from Jesus.[5]

The question arises as to the nature of the anticipation reflected in the two reports of Jesus' words. It is unsatisfactory to describe 13:2 as envisaging a purely historical event while 14:58 looks for an eschatological one; the two categories are not mutually exclusive in Jewish thought. Loisy's interpretation of Mark 14:58 assumes an apocalyptic future event wherein the temple would be engulfed in the destruction of the world and a new one would replace it in a new world.[6] But in view of related utterances of Jesus concerning disaster upon Jerusalem and its people (see below), it is unlikely that these sayings were intended to communicate such a notion. An apocalyptic parallel for the idea of a new temple more in harmony with the teaching of Jesus lies closer at hand in the Qumran concept of the renewed people of God as the true temple, as L. Gaston has elaborately demonstrated.[7] In harmony with this A. Vögtle acknowledges that Mark will have understood 14:58 as having a quite different significance than 13:2; the former is concerned with the abrogation of the old order of temple worship, sacrifice, and covenant, and their replacement by a new order in virtue of the redeeming sacrifice of Christ, as Mark's report on the tearing of the temple curtain (15:29) indicates.[8] W. Schmithals actually interprets 13:2 as possessing the identical notion: the destruction of the temple is held to signify the end of the Jewish worship, both that of the temple and synagogue, and its replacement by the eschatological worship of the new age, hence of Christianity and the church.[9]

While it is evident that such ideas may be included in the logical consequences of Mark 13:2, they should not be viewed as falling within the intention of the saying. The prophecy of 13:2 is an utterance of the

---

[5] G. Theissen, "Die Tempelweissagung Jesu," *TZ* 32 (1976): 145 n. 4.

[6] Contrary to his exposition in *Evangiles synoptiques*, 2:600–601; but Bultmann so understood Mark 14:58 (*The History of the Synoptic Tradition*, 2d ed. [ET New York, 1968], 120–21).

[7] L. Gaston, *No Stone on Another: Studies in the Significance of the Fall of Jerusalem in the Synoptic Gospels*, NovTSup 23 (Leiden, 1970), especially 126–28, 168–76.

[8] A. Vögtle, "Das markinische Verständnis der Tempelworte," in *Die Mitte des Neuen Testament*, Festschrift E. Schweizer, eds. U. Luz and H. Weder (Göttingen, 1983), 362–64.

[9] W. Schmithals, *Das Evangelium nach Markus*, Ökumenischer Taschenbuchkommentar zum Neuen Testament (Gütersloh, 1979), 557–59. T. Geddert emphatically affirms a like view (*Watchwords: Mark 13 in Markan Eschatology*, JSNTSup 26 [Sheffield, 1989], 138.

doom of the temple. Its relation to 14:58 is plain, but its distinction from it is equally clear, having a more limited and strongly expressed range of meaning. J. Ernst is surely right in maintaining that the linguistic differences between 13:2 and 14:58 tell against the former being a variant of the latter.[10] There are other declarations of Jesus concerning the fate of Jerusalem and its people which, while often differing in form, have the same explicit purpose as 13:2.

The most remarkable of these parallels to Mark 13:2 is offered in Luke 19:44, as J. Dupont has emphasized.[11] In this lament of Jesus over Jerusalem it is stated: "They will bring you to the ground, you and your children within your walls, and not leave you one stone standing on another." The coincidence of language in the last clause is notable: *ouk aphēsousin lithon epi lithon en soi*. Mark has the same terms, but with the verb in the passive: *ou mē aphethē ōde lithos epi lithon*. The short statement common to Luke 19:44 and Mark 13:2 is sufficiently striking to have warranted its circulation in the early church; but whereas in Luke it relates to the city, in Mark 13:2 it explicitly refers to the temple. Dupont in his article declined to pronounce a decision on this issue; Gaston argued strongly for the originality of Luke 19:44 and the application of the saying to the city, whereas Hartman viewed all three passages (Mark 14:58 with the other two) as variants of a single saying.[12] When Pesch came to write his commentary on Mark, he was persuaded by Dupont's arguments on the affinity of Mark 13:2 with Luke 19:44, but he now considers both to be independent sayings; with many other commentators he adopts the view that the exclamation of the disciple in Mark 13:1 could be an expression of the sentiment that such huge stones and structures as were in the temple would surely never be destroyed, whereupon Jesus declared that even these buildings would be destroyed and these stones be torn from their places.[13]

This interpretation is admittedly particularly plausible in the Matthean version of the discourse, since the prophecy of the ruin of the temple follows immediately upon the declaration of the judgment of God on the contemporary generation (Matt 23:34–36) and the lament over Jerusalem, with its terrible utterance: "Look, your house is abandoned to you—desolate" (23:38). Interestingly, this latter statement is one in which it is peculiarly difficult to be certain whether "house"

[10] J. Ernst, *Das Evangelium nach Markus*, RNT (1981), 369.
[11] J. Dupont, "Il n'en sera pas laissée pierre sur pierre (Mc 13,2; Luc 19,44)," *Bib* 52 (1971): 301–20.
[12] Gaston, *No Stone on Another*, 66–67; Hartman, *Prophecy Interpreted: The Formation of Some Jewish Apocalyptic Texts and of the Eschatological Discourse Mark 13 Par.*, ConBNT 1 (Lund, 1966), 219–20.
[13] R. Pesch, *Das Markusevangelium*, 2 vols., HTKNT (Göttingen, 1976–77), 2:271.

means city or temple since each entails the other.[14] OT prophetic utterances sometimes emphasize the one, sometimes the other, and frequently conjoin the two. In Ezekiel 9—11 the prophet, with characteristic detail, describes how the divine glory abandons first the temple, which has been profaned, and then the city, so leaving temple and city and nation to their fate. The prophecy of Jeremiah against the temple (Jer 7:1–20) similarly singles out the temple for destruction, but adds that the people and city will also experience the divine wrath (vv. 14–20). The prophecy is repeated in Jeremiah 26, explicitly relating to the temple and city, which leads to the recollection of the doom prophecy of Micah by certain of the elders (in defense of Jeremiah for proclaiming such a message):

> On your account
> Zion shall become a ploughed field,
> Jerusalem a heap of ruins,
> and the temple hill rough heath.[15]

The linking of temple, city, and people in the anticipated judgment of God is comprehensible, in that the destruction of the temple could not be accomplished without the devastation of the city, nor that of the city without the ruin of the temple, and in either case the populace would suffer virtual decimation. Hence the logic of the prophecy uttered by Jesus son of Ananus shortly before the Jewish War:

> A voice from the east,
> a voice from the west,
> a voice from the four winds;
> a voice against Jerusalem and the temple,
> a voice against the bridegroom and the bride,
> a voice against the whole nation![16]

The interpretation of Mark 13:2, accordingly, as relating to the temple as the center of Israel's life and a symbol of God's relation to the nation, is well grounded in the prophetic tradition of the OT. The broken relationship to God occasions a rejection of the place which serves as the visible embodiment of God's presence with and favor to the people, hence a judgment on the nation itself. But this is wholly in accord with Mark's distinctive viewpoint also. His account of the ministry of Jesus in Jerusalem begins with the tumultuous welcome of Jesus into the city, after which he at once makes his way into the temple and "looks around at everything" (11:11). The next day Jesus throws the merchants out of

---

[14] So Schulz comments on Matt 23:38: "The city as the house of Israel will be forsaken by God, in that he gives up the temple of Zion as his dwelling" (*Die Spruchquelle der Evangelisten* [Zürich, 1972], 356). Similarly, D. Hill, *The Gospel of Matthew*, NCBC (London, 1972), 316.

[15] Mic 3:12, which is cited in Jer 26:17–19.

[16] Cited by Josephus, *War* 6.301.

the temple. By his reference to Jer 7:11 in his address to the offending merchants and others, he makes it plain that his action is less a purification than a condemnation and threat of judgment. In Jer 7:11 the desecration of the temple to become "a den of robbers" is followed with the declaration: "I will do to the house which is called by my name, in which you trust, and to the place which I gave to you and to your ancestors, just what I did to Shiloh. And I will cast you out of my sight, just as I cast out all your kinsfolk, all the offspring of Ephraim."

Further, Mark has placed the account of the temple cleansing within his narrative of the withering of the fig tree (11:12–14, 20), which he clearly wishes to be understood as an act of prophetic symbolism, setting forth the impending judgment of God on the "fruit-less" nation (cf. Hos 9:10–10:2).[17] The two actions thus have one fundamental significance. The challenge of the Jewish leaders in the temple as to the authority of Jesus so to act is then described. In his reply Jesus recounts the parable of the Wicked Tenants (12:1–12), which exposes the root of the opposition of Israel's leaders to him as nothing less than rebellion against God, which will lead to inevitable judgment upon them. So follow the controversies of ch. 12, wherein the rulers seek in vain to discredit Jesus. The narrative concludes by Jesus leaving the temple, and uttering his prophecy of its destruction on the way out. So the ministry of Jesus in Jerusalem begins with a sign of the judgment of God on the temple and ends with a prophecy of the temple's destruc-tion. Never again is Jesus reported to have entered the temple precincts. His final departure may well be seen as symbolic of the departure of God from it, leaving the temple to its ultimate fate.

It is difficult, accordingly, to agree with those exegetes who view the prophecy of 13:2 as a simple prediction of what shall one day happen, without any threat of judgment within it.[18] On the contrary, both the precedents for the temple prophecy in the OT and the related sayings in the Gospel tradition lead to the view that the statement in v. 2 is viewed as a judgment on the nation in whose midst the temple stands. The two closest Gospel parallels to 13:2 are 14:58 and Luke 19:43–44; the former implies the rejection of the old temple in order that another may replace it which will more truly serve the praise of God; the latter tells of the impending desolation of the city and people "because you did not recognize God's moment when it came." The closest OT parallel to Mark 13:2 is Amos 9:1:

---

[17] See W. R. Telford, *The Barren Temple and the Withered Tree* (Sheffield, 1980), 216–17. In view of the connection between the withering of the fig tree and the temple cleansing Geddert urges that the former is viewed as a sign of the judgment on Israel's leaders rather than on the nation (*Watchwords*, 126–29).

[18] Pesch, *Naherwartungen*, 93–96; Zmijewski, *Eschatologiereden*, 83; Lühr-mann, *Das Markusevangelium*, HNT 3 (Tübingen, 1987), 218.

Strike the capitals so that the whole porch is shaken;
I will smash them all into pieces
and I will kill them all to the last man with the sword.

Admittedly the latter is directed to the temple at Bethel rather than
that in Jerusalem, but the divine wrath is called forth not by the location
of the shrine but by the sinfulness of the people. It is noteworthy that
after the fall of Jerusalem there were not lacking Jewish teachers who
acknowledged the sin of their people as calling forth the judgment of
God upon the nation. It is recorded in p. *Yoma* 11, 38c, 57: "Someone
asked R. Eliezer [ca. 90]: 'Were the later generations [at the time of the
second temple] more pious than the earlier [i.e., at the time of the first
temple]?' He replied, 'Let your witness, the temple, give you the proof.
Our fathers [at the time of the first temple] have removed the roof beams
(see Isa 22:8, He has lifted the covering of Judah); but we have broken
the walls [to the ground] (see Ps 137:7, "They cried, 'Tear it down, tear
it down, tear it down to the ground' ").' "[19]
There are, accordingly, very good grounds for interpreting the
prophecy of Mark 13:2 as making known a judgment of eschatological
proportions, a "day" of the Lord on the temple, city, and people. The
other dominical passages cited, however, indicate that what is held in
prospect is not the dissolution of the universe but a disaster on the
plane of history. As in days of old a nation will become the scourge of
God to carry out his judgment. The passage from prophecy to apocalyptic, especially on the lips of Jesus, does not necessarily entail the
annihilation of history, but rather raises the eyes to the Lord of all
history. Accordingly Schulz has rightly observed in connection with
the related saying, Matt 23:38: "For the community . . . the departure
of God from Jerusalem is to be equated with the abandonment to its
political enemies, and thus the apocalyptic and the historical-political
aspects of this preaching of doom are not to be separated."[20]
In comparison with the issues which we have been considering,
the question of the immediate context of the prophecy (in v. 1) is of
secondary importance. Bultmann viewed vv. 1–2 as a biographical
apophthegm; to him the address of v. 1 sounded as if it were formed for
the purpose of evoking the prophecy of v. 2c; the latter could be
assigned to the Palestinian community, and even perhaps to Jesus
himself, but the context to the hellenistic community.[21] Both Lambrecht and Pesch subjected the passage to detailed linguistic analysis,

---

[19] See Str-B, 1:946. Of other warnings by Jews of judgment on their nation
the best known is that of Johannan ben Zakkai: "O Galilee, Galilee, thou dost hate
the Torah; thy end will be seizure by the Romans." See further b. *Yoma* 39b, 43c, 61.
[20] Schulz, *Spruchquelle*, 356–57.
[21] Bultmann, *History of the Synoptic Tradition*, 36, 60.

which led them to affirm its specifically Markan character, and so its creation by Mark.[22] With that position a considerable number of exegetes agree.[23] Pesch's subsequent investigations into the Gospel of Mark, however, led him to postulate that 13:1–2 is to be included in the pre-Markan passion story, hence that Mark did not compose the passage, and that there are indications that the setting is historical and not secondary.[24] F. Neirynck has examined Pesch's claim that the material of the passion story in Mark is stylistically removed from the rest of the Gospel and concluded that such a deduction cannot be drawn from the evidence.[25] It is to be hoped, however, that redaction critics will not press too hard the notion that everything in the Gospels which bears the stamp of the author's style is thereby to be viewed as creations of the evangelists. It is of interest that nowhere else in Mark do we read of a single unnamed disciple addressing Jesus; the remark which he is said to have made is not unreasonable from a disciple of Jesus, despite the comments of exegetes to the contrary.[26] It is easy to overlook that the temple complex in Jerusalem was probably the most awesome building in the ancient world. We have also noted the possibility that the disciple's exclamation was in response to utterances of Jesus indicating coming judgment on Jerusalem and its temple, and his incredu-

---

[22] Lambrecht, *Die Redaktion des Markus-Apokalypse: Literärische Analyse und Strukturuntersuchung*, AnBib 28 (Rome, 1967), 68–72, 79; Pesch, *Naherwartungen*, 84–86.

[23] See, e.g., E. Lohmeyer, *Das Evangelium des Markus*, MeyerK (Göttingen, 1963), 267–68; D. E. Nineham, *St. Mark*, Pelican Gospel Commentary (Harmondsworth, 1963), 344; L. Gaston, *No Stone on Another*, 10–11; A. M. Ambrozic, *The Hidden Kingdom: A Redaction-Critical Study of the References to the Kingdom of God in Mark's Gospel*, CBQMS 2 (Washington, D.C., 1972), 225; W. Kelber, *The Kingdom in Mark* (Philadelphia, 1974), 111–12; E. Schweizer, *The Good News according to Mark* (ET Atlanta, 1970), 267; J. Dupont, "Il n'en sera pas laissé pierre sur pierre (Marc 13,2; Luc 19,44)," *Bib* 52 (1971): 304–6; Zmijewski, *Eschatologiereden*, 80; H. Anderson, *The Gospel of Mark*, NCBC (London, 1976), 290.

[24] Pesch sees a pointer to the pre-Markan origin of the setting in the commencement of the passage with a genitive absolute (*kai ekporeuomenou autou ek tou hierou*, v. 1); he affirms that pericopae beginning with a genitive absolute are found in Mark only in pre-Markan connecting verses (5:21; 10:17) and in material of the pre-Markan passion story (14:3, 22, 43, 66), apart from connections of time (1:32; 14:17, 33, 42; 16:1), but even of this last group the last four are from the pre-Markan passion story! (*Markus*, 2:268–71).

[25] F. Neirynck, "L'Evangile de Marc, à propos du Commentaire de R. Pesch," *Analecta Lovaniensa Biblica et Orientalia*, Sevr. V Fasc. 38 (1979), 8–27; see especially the conclusion on p. 27.

[26] Note, e.g., the oft-cited comment of Lohmeyer: "The admiring exclamation, which would be comprehensible from the mouth of strangers or pilgrims, but strange from a disciple who has been staying in Jerusalem for at least three days, surely serves simply to prepare for the prophetic saying of Jesus" (*Markus*, 268).

lity at the prospect of such huge buildings being destroyed and such enormous stones being overthrown.[27]

One can but weigh probabilities. Mark could have supposed that the prophecy of the temple was uttered by Jesus in the temple itself, at a point where the structures were most clearly seen; or he could have received with the tradition of the prophecy an intimation that it was made to an unnamed disciple on leaving the temple shortly before the Passover. In any case the observation of K. L. Schmidt on the passage is incontrovertible: "Here the announcement of place is naturally firmly anchored in the saying itself."[28]

Mark 13:3–4

This short pericope connects the prophecy of v. 2 with the discourse which follows. We have recognized that the discourse was composed by Mark. Did he compose the introduction also? The ambiguity of the question should be observed. It asks whether the evangelist created the scene in order to effect the transition from the prophecy of v. 2 to the following address, or whether he composed it on the basis of a tradition he had received.

The former alternative is adopted by most critical exegetes of this century. In their view it accords with Mark's frequent representations of Jesus giving instruction to his disciples in private, particularly in response to questions concerning his teaching.[29] It is in harmony with the esoteric nature of apocalyptic writings.[30] Its location is ideal for an apocalyptic revelation—on a mountain, and above all on the Mount of Olives.[31] It bears the imprint of Mark's style.[32] In addition the questions

---

[27] This understanding of the saying has been expressed by exegetes and critics through the years; see, e.g., H. A. W. Meyer, *Kritisch-exegetisches Handbuch über das Evangelium des Matthäus,* 3d ed. (Göttingen, 1853), ad loc.; T. Zahn, *Das Evangelium des Matthäus,* Kommentar zum Neuen Testament 1 (Leipzig, 1903), ad loc.; A. Schlatter, *Das Evangelium nach Matthäus,* Erläuterungen zum NT 1 (Stuttgart, 1947), 351; H. B. Swete, *The Gospel according to St Mark,* 3d ed. (London, 1927), 295; Bultmann, *History of the Synoptic Tradition,* 121; C. E. B. Cranfield, *The Gospel according to Saint Mark,* CGTC, 3d ed. (Cambridge, 1966), 391; Pesch, *Markus,* 2:270.

[28] K. L. Schmidt, *Der Rahmen der Geschichte Jesu* (Berlin, 1919), 290.

[29] See especially Mark 4:10–12; 7:17–23; 9:11–13, 28–29; 10:10–12; and F. Neirynck, *Duality in Mark* (Louvain, 1972), 53.

[30] "The fiction of secret information . . . corresponds to the apocalyptic style" (G. Hölscher, "Der Ursprung der Apokalypse Mk 13," *TBl* 12 [1933]: 193).

[31] See especially K. L. Schmidt, *Der Rahmen der Geschichte Jesu,* 290; E. Lohmeyer, *Markus,* 268. R. Pesch cites a number of passages in Gnostic and other apocryphal writings which speak of Jesus giving revelations and eschatological instruction on the Mount of Olives (*Markus,* 2:274).

[32] For the expression *eis to oros* see C. H. Turner, JTS 25 (1924): 19; for *epērōta* cf. idem, JTS 29 (1928): 360; on *kai kathēmenou* see Zerwick,

of v. 4 reflect the content of the discourse which is supposed to answer them; that is, they have been framed in the light of the answers already contained in the materials of the discourse.

The last two points are to be given due weight. The wording of the paragraph is undoubtedly Mark's, and the precise form of the questions is due to him. The implications of the other observations are less clear. It is not immediately apparent why a suggestion that Jesus gave instruction to his disciples apart from the crowds should be suspect. According to Mark, Jesus "appointed twelve that they should be with him, and that he might send them forth" (3:14); also on one occasion, when passing through Galilee, Jesus "did not want any one to know, because he was teaching his disciples" (9:30–31). Further, we know that Jewish rabbis were in the habit of explaining their public teaching to their pupils alone.[33] Testimony to a similar procedure on the part of Jesus could well have been present in the tradition received by Mark; if so it is comprehensible that he may have stylized it.[34] Yet if any utterance of Jesus was calculated to set the disciples questioning and burning to ask about it, the prophecy of v. 2 was such a statement.

It is needful to bear in mind that Mark had before him not only the prophecy about the ruin of the temple, but also traditions of Jesus' eschatological teaching, some of which we postulated had already gravitated together. In particular we suggested that at an early date the prophecy of v. 2 was linked with the passage concerning the abomination of desolation and the tribulation of Israel, vv. 14–20. We also gave reason to believe that this group of sayings later became linked with teaching on false messiahs and the true Messiah (vv. 6, 22) 21, 24–27. The need for a context which could include extended teaching on the

---

Untersuchungen zum Markus-Stil (Rome, 1937), 10. Zerwick notes that the word order of the main sentence in v. 3 accords with Mark's general usage (p. 91). The double question, as in v. 4, is frequent in Mark (e.g., 1:27; 2:7, 9; 6:2, 3; 7:18; 8:17, 18; 9:19; 11:28; 14:37). Zerwick further points out that when the disciples or Pharisees question the Lord, and so give occasion for a word of the Lord or a longer address, the rule is that these questions are formulated in direct speech; fourteen times this is observable, in 2:18, 24; 7:5, 9, etc. Strangely, the three exceptions are 4:10; 7:17; 10:10, which deal with a favorite thought of Mark: the emphasis on the distinction between public teaching of people and private instruction of the disciples! See ibid., 24–29. The position of *panta* at the end of v. 4 is an example of stress falling at the conclusion of a sentence, as in 2:28; 7:19, 27; 9:45; 10:13, 43, 44; 11:14 (ibid., 118–19). For further comments on the Markan style of 13:3–4 see the discussions in Lambrecht, *Redaktion*, 80–87; Pesch, *Naherwartungen*, 96–97, 101–2; and Neirynck, *Duality in Mark*, 54–55.

[33] So D. Daube, "Public Pronouncement and Private Explanation in the Gospels," *ExpT* 57 (1945): 175–77, reproduced in *The New Testament and Rabbinic Judaism* (London, 1956), 141–50.

[34] See especially the discussion on this feature by Neirynck, *Duality in Mark*, 53–54.

fate of Israel and the end of the age would have been pressing. It is at least a plausible suggestion that vv. 3–4 provided a desired connection between the temple prophecy and a core of discourse material relating to Israel's tribulation and the parousia of the Son of man.[35]

The suitability of the context for a revelation discourse on the end of the age is not in doubt—so fitting, indeed, it is not to be wondered at that references abound in later apocryphal literature to Jesus giving revelations on the Mount of Olives, in dependence on Mark's narrative.[36] It is, we may recall, as suitable for the delivery of an eschatological address as Matthew's picture of Jesus seated on a mountain, enunciating a new Torah, a greater than Moses addressing a new Israel (Matt 5:1ff.). Matthew has not so much created that scene as exploited a context provided by Mark (3:13), and possibly alluded to in Q (cf. Luke 6:12, 17, 20), in the interests of his understanding of the mission of Jesus and as an impressive mode of presenting the catechesis he had for the church. The same could apply to Mark, as he sought to transmit traditions he had received concerning the distress of Israel, the trials and the mission of the church, and the coming of the Son of man. If the scene of vv. 3–4 had been passed on to the evangelist as the setting for some of the materials of the chapter, he saw what a superb context it gave for a full-scale eschatological address: Jesus seated on Olivet, with the panorama of Jerusalem, dominated by its temple, before him! It was an ideal setting for the one great discourse of Jesus in his Gospel, placed at the end of his account of the ministry and forming the transition to the passion narrative.

As to the questions of the disciples in v. 4, their form will be due to Mark, who has to make them introduce not simply a paragraph relating to the fate of Jerusalem and its people, but an assemblage of eschatological sayings leading to a description of the end of the age.

The disciples' questions concerning the prophecy of v. 2 extend into two parallel clauses, in which the second member elaborates the first:

> pote tauta estai
> ti to sēmeion hotan mellē tauta synteleisthai panta.

The plural tauta instead of the singular touto in the first clause reflects an assumption that the ruin of the temple will form part of a complex of events. That is underscored in the tauta panta of the second clause; it voices an expectation that something will be said about the circum-

---

[35] While Pesch formerly considered that Mark composed vv. 3–4 as an ideal scene for the discourse, he later concluded that as Mark had before him a fully formed eschatological discourse it must have possessed an introduction, which probably posed a question to which the discourse formed an answer; that introduction was virtually vv. 3–4, shorn of its specifically Markan features (Markus, 2:273–74).

[36] Pesch provides examples in Markus, 2:274–75.

stances in which the destruction of the temple will take place. Accordingly, the simple question concerning when the ruin of the temple will happen is supplemented by a request for a sign; in a Jewish setting that is comprehensible, for the question "when" is not intended to extricate a date, but a knowledge of events that will warn the faithful when the catastrophe may be expected, and so to escape its horrors.

The replacement of the innocent verb *estai* by the more complex *mellē synteleisthai* is reminiscent of a question and answer in Dan 12:6–7 that has a curious affinity with the situation of Mark 13:3–4. After prophecies which tell of the terrors of the abomination of desolation in the temple of Jerusalem and unheard-of tribulation of the Jewish nation, the seer asks an angel guide, "How long will it be before these portents come to an end?" (LXX *pote oun synteleia hōn eirēkas moi tōn thaumastōn?*). The answer is given, "It shall be for a time, times, and a half. When the power of the holy people ceases to be dispersed all these things shall be accomplished" (LXX *syntelesthēsetai panta tauta*). The coincidence of language in such related contexts can hardly be accidental. It has led to a conviction, widely held, that the differently formulated questions in v. 4 have in view two quite different issues: the first looks back to the prophecy of the destruction of the temple in v. 2; the second looks onward to the prophecy of the end of the age in the discourse that follows.[37]

There are variations possible on this interpretation. The disciples, as representatives of Jews generally, assume that the destruction of the temple can take place only at the end of the age (the *synteleia tou aiōnos*, Matt 28:20); Mark has so arranged the narration of the signs of the end as to correct that misunderstanding, and so clearly distinguishes the two expectations. This also suits well the belief that a "little apocalypse" was available to Mark, who corrected its overly apocalyptic emphases with traditions of sayings of Jesus suitably ordered. Some exegetes strengthen this view by postulating that Mark looks back on the calamity of Jerusalem in AD 70 and views the whole range of signs in vv. 5–23, along with the prophecy of the temple's destruction, as fulfilled; the one vital issue then is the question in the second clause, since that remains unfulfilled, and the answer to it is given in the description of the cosmic signs which announce the coming of the Son of man (vv. 24–27). On this view no more signs in history are to be expected—only the heavenly portents of the glory of the exalted Christ at his appearing.[38] On this basis it was possible for Rudolf Pesch to speak of the *anti*-apocalyptic eschatological discourse.[39]

---

[37] So explicitly Schmithals, *Markus,* 2:570.

[38] See especially Brandenburger, *Markus 13 und die Apokalyptik,* FRLANT 134 (Göttingen, 1984), 87–105.

[39] Pesch, *Naherwartungen,* 225.

This distinction between the significance of the two clauses of v. 4 is certainly feasible, and it can be a helpful tool in the elucidation of the discourse. Nevertheless, a simpler interpretation of v. 4 lies at hand, namely that the two clauses are in strict parallelism, the second one explaining through expansion the sense of the first. On this interpretation the prophecy of v. 2 is illuminated by Dan 12:6–7, just as Mark 13:19 is by Dan 12:1: the calamity of the temple, like that described in Daniel, denotes the day of the Lord on Jerusalem and the Jewish nation. Despite the language frequently used to describe it, the day of the Lord is by no means to be equated with the end of the world. Most announcements of the day describe a judgment upon a people without indication of consequences that follow. Occasionally the destruction threatened is described as total (e.g., of Edom in Isaiah 14), more commonly it is not, and sometimes it is even followed by a promise of restoration (as of Egypt in Isaiah 19). Frequently the instruments of God's judgment on (the) day of the Lord are declared to be armies; in Jer 25:9 the Babylonians are the means of punishing Israel (Nebuchadnezzar is called "my servant"!), whereas in Isaiah 13 a day of the Lord is announced upon Babylon, in which the armies of the Medes are the appointed scourge of God. The description of the day of the Lord in Isaiah 34 is notable, inasmuch as it begins with an announcement of the day on "all nations," and it is accompanied by overwhelming cosmic signs: "All the host of heaven shall crumble into nothing, the heavens shall be rolled up like a scroll, and the starry host fade away," yet the oracle of judgment is directed solely against Edom, which is doomed to destruction like Sodom and Gomorrah. In Daniel the description of Israel's tribulation is assumed to give way to the nation's restoration in the kingdom of God. The form of the second clause of the disciples' question in Mark 13:4 leaves open eschatological possibilities of the circumstances surrounding the ruin of the temple and the events which are to follow it. The discourse will describe their nature.

The disciples' terms *pote*, *tauta*, and *tauta panta* will all recur later in the discourse; their connections with the questions will be determined in the light of the context of these terms (especially in vv. 29, 30, 35).

One final observation: the emphasis on signs is consonant with a feature in the discourse that Mark may well have created. The events described in vv. 5–23, while differentiated in their nature and significance, are all brought under the aspect of signs of the end (note the *tauta* of the Fig Tree parable, v. 29). The discourse, accordingly, goes beyond the question of the disciples, and beyond the prophecy which called it forth, for while the prophecy in v. 2 is expounded on the understanding of the temple's destruction as the day of the Lord upon Israel, the discourse proceeds on the assumption that the really important event is not the temple's ruin but the coming of the Son of man. In interpreting the various strands in the discourse it is important to bear in mind the observation of D. A. Koch: "In his editing of the apocalyptic traditions in ch. 13 Mark consciously carries through a distinction between historical and final events."[40] That we shall seek to recognize in our further exposition.

Mark 13:5–6, 21–22, 7–8

The statements here grouped are bound together by a common theme: they constitute a series of warnings not to be led astray by claims that the end of the age has already begun and the parousia of the Christ is immediately at hand.

The opening word *blepete* ("Watch!") is the most characteristic term of the discourse, and more than any other points to the nature of the discourse. It occurs again at the commencement of the second paragraph, which describes the task of the church in the present age (v. 9); it concludes the section on signs (v. 23); and it is the first word of the final paragraph (v. 33), which is dominated by the related term *grēgoreite*, "Be vigilant!" Since it is found also in 4:24; 8:15; 12:38, and in nonimperatival forms in 4:12; 5:36; 8:18, 23; 12:14, it is clearly a significant term for the evangelist. The only time Matthew uses *blepete* in this manner is in his citation of the opening word of the discourse, Matt 24:4. Luke does the same, but also employs it when reproducing Mark 4:24. The two other Synoptic evangelists thus do not allow the term to function in the discourse in the manner of Mark.[41]

If we ask what has led Mark to introduce this word so frequently in the address, it would seem to be to strengthen a fundamental idea which he finds already present in his sources in the light of the special nuance which he imports to the term. Here we recall the suggestion of T. Geddert that in the Gospel of Mark, *blepete*, which has the simple basic meaning of "Look," is consistently linked with a call to discernment.[42] Without doubt this fits the extended section vv. 5–23. Mark has placed in this section all the material he has inherited relating to signs (other than the Fig Tree parable of vv. 28–29, which looks back on it). It is generally agreed among recent exegetes that Mark has deliberately begun and concluded this passage with warnings about false messiahs and false prophets, who claim that the end is upon the world, and that Mark's stratagem was due to the activities of such persons in the critical

---

[40] D. A. Koch, "Zum Verhältnis von Christologie und Eschatologie im Markus-evangelium," in *Jesus Christus in Historie und Theologie*, Festschrift H. Conzelmann, ed. G. Strecker (Tübingen, 1975).

[41] *Blepete* does not occur at all in the Fourth Gospel.

[42] T. Geddert, *Watchwords*, 60.

time when his Gospel was written. The employment of *blepete* was eminently suitable to Mark's purpose. On this Geddert comments: "Both in 13:5 and 23 *blepete* is a call to see past the externals and recognize the deceptions that lurk beneath the persuasive words and deceptive signs."[43]

It is not impossible that in v. 5 Mark's source began with the simple statement, "Let nobody deceive you," and that by the mere addition of *blepete* he strengthened the meaning of the statement without modifying the sentence, and at the same time sounded the keynote for the entire discourse. In the next occurrence of *blepete*, v. 9, Matt 10:17 has a different equivalent: "Beware of men" (*prosechete apo tōn anthrōpōn*). Has Matthew changed Mark's word, or did he use a different source (e.g., Q?) for at least some of his material in 10:17–23? If the latter is correct, then Mark will have set his favorite term in place of another equivalent. In the concluding paragraph of the signs section Mark could suitably have commenced v. 21 with another *blepete*, just as in v. 5; instead he chose to set the verb in v. 23, so underscoring the appeal of vv. 21–23 and the call that sounds through the whole section of vv. 5–23. Its last occurrence in the chapter, v. 33, reinforces the term *agrypneite*; the sentence forms the burden of the closing paragraph, and is at the same time a feature of early Christian catechesis. Thus through his use of the term *blepete* Mark has emphasized a feature which was already embodied in the material of the discourse and has given to the whole the character of a call to spiritual discernment and alertness.

The two passages vv. 5–6 and 21–22 are so closely related that they are frequently regarded as doublets. Lambrecht considers that the starting point of these sayings is the Q statement, Matt 24:26/Luke 17:23; in his view Mark 13:21 is Mark's version of the Q saying, and Mark expanded it with v. 22; v. 6 is considered to be a different modification of the Q saying by Mark, but with the aid of vv. 21–22.[44] Pesch has put forward different views of the relation of vv. 5–6 and 21–22. He first suggested that Mark composed v. 21 in order to show that the parousia would not immediately follow the appearance of the abomination of desolation, and that vv. 6 and 22 originally formed a single, shorter saying, which Mark split up and expanded in order to form the "inclusion" of vv. 5–6, 21–23.[45] When Pesch produced his commentary he abandoned this view of the origin of the passage;

---

[43] Ibid., 86.

[44] Lambrecht, *Redaktion*, 104. Hahn has a closely similar view: vv. 5–6 were written in a different style from vv. 21–22; they were formed by Mark on the analogy of vv. 21–22 ("Die Rede von der Parusie des Menschensohnes," in *Jesus und der Menschensohn*, Festschrift A. Vögtle, ed. R. Pesch and R. Schnackenburg [Freiburg, 1975], 244).

[45] Pesch, *Naherwartungen*, 108–17.

probably influenced by Hahn, he recognized v. 21 as a parallel to Q, and considered v. 6 to be formed from v. 22.[46]

Pesch was surely right to reject the notion that Mark composed v. 21; in view of its close similarity to Matt 24:26/Luke 21:23 it should be viewed as one of the Markan doublets to the Q sayings. It was also right for Pesch to let his earlier view die—i.e., the coalescing of vv. 6 and 22, and eliminating the phrase "in my name" from v. 6; both v. 21 and the Q saying distinguish between the pseudochrists and the pseudoprophets who support them;[47] in v. 6 the claims are made by the messianic pretenders themselves, and the emphasis is on what they say; in v. 22 the would-be messiahs and the false prophets operate together, and the emphasis is on the miraculous deeds they perform.[48]

Verse 6

The many who come "in my name" (epi tō onomati mou) are to be understood not as claiming authority as the representatives of Jesus, but as claimants to the name which belongs to him, hence the explanatory addition, "saying that I am (he)."[49] The precise connotation of "I am" is uncertain. While some exegetes are attracted to the idea that the divine name is in view ("They come in my name, in that they utter the name, 'I am' ") and others understand the formula as a claim to be the returned Jesus, it is altogether more likely that the saying affirms a claim to be what Jesus is, namely the Messiah.[50] There may, however,

---

[46] See n. 44 above; cf. Pesch, Markus, 2:278–79.

[47] Lambrecht urges that in vv. 5–6 and 21–22 Mark thinks much more about the pseudochrists than about the pseudoprophets (Redaktion, 105).

[48] See Zmijewski, Eschatologiereden, 107–10. Note the instructive parallel in Rev 13:11–14, where the second beast is the "prophet" of the Antichrist, performing great signs and leading astray those who dwell on the earth.

[49] In his classic study Heitmüller affirmed that to interpret in this passage epi tō onomati mou as "on the ground or authority of my name" is inadmissible; it here denotes the requisitioning or claiming of the name, more briefly "with my name" (Im Namen Jesu, FRLANT I/2, Göttingen [1903], 63). Bietenhard made the same point: "False christs do not appeal to Jesus Christ but claim the name of Christ. One should thus translate 'under my name' " (TDNT, 5:277 n. 224).

[50] For the first, see, e.g., Lohmeyer, who thought it a traditional formula for the eschatological Redeemer (Markus, 270); see further D. Daube, New Testament and Rabbinic Judaism, 325ff.; W. Grundmann, Das Evangelium nach Markus, THKNT 2 (Berlin, 1959), 263; J. Ernst, Das Evangelium nach Markus, RNT (Regensburg, 1981), 373; J. Gnilka, Das Evangelium nach Markus, 2 vols., EKKNT (Neukirchen, 1978–79), 2:186–87. For the second, see, e.g., Nineham, Mark, 345; Schweizer, Mark, 268–69; W. Kelber, Kingdom in Mark, 115; W. Harrington, Mark, NT Message, vol. 4 (Dublin, 1979), 201; D. Lührmann, Markusevangelium, 219; F. W. Burnett, The Testament of Jesus-Sophia (Washington, D.C., 1979), 236, 246, 270–71. The majority of exegetes favor the third, e.g., A. H. McNeile, The Gospel according to St. Matthew (London, 1915), 345; J. Schnie-

be a nuance in the statement that would be of considerable importance to Mark. The affirmation "I am he," since it relates to the Messiah who comes with his kingdom (or who comes again in his kingdom) almost certainly carries with it the implication that the last times have now arrived and the apocalyptic denouement has begun.[51] It was precisely this assertion against which 2 Thess 2:1–12 was directed. In the period of Mark's writing, when events in Palestine were taking place which appeared to many to be the beginning of the end, it is comprehensible that such voices were being heard and were causing agitation and confusion and sharp division. This would explain why Mark separated vv. 6 and 22 and placed them at the beginning and the conclusion of the section on signs: the activity of such false prophets and "messiahs" is seen as the most urgent of the dangers against which Jesus warned; the great lie must be exposed, and the church turn a deaf ear to its advocates.

Verse 21

A consideration of v. 21 should begin with a comparison with the Q logion, so similar to it:

Matt 24:26   Luke 17:23

*ean oun eipōsin hymin idou en tē   kai erousin hymin, idou ekei: ē idou
erēmō estin, mē exelthēte: idou en   ōde: mē apelthēte mēde diōxēte
tois tameiois, mē pisteusēte*

Matthew's *en tē erēmō . . . en tois tameiois* echoes the Hebrew *miḥûṣ ûmēḥadārîm* (or *mibayit ûmiḥûṣ*), meaning "without and within" (for examples see Gen 6:14; Deut 32:25).[52] The statement alludes to the contemporary Jewish doctrine of the hidden Messiah—he will be born and will be unknown until the day of his manifestation. It is unlikely that Matthew has taken a simpler version of Q in order to express a "See here" or "See there" in a more complicated fashion; his version must be viewed as more original in this respect.[53] Whether his version of the

---

wind, *Das Evangelium nach Markus*, NTD (Göttingen, 1944), 167; Cranfield, *Mark*, 395; E. Stauffer, *TDNT*, 2:353; J. Schmid, *Das Evangelium nach Markus*, RNT (Regensburg, 1958), 188; V. Taylor, *The Gospel according to St. Mark* (London, 1952), 503–4; W. L. Lane, *The Gospel of Mark*, NICNT (Grand Rapids, 1974), 456; Pesch, *Naherwartungen*, 111; H. Anderson, *Mark*, 292.

[51] So W. Manson, *Christ's View of the Kingdom of God* (London, 1918), 176–78; idem, "The *Egō eimi* of the Messianic Presence in the New Testament," *JTS* 48 (1946): 137ff.; Pesch, *Naherwartungen*, 110–11.

[52] For a discussion on this see my *Commentary on Mark Thirteen* (London, 1957), 84–85.

[53] See Schulz, *Die Spruchquelle der Evangelisten*, 278; Lambrecht, *Redaktion*, 101–3; Zmijewski, *Eschatologiereden*, 410–11; I. H. Marshall, *The Gospel of Luke*, NIGTC (Grand Rapids, 1978), 659–60.

first and last lines is more primitive than Luke's, or whether he has accommodated both to Mark's version, is difficult to decide, but neither is the issue important. The message of all three versions is a warning against being drawn into the following of false claimants to messiahship.

It is to be observed that the Q version supplies an answer to the unspoken question, "How can it be known that these are *false* messiahs?" The answer is given: they cannot be God's Messiah, since his appearing will be as sudden and as evident as a lightning flash from heaven (Matt 24:27/Luke 17:24). It is likely that v. 21 in Mark's source had precisely the same concept; for if it be so that Mark himself separated v. 22 from v. 6, inserted v. 22 in its present position, and completed the signs section with v. 23, v. 21 will earlier have been directly followed by the description of the coming of the Son of man in the context of a theophany (vv. 24–27). The true Messiah is hidden not on earth but in heaven, and the revelation of his presence is comparable to that of the divine glory made known in the exodus and at Sinai, and awaited in the last day.[54]

Verse 22

Whereas the previous saying warns against listening to followers of pretended hidden messiahs, this passage represents the pseudomessiahs as operating in the open: they and the pseudoprophets seek to accredit themselves by performing "signs and portents." The impression made by such prodigies is so powerful that even the elect would succumb to their seductions were it not for the overruling mercy of God. The thought is not dissimilar to that of v. 20: as it is through the merciful intervention of God in shortening the period of Israel's tribulation that the elect are delivered, so the operation of the false messiahs and false prophets is neutralized in the elect by the overruling grace of God.[55]

It is instructive to compare these descriptions of pseudomessiahs and pseudoprophets with the picture given in 2 Thess 2:1–12. As in Mark 13:6, some in the Thessalonian church allege that the day of the Lord has already dawned. In the discourse the pretenders are pseudochrists and pseudoprophets; in 2 Thess 2:1–12 the pretender is strictly an antichrist; he embodies in himself the rebellion against God, and he "takes his seat in the temple and declares that he himself is a god." In

---

[54] This understanding of v. 21 is acknowledged by Hahn, "Die Rede von der Parusie des Menschensohnes des Markus 13," in *Jesus und der Menschensohn, Festschrift A. Vögtle,* ed. R. Pesch and R. Schnackenburg (Freiburg, 1975), 248; and following him, Pesch, *Markus,* 2:298.

[55] For the care of God for the elect in the last times note the parable of the Widow and the Unjust Judge, Luke 18:1–8.

the discourse the pseudochrists and pseudoprophets alike work prodigies to draw people after themselves, whereas in the Pauline discourse it is the Antichrist who works "powerful signs and miracles of the Lie." Clearly, there is a common tradition here which is being put to various uses. The distinction between the pseudochrists and pseudoprophets is maintained in Revelation 13, where it is the false prophet who performs the signs and portents on behalf of the Antichrist. In the Markan discourse these personages are subordinated to the fearful power represented by the "abomination of desolation."[56] It is possible that Paul has combined the picture of the opposition into one great personage in whom the features of everything that is counterfeit and evil is embodied.[57]

Verses 7–8

We have here a little paragraph incorporated by Mark with the section on false messiahs and false prophets. The association is fitting, for Mark's intention is to correct current misunderstandings relating to events which were both happening and believed to be imminent, and which were regarded as portents of the end of the age.

Wars, earthquakes, and famines are traditional elements in prophetic and apocalyptic representations of the end and of the times preceding it.[58] In the OT these are viewed less as preliminary signs of the end than as elements of the judgments of God experienced in a (or the) day of the Lord. Compare Ezekiel's description of the "four sore judgments" of the Lord (sword, famine, evil beasts, pestilence, Ezek 14:21) which he brings upon evil nations; whereas these are characteristic of God's judgments on a day of the Lord which he intends to bring on Jerusalem, the items mentioned in vv. 7–8 are preliminary to the great disaster which threatens the city and people of God.

Verse 7 singles out wars that will occur in the world. They form the most characteristic feature in prophetic descriptions of the day of the Lord, and understandably so, since the day of the Lord originally denoted a day in which the Lord went forth to battle with Israel's enemies.[59] One may note how the overwhelming defeat of Midian

---

[56] According to Loisy, they are the precursors, the auxiliaries of that which is to come, *Marc*, 379.

[57] On this see Hartman, *Prophecy Interpreted*, 104.

[58] Pesch describes them as belonging to the "repertoire of Jewish and Christian apocalyptic, inspired by the prophetic prophecies of doom" (*Markus*, 2:280).

[59] Note the dictum of von Rad: "Whenever and wherever great political complications were to be seen on the horizon, especially when hostile armies approached, a prophet could speak of the coming Day of Yahweh" ("The Origin of the Concept of the Day of Yahweh," *JSS* 4 [1959]: 107). See also idem, *TDNT*, 2:944.

through Gideon (Judges 7–8) came to be known as "the day of Midian," i.e., the day when God brought catastrophe on Midian, and how that deliverance of the nation is linked with that awaited on the day of the Lord for the kingdom of God (Isa 9:4). So the descriptions of the day of the Lord are replete with the imagery of battle (cf., e.g., Isaiah 13 and 34; Jeremiah 46–51; Ezekiel 7). As we have pointed out before, these judgments were by no means necessarily thought of as leading to the conclusion of history, as is apparent in Jeremiah's reiterated descriptions of the doom that is to befall Israel (e.g., chs. 6, 8, 9, 15, 18; see also Lam 2:22, wherein the fall of Jerusalem in 586 BC is referred to as the day of the Lord on the nation). That such days were viewed in hope as preceding the era of God's merciful restoration and rule is clear, and so they came to be regarded as premonitory signs of the end, as well as integral to the end itself. The language of v. 7 is probably traditional, and echoes such passages as Jer 51:46 and Dan 11:44.[60]

The opinion is increasingly being expressed that in the light of the prophecy of Mark 13:2 the statement about wars in v. 7 must have the Roman-Jewish War in mind. The scripture thought to be in view is Dan 9:26: "An anointed one shall be cut off and shall have nothing, and the troops of the prince who is to come shall destroy the city and the sanctuary. Its end shall come with a flood, and to the end there shall be war. Desolations are decreed" (NRSV). It is suggested that this had already taken place when Mark wrote: the war had been fought, the city taken, and the temple destroyed, and so an apocalyptic fever developed, fanned by false prophets. Hence Mark added, "Do not be alarmed. Such things are bound to happen; but the end is still to come."[61] While the tempering of eschatological expectation is clear enough, the bringing in of Dan 9:26 at this point is implausible. On the one hand the whole prophetic and apocalyptic tradition emphasizes wars as a feature of history under the judgment of God; there is no ground for maintaining that Dan 9:26 is in mind in Mark 13:7, especially as there is no contact in the language used. On the other hand that passage is unmistakably in mind in v. 14, where the abomination of desolation is named and the catastrophe upon Jerusalem is specifically in view. "Wars and reports of wars" most naturally relates to a plurality of conflicts, and that in a variety of areas. The added injunction, "Do not be alarmed. Such things are bound to happen, but the end is not yet," confirms that v. 7a is a generalizing statement. If we are concerned to know what Mark had in mind, v. 8 surely allows of no other interpretation:

---

[60] For passages in the apocalyptic writings which relate to the evils of the last times see the discussion by Hartman, *Prophecy Interpreted*, 30–32, and the detailed classified lists of references in ibid., nn. 30–54.

[61] So, e.g., Pesch, *Naherwartungen*, 121–22; idem, *Markus*, 2:280; Schmithals, *Markus*, 2:572; Gnilka, *Markus*, 186–88.

Nation will make war upon nation,
kingdom upon kingdom;
there will be earthquakes in many places;
there will be famines.

Here the war motif is taken up and explicates what is in mind in
v. 7. Like the earthquakes, the wars are "in many places"—"Nation
against nation, kingdom against kingdom." A confusion in all kinds of
lands is being described. Verse 8ab takes up and conflates two well-
known OT passages. Isaiah 19:2 tells of what takes place when the Lord
rides upon his swift cloud to Egypt:

I will set Egyptian against Egyptian,
and they shall fight one against another,
neighbour against neighbour,
city against city and kingdom against kingdom.

That language is employed in 2 Chron 15:6: "At those times there
was no safety for people as they went about their business; the inhabitants of every land had their fill of trouble; there was ruin on every side,
nation at odds with nation, city with city, for God had harassed them
with every kind of distress."

Whatever be thought about the date of Mark's composition of the
discourse, it is plain that for him vv. 7–8 primarily have in view a state
of affairs in the world that existed prior to the events described in vv.
14–20—and will doubtless continue. There is no justification for relating the two passages to a single situation within the land of Israel.

The exhortation in v. 7, "Do not be alarmed," would appear to refer
not so much to fear for one's safety by reason of the wars, as to fear that
the wars indicate that the end is upon the world; accordingly it is
emphasized, "the end is not yet." In its present context the statement
presumably contradicts the false messiahs and false prophets of v. 6,
who proclaim that the end has come.

It is noteworthy that the only passage outside the Synoptic discourse wherein the term *throeisthai* occurs is in the closely parallel
2 Thess 2:2, where Paul bids the Thessalonians not to "lose their heads"
(REB) through allegations that the day of the Lord has set in. "Such
things are bound to be," continues v. 7: in Greek, *dei genesthai*. This
phrase, constantly regarded as betraying a hellenistic environment
(there is no word for "must" in Hebrew and Aramaic), reflects rather
the rendering of a simple Aramaic future in a bilingual congregation
which understands how to translate language expressive of the divine
will: if God says that something shall be, then it must be![62] That is why
the LXX renders a simple future in Hebrew by *dei* in Lev 5:17 and Isa
30:29, and an Aramaic future by the same term in Dan 2:28 and 29

---

[62] See my *Jesus and the Kingdom of God*, 238–39.

(contrariwise Symmachus does the same thing in Dan 2:45, whereas LXX uses the ordinary future there). It is therefore reading more than is warranted in describing *dei* in v. 7 as "an apocalyptic must"; to represent it as the "necessity" of the eschatological event[63] is perhaps closer to Mark, but the main thought is of the historical process in a world that exists under the judgment of the sovereign Lord (cf. Rom 1:18ff.). This would emphasize the pertinence of the last clause in v. 7: "the end is still to come." In the will of God the end is not a bloodbath.

Verse 8 extends the description of the wars in v. 7 with far-ranging strife, accompanied by earthquakes in many places, and famines. Like wars, the earthquakes originally were an integral feature of the last day; they denoted the terror of creation before the coming of the Creator (cf. Mic 1:3–4; Hab 3:6, 10) and so were a standing element of descriptions of the day of the Lord. Since the same mode of portraying the coming of God in his interventions in history was earlier than their eschatological application (see, e.g., Judg 5:4–5; Ps 97:1–5), it was natural to include them in descriptions of the judgments of God on a rebellious world. Famines were regular accompaniments of wars, and insofar as the latter were represented as judgments on nations, the former were also similarly viewed. Since pestilence or plague was yet another grim consequence of wars, many prophetic passages link wars, famines, and pestilence together in descriptions of divine judgments (cf. Jer 14:12; 21:7; Ezek 5:12; 14:12–23), and Luke in his version of v. 8 includes pestilence with the other three (Luke 21:10–11).[64]

The purpose of Mark's inclusion of vv. 7–8 at this point in the discourse is tolerably clear. The evangelist has positive and negative observations to include. The *dei genesthai* of v. 7 implies a recognition of the lordship of God over history, even when history appears to go berserk. The restraining and judging hand of God is never removed from the course of this world's events. The too ready identification of contemporary events as the harbingers of the immediate end, particularly with respect to wars and natural calamities, is corrected: "the end is still to come." Yet it is not maintained that the hand of God cannot be discerned in the disturbances of the present, still less that the end is far off: "These things are the beginning of the birthpangs." That appears to affirm that contemporary happenings have eschatological significance, for they are the beginning of the passing of the old age and the heralds of the new, but they do not signify the transition point itself; they are the early harbingers of the end, not the finale.[65]

---

[63] For the former see W. Grundmann, *Markus,* 263; for the latter, see idem, *TDNT,* 2:23.

[64] Cf. my *Commentary on Mark Thirteen,* 36–37; and Hartman, *Prophecy Interpreted,* 80.

[65] So F. Mussner, *Christ and the End of the World,* 26; F. Flückiger, "Die

Accordingly "these things" are to be interpreted as signs of the judging presence of God in that history which is moving to the end which he has purposed; they are not the sign which the disciples requested (v. 4).

Mark 13:9–13

The paragraph is introduced by the Markan *blepete*, "Watch yourselves," which binds the passage to the rest of the discourse. Luke has no equivalent, whereas Matthew reads, "Beware of men" (*prosechete apo tōn anthrōpōn*), which introduces the equivalent section in Matt 10:17–23. Has Matthew varied Mark's language, or did he have a parallel source here? Or did Mark change an original *prosechete* to maintain a consistency of appeal in the discourse? We cannot tell.[66]

Verses 9 and 11 are closely related; together they form Mark's parallel to the single Q saying, Luke 12:11–12 (Matthew has conflated Mark and Q in his version, Matt 10:17–18). Mark 13:10 has been inserted between the two sentences, presumably by Mark himself; it performs the function of expanding the thought of witness briefly hinted at in the phrase *eis martyrion autois*. Mark treats vv. 12 and 13a as a continuous sentence, and the paragraph is brought to a conclusion by v. 13b.[67]

The separate sayings in the section are bound together in a twofold way, indicating how the evangelist would have his readers understand the passage. The verb *paradidonai*, "to hand over," occurs at the beginning of vv. 9, 11, 12. As to its first appearance, Luke has no intimation of it in his report of the Q equivalent, Luke 12:11–12. In Mark 13:11 its participial use may be thought to be superfluous. In v. 12, however, it may well have been found in Mark's source. The Targum of Jonathan on Mic 7:2ff., which supplies the basis of Mark 13:13, reads, "A man delivers up his brother to destruction"; since the same Targum appears to have influenced the conclusion of the sentence, it would appear to have provided the form of vv. 12–13a known to Mark,[68] and suggested the adoption of *paradidonai* in the earlier two sayings. The term *paradidonai*, however, is a loaded one in early Christian usage; it appears

---

Redaktion der Zukunftsrede," *TZ* 26 (1970): 401–2; T. Weeden, *Mark: Traditions in Conflict* (Philadelphia, 1971), 90–97; Pesch, *Naherwartungen*, 118–25; J. Ernst, *Markus*, 372; V. K. Agbanou, *Le discours eschatologique de Matthieu 24–25: Tradition et Rédaction* (Paris, 1983), 63–66.

[66] See the discussion in Lambrecht, *Redaktion*, 119, and 102 n. 1.

[67] C. F. Burney describes the structure of vv. 9–11 as a couplet (v. 9) followed by two quatrains (vv. 11, 12–13). When *eis martyrion autois* and v. 10 are omitted a rhythmic and parallelistic structure is obtained which marks off the paragraph from the rest of the chapter (*Poetry of Our Lord* [Oxford, 1925], 118).

[68] See Hartman, *Prophecy Interpreted*, 168–69.

in Mark's second passion prediction (9:31), it occurs no less than ten times in the passion narrative (chs. 14—15), and it appears in the confessional statement about Christ's death in Rom 4:25 and in Paul's own language of God's handing over Jesus to death in Rom 8:12. The term accordingly can include the handing over of Jesus for death both by men and by God. It is more than likely that Mark wished to parallel the fate of the disciples at the hands of hostile people—by permission of God—with that of Jesus in his passion.

A similar notion is hinted at in the second connective feature of the passage: each of the two pairs of sayings has the equivalent expression of "for my sake" (v. 9, *heneken emou*; v. 13, *dia to onoma mou*). By this means it is shown that the persecutions described are caused by the attachment of the disciples to Jesus. They are brought before courts and suffer among their kinsmen for one reason: their confession of Jesus as the Christ. We are inevitably reminded of the sayings regarding discipleship in 8:34–38: to follow the Lord who advances to Golgotha calls for willingness to shoulder a cross after him and courage to confess him before people, whatever the consequences.

The connection between the sayings in Mark 13:9–13 and those relating to cross bearing was perceived by the framers of the Gospel traditions. The Q equivalent of Mark 8:38 in Luke 12:8–9 is followed by the Q equivalent of Mark 13:9 and 11 (Luke 12:11–12), so suggesting that the confession of Jesus before people is to be made before courts of judgment, even as he made his confession in like circumstances (the inspiration to first-century Christians of the fearlessness of Jesus on trial is evidenced in 1 Tim 6:12–13). The Q equivalent of Mark 13:12 is placed by Matthew (10:34–36) immediately following his Q version of the cross-bearing saying (10:37–38), and then by the logion about losing life to find it (10:39), which is similar in thought, though not in form, to Mark 13:13b. This is no new discovery: it was the major thesis of F. Busch in his work on Mark 13 that the discourse has the same fundamental outlook as 8:29—9:1.[69] We have seen how D. A. Koch developed this insight: 8:29—9:1 presents Jesus as the Son of man, suffering death for the redemption of the kingdom of God and its returning Lord; in 13:9–13 this orienting to the Son of man as the Crucified and the Judge has the effect of inspiring disciples to accept their situation of suffering as in accord with the nature and calling of the church.[70]

---

[69] F. Busch, *Zum Verständnis der synoptischen Eschatologie,* especially 52–54. R. H. Lightfoot presented a related understanding of Mark 13 in *The Gospel Message of St. Mark* (Oxford, 1950), 45–59. C. B. Cousar freshly expounded the viewpoint in "Eschatology and Mark's Theologia Crucis: A Critical Analysis of Mark 13," *Int* 24 (1970): 321–35; see also T. Geddert, *Watchwords,* 149–76.

[70] Koch, "Zum Verhältnis," 407–8.

There are yet further implications for the context in which vv. 9–13 are set. By placing the *thlipsis* of the church in conjunction with that of the world (vv. 7–8) and of Israel (vv. 14–20), Mark shows the church as bound with humankind in its trials, and it suffers not only with them but for them. In so doing it treads in the footsteps of its Lord. In suffering for the name of Jesus the church shares his sufferings on behalf of the world. More particularly, the sufferings of Christians, when set in this context, are viewed as among the signs of the *kairoi* which lead to the end. They are provoked by confession of Christ in Christian witness and lead to further occasions of witness in law courts. Here lies at least one aspect of the significance of v. 10: every trial provides an opportunity for witness to the faith before people (so perhaps Luke 21:13; cf. 1 Pet 3:15; 4:14–16) and for the advancement of the gospel in the world (Phil 1:12–14), so pressing forward to the time when the "fullness of the Gentiles" comes in (Rom 11:25). The apocalyptic-eschatological faith provides an extra dimension to the urgency of the disciples' mission.

Verses 9–11

The call *blepete de hymeis heautous* ("You watch yourselves") contrasts with the appeal which begins the discourse (v. 5). There the disciples are bidden to watch others, i.e., claimants to messianic status, lest they be led astray by their deluded claims; here they must watch themselves, to ensure on the one hand that they do not fail to grasp the profound import of their mission to the world, and on the other that they do not fail in their faith and in their task.

The relation of vv. 9 and 11 to the Q saying, Luke 12:11–12, is not easy to determine. Lambrecht suggested that either Mark reproduced the Q saying faithfully in v. 11 and anticipated it with great freedom in v. 9, or that Mark had access to a fuller form of Q, reproduced by Matthew in Matt 10:17–23, and drew heavily on it in the whole of Mark 13:9–13; in the latter case Mark will have been less radical in his editing of his material than on the former postulate, and it is to this view that Lambrecht inclines.[71] Certainly the contacts between Mark's v. 11 and the Q version are close; the comparisons suggest, however, that Matthew conflated a Q version with Mark, rather than that Mark reproduced a version of Q almost identical with Matt 10:17ff. It is plausible to assume that Mark's source contained an independent version of the saying embodied in Q, and that it was fuller in its opening clauses than the version in Luke 12:11a.

The disciples are to be hauled before various courts.[72] They will be "handed over" to Jewish councils (sanhedrin) and beaten in syn-

---

[71] Lambrecht, *Redaktion*, 119–20.
[72] For a discussion on the nature of these courts, both in Palestine and in

agogues; i.e., they will be treated as offending Jews, subject to the discipline of Jewish courts, on the ground of their disturbing the peace and propagating heretical beliefs. The "governors and kings" before whom they will appear will be Roman procurators and kings of Israel, i.e., the Herods. A Palestinian provenance is in mind, and the book of Acts supplies abundant illustrations of the process. The language can, of course, be applied to areas outside Palestine, and Mark will doubtless have so extended its application. Apart from the existence of Jewish courts in the diaspora Mark will also doubtless have had in mind the terrible experiences of Christians in Rome during the Neronic persecution.

The opposition suffered by disciples of Jesus will occur *eis martyrion autois*, "for testimony to them." Strathmann's interpretation of this phrase is well known: *martyrion* denotes not the act of witness, which is rather *martyria*, but the evidence attested, and in the Gospels that commonly signifies evidence which demonstrates the guilt of those addressed; such, it is claimed, is the meaning of *martyrion* in this passage: the disciples' witness will serve in the last judgment as proof of the guilt of their incriminators.[73]

This interpretation is highly questionable. Mark's addition of v. 10 shows that he must have viewed the *martyrion* as having positive as well as negative import, depending on the response of the hearers. Strathmann applied the negative meaning of *martyrion* even to its use in Matthew's version of Mark 13:10: "This gospel of the kingdom will be proclaimed throughout the earth *eis martyrion pasin tois ethnesin*" (Matt 24:14). But it is an impossible notion that Matthew meant by the use of this phrase that the worldwide proclamation of the gospel is to serve the purpose of deepening the guilt of humankind; on the contrary, Matthew will have looked on the Christian mission as having the aim of giving to the nations the possibility of entrance into the kingdom of God (it is the "good news of the kingdom" that is to be preached to them), and the same will have been in Mark's mind. For him this process has to happen in all places and in all the time that remains to this age; it will lead to the arrest and trial of the Christian witnesses, but such occasions, far from silencing the preaching will but create further opportunities for it. As is frequently pointed out, persecutions of Christians become occasions for renewed proclamation: so W. Harrington affirmed, "Christian suffering is itself that proclamation; by suffering as Jesus suffered they are making him present to the world."[74]

---

the Diaspora, see D. R. A. Hare, *The Theme of Jewish Persecution of Christians in the Gospel according to St. Matthew*, SNTSMS 6 (Cambridge, 1967), 101–9.

[73] Strathmann, *TDNT*, 4:508–9. See further Cranfield's critique of Strathmann in *Mark*, 397–98; idem, *SJT* 6 (1953): 291–93.

[74] W. Harrington, *Mark*, 203.

For Mark this was prophecy fulfilled in the entire story of the church's progress—it anticipated the experience of Christians in their witness from the earliest days of the church in Palestine to the current situation of the church in Rome. There was therefore no stumbling block in the idea that the trials and sufferings of Christians were *eis martyrion autois*. It belongs to the imperative of the proclamation announced in v. 10, and for it the aid of the Spirit is made known in v. 11. In modern terms this is mission under the cross; it is mission set in the context of 8:34–38.

It will not be overlooked that even without 13:10 the importance of witness is assumed in vv. 9 and 11. The Spirit is the Spirit of prophecy,[75] and he is to inspire such witness in the trials of the disciples as makes the word of the Lord effective. His inspiration is conceived of not as enabling the disciples to demonstrate their innocence, but as empowering them to testify concerning the Christ for whose sake they stand on trial. The new feature in v. 10 is the extension of the witness of the gospel to all nations, and not simply to the Jews. It is an attractive suggestion that Mark's original source read as Matt 10:18: the disciples are to stand before governors and kings *eis martyrion autois kai tois ethnesin*, "for testimony to them and to the Gentiles." A number of manuscripts actually read Mark's version in this manner; the disciples are brought to trial *eis martyrion autois kai eis panta ta ethnē*; the particle *de* is then placed after *prōton*, making the sentence in v. 10 read, "But first the gospel must be preached."[76] Since the "first" relates to the coming of the end, the preaching of the gospel to the nations before the parousia would then be expressed in a terse but forceful manner. The same presupposition as to Mark's source has led others to assume that it caused Mark to expand the double phrase into

---

[75] So Str-B, 2:127–28, with illustrations, 129.

[76] F. C. Burkitt favored this textual tradition; see his discussion in *Christian Beginnings* (London, 1924), 145–47. G. D. Kilpatrick followed up Burkitt's view by proposing a different punctuation of Mark 13:9–10. Based on the observation that Mark's word order predominantly places the verb first in a sentence, he proposed that the clauses of v. 9 be viewed as beginning with the verbs *paradōsousin . . . darēsesthe . . . stathēsesthe, . . .* the last one ending with *eis martyrion autois kai eis panta ta ethnē*. Verse 10 then consists only of *prōton dei kērychthēnai to euangelion.* See Kilpatrick, "The Gentile Mission in Mark and Mark 13:9–11," in *Studies in the Gospels,* Festschrift R. H. Lightfoot, ed. D. E. Nineham (Oxford, 1955), 145–58. Kilpatrick's suggestion has not found general acceptance; see, e.g., the discussions in Cranfield, *Mark,* 398; Pesch, *Naherwartungen,* 126; Lambrecht, *Redaktion,* 133–35 (also my *Commentary on Mark Thirteen,* 42–44). By contrast, Pesch followed a quite different suggestion of C. H. Turner, that the verbs of v. 9 should be read as concluding the clauses in which they stand (*Naherwartungen,* 126); for criticism of this procedure see Lambrecht, *Redaktion,* 122 n. 1.

the present form of v. 10, so making him responsible for this form of missionary command.[77]

While toying with this interpretation formerly, I now think that it was precisely owing to v. 9 ending with the phrase *eis martyrion autois* that Mark adduced at this point the statement of v. 10, which he already possessed in his sources. Hahn is right in maintaining, contrary to Marxsen and others, that there is nothing specifically Markan in the language of v. 10, in the sense that it could not have existed in the tradition apart from him; *panta ta ethnē* is a well-known OT expression, which frequently occurs in OT citations in the NT (e.g., Mark 11:17; Acts 15:17; Rom 15:11); *euangelion* occurs in the catechetical summary of the preaching of Jesus in Mark 1:15; *kēryssein* is a common term in the early Christian mission, and we have seen the use of *dei* in sayings of Jesus circulating in bilingual Palestinian churches.[78]

Diverging from Hahn, I would be prepared to recognize the possibility of Mark's hand in *prōton*: the gospel must *first* be preached, for if that term emphasizes the necessity of the proclamation in the time prior to the end of the age, thereby indicating the task of the church in the period between the resurrection and the parousia, it does match with the *oupō to telos* of v. 7 and the *archē ōdinōn* of v. 8; that is to say, it implies a retarding moment with respect to those who are looking for the parousia to take place tonight, or tomorrow at the latest. It does not import into the saying an alien element, and it is consistent with Mark's aim in reproducing the discourse. The *prōton* does not introduce a "delay of the parousia" motif, in the sense of seeking to explain why the parousia has not happened. Rather it presents an urgent task to be done before it does happen, a task which has a vital place in God's purpose for the nations in relation to his saving sovereignty. For Mark in Rome the proclamation of the gospel to all nations does not signify an indefinitely long delay; the gospel has already gone far and wide, and knowledge of the *oikoumene* was very limited in his day.[79] Never-

---

[77] So, e.g., Lambrecht, who considered that $Q^{mt,mk}$ included the double phrase, as in Matt 10:18 (*Redaktion*, 124).

[78] This use of *euangelion* was first suggested by Lohmeyer, *Markus*, 29–30, and developed by W. Trilling, *Christus Verkündigung in den synoptischen Evangelien*, Biblische Handbibliothek 4 (Munich, 1969), 53. On *kēryssein* see Hahn's discussion of Mark 13:10 in *Das Verständnis der Mission im Neuen Testament*, WMANT (Neukirchen-Vluyn, 1963), 60–62.

[79] Cf. Rom 15:19–24 and especially the striking statement in Col 1:23. The conviction that the worldwide proclamation of the gospel does not imply (in the thought of the early church) a lengthy period of time was already maintained in relation to Mark 13:10 par. by W. C. Allen, *A Critical and Exegetical Commentary on the Gospel according to St. Matthew*, ICC, 3d ed. (Edinburgh, 1912), lxix; A. H. McNeile, *Matthew*, 347; A. W. F. Blunt, *The Gospel according to Saint Mark*, Clarendon Bible (Oxford, 1929), 236–37. For a restatement of this view in the

theless, it was evident, even to Mark, that the command of the Lord had not been fully carried out, and Mark would call his starry-eyed fellow Christians to cease gazing into heaven for intimations of the parousia and to further the witness to Christ in a world that continues to be hostile to the gospel.

The role of the Spirit in the disciples' witness is notable, partly by reason of the fewness of sayings of Jesus regarding the Spirit, and partly through the striking similarity between v. 11 and the teaching on the Paraclete in the Fourth Gospel, for v. 11 enshrines the basic thrust of the Paraclete sayings in that Gospel (notably John 15:26–27). This link between v. 11 and the Johannine sayings reflects favorably on the merit of the Johannine tradition in this respect, rather than on the demerit of the Markan logion. There is no need to set the saying to the account of the early community on the ground of its approximation to the experiences of the early proclaimers of the gospel,[80] any more than it is right to discount the cross-bearing sayings on the basis of the sufferings of Christians in the first century AD. The concept within the saying is relatively undeveloped, it is in line with the OT prophetic tradition, and it is strictly related to the occasions of need specified in the text.[81]

The Lukan variant ("I will give you a mouth and a wisdom which no opponent will be able to resist or refute," Luke 21:15) is almost certainly secondary,[82] and anticipates Luke's record of Stephen's powerful witness to the gospel (Acts 6:10). Luke's version of the saying, however, brings out a feature which is probably latent in Mark 13:11, namely the promise to Moses when he feared to embark on his mission to free the Israelites from the Egyptian power: "Go now, I will be with your mouth and teach you what you shall speak"; and again, extending the assurance to both Moses and Aaron: "You shall speak to him and put the words in his mouth; and I will be with your mouth and with his mouth, and will teach you what you shall do. He shall speak for you to the people; and he shall be a mouth for you, and you shall be to him as God" (Exod 4:12–16). The concept in this passage is remarkably similar to that in Mark 13:11, given the development of the idea of inspiration by the Spirit of God instead of by the direct action of God.

---

light of redaction criticism see Marxsen, *Mark the Evangelist,* 175–77; Pesch, *Naherwartungen,* 129–30; Zmijewski, *Eschatologiereden,* 145.

[80] Contrary to Grässer, *Das Problem der Parusieverzögerung in den synoptischen Evangelien und in der Apostelgeschichte,* BZNW 22 (Berlin, 1957), 158; Pesch, *Naherwartungen,* 132, idem, *Markus,* 2:287.

[81] The limited application of the saying is stressed by Lohmeyer, *Markus,* 273; V. Taylor, *Mark,* 509; C. K. Barrett, *The Holy Spirit in the Gospel Tradition* (London, 1947), 139; E. Schweizer, *TDNT,* 6:6. With this proviso the saying is viewed as dominical by these writers, other than Barrett (see next note).

[82] The contrary is maintained by C. K. Barrett, *Holy Spirit,* 131–32, followed by L. Gaston, *No Stone on Another,* 21 n. 1.

Verses 12–13

Wellhausen's comment on v. 12 is frequently cited: "Since Micah 7, this feature is a commonplace of Jewish apocalyptic in the description of the messianic woes."[83] Wellhausen observed, however, that its application in v. 13 is not what is meant by the general dissolution of the family bonds, and the observation is correct. But if one asks whether it is right to bring v. 13 into the picture conveyed by v. 12, the answer apparently must be yes, for the first line of v. 13 also belongs to the thought of Micah 7. L. Hartman drew attention to the targumic interpretation of Micah 7, which appears to sound through the Markan text.[84] As we mentioned earlier, Targum Jonathan reads, "A man delivers up his brother to destruction," as in Mark 13:12a, and it renders the clause in Mic 7:6, "a man's enemies are his own household," by "those who hate a man are the men of his own house." This makes it evident that Mark 13:13a, "You will be hated by all because of my name," relates to the kinsfolk mentioned in v. 12. Interestingly, the LXX of the same clause in Mic 7:6 reads, "A man's enemies are all the men in his house." There is thus strong precedent for regarding the sentence of Mark 13:12 as continuing into v. 13a, as do recent printed editions of the Greek NT and some translations of the Bible.

This procedure has two consequences. The conflict within families described in vv. 12–13a is not intended to represent a general anarchy in society through a universal disintegration of the family, but the antagonism which will arise in families wherein one or more members confess Jesus as the Christ (it arises *dia to onoma mou*). This mode of applying Mic 7:6 is more strongly expressed in the Q saying, Matt 10:34–36/Luke 12:51–53, where Jesus, prior to quoting the saying from Micah, is represented as saying, "I came to bring division" (so Luke; Matthew reads, ". . . a sword"), and further, as in Matthew, "I came to divide a man against his father." This intimates that Jesus saw it as part of his mission to create the apocalyptic conditions described by Micah. Whether the saying be regarded as ironical in intent, or expressing result as purpose, or even intended as unvarnished purpose, it is clear that v. 12 should not be dismissed as "an apocalyptic commonplace," as though it had nothing in common with Jesus. On the contrary, it appears to be integral to the ministry which moved to its climax in rejection and death, and which warned that whoever fol-

---

[83] Wellhausen, *Das Evangelium Marci* (Berlin, 1903), 102. For references in apocalyptic literature see 1 Enoch 100:1–2; Jub 23:19; 4 Ezra 5:9; 6:24. It is attested also in rabbinic literature; see the citations in Str-B, *Kommentar aus Talmud und Midrasch*, 4/2:982.

[84] Hartman, *Prophecy Interpreted,* 168–69.

lowed such a Leader and shared in his proclamation must expect to experience treatment comparable with that meted out to him.

A less important observation on the recognition of the unity of v. 12 with v. 13a is the independence of the statement in relation to v. 8. Many exegetes would join v. 12 with v. 8 as part of the "little apocalypse" which they consider Mark used. Admittedly there is a link between the two sayings via the OT, since Isa 19:2 conjoins the conflict of kingdom against kingdom with every man fighting against his brother. Nevertheless, v. 8 has in view distresses in the world at large, whereas vv. 12–13, like vv. 9–11, have the *thlipsis* of the followers of Christ in mind as they seek to serve him in a society which rejects him.[85] While this prophetic background is clear, Hengel suggests that Mark could hardly have reproduced vv. 12–13 without being reminded of the contemporary *odium humani generis* for Christians. The famous phrase of Tacitus is illustrated in his report of Nero's fastening the guilt for the fire of Rome on "a class hated for their abominations, called Christians by the populace."[86] That was followed by the first mass killing of Christians. It is not for nothing that Mark is the first person in the NT to speak of universal hatred of Christians.[87]

The last sentence of the paragraph, Mark 13:13b, following as it does the citation of Mic 7:6, could conceivably be a conscious echo of Mic 7:7: "As for me I will look to the Lord, I will wait for the God of my salvation" (LXX *hypomenō epi tō theō tō sōtēri mou*).[88] There are various echoes of the thought in words of Jesus. Luke's version of v. 13b, "By standing firm [*en tē hypomonē hymōn*, literally 'by your endurance'] you will win true life for yourselves," emphasizes that the salvation of Mark 13:13b denotes life in the kingdom of God, not simply survival of the tribulations to their limit. Luke's language moreover is reminiscent of his version of Mark 8:35: "Whoever seeks to gain (*peripoiēsasthai*) his life will lose it, and whoever loses it will save it, and live (*zōogonēsei*)" (Luke 17:33).

Fittingly, therefore, we come back to a saying which belongs to the complex of Mark 8:34–38: "Whoever wishes to save his life will lose it, but whoever will lose his life for my sake and for the gospel will save it." The endurance which wins life in the kingdom of God is that which does not fear those who can kill the body but fears rather him who has

---

[85] So Lagrange, *L'Evangile selon Saint Marc* (Paris, 1910), 339; Schniewind, *Markus,* 170; Lohmeyer, *Markus,* 273–74; Pesch, *Markus,* 2:286.

[86] Tacitus, *Annals* 15.44.2, 4.

[87] See Hengel's discussion of Mark 13:9–13 in *Studies in the Gospel of Mark* (ET London, 1985), 222–26.

[88] Hartman, *Prophecy Interpreted,* 168; and Pesch, *Markus,* 2:286, would add to Mic 7:7 passages from Daniel, viz., 11:32, 35; 12:11, 12; but these seem less likely in the context than the Micah passage.

power over both body and soul at the judgment (Matt 10:28/Luke 12:4–5). It is endurance in the way of Jesus, bearing the weight and the shame of his cross, emulating his fearless witness, even in trials, and looking to the day of his appearing.

Busch concluded his treatise on Mark 13 with the statement: "The great paradox of the chapter—a possibility of life between cross and parousia—was and is no riddle to the Christian church."[89] They know it best for whom it is the beating heart of the church's existence in mission.

Mark 13:14–20

The sayings of this pericope are bound together by their relation to the distress which is to fall upon Jerusalem and the Jewish people in Palestine. To what extent the sayings formed an original unity, or how early they were brought together, is a difficult problem, on which we have already made some tentative suggestions.[90] The greatest uncertainty attaches to vv. 15–16, since they are found in the Q apocalypse at Luke 17:31.[91] The matter is of secondary importance, however, since the content of vv. 15–16 more naturally sets them in a context of flight from the perils of war than in a context of expectation of the parousia (as they are placed in Luke 17:31). Mark's context is right according to subject, even though the sayings did not originally occur in sequence after 13:14.

The *hotan* which begins v. 14 calls to mind the *hotan* of v. 7; the latter, however, introduces events which are explicitly stated not to be the signs heralding the catastrophe prophesied in v. 2, whereas v. 14 appears directly to answer the disciples' question in v. 4 concerning the sign of the impending fulfillment of the prophecy. The passage which follows in vv. 15–20 does not describe the process by which the temple is destroyed or the sufferings in which the people will be engulfed; it emphasizes only the dread nature of the agonies. Israel's tribulation will climax human suffering in history.

It is to be observed that the statements which most clearly speak of the distress of the city and nation, vv. 14 and 19, echo OT passages, notably in the book of Daniel, which portray the tribulation of Jerusalem and Israel in the last times. There is not a syllable which reflects knowledge of events which took place in the Jewish War, still less of the actual destruction of the city and temple. Verse 14 is wholly determined by OT prophecy and the prophetic insight of the speaker, not by the history of the sixties (or seventies!) of the first century AD.

---

[89] Busch, *Zum Verständnis der synoptischen Eschatologie*, 157.
[90] See pp. 357–61.
[91] Compare the discussion in J. Zmijewski, *Eschatologiereden*, 473–78.

Indeed, the call to flee to the mountains when the abomination of desolation appears is difficult to reconcile with the course of events of the Jewish War. On this M. Hengel commented:

> The section Mark 13:14–19 . . . does not fit at all into the situation at or after the destruction of the temple and the city or in the time of the siege, from July to September 70. The occupation and destruction of the city had been preceded long beforehand by the gradual occupation of Judaea—with the exception of the fortress of Herodion and Massada. As early as 68, before the murder of Nero on June 9, Vespasian largely had Judaea under control and isolated Jerusalem. At that time an invitation to the inhabitants to flee into "the mountains" of the wilderness of Judah must have seemed nonsensical, for the fugitives would run into the hands of either the Romans or the Sicarii in and around Massada; the latter were no less murderous. Rather, the country people fled into the city, in which a bloody civil war was raging, only ended by the advance of Titus.[92]

Significantly, to judge from v. 20, the time of the destruction of the city is not only unknown but subject to the sovereign control of God in the future. The vagueness of the prophecy, the lack of clarification in the light of events that took place about AD 70, not least the lack of reference to the fact that the populace fled into the city and not away from it, thereby ensuring their doom, all combine to question the current trend of exegetes to affirm that Mark wrote this paragraph after the destruction of Jerusalem had taken place. For this speculation there appears to be no evidence.

Verse 14

The appearance of the abomination of desolation is to be a sign for flight. The nature of the "abomination" is the most puzzling element in the discourse, and has occasioned a wide variety of explanations.[93]

The phrase appears three times in Daniel (9:27; 11:31; 12:11). The most significant of these is the first, since it provides a context for the appearance of the "abomination": " He [the prince who is to come] shall make a strong covenant with many for one week, and for half of the week he shall make sacrifice and offering cease; and in their place shall be an abomination that desolates, until the decreed end is poured out upon the desolator" (NRSV).[94]

---

[92] Hengel, *Studies in the Gospel of Mark,* 16–17.

[93] For a comprehensive examination of the interpretation of the abomination of desolation see D. Ford, *The Abomination of Desolation in Biblical Eschatology* (Washington, D.C., 1979).

[94] The first occurrence of the expression "abomination of desolation" in Daniel (9:27) creates some uncertainty as to its meaning. J. A. Montgomery translates, "upon the wing [i.e., of the temple] shall be an Abomination-Appalling" (*A Critical and Exegetical Commentary on the Book of Daniel,* ICC [New

First Maccabees provides the historical background to this state-ment. Antiochus Epiphanes, on returning from his conquest of Egypt, entered Jerusalem and plundered the temple. He later sent an official, who by guile attacked the Jews, plundered Jerusalem, and set it ablaze. Orders were given that sacrifices in the temple should cease and the ancestral law no longer be observed. Altars, idols, and sacred precincts were to be established, and "swine and other unclean beasts" were to be offered in sacrifice. This reached its climax on the fifteenth day of Kislev, 167 BC: "the abomination of desolation was set up on the altar. . . . On the twenty-fifth day of the month they offered sacrifice on the pagan altar which was on top of the altar of the Lord" (1 Macc 1:54, 59).

The Hebrew expression *šiqqûṣ šōmēm* for "abomination of deso-lation" is ambiguous. *šiqqûṣ* is a detestable thing or person, most commonly in the OT an idol. The verb *šāmēm* means to be desolated, frequently of the devastation of countries (cf. Ezek 33:28–29), but also to be appalled (e.g., in Jer 4:9). Most commonly the latter meaning of the term has been adopted for this context, so that "abomination of desolation" has been viewed as a detestable thing that causes horror. Following the Maccabean account, the Danielic expression is viewed as denoting a pagan altar, whereon unclean sacrifices were offered to a pagan god, thereby transforming the temple of God into a heathen temple and causing "desolation"—whether of the Jews' spirit or the desertion of the temple. The expression "abomination of desolation" entails a typical Jewish wordplay. The name *ba'al šāmayim* means Lord of Heaven, often equated with Zeus Olympos. *Ba'al* was replaced by the term *šiqqûṣ* (an idol), and *šāmayim* (heaven), often pronounced *šāmēm*, became *šōmēm*, "desolating." Hence "Lord of Heaven" became "a de-testable idol that horrifies"![95]

There is, however, more to the expression than this. On the one hand there is evidence that Antiochus ordered not only a pagan altar to be placed on the altar of the Jerusalem temple but also an image of Zeus made in his own likeness.[96] This is reflected in Dan 9:27 itself: "there

York, 1927], 385). The Greek versions (LXX and Theodotion) read *kai epi to hieron bdelygma tōn erēmōseōn*, "upon the temple shall be an abomination of desola-tions." A. Lacocque sees the possibility of a double wordplay in the phrase "upon the wing of abominations": the "wings" of the abomination could mean the horns of the altar; the Baal Shamem of the Syrians was frequently depicted in the form of an eagle; the plural "abominations" could even represent the plural form of God (Elohim) rather than a plurality of abominations; hence Lacocque under-stands Dan 9:27 as meaning, "upon the horns of the altar and the wings of the abomination shall be one who desolates," so bringing the first occurrence of the phrase into line with the later two (*The Book of Daniel*, 23 [Atlanta, 1979], 198–99).

[95] E. Nestle, "Der Greuel der Verwustung," *Zeitschrift für die alttesta-mentliche Wissenschaft* 4 (1884): 248.

[96] See my *Commentary on Mark Thirteen*, 54–55; Str-B, 1:945 and 951; B.

shall be an abomination that desolates until the decreed end is poured out upon the desolator." The abominable idol represents the abominable person who creates the desolations. It is likely that a similar thought is in view in Mark 13:14, where the neuter *to bdelygma* is followed by a masculine participle, *hestēkota,* "standing where he ought not."

Further, it is unjustifiable to restrict the meaning of *šōmēm* to "causing horror." The term equally conveys the meaning of causing devastation and ruin. This is what the LXX translators had in view when they rendered *šiqqûṣ šōmēm* as *to bdelygma tēs erēmōseōs.* The latter term is derived from *erēmoō,* which signifies to lay waste, make desolate, bring to ruin. The translators evidently interpreted the Hebrew phrase as denoting an abomination which causes *destruction.* The OT prophetic background virtually compels the inclusion of this thought. The author of Daniel, like all apocalyptists, continued and interpreted the work of the prophets. We recall that Dan 9:27 is the conclusion of a reinterpretation of a prophecy of Jeremiah, which declares that Israel will be laid waste and serve Babylon for seventy years, and after that will be restored (Jer 25:8–12; 29:10–14). Time and again Jeremiah proclaimed coming destruction upon the cities of Israel because of their abominations. See, e.g., Jer 4:1–8; 44:22; and note especially 7:30–34: "The people of Judah have done evil in my sight, says the Lord; they have set their abominations in the house that is called by my name, defiling it . . . the land shall become desolate."

Ezekiel uttered a prophecy in a similar vein: "Therefore as I live, says the Lord God, surely because you have defiled my sanctuary with all your detestable things and with all your abominations—therefore I will cut you down; my eye will not spare, and I will have no pity. . . . Moreover I will make you a desolation and an object of mocking . . . a taunt, a warning and a horror to the nations around you, when I execute judgments on you in anger and fury and with furious punishments—I the Lord have spoken" (Ezek 5:11–15). It will be observed that in this passage the concepts of abominations, desolation, and horror come together. That the author of Daniel had such a prospect in view in his prophecy is shown by the context of his first saying on the abomination of desolation. Daniel 9:27 is immediately preceded by the statement: "the troops of the prince who is to come shall destroy the city and the sanctuary. Its [or his] end shall come with a flood, and to the end there shall be war."

It seems indubitable that the reinterpretation of Jeremiah's prophecy in Dan 9:24–27 has in view the coming of one who acts both

---

Rigaux, "*bdelygma tēs erēmōseōs,*" *Bib* 40 (1959): 675–76, and literature there mentioned; the commentaries on Daniel, ad loc.; D. Ford, *Abomination of Desolation,* 150–51.

blasphemously and destructively, causing devastation in the city and the temple and horror among the people. Whatever reinterpretation may be involved in the allusion to this passage in Mark 13:14, it should be acknowledged that the notion of horror by reason of blasphemy and devastation of city, temple, and land, as in Dan 9:26–27, are retained.[97] That is the assumption of the statements that follow in Mark 13:15–20, which appear to have in view the necessity of flight from an invading army and terrible distress of the people. It has an important consequence for our understanding of the relation of v. 14 (and by inference, of the whole discourse) to the prophecy of v. 2. Throughout the twentieth century a continuing line of scholars has maintained that the entire discourse is out of relation to the prophecy with which it begins, since the latter declares that the temple will be destroyed, whereas the discourse has in view merely its desecration.[98] Contrary to all such interpretations, it would appear that v. 14 has in view a blasphemous event which will entail the destruction of the temple and the city, and will thus be the means by which the prophecy of v. 2 will be fulfilled. Verse 2, far from being alien to the discourse, is its presupposition throughout.

The address to the reader ("Let the reader understand") could have stood in Mark's source, but it is more likely to be a parenthesis inserted by Mark, calling attention to the importance of grasping the significance of the scriptural expression, both in Daniel and in the light of its precedents in the earlier prophets. The call to "understand" is reminiscent of the many references in Daniel to understanding the secrets of divine revelation (see especially Dan 8:15–17; 9:22–23; 11:33; 12:10), but also of Mark's allusions to the privilege and responsibility of understanding the revelations of Jesus (e.g., Mark 4:11–12; 7:18; 8:17–18); the Seer of Revelation similarly calls for a like understanding of apocalyptic mysteries (cf. Rev. 13:18; cf. 17:9ff.).[99]

---

[97] Such is the interpretation of the *bdelygma* in Klostermann, *Markus*, 135; Lohmeyer, *Markus*, 17; Grundmann, *Markus*, 266; V. Taylor, *Mark*, 511–12; Lambrecht, *Redaktion*, 149–52; Pesch, *Naherwartungen*, 142–43; idem, *Markus*, 2:292; Hartman, *Prophecy Interpreted*, 151–52; Zmijewski, *Eschatologiereden*, 192–99; Ford, *Abomination of Desolation*, 148–51; see also the interesting attempts to render the Danielic expression in Third-World languages, cited by R. Bratcher and E. A. Nida in *A Translator's Handbook on the Gospel of Mark* (Leiden, 1961), 406.

[98] For example, Wellhausen sought to strengthen this view of v. 14 in the light of the oracle preserved in Rev 11:1–2: Jerusalem will be sorely oppressed, but the city and temple will be rescued by the Son of man at his appearing (*Marci*, 100; idem, *Einleitung in die drei ersten Evangelien*, 97).

[99] J. Weiss, *Das älteste Evangelium* (Göttingen, 1903), 77–78; and Lührmann, *Markus*, 222, explicitly conjoin these references to the scripture. Cf. also V. Taylor, *Mark*, 511–12; Cranfield, *Mark*, 403; R. H. Gundry, *Matthew: A Commentary on His Theological and Literary Art* (Grand Rapids, 1982), 481; and

When the abomination appears, "Those who are in Judea should flee to the mountain country." This is the reverse of what Jews would normally do, for instinctively they would tend to flee for refuge into the city wherein is the temple where God has "set his name," and which he would surely protect. On the contrary, they are bidden to flee to the mountain country, which was an ideal area for fugitives.[100]

The change from the second person at the beginning of the sentence, "When you see . . . ," to the third person, "Those who are in Judea should flee . . . ," is remarkable. It is not impossible that an original *pheugete*, "flee," has been changed to a third person imperative to fall in line with vv. 15–16, for the second person appears again in v. 18. Pesch, however, found in the text confirmation of the belief that here is the oracle to which Eusebius refers in his report of the flight of the Christians from Jerusalem to Pella in Transjordan: the Jerusalem church passes on the directive to the Christian Jews in the surrounding Judean territory.[101] The notion is not incompatible with the fact that the flight motif is frequently met in contexts of the day of the Lord (cf. Amos 5:19–20); note also the escape of Mattathias and his sons to the mountains in the uprising against the forces of Antiochus (1 Macc 2:28). Luke's use of Mark 13:15–16 in Luke 17:31, however, clearly has in view the command to Lot and his family to flee to the hills (Gen 19:17); such an association reflects a typology which views Jerusalem as another Sodom, and the impending destruction of the temple and city as a judgment of God, comparable to that on Sodom.[102]

There is, however, uncertainty as to the reliability of the Eusebian report. Pesch finds further substantiation of its historicity in the call to inhabitants of Jerusalem to flee to "the mountain country," since Jerusalem is in such territory; he suggested that a move out of the mountain country of Judea into the mountain area of Transjordan was in view.[103] Hengel demurs; while agreeing that there are no historical grounds for denying the report of the flight to Pella, he points out that Pella was not in the hills but in the northern rift of the Jordan, and that v. 14b is irrelevant to the issue.[104] F. Neirynck subjected the evidence of Eu-

---

notably R. E. Clements, "Apocalyptic, Literacy and the Canonical Tradition," 15–27, especially 17.

[100]BAGD, 582, cites by way of illustration Plutarch, *Moralia* 869B: *hoi anthrōpoi kataphygontes eis ta orē diesōthēsan* ("The men, by fleeing to the mountain country, found safety").

[101]Pesch, *Markus*, 2:292. The report in Eusebius runs as follows: "The whole body of the church at Jerusalem, having been commanded by a divine revelation given to men of approved piety there before the war, removed from the city, and dwelt at a certain town beyond the Jordan, called Pella" (*Eccl Hist* 3.5).

[102]So Hartman, *Prophecy Interpreted*, 151–52; Pesch, *Markus*, 2:293.

[103]Pesch, *Markus*, 2:292.

[104]Hengel, *Studies in the Gospel of Mark*, 130 n. 111.

sebius to careful examination and concluded that the historical basis of the report is so uncertain that to view it as a means of interpreting the discourse (as Pesch has done) is a highly dubious procedure.[105] J. Verheyden has devoted a book to the same issue; his researches led him to the conviction that Eusebius' account of the flight to Pella represents a theological judgment rather than a historical report.[106]

Our one comment on this debate is that, in the light of the uncertainty of the Eusebian account of the flight of the Jerusalem church to Pella, we cannot with confidence view Mark 13:14–20, still less the whole discourse, as (in Eusebius' language) "a divine revelation given to men of approved piety there before the war."

In the light of the foregoing considerations, how are we to interpret the "abomination of desolation" and the consequences of its/his appearance? The problem has been endlessly discussed; we can but briefly set forth the varied interpretations and refer the reader to more compendious treatment elsewhere.[107]

The classic view of the abomination sees therein a representation of the antichrist. Stress is laid on the masculine participle *hestēkota* ("standing"), on the active element in *erēmōseōs* ("one who creates desolation"), and above all on the close parallel with Paul's description

---

[105] See Neirynck, "Marc 13. Examen critique de l'interprétation de R. Pesch," in *L'Apocalypse johannique et l'Apocalyptique dans le N.T.*, ed. J. Lambrecht, BETL 53 (1980), 369–401. Pesch responds to Neirynck in ibid., "Markus 13," 363–65.

[106] Verheyden, *De Vlucht van de Christenen naar Pella, Onderzoek van het Getuigenis van Eusebius en Epiphanius* (Brussels, 1988). A summary of the book in English appears in "The Flight of the Christians to Pella, A Study of the Testimony of Eusebius and Epiphanius," *ETL* (1990): 241–44. Verheyden considers that Eusebius had a theological rather than a historical view of the Jewish War. The inspiration for his story was provided by Luke 21:20–24, especially v. 21a. According to Eusebius the presence of the Christians preserved Jerusalem from decline. "One who, like Eusebius, wants to describe the complete destruction of Jerusalem and Judea, inevitably has to answer the question what happened to the Christians. Eusebius solved the problem by having the Christians flee to Pella. That way they also play a decisive role in the execution of the punishment. In this account of the punishment the flight of the Christians is the condition for the final destruction of the Jews. . . . At the moment the Jews enter the city they believe to be safe the Christians, being the true defenders of Jerusalem, flee from it" (ibid., 243). So the flight of the Christians was the condition for the final destruction of the Jews. Why Pella was chosen is, in Verheyden's view, of secondary importance. Josephus mentions the case of a woman from Perea, who fled to her ruin in Jerusalem at the time when Eusebius claims the Christians fled to Pella in Perea. From references in Eusebius' *Onomasticon* it appears that Pella was an important city in Perea.

[107] An extended note on "The History of Interpretation of the BDELYGMA ERĒMŌSEŌS" is given in my earlier *Commentary on Mark Thirteen*, 59–72. Since that time D. Ford has provided a detailed examination of the subject in his *Abomination of Desolation*.

of the Man of Lawlessness in 2 Thess 2:3–12.[108] The major difficulty of this view is that Mark speaks of pseudomessiahs and pseudoprophets in addition to the "abomination," and even of their coming on the scene after the appearance of the abomination, vv. 21–22. We have noted the possibility that v. 21 in Mark's source was the immediate predecessor to the description of the parousia in vv. 24–26: it was *Mark* who edited his materials to emphasize that according to a word of Jesus (v. 21) the parousia itself will reveal the falsity of the pseudomessiahs and the pseudoprophets who support them! I cannot see how Mark himself could have viewed the abomination of desolation as the last antichrist. The concept in 2 Thessalonians 2 is in the nature of an expansion of the earlier tradition in Mark 13 (e.g., that the antichrist sits in the temple of God is likely to signify the heavenly temple rather than that in Jerusalem); it could well be that Paul has extended the central concept of Mark 13:14, as known to him, with the aid of Daniel 11, or it may be a parallel conception, with the kind of contact inevitable in view of Paul's knowledge of traditional elements embodied in the Markan discourse. As an instrument of destruction, the abomination could have been viewed by Mark as *an* antichrist, somewhat in the spirit of 2 Thess 2:7a and 1 John 2:18; but the authors of both those works will have viewed the contemporary manifestations of opposition to God's Christ as predecessors of the last antichrist, not the final reality itself.[109]

From early times it has been believed that the abomination prophecy related to the erection of an idol in the temple, just as Antiochus had done. This has been championed from at least Jerome onward,[110] in recollection of Hadrian's erection of a statue of the Capitoline Jupiter on the site of the ruined temple. More recently it has been popular to view the abomination prophecy in the light of Caligula's aborted attempt to place a statue of himself in the Jerusalem temple in AD 40. A corollary of this view is often drawn that the passage, and indeed the whole discourse, took its rise from this event. More recently it has been suggested that the apocalypse which was inspired by the horror of the

---

[108]The interpretation is especially popular among German scholars. See J. Weiss, *Das älteste Evangelium*, 77–78; Loisy, *Marc*, 374; McNeile, *Matthew*, 348; Busch, *Verständnis*, 92–94; Klostermann, *Markus*, 135; Schniewind, *Markus*, 171; Lohmeyer, *Markus*, 275–76; W. Foerster, *TDNT*, 1:600; Marxsen, *Mark the Evangelist*, 181; Harder, "Mark 13," *Theologicum Viatorum* 4 (1952): 82; Rigaux, "*bdelygma tēs erēmōseōs*," *Bib* 40 (1959): 682; Walter, "Tempelzerstörung," *ZNW* 57 (1966): 43; G. Minette de Tillesse, *Secret Messianique*, 427–29; Grundmann, *Markus*, 260; Haenchen, *Weg Jesu*, 447; Mussner, *Christ and the End of the World*, 36–37; Schweizer, *Mark*, 272; Gnilka, *Markus*, 193–96.

[109]See further Dodd, "The Fall of Jerusalem and the Abomination of Desolation," *JRS* 37 (1947): 53 n. 10; Lambrecht, *Redaktion*, 151–52; Pesch, *Naherwartungen*, 140; Zmijewski, *Eschatologiereden*, 197; Lührmann, *Markus*, 222.

[110]Jerome *Comm. in Ev. Matt* ad loc.

Caligula affair was freshly applied in the light of the Jewish War of 66–70. That the crisis of AD 40 could have occasioned an assemblage of existing traditions, such as we have in Mark 13, is perfectly possible; but the idea that it led to the creation of a short apocalypse centering on v. 14 entails the difficulties that we have reviewed in the little apocalypse hypothesis.[111]

Another long-established interpretation of the abomination in Mark 13:14 is its identification with the desolating and destructive Roman forces. This interpretation is as old as Luke's "translation" of the Danielic expression: "Jerusalem surrounded by armies" (21:20). It may be viewed as a natural—some would say inevitable—interpretation in the light of the connection between vv. 2 and 14, together with the following vv. 15–20. Most exegetes who adopt it are led to view the place where the abomination "ought not" to stand as the Holy Land, not the temple. It may be questioned, however, whether the term "abomination," of itself, is suitable to apply to an army without further explanation. We recall the qualifying phrase with the masculine participle: "standing where *he* ought not"!

It is tempting to assay a synthesis of these interpretations and to see in the *bdelygma* a prophecy of an antichristian commander of Roman armies planting in a (or the) holy place a Roman standard, with its idolatrous images of the emperor affixed, and proceeding to conquer and destroy the city, temple, and people.[112] The question arises, however, whether it is methodologically justifiable to look for an exact

---

[111]The belief that v. 14 was inspired by the Caligula affair was first propounded by Pfleiderer, *Das Urchristentum* (1897), 404. It was taken up by Holtzmann, *Die Synoptiker*, 168; P. Schmiedel, *En.Bib.* 2 (1857); J. Weiss, *Das älteste Evangelium*, 78; it became popularized through Piganiol, "Observations sur la date de l'apocalypse synoptique," *RHPR* (1924): 247ff., which in turn influenced G. Hölscher, with whom the theory is especially associated, "Der Ursprung der Apokalypse Mark 13," *TBl* 12 (1933): 193ff. For further developments of this view in the English-speaking world see my *Commentary on Mark Thirteen*, 65–66.

[112]Lührmann suggested that in the Markan context the abomination in the masculine form signified the Roman commander or his army as the "abominable desolator" (*Markus*, 222). A. Merx pointed out that the Syriac tradition generally presupposes *to sēmeion tou bdelygmatos* ("the sign of the abomination") for *to bdelygma tēs erēmōseōs* (*Das Evangelium Matthäus nach der syrischen im Sinaikloster gefundenen Palimpsesthandschrift*, ad loc.). This would strengthen the link of the abomination with the Roman army, not least since *sēmeion* frequently translates the Hebrew *nēs*, i.e., ensign. This led me earlier to identify the abomination particularly with the idolatrous Roman ensign, which, in view of intense Jewish hostility to its idolatrous nature, was never brought into the temple area; its appearance in the vicinity of Jerusalem could only be with hostile intent, i.e., for war; see my *Jesus and the Future*, 255–58. I would not now adhere to this interpretation, but I do see the association of the Roman army with its idolatrous ensigns as significant.

correspondence of this kind between a prophecy and a particular feature of history. While having ideas as to possible solutions of the riddle of the abomination in line with the opening sentence of this paragraph, Adolf Schlatter protested at the notion that Jesus has to give a closely defined historical prediction, as though prophecy supplied detailed accounts of events that are to take place in the future.[113] In support of this one should bear in mind that ancient prophecies are frequently viewed in the NT in a far from literal manner, and even more so in apocalyptic literature, which displays a special interest in the reinterpretation of prophecies.[114]

We have seen that the prophecy concerning the abomination of desolation in the book of Daniel was itself the product of meditation on earlier writings in the OT, and from them a new prophetic application to the situation of his time was made. On this D. Ford made a perceptive comment: "Daniel's presentation of the *shiqqutz shomem* is a welding of elements already existing in the historical and prophetic books. He merely consummates themes emphasized long before. And what Daniel did with motifs from his predecessors, Christ did with Daniel."[115] If this be so we need to exercise restraint in our attempts to interpret the precise meaning of Mark 13:14. We saw that a twofold significance regularly adheres to the expression "abomination of desolation," namely something or someone or even action that is detestable to God and that produces horror and destruction among humankind. It is likely that such a connection inheres in the use of the expression in Mark 13:14: a fearful sacrilege and blasphemy against God, which results in terrible destruction; the link with v. 2 indicates that the destruction will include the temple; the connection with vv. 15–20 indicates that the calamity will entail dreadful sufferings for the people of God. More than that we can hardly affirm with confidence; less than that we need not say.

Verses 15–16

The necessity for instant flight at the appearance of the "abomination," already mentioned in v. 14, is here emphasized. Whoever is on the flat roof of the house when the abomination appears, whether

---

[113]Schlatter, *Der Evangelist Matthäus* (Stuttgart, 1948), 703.

[114]For an example note the use made of Ezekiel's prophecy of the river of living water (47:11–12) in John 7:37–38 and Rev 22:1–2. In Ezekiel the river flows from the temple to the Dead Sea; in John 7:37 it issues from the Christ to the believer; in Revelation 22 it flows from the throne of God and the Lamb through the street of the city of God. In both NT passages, however, the river represents the life of the kingdom of God (interpreted in John 7:39 as mediated through the Holy Spirit).

[115]Ford, *Abomination of Desolation*, 309.

working or resting or meditating on the scriptures, has no time to go down the stairs of the courtyard to enter the house, select goods to take with him, climb up the stairs, and then go down the outer stairway. Similarly, anyone in the field, whether working or engaged in any other pursuit, should not turn back to fetch even his coat, needful as it is for a blanket at night as well as covering by day. The necessity for flight is too urgent.

Luke has the sayings in a context relating to the parousia (Luke 17:31), in the so-called Q apocalypse. He prefaces the sayings with the phrase "in that day," which refers to the day when the Son of man is revealed (Luke 17:30). Luke 17:31, like vv. 32–33, in all likelihood is from Q, not from Mark.[116] The application to the parousia can hardly be original; since possessions will be irrelevant in the day of the Lord's appearing, it is hardly necessary to tell one not to go down from the roof into the house to fetch one's belongings, or to turn back from the field to collect one's coat. In such a context the language has to be taken in a purely figurative manner, but in the Markan context it speaks vividly to the need of the occasion. The language of Mark 13:16, "He who is in the field must not turn back," is reminiscent of Gen 19:17: "Do not turn back, and do not stop in the surrounding country." By omitting the phrase "to take his coat," Luke makes a closer link with his next sentence, "Remember Lot's wife." The connection of thought, even without the explicit appeal of Luke 17:32, is apparent in Mark also: as Lot and his family had to hasten to escape from Sodom, so the people of God must flee to escape the doom of Jerusalem and its environs. Observe that in Rev 11:8 Jerusalem is named "spiritually" as Sodom.

Verses 17–18

These sayings continue the motif of flight in time of war in Palestine; they are bound together by the expression of compassion for those in peculiar difficulty in such a situation. Clearly they are not intended to be understood in a referred sense (any more than vv. 15–16). Their presence here illustrates the limits of Mark's redactional activity in the whole section, for although they have no pertinence for Mark's congregation(s), he reproduces them without change. The lament for pregnant women and nursing mothers is comprehensible in face of the advance of an invading army: such women cannot make haste like others. So also the call to pray that the flight may not take place in the winter plainly is not for the purpose of avoiding discomfort; it has in view a country in which wadis, which have little or no

---

[116] So T. W. Manson, *The Sayings of Jesus* (London, 1937), 144–45; A. Polag, *Die Christologie der Logienquelle* (Neukirchen-Vluyn, 1977), 100 n. 313; Marshall, *Luke,* 664–65; Lambrecht, *Redaktion,* 157; and see above, 318–19.

water in the summer, and even the Jordan itself, become swollen through winter rains, and so make escape difficult or even impossible.[117]

Verses 19–20

It is frequently suggested that Mark interprets the *thlipsis* ("distress") of "those days" (v. 19) as denoting not the tribulation of the Jews in Palestine but that of the Christians in Rome; this is supported by appeal to the phrase "unto this day," i.e., Mark's own day, and to the shortening of the days "for the sake of the elect," v. 20, which is believed to refer to Christians.[118] On the contrary, this would appear to be an example of overzealous application of the redaction-critical principle that every word of the Gospels must be related to the situation of the readers. It is evident that Jerusalem and the Jews of Judea are in mind in vv. 14–18, without reference to Christians of Rome or anywhere else in the gentile world; it would be unreasonable to leap from Judea and its people in vv. 14–18 to Rome and its Christians in vv. 19–20 without any hint of a change of subjects, or place or time. Moreover, v. 19 appears to follow on vv. 17–18 without a break and combines with v. 20 to form the climax of the description of Israel's tribulation, when its temple and city fall. Similar considerations apply to the notion that vv. 19–20 advance from the situation of the Jews in Palestine to a worldwide tribulation in the last days.[119] Verse 14 employs a Danielic image of Israel's distress in relation to the prophecy of v. 2; another Danielic text relating to the same distress is used in v. 19, and v. 20 underscores the gravity of that time of trouble; it is accordingly one continuing historical situation which is in view in the source and doubtlessly in Mark's understanding also.[120]

The language of v. 19, as also of Dan 12:1, which it cites, uses traditional expressions to denote severe tribulation, not simply of Israel

---

[117]Pesch (*Markus,* 2:293–94) calls attention to a report of Josephus concerning Jewish refugees from Gadara, who attempted to escape to the territory east of the Jordan in AD 68. The Romans pursued them to the river, which was swollen because of heavy rains and could not be crossed, and so slew the fleeing Jews (*War* 4.7.5).

[118]See Pesch, *Naherwartungen,* 151–54; Schrenck, *TDNT,* 4:188–89; V. Taylor, *Mark,* 514; Grundmann, *Markus,* 267.

[119]So V. Taylor, *Mark,* 514; Rigaux, *L'Antéchrist,* 243. Ford thinks that the aggression of the Romans against the Jews in Palestine is viewed as extending to the whole world, as Luke shows in Luke 21:20–24 (*Abomination of Desolation,* 76–79). Geddert considers that both the distress of the Jews in Jerusalem and a universal tribulation in the last times are in view in vv. 19–20 (*Watchwords,* 231–39).

[120]Lane comments, "It is characteristic for oracles of judgment to be couched in language that is universal and radical. The intention is to indicate that through human events God intervenes powerfully to modify the course of history" (*Mark,* 471).

but of other peoples also. We recall the descriptions of the Egyptian plagues recorded in the book of Exodus (a fitting comparison, in view of their serving as models of messianic judgments in the apocalyptic tradition, as in Rev 8:6—11:19 and 16:1–21). The hailstorm sent on the Egyptians is "such as has never been in Egypt from its first beginnings until now" (Exod 9:18). The locust plague is described in stronger terms: "They settled on all its territories in swarms so dense that the like of them had never been seen before, nor ever will be again" (Exod 10:14). So also when the slaying of the firstborn of the Egyptians takes place, "All Egypt will send up a great cry of anguish, a cry the like of which has never been heard before, nor ever will be again" (Exod 11:6). Josephus uses similar proverbial language when describing the sufferings of the Jews in the destruction of Jerusalem: "The misfortunes of all men, from the beginning of the world, are not so considerable as theirs were."[121] Curiously, such language is found in Plato's writings also: *oute gar gignetai, oute gegonen, out' oun mē genētai*, "It neither is, nor has happened, nor will happen."[122] The significance of the saying for Mark is its recognition of the eschatological nature of the distress of Jerusalem. The employment of the Danielic language categorizes the calamity upon Israel as the day of the Lord on the city and people which rejected the word of God and the Messiah sent by God. Lührmann, however, observes that the statement that the distress will be more terrible than in any previous time, and any that comes after, shows that there is yet another time to follow after the day of the Lord on Jerusalem, and in that respect the addition corresponds to "the end is not yet" of v. 7.[123]

The motif of the shortening of the days (v. 20) has analogies within the apocalyptic literature of Judaism, but no real parallels.[124] It ex-

---

[121]Josephus, *War* Proem 4.

[122]Plato, *Republic* 6, p. 492E.

[123]Lührmann, *Markus,* 223.

[124]The contrary has been constantly affirmed from Bousset on through his *Antichrist Legend*, 218–19. The evidence, however, does not allow the deduction. Pesch cites 1 Enoch 80:2; 4 Ezra 4:26; 2 Bar 20:1 as indicating that the shortening of days was "a well-known apocalyptic feature" (*Naherwartungen,* 153–54). 1 Enoch 80:2 says, "In the days of the sinners the years will be shortened"; but this describes a perversion of the natural order by the sins of human beings, so that sinners will die sooner—a meaning opposite to that of Mark 13:20. 4 Ezra 4:26 states, "The end is hastening fast to its end," speaking merely of the speedy coming of the end of the age. Only 2 Bar 20:1 can be said to be related to Mark 13:20:

Therefore behold, the days come,
And the times shall hasten more than the former,
And the seasons shall speed on more than those that are past
And the years shall pass away more quickly than the present,

presses the thought of God's mercy upon the disobedient nation, which yet contains within it a remnant of faithful people, the "elect whom he has chosen." There is no need to assume that Mark added the second sentence of v. 20 to his source.[125] Nor is it likely that the evangelist looked upon the shortening of the tribulation as a further "pause for breath" given to the church to complete its mission prior to the end.[126] The second sentence emphasizes and explains the first: God will not allow his people to be exterminated, however sinful and rebellious they have been; he will himself intervene to bring to a speedy end the agonies of those days for the sake of the faithful among them, whom he has elected to salvation. The simple idea of the text is comprehensible within its context: Mark, as well as Paul, was a Jew (Rom 11:1)!

Mark 13:23

This statement, which is truncated in Matthew (24:25, "See, I have told you beforehand"), and is omitted by Luke, forms a closely related counterpart to the opening of the discourse and the question which sparked it off. The *hymeis de blepete* of v. 23a balances the first word of the discourse, *blepete* (v. 5); *proeirēka hymin*, "I have told you beforehand," corresponds to the request in v. 4a, *eipon hēmin*, "tell us"; and the concluding *panta*, "all things," of v. 23 responds to the concluding *panta* of v. 4. Inasmuch as the saying follows immediately on the warning against the pseudomessiahs and pseudoprophets of vv. 21–22, and the *blepete* of v. 5 introduces the first warning against such people, it is clear that v. 23 is the final member of the inclusion which holds together the section of the discourse vv. 5–23.[127] In the light of the question of the disciples in v. 4, the saying indicates that all that they needed to learn has been spoken (as distinct from all that they would have liked to know!). They have been told of events in the world which could needlessly panic them (vv. 7–8), of false messiahs and false prophets who could deceive them (vv. 6, 21–22), of persecutions on

---

Therefore have I now taken away Zion
That I may the more speedily visit the world in its season.

In this passage Zion has already been "taken away," i.e., destroyed; the times are to be "hastened," in that the judgment of the nations may come and with it the new age. It is a mode of expressing the nearness of the end, with its judgment of the wicked and revelation of the kingdom of God, but again having a quite different concern in view from that of Mark 13:20. See further Lambrecht, *Redaktion*, 164.

[125] As Pesch, *Naherwartungen*, 153.
[126] So Zmijewski, *Eschatologiereden*, 202.
[127] So Lambrecht, *Redaktion*, 172; Pesch, *Naherwartungen*, 156.

account of their confession of Jesus as the Christ (vv. 9, 11–13), of their duty to declare to all the good news of the kingdom of God, despite the opposition they are to experience (v. 10), and of the dire fulfillment of the prophecy of v. 2 and an indication of the sign which forms its prelude (vv. 14–20). With v. 23 therefore a conclusion of the answer to the disciples in relation to the prophecy of v. 2 is reached. As Lambrecht remarked: "The *proeirēka hymin panta* brought the address to rest; from the literary and structural viewpoint (if not also of content) it could have been a genuine conclusion."[128]

Pesch compares the role of the statement in the discourse to the prophetic formulae of conclusion such as we find in Isaiah, e.g., "The Lord, the God of Israel has spoken it" (Isa 1:20; 4:5; 58:14; cf. also the related formulae in Isa 21:17; 24:3; 25:8).[129] The analogy is illuminating. Prophetic concluding formulae are, of course, generally followed by further oracles! So also here, the last word about God's purpose for the world has obviously not been spoken in vv. 5–22. The prophecy of v. 2 pronounces doom upon the temple and people of Israel, but the OT has much to say beyond descriptions of the day of the Lord, and the message of Jesus as a whole is mainly concerned with that "beyond." It is unthinkable therefore that the final word of God through Jesus could end with the word of judgment given in vv. 14–20 and the warning about pseudomessiahs and pseudoprophets in v. 22. More must be said of what lies beyond the doom proclaimed, and more in fact follows at once in the description of the parousia of the Lord. Nevertheless, Mark is concerned at this point to ensure that his readers grasp the purpose of the discourse; accordingly, before he relates the description of the parousia in his sources, he sets this summary of the instruction of Jesus before his readers: "Be on your guard! You have been told all you need to know!"[130]

While the saying relates to the whole discourse thus far, its attachment to vv. 21–22 makes it plain that the danger to the community of the activity of pseudomessiahs and pseudoprophets is especially in view. Both in Judea and in Rome the peril posed by these impostors is recognized as acute, and therefore Mark prominently sets it forth.

---

[128]Lambrecht, *Redaktion,* 174. Lane makes the same point: "From this structural perspective the response to the question of verse 4 is complete with verse 23. All that remains is to announce the final victory of the Son of Man" (*Mark,* 473).

[129]Pesch, *Naherwartungen,* 155 n. 591. The verb *prolegō,* "tell beforehand," occurs elsewhere in NT prophetic declarations, e.g., in Acts 1:16; Rom 6:29, and also with reference to earlier statements made by writers, e.g., 2 Cor 7:3; 13:2, etc.

[130]It is likely therefore that the saying is due to Mark's redaction; so A. E. J. Rawlinson, *Mark,* 189; Taylor, *Mark,* 517; Grundmann, *Markus,* 268; Lambrecht, *Redaktion,* 171–72; Pesch, *Naherwartungen,* 155.

While assurance is implied in v. 22 that the powerful "signs and omens" will not suffice to lead astray the genuine "elect," v. 23 underscores that the readers need to "make their calling and election sure."[131]

Mark 13:24–27

The first observation to make on this description of the parousia is that it is a fragment.[132] Like many other elements in the discourse, it will have circulated at one time as a unit, and then at an early date will have been grouped with other similar sayings. It is therefore virtually certain that the two opening phrases, "But in those days, after that tribulation," were added at some point in the development of the tradition to connect with a preceding context. One could conceive of that happening at various stages. One suggestion deserving of consideration is that the first phrase, "in those days," was added prior to Mark, and that the evangelist was compelled to insert the second to avoid misunderstanding when he set the text in its present place.[133] This is the more plausible on consideration that "in those days" is a common expression in the OT for the last days.[134] Such a generalizing expression would not necessarily refer to a precise point of time or to a particular event (e.g., the destruction of the temple in Jerusalem). When, however,

---

[131]So Walter: "It may be so indeed that the *eklektoi* cannot be led astray to apostasy; but Mark appeals to his readers: 'You take care!' That means: It will be made plain only later who really belongs to the elect" ("Tempelzerstörung," *ZNW* 57 [1966]: 39 n. 6). Accordingly the "elect" of v. 22 are not necessarily identical with those addressed in v. 23. The comment of Rawlinson is to the point: "The Evangelist has been copying a source which spoke in general terms of the elect: he here addresses himself directly to his readers, i.e. to the Christian community, sc. 'But you take heed! The warning of Jesus is meant for you! He has forewarned you of everything, so that there is no excuse for being misled!' " (*Mark,* 189).

[132]So Lohmeyer, *Markus,* 279; A. Vögtle, *Das Neue Testament und die Zukunft des Kosmos* (Düsseldorf, 1970), 70–71.

[133]This was maintained by Pesch in his earlier work, *Naherwartungen,* 157, citing in agreement E. Wendling, *Die Entstehung des Markus Evangeliums* (Tübingen, 1908), 160; and G. Neville, *The Advent Hope* (London, 1961), 64. Marxsen appears to hold the same view (*Mark,* 167). Pesch observed that the doubling of the temporal phrase is characteristic of Mark's style, as evidenced in tables given by Sir John Hawkins, *Horae Synopticae* (Oxford, 1899), 139–41; so also Lambrecht, *Redaktion,* 192–93. In his commentary on Mark, however, Pesch withdrew his adherence to this view; he now holds that the double phrase could as well have stood in the pre-Markan apocalypse and makes the surprising deduction that "in those days" relates to the days "after that distress," so identifying the reference of the two phrases (*Markus,* 2:301).

[134]See, e.g., Jer 3:16–18; 5:18; 31:29; 33:15–16; 50:4; Joel 2:29; 3:16; 3:1–3 (MT 4:1–3); Zech 8:23. The phrase is clearly related to the frequent prophetic expression "the days come," which again relates to the "latter days," which may be for weal or for woe.

Mark ordered the paragraph in its present context, the temporal phrase will have gained a narrower meaning than that which was intended. It is feasible therefore that he inserted the second phrase, "after that tribulation," in order to make it plain that the parousia was not being represented as the high point of Israel's distress; it would happen only "after that tribulation."

The recognition of the secondary origin of the two phrases is of no little importance in the interpretation of the discourse. Apart from the distinction between Mark's redaction and the tradition available to him on a crucially important matter, it throws light on his understanding of the tradition, and possibly also on the date of the discourse. Whereas the text leaves the impression that the parousia is expected to occur "in those days" of tribulation, Mark's redaction had a quite different purpose; he had plainly recorded in v. 7, "the end is not yet," i.e., it does not come with war. He further emphasized the preaching of the gospel to the nations before the end comes. That does not imply a far, as distinct from a near, expectation, but rather that which is expressed in vv. 32–37, namely nearness beyond all bounds of definition.

The bearing of this on the date of the discourse is less clear. The desire to distinguish between the tribulation of Israel and the parousia would have been equally urgent when the tribulation was in progress as afterward, since Jerusalem's fate is decreed by God. While Pesch, like many others, decided on a date after AD 70 for Mark's redaction of the discourse, and while Marxsen set it in the period of Jerusalem's tribulation,[135] it should not be overlooked that the distinction is just as conceivable in advance of the tribulation, as Matt 23:39, following on Matt 23:34–36, suggests.

Verses 24–25

It is evident that the passage consists of reminiscences of OT descriptions of the day of the Lord. It is less a series of citations than a conflation of allusions to that day, drawn from well-known passages of the Prophets.[136] Verse 24 reflects language used in Isa 13:10; v. 25a echoes Isa 34:4; v. 25b appears to mix Isa 34:4 with Joel 2:10 and 3:15–16 (= MT 4:15–16). Such an interweaving of OT allusions is unique in the tradition of the sayings of Jesus; it confirms not a few in assigning it to an apocalyptic source, and the clear reflection of the LXX at various points appears to support this judgment.[137] It must, however, be ac-

---

[135]Pesch, *Naherwartungen*, 220; Marxsen, *Mark*, 167–68; cf. 193–94.

[136]See T. W. Manson, "The OT in the Teaching of Jesus," *BJRL* 34 (1951–52): 316; Lambrecht, *Redaktion*, 176–78; Hartman, *Prophecy Interpreted*, 157–58. Pesch favors the term *Kontamination* of scripture passages (e.g., *Markus*, 2:302).

[137]So, e.g., T. F. Glasson: "It is incredible that this passage of Mark xiii (24–27)—a patchwork of O.T. testimonies, partly in LXX language—can be the

knowledged that if one is to speak of the day of the Lord it is natural to use the descriptive language of the prophets regarding it, just as it is to use the pictorial language of Dan 7:13 when one speaks of the parousia. It is also to be expected that Mark's Greek source would use the language of the Greek Bible when referring to OT texts and concepts; the Hebrew texts behind the allusions in Mark 13:24–25 convey exactly the intention that is desired.

The idea itself is of vital importance. The combination of OT recollections of the day of the Lord in conjunction with the parousia sayings of v. 26 serves to underscore the nature of the parousia as a theophany. It is virtually impossible to talk about a theophany without calling on the language of the OT in which it is expressed. It is a curious fact that the term with which v. 25 concludes, *saleuthēsontai*, "will be shaken," occurs in none of the passages from the LXX cited above, but it is a standard term in OT descriptions of theophany (e.g., Judg 5:5; Amos 9:5; Mic 1:4; Isa 64:11 [Theodotion]; Hab 3:6; Nah 1:5; Ps 18:7; 114:7; Job 9:6). A dozen texts other than those alluded to in Mark 13:24–25 would have done equally well to express the idea in mind. If this collocation of OT reminiscences is unique in the teaching of Jesus, the concept is not. It occurs in the parallel which we adduced to the conjunction of vv. 21 and 24–26, namely Luke 17:23–24, for the comparison of the lightning flash with the Son of man in his day recalls the fundamental idea of theophany, specifically, the stepping forth of the Lord of the storm into this world (cf., e.g., Exod 19:16; Hab 3:11; Ps 18:13–15; Zech 9:14–16).

A major factor in the strangeness of the representation of the parousia in Mark 13:24–27, not to say the revulsion which modern exegetes frequently express toward it, is due to their neglect of the notion of theophany in the OT. It has led to some extraordinary expositions of the passage, on the assumption that a theophany entails the dissolution of the universe. For example, H. E. Tödt wrote: "At the very moment when the earth is dissolving amidst cosmic convulsions the Son of Man shows himself with great power and glory and commands his angels to rescue his elect from the desolation."[138] A glance at the OT theophany concepts in the above-mentioned sayings shows how far removed from Jewish thinking on theophany and the day of the Lord that comment is. Let the reader compare Isaiah 34 with Habakkuk 3 and one will instantly see what the prophets have in mind: the heavens

---

teaching of Jesus" (*Second Advent*, 187). See further idem, "Mark xiii and the Greek Old Testament," *ExpT* 69 (1957–58): 213–14; and J. A. T. Robinson, *Jesus and His Coming* (London, 1957), 119–20. Hartman considers that Glasson overpressed his point (*Prophecy Interpreted*, 157 n. 38).

[138]Tödt, *The Son of Man in the Synoptic Tradition* (London, 1965), 34. Similar language with reference to Mark 13:24–25 is used by Loisy, *Marc*, 380–81.

above and the earth beneath are pictured as in terror and confusion before the overwhelming might of the Lord of Hosts when he steps forth into the world to act in judgment and salvation. None of the descriptions of theophany in the OT envisages the destruction of the universe at the coming of God. The same applies to NT descriptions of theophany at the end of the age, other than the possible exception of the depiction of the last judgment in Rev 20:11, but I do not believe that even that is an exception. That heaven and earth want to flee from him who sits on the throne but have nowhere to hide vividly expresses the basic theophanic idea of the terror of the universe before the appearance of the Creator; it is possible, however, that this ancient language is applied in Revelation 20 to the desire of humankind to escape from the presence of the all-holy God in the judgment day. At all events, when the language of theophany is used in relation to the parousia, there is no suggestion that the Son of man comes to destroy the world; the function of this ancient mythological language is purely to highlight the glory of that event and set it in its proper category: it represents the divine intervention for judgment and salvation.[139]

The most impressive section in Pesch's *Naherwartungen* is his lengthy discussion of this very theme, wherein he sought to bring to light the significance of the symbolism employed in Mark 13:24–25. "In these pictures we have to do with cosmological metaphors which describe a theological content"; and he rejected attempts to view them "realistically."[140] Unfortunately Pesch has been persuaded, through reading Hahn's criticism of this interpretation, to abandon his position, and to do exactly what he denied should be done—to interpret the language "realistically."[141] Hahn objected to viewing vv. 24–25 as employing metaphorical language on the ground that NT eschatology embraces humanity and the cosmos also; the parousia of the Son of man brings to a climax not only the history wherein antichrist appears and the gospel is preached to the whole world, but the end of this world and the perfection of the next.[142]

This interpretation of NT eschatology is not wrong, but it fails to take into account the complexity of NT presentations of the end. The denial of the pictorial nature of biblical descriptions of the climax of

---

[139]So A. Vögtle, *Das Neue Testament und die Zukunft des Kosmos,* 70–71. The whole work is an exposition of this understanding of the NT teaching on the cosmic accompaniments of divine interventions. Cf. also R. Schnackenburg, *Mark,* 101.

[140]Pesch, *Naherwartungen,* 158–66.

[141]Pesch, *Markus,* 2:303.

[142]Hahn, "Die Rede von der Parusie des Menschensohnes Markus 13," in *Jesus und der Menschensohn,* Festschrift A. Vögtle, ed. R. Pesch and R. Schnackenburg (Freiburg, 1975), 164–66.

the ages overlooks that in the OT theophanic language is used of historic events of the past, in a manner that cannot possibly be interpreted literally. This applies particularly to references to the exodus. Deborah's song tells of God's coming at the exodus in the same kind of way that prophets speak of the onset of the day of the Lord (Judg 5:4–5). Not only so, the poem in Habakkuk 3, with its extraordinary description of the coming of God, appears to relate primarily to the coming of God at the exodus, viewed as a pattern for the coming of God in the day of the Lord.

With respect to the portrayal of the parousia in Mark 13:24–27, it seems that some exegetes read it with the silent assumption that the discourse is an apocalypse which tells all. On the contrary, the discourse no more informs us as to what happens at the parousia than it tells us what happens to the forces which destroy Jerusalem, or how the nations are judged, or how the redeemed participate in the feast of the kingdom of God. The darkening of sun and moon is not remotely connected with the notion of their destruction, nor the shaking of the powers of the heavens with their disappearance. The falling stars alone could tally with such notions, but not in the light of Isaiah 34.[143]

The clearest indication we have of the way Mark 13:24–25 would be understood in the primitive church is the employment of similar language in the book of Revelation. In Rev 6:12 we have an almost identical reproduction of the same OT passages, but it goes even further in its use of hyperbole: "I watched as he broke the sixth seal. And there was a violent earthquake; the sun turned black as a funeral pall, and the moon all red as blood; the stars in the sky fell to the earth, like figs shaken down by a gale; the sky vanished, as a scroll is rolled up, and every mountain and island was moved from its place." On the basis of a "realistic" interpretation, that passage should describe the total dissolution of the universe.

But we read on: "Then the kings of the earth, magnates and marshals, the rich and the powerful, and all men, slave or free, hid themselves in caves and mountain crags; and they called out to the mountains and the crags, 'Fall on us and hide us from the face of the One who sits on the throne and from the vengeance of the Lamb.' For the great day of their vengeance has come, and who will be able to stand?" Clearly the two pictures do not comport. But why should they? John is writing an apocalypse! Later he will recount the song of the victors over the beast and its image: "All nations shall come and worship thee, for thy judgments have been revealed" (15:4). That event he expects to take place on this solid earth, after a parousia of "Faithful

---

[143]Compare R. H. Gundry's comment: "The falling of the stars refers to a shower of meteorites, and the shaking of the heavenly powers to God's displacing 'the spiritual forces of wickedness in the heavenly places (Eph 6:12)'" (*Matthew*, 487). Such a mixture of realistic and allegorical interpretation is clearly at fault.

and True," riding on a white horse, followed by armies of heaven on white horses, who watch him as he treads the winepress of the fury of the wrath of God the Almighty (19:1ff.). This, too, is theophanic language. Its setting in the context of an opened heaven, with the King of kings riding at the head of innumerable cavalry of heaven seated on winged pegasi, is as literally intended as the shattered heaven and earth in the day of God in ch. 6. Is it not abundantly clear that the ancient tradition of the unimaginable theophany was vividly maintained in the NT community? It is in that light that we should interpret Mark 13:24–27.[144]

Verse 26

In view of the Danielic citations in vv. 14 and 19, the statement invites comparison with Dan 7:13 and Mark 14:62. Tödt suggests that Mark 13:26 cites directly Dan 7:13, but that the concept of the Son of man is determined by the Similitudes of Enoch rather than by Daniel.[145] There can be no reasonable doubt that Dan 7:13 is reflected in Mark 13:26, but there is no justification for bringing in the Enoch tradition on behalf of the Son of man concept here. We have no evidence that the Similitudes of Enoch were known to Jesus, or that they circulated among the first-generation church.[146] Moreover, there is no parousia concept in the Similitudes.[147] It is noteworthy that our saying commences with *opsontai*, "they shall see," which is only faintly represented in Dan 7:13 by the opening word of the seer, "I saw," but which appears in the second person in Mark 14:62, "You will see." Curiously, while both Dan 7:13 and Mark 14:62 speak of the clouds of heaven, the latter term is missing in Mark 13:26.

It has therefore been proposed that Mark 13:26 represents an interpretation of 14:62 in the light of Dan 7:13–14, or that Mark 13:26 modifies Dan 7:13 in the light of Mark 14:62. Such is the belief of L. Gaston, who sees Mark 14:62 as a Christian interpretation of the resurrection of Jesus with the aid of Dan 7:13, and Mark 13:26 as the result of the midrash of the early church.[148] Lambrecht has a related view,

---

[144]G. Volkmar, commenting on this passage, suggested that it be viewed as deliberate quotation, with the implication: "After the tribulation of those days the Scriptures will be fulfilled which speak in this manner; then shall the advent take place" (*Jesus Nazarenus und die erste christliche Zeit* [1882], 285). The reminder that we are here dealing with an ancient Semitic tradition is right.

[145]Tödt, *Son of Man*, 35.

[146]We cannot be so sure about the *second*-generation church, notably that of Matthew. The possibility of Matthew's knowledge of the Similitudes arises particularly with respect to Matt 19:28 and 25:31. See the discussion in my *Jesus and the Kingdom of God*, 308–12, and references in nn. 378–79, pp. 408–9.

[147]So Brandenburger, *Markus 13 und die Apokalyptik*, 61–63; see above, pp. 304, 307–9, for comments on this issue.

[148]Gaston, *No Stone on Another*, 388–89.

seeing Mark 13:26 in the light of Mark 8:39—9:1 and 14:62, but all as due to Markan redaction.[149] It all sounds very complex and sophisticated, but it is less well founded than it appears, for a sound exegesis of 14:62 does not permit viewing it as primarily an interpretation of the resurrection of Jesus.[150] If, on the other hand, 13:26 depends on 14:62, why has it wholly neglected the exaltation of Jesus, which is so important to the trial saying?[151] Mark 13:26 should be allowed to stand on its own feet as an independent expression of the parousia tradition.

Every item in the saying has been scrutinized for its contribution to the significance of the whole. Pesch has interpreted the opening word *opsontai*, "they shall see," in the light of the *opsesthe*, "you shall see" of 14:62; the latter is addressed to the judges of Jesus, and suggests that they are to see Jesus coming as Judge; taking into account also 8:38, Pesch affirms that for Mark, "to see" the coming Son of man is to experience the coming for judgment.[152] That is surely pressing the term beyond what is warranted; for the implication of "seeing" the coming of the Son of man in 14:62 as a coming for condemnation is due to the attitude of those addressed: they are in the act of rejecting the Son of man with a view to procuring his death; hence it is relevant to cite 8:38 in this context. But 8:38 is a truncated saying, abbreviated because of Mark's emphasis in the context wherein it appears. Mark knows that when Jesus is confessed before people there will be a corresponding confession by the Son of man before the angels of God, and for such confessors the "seeing" of the Son of man will be for salvation, not for judgment, as is plainly implied in the Q version of the logion, Luke 12:8–9.

Accordingly, for God's "elect" (Mark 13:27) to "see" the Son of man coming is the same as seeing the kingdom of God come with power (9:1), and it is not unrelated to seeing Jesus in the resurrection (16:7).

---

[149]Lambrecht, *Redaktion*, pp. 181–84, 189–93.

[150]See further my *Jesus and the Kingdom of God*, 298–303.

[151]Zmijewski raises this question with a like motive (*Eschatologiereden*, 238).

[152]Pesch, *Naherwartungen*, 170. Similarly Gnilka, *Markus*, 199–200. Ernst claims that Dan 7:14 and especially 1 Enoch 62:2, 13 are significant for understanding the parousia; in the latter passage the destruction of sinners and the homecoming of the elect are mentioned together; "seeing" the Lord at his parousia has to do with judgment, for such persons are the "enemies, the wicked and sinners" who meet with judgment and are spoken of (in v. 26) with an impersonal future (*Markus*, 386). This is true of 1 Enoch 62 but not of Mark 13:24–27. The former has a lengthy account of the punishment of the "sinners, oppressors, kings, governors, high officials, and landlords"; when they see the Son of man on his glorious throne they are seized with panic and rush from his presence, but are delivered by the Son of man to angels for execution of vengeance and punishments. The whole representation is far from Mark 13:24–27; how Ernst can equate "the impersonal future" ("they shall see") of Mark 13:26 with the Enochic picture I fail to understand.

Both aspects of the "seeing" may be comprised in the *opsontai* of 13:26, for that is evidently a generalized use of the term, and could even be considered as an impersonal middle voice, used as an equivalent for the passive. In either case there is a certain advance in the representation of the parousia in 13:26 over 14:62; for the third person plural suggests that the coming of the Son of man will be a universal event, experienced by all, not simply by the followers of Jesus or by his opponents. In the context of the discourse, 13:26 also represents an advance over Dan 7:13, since the Son of man who is "coming" is the Messiah Jesus, hence the coming signifies his returning.[153] The unacknowledged, rejected, and finally slain Son of man comes to complete the work of establishing the sovereignty of God which he began in his ministry. In the discourse, set as it is immediately prior to the passion narrative, the parousia of the Son of man gains a unique significance which it could not have had in any Jewish apocalypse, including Daniel.

That the Son of man comes *en nephelais, in* the clouds, instead of *with* the clouds, as in Daniel (*meta tōn nephelōn*, Theodotion; *epi tōn nephelōn*, LXX) has been rather heavily discussed, as though a distinction were being made between the Almighty One traveling with the clouds and the movement of lesser beings in the clouds.[154] The scruples are needless. The saying in its context denotes a theophany; the OT also speaks of God descending *en nephelē* (e.g., Exod 34:5). Mark's change of preposition is almost certainly due to stylistic considerations; his source is before him, and he is about to write *meta dynameōs pollēs doxēs*, "with great power and glory," and he naturally would not wish to use *meta* twice.[155]

Neither Dan 7:13 [14] nor Mark 14:62 states that the coming of the Son of man is with great power and glory, as in Mark 13:26, but the idea is present in both passages. Dan 7:13[14] records, "And to him was given dominion and glory and kingdom," which is very close to Mark's phrase, though strangely neither Theodotion nor LXX uses Mark's term (Theodotion: *kai autō edothē hē archē kai hē timē kai hē basileia*; LXX: *kai edothē autō exousia*). The power and glory may be considered to be represented in Mark 14:62 by the allusion to Ps 110:1: *ek dexiōn kathēmenon tēs dynameōs*, "sitting at the right hand of the power." It is an interesting example of a single concept being represented in three different ways. In Mark 13:26 the phrase may well be viewed as having the function of interpreting the significance of the coming in the clouds,

---

[153] See Lambrecht, *Redaktion*, 181–82.

[154] So Dalman, *Words of Jesus* (ET Edinburgh, 1902), 241; W. O. E. Oesterley, *The Doctrine of the Last Things* (London, 1909), 148. See also my *Commentary on Mark Thirteen*, 91–92.

[155] Similarly Lambrecht, *Redaktion*, 182–83.

for to "come" in such a manner is to come with the glory and power of God himself.[156]

And that, in truth, is what is represented in Mark 13:26: Jesus, the representative of the kingdom of God in his ministry, is to come back as the representative of the kingdom of God in theophanic glory. A theophany is always from heaven to the world of humankind; that rules out any idea that 13:26 denotes the concept of the coming of the Son of man to God in heaven.[157] Precisely the opposite is set forth in this passage: the representative of heaven "comes" from heaven to accomplish God's purpose in the world.

But what is that purpose? Is it to achieve salvation? Or is it to execute judgment? Generally the former view has been maintained, since vv. 26–27 make no mention of the Son of man as the executor of the divine wrath; he gathers the elect of God for his kingdom. Pesch, on the contrary, considers that the very notion of the Son of man coming in the manner of the theophany comports with his being seen by his adversaries for judgment: the Son of man comes as the Judge.[158] If that last term is recognized to be neutral it is acceptable; otherwise it is misleading. Pesch acknowledges that the Son of man comes for judgment and salvation, and that Mark's real interest is in the latter, as is seen from v. 27.[159] Without doubt the representations of theophany in the OT have both ideas in view, some passages stressing the coming for judgment, as Isaiah 19, and others the coming for deliverance. The earliest prophetic declaration of a theophany falls in the latter category, namely Judg 5:4–5 (virtually repeated in Ps 68:7–8; cf. also Ps 18:6–18 and Isa 40:9–11). The classic passage Hab 3:2–16 is largely taken up with the coming of God for judgment, but at the same time it shows that the real purpose of the theophany is for the deliverance of God's people (Hab 3:13). It may fairly be said that so far as the interest of the eschatological discourse is concerned, the prime purpose of the theophanic parousia is for the deliverance of the people of God, but that cannot be imagined without the exercise of judgment. By accident or design, however, the discourse is silent on the latter aspect.[160]

---

[156]So Vögtle, "Exegetische Erwägungen," in *Gott in Welt*, Festschrift Karl Rahner, 2 vols. (Freiburg, 1964), 1:647; Pesch, *Naherwartungen*, 171; idem, *Markus*, 2:304; Lambrecht, *Redaktion*, 184.

[157]Contra Jeremias, *New Testament Theology* (ET London, 1971), 274; T. Weeden, *Mark*, 129–31. See further the related discussion on Dan 7:13 and Mark 14:62 in my *Jesus and the Kingdom of God*, 28–20, 299–302.

[158]Pesch, *Naherwartungen*, 171.

[159]Ibid., 172; idem, *Markus*, 2:303–4.

[160]In Lohmeyer's view the chief theme of Mark 13, unlike that of apocalypses generally, is the coming of the Son of man, not in judgment on the world but for the gathering of the saints, i.e., for the formation of the eschatological community (*Markus*, 278). So too Dupont observes that the theophanic setting of

One final issue may be briefly dealt with, namely the relation of Mark 13:26 in its present context to the authentic teaching of Jesus. We have already seen that the passage is frequently regarded as a community formulation, molded in the course of the Gospel traditions; some see it as a Christian prophetic utterance, others as an excerpt from a Jewish apocalyptic source, and still others as a composition of Mark. Clearly it is impossible to demonstrate the validity of one line of argument, like one well-aimed ball that sends all the pins in the alley flying to the back. I can but express the conviction that the objections to the dominical origin of the saying are less convincing than is commonly represented.

On the assumption that 13:24–27 is derived from a Jewish apocalyptic flyleaf, Vögtle asserted that the passage "as good as certainly" is not an utterance of Jesus.[161] He was building on the findings of his former pupil, Pesch; but Pesch has since become convinced that the source of Mark 13 was Christian, not Jewish. On my reading of the evidence there is nothing to be said in favor of viewing the basis of the discourse as a Jewish apocalypse, not least in view of the lack of a parousia doctrine in Jewish apocalypses prior to the end of the first century AD. Tödt rejected Mark 13:26 since, on his view, no authentic statement of Jesus refers to a scriptural saying of the Son of man;[162] this, too, is bound up with Tödt's unduly restricted view of the origin of the Son of man sayings in the Gospels, including their supposed dependence on the Similitudes of Enoch, a position that is becoming increasingly difficult to justify. Vermes dismissed the saying on the ground that utterances relating to the parousia of the Son of man-Jesus assume that Jesus regarded himself as Messiah, and Jesus entertained no such self-understanding;[163] that flies in the face of the teaching of Jesus on the kingdom of God, particularly its presence, which intimates that he is the mediator of the kingdom of God. Gaston's objection depends on his understanding of the evaluation of Mark 13:26 and 14:62 and the meaning of Dan 7:13, all of which is highly questionable.[164]

And so we could go on, knocking down one pin after another, while someone else quietly puts them up again! Perhaps one may be permitted to observe that a comprehensive investigation of the sayings

---

the parousia of the Son of man, far from representing the parousia as a massacre, emphasizes its purpose as for the gathering of the elect; the discourse is "a pure message of hope" ("La ruine du temple et la fin des temps dans le discours de Marc 13," in *Apocalypses et Théologie de l'espérance,* LD 95 [Paris, 1977], 250–54).

[161]Vögtle, *Die Zukunft des Kosmos,* 69–70.
[162]Tödt, *Son of Man,* 35–36.
[163]G. Vermes, *Jesus the Jew* (New York, 1973), 183.
[164]Gaston, *No Stone on Another,* 388–89.

of Jesus on the kingdom of God, and of the Son of man sayings in relation to his ministry, death, resurrection, and parousia, tends to a positive evaluation of the essential content of Mark 13:24–26. That the passage contains the ipsissima verba of Jesus it is not necessary to maintain; but that its content is harmonious with the eschatological teaching of Jesus is well grounded.[165]

Verse 27

The climax of the parousia description is the gathering of the "elect" at the command of the Son of man, unquestionably in order that they may participate in the kingdom of God. This represents the fulfillment in a new key of the ancient hope of the reunion of Israel's scattered tribes, as stated in such passages as Isa 11:12; 27:12–13; 60:1–9. The language in which our text expresses this hope is drawn primarily from Zech 2:6 (MT 10) and Deut 30:3, possibly with Isa 43:6 in mind, but also under the unexpressed assumption that the angels of Dan 7:10 are at the behest of the Son of man.[166] The text of Zech 2:6 is uncertain. The MT (2:10) reads, "I have spread you abroad as the four winds of heaven," but LXX has, "I will gather you from the four winds of heaven" (ek tōn tessarōn anemōn tou ouranou synaxō hymas). The LXX rendering can hardly be due to a misunderstanding of the MT. It would seem that the translators read mēar:ba (from the four winds) instead of kear:ba (to the four . . .) and some such verb as āsap:tî (I have gathered) instead of pēras:tî (I have spread abroad). On this D. Winton Thomas wrote, "The LXX rendering is more in accord with the context, where the prophet is thinking of the gathering in of the Jews still outside Palestine, than is the M.T., which refers to the spreading abroad of the Jews all over the world."[167] There is no doubt about the text and

---

[165]It is significant that while Lambrecht labors to demonstrate that vv. 24–27 were composed by Mark, he emphasizes that Mark is the author (Verfasser) of the paragraph but not the originator (Verfertiger) of its elements. "It is not really thinkable that the content of this pericope does not ultimately go back to an authentic teaching of Jesus. Nevertheless, it is another question whether, e.g., Mark 13:26 is a genuine saying of Jesus" (Redaktion, 193).

[166]For angels accompanying the Son of man at the parousia see Mark 8:38, and for their carrying out a like task as emissaries of the Son of man see Matt 13:41.

[167]IB, 6:1065. Such is the view of many OT scholars, including Wellhausen, Die Kleinen Propheten, 4th ed. (Berlin, 1963), 180; K. Marti, Das Dodekapropheten (Tübingen, 1904), 406; W. Nowack, Die Kleinen Propheten (Göttingen, 1922), 337; E. Sellin, Das Zwölfprophetenbuch (Leipzig, 1930), 491; and Kittel in BHK. H. G. Mitchell adhered substantially to the MT (A Critical and Exegetical Commentary on Haggai, Zechariah, Malachi, and Jonah, ICC [Edinburgh, 1912], 145), and A. Petitjean emphatically so Les oracles du Proto-Zacharie [Paris, 1969], 97–98).

meaning of Deut 30:3. The passage is striking in the kinship of its thought to that of the discourse. It comes at the conclusion of the long prophetic statement in Deuteronomy 28—30, which warns Israel of what will happen to the people if they cease to listen to the voice of the Lord: like an eagle, a nation will come from afar; it will besiege and destroy Israel's towns, and the people will be scattered among the nations; when, however, Israel returns to the Lord, he will gather them again from all the countries to which he scattered them: *ean ē hē diaspora sou ap' akrou tou ouranou heōs akrou tou ouranou ekeithen synaxei se kyrios ho theos sou*, "If your outcasts are in the uttermost parts of heaven, from there the Lord your God will gather you" (Deut 30:4 LXX). With the last line one should compare the language of Deut 13:8 LXX: *ap' akrou tēs gēs heōs akrou tēs gēs*, "from the end of earth to the end of earth."

Mark has given an unusual conflation of the two modes of expression in v. 27: "from the end of earth to the end of heaven." It has also led to some strange interpretations, like that of Lohmeyer, who considered that the elect are conceived of as being united on the peak point of earth, i.e., "the holy and high midst of earth, and from there they are brought up to the highest point of heaven, where God is enthroned."[168] Menzies understood it to mean the farthest east (the extremity of earth for the Jews) to the farthest west (where the sky dips down on the ocean).[169] McNeile pointed out that since the vault of heaven rested on the earth, the *akra*, the "extremities," touched each other, but he did not indicate why that understanding was expressed in terms of v. 27.[170] Probably we are merely presented with a pleonasm, which is also, as Lambrecht put it, a brachyology, signifying the gathering of the elect from the farthest reaches of earth and of heaven.[171]

The language is tantalizingly brief. Is a resurrection of the people of God assumed in our text? Is a doctrine of reunion of the living who hope in God with the resurrected faithful envisaged? Paul almost certainly drew his teaching in 1 Thess 4:15–17 from an early tradition of the saying reproduced in Mark 13:24–27. Yet not a hint of an allusion to resurrection of the dead is given in the context. Who are the elect of v. 27? In v. 20 they appear to denote the faithful in Israel, yet in v. 27,

---

[168]Lohmeyer, *Markus*, 279.

[169]Menzies, *The Earliest Gospel: A Historical Study of the Gospel according to Mark* (London and New York, 1901), 240.

[170]McNeile, *Matthew*, 353.

[171]Lambrecht, *Redaktion*, 189. It should be noted that the phrase is not without parallel. A similar expression occurs in Philo: *apo gēs eschatōn achris ouranou peratōn* (*Migr. Abr.* 181; and, with the same phrase in reverse order, in *Cherb.* 99). In 1 Enoch 57:2 the Hesychian group of mss. read, concerning the exiles returning homeward on their wagons, "the sound thereof was heard from the end of the earth to the end of the heaven."

which will have originated in another context, the faithful followers of the Son of man will primarily have been in mind (cf. 8:38 and the Q parallel Luke 12:8–9). Interestingly, Zech 2:6, which is especially in mind in our saying, is followed by the extraordinary declaration of v. 11: "Many nations shall come over to the Lord on that day and become his people, and he will make his dwelling with you." The unity of Gentiles and Jews in one people of the kingdom of God is a highly unusual expectation in the OT. That Jesus himself looked for Gentiles to stream from the ends of the earth into the kingdom of God, while "sons of the kingdom" would be excluded, is evident from Matt 8:11–12/Luke 13:28–29. The universal implications of Mark 13:27 could well envisage the gathering of the elect of all nations along with the penitents of Israel into a single community under the lordship and in the fellowship of the Son of man. If that is the sole task of the Son of man in his parousia which Mark or his source explicitly mentions, that may be because it was viewed as of supreme importance; through it he becomes, as Gloege put it, "the Christ in his perfected absoluteness."[172]

Mark 13:28–29

This short parable of the Fig Tree has generally been viewed as substantially authentic.[173] In recent times, however, its authenticity has been questioned; by some it is considered to be wholly due to Mark's composition, by others as heavily redacted by Mark.[174] It is desirable to examine the grounds for these views.

Both Pesch and Lambrecht consider the introductory phrase in v. 28a, *apo de tēs sykēs mathete tēn parabolēn*, "From the fig tree learn the lesson," to have been composed by the evangelist as a transition to the parable. Pesch accepts v. 28b as an authentic reminiscence of the teaching of Jesus, although the original utterance probably did not take the form of a parable.[175] Lambrecht is doubtful about v. 28b; for him it is not possible

---

[172]Gloege, *Reich Gottes und Kirche im Neuen Testament* (Gütersloh, 1929), 191.

[173]See, e.g., McNeile, *Matthew*, 354; Otto, *Kingdom of God and Son of Man*, 148; Dodd, *Parables of the Kingdom*, 137; Klostermann, *Markus*, 137; Lohmeyer, *Markus*, 280–81; Jeremias, *The Parables of Jesus*, rev. ed. (ET London, 1963), 119–20; Schniewind, *Markus*, 175; Grundmann, *Markus*, 170; V. Taylor, *Mark*, 520; Grässer, *Parusieverzögerung*, 152; Kümmel, *Promise and Fulfilment*, 20–22; E. Schweizer, *Mark*, 278; Anderson, *Mark*, 299. Bultmann speaks with divided voice in *History of the Synoptic Tradition*: for authenticity, 123; against it, 125; in *Jesus and the Word*, 30, he treats it as authentic. Hahn is sure of the authenticity of v. 28, but uncertain of the application in v. 29 ("Die Rede von der Parusie," 258).

[174]For the former see, e.g., Lambrecht, *Redaktion*, 201; for the latter see, e.g., Pesch, *Naherwartungen*, 176–81.

[175]Pesch, *Naherwartungen*, 176.

to determine whether it is authentic, but one consideration carries weight with him: "If Mark is responsible for the structure and composition of the first two parts of the address (vv. 5–27), his share in the redaction, whether newly created or newly drafted, is considerable."[176]

Both Lambrecht and Pesch think that the evangelist composed v. 29. In this they are not alone,[177] but they provide more substantial grounds than others. They make the following points: *houtōs* is frequent in Mark, and in particular *houtōs kai hymeis* is reminiscent of Mark 7:18; *hotan idete* is formulated with an eye on vv. 4, 14, 30; *tauta ginomena* harks back to previous elements of the discourse, whether specifically to vv. 14–20 (so Lambrecht), or to vv. 4, 14 and in anticipation of v. 30 (so Pesch);[178] *ginōskete hoti engys estin* is taken from v. 28; *epi thyrais* is added by Mark, with an eye on the later parable of the Doorkeeper and the return of the Master; both writers cite Jeremias as indicating that the phrase is a hellenistic expression ("The use of a spatial image to denote time is Hellenistic") and that the plural for door (*thyrai*) is classic.[179]

These contentions do not have an identical degree of plausibility. For example, the mere fact of the presence of the parable within the discourse is a most inadequate reason for affirming its inauthenticity;[180] and the presence of redactional elements in reports of parables of Jesus by no means signifies that the parables themselves are secondary, as the work of Jeremias abundantly illustrates. The moot question is how extensive the redactional elements are.

The origin of the opening phrase of v. 28 is uncertain. The parables of Jesus do not normally begin in this manner. Lohmeyer suggested that the original beginning may have followed the model of other parables of Jesus: *homoia estin hē basileia tou theou dendrō* ("The kingdom of God is like a tree"); or it could have commenced with a simple *ōs* or *ōsper*, as in the parable of the Talents, Matt 25:14.[181] If there was such an introduction, mention must have been made of the fig tree in the main sentence, since it is the blossoming of this tree to which the parable draws attention.[182] Perhaps, however, we should be content to

---

[176]Lambrecht, *Redaktion*, 201.

[177]See, e.g., N. Perrin, *Rediscovering the Teaching of Jesus*, 202; Nineham, *Mark*, 359; Hartman, *Prophecy Interpreted*, 223; Zmijewski, *Eschatologiereden*, 261; Hahn, "Die Rede von der Parusie," 258.

[178]Lambrecht, *Redaktion*, 199; Pesch, *Naherwartungen*, 179.

[179]Jeremias, *TDNT*, 3:173–74 and n. 8.

[180]Lambrecht himself admitted this: "A Markan formation . . . can no longer surprise us. But this is not a strong argument, for it is very possible that in the construction of the discourse several verses as wholes were used without editing" (*Redaktion*, 221).

[181]Lohmeyer, *Markus*, 280.

[182]Lagrange pointed out that most of the trees in Palestine were evergreen.

acknowledge the Semitic background of *parabolē* in *māšāl* and recall its enigmatic implication: "From the fig tree learn the veiled meaning it has to teach," which is a perfectly comprehensible introduction to a parable.[183]

There appears to be insufficient reason for rejecting the substance of v. 28b, as the great majority of exegetes agree. Yet the statement in its present form could not have been uttered alone. The calling attention to the fig tree's bursting into leaf as a sign of the nearness of the summer is likely to have been the basis of a comparison, and in the light of the teaching of Jesus generally that comparison in all probability related to the kingdom of God. Mark has given just such a clause in v. 29, and it makes explicit the comparison implicit in the first section of the sentence (v. 28). Verse 29 can be ruled as secondary only if it be demonstrated that (a) the form of v. 28 has been transformed from an independent sentence which carries its own comparison, or (b) the Markan linguistic features in v. 29 have wholly determined the sense of the statement. The former is improbable; the latter we have yet to examine.

In v. 29 the phrase *houtōs kai hymeis* could certainly be redactional, in view of its appearance in 7:18; but to import into v. 29 the meaning which it has in 7:18 would make the statement very strange. It is possible that a simple *houtōs* or *houtōs kai* was in the source (it is the *hymeis* which causes perplexity to interpreters); but it is more plausible to assume that *houtōs kai* represents the familiar w^{e}kēn, and so *kai* will go with the whole sentence and not simply with *hymeis* (cf. NRSV: "So also, when you see these things taking place").

Hotan idēte tauta ginomena ("When you see these things happening") in the present context links the parable with the foregoing discourse. The notion that *tauta* refers to the cosmic signs in vv. 24–25, despite its enthusiastic advocacy by Brandenburger,[184] is implausible; on the one hand the "signs" of a theophany are typically consequences of the appearing of God, not its precedents, and on the other hand they are so completely one with the event that they cannot be viewed as premonitory signs. Mark will have expected his readers to recognize that the *tauta* must represent forerunners of the end and not the end

---

"The fig tree, which is very common and which begins before the vine, although after the almond tree, truly gives the sign of spring, for if the cold sometimes surprises the almond trees in flower, it does not return when the leaves of the fig tree have appeared" (*Marc*, 347).

[183] So W. R. Telford, *The Barren Temple and the Withered Tree* (Sheffield, 1980), 213.

[184] Brandenburger, *Markus 13 und die Apokalyptik*, FRLANT 134 (Göttingen, 1984), 101–2. See further the excellent treatment of this theme in Jörg Jeremias, *Theophanie: Die Geschichte einer alttestamentlichen Gattung* (Neukirchen-Vluyn, 1964), 7.

itself. While the *hotan* inevitably recalls v. 4, it more obviously picks up v. 14, plus the paragraph which that verse begins, but it could also gather into itself other elements such as vv. 7–8, 9–13, and 21–22. If we are discussing the authenticity of the parable these elements of the context are, of course, irrelevant, since the parable will have circulated in the tradition alone. The question is whether its original context was in any sense comparable to its present one, and whether the placing of it here has distorted the parable.

The repetition of *ginōskete hoti engys estin* ("know that he [it] is near") in v. 29 after its appearance in v. 28 is unusual. Nevertheless, *ginōskete* as part of the application of the comparison stated in v. 28 is not unfitting, particularly if the first *ginōskete* is read as an indicative and the second as an imperative, which would balance the *mathete* of v. 28 well ("learn the veiled meaning of the fig tree . . . know that he is near").[185]

Engys stands here only in Mark. In sayings of Jesus in Matthew and Luke it occurs only in their versions of this parable, other than in Matt 26:18. It can hardly be said to be a key term in early Christian eschatological proclamation (it is found in Phil 4:5; Rev 1:3; 22:10; cf. also Rom 13:11–12), but the idea in the term was important. This is not an instance in which a concept common to Jesus and his church can be put to the account of the church; its central presence in the proclamation of Jesus is firmly attested, both in statement and in parable, and this it is which gave rise to its place in the teaching of his followers. (*Engys*, of course, is related to *engizein* in the tradition of our Lord's teaching, e.g., Mark 1:15; 14:42, and to the sayings and parables of Jesus expressing a near expectation.)

Various scholars, including some who acknowledge the parable to be authentic, have viewed *epi thyrais* as due to Mark's redaction.[186] For example, Rigaux believed that it was due to Mark's redundant style.[187] Again we find ourselves in uncertainty, but in the interests of accuracy it should be pointed out that Jeremias's assertion that the use of a spatial image for a statement of time is Hellenistic is of dubious validity. Is not

---

[185] *Ginōskete* in v. 29 is read as imperative by Klostermann, *Markus,* 139; V. Taylor, *Mark,* 520; Cranfield, *Mark,* 408; Pesch, *Naherwartungen,* 178; Zmijewski, *Eschatologiereden,* 263; Gnilka, *Markus,* 203. It is to be observed that the structure of this parable is not unlike that of the parable of the Burglar, Matt 24:42–44/Luke 12:39–40. Apart from the *houtōs* which occurs at the beginning to impress the lesson on the hearers, there is a relatively firm parallelism between the first and second members of the comparison, closer in Luke than in Matthew but without change of meaning.

[186] So, above all, Jeremias, *Parables,* 119–20.

[187] Rigaux, *Témoignage de l'évangile de Marc* (Louvain, 1965), 90. It is included by Sir John Hawkins in his list of duplicated expressions in Mark (*Horae Synopticae,* 139–42).

the use of *engys* and *engizein* itself an employment of "spacial image as indication of time"? Both adverb and verb are frequently used in the NT for space and for time. *Epi thyrais* is of the same order of picture thinking in relation to time as *engys*. Some OT passages appear consciously to apply the figure of near and far distance to statements relating to time, e.g., Isa 46:12–13:

> Hearken to me, you stubborn of heart,
> you who are far from deliverance:
> I will bring near my deliverance, it is not far off,
> and my salvation will not tarry.

One wonders whether there is any difference of concept, let alone milieu, between Jas 5:8: *hē parousia tou kyriou ēngiken* ("The coming of the Lord has drawn near") and Jas 5:9: *ho kritēs pro tōn thyrōn hestēken* ("The judge stands before the door"), other, that is, than the fact that the former speaks of the Lord drawing near and the other of the Lord standing near. If there is no distinction of mode of thought between them, is there any in Mark 13:29, where the two ideas are juxtaposed: *engys estin epi thyrais*?

The statement that the plural *thyrai* ("doors") for the singular *thyra* ("door") is "classic" is puzzling, if by "classic" is meant "not current in Koine or Biblical Greek." For the usage is frequent enough in the LXX. Admittedly it is difficult to find an example where the plural *thyrai* is incontestably used for a single door, as distinct from double doors; but in Exodus and Leviticus the LXX renders the term *petah*, the door of the tent of meeting, by the singular and plural of *thyra* without change of meaning, and apparently without reason for change.[188]

Our conclusion on the redaction of the parable is that while the redactor's hand is certainly to be discerned at various points, these of themselves are insufficient to determine its origin or meaning. There appears to be no adequate reason for denying the early formation of the parable in its essential content. In relation to content we may speak more positively: in view of the harmony of the parable with Jesus' proclamation of the kingdom of God, we are strongly of the opinion that there are no grounds for denying the parable to him. This we must examine further.

The main thrust of the Fig Tree parable is the comparison between the appearance of the fig tree's leaves as a harbinger of summer and

---

[188] Apart from a number of instances of *thyra* in the singular (e.g., Exod 12:26; 33:9–10) and in the plural (e.g., Exod 29:4, 11, 32, 42) for *petah*, we find the usage varying in the same context (Exod 40:5 singular; 40:6 plural; Lev 1:3 singular; 1:5 plural), and such changes occur willy-nilly with prepositions (Lev 4:4, *para tēn thyran*; 4:7, *para tas thyras*; 15:14 and 17:7, *epi tas thyras*; 15:29 and 17:4, *epi tēn thyran*).

events that serve as harbingers of the parousia or kingdom of God. It is a nature parable of a similar order to the parables of the kingdom which form the substance of Mark 4. Scholars now generally recognize that those three parables portray the kingdom of God as a process initiated in and through the ministry of Jesus, and that in them there is contrast between its beginnings and its end. Each parable makes a distinct contribution to the understanding of the kingdom.

The parable of the Seed Growing Secretly emphasizes the growth of the seed "by itself," *automatē*, better rendered "without visible cause," "incomprehensibly," even "effected by God." Applied to the kingdom of God the parable means that a sowing has taken place which must issue in the final harvest of the judgment and kingdom of God because it has God Almighty behind it—alike at its beginning and in its continuance and at its end. The Mustard Seed parable contrasts the beginning and the end of the process of growth—"a midget of a seed among seeds, but a veritable tree among herbs."[189] But there is more than beginning and end; there is a silent presumption of growth over which God presides. On this N. A. Dahl commented: "To Jews and Christians organic growth was but the other side of what was essentially the creative work of God who alone gives growth."[190] The parable thus illuminates the kingdom of God as a single event, of beginning, end, and whatever lies between. The kingdom is God ever active in his sovereign working in judgment and salvation.

The distinctiveness of the parable of the Sower lies in its representation of God's kingdom initiated and continuing in face of resistance to the word of the kingdom. That word meets obstacles and opposition of many kinds, all of which, however, are as inevitable as those encountered by anyone who sows a field. Such a person has to reckon with birds of the air, thorns and thistles, paths where people tread, shallow earth and scorching sun; but despite them all, the farmer labors in confidence that harvest will come, and that there may even be a bumper crop (thirtyfold, sixtyfold, a hundredfold)! The parable is a reminder that the saving sovereignty of God operates in a fallen world— that is its raison d'être: the kingdom of God is God's *saving* sovereignty! When therefore the Christ of God came to inaugurate it he could not but be aware that opposition and suffering were unavoidable in the mission of the kingdom, and he sought to ensure that those who labored with him should also know it, and accept it, and be confident in the sure fulfillment of God's purpose.

It is evident that the parable of the Fig Tree manifests the same fundamental order of thinking as the parables of Mark 4. Exegetes have

---

[189]C. W. F. Smith, *The Jesus of the Parables*, rev. ed. (Philadelphia, 1975), 53.
[190]Dahl, "The Parables of Growth," *ST* 5 (1951): 147.

commonly seen in the signs to which 13:29 refers those performed by
Jesus in his ministry, revealing his judgment on the situation at that
time, whether it be the developing crisis precipitated through his
ministry, or the impending perfection of the kingdom which he initiated.[191] In either case the "signs" of the kingdom are contrasted with
the Markan context of trials and tribulations described in the discourse.
Indeed, Jeremias objected to Mark's relating the parable to the "horrors
of the end," as he described them, on the ground that the simile of the
blossoming fig tree is more suitable to the signs of the time of salvation.
He interpreted as follows: "Its shoots, bursting with life out of death . .
. herald the summer. In like fashion, says Jesus, the Messiah has his
harbingers. Consider the signs: the dead fig tree is clothed with green,
the young shoots sprout, winter is over at last, summer is at the
threshold, those destined to salvation awake to new life (Mt 11:5), the
hour is come, the final fulfilment has begun."[192]

This interpretation, attractive as it appears, requires modification
in two respects. First, Jeremias, with so many other exegetes, has failed
to take into account the future tense implied in the *hotan idēte* of v. 29:
"When you see [in times ahead] these things happening" (cf. the similarly unmistakable future reference of *hotan* plus the subjunctive in vv.
7, 9, 14). There is thus a fundamental shift of emphasis in the parable
which distinguishes it from the parables of growth generally. Granting
that the promised kingdom of God has been inaugurated through the
mission of Jesus, the emphasis of the parable is wholly on its future.
The structure of the parable posits events which point to the approach
of the perfected kingdom of God which will take place at the parousia
of the Lord. Second, Jeremias has pressed the imagery of the parable to
an unwonted extent, as though the "summer" must image the kingdom
of God without judgment, an idea remote from Jesus and from Mark.
The language of v. 29 is admittedly ambiguous: "When you see these

---

[191]For the former see Dodd, *Parables of the Kingdom*, 137; Nineham, *Mark*,
359; N. Perrin, *Rediscovering the Teaching of Jesus*, 202; Zmijewski, *Eschatologiereden*, 261. Perhaps the majority of exegetes favor the latter; cf. Otto,
Kingdom of God and Son of Man, 148; B. T. D. Smith, *The Parables of the
Synoptic Gospels* (Cambridge, 1937), 29–31; Bultmann, *Jesus and the Word*, 30;
V. Taylor, *Mark*, 520; Grässer, *Parusieverzögerung*, 165; C. H. Hunzinger, *TDNT*,
7:757; Kümmel, *Promise and Fulfilment*, 21–22; Hartman, *Prophecy Interpreted*,
223; Pesch, *Markus*, 2:307.

[192]Jeremias, *Parables*, 119–20. In this view of the parable Jeremias was
anticipated fifty years by E. Haupt in *Die eschatologischen Aussagen Jesu in den
synoptischen Evangelien* (Berlin, 1895), 27–29. Lohmeyer advocated a variation
of Jeremias's interpretation: "As from a bare tree the fresh green shoots out, so
from the dryness of the time come the blossoms of the eschatological consummation. The end time is the summer of the world time, the world time of the
preceding stormy and fearful winter. The diversity and yet persisting continuity
of the world time and end time is thereby intelligibly illustrated" (*Markus*, 281).

things happening, know that *engys estin epi thyrais.*" This latter clause could conceivably relate to the parousia, or the judgment, or the kingdom, but, as J. Ernst rightly observed, "The picture of the door gives the personal interpretation a certain precedence."[193] In that case the parable anticipates the Lord in his coming for the salvation and the judgment of the kingdom of God, as is implied in vv. 24–27 and in the parable of the Porter, vv. 34–36.

There is, moreover, an interesting link between the parable of the Fig Tree and the withering of the fig tree, described in 11:12–14. The latter provides the context for the cleansing of the temple, and it is evident that the reader is expected to see both events as signs of judgment. The parable of the Fig Tree is recounted after Jesus has made his final exit from the temple. The suggestion of Wellhausen and Schwartz may be recalled, that the withering of the fig tree and the parable of the Fig Tree are reflections of an aetiological legend about a particular fig tree, said to have been withered at the word of Jesus: "No man shall eat any fruit of you till I come."[194] The notion is thoroughly implausible, but W. R. Telford has suggested that Mark wished his readers to perceive a connection between the two episodes concerning the fig tree sign and parable:

> [T]he fig-tree's *withering* in Chapter 11 was intended in our view to be seen as an eschatological sign prefiguring an imminent *judgement* upon the Jewish people, but in particular upon their Temple. In Chapter 13, the disciples, and hence the readers, are invited to look upon the fig-tree's blossoming as a sign likewise prefiguring an eschatological event, viz., the coming Age of both *blessing* and *judgement.* Here, then, Mark may perhaps be seen reflecting the two different sides of the fig-tree's eschatological symbolism, that is, its withering as a sign of judgement, its blossoming as a sign of blessing (at least for Christians).[195]

The parable of the Fig Tree is clearly of no little significance for understanding the discourse. Hahn regarded it as "the genuine key passage of the discourse." He actually considered the parable to be the "crystallization-nucleus" of the discourse, around which the discourse was formed.[196] That is a doubtful notion, for it is likely that the prophecy of v. 2 determined in no small measure the content of the discourse. But it is true that the course of history between the initiation of the kingdom of God through Jesus and its consummation at the parousia is viewed as "eschatological time," subject to the sovereignty

---

[193]Ernst, *Markus,* 389. Interestingly, the Syriac version (Sinaiticus) presumes the reading *engys eimi tē thyra.*

[194]See J. Wellhausen, *Marci,* 106; E. Schwartz, "Der verfluchte Feigenbaum," *ZNW* 5 (1904): 80–84.

[195]Telford, *Barren Temple,* 216.

[196]Hahn, "Die Rede von der Parusie," 257.

of God, so that events in the wider world, in the church, and in Israel may be viewed as signs of the kingdom of God. V. K. Agbanou expressed this conviction in the dictum, "The time of the church constitutes the premonitory sign of the advent of Christ."[197] The statement is right, but the discourse has a broader vision, for it takes into account the turbulent events among the nations, and the distress of Israel as well as of the church.

Here we remind ourselves of the nature of the "signs" in the discourse. Why are they all so negative? For two reasons above all: the discourse sets out from a prophecy of the destruction of the temple and questions by the disciples as to time and sign; the prophecy represents God's judgment on his people's rejection of his word, his Messiah, his kingdom, and its proclaimers. As Mark writes, the fulfillment is on its way. Second, the followers of Jesus are experiencing the consequences of being the church of the crucified Messiah: in pursuing the mission committed to them they are sharing the "woes of the Messiah" in a manner never anticipated by any Jewish apocalyptist. They are sharing his sufferings that the world might know the blessings of the kingdom. In both respects the discourse is true to the message and destiny of Jesus. Standing in the tradition of Israel's prophets, Jesus declared God's judgment on God's rebellious people (cf. Matt 10:34–36/Luke 12:51–53; Matt 10:14–15/Luke 10:10–12; Matt 11:21–23/Luke 10:13–15; Luke 13:1–5, and 6–9—another Fig Tree parable!). He also spoke of his own destiny to suffer rejection and death in the service of the kingdom of God (Luke 12:49–50; Mark 8:31; 9:31; 10:45; 14:22–25) and of his disciples' involvement in his suffering (Mark 8:34–37).

In the late sixties AD there was nothing the Christians in Rome needed more urgently to know than that God was working his purpose out in the world, in Palestine, and in the church of the empire, not least in view of their having lately come through the most appalling persecution that the church had known to that time or was to know. They had seen and suffered the "horrors of the end," to cite Jeremias, and through the parable of the Fig Tree they were encouraged to recognize in them signs of the presence and impending victory of the kingdom of God. They would have approved of Hahn's thought about the parable: to those sharing in the sufferings of the Christ the parable of the Fig Tree is "the key to the discourse." In that conviction they continued faithfully to proclaim to all the kingdom of God that came in the living, dying, and rising of Jesus the Christ and is to be revealed in his parousia.

---

[197] Agbanou, *Discours eschatologique,* 116, with appeal to H. Kahlefeld, *Paraboles et Leçons d'Evangile* (Paris, 1969), 1:36.

Mark 13:30

It is of interest that, in contrast to the wide variety of interpretations that have been accorded to Mark 9:1 and Matt 10:23, the majority
of exegetes through the centuries to the present day have viewed Mark
13:30 as relating to the events leading up to and including the parousia
of Christ.[198] The interpretation of the saying in relation to the fall of
Jerusalem did not become widely adopted until the time of the Protestant Reformation, when Calvin's great influence led many so to interpret it. Luther and Zwingli, however, adhered to the traditional view,
as did their opponents in the Counter-Reformation. Since that time the
two views have been promulgated side by side, with the majority
adhering to the older view.[199]

The latter interpretation was possible for the church in the period
prior to the rise of critical study of the NT on the basis that *genea*
(generation) denotes something other than the contemporaries of Jesus.
While Origen extended it to include the generation of the NT, it was
more common to think in terms of the "generation" of the church, or of
the Jewish nation, or of humankind as a whole.[200] It was Reimarus who
drew attention to the illegitimacy of interpreting *genea* in these ways,
and he drew the corollary that if the saying relates to the parousia, it
sets the end time within the bounds of the first-generation church.[201]
Such indeed is the majority view among critical scholars today, though
not without strong dissent. The urgent points of debate at the present
time relate to the origin of the saying (whether it is authentic to Jesus,
or from an apocalyptic source, or a modification of a saying in the Jesus
tradition, or a saying ascribed to him by a Christian prophet) and the
scope of the saying (whether it refers to the end of the age or to
significant events prior to the end). Both the origin and scope of the
saying can be determined only by examining its components.

The saying is introduced in all its versions by the phrase *amēn
legō hymin*. The use of "amen" to affirm a statement in this manner is
characteristic of Jesus. Jeremias claims that it is without parallel in

---

[198] A brief but extraordinarily compact review of the history of interpretation of Mark 13:30 is provided by M. Kunzi in an appendix to his work, *Das
Naherwartungslogion Markus 9:1 par* (Tübingen, 1977), 213–24. From Kunzi's
account it is evident that the understanding of the saying in relation to the
parousia prevailed among both the Eastern and Western Fathers, as also in the
Middle Ages. It goes without saying that the parousia was then viewed as lying
at a distance, at least from the time of Jesus and the apostolic age.

[199] For references concerning the views of scholars in the various epochs of
the church's history see Kunzi, *Naherwartungslogion*, 214–21.

[200] Illustrations in ibid., 214–15.

[201] Reimarus, *Fragmente* (Braunschweig, 1778), 5th ed., 85–87, 95–96.

Jewish literature and is thus a mark of the authentic voice of Jesus.[202] Unfortunately, it is difficult to utilize this fact as a test of authenticity in individual sayings; it was such a well-known feature of Jesus' speech that it would have been natural for one formulating a saying as from Jesus, or refashioning one in the Jesus tradition, to employ it. This is commonly thought to have happened in the case of Mark 9:1, which also commences with *amēn legō hymin* and which may be a reformulation of this very saying. Curiously enough, Jeremias himself appears to have doubts about the authenticity of Mark 13:30, but on different grounds.[203]

The phrase "this generation" should cause no difficulty for interpreters. While admittedly *genea* in earlier Greek meant birth, progeny, and so race, in the sense of those descended from a common ancestor, in the LXX it most frequently translated the Hebrew term *dôr*, meaning age, age of humankind, or generation in the sense of contemporaries.[204] The expression "this generation" is often found on the lips of Jesus in the Gospels, but rarely elsewhere in the NT.[205] In sayings attributed to Jesus the term appears to have a twofold connotation: on the one hand it always signifies his contemporaries, and on the other hand it always carries an implicit criticism.[206] Jeremias described the latter feature in a more emphatic manner; these logia, he says, are "sayings of extreme rebuke," though he views Mark 13:30 as an exception in this regard.[207]

The latter suggestion I find puzzling. The other four occasions in Mark wherein "this generation" occurs conform to the pattern elsewhere observable in the Gospels (Mark 8:12a, 12b, 38; 9:19), and there appears to be no reason for viewing 13:30 in any other light.[208] So far as Mark himself is concerned, he will have regarded 13:30 as having a similar import as the rest of the sayings about "this generation," since he has related the eschatological discourse to the prophecy of the overthrow of the temple, and he will have viewed this as a prophecy of judgment upon the nation. Moreover, the language of v. 30 is reminiscent of the disciples' question in v. 4 as to the time when the catastrophe is to take place, thereby closely relating the two passages. Admittedly, when Mark was writing his Gospel the limits of the lifetime of the contemporaries of Jesus were rapidly being reached, but if it is true that

---

[202]Jeremias, "Characteristics of the ipsissima vox Jesu," in *The Prayers of Jesus*, SBT 2/6 (ET London, 1967), 112–15. The evidence is briefly stated in idem, *New Testament Theology*, 35–36.

[203]Jeremias, *New Testament Theology*, 139 n. 2.

[204]So Büchsel, *TDNT*, 1:662–63.

[205]The occurrences in sayings of Jesus are Mark 8:12a and 12b; 8:38; 9:19; Matt 11:16 par.; 23:39 par.; 11:30; 17:25. See further Acts 2:40; Heb 3:10.

[206]So Büchsel, *TDNT*, 1:663.

[207]Jeremias, *New Testament Theology*, 134.

[208]So Zmijewski, *Eschatologiereden*, 278.

he composed the discourse during the Jewish-Roman War (AD 66–70), he will have had reason to believe that he was living close to the limits of the very crisis of which Jesus spoke, and to expect the fulfillment of the prophecies of vv. 2 and 14–20 shortly.

The logion states that this generation will not "pass away," *ou mē parelthē*. Pesch felt unhappy about this use of *parerchesthai* and viewed it as an indication that the statement was contrived. He claimed that the application of the verb to convey the meaning intended was unnatural, and that it was possible only because of the juxtaposition of the sentence with v. 31, wherein the term twice appears: "heaven and earth will pass away, but my words will not pass away." Pesch commented: "The parallels from the LXX show . . . that the mode of speaking about passing away or not passing away of words is frequent. . . . The passing away of human beings, or a generation, is never spoken about outside Mark 13:30."[209] If this is spoken about the use of the term in the LXX it is strictly correct, but it is misleading, and it is not true outside the LXX. In the LXX *parerchesthai* has a variety of usages, among which is a characteristic one of denoting the transience of human life and of everything connected therewith. For example, we read: "My days die away like an echo" (*parēlthon en bromō*, Job 17:11); "Our life will pass away (*pareleusetai*) like the last vestige of a cloud" (Wisd 2:4); sons of men are said to be "like a dream at daybreak, like the grass which springs up in the morning and passes away" (*parelthoi*, Ps 90:6–7 [LXX Ps. 89:5–6]). That the verb is not actually used with a human being as subject may well be accidental in view of the tenor of these statements. This is illustrated in the allusion to Ps 90:6–7 in Jas 1:10, where the rich man is ironically bidden to rejoice in his coming humiliation, "because as a flower of the field he will pass away." Clement of Rome, still (presumably) in the first century AD, provides an unambiguous parallel to the usage in Mark 13:30: "All the generations from Adam unto this day have passed away" (*hai geneai pasai apo Adam . . . parēlthon*, 1 Clem 50:3). There is accordingly no need to look to Matt 5:18 or Mark 13:31 to justify the appearance of *ou mē parelthē* in relation to "this generation"; it is harmonious with biblical thought and usage.

The burning question in Mark 13:30, however, is what is expected to happen before "this generation" passes away. Mark records that it will not do so until "all these things happen" (*tauta panta genētai*). It is generally acknowledged that *tauta panta* ("all these things") in this passage has its precedents in both the immediate and the more remote context. *Tauta* appears in the immediately preceding parable of the Fig Tree (v. 29: "When you see these things happening," *hotan idēte tauta ginomena*), and both *tauta* and *tauta panta* occur in the disciples'

---

[209]Pesch, *Naherwartungen*, 184.

question in v. 4, from which the discourse ostensibly takes its rise: *pote tauta estai; kai ti to sēmeion hotan mellē tauta synteleisthai panta;* "When will these things be? And what will be the sign when all things will be accomplished?" Hahn suggests that in v. 29 the *tauta* refers to the signs narrated in the discourse, but the *tauta panta* of v. 30 to the parousia passage in vv. 24–27.[210] We have already observed (in our exposition of v. 4) that if the *tauta panta* of v. 30 really does hark back to the *tauta panta* of v. 4b, the significant connection thereby made lies in the verb *synteleisthai*, for its citation of Dan 12:7 categorizes the prophesied destruction of the temple as falling within the day of the Lord on Jerusalem and the nation. It is an eschatological action of God, but it by no means necessarily falls within the end time any more than the majority of prophecies of the day of the Lord in the OT are thought to do. Despite the concurrence of many scholars with the judgment of Hahn that v. 30 includes the parousia within its scope,[211] we shall defer decision on the issue until we have considered the origin of the logion and its relation to v. 32.

Inevitably the question is pressed whether Mark's setting of the saying is in harmony with its original intention, or whether its present position has obscured its meaning. Pesch is convinced that the former is true. He urges that the difficulty of understanding the saying as an isolated logion and its suitability to its present context suggest that the saying was constructed for this context. While earlier holding that Mark 9:1 provided the model for its structure, recently he has viewed the inspiration of the saying as provided in such "amen" sayings as 9:1; Matt 10:23; 23:36, with Mark 13:31 supplying the language regarding the passing away of this generation.[212] There is, on the contrary, reason for believing that Mark 13:30 was the source from which 9:1 was

---

[210]Hahn, "Die Rede von der Parusie," 247.

[211]So A. Loisy, *Evangiles synoptiques*, 2:435; McNeile, *Matthew*, 355; Lohmeyer, *Markus*, 281; Kümmel, "Eschatological Expectation in the Proclamation of Jesus," in *The Future of Our Religious Past*, Festschrift R. Bultmann, ed. J. M. Robinson (London, 1971), 30; O. Cullmann, *Salvation in History* (ET London, 1967), 214; B. Rigaux, *La seconde venue*, 197–98; R. Schnackenburg, *God's Rule and Kingdom*, 207–8 (in the present context, not necessarily so originally); J. Dupont, "La ruine du temple," 217–18. C. S. Mann acknowledges that the saying refers to the description of the parousia in vv. 24–26, but he interprets it of the fulfillment by Jesus of his vocation to initiate the kingdom of God through his death and resurrection, which vocation will be consummated at the end of time (*Mark*, 537). While this understanding of the saying is not without supporters, it is difficult to view it as an objective interpretation of the parousia passage.

[212]Pesch, *Naherwartungen*, 181–90; idem, *Markus*, 2:308–9. In his later view of Mark 13:30 Pesch has modified the position of L. Gaston, who, however, regards 9:1; 13:30; Matt 10:23; and 23:39 as four variants of a single (nondominical) saying (*No Stone on Another*, 451–52). V. K. Agbanou argues that Mark 9:1 and 13:30 are different applications of an earlier logion (*Discours eschatologique*, 110).

constructed.[213] If we are to look for any dominical saying which may throw light on the meaning of 13:30, the Q saying Luke 11:51/Matt 23:36 is closest of all. The whole passage, Luke 11:49–51/Matt 23:34–36, is of considerable importance, since it supplies reason why the contemporary generation is to experience the events indicated by the ambiguous *tauta panta*. We reproduce here the Lukan version, since it seems more closely to adhere to the original Q tradition.[214]

> Therefore also the Wisdom of God said, "I will send them prophets and messengers, and some of them they will kill and persecute; that the blood of all the prophets, shed from the foundation of the world, may be required from this generation, from the blood of Abel to the blood of Zechariah, who perished between the altar and the sanctuary. Yes, I tell you, it shall be required of this generation" (*nai, legō hymin, ekzētēthēsetai apo tēs geneas tautēs*).

The saying is introduced as an utterance of Wisdom, wherein Wisdom declares its resolve to send to God's people "prophets and messengers," but their mission will be in vain, for they will be rejected, persecuted, and even slain. Strangely, the exegetes have largely ignored the question where Wisdom's utterance ceases, whether it is confined to v. 49 or whether it extends to the whole passage. The REB and the NRSV assume that the former is the case, and so they set v. 49 alone within quotation marks. On that interpretation v. 49 employs a wisdom saying to characterize the obtuseness of the people in their rejection of the messengers sent by God (a familiar theme in Wisdom literature), and this conduct is cited as a reason for the judgment of God that is to fall on "this generation." That the blood of all the prophets shed throughout the sacred history is to be demanded of this generation (from Abel to Zechariah connotes the first and last killings of men of God recorded in the OT scriptures, Gen 4:8; 2 Chron 24:20–22) implies that "this generation," like its predecessors, also has rejected the messengers of God and his message sent through them. More specifically, it implies that this generation has brought to a climax the evil of rejecting the messengers of God, since it has repudiated his supreme representative, the Bearer of the word of the kingdom and the kingdom itself; hence it will endure the wrath of God to the full. Luke's twofold declaration: "The blood of all the prophets will be required of this generation. . . . Yes, I tell you, it will be required of this generation," is striking; it drives home the inescapability of the judgment which "this

---

[213]The relation between Mark 13:30 and 9:1 continues to be disputed. The majority view in seeing 13:30 as dependent on 9:1 is reversed by Haenchen, *Weg Jesu*, 452; H. Schürmann, *Das Lukasevangelium*, HTKNT (Freiburg, 1969), 1:551.

[214]See the detailed discussion of the text by S. Schulz, *Q—Die Spruchquelle der Evangelisten* (Zürich, 1972), 336–39; and Marshall, *Luke*, 502–6.

generation" will suffer. It is to be observed, however, that Matthew's statement (Matt 23:36), "Amen, I tell you, all these things will come upon this generation," *amēn legō hymin, hēxei tauta panta epi tēn genean tautēn*, is closer to the wording of Mark 13:30.

The closeness of relation between the Q tradition and Mark in this passage is undeniable. It has led some to suggest a dependence of Mark 13:30 on the Q saying. For example, L. Hartman considers that v. 30 "combines the Markan tradition with Matt 23:36 and 5:18"; and he further suggests, "A logion of judgment against the Jews is interpreted as of the fall of Jerusalem."[215] It may well be rather that Mark 13:30 represents the form which the Q saying took when it was repeated apart from its context and became an isolated saying.

If Mark 13:30 is a variant of the Q saying its meaning is evident. In the intention of Jesus it relates to the doom which is to fall on the nation Israel in the near future, on the generation contemporary with Jesus. If Mark recognized this meaning he would have specifically related it to the ruin of the temple and all that is bound up with it within the discourse. But he has placed the saying after the description of the parousia in vv. 24–27. Did he then wish his readers to understand that the parousia and the triumph of the kingdom of God would also take place within the contemporary generation? The question is answered in the affirmative by the majority of critical scholars, including some who also consider that this was according to the mind of Jesus. For years I adhered to this interpretation, compelled by the apparently irresistible logic of the passage. More recently, however, other factors have caused me to query this conclusion.

(1) The significance of the connection with the Q saying Matt 23:36/Luke 11:51. It is one of the pointers to Jesus viewing the catastrophe to which Israel was heading as the day of the Lord on the nation and its city.

(2) In the OT prophetic literature the day of the Lord on a city or people most commonly signifies an act of God in judgment, not the immediate precursor of the kingdom of God.

(3) It is Mark himself who placed 13:32 in this context. He presumably found it as an independent saying (as also vv. 30 and 31).[216] When

---

[215]Hartman, *Prophecy Interpreted*, 225. Lambrecht has similarly expressed himself (*Redaktion*, 203–4), while also recognizing that Mark 13:30 and 31 could have been wholly constructed on the basis of Matt 5:18.

[216]So, e.g., T. W. Manson, *Sayings of Jesus*, 333; Lohmeyer, *Markus*, 280; V. Taylor, *Mark*, 219; Grässer, *Parusieverzögerung*, 129; Kümmel, "Eschatological Expectation," 38; W. Michaelis, *Der Herr verzieht nicht die Verheissung* (Bern, 1942), 33 (with hesitation); Cullmann, *Salvation in History*, 214; Dupont, "La parabole du maître qui rentre dans la nuit," 34–36, in *Mélanges Bibliques*, Festschrift B. Rigaux, ed. A. Descamps and R. P. André (Gembloux, 1970), 90.

viewed by itself the verse's meaning is unambiguous: the time of the end, therefore of the parousia and consummation of the kingdom of God, is unknown to all humanity, including the Son of God; only the Father knows it. This I earlier failed to take as seriously as the saying demands, for I viewed v. 32 always in the light of v. 30, as though Mark (and Jesus) meant that while the end would fall within the contemporary generation its closer definition of time is beyond the bounds of knowledge. But that is an illegitimate interpretation of v. 32 (see the exposition of the saying below).

(4) The interpretation of v. 30 as affirming that the time of the end is to fall within the generation of Jesus entails Mark in a contradiction of interests. If he was writing during the Jewish-Roman War, ca. AD 68, the generation of Jesus and the apostles was already at its limit; accordingly, if he was representing that the parousia was to happen before the end of that generation, then he was looking for it to take place in the very near, if not immediate, future. But to oppose that notion was one of Mark's primary emphases in his redaction of the discourse; whereas he sought to diminish the eschatological fever of his contemporaries, and of the false prophets in particular, on this reading of the evidence there was little or no difference between his "near expectation" and that of the people he was opposing.

Accordingly, the most plausible solution of the problem which Mark has posed for his readers in bringing vv. 30–32 together is that he views them as setting forth the times of fulfillment of the prophecies in vv. 1–27. Verse 30 relates primarily to the prophecy of v. 2 and the signs in the discourse related to it. Whereas virtually everything in vv. 5–23 can fall within the scope of v. 30, its chief pertinence is to the sayings on the judgment and tribulation of Israel.

It may finally be remarked that since the saying is closely linked with the teaching of Jesus in both content and language, there is no sufficient ground for denying it to be an authentic utterance of Jesus.[217]

Mark 13:31

This statement, which from Colani on has frequently been viewed as the conclusion of the apocalypse embodied in the discourse, is now widely acknowledged to be an isolated saying, set at this point in order

---

[217] So, e.g., McNeile, *Matthew*, 354–55; Rawlinson, *Mark*, 192; W. Manson, *Jesus the Messiah*, 65; T. W. Manson, *Sayings of Jesus*, 333–34; cf. also idem, *Teaching of Jesus*, 277–84; G. Harder, "Das eschatologische Geschichtsbild d. Mark. 13," *Theologica Viatorum* 4 (1953): 2; Kümmel, *Prophecy and Fulfilment*, 91; idem, "Eschatological Expectation," 39; Lohmeyer, *Markus*, 281; Cullmann, *Salvation in History*, 215; Bonnard, *Matthieu*, 353; Kunzi, *Naherwartungslogion*, 224; D. Hill, *Matthew*, 323; Zmijewski, *Eschatologiereden*, 276–77; Marshall, *Luke*, 780.

to authenticate the teaching given within the discourse.[218] While it is conceivable that the saying was already joined with v. 30 in Mark's source,[219] it is more likely that the evangelist himself was responsible for the conjunction of vv. 30, 31, and 32. Virtually all investigators admit that v. 32 formed no part of a pre-Markan apocalyptic source. Verse 31 was placed at this point, first because of the twofold occurrence within it of the term *pareleusontai* ("will pass away"), which occurs also in v. 30 (*parelthē*), and second because it makes an impressive confirmation of the truth of v. 30, yet at the same time prepares for v. 32, which is an equally important statement relating to the time of the end. Since therefore vv. 30 and 32 are intrinsically unrelated but are bound together through v. 31, it is reasonable to assume that all three statements were at one time independent sayings, and that Mark himself ordered them within this context in the discourse.

Before discussing the meaning of the statement it is necessary to consider its relation to the Q saying found in Matt 5:18/Luke 16:17.

Matt 5:18	Luke 16:17
Amen I say to you,	
until heaven and earth	It is easier for heaven and earth
pass away (*parelthē*)	to pass away (*parelthein*)
one jot or one stroke	than for one stroke of the law
will not pass from the law	to fall.
until all be fulfilled.	

Here is a strong asseveration of the permanence of the law in relation to that of heaven and earth, whether it is interpreted as meaning that the law continues in force till heaven and earth disappear and are replaced by the new creation (Matthew), or that the validity of the law is as firm as the steadfastness of creation (Luke). We are not concerned with the question of the priority of the Matthean or Lukan versions in relation to each other,[220] but the relation of an utterance

---

[218]Those who view it as a conclusion include Colani, *Jésus Christ et les croyances messianiques*, 202–3; W. Weiffenbach, *Der Wiederkunftsgedanke Jesu* (Leipzig, 1893), 152–53; H. J. Holtzmann, *Die Synoptiker*, 170; R. H. Charles, *A Critical History of the Doctrine of a Future Life*, 2d ed. (London, 1889), 381–82; W. Bousset, *Kyrios Christos*, 2d ed. (Göttingen, 1921), 43; Hahn, "Die Rede der Parusie," 243; Pesch, *Markus*, 2:304, 309. Those who see it as an isolated saying are Wellhausen, *Marci*, 107; Rawlinson, *Mark*, 192; E. Wendling, *Entstehung des Markus*, 155–56; Schniewind, *Markus*, 176; J. Schmid, *Markus*, 193; Lohmeyer, *Markus*, 280; V. Taylor, *Mark*, 521; Cranfield, *Mark*, 410; Grundmann, *Markus*, 260; Kümmel, *Prophecy and Fulfilment*, 91; Pesch, *Naherwartungen*, 189; idem, *Markus*, 2:309; Marshall, *Luke*, 781.

[219]Marxsen, *Mark*, 162, 187.

[220]Lambrecht considers Luke 16:17 on the whole more primitive than Matt 5:18 (*Redaktion*, 216–20). Schulz thinks Matt 5:18 more primitive than Luke

concerning the law and another concerning the teaching of Jesus, both given in strikingly similar terms, must be faced.

Lambrecht has lengthily considered the matter, and concluded that Mark 13:31 is dependent on the Q saying; for while it is abstractly possible that Jesus could have used this mode of speech, first with respect to the law and then with respect to his own words, "in content the two affirmations are not easily united, on the contrary they exclude one another."[221] He proposed two alternative solutions to account for the Markan saying: either it was based on the Lukan version, and Mark changed it by replacing the reference to the law with reference to the words of Jesus, or Mark knew the saying as in Matthew and divided it into two sentences, first using the saying to form v. 30, and then using it again to form v. 31. Of the two suggestions Lambrecht appears to prefer the second.[222]

Now, while various writers favor this solution, in a simpler form,[223] it appears doubtful to me. If we may take Luke's language to be the more original form of the Q saying, it is clearly not an assertion regarding the nature of the universe, but pictorially represents the authority and the continuance of the law of God, and the language is not to be pressed.[224] But it is also true that Mark's saying is not intended to provide an apocalyptic utterance concerning the future of the universe but is an affirmation of the authority of Jesus' words. Why should it be viewed as out of the question for Jesus to refer both to the importance of the law, as an inspired expression of the will of God, and also to the importance of the word which God sent him to proclaim to Israel? There is no inconcinnity between the two affirmations, nor equivalence of images employed in them. Indeed, so characteristic is the Markan saying of the instruction of Jesus, in relation both to the law (cf. the antitheses of Matt 5:21–48) and to the kingdom of God, we should have to say that if any doubt attached to either saying through alleged contradiction, it would have to be the Q saying which yielded to the Markan, since the tradition is strong that the destiny of human beings is determined through their response to Jesus in his word.[225] But again, let it be repeated, the sayings which we are

---

16:17 (*Spruchquelle*, 114). Lambrecht provides a reconstruction of the saying from both versions: "It is easier for heaven and earth to pass away than for a jot or a stroke to fall from the law" (*Markus-Apokalypse*, 220).

[221] Lambrecht, *Redaktion*, 221; see 211–27.

[222] Ibid., 224–26.

[223] So Hartman, *Prophecy Interpreted*, 225; Schweizer, *Mark*, 279; Vögtle, *Zukunft des Kosmos*, 101–2.

[224] See Polag, *Die Christologie der Logienquelle* (Neukirchen-Vluyn, 1977), 79: "The saying, according to its *Gattung*, is a proverb with hortatory character; it must therefore not be pressed in its affirmation."

[225] Such is Kümmel's conviction. He holds that Matt 5:18–19 is irreconcilable with the general teaching of Jesus concerning the law and considers the sayings to be Judaistic additions to the tradition of Jesus' teaching ("Jesus und

considering are not in conflict. Moreover, on the basis of the Lukan saying it is unjustifiable to draw distinctions between the Q saying and Mark 13:31, as for example that the law is assumed to be valid for the period prior to the coming of the kingdom, whereas the words of Jesus are eternally valid, because they last into the kingdom. That is to treat the pictorial language of Luke 16:17 in an illegitimate manner and to offset two sayings which have different intentions.

It may, however, be objected that we have proceeded too quickly in our treatment of Mark 13:31, since we have not defined what is meant by "my words." What is envisaged as more permanent than heaven and earth? A difference of opinion is involved, depending on whether the saying is viewed in relation to Mark's context or is considered independently of the context. In the former case it is on the one hand likely that Mark saw v. 31 as embracing the whole discourse, but as having particular reference to v. 30, just as he placed v. 23 in order to bring to a climax all that had been said to that point, and yet with special reference to vv. 21–22.[226] On the other hand nothing in the content of the saying demands an eschatological context, or any other special element of the instruction of Jesus. From this point of view it is more general even than Matt 5:18 and Luke 16:17, since the Q saying refers to the moral demands of the law, whereas there is no such limitation in the saying concerning the words of Jesus.[227] Nevertheless, since the all-embracing theme of Jesus' preaching was the kingdom of God, one could with probability relate the saying to the authority of Jesus as the representative of the divine sovereignty. It is in this area that an emphatic statement of this kind would fittingly be called forth, for it is above all in the context of the judgment and the vindication before God that the authority of Jesus and his mission is declared (Luke 12:8–9/Mark 8:38).[228]

Hesitation has sometimes been expressed as to the likelihood of Jesus' uttering a statement in these terms, precisely because in the related Mark 8:38 the phrase "and of my words" is suspect as a Markan

---

der jüdische Traditionsgedanke," *ZNW* 33 [1934]: 127–28).

[226] So Lambrecht, *Redaktion*, 212. Some exegetes relate the saying only to v. 30, as, e.g., Klostermann, *Markus*, 138; Schmid, *Markus*, 193 (in the present setting of the saying); Marxsen, *Mark*, 187 n. 140; Lane, *Mark*, 480; Marshall, *Luke*, 780–81. Pesch strictly relates v. 31 to vv. 30 and 32 (*Naherwartungen*, 190); so also Zmijewski, *Eschatologiereden*, 279.

[227] The majority of exegetes have related v. 31 to the teaching of Jesus generally; so, e.g., Wellhausen, *Marci*, 107; Swete, *Mark*, 325; Lagrange, *Marc*, 348–49; Bertram, *TDNT*, 4:838; Schmid, *Markus*, 193; T. W. Manson, *Teaching of Jesus*, 291; Traub, *TDNT*, 5:515–16; Bonnard, *Matthieu*, 353; Lane, *Mark*, 480; Anderson, *Mark*, 300.

[228] So E. Schweizer: "The statement is meaningful only if Jesus' words—or the law—are declared to be the standard by which everything will be decided after heaven and earth have passed away, i.e. in the last judgment" (*Mark*, 279).

addition; the question is asked whether the motive which prompted the insertion of that phrase in 8:38 could also have led to the affirmation of the supreme authority of Jesus' words in 13:31. In my judgment that is an unlikely suggestion. The expansion in 8:38 is a typical Markan repetition which brings out the meaning of the saying; it is thereby made clear that to be ashamed of Jesus is to repudiate him as the bearer of the word of God, and so to deny the truth of his proclamation of the kingdom of God. In 13:31, however, the "words" of Jesus form the key element of the saying, and without the term there is no statement at all, other than the purely introductory first clause, which nevertheless has place only because it is contrasted with the main clause.

If the fundamental idea of 13:31 is the eternal truth of the words of Jesus, it has a close parallel in the Q parable at the conclusion of the great sermon, Matt 7:24–27/Luke 6:47–49, wherein Matthew's version, including his reference to the "words" of Jesus as of crucial importance, is generally viewed as more primitive than Luke's. A related, though very different, expression of the importance of the message of Jesus is seen in Mark 6:11–12. These sayings may be viewed as a bridge between 8:38 and 13:31.[229] As an expression of the authority of the message of Jesus, 13:31 may be viewed as the corollary of Jesus' entire proclamation of the kingdom of God and of his relationship to the divine sovereignty. Such was the conviction of Lohmeyer: "The eternity of these words is grounded in the thought of the Son of man as the eschatological fulfiller. . . . In what he speaks everything is comprehended because he speaks it; he is the consummator because he is the teacher of these imperishable words, he is the teacher because he is the consummator."[230]

Mark 13:32

There is general agreement that this logion was an independent saying in the tradition and that it owes its present position to Mark.[231]

---

[229]On the authenticity of Mark 13:31 see especially Kümmel: "The saying ascribes to the perishable sayings of Jesus an imperishable duration in contrast to the imminent passing away of the visible world. This estimation of Jesus' sayings corresponds in its essence altogether with Jesus' claim elsewhere that his decision represents the will of God absolutely (Matt 5:21ff.), so that there is no reason to consider this saying to have been formulated by the early Church" (*Prophecy and Fulfilment*, 91).

[230]Lohmeyer, *Markus*, 282. C. S. Mann commented on v. 31 in a very similar tone: "Whether this is a genuine saying of Jesus or not the plain sense is that he who has spoken will be the Agent of the New Age, the initiator of the redemption spoken of in the saying about The Man, and that in him there will be the fulfillment of which he spoke in Matt 5:17–18" (*Mark*, 538).

[231]B. Rigaux viewed vv. 30–32 as "an assemblage of separate logia" (*Seconde venue*, 214). Kümmel considers, "This [v. 32] is a detached saying showing no connexion with what precedes or follows it" (*Promise and Fulfilment*, 40).

The idea that the statement may have concluded the Jewish apocalypse, viewed as the basis of the discourse, has not commended itself.[232] While it is frequently recognized that v. 32 anticipates the parabolic sayings which follow in vv. 33–37, and that it may have drawn to itself these sayings of like theme, Lambrecht has taken a less common path of suggesting that Mark composed the logion for the context with the aid of vv. 33–37 (e.g., "no one knows" of v. 32 is thought to have been prompted by the "you do not know" of vv. 33 and 35).[233] He qualifies this judgment, however, by stating, "It is not in the least thereby suggested that the content of 13:32 could not be authentic."[234] One would have thought, nevertheless, that the striking nature of the saying indicates the probability of dependence in the other direction; that is, to use Ambrozic's expression, that vv. 33 and 35–36 "spell out the message of v. 32."[235] Just as the idea of passing away and not passing away has caused vv. 30 and 31 to be associated, so vv. 32 and 33–36 have been linked by their employment of the catchword "know." While some scholars have viewed v. 32 in its entirety as a product of *Gemeindetheologie*,[236] the great majority have been and are ready to acknowledge the authenticity of the utterance in its essential content; its difficulty for believers on the one hand (regarding the ignorance of Jesus as to the time of the end, as evidenced by the number of manuscripts and church fathers omitting "neither the Son" from Matt 24:36) and its harmony with the attested teaching of Jesus on the other (e.g., Luke 17:20–21 and the parables of watching) point in this direction.

See further Lohmeyer, *Markus*, 280; V. Taylor, *Mark*, 522; Cullmann, *Salvation in History*, 205; van Iersel, *Der Sohn* (Leiden, 1961), 121; Schweizer, *Mark*, 279; Grundmann, *Markus*, 270; Hahn, "Die Rede von der Parusie," 243–44; M. Horstmann, *Studien zur Markinischen Christologie* (Munich, 1969), 53; Kelber, *Kingdom in Mark*, 125; Pesch, *Naherwartung*, 190–91; idem, *Markus*, 2:309.

[232]Contra Bultmann, *History of the Synoptic Tradition*, 123; Harder, *Theologia Viatorum* 4 (1953): 95; Klostermann, *Markus*, 138 (apparently).

[233]Lambrecht, *Redaktion*, 236. Lambrecht was, however, anticipated by Wendling, who also thought that "no one knows" was suggested by the statement "You do not know" of vv. 33 and 35, and that the saying was produced in imitation of Matt 11:27 (*Entstehung des Markus*, 164–65). Similar ideas were voiced by Wellhausen, *Marci*, 107; and A. T. Cadoux, *Sources of the Second Gospel* (New York, n.d.), 226 (in the opinion of Cadoux v. 32 was originally a comment on v. 33 and later incorporated into the text).

[234]Lambrecht, *Redaktion*, 238.

[235]Ambrozic, *Hidden Kingdom*, 223.

[236]Bousset thought that Mark 13:32 was composed "under the impression of the delayed parousia," (*Kyrios Christos*, 52). See also Loisy, *Evangiles synoptiques*, 2:438; C. Clemen, *Religionsgeschichtliche Erklärung des N.T.* (Giessen, 1924), 77; Grässer, *Parusieverzögerung*, 81–82; Anderson, *Mark*, 301 (possibly).

Not a few critics have doubted the originality of the concluding phrase, especially "not even the Son," on the ground that this could have been an addition in the spirit of Matt 11:27.[237] Discussion about the origin and significance of this language about "the Son" and "the Father" must be reserved till later; suffice it to say at this juncture that the arguments are by no means all on one side,[238] and the discussion has entered on a new stage in the light of recent investigation into the relation of the concepts of "the Son," "Son of God," and "Son of man." It is desirable to separate the issues of the limits of Jesus' knowledge concerning the eschaton and the relation of Jesus to the Father. Even van Iersel, who was chiefly concerned about the latter issue, pointed out that the reference to the Son-Father relationship is incidental to the saying and not its intention: "Only in passing does he describe himself as 'the Son' and God as 'the Father.' What he stresses in this saying could have been said without the use of these two expressions. The Father-Son relationship therefore is not the object of Jesus' statement."[239] It is desirable to clarify this point, that we not be deflected from grasping the significance of this saying for the eschatological teaching of Jesus.

"But about that day or hour nobody knows . . . only the Father." The statement is not without parallel in the OT and in Jewish apocalyptic literature.[240] In Mark's context there is little doubt as to what "day

---

[237]Dalman viewed the saying as authentic apart from the concluding phrase "nor the Son, but the Father only" (*Words of Jesus*, 194). Most who have doubts about the phrase would omit simply "nor the Son"; so, e.g., Merx, *Matthäus*, ad loc.; B. T. D. Smith, *Matthew*, 188; Kümmel, *Promise and Fulfilment*, 42; Oepke, *TDNT*, 5:867; Schrenk, *TDNT*, 5:989; Bornkamm, *Jesus of Nazareth* (ET London, 1960), 226; Jeremias, *New Testament Theology*, 131; A. J. B. Higgins, "The Old Testament and Some Aspects of N.T. Theology," *CJT* 6 (1960): 204; Horstmann, *Studien*, 54.

[238]See, e.g., van Iersel, *Der Sohn*, 122–23; Lohmeyer, *Markus*, 283; Grundmann, *Markus*, 271; V. Taylor, *Mark*, 522; Cullmann, *Christology of the New Testament*, 2d ed. (ET Philadelphia, 1959), 287ff.; A. Moore, *Parousia*, 99; Schnackenburg, *God's Rule and Kingdom*, 210; Rigaux, *Seconde venue*, 183; Vögtle, "Exegetische Erwägungen," 640. Schweizer appears uncertain about the reference to the Son (*TDNT*, 7:366, 372; idem, *Mark*, 279).

[239]Van Iersel, *Der Sohn*, 122–23.

[240]Strobel makes the extraordinary claim, "The theologoumenon of the unknown end appears clearly in the entire apocalyptic literature between 200 BC and AD 100 as an apocalyptic central assertion" (*Kerygma und Apokalyptik*, 85); the evidence he adduces, however, does not substantiate that claim. The solitary knowledge of God as to the time of the end is adumbrated in Zech 14:7, "There shall be continuous day (it is known to the Lord)," LXX *kai hē hēmera ekeinē gnōstē tō kyriō*; Pss Sol 17:2, "See Lord, and raise up for them their king, the son of David, to rule over your servant Israel in the time known to you, O God." Fourth Ezra 4:51–52 is a closer parallel to the thought of Mark 13:32 but less explicit: "I prayed and said, 'Do you think that I shall live until those days? Or

or hour" is in view: it is the time of the parousia, described in vv. 24–27, to which Mark has related the parable of the Fig Tree in vv. 28–30. If the evangelist viewed the fall of the temple as the chief precursor of the end, as the eschatological language in vv. 4 and 14–20 suggests that he did, then he could conceivably have linked vv. 30 and 32 together, on the understanding that the generation of Jesus has not yet wholly passed, but the time indicated in the phrase "that day or hour" remains unknowable. This has the effect of producing a strong near expectation of the end, but one which excludes calculations, since the times are in God's hands. It entails interpreting v. 32 in the light of v. 30, which is what the majority of modern exegetes do. So Ambrozic wrote: "The kingdom is near, it is coming within the lifetime of this generation, but no one knows the moment of its arrival; men must therefore be continually on the alert."[241] I myself expressed the same view forty years ago and many times since, defining v. 32 in relation to v. 30 as signifying "a narrower limitation of time over against a broader period,"[242] and in doing so I believed that this represented not only Mark's interpretation but the intention of Jesus also. This appeared to me to be demanded by the expansion in v. 32 of "that day" with the words "or hour"; the latter seemed to give a more precise connotation to the simpler expression; in relation to v. 30 the total phrase appeared to allude to a specific point of time within the generation of Jesus.

Adopting the same view, P. Schwartzkopff sought to press it home by illustrating the effect that such language as that in v. 32 would have upon people in our own times. He urged that anyone who said, "I cannot tell the day or hour in which France will perish," or "in which the earth would become a mass of ice," would appear ridiculous, for that would be a misapplication of language that properly relates to a precise expectation.[243] It would seem, however, that Schwartzkopff, as I myself also, insufficiently appreciated the difference between modern Western and ancient Semitic uses of the terms involved. Substitute for

---

who will be alive in those days?' He [the angel interpreter] answered me and said, 'Concerning the signs about which you ask me, I can tell you in part, but I was not sent to tell you concerning your life, for I do not know.' " Apoc. of Ezra 3:3–4 is hardly relevant, since it is a Christian composition, dated AD 150–850, and the passage is believed by its translator to be self-contradictory; see *OTP*, 1:563. Schlatter cites Mek. on Exod 16:32: "Nobody knows when the kingdom of the house of David will return to its place" (*Matthäus*, 713).

[241] Ambrozic, *Hidden Kingdom*, 218. See further Loisy, *Evangiles synoptiques*, 438; Moffatt, *Theology of the Gospels*, 44; T. W. Manson, *Teaching of Jesus*, 278; Guignebert, *Jesus*, 345; Kelber, *Kingdom in Mark*, 126.

[242] See especially my earlier work *Jesus and the Future*, 260–63.

[243] Schwartzkopff, *Die Weissagungen Jesu Christi von seinem Tode, seiner Auferstehung und Wiederkunft und ihr Erfüllung*, 178.

"France" the name "Babylon," and one could imagine an OT prophet expressing himself thus:

> The day comes,
> the hour draws near,
> known it is to the Lord alone.
> In that day Babylon shall be laid waste,
> and in that hour the land shall become a desolation.

The feature which makes the difference is the peculiar connotation of "the day" and "the hour," still more of "that day," in the literature of Israel's prophets and apocalyptists; either term can denote the day of the Lord, the time of God's "coming" to enact judgment and/or salvation among humankind. For this reason there can be little doubt that Mark 13:32 must have been spoken originally in an eschatological context, wherein the end known only to God was the subject in mind. Mark was justified therefore in setting the saying in a context related to the parousia.

To satisfy oneself about this matter one needs only to consult a concordance and observe how the terms "day" and "hour" are used in the Bible. In Ezek 30:2–3, for example, the prophet employs the term "day" solitarily to denote the day of the Lord, and then follows it with the fuller expression:

> Woe, woe for the day!
> for a day is near,
> a day of the Lord is near,
> a day of cloud, a day of reckoning for the nations.

Similar usage is seen in Zeph 1:7–13; 3:11–20; Zech 9:14–16; 12:1–13:6; 14:4–5, while Isaiah 27 has examples of separate oracles commencing with the phrase "on that day" without need of amplification or explanation. It is important to observe that the Hebrew terms yôm (day) and 'ēṭ (time) can be used virtually synonymously in eschatological contexts in the OT prophets, and that in the Greek versions of the OT both terms can be rendered by hēmera (day), hōra (hour), and kairos (time) without appreciable difference of meaning. For example, the phrase bā'ēṭ hahî' ("at that time") is rendered on several occasions by en tē hēmera ekeinē (for noneschatological contexts cf. Josh 6:25 [MT 26]; for eschatological, Zech 1:12) and much more often by en tō kairō ekeinō (e.g., Gen 38:1; Jer 3:17). In Esth 8:1 the phrase bayyôm hahû' ("in that day") is rendered in the LXX ms. S by en tautē tē hōra ("in that hour") and in the mss. A and B by en tautē tē hēmera ("in that day"). Terminology for the last day is frequently met in the book of Daniel. In Dan 11:40 the "time of the end" ('ēṭ qēṣ) is rendered by hōra synteleias, in 12:4 by kairou synteleias. In 12:1 the time of tribulation in the LXX is introduced by kata tēn hōran ekeinen, and is defined as *hēmera thlipseōs*, but in Theodotion as *kairos thlipseōs*. Thus, the three terms may be variously combined in expressions relating to the end, as in Dan 8:19; 12:13.

It is striking that these three terms, *hēmera*, *hōra*, and *kairos*, appear in successive statements relating to the end in Mark 13:32–33: in v. 32 "that day," "(that) hour," in v. 33 "the time" (*kairos*). Admittedly v. 32 is an isolated saying, and the same is probably true of v. 33, which forms a bridge to the parabolic sayings that follow. This conjunction of terms, however, suggests that Mark was fully conscious of the significance of the words he was using. For "that day or hour" is a fulsome expression, in which both terms have an identical meaning. Either of them, standing alone in this sentence, could convey the idea of "the day when the Son of man appears" (Luke 17:30). Their conjunction would seem to draw attention to the time when the last day occurs, rather than to the content of the event. Jesus would never have said that neither he nor anyone else knew anything about the nature of the last day, for its character as revelation for judgment and the salvation of the kingdom of God is basic to his proclamation.[244] To state that none knows "that day or hour"—neither human being, nor angel, nor Jesus, but God alone—is to affirm a universal ignorance of the time when "the day" will break, or when "the hour" will strike.

In the light of this evidence it would appear that v. 32 is not to be interpreted as affirming the inability of human beings, angels, and Jesus to declare the time within the contemporary generation when the kingdom of God will come. The primary intention of v. 30, as we saw, is not to set a date but to declare the doom which the contemporaries of Jesus cannot escape. That such a statement has implications for the time of the end is due to its nature as the day of the Lord on Jerusalem, hence an eschatological event, but in the tradition it is clearly distinguished from the parousia and coming of the saving sovereignty of God. Despite the protests of many exegetes, accordingly, we surely misconstrue the denotation of v. 32 if we attempt to force it into the context of v. 30. This means that we must allow v. 32 to stand on its own feet and not subordinate it to v. 30, as is so constantly done in contemporary exposition.[245]

Even proceeding on the basis of this understanding of v. 32, the precise meaning of the saying is by no means settled. How far are we to

---

[244]Contra T. Geddert, who writes: "Mark 13:32 says only that there is something about 'That Day' or 'The Hour' which is known only to the Father. It is concerning the final eschatological events . . . that humans, angels and the Son alike share ignorance. Without 13:33 we could not be sure that one of the main unknown features is the timing" (*Watchwords*, 246).

[245]Similarly Lagrange, *Marc*, 350; Kümmel, *Promise and Fulfilment*, 150; Michaelis, *Der Herr verzieht nicht*, 45; Schnackenburg, *God's Rule and Kingdom*, 211.

take the thought that Jesus does not know when the last day will come? Is his ignorance of the time of the end "absolute," to use a term frequently applied to this statement? B. Rigaux has no doubt as to the answer: "We understand the saying of Jesus in the sense of an ignorance bearing absolutely on the date of the Day of Yahweh and not . . . of a relative ignorance."[246] Vögtle similarly writes that v. 32 "affirms an absolute ignorance relative to the point of time of the parousia."[247] Both scholars regard v. 32 as a cornerstone of the eschatological instruction of Jesus, a kind of yardstick for the reconstruction of his teaching. Wellhausen apparently agreed with this sentiment, without being sure about the attribution of the saying to Jesus; but he saw v. 32 as relegating the parousia hope into the background to such an extent as to make it superfluous, or at least robbed of all actuality.[248] J. Schreiber followed in the same steps; in his view v. 32 effectually dismisses the question of v. 4 as a matter not worth the Christian's knowing—indeed, v. 32 radically repudiates the question of time, and with it every Jewish-Christian near expectation.[249] E. Grässer sees a similar implication in v. 32, and therefore denies that it could have come from Jesus: "Should Jesus, who elsewhere proclaimed with such unremitting earnestness the nearness of the kingdom, have questioned the certainty of his expectation in this manner? For this pointed declaration of ignorance means nothing less than that."[250]

Such interpretations of v. 32 proceed from a misunderstanding of the logion. Grässer is justified in protesting that one cannot evade the near expectation of Jesus, and so he rejects the authenticity of the saying as implying a delay of the parousia. But does it imply a delay? In itself the saying affirms neither a near expectation nor a far expecta-tion. But if one is to press the absoluteness of the ignorance of Jesus concerning the end, he has no idea whether it be near or far—he knows *nothing* about it! Interestingly both Rigaux and Vögtle expressly denied that Jesus held a far expectation of the end, and they declared their belief that Jesus looked for the fulfillment of the promise of the kingdom in the near future. But this expectation is to be distinguished from "knowledge." Rigaux sought to explain the difference by distinguishing between the expectation which Jesus cherished concerning the coming of the kingdom of God and the teaching which he gave relative to it; since v. 32 is the "fundamental text for eschatological exegesis," and it excludes knowledge of the time of the end, what Jesus said about that time must be viewed under the former heading; it expresses a hope

---

[246]Rigaux, *Seconde venue,* 191 n. 1.
[247]Vögtle, "Exegetische Erwägungen," 610.
[248]Wellhausen, *Marci,* 107.
[249]Schreiber, *Theologie des Vertrauens,* 128.
[250]Grässer, *Parusieverzögerung,* 82.

which inspires exhortation to be ready for it, not teaching which declares the time.[251] The instinct is right, the language inadequate, like the term "absolute" in relation to the ignorance of Jesus relating to the end.

It is difficult to maintain that Jesus did not teach in ways that intimated the nearness of the end. We recall the parable of the Fig Tree (with or without the application in Mark 13:29) and the parable of the Widow and the Judge, wherein Jesus gave assurance that God will vindicate his chosen ones "speedily" (Luke 18:8—though significantly the "assurance" is given in the form of a question!). The parables of the kingdom generally assume that the incursion of the saving sovereignty of God in the ministry of Jesus moves to a climax for which his contemporaries must prepare themselves. By contrast, the modern church has so completely lost any sense of near expectation, it is difficult for us objectively, yet sympathetically, to put ourselves into the shoes of our earliest forebears. We are more at home with the sentiment of William Temple's well-known dictum: "If Christianity is the final religion, the Church is still in its infancy. Two thousand years are as two days. The appeal to the 'primitive Church' is misleading; we are the primitive Church."[252]

Encouraging as that thought may be, we should freely acknowledge that it reflects a vastly different world of thought from that of Jesus. His was a world dominated by the thought of the new world, powerfully breaking into this world in the present and destined to loose the flood gates of divine judgment and glory in a future which surely will not tarry. That "new world," namely the kingdom of God, no longer dominates the church. Not that Jesus awaited its revelation tomorrow. His references to the doom of Israel, its city and temple, anticipate a history unfolding after his own death. And if the mission to Israel's cities is not completed before the Son of man comes (Matt 10:23), Jesus nevertheless anticipated a change of heart on the part of his people by the time the parousia occurred (Matt 23:39), which presumably proceeds from a continuance of the mission after Israel's distress. All this justifies Oepke's observation of "the tremendous tension which permeates Jesus' whole world of thought" in the sphere of eschatology, and which corresponds to the basic attitude of the NT generally, "that of both concentrated and extended expectation at one and the same time."[253]

That leads one to ask whether the distinction which Rigaux sought to make corresponds, in measure at least, to the difference between hope and dogma. To look for the fulfillment of the promise of the

---

[251]Rigaux, *Seconde venue*, 190, 198.

[252]W. Temple, "The church," in *Foundations*, ed. B. H. Streeter (London, 1912), 340.

[253]Oepke, *TDNT*, 5:867.

kingdom in ardent hope is not the same as laying down authoritatively at what time it shall come.[254] Vögtle agreed, and endeavored to relate that to the terms of our text: "Jesus reckoned with the coming of the Son of man soon, with the completion soon of that which had been begun; but he not only did not lay this down in express statements as to the time of the end, but expressly described this as the exclusive reserve of the Majesty of God."[255]

The last clause of that citation is worth pondering. If Jesus denied to all humankind and angels and himself knowledge of the end and stated that God alone had such knowledge, that is because God alone had the power to determine that day. The issue is related to Jesus' answer to the request of James and John for positions at either side of him in his glory: "To sit at my right or left is not for me to grant; it is for those to whom it has already been assigned" (Mark 10:40). The thought of Mark 13:32 is maintained in Acts 1:7: "The Father has set the times and seasons in his own authority." But Mark 13:32 includes a further thought: it is the part of the Son to leave them in the Father's hands, for the mark of the Son is to maintain unreserved obedience to the Father.[256]

Now Mark 13:32 raises in an acute form the relation of the concepts "the Son," "Son of God," and "Son of man," an issue which arises in other Synoptic sayings. Apart from its context in the eschatological discourse, the saying is eschatological in content; it is an apocalyptic utterance which excludes apocalyptic reckoning concerning the time

---

[254]So Schnackenburg; in his view the juxtaposition of Mark 13:30 and 32 provides a lesson, "namely to nourish a living eschatological hope from the urgent prophetic preaching of Jesus without drawing false conclusions about that prophecy from individual passages" (*God's Rule and Kingdom*, 212). Schnackenburg elaborates this in a later article: Jesus opened the eyes of his hearers to the future, not in the form of teaching but of warning, consolation, promise. It is "a prophetic message which is not intended to instruct about the point of time (cf. Mark 13:32), but to draw attention to the significance of the hour, the *kairos* of decision (cf. Luke 12:54–56), the pressure of the eschaton" ("Kirche und Parusie," in *Gott in Welt*, Festschrift K. Rahner [Freiburg, 1964], 2:568–69).

[255]Vögtle, "Exegetische Erwägungen," 651.

[256]On this issue Adolf Schlatter has an interesting and characteristic exposition. He suggests that from the relation to God which Jesus named Sonship Jesus drew two norms. The one was his consciousness of desiring the will of the Father, and from this proceed those sayings which express his certainty, for Jesus saw no hindrance in God which would postpone the perfection of his kingdom to a distant future. With this assurance a second norm was conjoined, no less binding than the former, which makes obedience the mark of the Son; that entails subordination to the sovereign will of God, and the renunciation of all reckonings and claims which would define beforehand what is coming in the future; that which is to come will come when the Father sends it. These two marks of Sonship are always united in Jesus; they create no uncertainty in his inner life, but give the double form to his teaching which both affirms and purifies the hope of his disciples (*Der Evangelist Matthäus*, 714).

of the end. One might have expected that the subject of the statement concerning the coming of the end would have been the Son of man, rather than the Son. Various endeavors have been made to incorporate that idea into the text, as for example the suggestion that "the Son" in the saying represents not Jesus himself but the heavenly Son of man, or that originally the text read "the Son of man," rather than "the Son," and in any case that the "trinitarian" formula Father, Son, and angels may originally have been God, Son of man, angels.[257] Such suggestions are believed to find support in the related Mark 8:38, where the Son of man, the glory of his Father, and the holy angels are juxtaposed. In 14:61 the high priest asks whether Jesus is the Messiah, "the Son of the Blessed One," to which Jesus replies, "I am; and you will see the Son of man . . ."; that saying appears to presuppose a tacit equation of Son of God and Son of man.

Few sayings in the Synoptic tradition illuminate the problem. In the Synoptics Jesus does not use the term "Son of God" in reference to himself, but two comparable passages need to be considered. In the parable of the Vineyard the owner sends as his last messenger his "beloved son" (Mark 12:6); it is probable that a parallel with the mission of Jesus is intended, but the description of the son in the parable cannot be viewed as a title; in the context of Jesus' instruction it may be viewed as relating to his role in the service of the divine sovereignty. Matthew 11:27 is the one other Synoptic saying which employs the absolute use of "the Father" and "the Son." While it has been common to view the logion as reflecting hellenistic religious categories, there is a strong tendency now to recognize the background of the saying as apocalyptic, with a marked affinity to the Thanksgiving Hymns of the Qumran community; rather than interpret the saying in terms of mystical knowledge, we are to see in it an expression of the Father's election and acknowledgment of the Son, who has the function of representing God in the world.[258]

Outside the Synoptic tradition examples are found of the title "Son of God," or even simply "the Son," in strongly eschatological contexts. 1 Thessalonians 1:10 is a saying drawn from early Christian tradition: "You turned from idols to be servants of the living God, and

---

[257]So, e.g., R. H. Fuller, *Mission and Achievement of Jesus*, SBT 1/12 (London, 1954), 83; idem, *Foundations of New Testament Christology* (London, 1965), 114. Schweizer is content to affirm, "Mark 13:32 is rooted in the Son of man Christology" (*TDNT*, 8:372). So also Pesch, *Markus*, 2:310; Schmithals, *Markus*, 580–81. Brandenburger thinks that "neither the Son," coming after the angels, cannot refer to the earthly Son but must refer to the preexistent Son who is Mediator of creation (*Markus 13 und die Apokalyptik*, 123).

[258]So, e.g., Schweizer, *TDNT*, 8:373; W. D. Davies, *The Setting of the Sermon on the Mount* (Cambridge, 1964), 206–7; Hahn, *The Titles of Jesus in Christology* (ET London, 1969), 373.

to wait expectantly for the appearance from heaven of his Son Jesus . . . our deliverer from the terrors of judgment to come." As with Mark 13:32 it has been suggested that this saying may originally have been spoken of the Son of man,[259] but the suggestion is implausible; apart from the problem of nondominical Son of man sayings circulating in the primitive church, of which we have no proof, the evidence of the citation as exemplifying the eschatological overtones of the concept "Son" in primitive Christianity should not be so cavalierly set aside; at most one could view it as an indication of the effect of the Son of man sayings on the concepts of "Son" and "Son of God."[260] The same applies to 1 Cor 15:24–28; the risen Christ is to come at the end of the age for the resurrection of those who belong to him: "Then comes the end, when he delivers up the kingdom to God the Father," at which point, "the Son himself will also be subjected to God who put all things in subjection to him." So the Son must reign until all that opposes God in the world is subject to him, and then he submits the sovereignty to the Father. The two terms "the Son" and "the Father" are not set alongside each other so explicitly as in Mark 13:32, but they are there, and once more the eschatological significance of the Son is marked, little differentiated from Son of God and Son of man, save that "the Son" is more fittingly used in association with "the Father."

What is most surprising is the way in which "the Son," "the Son of God," and "the Son of man" appear in the Johannine writings, particularly in the Fourth Gospel. All three terms and their attributes occur interchangeably in John 5:19–29: "As the Father raises the dead and gives them life, so the Son gives life to those whom he wishes. Indeed, the Father judges no one, but he has given all judgment to the Son. . . . The hour is coming and now is when the dead will hear the voice of the Son of God, and they who hear will live. For as the Father has life in himself, so also he has granted the Son to have life in himself; and he gave him authority to pass judgment because he is the Son of man." It is evident that in this passage the functions of the Son, the Son of God, and the Son of man are identical. The Son (of God) has been appointed to fulfill the role of the Son of man.

What are we to deduce from these expressions of the relatedness of the concepts "Son," "Son of God," and "Son of man"? Clearly the "Son of man" is the dominant expression in the teaching of Jesus,

---

[259]Schweizer, *TDNT*, 8:370.

[260]So Hahn, who posits a fusion of Son of God with the Son of man tradition here, the like applying also to the function of Jesus as Redeemer from "the wrath to come"; nevertheless, he adds, "The Son of God title remains decisive; in this we can see how the Messiah conception, far from being a general designation, was used especially to describe the eschatological office of Jesus" (*Titles of Jesus*, 286).

whereas (in the Synoptic tradition) the "Son" is rarely mentioned, and "Son of God" not at all on his lips (though note Mark 14:61–62). Should we then postulate that the "Son of God" concept is rooted in that of the "Son of man"? Such is the conviction of not a few scholars. Ernst Lohmeyer stated, with reference to Mark 13:32: "It is scarcely accidental that it [the title 'the Son'] emerges in an apocalyptic connection, as all designations of the dignity of Jesus are of this origin; and it is yet less critical to suspect it, for what conceivable reason exists that the primitive Christian faith should exclude its Lord from this knowledge? Hence one may say that the designation 'Father and Son' belongs not only to the oldest tradition, but also to the preaching of Jesus, for it is also the pure consequence of taking over the title Son of Man."[261]

On this view several comments may be made. The affirmation that "all designations of the dignity of Jesus" originate in apocalyptic is too narrow a basis for the Christology implied in the teaching of Jesus. The concept "Son of God" has deep roots in the OT and late Jewish tradition; since it was applied to the nation, its king, and the Messiah, it is unlikely that it would ever follow as a secondary application of the "Son of man" concept. We must also remember the importance to Jesus of the address to God as *Abba*. It would appear that we have to recognize three different concepts—the Son, the Son of God, the Son of man— which have different roots, but which were capable of being closely related and of being interpenetrated by one another.

The "Son of God" finds its primary application to the nation Israel in Exod 4:22–23: Israel is God's firstborn son; if Pharaoh will not release God's firstborn, he will lose his own firstborn son. In Nathan's message to David, 2 Sam 7:14, the king is spoken of as God's son: "I will be his father, and he shall be my son." That is echoed in Ps 89:26–27, which stresses the personal relation of the king to God: "He will say to me, 'You are my father, my God, my rock and my safe refuge.' And I will name him my firstborn, highest among the kings of the earth." Here salvation as well as privileged status is included in the relation of son to God. In Ps 2:7 the language approximates more closely the Oriental view of the king as son of God, but even here the notion of legitimation does not exclude that of salvation.[262]

---

[261]Lohmeyer, *Markus*, 283. For comparable views see Sjöberg, *Der verborgene Menschensohn*, 187ff.; Schweizer, *TDNT*, 8:372. C. F. D. Moule holds that in Daniel 7 the "Ancient of Days" represents the Father, and the "one like a son of man" the Royal Son, and adds, "It is organic to the ministry of Jesus that the Son of God shows himself as the frail and vulnerable Son of Man. The two are identical in reality" (*The Origin of Christology* [Cambridge, 1977], 24–27). This interpretation is expounded in detail by Seyoon Kim, *The Son of Man as Son of God*, WUNT 30 (Tübingen, 1983), 36.

[262]Hengel cites H. Gese for the view that "You are my Son" represents a realized promise of salvation which is further strengthened by the addition of

We have already noticed that the concept of nation, king, and Messiah as Son of God did not become lost in later Judaism, but remained alive in varied ways. Ps 2:7 and the promise to David in 2 Sam 7:14 were interpreted messianically among the Jews. The latter passage assumed considerable importance in the Qumran community. Its use in 4QFlor 1.6–7, along with the regulations for seating at the feast in 1QSa 2.11ff. and the references to the Son of God in the Daniel apocryphon of Cave 4, make it highly probable that the covenanters viewed the royal Messiah as Son of God.[263]

The extension of this expression to specially worthy or gifted Israelites is also significant for understanding the Jewish mind in the age of Jesus. The righteous among the Jews were singled out as sons of God, as may be seen in Sir 4:10; Jub 1:24–25; and Wisd 2:18.[264] The last is especially important because of the representative nature of the figure described. The charismatic miracle worker and the mystic were similarly viewed as sons of God par excellence.[265] It is clear that the concept "son of God" was much more familiar in the era of late Judaism than has been customarily acknowledged. This familiarity would have operated, at least in measure, to offset the natural reserve of the rabbis to apply the "Son of God" concept to the Messiah (out of reverence to God and in resistance to pagan notions of divinized men). It will also be appreciated that Jesus could have been regarded as Son of God by

---

the clause, "today I have begotten you." "The enthronement of the Davidic king on Zion is understood as birth and creation through God" (*The Son of God: The Origin of Christology and the History of Jewish-Hellenistic Religion* [ET Philadelphia, 1976], 23). The citation from Gese is from *Probleme biblischer Theologie, Festschrift G. von Rad,* ed. H. W. Wolff (Munich, 1971), 82.

[263]H. Braun was prepared to affirm that in the Qumran literature the Messiah is regarded as Son of God, and with van der Woude that this understanding of the Messiah is not unique to Qumran, but is simply Jewish (*Qumran und das Neue Testament* [Tübingen, 1966], 76).

[264]Sirach 4:10: "Be a father to orphans, and like a husband to their mother; then the Most High will call you his son, and his love for you will be greater than a mother's." Jubilees 1:24–25: "I will be their father and they shall be my sons. And they shall be called sons of the living God, and every angel and every spirit shall know . . . that these are my sons, and that I am their Father in uprightness and righteousness, and that I have loved them." Wisdom 2:18: "If the just man is God's son, God will stretch out a hand to him and save him from the clutches of his enemies."

[265]This theme is discussed in D. Flusser, *Jesus* (New York, 1969), 93–94; G. Vermes, *Jesus the Jew,* 206–10; Hengel, *Son of God,* 42–43, in all of which examples are given. Rabbi Hanina ben Dossa, living a generation after Jesus, was famous for his miracles of healing; a heavenly voice said of him, "The whole world will be nourished because of my son Hanina—and a morsel of John's bread will satisfy my son Hanina for a week" (b. *Ta'an.* 24b). Ishmael b. Elisha is said to have had a vision of Yahweh, who addressed him, "Ishmael, my son, bless me" (b. *Ber.* 7a).

the common people without thereby necessarily identifying him with the King-Messiah.

As to Jesus himself, we must never forget his own characteristic mode of addressing God as *Abba,* and the implications which that has for his understanding of his relationship to God. It would be unreasonable to view it as primarily reflecting a consciousness of function as King-Messiah, in the tradition of 2 Sam 7:14; Ps 2:7 etc., or of his self-estimate as a wonder-worker or the like. It is surely an expression of his experience of God, of his understanding of God, and of his relation to God. Naturally, in the setting of Judaism this cannot have been divorced from a consciousness of relation to the people of God, who are both elect and beloved of God and called to faithful and obedient service. To be set in relation to God and to be set to service for God are propagated together in Israel's history, as Exod 19:4–6 illustrates. For Jesus, therefore, the consciousness of God-relatedness will have been accompanied by a sense of vocation and of representation. This finds clear expression in the controverted Matt 11:27, where the notion of choice of the Son by the Father is bound up with the Son's vocation to reveal him and with his accompanying authority and power to do so. Status, commission, and authority belong together in this declaration of the Son's relation to the Father, and it remains firmly set within Israelite tradition. Given the context of the message and ministry of Jesus in Israel, the severe limitation of the authority of the Son in Mark 13:32 is surprising, and yet it is so harmonious with that message and ministry that objections to the authenticity of the saying are implausible. Rarely have these taken into account the eschatological significations of "Son" and "Son of God," or the relation of both to the "Son of man," or the fundamental element of obedience and subordination in the notion of "Son" within Israel.

All this suggests that a conviction of Jesus that he stood in relation to God as Son, understood within the context of the service of the kingdom of God which was at the center of his life, would readily coalesce with a sense of vocation to carry out the function of the Son of God, as interpreted within the tradition of his people. The "Son of God" concept would in turn be modified by his understanding of the relation of the Son to the Father, and of the nature of ministry set within that context. That would include a combination of authority from the Father and obedient service due to the Father from the Son. To that understanding the "Son of God" concept adds the notion of representation regarding the rule of God and the firstborn people of God.

All this could be said without taking into account the Son of man. But our consideration of the Son of man passages in the Gospels has shown us a figure who is also representative, serving the rule of God in all its aspects. The Son of man is charged with authority to act for God in the service of his saving sovereignty (Mark 2:10), yet he also represents the people to whom the rule is promised (2:28). His service includes the function of suffering, so that the rule of God may be salvation for the world (8:31, etc.), but he also acts as the agent of its consummation in judgment and salvation (8:38; Luke 12:8–9; Mark 14:62, etc.). In his service of suffering and consequent exaltation the Son of man fulfills the roles of the rejected Prophet, the Righteous Sufferer, the Servant of the Lord, and the Martyr for God's cause—figures which are all closely related to the Son of God motif in Israel.[266] In these circumstances it would be astonishing if there had been no trace in the teaching of Jesus of a coalescence of the representative figures of the Son, the Son of God, and the Son of man. As it is, we have seen evidences of the eschatological functions of the Son of man strengthening the eschatological elements already attaching to the concepts of "Son" and "Son of God." Such mutual influence of the three concepts would have been encouraged through reflection on the primary passage for the eschatological Son of man in the OT, namely Dan 7:13; for there the one like a son of man receives authority and dominion from the Ancient of Days in a representative capacity—he represents the sovereignty of God and the people to whom it is conveyed. The messianic understanding of the vision, unquestioned in the era of Jesus, matches the traditional view of the royal Son of God so closely that Jewish readers of Daniel would naturally assume that the Son of man is the Son of God; or, otherwise expressed, they would view the passage as depicting the Son of God in the guise of the Son of man.[267]

We conclude that while the christological figures of the Son, the Son of God, and the Son of man are distinguished in the tradition, there was no little overlap in the concepts and in the function associated with them. All are representative as well as individual figures, and the functions which they fulfill relate to the service of the kingdom of God, both in its inauguration and in its consummation. Accordingly they denote the present and the future status and function of him who bears these names: Jesus is the Son, and as the obedient Son he will share the Father's glory when it pleases the Father to reveal the kingdom; he is the Son of God, and with the kingdom will appear as Judge and

---

[266]For an elaboration of this statement see my *Jesus and the Kingdom of God*, 237–47.

[267]This is the element of truth in the observation of Schrenk: "The combination of the Ancient of days and *bar nasha* in [Dan 7:13] (which was combined with Ps. 2:7 and 110:1) undoubtedly demanded the interrelating of Father and Son. This vision was well adapted to express both the sovereignty of the Father and also the commission of the Son" (*TDNT*, 5:989). This is true because of the prior existence of the concepts of Father and Son in relation to the kingdom of God, not because the reading of Daniel 7 gave rise to them.

Redeemer; he is the Son of man, and at the end will complete the tasks of the Son of man for God and the redeemed.[268]

Mark 13:33-37

It is common to view the closing paragraph of the discourse as a loosely attached appendage, not least in view of the differing ways in which Matthew and Luke conclude their versions of the discourse. However, on the one hand, Hartman acknowledges that the hortatory material was linked with the essential elements of the address in the pre-Markan tradition, though not so closely bound with it as the other material.[269] Dupont, on the other hand, protests against the frequent diminution of the importance of this section; rather than viewing it as an appendage he sees it as deeply significant for the purpose of the discourse; the passage shows that the time is short, and that it is necessary above all to maintain vigilance. Accordingly, "These verses throw light on the interpretation which the evangelist gives to the discourse taken as a whole."[270]

Where has this material come from? Gaston describes it as "pure parenesis," almost every phrase of which can be paralleled in the epistles of the NT as well as in the parable of Watchfulness: "It seems that both the exhortations of the epistles and this section of Mark echo the language of parables without being such themselves."[271] Vincent Taylor found in the passage "a homiletical echo of several parables."[272] Lambrecht is more specific: he considers that this passage has points of

---

[268]A highly significant article on this theme has been written by W. R. G. Loader, "The Apocalyptic Model of Sonship: Its Origin and Development in New Testament Tradition," *JBL* 97/4 (1978): 525–54. The thesis is maintained that the terminology "Father-Son," which has its roots in Jesus' use of *abba*, features especially in contexts and sayings which refer to Jesus' future apocalyptic function, mostly as Son of man. This results in a tendency for the word "Son" not only to be used in such contexts, but also itself to take up into its meaning apocalyptic connotations. In this way the description of Jesus as Son comes to carry with it the idea of Jesus exercising the kind of apocalyptic functions mostly associated with the Son of man motif. Developed in this way the apocalyptic model of sonship comes to be the predominant meaning of Jesus' sonship. This position is close to that which I have represented in the foregoing discussion, but Loader has not given the same recognition to the early eschatological associations of the terms "Son" and "Son of God," nor has he recognized the place of all three terms in the whole process of the coming of the kingdom of God, as reflected in the teaching of Jesus.

[269]Hartman, *Prophecy Interpreted*, 175.

[270]Dupont, "La parabole du maître qui rentre dans la nuit," in *Mélanges Bibliques*, Festschrift B. Rigaux, 90–91.

[271]Gaston, *No Stone on Another*, 39–40.

[272]V. Taylor, *Mark*, 524. Similarly Pesch, *Markus*, 2:313.

contact with four parables: the Watching Servants (Luke 12:35–38), the Thief in the Night (Luke 12:39–40/Matt 24:42–44), the Good and Bad Servant (Luke 12:42–46/Matt 24:45–51), and the Talents/Pounds (Matt 25:14–30/Luke 19:12–27). Since these parables occur in various places in Matthew and Luke, Lambrecht feels that the only reasonable explanation for Mark's text is that it is a secondary combination of them: "Mark knew these Q parables; with fragments of them—words and ideas—he has created a secondary parable."[273] The contacts are undeniable, but the extent to which Mark was responsible for creating the parable is less clear. There is much to be said for the view that, taking into account all the redactional elements in Mark 13:33–37, we have an authentic parable in vv. 34–36, provided with an introduction in v. 33 and a summary exhortation in v. 37. The closest parallel in the Gospel tradition to vv. 34–36 is the parable of the Watching Servants in Luke 12:36–38. In all probability the two parables have come down in the tradition as variants of a single parable and have been differently edited by the two evangelists.[274]

Verse 33

With A. Weiser we may agree that there is no reason for postulating an original link with v. 32; the ground for the appeal to "watch" is given in v. 33b: "for you do not know when the time is."[275] It is uncertain, however, whether Weiser is right in affirming that there is no link between v. 33 and the parable that follows.[276] Admittedly the statement has essentially "a transitional function." Pesch likewise views v. 33 as a redactional introduction to the parable of v. 34, just as v. 28a is to the parable of v. 28b.[277] We grant that the characteristic *blepete* at the beginning of v. 33 is due to Mark; it sets the tone for the whole paragraph, emphasizes the appeal of v. 33, and binds it to the entire previous discourse. Nevertheless, it is conceivable that v. 33 from *agrypneite* onwards was in the pre-Markan tradition.[278] It suits the parable of vv. 34–36 perfectly, especially when the latter is pruned of

---

[273]Lambrecht, *Redaktion,* 249–51.

[274]So Dodd, *Parables of the Kingdom,* 161–62; Jeremias, *Parables,* 53–54; Kümmel, *Prophecy and Fulfilment,* 54; Dupont, "Parabole du maître," 106; J. D. Crossan, *In Parables: The Challenge of the Historical Jesus* (New York, 1973), 98; A. Weiser, *Die Knechtsgleichnisse der synoptischen Evangelien* (Munich, 1971), 139.

[275]Weiser, *Knechtsgleichnisse,* 131.

[276]Ibid., 132.

[277]Pesch, *Naherwartungen,* 195–96; idem, *Markus,* 2:313; similarly Bultmann, *History of the Synoptic Tradition,* 130; Schmid, *Markus,* 249; Grässer, *Parusieverzögerung,* 85; Dupont, "Parabole du maître," 90; Weiser, *Knechtsgleichnisse,* 131–32; Zmijewski, *Eschatologiereden,* 295.

[278]So Pesch, *Markus,* 2:314, 316.

its secondary additions, and its emphasis on "You do not know the time" gives it an excellent link with v. 32. We may be prepared to leave the origin of the saying *sub judice*.

Verses 34–36

Jülicher has pronounced this passage to be "a distorted and confused jumble of motifs" from the longer parables of Matthew and Luke, containing nothing which appears as an authentic word of Jesus.[279] In reality the "jumble" is not so great as is alleged, and the contacts with other parables are traceable with reasonable clarity. Dupont has rightly stated, "The first elements of v. 34 present an incontestable kinship with the beginning of the parable of the Talents."[280] Curiously, however, on reflection the nature of the "kinship" is not so clear as the fact. It is frequently assumed without question that Mark has borrowed his sentence from Matthew's parable of the Talents. For Augustine and moderns who assume the priority of Matthew over Mark that is a natural assumption,[281] but when the priority of Mark is accepted that assumption is less obvious. And are we sure that Mark knew Q? The question needs to be sharpened, for the contact is between Mark and the Matthean parable of the Talents, not between Mark and Luke's parable of the Pounds. It is not impossible that Mark's parable was enriched with a reminiscence of the Q parable in the pre-Markan tradition and that Matthew, having read Mark's parable, adjusted his version of the parable to Mark's language.[282]

The rest of the parable, as we have noticed, is especially close to that of the Watching Servants in Luke 12:36–38. Luke is probably right in representing the master as going to a banquet and returning home the same night. Mark's *apodēmos* indicates a considerable journey; with that the assignment of authority to the servants is consonant, but hardly the instruction that the porter must remain vigilant and not sleep, since the master could return at any hour of the night. Mark's parable will perhaps have earlier begun: *hōs anthrōpos apheis tēn oikian autou tō thyrōrō eneteilato hina grēgorē*, i.e., "The situation is as when a man leaves his house and commands the porter to watch."[283] The continua-

---

[279]Jülicher, *Die Gleichnisreden Jesu*, 2 vols., 2d ed. (Tübingen, 1910), 1:170–71.

[280]Dupont, "Parabole du maître," 97.

[281]C. S. Mann remarked on vv. 34–36: "If anything betrays the character of Mark's gospel as a conflated document, a digest of Matthew and Luke, then this parable does" (*Mark*, 540). David Wenham's investigation of Mark 13 starts with this parable, since in it the Markan dependency on Matthew seems to him so very plain; see *The Rediscovery of Jesus' Eschatological Discourse*, Gospel Perspectives 4 (Sheffield, 1984), 15–49.

[282]See Dupont, "Parabole du maître," 97.

[283]Weiser, *Knechtsgleichnisse*, 137.

tion of the parable in v. 35, however, is expressed in the second person, and so has been accommodated to the readers: "Keep awake, then, for you do not know when the master of the house is coming." Rather than view the statement as an extraneous application added to the parable of v. 34, the parallel in Luke 12:37–38 suggests that this is a modification of an original continuation stated in the third person: "He will watch, for he does not know when the master of the house is coming . . . lest coming suddenly he find him sleeping."[284]

Mark's statement of the time in terms of the fourfold division of the night, according to the Roman custom and enumeration, is similarly likely to be a later variant of the threefold division which is given by Luke (12:38). It is, however, pressing the language unduly to assert that Mark's change is due to reflection on the delay of the parousia.[285] There is no hint of the passing of the night hours, nor a call to wake out of sleep, as, e.g., in Rom 13:11–14. On the contrary, the emphasis in v. 35 falls on the incalculability of the time of the master's return and its suddenness, as v. 36 proceeds to show ("lest coming suddenly he finds you sleeping"). This gives a genuine echo of the teaching of Jesus, such as that contained in the parable of the Burglar (Matt 24:43–44/Luke 12:39–40), in the parable of the Wise and Foolish Maidens (Matt 25:1–13), and in the Q apocalypse (Luke 17:24, 26–30). There is good reason, accordingly, to view the core of the parable as an authentic reminiscence of the teaching of Jesus.[286]

Having considered the origin of the parable we now inquire as to its intention. It is well known that both Dodd and Jeremias viewed the parable as one of the parables of crisis. It was basic to Dodd's interpretation of the teaching of Jesus that the crisis was precipitated through the ministry of Jesus, whose proclamation of the kingdom of God was rejected by the nation as a whole. "If He said to the general public, 'Be like men awaiting their master,' he may have meant 'Be alert and prepared for any development in this critical situation.' If He addressed His own disciples, then we may compare the words which He spoke to them in Gethsemane: 'Watch and pray, that ye enter not into temptation' (Mk. xiv. 38)—the 'temptation,' or more properly 'testing time,' being in that case the immediately impending attack upon Him and His followers."[287]

---

[284]Ibid., 142.

[285]Contrary to Grässer, *Parusieverzögerung*, 88.

[286]So Weiser, *Knechtsgleichnisse*, 138. He subjects vv. 35–36 to a detailed investigation to determine what is traditional and what is redactional in the passage (pp. 139–44). His examination of the language and style leads him to conclude: "The evangelist has received from the tradition the basic elements of vv. 35–36 that belong to the parable. His redactional activity consists in adapting this traditional content in a direct application to his community. Corresponding to the form of v. 35 he has also given v. 33 its form and set it before the parable."

[287]Dodd, *Parables of the Kingdom*, 2d ed. 1936, pp. 165–66 (3d ed. 1961,

Jeremias had an interpretation similar to that of Dodd, except that he allowed for the development of the contemporary situation into an ultimate crisis in the future, albeit an immediately impending one. He, too, refers to the appeal in Gethsemane, but with respect to the final testing time of the great distress. If the parable was addressed to the crowd it was a call to be prepared for the coming calamity, which would descend as suddenly and devastatingly as Noah's flood; probably, however, it was intended for the scribes, calling on them not to sleep when the crisis arrived.[288]

The reference to the Gethsemane narrative is frequently made in connection with the parable; that the parallel was seen from earliest times is apparent in the longer reading of v. 33 in the majority of manuscripts: *agrypneite kai proseuchesthe*, "Watch and pray." The addition, nevertheless, is clearly secondary. When the shorter reading is adopted the parallel consists of a call to remain on the alert and not to fall into a state of spiritual torpor. The Gethsemane narrative depicts the unhappy situation of a group of disciples who slept instead of maintaining wakefulness in prayer with their master. That, as Dupont observed, suggests that the narrative of Gethsemane has become an illustration of the "keep watch" of 13:36.[289] It does not justify interpreting the parable in terms of the Gethsemane experience.

The event in view in the parable of the Porter will be linked with the great theme of Jesus' proclamation and instruction, namely the coming of the kingdom of God and the judgment which accompanies it. The fitness of this being represented in a parable about the absence and return of a master of a household is seen in the inseparable association in Jewish thought of the judgment and the kingdom of God with the coming of God. Significantly, in the parable of the Vineyard and the Wicked Tenants the judgment of God is represented by the coming of "the lord of the vineyard" (Mark 12:9), by which the coming of God was clearly intended. The same holds good of the entry of the king into the marriage banquet of his son (Matt 22:11–14). Does the same hold good of the parable of the Porter? Dupont is strongly convinced that it does:

> If we properly understand the intention of Jesus in these parables, they do not aim to give an understanding of the role to which Jesus will have to revert in the last day in virtue of his position as Son of man, nor of the future function which will be given him to fulfill, but of the significance of the mission which he actually accomplishes. To give the true sense to the ministry of Jesus is to recognize in it the first act of the coming of the

---

pp. 131–32).
[288]Jeremias, *Parables*, 55.
[289]Dupont, "Parabole du maître," 99.

reign of God, the signal harbinger of the judgment which will decide admission into the kingdom.[290]

It seems to me that this exposition makes an unreal distinction between the mission of Jesus in relation to the inauguration of the reign of God and the action of God in relation to its consummation. In all the instruction of Jesus relative to the kingdom it is God who acts in and through him to establish the kingdom, whether in his ministry or in the anticipated future. The Q saying in Luke 11:20/Matt 12:28 is a crucial example of the understanding of Jesus as to his role in the kingdom of God: "If it is by the finger of God that I cast out the demons, then the kingdom of God has come upon you." The liberating power of the saving sovereignty of God, operative through the mighty Spirit of God, is the means by which Jesus performs his exorcisms and is victor over Satan, and so brings the kingdom of God among humankind. He is the instrument through which the saving sovereignty of God is at work in the world. Or, in our more commonly used terminology, he is the Bearer of the kingdom of God, its Representative, its Mediator.

This is equally apparent in such utterances as Matt 11:5, 12; Mark 2:18–19; Luke 4:16–21; 17:20–21, to say nothing of the parables of the kingdom. The latter are particularly important, especially the parables of growth, since they all depict the kingdom of God initiated through Jesus as pressing on to its manifest consummation. There can be no doubt that Mark, in setting the parable of the Porter after his portrayal of the parousia and the parable of the Fig Tree, interpreted the master of the house, returning at an unknown hour, as the exalted Christ in his parousia.[291] What, after all, is the parousia of the Son of man but the coming of the representative of the kingdom of God to complete the process of the coming of the kingdom? The parousia of the Son of man is strictly parallel to the coming of the kingdom of God, for both represent the action through which the saving sovereignty of God is operative in the world. So it is that the Son of man sends the angels of God to gather the elect of heaven and earth into the kingdom of God (13:27). The Christ, the Son of man and Son of God, is the one through whom God acts in his sovereign power, in both the beginning and the end of the achievement of his redeeming purpose.

When Matthew replaced Mark's little parable of the Porter with the Q apocalypse (Matt 24:37–42), the parables of the Burglar (24:43–44), the Faithful and Unfaithful Servant (24:45–51), the Ten Maidens (25:1–13), and the Talents (25:14–30), and brought all to a climax in the vision of the last judgment (25:31–46), he was but elaborating the

---

[290]Ibid., 115. Weiser expresses very similar ideas (*Knechtsgleichnisse*, 149).
[291]So Kümmel, *Prophecy and Fulfilment*, 54–56, and the majority of commentators.

essential meaning of the Markan parable, for the mission of Jesus was and is to be God's agent, in whom God acted, acts, and will act to fulfill his redeeming will in its totality. The kinship of the primitive confession to the word and deed of Jesus is evident: "God in Christ was reconciling the world to himself" (2 Cor 5:19), for it was God who effected the coming of the kingdom in the word and acts of Jesus in his ministry, in the sacrificial offering of his life, and in his resurrection to the position of power and authority, and he will also effect the judgment and salvation of the kingdom in the coming of the Son of man. The difference between the coming of God in the lowly service of Jesus and in the parousia at the end is that between hiddenness and manifestation. But the theophany of the Father and of the Son is one. The coming of God for the consummation of his kingdom takes place in the coming of the Son of man. The return of the master of the house in the parable of Mark 13:34–36, accordingly, is actualized in the parousia of the Christ.

Verse 37

In the context of the discourse the appeal to "all" to be watchful should strictly relate to the rest of the twelve disciples (cf. 14:29, 31), but no such restriction can have been intended by Mark. By a curious coincidence Luke follows the variant parable of the Watching Servants and that of the Burglar with the question of Peter, "Lord, are you speaking this parable to us or to all?" (Luke 12:41). In Mark's view "all" naturally includes in its scope all believers. As Lambrecht observed, on the plane of Markan redaction the *pasin legō* depicts the opposite pole to the *kat' idian* in v. 3.[292] It makes explicit the hints scattered through the discourse that in the instruction delivered to the disciples the church is being addressed. The final lesson of the discourse is now applied to all disciples of the Lord: The end is near but incalculable; consequently all must at all times be "awake."

Precisely what does that signify for the church? Essentially the attitude of spiritual alertness, i.e., readiness for God at every moment in the rendering of what Paul calls the obedience of faith (Rom 1:5). It is the opposite of the depiction of the disciples in Acts 1:10 as they gazed into heaven, straining eyes to see Jesus. The parables of Matthew 24—25 which replace Mark's parable of the Porter suggest that spiritual alertness is expressed in faithful service in the Master's house, diligent use of talents bestowed, and doing the works of God and his Christ in feeding the hungry, giving drink to the thirsty, welcoming the stranger, ministering to the ill and to those in prison. Mark hinted at the same idea in his inclusion of the clause "he gave to his servants authority, to

---

[292]Lambrecht, *Redaktion,* 248.

each one his task" (13:34). Schmithals rightly observed that "waiting" for the Lord is an active pursuit, which, in the light of v. 10, includes the duty of all the Lord's servants to labor in their own way in the spread of the gospel.[293]

So the discourse concludes with an expression of a near expectation, qualified by the recognition that the times of the divine-human story are in the hands of God. It is a near expectation which inspires service of the kingdom in the spirit of him through whom the kingdom came and is to come. Such an expectation is finely defined by Pesch as

> the eschatological attitude of those who stake their all on the sovereignty of God in the sovereignty of Jesus Christ and, like Jesus himself, in his Spirit, enable the powers of God's sovereignty to be perceived, and cause God's sovereignty to reach human beings in its healing power—and at the same time to await its fulfillment from God through Jesus Christ. . . . It is realized and concretized on the way of following in cross bearing (Mark 8:34–38), on the path that is free from anxiety because it is radical trust in God and his Son Jesus Christ in the power of the Holy Spirit (13:9–11), a way which leads to death and to the hoped-for resurrection promised in Jesus Christ.[294]

---

[293]Schmithals, *Markus,* 582. See also Anderson, *Mark,* 301–2; Schweizer, *Mark,* 283–84.

[294]Pesch, *Naherwartungen,* 201–2.

SELECT BIBLIOGRAPHY

Achtemeier, P. *Mark, Proclamation Commentaries.* Edited by G. Krodel. Philadelphia, 1975.

Agbanou, V. K. *Le discours eschatologique de Matthieu 24–25: Tradition et
Rédaction.* Etudes Bibliques. Nouvelle Série 2. Paris, 1983.

Allen, W. C. *A Critical and Exegetical Commentary on the Gospel according to
S. Matthew.* ICC. Edinburgh, 1907. 3d ed. 1912.

_____. "The Gospel according to Saint Mark with introduction and notes."
Oxford Church Biblical Commentary. London, 1915.

Althaus, P. *Die Letzten Dinge.* (1st ed. 1922). 5th ed. Gütersloh, 1949.

Ambrozic, A. M. *The Hidden Kingdom, A Redaction-critical Study of the
References to the Kingdom of God in Mark's Gospel.* CBQMS 2. Washington, D.C., 1972.

Anderson, H. *The Gospel of Mark.* New Century Bible. Edited by M. Black.
London, 1976.

Andrews, H. T. "The Significance of the Eschatological Utterances of Jesus."
London Theological Studies. London, 1911.

Aune, D. E. *Prophecy in Early Christianity and the Ancient Mediterranean
World.* Grand Rapids, 1983.

Bacon, B. W. *The Gospel of Mark: Its Composition and Date.* New Haven, 1925.

Baldensperger, W. *Das Selbstbewusstein Jesu im Lichte der messianischen Hoffnungen seiner Zeit.* Strassburg, 1888.

Barnes, E. W. *The Rise of Christianity.* London, 1947.

Bartlet, J. V. "The Meaning and Task of Christology." *The Lord of Life.* London,
1929.

Batiffol, P. *L'Enseignement de Jésus.* Paris, 1909.

Baur, F. C. *Kritische Untersuchungen über die kanonischen Evangelien.* Tübingen, 1847.

Beare, F. W. *The Earliest Records of Jesus.* Oxford, 1962.

Beasley-Murray, G. R. *Jesus and the Future.* London, 1954.

_____. *A Commentary on Mark Thirteen.* London, 1962.

_____. *The Book of Revelation.* New Century Bible. London, 1974.

_____. *Jesus and the Kingdom of God.* Grand Rapids and Exeter, 1986.

Bengel, J. A. *Gnomon Novi Testamenti*. 2d ed. 1763; ET from 3d ed. of J. Steudel. Edinburgh, 1857.

Beyschlag, W. *New Testament Theology*. (German, 1891). Edinburgh, 1895.

Black, M. *An Aramaic Approach to the Gospels and Acts*. Oxford, 1946.

Bleek, F. *Synoptische Erklärung der drei ersten Evangelien*. Edited by H. Holtzmann. Leipzig, 1862.

Blunt, A. W. F. "The Gospel according to Saint Mark." *The Clarendon Bible*. Oxford, 1929.

Boismard, M.-E. "La 'Two-Gospel Hypothesis': Le discours eschatologique de Matthieu 24 et parallèls." In *The Interrelations of the Gospels*. Edited by D. L. Dungan. BETL 95. Pages 265–88. Louvain, 1990.

Boring, M. E. *Sayings of the Risen Jesus. Christian Prophecy in the Synoptic Tradition*. SNTSMS 46. Cambridge, 1982.

Bornkamm, G. "End Expectation and Church in Matthew." In G. Bornkamm, G. Barth, and H. J. Held. *Tradition and Interpretation in Matthew*. Pages 15–51. Philadelphia, 1963.

_____. "Die Vorgeschichte des sogennanten Zweiten Korintherbriefes." In *Geschichte und Glaube*, Part 2, Gesammelte Aufsätze 4, 1968. Pages 162–94, abbreviated in "The History of the Origin of the so-called Second Letter to the Corinthians," *NTS* 8 (1962): 258–64.

Bouquet, A. C. *Jesus: A New Outline and Estimate*. Cambridge, 1933.

Bousset, W. *The Antichrist Legend*. 1895. ET London, 1896.

_____. *Jesus*. ET London and New York, 1906.

_____. *Die Religion des Judentums im späthellenistischen Zeitalter*. 3d ed. Edited by H. Gressmann. Tübingen, 1926.

Bowman, J. W. *The Gospel of Mark, The New Christian Jewish Passover Haggadah*. Leiden, 1965.

Brandenburger, E. *Markus 13 und die Apokalyptik*. FRLANT 134. Edited by W. Schrage and R. Smend. Göttingen, 1984.

Brandon, S. G. F. "The Apologetic Factor in the Markan Gospel." In *Studia Evangelica* II. Edited by F. L. Cross. Pages 34–46. Berlin, 1964.

_____. *The Fall of Jerusalem and the Christian Church*, London, 1951.

_____. "The Date of the Markan Gospel." *NTS* 7 (1960–61): 126–41.

Branscomb, H. *The Gospel of Mark*. MNTC. London, 1937.

Briggs, C. A. *The Messiah of the Gospels*. Edinburgh, 1894.

Bruce, A. B. "The Synoptic Gospels." *The Expositor's Greek Testament*. London, 1912.

Bultmann, R. *Die Geschichte der synoptischen Tradition*. 2d ed. Göttingen, 1931.

_____. *History of the Synoptic Tradition*. ET London, 1963.

_____. *Jesus and the Word*. London, 1935.

_____. *Jesus*. Berlin, 1926.

Bundy, W. E. *Jesus and the First Three Gospels. An Introduction to the Synoptic Tradition*. Cambridge, Mass., 1955.

Burkill, T. *Mysterious Revelation. An Examination of the Philosophy of St. Mark's Gospel*. New York, 1963.

Burkitt, F. C. *Jesus Christ. An Historical Outline*. London, 1932. (Reprint, with additions, of article in *A History of Christianity in the Light of Modern Knowledge*. London, 1929).

_____. *Christian Beginnings*. London, 1924.

_____. *The Earliest Sources for the Life of Jesus*. 2d ed. London, 1922.

_____. "The Use of Mark in the Gospel according to Luke." In *The Beginnings of Christianity*. Vol. 2. Edited by F. J. F. Jackson and K. Lake. London, 1922.

_____. *The Gospel History and Its Transmission.* Edinburgh, 1906. 3d ed. 1911.

_____. "The Eschatological Idea in the Gospel." From the volume, *Essays on some Biblical Questions of the Day by members of the University of Cambridge.* Edited by H. B. Swete. London, 1909.

Burnett, F. W. *The Testament of Jesus-Sophia. A Redaction-Critical Study of the Eschatological Discourse in Matthew.* Washington, D.C., 1979.

Burney, C. F. *The Poetry of Our Lord.* Oxford, 1925.

Busch, F. *Zum Verständnis der synoptischen Eschatologie; Markus 13 neu untersucht.* Gütersloh, 1938.

Cadman, W. H. *The Last Journey of Jesus to Jerusalem.* Oxford, 1923.

Cadoux, A. T. "The Historic Jesus." In *The Lord of Life.* London, 1929.

_____. *The Sources of the Second Gospel.* London, 1935.

_____. *The Theology of Jesus.* London, 1940.

Carpenter, J. Estlin, *The First Three Gospels, their Origin and Relations.* 3d ed. London, 1904.

Case, S. J. "The Alleged Messianic Consciousness of Jesus." *JBL* 46 (1927).

_____. *Jesus, A New Biography.* Chicago, 1927.

Charles, R. H. *A Critical and Exegetical Commentary on the Revelation of St. John.* ICC. Edinburgh, 1920.

_____. *A Critical History of the Doctrine of a Future Life.* 1st ed. 1899; 2d ed. 1913.

Charnwood, Lord. *According to St. John.* London, 1925.

Cheyne, T. K. "Abomination of Desolation." In *Encyclopaedia Biblica,* Vol. 1, cols. 21–23. London, 1899.

Clements, R. E. "Apocalyptic, Literacy, and the Canonical Tradition." In *Eschatology in the New Testament.* Festschrift G. R. Beasley-Murray. Edited by W. H. Gloer. Pages 15–27. Peabody, Mass., 1988.

Clogg, F. B. *An Introduction to the New Testament.* London, 1937. 2d ed. 1940.

Colani, T. *Jésus Christ et les croyances messianiques de son Temps.* 2d ed. Strasbourg, 1864.

Conzelmann, H. "Geschichte und Eschaton nach Mc 13." *ZNW* 50 (1959): 210–21.

Cousar, C. B. "Eschatology and Mark's Theologia Crucis. A Critical Analysis of Mark 13." *Interpretation* 24 (1970): 321–35.

Cranfield, C. E. B. *The Gospel according to St. Mark.* CGT Commentary. Edited by C. F. D. Moule. Cambridge, 1959.

_____. "St. Mark 13." *SJT* 6 (1953): 189–96, 287–303; 7 (1954): 284–303.

Creed, J. M. *The Gospel according to St. Luke.* London, 1930.

Cullman, O. *Christ and Time.* London, 1951.

_____. *The Christology of the New Testament.* London, 1959.

_____. *Le Retour du Christ, espérance de l'Eglise, selon le Nouveau Testament.* Neuchâtel, 1948.

_____. *Salvation in History.* London, 1967.

Curtis, W. A. *Jesus Christ the Teacher.* London, 1943.

Dalman, G. *Jesus-Jeschua.* London, 1929.

_____. *Sacred Sites and Ways.* London, 1935.

_____. *The Words of Jesus.* Edinburgh, 1909.

Darby, J. N. *Synopsis of the Books of the Bible.* Vol. 3. 3d. ed. London. 1877.

Daube, D. "The Abomination of Desolation." *The New Testament and Rabbinic Judaism.* London, 1956.

_____. "Public Pronouncement and Private Explanation in the Gospels." *ExpT* 57 (7, 1946).

Davidson, S. *Doctrine of the Last Things contained in the N.T.* London, 1882.

Davies, J. Newton. "Mark." *The Abingdon Bible Commentary.* Edited by F. C. Eiselen, E. Lewis, and D. G. Downey. New York, 1929.

Dehn, G. *Der Gottessohn, Die Urchristliche Botschaft.* Vol. 2. Hamburg, 1953.

Denney, J. *Jesus and the Gospel.* 4th ed. London, 1913.

De Pressensé, E. *Jesus Christ: His Times, Life and Work.* 7th ed. London, 1879.

Dewar, F. "Chapter 13 and the Passion Narrative in St. Mark." *Theology* 64 (1961): 99–107.

Dewick, E. C. *Primitive Christian Eschatology.* Cambridge, 1912.

Dibelius, M. *A Fresh Approach to the New Testament and Early Christian Literature.* London, 1936.

_____. *Gospel Criticism and Christology.* London, 1935.

_____. *Jesus.* ET Philadelphia, 1949.

Dieterich, A. *Nekyia: Beiträge zur Erklärung der neuentdeckten Petrusapokalypse.*

von Dobschütz, E. *The Eschatology of the Gospels.* London, 1910.

Dodd, C. H. *The Apostolic Preaching and its Developments.* London, 1936. 2d ed. 1944.

_____. *The Coming of Christ.* Cambridge, 1951.

_____. "The Fall of Jerusalem and the 'Abomination of Desolation.' " *Journal of Roman Studies* 37 (1947).

_____. *History and the Gospel.* London, 1938.

_____. *The Parables of the Kingdom.* London, 1935, rev. 1936.

_____. "The 'Primitive Catechism' and the Sayings of Jesus." *More New Testament Studies.* Pages 11–29. Manchester, 1968.

Donahue, J. R. *Are you the Christ?* SBLDS 10. Pages 128–35, 168–71. Missoula, 1973.

Dougall, L. and C. W. Emmet. *The Lord of Thought.* London, 1922.

Drewermann, E. *Das Markusevangelium.* Vol. 2: Mk 9,14—16,20. Olten and Freiburg im Breisgau, 1988.

Driver, S. R. "Abomination of Desolation." *A Dictionary of the Bible,* 1:12–13.

Duncan, G. S. *Jesus, Son of Man.* London, 1947.

Dungan, D. L. *The Interrelations of the Gospels, A Symposium.* Edited by D. L. Dungan. BETL 95. Louvain, 1990.

Dupont, J. "Il n'en sera pas laissée pierre sur pierre (Mc 13,2; Luc 19,44)." *Biblica* 52 (1971): 301–20.

_____. "La parabole du maître qui rentre dans la nuit (Mc 13, 34–36)." *Mélanges Bibliques au B. Rigaux.* Edited by A. Descamps and A. de Halleux. Pages 89–116. Gembloux, 1970.

_____. "La ruine du temple et la fin des temps dans le discours de Marc 13." *Apocalypses et Théologie de L'espérance.* Lectio Divina 95. Pages 207–70. Paris, 1977.

Easton, B. S. *Christ in the Gospels.* The Hale Lectures, 1929–30. New York and London, 1930.

_____. *The Gospel according to St. Luke. A Critical and Exegetical Commentary.* ICC. Edinburgh, 1926.

Edersheim, A. *The Life and Times of Jesus the Messiah.* London, 1883. 2d ed. 1884.

Eisler, R. *The Messiah Jesus and John the Baptist.* London, 1931.

Emmet, C. W. *The Eschatological Question in the Gospels.* Edinburgh, 1911.

Ernst, J. *Das Evangelium nach Markus.* RNT. Edited by J. Eckert and O. Knoch. Regensburg, 1981.

Farrer, A. *A Study in St. Mark.* London, 1951.

Feine, P. and J. Behm. *Einleitung in das neue Testament.* 9th ed. Heidelberg, 1950.

Fiebig, P. *Der Menschensohn.* Tübingen and Leipzig, 1901.

Findlay, A. F. *Byways in Early Chrisitan Literature*. Edinburgh, 1923.

Fitzmeyer, J. A. *The Gospel according to Luke*. 2 vols. Anchor Bible 29, 29A. Garden City, New York, 1981–85.

Flew, R. Newton. *Jesus and His Church*. 2d ed. London, 1943.

Flückiger, F. "Die Redaktion der Zukunftsrede in Markus 13." *TZ* 26 (1970): 395–409.

_____. *Der Ursprung des christlichen Dogmas*. Zollikon-Zürich, 1955.

Ford, D. *The Abomination of Desolation in Biblical Eschatology*. Washington, D.C., 1979.

Frame, J. E. *A Critical and Exegetical Commentary on the Epistles of St. Paul to the Thessalonians*. ICC. Edinburgh, 1912.

France, R. T. *Jesus and the Old Testament. His Application of Old Testament Passages to Himself and His Mission*. London, 1971.

von Gall, A. F. BASILEIA TOU THEOU. *Eine religionsgeschichtliche Studie zur vorkirchlichen Eschatologie*. Heidelberg, 1926.

Gardner-Smith, P. *The Christ of the Gospels*. Cambridge, 1938.

Gaston, L. *No Stone on Another. Studies in the Significance of the Fall of Jerusalem in the Synoptic Gospels*. SNT 23. Leiden, 1970.

Geddert, T. J. *Watchwords. Mark 13 in Markan Eschatology*. JSNT Supplement Series 26. Sheffield, 1989.

Geiger, R. *Die Lukanischen Endzeitreden, Studien zur Eschatologie des Lukas-Evangeliums*. Europäische Hochschulschriften, Series 23. Theologie 16. Bern-Frankfurt a.M., 1973.

Geldenhuys, N. *Commentary on the Gospel of Luke*. NICNT. Grand Rapids, 1950.

Gess, W. F. *Christi Zeugnis von seiner Person und seinem Werk*. Basel, 1870.

Glasson, T. F. "Mark XIII and the Greek Old Testament." *ExpT* 69 (1957–58): 213–15.

_____. *The Second Advent*. London, 1945. 3d ed. 1963.

Gloege, G. *Das Reich Gottes im Neuen Testament*. Borna-Leipzig, 1928.

_____. *Reich Gottes und Kirche im Neuen Testament*. Neutestamentliche Forschungen. Edited by O. Schmitz. Gütersloh, 1929.

Gnilka, J. *Das Evangelium nach Markus*. EKK 2/2. Edited by J. Blank, etc. Neukirchen-Vluyn, 1978–79.

_____. "Markus 13 in der Diskussion." *BZ* (1969): 129–34.

Godet, F. "A Commentary on the Gospel of Luke." *Clarke's Foreign Theological Library,* 4th series, Vol. 45, 5th ed. (Translated from the 2d French ed. of 1870).

Goguel, M. *The Life of Jesus*. London, 1933. (Translated from *La Vie de Jésus*. Paris, 1932.)

Goodspeed, E. J. *A Life of Jesus*. New York, 1950.

Grant, F. C. *The Earliest Gospel*. New York, 1943.

_____. *The Gospel of the Kingdom*. New York, 1940.

Grässer, E. *Das Problem der Parusieverzögerung in den synoptischen Evangelien und in der Apostelgeschichte*. Supplement to *ZNW* 22. Berlin, 1957.

Grayston, K. "The Study of Mark 13." *BJRL* 56 (1974): 371–87.

Grob, R. *Einfuhrung in das Markus Evangelium*. Zürich, 1965.

Grundmann, W. *Das Evangelium nach Markus*. TKNT 2. Edited by E. Fascher. Berlin, 1959.

Guelich, R. "Mark 13: A Text under Scrutiny." Paper for SNTS Seminar on Mark. Cambridge, 1988.

Guignebert, C. *Jesus*. (Translated from the French.) London, 1935.

Gundry, R. H. *Matthew: A Commentary on His Literary and Theological Art*. Grand Rapids, 1982.

Gunkel, H. *Schöpfung und Chaos in Urzeit und Endzeit.* Göttingen, 1895.
_____. *Zum religionsgeschichtlichen Verständnis des Neuen Testaments.* Göttingen, 1903. 3d ed. 1930.
Gunther, J. J. "The Fate of the Jerusalem Church, The Flight to Pella." *ThZ* 29 (1973): 81–94.
Guy, H. A. *The New Testament Doctrine of the "Last Things."* London, 1948.
_____. *New Testament Prophecy. Its Origin and Significance.* London, 1947.
Haenchen, E. *Der Weg Jesu: Eine Erklärung des Markus-Evangeliums und der kanonischen Parallelen.* Berlin, 1966.
Hahn, F. "Die Rede von der Parusie des Menschensohnes Markus 13." In *Jesus und der Menschensohn.* Festschrift A. Vögtle. Edited by R. Pesch and R. Schnackenburg. Pages 240–66. Freiburg, etc., 1975.
Harder, G. "Das eschatologische Geschichtsbild der sogenannten kleinen Apokalypse Markus 13." *Theologia Viatorum* 4. Jahrbuch der kirchlichen Hochschule Berlin, 1952. Pages 71–107. Berlin, 1953.
Hare, D. R. A. *The Theme of Jewish Persecution of Christians in the Gospel According to Matthew.* SNTSMS 6. Cambridge, 1967.
Harnack, A. *The Date of the Acts and of the Synoptic Gospels.* London, 1911.
_____. "What is Christianity?" *Theological Translation Library* 14. London, 1901.
Harrington, W. *Mark. A Biblical-Theological Commentary.* NTM 4. Dublin and Wilmington, Delaware, 1979.
Hartman, L. *Prophecy Interpreted. The Formation of some Jewish Apocalyptic Texts and of the Eschatological Discourse Mark 13 Par.* Coniectanea Biblica NT Series 1. Lund, 1966.
Hase, C. *Leben Jesu.* Leipzig, 1829. 2d ed. 1835. 3d ed. 1840. ET from 3d and 4th editions, 1860.
Hastings, J., ed. *A Dictionary of Christ and the Gospels.* 2 vols. Edinburgh, 1906.
Hauck, F. *Das Evangelium des Markus. Theologischer Handkommentar zum Neuen Testament.* Leipzig, 1931.
Haupt, D. Erich. *Die eschatologischen Aussagen Jesu in den synoptischen Evangelien.* Berlin, 1895.
Headlam, A. C. *The Life and Teaching of Jesus the Christ.* London, 1923.
Heard, R. *An Introduction to the New Testament.* London, 1950.
Heitmüller, W. *Im Namen Jesu.* FRLANT. Edited by W. Bousset and H. Gunkel. Göttingen, 1903.
Hengel, M. *The Son of God. The Origin of Christology and the History of Jewish-Hellenistic Religion.* London, 1976. Studies in the Gospel of Mark. London, 1985.
Héring, J. *Le Royaume de Dieu et sa Venue.* Paris, 1937.
Hermann, I. *L'évangile de saint Marc.* Paris, 1969.
_____. "Die Gefährdung der Welt und ihre Erneuerung. Auslegung von Mk 13, 1–37." *BuL* 7 (1966): 305–9.
Hogg, A. G. *Christ's Message of the Kingdom.* Edinburgh, 1913.
Hofer, J. and K. Rahner, eds. *Lexikon für Theologie und Kirche.* 10 vols. 1906.
Holdsworth, W. W. *Gospel Origins.* London, 1913.
Hölscher, G. "Der Ursprung der Apokalypse Mk. 13." *Theologische Blätter.* Leipzig, July 1933.
Holtzmann, H. J. *Hand-Kommentar zum Neuen Testament, erster Band, die Synoptiker.* Freiburg, 1889.
_____. *Lehrbuch der historisch-kritischen Einleitung in das Neue Testament.* Freiburg, 1885.
_____. *Lehrbuch der neutestamentlichen Theologie.* Leipzig, 1897.

_____. *Die synoptischen Evangelien, ihr Ursprung und geschichtlicher Charakter.* Leipzig, 1863.

Holtzmann, O. *Leben Jesu.* Tübingen and Leipzig, 1901. ET *The Life of Jesus,* London, 1904.

Hooke, S. H. *The Kingdom of God in the Experience of Jesus.* The Colet Library of Modern Christian Thought and Teaching 8. London, 1949.

Hooker, M. *The Son of Man in Mark: A Study of the Background of the Term "Son of Man" and Its Use in St. Mark's Gospel.* London, 1967.

_____. "Trial and Tribulation in Mark XIII." *BJRL* 65 (1982): 78–99.

Hort, F. J. A. *Judaistic Christianity.* Cambridge and London, 1894.

_____. *The Apocalypse of St. John I–III.* London, 1908.

Horton, R. F. *The Growth of the New Testament.* London, 1913.

Hoskyns, E. C. and N. Davey. *The Fourth Gospel.* 1940. 2d ed. London 1947.

_____. *The Riddle of the New Testament.* 1st ed. 1931. 3d ed. London, 1936.

Howard, W. F. *Christianity according to St. John.* London, 1943.

Hunkin, J. W. *The New Testament, A Conspectus.* The Colet Library of Modern Christian Thought and Teaching 10. London, 1950.

Hunter, A. M. *The Gospel according to Saint Mark.* Torch Bible Commentaries. London, 1948.

Jackson, H. Latimer. *The Eschatology of Jesus.* London, 1913.

Jacobsen, A. *Untersuchungen über die synoptische Evangelien.* Berlin, 1883.

James, M. R. *The Apocryphal New Testament.* Oxford, 1924.

Jeremias, J. *Die Abendsmahlworte Jesu.* 2d ed. Göttingen, 1949.

_____. "Jesus als Weltvollender." *Beiträge zur Förderung christlicher Theologie.* Edited by A. Schlatter and W. Lütgert. Vol. 33, Heft 4. Gütersloh, 1930.

_____. *New Testament Theology, The Proclamation of Jesus.* London, 1971.

_____. *The Parables of Jesus.* Revised ed. London, 1963.

_____. *The Prayers of Jesus.* London, 1967.

Johnson, S. E. *The Gospel according to St. Mark,* Black's New Testament Commentaries. London, 1960. (= Harper New Testament Commentaries. New York, etc., 1961).

Jülicher, A. *Einleitung in das neue Testament.* Freiburg and Leipzig, 1894.

_____. "Die Religion Jesu und die Anfänge des Christentums bis zum Nicaenum." A Contribution to *Die christliche Religion.* Part 1; Section 4 of *Die Kultur der Gegenwart.* Edited by Paul Hinneberg. Berlin and Leipzig, 1906.

_____. *Die Gleichnisreden Jesu.* 2 vols. Tübingen, 1910.

Keck, F. *Die öffentliche Abschiedsrede Jesu in Lk 20, 45–21, 36. Eine redaktions- und motivgeschichtliche Untersuchung.* Forschung zur Bibel 25. Edited by R. Schnackenburg and J. Schreiner. Stuttgart, 1976.

Kee, H. C. *The Community of the New Age, Studies in Mark's Gospel.* Philadelphia, 1977.

Keim, J. *Geschichte Jesu von Nazara in ihrer Verkettung mit dem Gesammtleben seines Volkes.* Vol. 3. Zürich, 1872. ET *Jesus of Nazara,* Vol. 5. London, 1881.

Kelber, W. *The Kingdom in Mark, A New Place and a New Time.* Philadelphia, 1974.

Kelly, W. *An Exposition of the Gospel of Mark.* Edited with additions by E. E. Whitfield. London and Glasgow, 1907; 2d ed. 1927.

_____. *Lectures on the Gospel of Matthew.* London, 1868.

Kennedy, H. A. A. *St. Paul's Conceptions of the Last Things.* London, 1904.

Klausner, J. *Jesus of Nazareth*. (Hebrew) Jerusalem, 1922. ET London, 1925.

Klostermann, E. "Das Markusevangelium." *Handbuch zum Neuen Testament*. Founded by H. Lietzmann, Vol. 3. Tübingen, 4th ed. 1950.

Knopf, R., H. Lietzmann, and H. Weinel. *Einführung in das neue Testament*. 5th ed. Berlin, 1949.

Knox, W. L. *The Sources of the Synoptic Gospels*. Vol. 1. Edited by H. Chadwick. Cambridge, 1953.

Koch, D. A. "Zum Verhältnis von Christologie und Eschatologie im Markusevangelium." In *Jesus Christus in Historie und Theologie*, Festschrift H. Conzelmann. Edited by G. Strecker. Pages 395–408. Tübingen, 1975.

Kümmel, W. G. "Eschatological Expectation in the Proclamation of Jesus." In Essays for R. Bultmann, *The Future of our Religious Past*. Edited by J. M. Robinson. Pages 29–48. London, 1971.

_____. "Jesus und der jüdische Traditionsgedanke." *ZNW* 33 (1934): 105–30.

_____. *Promise and Fulfilment*. Revised ed. London, 1957.

_____. *Verheissung und Erfüllung*. Abhandlungen zur Theologie des alten und neuen Testaments 6. Basel, 1945.

Kunzi, M. *Das Naherwartungslogion Markus 9.1 par*. Beiträge zur Geschichte der Biblischen Exegese 21. Edited by O. Cullmann, etc. Tübingen, 1977.

Ladd, G. E. *The Presence of the Future. The Eschatology of Biblical Realism*. Grand Rapids, 1974. (A revision of *Jesus and the Kingdom*. New York, 1964).

_____. *A Theology of the New Testament*. Grand Rapids, 1974.

Lagrange, M. J. "L'Avènement du Fils de l'Homme." *Revue Biblique* (1906): 382ff.

_____. *Evangile selon Saint Marc*. Paris, 1911.

Lake, K. and S. *An Introduction to the New Testament*. London, 1938.

Lambrecht, J. "Die Logia-Quellen von Markus 13." *Biblica* 47 (1966): 321–360.

_____. *Die Redaktion der Markus-Apokalypse. Literarische Analyse und Strukturuntersuchung*. Analecta Biblica 28. Rome, 1967.

Lane, W. L. *The Gospel of Mark*. New International Commentary on the New Testament. Edited by F. F. Bruce. Grand Rapids, 1974.

Leckie, J. H. *The World to Come and Final Destiny*. Edinburgh, 1918.

Legasse, S. "Le discours eschatologique de Mc 13 d'après trois ouvrages récents." *BLE* 71 (1970): 241–61.

Levertoff, P. P. and H. L. Goudge. "The Gospel according to St. Matthew." *A New Commentary on Holy Scripture*. Edited by C. Gore, H. L. Goudge, A. Guillaume. London, 1928.

Lietzmann, H. *The Beginnings of the Christian Church*. ET London, 1937, revised 1949.

Lightfoot, R. H. *The Gospel Message of St. Mark*. Oxford, 1950.

_____. *History and Interpretation in the Gospels*. London, 1935.

_____. *Locality and Doctrine in the Gospels*. London, 1938.

Loader, W. R. G. "The Apocalyptic Model of Sonship: Its Origin and Development in New Testament Tradition." *JBL* 97 (1978): 525–64.

Lohmeyer, E. *Das Evangelium des Markus*. MeyerK 2. 2d ed. Göttingen, 1951.

Loisy, A. *L'Evangile selon Marc*. Paris, 1912.

_____. *The Origins of the New Testament*. London, 1950.

Lowrie, W. *Jesus according to St. Mark. An Interpretation of St. Mark's Gospel*. London, 1929.

Luce, H. K. *The Gospel according to S. Luke*. CGT. Cambridge, 1933.

Lührmann, D. "Markus 14,55–64: Christologie und Zerstörung des Tempels im Markusevangelium." *NTS* 27 (1981): 457–74.

_____. *Das Markusevangelium.* HNT 3. Edited by A. Lindemann. Tübingen, 1987.

McCown, C. C. "The Eschatology of Jesus Reconsidered." *Journal of Religion* 16 (1936).

MacCulloch, J. A. "Eschatology." *Encyclopaedia of Religion and Ethics,* Vol. 5. Edinburgh, 1912.

McGiffert, A. C. "Epistle to the Thessalonians." *Encylopaedia Biblica.* Vol. 4. London, 1903.

Mackinnon, J. *The Historic Jesus.* London, New York, and Toronto, 1931.

Mackintosh, H. R. *Immortality and the Future.* London, New York, and Toronto, 1915. 2d ed. 1917.

McNeile, A. H. *The Gospel according to St. Matthew.* London, 1915.

McNicol, A. J. "The Composition of the Synoptic Eschatological Discourse." In *The Interrelations of the Gospels.* Edited by D. J. Dungan. BETL 95. Pages 157–200. Louvain, 1990.

Maddox, R. *The Purpose of Luke–Acts.* FRLANT. Edited by W. Schrage and E. Wurthwein. Göttingen, 1982.

Major, H. D. A. "The Gospel according to St. Mark." In *The Mission and Message of Jesus.* London, 1937.

Mann, C. S. *The Gospel According to Mark.* Anchor Bible 27. New York, 1986.

Manson, T. W. *The Sayings of Jesus.* (Book 2 of *The Mission and Message of Jesus.*) London, 1937.

_____. *The Teaching of Jesus.* Cambridge, 1931.

Manson, William, *Christ's View of the Kingdom of God.* London, 1918.

_____. *The Gospel of Luke.* MNTC. London, 1930.

Marshall, I. H. *The Gospel of Luke: A Commentary on the Greek Text.* NIGTC. Exeter and Grand Rapids, 1978.

Martin, H. *The Necessity of the Second Coming.* London, 1928.

Marxsen, W. *Mark the Evangelist. Studies on the Redaction History of the Gospel.* Nashville, 1969.

Mathews, S. *The Messianic Hope in the New Testament.* Chicago, 1905.

Mauriac, F. *Vie de Jésus.* Collection l'Histoire. Edited by E. Flammarion. 2d ed. Paris, 1936.

Menzies, A. *The Earliest Gospel.* London, 1901.

Merx, A. *Die Evangelien des Markus und Lukas nach der syrischen im Sinaikloster gefundenen Palimpsesthandschrift.* Berlin, 1905.

_____. *Das Evangelium Matthäus nach der syrischen im Sinaikloster gefundenen Palimpsesthandschrift.* Berlin, 1902.

Meyer, A. *Jesus Muttersprache.* Freiburg and Leipzig, 1896.

Meyer, Ed. *Ursprung und Anfänge des Christentums.* Vol. 1. Stuttgart and Berlin, 1921.

Meyer, H. A. W. *Kritisch exegetisches Handbuch über das Evangelium des Markus und Lukas.* 3d. ed. Göttingen, 1855.

_____. *Kritisch exegetisches Handbuch über das Evangelium des Matthäus.* 3d ed. Göttingen, 1853.

Michaelis, W. *Einleitung in das neue Testament.* Bern, 1946.

_____. *Der Herr verzieht nicht die Verheissung; Die Aussagen Jesu über die Nähe des Jüngsten Tages.* Bern, 1942.

Micklem, P. A. *St. Matthew.* Westminster Commentaries. Edited by W. Lock. London, 1917.

Milligan, G. *The New Testament Documents. Their Origin and Early History.* London, 1913.

Minette de Tillesse, G. *Le Secret Messianique dans l'Evangile de Marc.* Paris, 1968.

Moffatt, J. *An Introduction to the Literature of the New Testament*. Edinburgh, 1911. 3d. ed. 1918.

_____. *The Theology of the Gospels*. London, 1912.

Monnier, H. *La Mission Historique de Jésus*. 2d ed. Paris, 1914.

Montefiore, C. G. *The Synoptic Gospels*. London, 1909. 2d ed. 1927.

Morgan, G. C. *The Gospel according to Matthew*. New York, etc.

Muirhead, L. A. "Eschatology." *A Dictionary of Christ and the Gospels*. Edited by J. Hastings, Vol. 1. Edinburgh, 1906.

_____. *The Eschatology of Jesus*. London, 1st ed. 1904, 3d ed. 1906.

_____. *The Terms Life and Death in the Old and New Testaments, and other Papers*. London, 1908.

Müller, E. F. K. "Wiederkunft Christi." In *Realencyklopädie für protestantische Theologie und Kirche*. Vol. 21. 3d ed. Leipzig, 1908.

Murray, J. M. *The Life of Jesus*. London, 1926.

Mussner, F. *Christ and the End of the World*. Contemporary Catechetics. Edited by J. Goldbrunner. Univ. of Notre Dame, 1965.

Nairne, A. "The Epistle of Priesthood." *Studies in the Epistle to the Hebrews*. Edinburgh,1913.

Neander, A. *The Life of Jesus Christ in Its Historical Connexion and Historical Development*. London, 1853 (from 4th German ed. 1st ed. 1837).

Neirynck, F. "Le Discours Anti-Apocalyptique de Mc. XIII." *ETL* 45 (1969): 154–64.

_____. *Duality in Mark. Contributions to the Study of the Markan Redaction*. BETL 31. Leuven, 1972.

_____. "The Eschatological Discourse." In *The Interrelations of the Gospels*. Edited by D. J. Dungan. Pages 108–24. BETL 95. Louvain, 1990.

_____. "L'Evangile de Marc, à propos du Commentaire de R. Pesch." *Analecta Lovaniensa Biblica et Orientalia*. Sevr. Fasc. 38 (1979) 8–27.

_____. "Marc 13. Examen critique de l'interprétation de R. Pesch." In *L'Apocalypse johannique et l'apocalyptique dans le Nouveau Testament*. Edited by J. Lambrecht. BETL 53. Pages 369–401. Leuven, 1980.

_____. "Note on the Eschatological Discourse." In *The Interrelations of the Gospels*. Edited by D. J. Dungan. BETL 95. Pages 77–80. Louvain, 1990.

Nineham, D. *Saint Mark*. The Pelican Gospel Commentaries. London, 1963.

Oesterley, W. O. E. *The Doctrine of the Last Things. Jewish and Christian*. London, 1909.

Olmstead, A. T. *Jesus in the Light of History*. New York, 1942.

Otto, R. *The Kingdom of God and Son of Man*. London, 1938 (ET of *Reich Gottes und Menschensohn*, 1934).

Papini, G. *The Story of Christ*. London, 1923.

Peake, A. S. *A Critical Introduction to the New Testament*.

Perrin, N. *Jesus and the Language of the Kingdom*. London, 1976.

_____. *The Kingdom of God in the Teaching of Jesus*. London. 1963.

_____. "Mark 14,62: The End Product of a Christian Pesher Tradition?" *NTS* 12 (1965–66): 150–55.

_____. *A Modern Pilgrimage in New Testament Christology*. London, 1974.

_____. *The New Testament, an Introduction*. New York, 1974.

_____. *Rediscovering the Teaching of Jesus*. London, 1967.

Perrot, C. "Essai sur le discours eschatologique (Mc 13, 1–37 parr)." *RScR* 47 (1959): 481–514.

Pesch, R. "Markus 13." In *L'Apocalypse johannique et l'apocalyptique dans le Nouveau Testament*. Edited by J. Lambrecht. Pages 355–68. Leuven, 1980.

_____. *Das Markusevangelium*. HTKNT. Freiburg, etc. Part 1, 1976. Part 2, 1977.

_____. *Naherwartungen, Tradition und Redaktion in Mk 13*. Düsseldorf, 1968.

_____. "Die Passion des Menschensohnes. Eine Studie zu den Menschensohnworten der vormarkinischen Passionsgeschichte." In *Jesus und der Menschensohn*. Edited by R. Pesch and R. Schnackenburg, Pages 166–95. 1975.

Pfleiderer, J. "Über die Composition der eschatologischen Rede, Mt. 24.4ff." *Jahrbücher für Deutsche Theologie*. Vol. 13. Gotha, 1868.

_____. *Das Urchristentum, seine Schriften und Lehren*. Berlin, 1887.

Piganiol, A. "Observations sur la date de l'apocalypse synoptique." *Revue d'Histoire et de Philosophie religieuses*. Strasbourg, 1924.

Plummer, A. *A Critical and Exegetical Commentary on the Gospel according to St. Luke*. ICC. Edinburgh, 1896. 5th ed. 1922.

_____. *An Exegetical Commentary on the Gospel according to St. Matthew*. London, 1909.

_____. *The Gospel according to St. Mark*. CGT. Cambridge, 1914.

Plumptre, E. H. "The Gospel according to St. Matthew, St. Mark and St. Luke." In *A Bible Commentary for English Readers*. Edited by C. J. Ellicott. London, 1897.

Polag, A. *Die Christologie der Logienquelle*. WMANT 45. Neukirchen-Vluyn, 1977.

Pünjer, G. C. B. "Die Wiederkunftsreden Jesu." *Zeitschrift für wissenschaftliche Theologie* 2, 1878.

Rawlinson A. E. J. *Christ in the Gospels*. Oxford, 1944.

_____. *St. Mark*. Westminister Commentaries. London, 1925.

Reese, A. *The Approaching Advent of Christ: An Examination of the Teaching of J. N. Darby and his Followers*. London, 1937.

Reimarus, C. H. S. *Fragments from Reimarus*. Edited by C. Voysey. London and Edinburgh, 1870. (ET of *Von dem Zwecke Jesu und seiner Jünger, noch ein Fragment des Wolfenbüttelschen Ungenannten*. Edited by G. E. Lessing. Braunschweig, 1778).

Renan, J. E. *L'Antéchrist*. *Histoire des Origines du Christianisme*. Vol. 4, 1873. ET *The Antichrist*. London, 1890.

_____. *La Vie de Jésus*. Berlin, 1863. ET London, 1935.

Rengstorf, K. H. *Das Evangelium nach Lukas*. Das neue Testament deutsch. Edited by P. Althaus and J. Behm. Vol. 3. 5th ed. Göttingen, 1949.

Réville, A. *Jésus de Nazareth*. Paris, 1897.

Reumann, J. *Jesus in the Church's Gospels*. Philadelphia, 1968.

Rigaux, B. "*Bdelygma tēs erēmōseōs*." *Biblica* 40 (1959): 675–83.

_____. "La seconde venue de Jésus." In *Messianisme et Eschatologie*. Edited by E. Massaux, etc. Rech Bib 6. Pages 173–216. Louvain, 1962.

Roark, D. M. "The Great Eschatological Discourse." *NovT* 7 (1964–65): 123–27.

Robertson, A. *Regnum Dei.* Bampton Lectures 1901. London, 1901.

Robinson, J. A. T. *In the End, God*. London, 1950.

_____. *Jesus and His Coming: The Emergence of a Doctrine*. London, 1957.

Robinson, J. M. *The Problem of History in Mark*. SBT 21. London, 1957.

Robinson, T. H. *The Gospel of Matthew*. MNTC. London, 1928.

Ropes, J. H. *The Synoptic Gospels*. Cambridge, Mass., 1934.

Rousseau, F. "La structure de Marc 13." *Bib* 56 (1975): 157–72.

Rowley, H. H. *The Relevance of Apocalyptic*. London, 1944. 2d ed. 1947.

Russell, J. S. *The Parousia. A Critical Enquiry into the New Testament Doctrine of our Lord's Second Coming*. London, 1878.

Salmond, S. D. F. *The Christian Doctrine of Immortality*. Edinburgh, 1895. 4th ed. 1901. 5th ed. 1903.

_____. *The Gospel according to St. Mark*. Century Bible. London.

Sanday, W. "The Apocalyptic Element in the Gospels." *Hibbert Journal* 10 (1, 1911).

_____. "Jesus Christ." *Dictionary of the Bible*. 2. Reprinted as *Outlines of the Life of Christ*. Edinburgh, 1905.

_____. *The Life of Christ in Recent Research*. Oxford, 1907.

Sanday, W., and A. C. Headlam. *A Critical and Exegetical Commentary on the Epistle to the Romans*. ICC. Edinburgh, 1895, 5th ed. 1902.

Schenkel, D. *Das Charakterbild Jesu. Ein biblischer Versuch*. Wiesbaden, 1864.

Schlatter, A. "Das Evangelium nach Markus und Lukas." *Schlatters Erläuterungen zum Neuen Testament*. Stuttgart, 1947.

_____. "Das Evangelium nach Matthäus." *Schlatters Erläuterungen zum Neuen Testament*. Stuttgart, 1947.

Schlink, Prof. E. "A Meditation on the Christian Hope." *Ecumenical Review*. Geneva, January 1952.

Schlosser J. "La Parole de Jésus sur la Fin du Temple." *NTS* 36 (1990): 398–414.

Schmid, J. "Das evangelium nach Markus." *Das Neue Testament*. Edited by A. Wikenhauser and O. Kuss. Vol. 2. Regensburg, 1950.

Schmidt, E. *Das Evangelium nach Markus*. RNT. Regensburg, 1981.

Schmidt, K. L. *Der Rahmen der Geschichte Jesu*. Berlin, 1919.

Schmidt, N. *The Prophet of Nazareth*. New York, 1905.

Schmiedel, P. W. "The Gospels." *Encyclopaedia Biblica*. Vol. 2. Cols. 1857, 1887–88. London, 1901.

Schmithals, W. *Das Evangelium nach Markus. Kapitel 9, 2–16, 18*. OTKNT. Edited by E. Grässer and K. Kertelge. Vol. 2/2, Gütersloh, 1979.

Schnackenburg, R. *Das Evangelium nach Markus*. Geistliche Schriftlesung, Düsseldorf, 1966.

_____. *God's Rule and Kingdom*. London, 1963.

_____. "Kirche und Parusie." In *Gott und Welt*. Festschrift K. Rahner. Vol. 1. Pages 551–78. Freiburg, 1964.

_____. "Naherwartung." *Lexikon fur Theologie und Kirche*. Vol. 7. Cols. 777–79.

Schniewind, J. "Das Evangelium nach Markus." *Das Neue Testament Deutsch*. 5th ed. Göttingen, 1947.

_____. "Das Evangelium nach Matthäus." *Das Neue Testament Deutsch*. 5th ed. Göttingen, 1950.

Schoeps, H. J. "Ebionitische Apokalyptik im Neuen Testament." *ZNW* 51 (1960): 101–11.

_____. *Theologie und Geschichte des Judenchristentums*. Tübingen, 1949.

Schräder, E. *Die Keilinschriften und das Alte Testament*. 3d ed. Revised by H. Zimmern. Berlin, 1903.

Schreiber, J. *Theologie des Vertrauens*. Hamburg, 1967.

Schulz, S. *Die Spruchquelle der Evangelisten*. Zürich, 1972.

Schwartz, E. "Der verfluchte Feigenbaum." *ZNW* (1904).

Schwartzkopff, P. *Die Weissagungen Jesu Christi von seinem Tode, seiner Auferstehung und Wiederkunft und ihr Erfüllung*. Göttingen, 1895.

Schweitzer, A. *The Quest of the Historical Jesus*. (*Von Reimarus zu Wrede*, 1906). ET London, 1910.

Schweizer, E. *The Good News according to Mark*. Richmond, Virginia, 1970.

Scofield, C. I. *The Holy Bible,* with a new system of connected topical references to all the greater themes of Scripture, with annotations, revised marginal renderings, summaries, definitions, chronology, and index. Oxford, 1909. 2d ed. 1917.

Scott, E. F. *The Kingdom and the Messiah*. Edinburgh, 1911.

_____. *"The Literature of the New Testament": Records of Civilisation.* Edited under the auspices of the Department of History, Columbia University. New York, 1932.

Selwyn, E. C. *The Oracles in the New Testament.* London, 1912.

_____. *The Teaching of Christ.* London, 1915.

Simkhovitch, V. G. *Toward the Understanding of Jesus.* New York, 1921.

Smith, B. T. D. *The Gospel according to S. Matthew.* CGT. Cambridge, 1927.

Smith, David. *The Days of His Flesh.* The Earthly Life of our Lord and Saviour Jesus Christ. London, 1905. 8th ed. 1910.

_____. *The Disciple's Commentary on the Gospels.* London, 1928.

Sneen, D. *Visions of Hope.* Minneapolis, Minn., 1978.

von Soden, D. F. H. *Urchristliche Literaturgeschichte.* Berlin, 1905.

Sowers, S. "The Circumstances and Recollections of the Pella Flight." *ThZ* 26 (1970): 305–20.

Stanton, V. H. *The Gospels as Historical Documents.* Part 2, *The Synoptic Gospels.* Cambridge, 1909.

Stevens, G. B. *The Theology of the New Testament.* 1st ed. 1901. 2d ed. Edinburgh, 1906.

Stonehouse, N. B. *The Witness of Luke to Christ.* London, 1951.

_____. *The Witness of Matthew and Mark to Christ.* Philadelphia, 1944.

Strack, H. L. and P. Billerbeck. *Kommentar zum Neuen Testament aus Talmud und Midrasch.* 5 vols. Munich, 1922.

Strauss, F. *Das Leben Jesu.* 2 vols. 1835–36. Translated from the 4th ed. by George Eliot, *The Life of Jesus Critically Examined.* London, 1846.

_____. *Das Leben Jesu für das deutsche Volk bearbeitet,* Leipzig, 1864. Translated as *A New Life of Jesus.* London, 1865.

Streeter, B. H. "The Historic Christ." *Essay in Foundations. A Statement of Christian Belief in Terms of Modern Thought.* London, 1912.

_____. *Studies in the Synoptic Problem by Members of the University of Oxford.* Oxford, 1911.

_____. *The Four Gospels.* London, 1924.

Suhl, A. *Die Funktion der alttestamentlichen Zitate und Anspielungen im Markusevangelium.* Gütersloh, 1965.

Swete, H. B. *The Apocalypse of St. John.* London, 1906. 3d ed. 1909.

_____. *The Gospel according to St. Mark.* London, 1898. 3d ed. 1909.

Taylor, V. "The Apocalyptic Discourse of Mark 13." *ExpT* 60 (4, 1949.

_____. *Behind the Third Gospel: A Study of the Proto-Luke Hypothesis.* Oxford, 1926.

_____. *The Gospel according to St. Mark.* London, 1952.

_____. *The Gospels: A Short Introduction.* London, 1930. 4th ed. 1938.

Telford, W. R. *The Barren Temple and the Withered Tree, A Redaction-critical Analysis of the Cursing of the Fig-Tree Pericope in Mark's Gospel and Its Relation to the Cleansing of the Temple Tradition.* JSNT Sup 1. Sheffield, 1980.

Theissen, G. "Die Tempelweissagung Jesu." *TZ* 32 (1976).

Thomas, G. "Jüdische Apokalyptik am Ende der ersten nachchristlichen Jahrhunderts." *Kairos* 11 (1969): 134–44.

Titius, A. *Jesu Lehre vom Reiche Gottes.* Vol. 1 of *Die neutestamentliche Lehre von der Seligkeit.* Freiburg and Leipzig, 1895.

Tödt, H. E. *The Son of Man in the Synoptic Tradition.* London, 1963.

Torrey, C. C. *Documents of the Primitive Church.* New York and London, 1941.

_____. *The Four Gospels.* London, 1933.

_____. *Our Translated Gospels.* London, 1937.

Trocmé, E. *The Formation of the Gospel according to Mark.* ET London, 1975.

Tuckett, C. M. "The Eschatological Discourse." In *The Interrelations of the Gospels*. Edited by D. L. Dungan. BETL 95. Pages 63–76. Louvain, 1990.

Turner, C. H. "The Gospel according to St. Mark." *A New Commentary on Holy Scripture*. Edited by C. Gore, H. L. Goudge, A. Guillaume. London, 1928.

Turner, C. H. "Marcan Usage: Notes, Critical and Exegetical on the Second Gospel." *JTS* 25–29 (1924–28).

Turner, N. *A Grammar of New Testament Greek*. Vol. 4, *Style*. Edinburgh, 1976.

van Iersel, B. M. F. *"Der Sohn" in den synoptischen Jesusworten*. NovTSup 3. 2d ed. Leiden, 1964.

Verheyden, J. *De Vlucht van de Christensen naar Pella. Onderzoek van het Getuigenis van Eusebius en Epiphanius*. Brussels, 1988. English summary in "The Flight of the Christians to Pella. A Study of the Testimony of Eusebius and Epiphanius." *ETL*, 1990.

Vermes, G. *Jesus the Jew, A Historian's Reading of the Gospels*. New York, 1973.

Vischer, Eberhard. *Die Offenbarung Johannis*. Leipzig, 1886.

Vögtle, A. "Exegetische Erwägungen über das Wissen und Selbstbewusstsein Jesu." In *Gott in Welt*, Festschrift K. Rahner. Vol. 1. Pages 608–67. Freiburg, 1964.

_____. "Das markinische Verständnis der Tempelworte." In *Die Mitte des Neuen Testaments*, Festschrift E. Schweizer. Pages 362–83. Göttingen, 1983.

_____. *Das Neue Testament und die Zukunft des Kosmos*. Kommentare und Beiträge zum Alten und Neuen Testament. Düsseldorf, 1970.

Volkmar, G. *Jesus Nazarenus und die erste christliche Zeit*. Zürich, 1882.

Volz, P. *Jüdische Eschatologie von Daniel bis Akiba*. Tübingen and Leipzig, 1903.

Walter, N. "Tempelzerstörung und synoptische Apokalypse." *ZNW* 57 (1966): 38–49.

Weeden, T. *Mark, Traditions in Conflict*. Philadelphia, 1971.

Weiffenbach, W. *Die Wiederkunftsgedanken Jesu*. Leipzig, 1873.

Weiser, A. *Die Knechtsgleichnisse der synoptischen Evangelien*. Munich, 1971.

Weiss, B. *Biblical Theology of the N. T.* 3d ed. 1879. ET Edinburgh, 1882.

_____. *Evangelium des Markus. Die Evangelien des Markus und Lukas*, 6th ed. 1878, Göttingen, 8th ed. 1892.

Weiss, J. *Das älteste Evangelium*. Göttingen, 1903.

_____. "Das Markus-Evangelium." In *Die Schriften des Neuen Testaments*. Edited by Joh. Weiss. 2d ed. Göttingen, 1906.

_____. *Die Predigt Jesu vom Reiche Gottes*. Göttingen, 1892.

_____. *Das Urchristentum*. Göttingen, 1917.

Weisse, C. H. *Die Evangelienfrage in ihrem gegenwärtigen Studium*. Leipzig, 1856.

_____. *Die evangelische Geschichte: Kritisch und philosophisch bearbeitet*. Leipzig, 1838.

Weizsäcker, C. *The Apostolic Age of the Christian Church*. ET London, 1895.

_____. *Untersuchungen über die evangelische Geschichte*. Tübingen, 1864.

Wellhausen, J. *Einleitung in die drei ersten Evangelien*. 2d ed. Berlin, 1911.

_____. *Das Evangelium Marci, übersetzt und erklärt*. 2d ed. Berlin, 1909.

Wendland, E. *Die Entstehung des Marcus-Evangeliums*. Tübingen, 1908.

Wendland, H. D. *Die Eschatologie des Reiches Gottes bei Jesus*. Gütersloh, 1931.

Wendt, H. H. *Die Lehre Jesu*. Göttingen, 1886.

Wenham, D. "Paul and the Synoptic Apocalypse." In *Gospel Perspectives, Studies of History and Tradition in the Four Gospels*, 2. Edited by R. T. France and D. Wenham. Pages 345–72. Sheffield, 1981.

_____. "Recent Study of Mark 13." In *TSF Bulletin*, nos. 71 and 72, 1975.

_____. *The Rediscovery of Jesus' Eschatological Discourse*. Gospel Perspectives 4. Sheffield, 1984.

_____. "'This Generation will not Pass . . .' A Study of Jesus' Future Expectation in Mark 13." In *Christ the Lord*, Festschrift D. Guthrie. Edited by H. Rowdon. Pages 127–50. London, 1982.

Werner, M. *Die Entstehung des christlichen Dogmas*. Bern-Leipzig, 1941.

Wernle, P. *The Sources of Our Knowledge of the Life of Jesus*. London, 1907. (ET of *Die Quellen des Lebens Jesu*. Tübingen.)

Wilder, A. N. *Eschatology and Ethics in the Teaching of Jesus*. Revised ed. New York, 1950.

Williams, N. P. *Studies in the Synoptic Problem by Members of the University of Oxford*. Oxford, 1911.

Winstanley, E. W. *Jesus and the Future*. Edinburgh, 1913.

Wohlenberg, G. "Das Evangelium des Markus." *Kommentar zum Neuen Testament*. Edited by T. Zahn. Vol. 2. Leipzig, 1910.

Wood, H. G. "Mark." *A Commentary on the Bible*. Edited by A. S. Peake. London, 1920.

Worsley, F. W. *The Apocalypse of Jesus*. London, 1912.

Wrede, D. W. *Das Messiasgeheimnis in den Evangelien*. Göttingen, 1901.

Zahn, T. "Das Evangelium des Matthäus." *Kommentar zum Neuen Testament*. Edited by T. Zahn. Vol. 1. Leipzig, 1903.

_____. *Introduction to the New Testament*. Edinburgh, 1909. (From 3d ed. of the German.)

Zerwick, M. *Untersuchungen zum Markus-Stil, Ein Beitrag zur stilistischen Durcharbeitung des N.T.* Rome, 1937.

Zmijewski, J. *Die Eschatologiereden des Lukas-Evangeliums. Eine traditions- und redaktionsgeschichtliche Untersuchung zu Lk 21, 5–36 und Lk 17, 20–37*. Bonner Biblische Beiträge. Edited by G. F. Botterweck and H. Zimmermann. Bonn, 1972.

INDEX OF MODERN AUTHORS

Agbanou, V. K., 398, 442, 446
Albright, W. F., 341
Allen, W. C., 135–36, 403
Althaus, P., 156–57, 158
Ambrozic, A. M., 198–200, 353, 383, 454, 456
Anderson, H., 327, 333–35, 383, 392, 434, 452, 454, 475
André, R. P., 448
Andrews, H. T., 122–23

Bacon, B. W., 87–90, 148, 154
Baldensperger, W., 45
Bammel, E., 170
Barrett, C. K., 404
Barth, G., 214, 351
Barth, K., 238
Bauer, W., 373
Baur, F. C., 2, 8–9, 171
Beasley-Murray, G. R., 76, 163, 224, 274, 302, 307, 308, 342, 353, 367, 373, 392, 396, 397, 402, 409, 413, 415, 427, 428, 429, 430, 456, 467
Behm, J., 158
Belo, F., 316
Bengel, J. A., 17, 18, 127–28, 129, 133
Bertram, G., 452
Beyschlag, W., 24, 25, 113–14
Bietenhard, H., 391
Billerbeck, P., 294, 382, 402, 405, 409
Blank, J., 282

Bleek, F., 10
Blunt, A. W. F., 403
Boismard, M.-E., 229, 230, 231, 233–36
Bonnard, P., 449, 452
Borg, M. J., 254
Borsch, F. H., 175
Boring, M. E., 220–24
Bornkamm, G., 162, 214, 215, 351, 352, 455
Bousset, W., 45, 57, 419, 450, 454
Bowman, J. W., 327
Brandenburger, E., 222, 303–9, 365, 374, 375, 387, 427, 436, 462
Brandon, S. G. F., 168–71, 190, 191
Branscomb, H., 90
Bratcher, R., 411
Braun, H., 465
Briggs, C. A., 129–31
Bruce, F. F., 198
Büchsel, F., 444
Bultmann, R., 65, 69–71, 220, 295, 318, 356, 378, 382, 384, 434, 440, 446, 454, 469
Burkitt, F. C., 139–41, 402
Burnett, F. W., 391
Burney, C. F., 398
Busch, F., 32, 101, 146–48, 164, 176, 179, 216, 286, 371, 399, 407, 414

Cadoux, A. T., 454
Cadoux, C. J., 152–53

Carrington, P., 350
Case, S. J., 86
Charles, R. H., 55, 57, 58–61, 133, 149, 450
Clemen, C., 454
Clements, R. E., 224–27, 367, 412
Colani, T., 1, 9, 13–20, 21, 22, 25, 28, 29, 30, 31, 32, 35, 46, 65, 66, 93, 104, 113, 128, 149, 334, 335, 365, 377, 450
Combs, W. W., 320
Conzelmann, H., 162, 179–81, 183, 200, 214, 215, 216, 286, 291, 293, 352, 353, 355, 389
Cousar, C. B., 191–95, 197, 208, 213, 399
Cranfield, C. E. B., 236–39, 240, 241, 384, 392, 401, 402, 411, 437, 450
Creed, J. M., 27
Cross, F. L., 169
Crossan, J. D., 319, 469
Cullman, O., 101, 155–56, 170, 446, 448, 449, 454, 455

Dahl, N. A., 193, 439
Dalman, G., 429, 455
Daube, D., 162, 214, 351, 385, 391
Davey, N., 100
Davies, W. D., 162, 214, 351, 462
De Pressensé, E., 128–29
Descamps, A., 448
Dibelius, M., 294
Dodd, C. H., 77, 79, 96–99, 162, 214, 215, 286, 350, 351, 355, 414, 434, 440, 469, 471, 472
Drewermann, E., 346–49
Duncan, G. S., 78–79
Dungan, D. L., 229
Dupont, J., 216–20, 281, 379, 383, 430, 446, 448, 468, 469, 470, 472
Dyer, K. D., 313–21

Easton, B. S., 67, 124
Eisler, R., 90–91
Ernst, J., 329–31, 379, 391, 398, 428, 441

Farmer, W. R., 229
Farrer, A., 159, 160
Feine, P., 158
Fitzmeyer, J. A., 307
Flückiger, F., 195–98, 205, 397
Flusser, D., 175, 465
Foerster, W., 414

Ford, D., 77, 220, 408, 410, 411, 413, 416, 418
France, R. T., 173, 247–49, 298, 319
Fuller, R. H., 462
Funck-Brentano, F., 22

Gaston, L., 219, 283–88, 307, 327, 353, 378, 379, 383, 404, 427, 431, 446, 468
Geddert, T. J., 309–13, 378, 381, 389, 390, 399, 418, 458
Geiger, R., 295
Geldenhuys, N., 112
Gerold, T., 19
Gese, H., 464, 465
Gess, W. F., 123–27
Glasson, T. F., 29, 30, 75–77, 173, 319, 423, 424
Gloege, G., 142–44, 145, 434
Gloer, W. H., 224, 367
Gnilka, J., 278, 329, 335–37, 369, 391, 395, 414, 428, 437
Godet, F., 112, 113, 115, 116
Goguel, M., 12, 71–72, 353
Goodspeed, E. J., 82
Gore, Bishop, 65, 66
Gore, C., 136
Goudge, H. L., 136
Grant, F. C., 30, 31
Grässer, E., 164–66, 404, 434, 440, 448, 454, 459, 469, 471
Grayston, K., 171, 205–8, 213, 363, 371
Grundmann, W., 319, 321–23, 353, 391, 397, 411, 414, 418, 421, 434, 450, 454, 455
Guelich, R., 227–29
Guignebert, C., 456
Guillaume, A., 136
Gundry, R. H., 411, 426
Guthrie, D., 298
Guy, H. A., 77–78

Haenchen, E., 325–27, 333, 414, 447
Hahn, F., 171, 210–13, 305, 329, 375, 390, 391, 393, 403, 425, 434, 435, 441, 442, 446, 450, 454, 462, 463
Hanson, P., 366
Harder, G., 163–64, 414, 449, 454
Hare, D. R. A., 401
Harmer, J. R., 34
Harrington, W., 391, 401
Hartman, L., 174, 200, 203, 206, 224, 262–66, 278, 281, 288, 307,

319, 327, 329, 344, 360, 379, 394,
    395, 397, 398, 405, 406, 411, 412,
    423, 424, 435, 440, 448, 451, 468
Hase, C., 5–6, 12, 18
Hauck, F., 61, 68–69, 368, 369
Haupt, D. E., 29, 32, 33, 137, 139,
    243, 440
Hawkins, J., 422, 437
Heard, R., 69, 78–79
Heim, K., 237, 238
Heitmüller, W., 105, 106, 391
Held, H. J., 214, 351
Hengel, M., 170, 364, 406, 408, 412,
    464, 465
Higgins, A. J. B., 455
Hill, D., 380, 449
Hölscher, G., 72–74, 90, 94, 95,
    181, 346, 384, 415
Holtzmann, H. J., 10–11, 16, 22, 23,
    24–25, 41–42, 47, 117, 148, 415,
    450
Holtzmann, O., 81–82
Hooke, S. H., 78–79
Hooker, M., 186–90, 366
Horstmann, M., 454, 455
Hoskyns, E. C., 100
Howard, J. K., 242–44
Howard, V., 281
Hunzinger, C. H., 440
Huxley, T. H., 30

Jackson, H. L., 29
Jeremias, J., 325, 356, 430, 434,
    435, 437, 440, 442, 443, 444, 455,
    469, 471, 472
Jeremias, Jorg, 248, 307, 436
Jülicher, A., 27–28, 470

Kahlefeld, H., 442
Käsemann, E., 174, 360
Keck, F., 295–98
Kee, H. C., 319
Keim, J., 23, 39, 113
Kelber, W., 171, 174, 203–5, 383,
    391, 454, 456
Kennedy, H. A. A., 114
Kertelge, K., 325
Kilpatrick, G. D., 402
Kim, S., 464
Kittel, R., 320, 432
Klausner, J., 80, 85–86
Kloppenborg, J. S., 318, 319
Klostermann, E., 411, 414, 434,
    437, 452, 454

Koch, D. A., 213–16, 352, 371, 389,
    399
Koch, K., 206, 226, 227, 334
Kümmel, W. G., 101–4, 158, 307,
    338, 434, 440, 446, 448, 449, 450,
    451, 453, 455, 458, 469, 473
Kunzi, M., 443, 449

Lacocque, A., 409
Ladd, G. E., 244–47
Lagrange, M.-J., 83–85, 406, 435,
    452, 458
Lambrecht, J., 173, 206, 266–73,
    274, 278, 286, 288, 307, 318, 319,
    353, 362, 363, 364, 382, 383, 385,
    390, 391, 392, 398, 400, 402, 403,
    411, 413, 414, 417, 420, 421, 422,
    423, 427, 428, 429, 430, 432, 433,
    434, 435, 448, 450, 451, 452, 454,
    468, 469, 474
Lane, W. L., 327–29, 392, 418, 421,
    452
Lightfoot, J. B., 34
Lightfoot, R. H., 87, 99–101, 157,
    159, 162, 354, 370, 371, 399, 402
Loader, W. R. G., 468
Lohmeyer, E., 101, 106–9, 111, 137,
    139, 176, 286, 322, 353, 383, 384,
    391, 403, 404, 406, 411, 414, 422,
    430, 433, 434, 435, 446, 448, 449,
    450, 453, 454, 455, 464
Loisy, A., 48–52, 54, 55, 65, 377,
    378, 394, 414, 424, 446, 454, 456
Lührmann, D., 343–46, 377, 381,
    391, 411, 414, 415, 419
Lütgert, K., 145
Luz, V., 378

Mack, B., 254, 365
Mackinnon, J., 145–46
Major, H. D. A., 82
Mann, C. S., 341–43, 355, 446, 453,
    470
Manson, T. W., 93–96, 97, 124, 307,
    350, 417, 423, 448, 449, 452, 456
Manson, W., 392, 449
Marshall, I. H., 220, 293, 307, 318,
    319, 392, 417, 447, 449, 450, 452
Marti, K., 432
Martin, H., 93
Marxsen, W., 162, 171, 174, 175–
    79, 180, 182, 219, 322, 404, 414,
    422, 423, 450, 452
Massaux, E., 241, 253

Mathews, S., 121–22, 125
Mattil, A. J., 293
McCown, C. C., 1, 2, 17, 18
McNeile, A. H., 391, 403, 414, 433, 434, 446, 449
McNicol, A. J., 230–33
Menzies, A., 433
Merx, A., 26–27, 82–83, 415, 455
Meyer, A., 80–81
Meyer, E., 61–62
Meyer, H. A. W., 9–10, 116, 384
Michaelis, W., 448, 458
Michaels, J. R., 254–56, 365, 366
Miller, W., 17, 18
Minette de Tillesse, G., 190–91, 199, 200, 414
Mitchell, H. G., 432
Moffatt, J., 29, 48, 55, 117, 149, 456
Montefiore, C. G., 54–55
Montgomery, J. A., 408
Moore, A. L., 239–42, 245, 455
Moule, C. F. D., 170, 464
Muirhead, L. A., 28, 29, 117, 148
Müller, E. F. K., 115–17
Müller, K., 175
Munck, J., 353
Mussner, F., 259–61, 288, 397, 414
Myers, C., 316

Neander, A., 72, 111, 112
Neil, W., 198
Neirynck, F., 207, 229, 233, 234, 235, 236, 283, 353, 363, 383, 384, 385, 412, 413
Nestle, E., 409
Neville, G., 257–59, 288, 422
Nida, E. A., 411
Nineham, D., 318, 323–25, 383, 391, 402, 435, 440
Nowack, W., 320, 432

Oepke, A., 455, 460
Oesterley, W. O. E., 67, 429
Oesterreicher-Mollwo, M., 347
Olmstead, A. T., 90
Otto, R., 91–92, 434, 440

Patsch, H., 325
Perrin, N., 172–75, 177, 270, 319, 435, 440
Pesch, R., 171, 174, 175, 200, 206, 210, 212, 214, 218, 219, 273–83, 288, 289, 290, 295, 325, 329, 333, 346, 353, 359, 362, 364, 375, 377, 379, 381, 382, 383, 384, 385, 386, 387, 390, 391, 392, 393, 394, 395, 398, 402, 404, 406, 411, 412, 413, 414, 418, 419, 420, 421, 422, 423, 425, 428, 430, 431, 434, 435, 437, 440, 445, 446, 450, 452, 454, 462, 468, 469, 475
Petitjean, A., 432
Pfleiderer, J., 35–38, 39, 40, 42, 118, 137, 368
Piganiol, A., 62–64, 67, 415
Plummer, A., 112
Polag, A., 307, 318, 319, 417, 451
Pünjer, G. C. B., 41–42

Rahner, K. , 241, 251, 253, 430, 461
Rawlinson A. E. J., 64–67, 69, 97, 202, 356, 421, 422, 449, 450
Reimarus, C. H. S., 19, 21, 443
Renan, J. E., 11–12, 13, 18, 19, 21, 41, 113
Rengstorf, K. H., 158
Réville, A., 25–26, 81
Rigaux, B., 241, 253, 254, 409–10, 414, 418, 437, 446, 448, 453, 455, 459, 460, 468
Robinson, J. A. T., 166–68, 171, 178, 182, 424
Robinson, J. M., 446
Rohde, J., 162
Roux, H., 237
Rowdon, H., 298–99
Rowley, H. H., 153–54

Salmond, S. D. F., 133
Sanday, W., 21, 22, 133–35
Schenkel, D., 12–13, 18
Schlatter, A., 59, 143, 154–55, 162, 328, 384, 416, 456, 461
Schlosser J., 377
Schmid, J., 158, 219, 392, 450, 452, 469
Schmidt, J., 329
Schmidt, K. L., 384
Schmidt, N., 31
Schmiedel, P. W., 415
Schmithals, W., 329, 337–40, 369, 378, 387, 395, 462, 475
Schnackenburg, R., 174, 175, 210, 249–54, 281, 375, 390, 393, 425, 446, 455, 458, 461
Schneider, A., 147
Schniewind, J., 147, 157–58, 175, 176, 391–92, 406, 414, 434, 450
Schoeps, H. J., 83, 171–72

Schräder, E., 66
Schreiber, J., 184–86, 459
Schrenk, G., 237, 418, 455, 467
Schulz, S., 318, 380, 382, 392, 447, 450
Schürer, E., 63
Schürmann, H., 251, 271, 307, 319, 325, 447
Schwartz, E., 71, 72, 441
Schwartzkopff, P., 25, 32, 59, 131–33, 139, 456
Schweitzer, A., 28, 29, 40, 46, 47, 52, 56, 140, 141, 195, 284
Schweizer, E., 219, 318, 327, 331–33, 378, 383, 391, 404, 414, 434, 451, 452, 454, 455, 462, 463, 464, 475
Sellin, E., 320, 432
Selwyn, E. G., 350
Sjöberg, E., 464
Smith, B. T. D., 78–79, 440, 455
Smith, C. W. F., 439
Smith, D., 82, 141
Sowers, S., 328
Spitta, F., 63
Stauffer, E., 392
Stevens, G. B., 114
Strack, H. L., 294, 382, 402, 405, 409
Strathmann, H., 401
Strauss, D. F., 2–5, 7, 8, 11, 12, 18, 19, 20–22, 23, 28, 29, 110, 111, 123, 128 (F. Strauss in bib)
Strecker, G., 214, 352, 389
Streeter, B. H., 55–58, 136, 152, 233, 460
Strobel, A., 178, 293, 455
Suhl, A., 181–82
Sundwall, J., 176
Swete, H. B., 140, 141, 384, 452

Taylor, V., 68, 104–6, 111, 124, 219, 318, 356, 392, 404, 411, 418, 421, 434, 437, 440, 448, 450, 454, 455, 468
Telford, W. R., 381, 436, 441
Temple, W., 460
Theissen, G., 377, 378
Thomas, D. W., 76, 320, 432
Titius, A., 32, 133, 139
Tödt, H. E., 424, 427, 431
Torrey, C. C., 89, 148–52, 306, 366
Traub, H., 452
Trilling, W., 403

Trocmé, E., 208–10
Tuckett, C. M., 230, 231
Turner, C. H., 56, 136–37, 286, 363, 384, 402
Turner, N., 363

van der Woude, A. S., 465
van Iersel, B. M. F., 454, 455
Vassiliadis, P., 319
Verheyden, J., 413
Vermes, G., 175, 431, 465
Vielhauer, P., 283, 318
Vögtle, A., 174, 210, 211, 241, 253, 254, 281, 375, 378, 390, 393, 422, 425, 430, 431, 451, 455, 459, 461
Volkmar, G., 23–24, 41–42, 113, 427
von Dobschütz, E., 32
von Rad, G., 238, 394, 465

Walter, N., 182–84, 353, 414, 422
Waetjen, H., 316
Weder, H., 378
Weeden, T., 174, 200–203, 205, 398, 430
Weiffenbach, W., 21, 22–23, 32, 38–41, 42, 105, 131, 450
Weiser, A., 282, 469, 470, 471, 473
Weiss, B., 116, 117
Weiss, J., 29, 38, 54, 116, 117–21, 130, 151, 368, 411, 414, 415
Weisse, C. H., 2, 6, 7, 8, 9, 11, 18, 19, 49, 137–39
Weizsäcker, C., 23, 32–35, 37, 38, 50, 90, 115
Wellhausen, J., 2, 27, 28, 52–54, 65, 147, 320, 405, 411, 432, 441, 450, 452, 454, 459
Wendland, H. D., 144–45, 288, 375, 376
Wendling, E., 45, 47–48, 422, 450, 454
Wendt, H. H., 40, 41, 42–44, 45, 49, 50, 58, 112–13, 121, 137
Wenham, D., 298–303, 321, 470
Werner, M., 29, 47, 195
Wohlenberg, G., 126
Wolff, H. W., 465

Zahn, T., 123–27, 384
Zimmern, H., 66
Zerwick, M., 286, 363, 384, 385
Zmijewski, J., 219, 288–95, 297, 307, 318, 377, 381, 383, 391, 392, 404, 407, 411, 414, 420, 428, 435, 437, 440, 444, 449, 452, 469

INDEX OF ANCIENT SOURCES

OLD TESTAMENT

Genesis

4:8	447
6:14	392
19	265
19:17	265, 275, 412, 417
38:1	457

Exodus

4:12–16	404
4:22–23	464
9:18	419
10:14	419
11:6	419
12:26	438
19:4–6	466
19:16	424
29:4	438
29:11	438
29:32	438
29:42	438
33:9–10	438
34:5	429
40:5	438
40:6	438

Leviticus

1:3	438
1:5	438
4:4	438
4:7	438
5:17	76, 396
15:14	438
15:29	438
17:4	438
17:7	438

Deuteronomy

13:1–5	359
13:7	76
13:7 (LXX 8)	76
13:8	433
28—30	433
30:3	432, 433
30:3–4	265, 320
30:4	76, 248, 433
32:25	392

Joshua

6:25	457

Judges

5:4–5	248, 307, 320, 375, 397, 426, 430
5:5	424
7–8	395

2 Samuel

7:13	196
7:14	464, 466

1 Kings

17:1	294
18:1	294

2 Chronicles

15:6	264, 396
24:20–22	447

Esther
8:1   457

Job
9:6   424
17:11   445

Psalms
2:7   464, 466, 467
18:3–19   308
18:6–18   430
18:7   424
18:13–15   424
68:7–8   430
77:14–16   375
77:16–18   308
89:26–27   464
90:6–7   445
97:1–5   397
110:1   175, 429, 467
114:1–8   375
114:7   424
137:7   382

Isaiah
1:19–20   187
1:20   421
2:2   151
4:5   421
8:23   172
9:4   395
10:22–23   90
11:12   432
13   197, 388, 395
13:4   197
13:8   264
13:9–10   181
13:10   247, 265, 319, 423
13:13   151
13:17   197
14   388
15–16   197
17   197
19   197, 388, 430
19:2   264, 396, 406
21:3   264
21:17   421
22:8   382
23–24   197
24:3   421
24:17   297
24:18–19   264
24:19f.   151
24—27   366
25:8   421

27   457
27:12–13   432
27:13   265
28:22   90
29:6   264
30:29   76, 396
34   239, 388, 395, 424,
                       426
34:4   75, 247, 265, 319,
                       423
40:9–11   430
41:12   150
43:6   432
45:1   150
45:14   150
46:12–13   438
49:22–23   150
58:14   421
59:15–20   360
60:1–9   432
63:15—64:13   187
64:11   424
65—66   366
66:19–20   150

Jeremiah
3:16–18   422
3:17   457
4:1–8   410
4:9   409
4:13–20   264
5:18   422
6   395
6:22–26   264
7:1–15   187
7:1–20   380
7:11   310, 381
7:14–20   380
7:14–34   187
7:30–34   410
8   395
8:13   185
9   395
14:12   264, 397
15   395
18   395
21:7   397
25   197
25:8–12   410
25:9   388
26   197, 380
26:17–19   380
29:10–14   410
31:29   422

33:15–16	422		7:13	6, 37, 53, 123, 175, 187, 189, 196, 247, 252, 272, 284, 287, 316, 337, 341, 342, 346, 424, 427, 429, 431, 467
44:22	410			
46	197			
46—51	395			
47	197			
48	197			
49	197		7:13–14	150, 265, 272, 287, 320, 427
50–51	197			
50:4	422		7:14	428
51:46	395		7:21–22	167
			7:22	287
Lamentations			7:25	264, 294
1:12	296		7:28–29	342
1:21	296		8:9–26	262
1:22	296		8:11	265
2:1	296		8:13	294
2:22	395		8:15–17	411
4:6	265		8:19	458
			9	229
Ezekiel			9:24–27	262, 410
5:1–	77		9:26	77, 395
5:11–15	410		9:26–27	126, 191, 219, 256, 287, 357, 411
5:12	397			
7	395		9:27	37, 77, 183, 265, 357, 408, 409, 410
9—11	380			
13:5	296		11	126, 191, 414
14:12–23	397		11:1–39	191
14:13	264		11:21–12:4	262
14:21	394		11:30–39	125
25	197		11:31	191, 265, 357, 408
26–28	197		11:32	406
29–30	197		11:33	411
30:2–3	457		11:35	90, 406
32:7–8	319		11:40	457
33:28–29	409		11:40–41	191
34:12	296		11:40–45	164
47:11–12	416		11:44	395
47:1f.	151		12:1	90, 265, 343, 344, 357, 388, 418, 457
Daniel			12:1ff.	361
2:28	76, 174, 344, 345, 396		12:4	457
			12:6–7	231, 294, 387, 388
2:28–29	264		12:7	150, 328, 446
2:29	76, 345, 396		12:10	411
2:31–45	262		12:11	37, 183, 265, 357, 406, 408
2:45	76, 345, 397			
2:45 [Theod]	264		12:13	458
7	14, 161, 304, 464, 467			
			Hosea	
7:7–27	262		9:10—10:2	381
7:9–13	167			
7:9ff.	248		*Joel*	
7:10	432		2	239
7:11	265		2:2	265
			2:10	265, 423

2:29	422
2:30–31	150
2:31	319
3:1–3	422
(MT 4:1–3)	
3:4	150, 319
3:15–16	423
(MT 4:15–16)	
3:16	422
4:15	265
4:18	151

Amos

1:2	308, 375
5:16–27	197
5:18–20	243
5:19–20	412
9:1	381
9:5	424

Micah

1:3–4	308, 397
1:4	151, 320, 424
3:6–12	187
3:12	380
7	405
7:2ff.	398
7:6	405, 406
7:7	406

Nahum

1:2–6	308
1:5	424
2–3	197

Habakkuk

2:3	259
3	248, 424, 426
3:2–16	430
3:3–6	375
3:3–13	181, 308
3:6	320, 397, 424
3:10	397
3:10–11	375
3:11	424
3:13	150, 430

Zephaniah

1:7–13	457
3:11–20	457
9:14–16	457
12:1—13:6	457
14:4–5	457

Haggai

2:6	260

Zechariah

1:12	457
2:6	75, 320, 331, 333, 432, 434
2:6 (MT 10)	432
2:10	248, 265
8:23	422
9:9	342
9:14–16	424
12:10ff.	175
12:12ff.	265
14:2	150
14:4	288
14:5	265
14:7	455
14:8	151

NEW TESTAMENT

Matthew

4:15	172
5—7	46
5:1ff.	386
5:11	368
5:17–18	453
5:18	269, 272, 324, 445, 448, 450, 452
5:18–19	451
5:21–48	451
5:21ff.	453
7:15–27	351
7:15ff.	351
7:22ff.	355
7:24–27	453
8:11	70
8:11–12	434
10	46, 47
10:5	300
10:5–16	47
10:14–15	442
10:17	390
10:17–18	398
10:17–19	300
10:17–20	48, 234, 271
10:17–21	244
10:17–22	47, 231, 232, 234, 235
10:17–23	119, 268, 271, 300, 398, 400
10:17–39	351
10:17ff.	260, 400
10:18	331, 402, 403
10:19–20	318
10:21	234

10:22a	234
10:22b	234
10:23	36, 46, 57, 79, 82, 115, 119, 122, 126, 131, 141, 235, 240, 245, 249, 254, 268, 271, 300, 358, 443, 446, 460
10:23a	232
10:24–25	59
10:28	407
10:34–36	399, 405, 442
10:37–38	399
10:37ff.	14
10:39	399
11:5	440, 473
11:5–6	372
11:11	15
11:12	473
11:16	444
11:20–24	372
11:21–23	442
11:25–27	327
11:27	48, 235, 454, 455, 462, 466
11:30	444
12:28	239, 473
13	46, 235
13:14–20	116
13:24ff.	352
13:36ff.	352
13:41	432
13:47ff.	352
15:1–13	69
16:27–28	235
16:28	5, 126
17:25	444
18:20	139
18:23–35	352
19:28	300, 427
21:30	364
21:43–44	124
22:7	114
22:7–8	124
22:7ff.	126
22:11–14	472
23:38f.	126
23:18	271
23:31–39	352
23:31ff.	132
23:34–36	198, 355, 370, 379, 423, 447
23:36	132, 165, 269, 291, 446, 448
23:37–39	346, 370
23:37—25:46	218
23:38	267, 379, 380, 382
23:38–39	60
23:39	423, 444, 446, 460
24	3, 8, 81, 144, 145, 230, 231, 233, 234, 244, 300, 352, 368
24—25	2, 5, 46, 301, 303, 352, 398, 474
24:1–3	9, 234
24:1–28	10
24:1–36	230
24:1–51	230
24:4	389
24:4–5	234
24:4–6	26
24:4–14	126
24:4ff.	35
24:6	125, 127
24:6–8	144
24:8	126
24:9	36
24:9–14	231, 232
24:10–12	231
24:14	113, 125, 208, 345, 369, 401
24:15	83, 91, 125, 232
24:15–28	83, 125
24:15–31	125
24:15a	232
24:15b	232
24:19	127
24:20	86, 171
24:22	127
24:23–24	357
24:23–25	234
24:25	420
24:26	234, 268, 271, 279, 318, 358, 390, 391, 392
24:26–27	119, 248, 265, 357
24:26–28	231, 233
24:27	318, 393
24:29	36, 116, 127
24:29–30	144
24:29–31	27, 235
24:29ff.	10
24:30	119, 122, 245, 304
24:30–31	235
24:30a	231, 235
24:30ab	119
24:31	145, 235
24:32–33	112

24:33	119
24:34	57, 126, 235
24:36	5, 16, 126, 235, 454
24:37—25:30	232, 233
24:37—25:46	230, 232
24:37–39	300
24:37–41	233
24:37–42	473
24:38	233
24:42	245, 299
24:42–43	233
24:42–44	437, 469
24:43	299
24:43–44	471, 473
24:43–51	231
24:44	235, 245, 250, 299
24:45–51	469, 473
24:50	235, 250
25	144, 145, 195, 245, 352
25:1–12	299
25:1–13	471, 473
25:5	113, 233
25:12	233
25:13	232, 233, 235, 299, 301
25:14	299, 435
25:14–15	233
25:14–30	195, 300, 469, 473
25:31	427
25:31–46	195, 300, 330, 473
25:32	145
25:46	144, 145
26:18	437
26:64	9, 114, 123
28:20	139, 387
Mark	
1	184
1—13	208, 210
1:1—8:29	202
1:2—3:6	274
1:8	255
1:9	184, 315
1:14	242
1:14–15	15, 177, 202, 255, 362
1:15	91, 116, 155, 177, 186, 255, 256, 276, 334, 437
1:27	385
1:32	383
2:1—3:6	309
2:7	385
2:9	385
2:10	466
2:18	385
2:18–19	473
2:18ff.	179, 181
2:19–20	202
2:20	184, 255, 315
2:24	385
2:28	385, 467
3:7—6:29	274
3:13	386
3:14	385
3:20–35	228
3:20—4:34	160
3:20ff.	161
3:22	372
3:22–26	160
3:28–30	161
3:31–35	161
4	195, 205, 207, 212, 227, 229, 327, 356, 363, 439
4:1–2	356
4:1–20	161
4:2–32	140
4:10	356, 385
4:10–12	64, 384
4:10–23	278
4:10ff.	89
4:11	70, 194
4:11–12	356, 411
4:12	61, 389
4:13	356
4:14–20	356
4:21–25	266, 356
4:24	389
4:26–29	161, 192
4:33–34	356
4:35	315
4:35–41	161
5:21	383
5:36	389
6:1–6	228
6:2	385
6:3	385
6:7–13	47, 266
6:11–12	453
6:30—8:26	274
7	227
7:5	385
7:6	61
7:9	385
7:17	385
7:17–23	384

7:17ff.	89
7:18	118, 385, 411, 435, 436
7:19	385
7:27	385
8—12	146
8:1	315
8:11	372
8:11–12	65, 372
8:11–13	309, 315
8:12	185
8:12a	444
8:12b	444
8:15	389
8:17	118, 385
8:17–18	411
8:18	61, 385, 389
8:22ff.	202
8:23	389
8:27–33	64, 214, 215, 352, 371
8:27—9:1	146, 214, 216, 322, 325, 352, 363, 371, 372
8:27—10:52	274
8:27ff.	323
8:29—9:1	399
8:31	76, 255, 325, 368, 442, 467
8:31–38	193, 334
8:31ff.	146, 194
8:34	146, 368, 371
8:34–37	179, 215, 352, 371, 442
8:34–38	187, 228, 399, 402, 406, 475
8:34—9:1	148, 215, 255, 266
8:34ff.	146, 179
8:35	193, 318, 406
8:35–38	255
8:38	48, 56, 136, 179, 185, 187, 201, 215, 316, 362, 399, 428, 432, 444, 452, 453, 462, 467
8:38—9:1	214, 215, 269, 272, 352, 371
8:39—9:1	428
9:1	56, 69, 79, 102, 122, 131, 134, 136, 141, 165, 182, 198, 240, 245, 249, 253, 255, 258, 269, 293, 326, 336, 341, 428, 443, 444, 446, 447
9:2–16:18	338
9:11–13	384
9:19	185, 385, 444
9:28–29	384
9:30–31	385
9:30–32	146
9:30–50	278
9:31	354, 368, 399, 442
9:33–37	146
9:38–39	48
9:45	385
9:48	61
10	46
10:10	385
10:10–12	384
10:13	385
10:17	383
10:17–23	390
10:18	276
10:24	48
10:29–31	228
10:32	353
10:32–34	146
10:35–45	146
10:35ff.	87
10:40	461
10:43	385
10:43–45	255
10:44	385
10:45	325, 442
11	227
11—12	187, 327, 335, 353, 363
11:1	316
11:1—12:44	274, 278
11:11	380
11:11–14	53
11:12–14	340, 353, 370, 381, 441
11:12–25	185
11:12ff.	72, 185
11:14	385
11:15–17	310
11:15–18	370
11:17	218, 353, 403
11:17–18	340
11:18	53
11:20	381
11:20–21	353, 370
11:22	316
11:27—12:1	267
11:28	216, 267, 385

11:29–32	170
11:49–51	170
12	227, 381
12:1–12	114, 353, 381
12:6	462
12:8	364
12:9	340, 472
12:10	61
12:14	389
12:25	70, 102
12:38	389
12:38–39	8
12:49–52	170
13:1	108, 176, 227, 231, 379, 382, 383
13:1a	303
13:1–2	47, 48, 52, 53, 59, 71, 74, 83, 88, 89, 103, 106, 203, 267, 287, 303, 305, 306, 316, 317, 335, 337, 353, 357, 362, 365, 382, 383
13:1–2a	69
13:1–2ab	274, 281
13:1–3a	267
13:1–4	40, 44, 53, 94, 164, 179, 195, 198, 199, 210, 211, 217, 234, 240, 263, 276, 300, 323, 325, 331, 335, 365
13:1–5	116
13:1–5a	108, 174
13:1–6	43, 74
13:1–8	85
13:1–20	6, 8
13:1–22	83
13:1–27	449
13:1–37	8, 230
13:1b–2	303
13:2	13, 39, 54, 70, 83, 102, 108, 132, 151, 163, 168, 170, 171, 176, 178, 179, 183, 186, 187, 190, 196, 198, 205, 209, 216, 220, 228, 229, 247, 248, 252, 255, 256, 266, 267, 271, 281, 283, 287, 291, 306, 310, 315, 317, 322, 324, 325, 331, 332, 334, 340, 343, 345, 356, 358, 360, 370, 373, 376, 388, 395, 407, 411, 415, 416, 418, 421, 441, 445, 449
13:2–3a	267
13:2–4	40
13:2ff.	40
13:2b	69, 70
13:2c	274, 278, 281, 382
13:3	70, 199, 227, 234, 267, 288, 385, 474
13:3–4	47, 48, 72, 108, 303, 305, 317, 325, 337, 338, 356, 358, 362, 365, 384, 387
13:3–5	82, 281
13:3–6	303, 315
13:3–8	89
13:3–27	53
13:3–31	66, 281
13:3–37	52, 100, 140, 303, 306
13:4	47, 50, 93, 105, 138, 147, 164, 176, 184, 190, 196, 199, 207, 209, 211, 213, 216, 218, 220, 231, 240, 243, 246, 248, 255, 267, 274, 289, 291, 303, 305, 307, 310, 316, 317, 325, 328, 331, 343, 355, 385, 388, 398, 407, 420, 421, 435, 437, 444, 446, 456, 459
13:4–5a	270, 273
13:4–6	121
13:4–23	270
13:4a	211, 213, 217, 273, 328, 338, 420
13:4b	211, 217, 228, 289, 328, 336, 446
13:5	138, 146, 147, 164, 199, 207, 217, 289, 310, 361, 362, 390, 400, 420
13:5–6	40, 43, 44, 48, 53, 55, 69, 92, 108, 118, 127, 165, 168, 176, 195, 203, 210, 211, 218, 223, 224, 228, 243, 305, 322, 331, 337, 343, 365,

	368, 369, 374, 389, 391	13:6–37	81
13:5–7	118, 192, 197	13:7	76, 101, 108, 119,
13:5–8	10, 33, 55, 88, 94,		127, 138, 174, 176,
	104, 105, 130, 188,		181, 182, 190, 195,
	209, 255, 256, 264,		197, 205, 208, 211,
	284, 323		217, 219, 228, 237,
13:5–13	35, 82, 126, 158,		244, 245, 255, 264,
	176, 178, 182, 247,		279, 280, 315, 326,
	252, 285, 322, 323,		331, 335, 338, 339,
	331		343, 345, 357, 361,
13:5–22	328, 421		374, 394, 397, 403,
13:5–23	137, 147, 148, 166,		407, 419, 423, 433,
	168, 170, 192, 199,		440
	200, 217, 236, 240,	13:7a	284, 285, 288, 395
	241, 257, 265, 270,	13:7b	201, 209, 277, 284,
	290, 298, 299, 343,		285, 335, 369
	345, 364, 365, 374,	13:7c	183
	375, 387, 390, 449	13:7–8	33, 35, 36, 38, 40,
13:5–27	69, 172, 209, 217,		47, 48, 53, 55, 60,
	257, 303, 323, 324,		64, 65, 68, 69, 73,
	331, 435		85, 86, 102, 104,
13:5–31	16, 32, 33, 93, 94,		126, 127, 144, 164,
	147, 328		165, 181, 182, 184,
13:5–37	54, 143, 240, 303		201, 210, 211, 217,
13:5a	207, 273		223, 224, 228, 236,
13:5b	207, 284, 285		243, 244, 260, 264,
13:5b–6	48, 217, 234, 266,		265, 275, 281, 282,
	268, 279, 303, 304,		289, 290, 292, 303,
	359		304, 306, 314, 317,
13:5b–8	108, 262, 264		333, 335, 337, 338,
13:5b–13	317		344, 348, 356, 361,
13:5b–22	304		362, 365, 369, 376,
13:5b–23	274		389, 394, 396, 397,
13:5b–27	174		400, 420, 437
13:5b–31	224	13:7–9a	38, 43, 121
13:5f.	37	13:7f.	95
13:5ff.	50, 72, 170, 194,	13:8	101, 108, 119, 120,
	197, 331		138, 160, 163, 170,
13:6	33, 39, 50, 74, 101,		176, 181, 190, 195,
	103, 104, 137, 138,		197, 207, 219, 244,
	168, 183, 186, 199,		245, 277, 280, 285,
	207, 209, 210, 222,		289, 292, 315, 326,
	223, 263, 265, 271,		331, 338, 357, 374,
	275, 277, 279, 281,		395, 397, 403, 406
	284, 285, 289, 331,	13:8a	264, 285, 331
	335, 345, 357, 359,	13:8ab	288, 396
	361, 362, 385, 390,	13:8b	285, 331
	393, 396, 420	13:8c	183, 209, 331, 335,
13:6–7	279, 306		369
13:6–8	50, 84, 116, 324	13:8d	201
13:6–13	244	13:9	36, 100, 101, 103,
13:6–14	97		104, 167, 174, 176,
13:6–18	84		181, 199, 206, 208,
			222, 264, 268, 271,

	276, 281, 322, 335, 340, 344, 354, 357, 358, 361, 362, 369, 389, 390, 398, 400, 402, 403, 421, 440		339, 340, 345, 357, 358, 360, 362, 369, 398, 400, 403, 421, 475
13:9–10	315, 402	13:11	48, 51, 90, 101, 103, 104, 120, 167, 176, 181, 205, 208, 264, 268, 271, 276, 289, 318, 319, 322, 335, 337, 340, 344, 354, 357, 358, 361, 369, 398, 400, 402, 404, 434
13:9–11	53, 69, 161, 164, 195, 197, 224, 234, 263, 266, 300, 331, 335, 375, 398, 400, 402, 406, 475		
13:9–13	10, 33, 35, 37, 40, 47, 48, 55, 58, 59, 65, 73, 74, 82, 84, 86, 88, 89, 94, 98, 104, 106, 108, 116, 118, 119, 126, 130, 138, 168, 170, 179, 181, 185, 187, 188, 193, 201, 202, 207, 209, 211, 215, 217, 228, 231, 234, 235, 243, 255, 256, 260, 264, 266, 268, 271, 276, 303, 304, 323, 324, 326, 329, 336, 339, 356, 360, 365, 368, 369, 374, 398, 400, 406, 437	13:11–12	93
		13:11–13	281, 362, 421
		13:11–13a	317
		13:11a	315
		13:11b	108, 285, 315, 324
		13:11d	315
		13:11d–13a	314
		13:12	47, 48, 50, 53, 68, 69, 73, 95, 102, 103, 167, 176, 181, 182, 195, 205, 234, 264, 266, 276, 277, 280, 288, 289, 315, 331, 335, 337, 340, 344, 357, 361, 398, 399, 405, 406
13:9–17	90	13:12–13	90, 104, 138, 161, 168, 300, 354, 398, 405, 406
13:9–20	98		
13:9–27	85, 86		
13:9a	47, 48, 90, 285, 303, 335, 337	13:12–13a	207, 358, 398, 405
		13:12–16	262, 264
13:9b	48, 285, 289, 337	13:12a	405
13:9b–10	90	13:13	53, 101, 103, 108, 119, 164, 181, 195, 197, 222, 268, 277, 289, 322, 324, 340, 361, 398, 399, 405
13:9b–11	48, 138		
13:9b–12	244		
13:9b–13	39, 43, 44, 121, 303		
13:9bc	51		
13:9bcd	120	13:13:14	74
13:9c	337	13:13:30	38
13:9ff.	194, 195, 197, 206, 207, 300, 322, 361	13:13:32	39
		13:13:4	44
13:10	36, 39, 42, 48, 53, 82, 101, 104, 108, 115, 118, 119, 165, 167, 168, 176, 180, 182, 184, 185, 193, 207, 211, 219, 232, 236, 245, 255, 256, 263, 268, 276, 281, 289, 290, 316, 322, 324, 331, 335, 337,	13:13–20	161
		13:13–22	181
		13:13a	48, 69, 90, 167, 176, 234, 276, 315, 335, 337, 357, 398, 405, 406
		13:13b	43, 48, 68, 90, 167, 176, 207, 234, 277, 285, 315, 335, 337, 357, 398, 399, 406

13:13b–14	50
13:13b–20a	47, 48
13:14	8, 17, 36, 37, 41, 49, 50, 52, 60, 65, 66, 73, 77, 83, 85, 88, 91, 101, 102, 108, 112, 118, 119, 127, 138, 149, 151, 152, 154, 165, 167, 169, 170, 173, 176, 178, 180, 182, 186, 190, 197, 198, 205, 208, 211, 217, 219, 224, 226, 228, 229, 237, 247, 252, 255, 256, 265, 268, 271, 275, 277, 280, 282, 284, 285, 289, 290, 304, 318, 328, 332, 335, 343, 345, 355, 357, 358, 360, 361, 363, 366, 367, 370, 395, 407, 408, 410, 411, 414, 416, 418, 427, 435, 437, 440
13:14–16	6, 195, 197, 206
13:14–18	219
13:14–18	82, 84, 194, 207, 220, 285, 322, 345, 418
13:14–19	77, 82, 285, 408
13:14–20	33, 35, 36, 38, 43, 44, 50, 54, 55, 59, 60, 65, 68, 73, 79, 82, 85, 92, 97, 99, 102, 104, 106, 107, 116, 121, 126, 163, 167, 168, 171, 172, 182, 188, 192, 201, 210, 212, 217, 223, 224, 228, 243, 256, 275, 280, 285, 288, 289, 300, 302, 307, 317, 319, 325, 327, 331, 333, 335, 337, 338, 340, 356, 358, 360, 362, 365, 385, 396, 400, 407, 413, 421, 435, 445, 456
13:14–20a	164, 277
13:14–21	314, 317
13:14–22	53, 68, 69, 169, 176, 211, 228, 247, 281, 292
13:14–23	10, 35, 41, 83, 90, 104, 105, 108, 125, 158, 209, 247, 252, 260, 317, 323
13:14–25	96
13:14–27	55, 86, 108, 125, 322
13:14–31	33
13:14a	150, 232, 338
13:14ab	90
13:14b	228, 338, 412
13:14c	89, 90
13:14f.	115
13:14ff.	37, 45, 66, 83, 94, 95, 125, 177, 178, 181, 191, 206, 209, 211, 213, 241, 247, 287, 290, 298, 322, 324, 331, 359
13:15–16	50, 51, 82, 89, 90, 92, 101, 108, 118, 119, 138, 167, 176, 207, 219, 256, 261, 266, 280, 285, 306, 307, 318, 319, 357, 358, 407, 412, 416, 417
13:15–18	265
13:15–20	261, 407, 411, 415, 416
13:16	417
13:16–17	161
13:17	7, 89, 90, 118, 127, 167, 184, 195, 197, 280, 315, 318, 358, 361
13:17–18	85, 108, 138, 256, 261, 418
13:17–19	50, 346
13:17–20	60, 119, 335
13:17ff.	59
13:18	7, 59, 63, 73, 167, 171, 195, 197, 206, 209, 277, 280, 332, 358
13:18–19	318
13:18–27	89
13:19	48, 92, 124, 197, 207, 265, 282, 285, 289, 290, 344, 345, 357, 358, 360, 361, 370, 388, 407, 418, 427
13:19–20	62, 68, 84, 85, 108, 138, 167, 195, 197,

	209, 211, 265, 289,	13:23	47, 53, 69, 147, 176,
	298, 300, 302, 418		190, 199, 206, 207,
13:19–20a	280		217, 222, 227, 279,
13:19–22	262, 264, 300		281, 285, 292, 303,
13:19–27	84		304, 310, 315, 317,
13:19b	292		328, 337, 362, 389,
13:19b–23	230		390, 393, 420, 422,
13:20	33, 34, 36, 50, 68,		452
	71, 90, 114, 118,	13:23a	420
	127, 138, 197, 207,	13:24	36, 101, 127, 128,
	211, 275, 285, 302,		138, 147, 180, 182,
	318, 348, 358, 361,		184, 207, 247, 257,
	393, 408, 418, 420,		269, 272, 275, 282,
	433		291, 294, 319, 336,
13:20–23	265		338, 370, 423
13:20–24	292	13:24–25	75, 99, 119, 173,
13:20–32	164		181, 189, 218, 247,
13:20b	48		248, 252, 256, 260,
13:21	51, 101, 108, 118,		269, 275, 282, 290,
	119, 168, 184, 205,		304, 305, 307, 309,
	206, 208, 211, 243,		321, 331, 336, 374,
	268, 271, 278, 279,		423, 426, 436
	285, 303, 307, 318,	13:24–25a	118
	319, 337, 357, 359,	13:24–26	98, 144, 168, 247,
	369, 385, 390, 393,		248, 271, 309, 358,
	414, 424		359, 375, 414, 424,
13:21–22	48, 73, 74, 165, 170,		432, 446
	182, 183, 186, 203,	13:24–27	6, 7, 10, 27, 33, 35,
	206, 210, 211, 223,		38, 41, 43, 44, 47,
	261, 263, 265, 266,		49, 53, 55, 60, 65,
	271, 279, 281, 290,		68, 69, 73, 75, 82,
	304, 305, 343, 345,		85, 94, 95, 98, 100,
	361, 362, 368, 374,		102, 106, 121, 127,
	389, 391, 414, 420,		137, 138, 147, 158,
	421, 437, 452		161, 163, 164, 166,
13:21–23	6, 33, 35, 36, 39, 40,		168, 171, 172, 176,
	43, 44, 48, 55, 73,		178, 182, 185, 188,
	74, 84, 92, 106,		195, 197, 199, 201,
	108, 116, 121, 137,		204, 206, 209, 212,
	138, 165, 168, 188,		217, 223, 224, 235,
	192, 195, 197, 199,		240, 242, 243, 248,
	217, 224, 234, 266,		249, 255, 257, 260,
	268, 279, 285, 303,		262, 264, 265, 268,
	331, 365, 390		270, 272, 274, 275,
13:21ff.	36, 37, 101, 103		277, 278, 280, 282,
13:22	39, 40, 64, 68, 77,		283, 285, 288, 290,
	108, 118, 119, 168,		292, 293, 298, 303,
	182, 201, 228, 243,		307, 314, 319, 321,
	275, 277, 279, 281,		323, 325, 326, 329,
	285, 289, 303, 309,		331, 333, 335, 337,
	314, 315, 318, 335,		343, 344, 349, 357,
	337, 359, 361, 385,		359, 361, 362, 364,
	390, 393, 421, 422		365, 385, 387, 393,
13:22–23	50, 68, 100, 359		422, 423, 424, 426,

	428, 431, 433, 441, 446, 448, 456
13:24–29	209
13:24–30	317
13:24–31	54, 116, 211, 281
13:24–32	228
13:24a	219, 311, 370
13:24b–25d	276
13:24b–27	50, 370
13:24f.	115
13:24ff.	36, 85, 117, 177, 210, 252, 323
13:25	75, 138, 319, 320, 424
13:25–28	292
13:25a	269, 423
13:25b	423
13:25b–27	118
13:26	31, 65, 99, 101, 122, 161, 174, 175, 187, 189, 208, 214, 228, 247, 265, 269, 276, 290, 304, 316, 320, 337, 341, 357, 359, 424, 427, 432
13:26–27	269, 272, 331, 333, 336, 430
13:27	68, 73, 75, 76, 93, 101, 176, 197, 208, 218, 230, 248, 269, 272, 276, 290, 304, 320, 324, 331, 357, 428, 430, 432, 434, 473
13:28	53, 54, 69, 147, 207, 290, 434, 437
13:28–29	33, 39, 41, 43, 44, 48, 51, 53, 54, 72, 83, 108, 112, 117, 121, 125, 127, 138, 164, 165, 176, 184, 186, 188, 206, 207, 211, 213, 217, 236, 248, 258, 266, 285, 305, 309, 311, 315, 321, 337, 339, 356, 357, 365, 372, 374, 389, 434
13:28–30	6, 85, 211, 224, 244, 456
13:28–31	84, 94, 199, 210, 211, 217, 240, 362
13:28–32	35, 36, 41, 106, 195, 199, 263, 303, 336
13:28–36	303
13:28–37	74, 104, 105, 118, 137, 172, 174, 217, 239, 243, 270, 274, 285, 323, 325, 331, 364, 365
13:28a	207, 276, 290, 434, 469
13:28a–29	305
13:28b	305, 434, 436, 469
13:28bc	276
13:28f.	92, 157
13:28ff.	36, 37, 170
13:29	43, 44, 53, 54, 69, 126, 132, 139, 147, 185, 190, 199, 207, 209, 211, 213, 217, 236, 237, 240, 245, 248, 250, 273, 276, 290, 312, 328, 336, 388, 434, 438, 440, 445, 446, 460
13:29–30	328
13:29–37	270, 273
13:30	10, 11, 43, 47, 48, 53, 54, 57, 69, 100, 113, 117, 121, 126, 131, 132, 147, 156, 158, 165, 166, 170, 176, 182, 184, 186, 199, 201, 208, 211, 217, 222, 235, 239, 241, 244, 246, 248, 250, 253, 255, 258, 261, 269, 276, 290, 291, 293, 298, 305, 311, 321, 324, 326, 336, 337, 341, 357, 388, 435, 443, 452, 454, 456, 458, 461
13:30	240
13:30–31	38, 42, 43, 50, 60, 104, 207, 266, 272, 315, 317, 337
13:30–32	65, 108, 121, 176, 188, 273, 276, 365, 449, 453
13:31	6, 16, 38, 42, 48, 53, 69, 158, 176, 186, 214, 222, 249, 256, 258, 261, 272, 273, 276, 322, 324, 336, 337, 357, 445, 446, 448, 454

13:31–37   317   282, 299, 301, 337,
13:32   5, 6, 16, 35, 40, 48,   339, 357, 359, 362,
              51, 53, 54, 65, 69,   375, 441, 469, 470,
              72, 86, 113, 114,   474
              117, 118, 121, 126,   13:34–37   232
              127, 131, 132, 135,   13:34a   166
              138, 147, 157, 158,   13:34ff.   194
              165, 166, 170, 176,   13:35   48, 113, 157, 185,
              178, 184, 186, 190,   233, 285, 315, 388,
              199, 201, 207, 210,   454, 471
              227, 230, 235, 237,   13:35–36   199, 232, 276, 454,
              241, 245, 248, 250,   471
              253, 254, 256, 259,   13:35–37   65, 231, 315
              276, 291, 293, 299,   13:35a   303
              311, 313, 315, 317,   13:36   471, 472
              322, 324, 326, 334,   13:36–37   233
              336, 356, 357, 361,   13:36a   292
              372, 446, 448, 450,   13:37   48, 77, 118, 194,
              452, 459, 461, 464,   199, 207, 227, 245,
              466, 469, 470   273, 276, 285, 299,
13:32–33   68, 100, 131, 337,   303, 317, 337, 357,
              417, 458   362, 469, 474
13:32–37   6, 43, 44, 53, 73, 74,   13:37–38   198, 355
              84, 93, 94, 116,   13:38   214, 291, 352, 434
              121, 161, 217, 240,   13:39   198
              266, 328, 423   14   100, 363
13:32ff.   217   14—15   100, 146, 187, 399
13:33   48, 118, 194, 199,   14—16   161, 208, 210, 335,
              207, 227, 232, 245,   354
              285, 291, 299, 301,   14:1—16:8   274
              303, 313, 315, 317,   14:3   383
              359, 389, 390, 454,   14:9   255
              458, 469, 471, 472   14:10   354, 368
13:33–35   206   14:17   315, 383
13:33–36   273, 285, 303, 361,   14:18   354
              454   14:21   354
13:33–37   33, 39, 40, 51, 69,   14:22   383
              74, 158, 164, 166,   14:22–25   325, 442
              176, 192, 193, 200,   14:25   15, 70, 315
              210, 218, 232, 233,   14:27   61
              246, 248, 253, 258,   14:28   172, 202, 255
              261, 285, 291, 299,   14:29   474
              301, 310, 311, 355,   14:31   474
              356, 359, 365, 376,   14:32–42   310
              454, 468, 469   14:33   383
13:33a   233, 362   14:33–42   193
13:33b   232, 233, 357, 469   14:34   355
13:33ff.   48, 193, 217, 266,   14:36   185
              324, 359, 361   14:37   315, 385
13:34   199, 233, 276, 282,   14:38   471
              315, 469, 471, 475   14:41   315, 368
13:34–35   276, 299   14:42   383, 437
13:34–36   48, 165, 188, 201,   14:43   383
              228, 232, 245, 261,   14:50   207

14:55–64	72, 343, 344, 377
14:58	53, 83, 176, 196, 198, 252, 267, 271, 274, 281, 310, 324, 327, 344, 377, 379, 381
14:58–59	169
14:61	462
14:61–62	464
14:62	15, 56, 59, 79, 97, 99, 100, 103, 122, 131, 136, 167, 175, 181, 185, 187, 189, 209, 247, 255, 269, 272, 293, 316, 334, 340, 342, 354, 427, 431, 467
14:66	383
14:72	315
15	100, 184
15:1	354, 368
15:10	368
15:15	354, 368
15:29	83, 196, 267, 310
15:33	310
15:34	185
15:38	310, 316
15:39	316
16:1	383
16:7	172, 202, 428
16:7–8	204
16:8	254, 363
16:9–20	172
Luke	
1:3	124
4:16–21	473
4:25	294
6:12	386
6:17	386
6:20	386
6:22	368
6:47–49	453
9:24	318
10:3–12	47
10:10–12	442
10:12	135
10:13–15	442
10:13–16	170
11:20	473
11:31–32	135
11:49	447
11:49–51	355, 447
11:51	447, 448
12	231, 302
12:11–12	90, 207, 231, 268, 271, 318, 357, 358, 369, 398, 400
12:11a	358, 400
12:22–34	302
12:28	302
12:34–36	300
12:35	124, 299
12:35–36	294
12:35–38	195, 231, 243, 469
12:35–48	230, 301, 303
12:35ff.	294
12:36–38	232, 299, 301, 469, 470
12:37–38	471
12:38	166, 471
12:39	42
12:39–40	294, 437, 469, 471
12:39–46	231
12:4–5	407
12:40	250
12:41	299, 301, 474
12:42–44	299
12:42–46	469
12:45–46	294, 300
12:46	250
12:49–50	442
12:51–53	90, 405, 442
12:54–56	372, 461
12:54ff.	90
12:7	90
12:8	330
12:8–9	170, 287, 362, 399, 428, 434, 452, 467
13:1–5	355, 362, 370, 442
13:1ff.	164, 170
13:6–9	442
13:23	218
13:28–29	434
13:35	267
16:17	272, 450, 452
17	16, 230, 231, 233, 270, 300, 302
17:20	54, 91, 250, 373
17:20–21	71, 102, 218, 241, 300, 302, 372, 373, 454, 473
17:20–23	300
17:20–37	230, 288, 295, 377
17:20ff.	71, 81, 157, 325
17:21	301, 302
17:22	124, 245
17:22–23	135

17:22–24	233	21:6	284, 291
17:22–30	233	21:8	306
17:22–37	118, 167, 236, 300, 301, 303, 340	21:8–9	234
		21:8ff.	292
17:22ff.	10, 15, 219, 324, 352	21:9	128
17:23	138, 234, 268, 271, 279, 318, 357, 390, 392	21:10	167
		21:10–11	397
		21:10–28	296
17:23–24	106, 167, 168, 213, 231, 248, 265, 307, 358, 424	21:10–36	67
		21:10b–11	296
		21:11	308, 331
17:23–25	42	21:12	231
17:24	318, 340, 362, 372, 393, 471	21:12–19	67, 68, 231, 232, 234
		21:13	208, 232, 400
17:25	59	21:14a	231
17:26–27	300	21:15	404
17:26–30	250, 362, 372, 471	21:16–17	68
17:26–35	42, 233	21:16b	231
17:26–37	300	21:17	201, 208
17:27	233	21:20	105, 112, 124, 151, 232, 235, 364, 415
17:30	340, 417, 458		
17:31	50, 77, 82, 90, 95, 138, 207, 219, 280, 306, 318, 319, 357, 407, 412, 417	21:20–21	150
		21:20–24	10, 67, 94, 96, 99, 105, 183, 296, 413, 418
17:32	417	21:20–28	235
17:33	318, 406	21:20–36	68
17:34–35	77, 250	21:20ff.	94, 95
17:37	77	21:21	318, 357
18:1–2	113	21:21a	68, 413
18:1–8	195, 245, 393	21:21b–22	235
18:8	460	21:21bc	95
19:11	245	21:22	292
19:12	113, 124	21:23	302, 391
19:12–27	469	21:23a	68
19:41–44	235, 362, 355, 370	21:23b	361
19:41ff.	170	21:23b–25	235
19:43–44	381	21:24	71, 112, 124, 126, 302
19:44	281, 284, 379, 383		
19:44ff.	286	21:25	98
19:47–48	296	21:25–26	308
19:47—29:44	296	21:25–28	296
20:24	296	21:26a	138
20:45	296	21:26b–27	68
20:45—21:36	295, 296	21:27	122
21	60, 67, 94, 230, 231, 233, 234, 235, 288, 292, 295	21:28	138, 235
		21:29	67
		21:29–33	68
21:5	296	21:31	85, 244
21:5–11	68	21:32	293
21:5–36	230, 288, 303, 377	21:33	16
21:5–7	234	21:34–36	232, 233, 292, 297, 361
21:5–9	67		
21:5–36	295	21:36	85, 232, 233, 292

21:37	71
21:37–38	296
22	146
22:26	64
22:30	135
23:27–31	355, 362
23:27ff.	170
23:29–31	89
23:29ff.	90

John
2:13–22	267
2:13ff.	267
2:18	267
2:19	267, 271, 339
2:19ff.	267
5:19–29	463
7:37	416
7:37–38	416
7:39	416
7:53—8:11	173
10:22–39	77
12:31–32	100
14—16	146
15	59
15:26–27	404
16:16	9
16:33	147
20	59
21:22	126

Acts
1:6–12	284
1:7	78, 79, 461
1:9	143
1:10	474
1:16	421
2:40	444
6:10	208, 404
6:13	83, 198
7	196
7:48	198
7:48–50	198
7:55	208
11:28	171
13:6	64
15:17	403
21:10	171

Romans
1:3–4	181
1:5	474
1:18ff.	397
4:25	399
6:17	351

6:29	421
8:32	399
9:28	90
11:1	420
11:25	361, 400
11:25–26	296
11:25ff.	198, 360
13:1	321
13:11–12	351, 437
13:11–13	360
13:11–14	285, 471
15:11	403
15:19–24	403
16:17ff.	351

1 Corinthians
7:28	361
7:29	361
13:9ff.	113
15:24–28	463
16:	351

2 Corinthians
4:5	361
5:19	474
5:9–11	181
7:3	421
13:2	421

Galatians
6:11–12	351

Ephesians
4:11	64
6:10–18	285, 360
6:10ff.,	351
6:11–12	360
6:12	426

Philippians
1:12–14	400
2:9ff.	181
3:2ff.	351
3:18–19	351
3:18–21	359
4:5	437

Colossians
1:23	361, 403
1:23–29	361

1 Thessalonians
1—3	361
1:6	355
1:9–10	181
1:10	462

2:13	350
2:14–16	198
2:16	205, 355, 361
2:24f.	67
3:1–4	355
4—5	351
4:1–8	350
4:13—5:11	355
4:15	191, 263, 282, 327
4:15–17	361, 433
4:15—5:11	359, 361
4:17	347
5:1–2	48
5:1–11	195, 285, 356
5:1ff.	361
5:3	355, 361
5:4ff.	361
5:6	77, 361
5:6–8	360
5:9	361

2 Thessalonians

1:4–7	355
1:5	195, 356, 361
1:6–10	359
2	57, 58, 73, 74, 94, 96, 97, 119, 125, 165, 170, 189, 260, 261, 324, 414
2:1	361
2:1–2	346
2:1–4	89
2:1–9	361
2:1–12	392, 393
2:1–15	285
2:2	305, 306, 361, 369, 396
2:2ff.	355
2:3–4	185, 361
2:3f.	232
2:3–10	256
2:3–12	414
2:4–10	184
2:4–12	359
2:4ff.	355
2:7a	414
2:8–12	359
2:9	361
2:13	361
2:15	350, 360
3:6	221, 350
4:15–18	359
5:1ff.	325

1 Timothy

4:1ff.	355
6:12–13	399

2 Timothy

2:12–13	361
4:1–5	361
4:1–8	359
4:1ff.	355

Hebrews

1:2	373
3:10	444
10:36–39	259

James

1:10	445
5:1–11	351
5:7ff.	285
5:8	438
5:9	438
5:17	294

1 Peter

1:13	195, 356
3:15	400
4:7	195, 285, 356, 360
4:12–19	355
4:14	324
4:14–16	400
5:5ff.	351
5:6ff.	351
5:8	195, 356
5:8–9	360
5:9	90
5:13	105

2 Peter

3:2ff.	351
3:3–7	359
3:3ff.	355
3:9	242
3:12	320

1 John

2:18	414
2:18ff.	263
4:1ff.	263

Jude

17ff.	351

Revelation

1:1	76
1:1–3	41
1:2	177
1:3	437
1:7	37, 175

1:9–19	41
2:9ff.	351
3:2ff.	356
4:1	76
5	181
6	60, 427
6:7–8	60
6:12	426
6:12–14	308
6:12–15	75
7:9	118
8:5	308
8:6—11:19	419
9—11	34
9:12	34
10:1–11	35
11:1–2	52, 364, 411
11:3–13	355
11:8	417
11:14	34
11:19	308
12:4–17	172
12:14	294
13	170, 355, 359, 394
13:5	375
13:6	45
13:9	326
13:11–13	355
13:11–14	391
13:18	118, 326, 411
14:1ff.	41
14:6–12	322
15:4	426
16:1–21	419
16:12ff.	355
16:15	325, 356
16:17	308
16:17–21	35
16:18	308
16:20	308
17	164
17—19	35
17:1ff.	355
17:9	326
17:9ff.	411
18:2	105
19:1ff.	427
19:11–21	359
19:11—20:3	359
20:11	308, 425
21:5	330
22	416
22:6	76
22:1–2	416
22:10	437
22:12	330

APOSTOLIC FATHERS

1 Clement
50:3	445

Barnabas
4:3	33, 90

Didache
16:3	351

Epiphanius, *Haer.*
29.7	171
30.2	171

Eusebius, *Eccl Hist*
3.5	35, 412
3.5.3	171

Jerome, *Comm. in Ev. Matt* | 414
1:37, 39	171
1:37	172

APOCRYPHA

1 Maccabees
1:54	409
1:59	409
2:28	412

Wisdom
2:18	465
2:4	445

Sirach
16:18–19	308
4:10	465

PSEUDEPIGRAPHA

Psalms of Solomon
17:2	455

1 Enoch
1:4–7	308
57:2	433
62	304, 337, 428
62:2	428
62:5	175
62:13	428
80:2	419
91—93	373
100:1–2	405

2 Baruch
20:1   419
29:3   342
30:1–2   342
53—74   373
54:1–5   373

4 Ezra
3:17–19   308
4:26   419
4:33–37   305
4:36–37   373
4:51–52   455
5:9   405
6:24   405
13   304

Apocalypse of Ezra
3:3–4   456

Assumption of Moses
7   353
10:3   308

Jubilees
1:24–25   465
23:19   405
45:14   353

Testament of Levi
3:9   308

Test. Twelve
  Patriarchs   353

DEAD SEA SCROLLS

1QDM   353

1QH
3:34–36   308

1QSa
2.11ff.   465

4QFlor
1.6–7   465

RABBINIC WRITINGS

b. Ber.
7a   465

b. Sanh.
97a   86
98a   342

b. Ta'an.
24b   465

b. Yoma
39b   382
43c   382
61   382

Mek. on Exod
  16:32   456

Midr. Ruth
  2:14   342

p. Yoma
11   382
38c   382
57   382

Seder Olam Rab.
17   294

Targum Jonathan
  on Mic 7:22ff. 264

JOSEPHUS

War
Proem 4   419
4.3.6–8   328
4.3.12   35
4.7.5   418
6.2.1   35
6.301   380

PHILO

Cherubim
99   433

Mig. Abraham
181   433

GRECO-ROMAN AUTHORS

Plato, *Republic*
6, p. 492E   419

Plutarch, *Moralia*
869B   412

Tacitus, *Annals*
15.44.2, 4   406

Printed in the United States
136498LV00001B/79/A